THE VICTORIAN G

How did realist fiction alter in the effort to craft forms and genres receptive to the dynamism of an expanding empire and globalizing world? Do these nineteenth-century variations on the "geopolitical aesthetic" continue to resonate today? Crossing literary criticism, political theory, and *longue durée* history, *The Victorian Geopolitical Aesthetic* explores these questions from the standpoint of nineteenth-century novelists such as Wilkie Collins, George Eliot, Gustave Flaubert, and Anthony Trollope, as well as successors including E. M. Forster and the creators of recent television serials. By looking at the category of "sovereignty" at multiple scales and in diverse contexts, Lauren M. E. Goodlad shows that the ideological crucible for "high" realism was not a hegemonic liberalism. It was, rather, a clash of modern liberal ideals struggling to distintricate themselves from a powerful conservative vision of empire while striving to negotiate the inequalities of power which a supposedly universalistic liberalism had helped to generate. The material occasion for the Victorian era's rich realist experiments was the long transition from an informal empire of trade that could be celebrated as liberal to a neo-feudal imperialism that only Tories could warmly embrace.

The book places realism's geopolitical aesthetic at the heart of recurring modern experiences of breached sovereignty, forgotten history, and subjective exile. The Coda, titled "The Way We Historicize Now", concludes the study with connections to recent debates about "surface reading", "distant reading", and the hermeneutics of suspicion.

The Victorian Geopolitical Aesthetic

Realism, Sovereignty, and Transnational Experience

LAUREN M. E. GOODLAD

UNIVERSITY PRESS

Great Clarendon Street, Oxford, OX2 6DP,
United Kingdom

Oxford University Press is a department of the University of Oxford.
It furthers the University's objective of excellence in research, scholarship,
and education by publishing worldwide. Oxford is a registered trade mark of
Oxford University Press in the UK and in certain other countries

© Lauren M. E. Goodlad 2015

The moral rights of the author have been asserted

First published 2015
First published in paperback 2017

All rights reserved. No part of this publication may be reproduced, stored in
a retrieval system, or transmitted, in any form or by any means, without the
prior permission in writing of Oxford University Press, or as expressly permitted
by law, by licence or under terms agreed with the appropriate reprographics
rights organization. Enquiries concerning reproduction outside the scope of the
above should be sent to the Rights Department, Oxford University Press, at the
address above

You must not circulate this work in any other form
and you must impose this same condition on any acquirer

Published in the United States of America by Oxford University Press
198 Madison Avenue, New York, NY 10016, United States of America

British Library Cataloguing in Publication Data
Data available

Library of Congress Cataloging in Publication Data
Data available

ISBN 978–0–19–872827–6 (Hbk.)
ISBN 978–0–19–879761–6 (Pbk.)

Links to third party websites are provided by Oxford in good faith and
for information only. Oxford disclaims any responsibility for the materials
contained in any third party website referenced in this work.

Acknowledgments

This book has been more than a decade in the making, years in which I was the fortunate beneficiary of many kinds of research support as a faculty member of the University of Illinois, Urbana. I began the project as a fellow of the Illinois Program for Research in the Humanities and the Center for Advanced Study and concluded it with the generous funding of a University Scholar award. As Director of the Unit for Criticism & Interpretive Theory between 2008 and 2014, it was my privilege to host conferences, symposia, and lectures with some of the world's most intellectually stimulating scholars—events that typically began as reading groups. There is not a single page in this book that has not gained from conversations with Unit for Criticism faculty and students and the invited scholars whose work brought us together.

My years directing the Unit gave me the opportunity to work closely with wonderful colleagues including Nancy Abelmann, Manisha Basu, J. B. Capino, Eleanor Courtemanche, Elena Delgado, Maggie Flinn, Zsuzsa Gille, Dara Goldman, Dianne Harris, Lilya Kaganovsky, Ellen Moodie, Justine Murison, Harriet Murav, Hina Nazar, Melissa Orlie François Proulx, Allyson Purpura, Jesse Ribot, Ricky Rodriguez, Kristin Romberg, Bruce Rosenstock, Michael Rothberg, Rob Rushing, Irene Small, Gabriel Solis, Siobhan Somerville, Anna Stenport, Ted Underwood, and Terri Weissman. In the English department, I am grateful for the advice and support of Curtis Perry, Martin Camargo, Peter Garrett, Gordon Hutner, Carol Neeley, Trish Loughran, Bob Markley, and Bob Parker, as well as for the outstanding collegiality of Julia Saville, who read multiple drafts of almost every chapter.

Excerpts from this book have appeared in *PMLA, Literature Compass, Novel, Victorian Literature and Culture,* and *Victorian Studies* and an early version of Chapter 4 appeared in *The Politics of Gender in Anthony Trollope's Novels*. I am grateful for the many kinds of editorial help I received on these germs of an evolving project.

The community of Victorian and nineteenth-century scholarship is an extraordinary web for vibrant interdisciplinary flourishing. There is almost no end of the thanks I would wish to express to—and for—this world-within-a-world. For their generosity in inviting me to share work-in-progress and learn from exacting readers and audiences I am grateful to Tim Dean, David Schmid, Rachel Ablow, and Carine Mardorossian at the University of Buffalo; Robert Caserio at Penn State; Talia Schaffer, Nancy Yusef, and Richard Kaye at the CUNY Graduate Center; John Kucich, Diane Sadoff, Jonah Siegel, David Kurnick, and Kate Flint at Rutgers; Amanda Claybaugh, Sharon Marcus, and Eileen Gillooly at Columbia; Ortwin de Graef at the University of Leuven; Nancy Henry at the University of Tennessee; Rachel Teukolsky at Vanderbilt; David Thomas and Chris vanden Bossche at Notre Dame; Kathy Woodward, Charles LaPorte, Kathleen Blake, Jane Lee, and George Behlmer, at the University of Washington; Ian Duncan,

Jos Lavery, and Mark Bevir at Berkeley; Dino Felluga and Emily Allen at Purdue; Jed Esty and the postcolonial and British literature graduate student groups at the University of Pennsylvania; Rachel Buurma, Peter Logan, Kate Thomas, and Priya Joshi in the Nineteenth Century Collective in Philadelphia; Helena Michie and Alexander Regier at Rice; Marie Pantojan, Hosanna Krienke, and Jules Law at Northwestern; Caroline Levine and Susan Bernstein at Wisconsin; and Regenia Gagnier, Margaret Markwick, and Deborah Morse at the Trollope conference in Exeter. For enabling me to share parts of the project outside Victorian studies proper, I thank Linda Zerilli at the Center for the Study of Gender & Sexuality at the University of Chicago, Chris Bush for inviting me to join his seminar at the ACLA, and David Palumbo-Liu for including perspectives from the geopolitical aesthetic in his panel on debt at the American Studies Association.

For invaluable commentary on draft chapters, both early and late, I am especially indebted to Bruce Robbins, John Kucich, Tanya Agathocleous, Nicholas Birns, Patrick Bray, Elaine Freedgood, Caroline Levine, Karuna Mantena, Andrew Miller, Andrew Sartori, Harry Shaw, Amanda Anderson, Steven Arata, Duncan Bell, Gordon Bigelow, Antoinette Burton, Jim Buzard, Frances Ferguson, Geoff Gilbert, Rae Greiner, Danny Hack, Nathan Hensley, Nancy Henry, Amy Kaplan, Ivan Kreilkamp, Carolyn Lesjak, Dana Polan, David Skilton, Martin Weiner, Julia Wright, Jeremy Varon, and Georgios Varouxakis. Former and current graduate students whose work became an inspiration for mine include Carrie Dickison, Liz Hoiem, Carl Lehnen, Zia Miric, Donghee Om, Austin Riede, Gautam Basu Thakur, Frederik van Dam, Terra Walston, and Dan Wong. Ben O'Dell and Thierry Ramais who provided crucial research assistance at various stages of the project, also belong to this group.

At Oxford University Press, Jacqueline Baker, Rachel Platt, and Nicholas Bromley have been unfailingly generous with their time and expertise.

My parents, Jerry and Cindy Eisenberg have never stopped helping me on a daily basis; my sons, Alex Goodlad and Edward (Teddy) Sammons, teach me every day to believe in the arc of the future; and my husband, Mark Sammons, is the center of gravity on which everything else depends. This book is dedicated to him.

Contents

List of Illustrations ix

    Prologue 1

1. Toward a Victorian Geopolitical Aesthetic 19

2. Imperial Sovereignty: The Limits of Liberalism and the Case of Mysore 39

3. Trollopian "Foreign Policy": Rootedness and Cosmopolitanism in the Mid-Victorian Global Imaginary 65

4. "India is 'a Bore'": Imperial Governmentality in *The Eustace Diamonds* 87

5. "Dark, Like Me": Archeology and *Erfahrung* in Wilkie Collins's *Armadale* and *The Moonstone* 110

6. The Adulterous Geopolitical Aesthetic: *Romola* contra *Madame Bovary* 161

7. Where Liberals Fear to Tread: E. M. Forster's Queer Internationalism and the Ethics of Care 208

8. The *Mad Men* in the Attic: Seriality and Identity in the Modern Babylon 242

    Coda: The Way We Historicize Now 268

Works Cited 295
Index 331

List of Illustrations

4.1.	"A living monument of English injustice"	99
4.2.	"New crowns for old ones"	107
8.1.	Paul Newman as Ari Ben Canaan and George Maharis as Yoav	255
8.2.	Lily Meyer and Yoram Ben Shulhai	256
8.3.	Ari Ben Canaan and Kitty Fremont dining in the "Rome of the Middle East"	257
8.4.	Don and Betty Draper dining in Rome	258
8.5a.	Joan looks at a caged bird	261
8.5b.	Walter Deverell's "A Pet" (1853)	262
8.6.	Don, fading in, listens to "Babylon" as Sally and Betty, playing dress-up, fade out	263
8.7.	Metaphors of physical discomfort (Season 3 publicity)	263

Prologue

Many people reading this book will remember a time (more likely, a series of times) when Victorianist scholars regarded the self-evident stage for their literary study as the English nation, the British Isles, or the British Empire. Over the last decade or so it has become usual to consider that "Victorian" literature, though written in English by authors who were typically British nationals, is the product of palpably transnational forces and global perspectives.[1] The importance of measuring this encompassing globality as we write about the Victorian past is an underlying assumption of this book. Studies like David Armitage's *The Ideological Origins of the British Empire* (2000), A. G. Hopkins's *Globalization in World History* (2002), Ellen Meiksins Wood's *Empire of Capital* (2003), C. A. Bayly's *The Birth of the Modern World* (2003), John Darwin's *The Empire Project: the Rise and Fall of the British World-System* (2009), and Paul Young's *Globalization and the Great Exhibition* (2009) have shown that *globalization*, a condition associated with the present day, is a process of capitalist expansion which has been unfolding for centuries. Theorists of global culture have explored how the "cosmopolitan character" of capital which Karl Marx and Friedrich Engels observed in 1848, embeds particular places, histories, and experiences in networks of transnational "inter-dependence" ("Manifesto" 476). Given the intensity of today's reflections on globalization, it is no surprise to find scholars drawn to terms like *postcolonial*, *transatlantic*, *black Atlantic*, *cosmopolitan*, *transnational*, or *international* to describe nineteenth-century history and culture.

While this turn toward the geohistorical and transnational has invigorated Victorian studies in many ways, it has only begun to imprint the study of nineteenth-century literature. Inspired by a vast body of multidisciplinary work on the global, literary scholars have begun to articulate the critical frameworks necessary to exploring literature as a fundamentally "worlded" phenomenon—formally as well as thematically. This study seeks to augment that process by offering a working theory of the Victorian "geopolitical aesthetic," the main

---

[1] Following the feminist geographer Hyndman, I use *transnational* to signify "not only relations that traverse political borders," but also "scales of analysis both coarser and finer than the nation-state" (316). To avoid proliferation of scare quotes, I use *Victorian* to signify the nineteenth-century decades that coincided with Victoria's reign and their legacies as well as a field of study that, in recent years, has turned away from the nation-state, narrowly defined, and toward postcolonial, transnational, transatlantic, and global perspectives. As P. Joshi argues, properly understood, the term "Victorian," should, like "globalization," capture "the unevenness intrinsic to transnational economic and cultural encounters" ("Globalizing" 38). For related commentary see, for example, Bristow, "Whether" ; Flint; Goodlad and Wright; and Marcus, "Same."

contexts for which are the transnational structures and experiences particular to the nineteenth century—though still resonant today—and the fictional experiments of Anthony Trollope, George Eliot, Wilkie Collins, E. M. Forster, and their French precursor, Gustave Flaubert. In its simplest shape, the book asks how realist fiction altered in its multiple efforts to craft aesthetic forms receptive to the dynamism of a fast-globalizing world.

The Victorian Geopolitical Aesthetic began as an exploration of the intersection between realism and the international and imperial dimensions of liberalism. My first book, *Victorian Literature and the Victorian State: Character and Governance in a Liberal Society* (2003), argued that nineteenth-century Britain's profoundly anti-statist culture required more nuanced accounts of liberalism and British literature than were likely to emerge from scholarship heavily indebted to Michel Foucault's analyses of modern discipline on the Continent. Foucault's later works on liberalism and "governmentality," I proposed, provided better guides for probing the paradoxes of governance which haunted novels like Frances Trollope's *Jessie Phillips: A Tale of the New Poor Law*, Charles Dickens's *Bleak House*, Anthony Trollope's *The Three Clerks*, and George Gissing's *The Nether World*. Since my focus was the metropolitan state, and my goal was to illuminate contrasts between Britain and the Continent, *Victorian Literature and the Victorian State* only intermittently discussed imperial practices and said little about transnational cultural and political formations. The starting point of the new book, therefore, was to focus literary analysis on border-crossing encounters such as liberationist movements in Europe and imperial expansion in South Asia.

The 2000s were an auspicious moment for this enterprise. Books like Edward Said's *Culture and Imperialism* (1993) had helped to ignite a vigorous interest in postcoloniality among critics of British literature. Scholars of "the new imperial history" were elucidating the complex shape of empire and its impact on every facet of Victorian life.[2] Political theorists such as Uday Singh Mehta, Jennifer Pitts, and (more recently) Karuna Mantena were making penetrating connections between liberal political philosophy and imperialism. Mehta's *Liberalism and Empire: A Study in Nineteenth-Century British Liberal Thought* (1999) described liberalism as an intrinsically dominatory ideology, the hallmark of which was imperviousness to the plurality of human experience. This view of liberalism as a philosophical and political machinery of objectification, abstraction, and self-aggrandizement resonated with classic postcolonial studies including Johannes Fabian's *Time and the Other: How Anthropology Makes its Object* (1983; 2002), and contemporaneous works such as Dipesh Chakrabarty's *Provincializing Europe: Postcolonial Thought and Historical Difference* (2000; 2007). Such scholarship showed how the self-congratulatory notion of Britain as a vanguard of universal liberty and enlightenment naturalized the geopolitics of a growing empire—a topic that could not but reverberate in the post-9/11 era of "liberationist" wars in the Middle East.

---

[2] Cooper and Stoler's *Tensions of Empire: Colonial Cultures in a Bourgeois World* (1997), Hall's *Civilising Subjects* (2002), Burton's *After the Imperial Turn* (2003), Lambert and Lester's *Colonial Lives across the British Empire* (2006), D. Bell's *The Idea of Greater Britain* (2007) and Sartori's *Bengal in Global Concept History* (2008) are among several historical studies of this kind which have influenced this book.

Yet, as I prepared to write on novelists including Trollope, Collins, Eliot, and Forster, as well as contemporaries like Benjamin Disraeli, Harriet Martineau, John Stuart Mill, and J. R. Seeley, it became increasingly clear that Victorian-era ethics, politics, and aesthetics were not adequately explained as a "liberal" tendency toward abstraction and instrumentalization. For one thing, "liberalism" itself is conceptually protean—a moving target that is notoriously difficult to historicize. If one obvious challenge for scholars of the nineteenth century is the simple fact that many influential contemporaries were not liberals (curtailing any wholesale equation between "liberal" and "Victorian"), a more subtle difficulty is that many Victorians who called themselves liberals embraced policies and beliefs that defenders of liberalism today would condemn. As Wendy Brown writes, liberalism is a "nonsystematic and porous doctrine subject to historical change and local variation" (*States* 141). Unsurprisingly, then, liberalism so-called has a different lineage in Europe than in the United States.[3] Indeed, the topic remains hard to pin down in our own day. Is liberalism's contemporary essence encapsulated in the New Deal's legacy? Does it live on in those regulatory, equalitarian, and redistributive agendas that self-described liberals defend from the back benches of mainstream US politics? Do liberal aspirations thrive on a global scale in the postcolonial projects Amartya Sen promotes in books such as *Development as Freedom* (1999)? Or has liberalism everywhere been captured by the economistic "neoliberalism" that, since the 1990s, has found Democrats like Bill Clinton and Barack Obama adopting many neoclassical doctrines dear to conservatives?[4]

With present-day liberalism eluding stable political categories, it is little wonder that the nomenclature familiar to Victorian readers has become obscure. General accounts of nineteenth-century liberalism tend to paper over distinctions between "advanced liberals," "philosophical radicals," political economists, utilitarians, radicals, Whigs, republicans, and, in the case of Anthony Trollope, "advanced, but still . . . conservative Liberal[s]" (*Autobiography* 147). Historicizing liberalism can thus lead, ironically, to the kind of undifferentiating assimilation of which liberalism itself is charged. Even when scholarship is admirably specific, as when Mehta approaches "liberal" imperialism through illuminating discussions

---

[3] The British Liberal Party famously split over home rule in Ireland at around the same time that progressive "New Liberals" were beginning to embrace explicitly social democratic, collectivist, and labor-oriented policies. Thus, left-leaning and socially democratic "liberals" in the United States have not had significant British counterparts since the early-twentieth-century rise of the Labour Party. As a result, British social democrats often use "liberal" to denote free-market ideologies, while American enthusiasts of the free market use the same descriptor to denote supporters of state welfare, regulation, and progressive taxation. In both cases, "liberal" is a term of opprobrium—but for very different reasons.

[4] For work that helpfully articulates *neoliberalism* today as distinct from the liberalisms of the past, see Brown, "Neo-Liberalism"; Clarke; and Duggan. I describe some of the difficulties of writing on Victorian liberalism in Goodlad, "'Character'" and Goodlad, "Liberalism." On the welfare state, see Robbins, *Upward* as well as *States of Welfare*, a special issue co-edited by Goodlad, Robbins, and Rothberg. Throughout this book, I insert quotation marks around liberal or liberalism to emphasize ironic, paradoxical, or ambiguous usages, reserving the term without quotation marks for neutral denotation. I capitalize the word "Liberal" when I am referring specifically to any position or person associated with the Liberal Party.

of James Mill, Thomas Babington Macaulay, and J. S. Mill, the tendency is to subsume differences in order to proffer synthetic analyses. For all the importance of exploring the imperial mentality that Mehta pinpoints, the history of Britain's multifarious global expansion confutes the thesis of a "singular and imperial 'logic', 'impulse', or 'urge'"(D. Bell, "Empire" 865; cf. Sartori, "British").

Liberalism is even less reliable as a vehicle for describing the fiction of this period. It is no accident that not one of the novelists considered in this book provides a stable "liberal" foundation—including Forster whom, as I shall argue, has been mistaken for liberalism's literary standard bearer (Ch. 7). That is true whether liberalism is defined as a democratic political philosophy; a theory of progress, freedom, equality, or tolerance; a universalizing perspective; a cosmopolitan ethics; a procedural ethics rooted in theories of democratic consent; an economic doctrine; or a basis for either promoting or rejecting imperial pursuits. Still less do the literary works considered in this book—including *The Warden* (1855), *Romola* (1862–3), *Armadale* (1864–6), *The Eustace Diamonds* (1871–3), and *Where Angels Fear to Tread* (1905)—evoke a continuous "liberal" aesthetic, formally or otherwise. To the contrary, such works so deeply problematize the idea of a singular liberal project that their most valuable lesson in this regard is to teach caution in wielding this freighted term.

In *Victorian Literature and the Victorian State*, the exploration of particular debates over governance enabled the framing of key tensions with relative ease. But, as I quickly learned, the task of exploring realist narrative's flexile aesthetic responses to an ongoing process of capitalist globalization posed greater methodological challenges. This was in one sense a question simply of historical complexity. How does one elucidate Victorian fiction's grappling with a project of global modernity which, in some sense, was "liberal," when liberalism itself is hydra-headed, when influential Tory alternatives were on the rise, and when the structures in which such politics were enmeshed are complicated and, at times, obscure? But the difficulty was, in another sense, fundamentally disciplinary. As the editors of a recent volume on world-systems theory note, the analysis of global capital, a topic that invites macrosociological methodologies, can pose significant challenges for the humanistic study of cultures (Palumbo-Liu et al., "Introduction"). At a time of "waning" individual and national sovereignties (W. Brown, *Walled*), what can a study of the "worlding" of nineteenth-century literature contribute to the more concretely political task of understanding the ongoing effects of capitalist globalization?

The Victorian Geopolitical Aesthetic approaches these problems in part by pursuing a twofold critical enterprise. That is, while most of this book is recognizably the work of a literary scholar writing on questions of nineteenth-century realist form and its aftermath, Chapter 2 engages questions and methods familiar to historians by way of considering the problem of imperial sovereignty from Tory as well as Liberal standpoints. The succeeding chapters are devoted to illustrating the "geopolitical aesthetic" at work in a range of formally diverse realist texts including Trollope's travel writings, Trollope's series novels, Collins's sensation novels, Flaubert's "serious imitation of the everyday," Eliot's historical fiction,

Forster's Italian tragicomedy, and, in the final chapter, the recent surge of serialized realism on television. Through these disparate engagements, I develop the "Victorian" geopolitical aesthetic as an approach to understanding literature's ongoing dialogue with globalization's *longue durée*.

TERMINOLOGY

In writing this book, I have sought supple language to articulate the political, ethical, and aesthetic stakes of the transnational imaginaries arising in response to unprecedented forms of global experience. The term *realism* is used to describe a diverse narrative fiction that stretches horizontally (to embrace mid-Victorian authors like Collins and Eliot at their most experimental and French contemporaries like Flaubert), as well as vertically (to the Forsterian cusp of Modernism and the neo-Victorianism of today's serial television). If this use of "realism" is deliberately loose—indeed, too loose for those who prefer hard distinctions between realism and sensation fiction—the wish to spur dialogue about realist form is firm and persistent.[5] Beginning in Chapter 1, I push against a still influential set of assumptions which holds that nineteenth-century realism, post-1848 realism, British realism, or realism *tout court*, are bankrupt forms of lifeless mimicry which lack narrative art and historical acuity. In actuality, none of the novels considered in this book adheres to a generic set of realist prescriptions. This includes the works of Trollope whose reputation as a classic realist is justifiable but, for that very reason, testimony to the formulaic expectations the label often invites. My point, then, is not to defend select novels on the grounds of their non-realism, but, rather, to show how confusion about what "realism" signifies remains an obstacle to critical understanding.[6]

---

[5] While this study recognizes substantial formal differences between Collins's fiction and, for example, Eliot's, Flaubert's or Trollope's, the category of realism is left sufficiently open to facilitate comparisons as well as contrasts. It is worth noting that even sophisticated contemporaries like Henry James lacked the firm definition of realism which scholarship on mid-Victorian fiction tends to enforce. Praising Disraeli's *Lothair* (1870) as a "work . . . abounding in the romantic element," James contrasted it to the "the hard, sordid, pretentious accuracy" of contemporaneous fiction and offered not only Trollope but also Collins to exemplify such "dreary realism" (Rev. of *Lothair* 251). Even in France, where *realism* was used to describe Flaubert's controversial naturalistic style in *Madame Bovary*, one finds Charles Baudelaire repudiating the term as a "degrading insult flung in the face of all analytical writers" and "a vague and overflexible term applied by indiscriminate minds to the minute description of detail rather than to a new method of literary creation" ("*Madame*" 406). As Wellek notes in an important 1961 essay, no self-identified "realist" movement existed in Britain until the Zola-influenced naturalism of George Moore and George Gissing (4). Wellek proposes a pragmatic definition of realism as the "objective representation of contemporary social reality" (10). More recently, Beaumont's *Adventures in Realism* (2007) collects a variety of essays on the topic which aim to historicize realism "from the perspective of . . . different disciplines and in a number of different registers" ("Introduction" 10)—precisely what this book also aims to achieve. For a worthwhile effort to consolidate realism's aesthetic around a concern with building suspense in order to put "mimesis to the test" see C. Levine, *Serious* (12).

[6] Trollope's status as the most classically realist of the authors described in this study explains why the first two literary chapters (3 and 4) are devoted to his works even though some of those works were published after the more formally hybrid Collins and Eliot fictions explored in Chapters 5 and 6, respectively.

Unsurprisingly, *imperialism* provides a crucial context for exploring Victorian literature's global provenance. Throughout this book, the term denotes the multiple practices of expansion and domination which gradually advanced capitalism's structurally multi-pronged determination to evolve into a global system. The conditions of possibility for such practices, so far from homogeneously "liberal," were layered, variable, and often specific to place and time. Thus, while *liberalism* is another key term for this study (in the multiplistic sense I have already described), the chapters that follow use it primarily to explain recurring crises over individual, national, and imperial sovereignty: crises precipitated when, for example, deeply felt ethico-political ideals clashed with imperial presumptions, practices, and goals.

The term *geopolitics* appears in these pages to describe the means and modes through which diverse world actors, including the British state, worked consciously and unconsciously to extend the imperatives of transnational capital, inside and outside imperial formations. "Geopolitics" thus designates the heterogeneous political framework for the evolving world-system theorized by Immanuel Wallerstein among others.[7] Geopolitics as such privileged nation-centric visions of the global, celebrating "free" trade, white settlement in temperate zones like Canada and Australia, as well as the supposed benefits of a British "civilizing mission" in the global south. But that is not to say that Victorian culture was built around a coherent idea of Britain as an imperial nation-state. To the contrary, the appealing notion of England as the archetypal *non*-empire—a maritime and commercial power diffusing progress without resort to political oppression—was the ideological heart of the early-Victorian era's "free trade imperialism."

According to Bernard Semmel, Britain's empire of free trade arose in the hundred years between 1750 and 1850 (*Rise*).[8] Since the shift to formal imperialism came about in the 1870s (with the 1876 Royal Titles Act being the first in a series of landmarks), the years from 1848 to 1876 were an intense period of transition—a point scholars of mid-Victorian literature often miss. Appreciating the "geopolitics" of this period entails grasping not only the diverse practices through which Britain's imperial borders burgeoned, but also the tendency of contemporaries to identify this process with the beneficent extension of "trade."

---

[7] As Wallerstein writes, "A world-system is not the system of *the* world, but a system *that is a* world and that . . . most often has been, located in an area less than the entire globe" (*World-Systems* 98). This meaning, as well as Jameson's similar usage of "geopolitics," is distinct both from early twentieth-century geography's invention of the term to describe "the influences of spatial environment on political imperatives" and from the present-day use as a euphemism for "power politics" (Howard para 2). My understanding is also informed by the *critical geopolitics* articulated by recent geographers such as Ó Tuathail who question "the logocentric infrastructures" that endow "geopolitics" with the status of a "natural" and "knowable" reality (68); Hyndman, who uses feminist tools to resituate critical analyses from partial and embodied perspectives; and Minca who explores the spatial underpinnings of new theories of sovereignty.

[8] Lynn describes free trade as "the quintessential characteristic of the early Victorian view of the world, combining moral commitment with material self-interest" (103). See also Semmel, *Liberal*, as well as Gallagher and Robinson. For an illuminating study of free trade's relation to romance genres such as maritime fiction see Çelikkol.

Consider, for example, Lord Palmerston, a leading Whig and the main arbiter of British foreign policy from 1830 until his death in 1865. In his well-known 1842 speech in favor of repealing the Corn Laws, Palmerston described free trade as "the interchange of mutual benefits engendering mutual kind feelings," a progressive practice that would lead "civilization with one hand and peace with another" (excerpted in Bourne 255). Yet, as foreign secretary or prime minister for most of the period between 1830 and 1865, Palmerston's policies included two Opium Wars with China as well as campaigns in Afghanistan and a full-scale war in the Crimea—both motivated partly to check Russian access to South Asia. Writing to the Governor General of India, Palmerston insisted that it "is the business of Government to open and to secure the roads for the merchant." Concerned that Europe's manufacturers were "fast excluding" British products from continental markets, he asserted the state's "unremitting" duty "to find in other parts of the world new vents for the produce of [British] industry" (qtd. in Davison 28). With free trade thus providing the official doctrine of the day, while territorial imperialism operated as an object of quiet government policy, it is no wonder that when the Sepoy "mutiny" broke out in 1857, sophisticated commentators like Martineau were prepared to declare that "India is no colony of ours," since Britain's "footing" there "began and extended without the national cognizance" (*Suggestions* 178). Such pervasive disavowal of imperial practice in the face of aggressive territorial advance explains Seeley's famous claim, in *The Expansion of England* (1883), that Britons seemed to have "conquered . . . half the world in a fit of absence of mind" (12).

In 1860, Britain was responsible for one quarter of the world's trade (double that of its nearest competitor) with staple industries like textiles both importing raw materials and exporting finished products. Throughout the 1860s, foreign markets were the destination for a third of Britain's woolens, 40% of its iron and steel, and two-thirds of its cotton textiles (B. Porter, *Britain* 16 and *passim*).[9] As classic Victorian literature richly attests—Thomas Carlyle's *Past and Present* (1843), Charles Dickens's *Little Dorrit* (1855–7), or John Ruskin's *Unto This Last* (1860), for example—the unregulated industrial and financial capitalism that underwrote this formidable export economy was often portrayed as a threat to cherished "heirloom" forms of individual, communal, and national sovereignty, and the kinds of experience they entailed. Such anxieties about the modern condition, moreover, were exacerbated by geopolitical effects that were palpable to the metropole, geographical distance and "absence of mind" notwithstanding. Thus, rubbing against the agreeable idea of British commerce as the engine of world peace and prosperity was the far less desirable awareness of a "free trade" reliant on the continuous exercise of military power. In addition to the two wars fought to open China's ports to British opium between 1839 and 1860, and the

---

[9] According to an 1861 article in *The London Review*, imperial "possessions" were "consum[ing] annually British produce and manufactures to the value of 43 ½ millions, thus taking close upon one-third of our whole exports, and nearly as much as all Europe buys of us"—a figure which was said to be "increasing annually in a most rapid ratio" ("Britain's Colonies" 580).

disastrous effort to subdue Afghanistan in 1839–1842, the territorial acquisitions that accompanied "trade" included annexation of Hong Kong in 1843, Labuan in Indonesia in 1846, the Orange River in South Africa in 1848, as well as numerous "princely states" in India—all "triggered by the need to secure existing frontiers and pacify internal dissent" (M. Taylor 148).[10] This was the kind of geopolitical activity J. S. Mill struggled to countenance in his labored allusions to imperialism in works such as *Considerations on Representative Government* (Ch. 2).

In fact, Britain's presence on the Indian subcontinent was hardly assimilable to a relation of trade or settlement, a reality more difficult to ignore after the "mutiny" that broke out in 1857. Whereas the emigration of British settlers to (supposedly) under-utilized land in North America or Australia conformed to capitalist norms of productivity, Britain's densely populated Indian "dependencies" originated in mercantilist policy and morphed into an anomalous empire of "tax and tribute" reminiscent of ancient Rome (E. Wood 111).[11] The notion of a "Greater Britain" spreading Anglo-Saxon blood, culture, and language to the world's temperate zones was an appealing face for a globalizing Britain; but the idea of "extended dominion over black subjects," as Trollope phrased it in 1875, was a different kettle of fish entirely (*Tireless* 200). Though neither the East India Company nor the British state wished to publicize the fact, British India was, in fact, a military and bureaucratic despotism of the kind Britons had long derided as the product of Continental cultures that lacked the Anglo-Saxon Protestant's supposedly deep and abiding commitment to liberty.

At stake in defining and defending these longstanding beliefs about Britain's global identity was the idea of *sovereignty*, a multivalent term used to stand for the political ideal of individual, local, and national self-governance. Recent critical discussions of the topic have centered on the influential political theory of Giorgio Agamben in works such as *Homo Sacer: Sovereign Power and Bare Life* (1998) and *State of Exception* (2005). For a number of reasons—not least his tendency to blur

---

[10] On the massacre of the retreating East India Company's army from Afghanistan in 1842 see Burton, *First Anglo-Afghan*.

[11] As India's "declaration of independence" made clear in 1930, the British deindustrialized India in order to impose their vision of an agrarian global south destined to provide raw materials and markets for an industrially advanced north all while levying taxes through the local elites who helped to maintain this quasi-feudal structure. On the East India Company's deliberate use of the Great Exhibition to portray its activities in India as "an empire of free labor and free trade," see Kriegel, "Pudding" 234; on tensions within discourse about India during the Exhibition, see Young, "'Carbon.'" According to India's declaration, "India has been ruined economically. The revenue derived from our people is out of all proportion to our income . . . Village industries, such as hand-spinning, have been destroyed . . . and nothing has been substituted," see <http://cs.nyu.edu/kandathi/swaraj.txt>. Of course, postcolonial theorists such as Loomba use the terms *colony* and *colonialism* to describe the nuanced relationships through which imperial powers like Britain "restructured the economies of" the countries they conquered, not only extracting wealth, but also "drawing them into a complex relationship with their own [economies], so that there was a flow of human and natural resources between colonized and colonial countries" (3). While such interconnection is undeniable, in this book I emphasize the Victorian rhetorical tendency to reserve "colony" for spaces of white settlement, while referencing non-settlement territories like India through alternative terms such as "possession" and "dependency"—a distinction that bolstered the illusion of a maritime empire of trade.

past and present—Agamben's analysis of modern government is of limited value to a materialist study of aesthetic forms which explores transformations over the long nineteenth century and beyond.[12] That said, Carl Schmitt's original conception of the sovereign as "he who decides on the exception" to the rule of law—is highly relevant to the globalizing structures this book describes (*Political* 5). The liberal ideal of a democratic sovereignty was especially vexed in the imperial arena where British rule was perforce subtended or displaced by extra-constitutional forms of power and violence (Ch. 2). Thus, in the Schmittian phrase that Agamben takes up, an empire of conquest was, by definition, a "state of exception" (*Political* 5 n. 1)—a perception that percolates through Victorian literature in a number of ways.[13] While breached metropolitan sovereignty is the focal point for naturalistic narratives of capitalist globalization including Flaubert's *Madame Bovary* and Trollope's *The Eustace Diamonds*, Eliot's focus in *Romola* is the sovereign citizen of a republic (Ch. 6), and Collins's, a plumbing of transnational experience to replace the convention of a singular and unified sovereign entity with one that is porous and pluralized (Ch. 5).

Fredric Jameson has coined the term *geopolitical aesthetic* to describe how particular artistic forms suggest "an unconscious, collective effort" to "figure out" the "the landscapes and forces" specific to global situations that are at once lived and beyond individual experience and cognition. By "geopolitical unconscious," he denotes the impact of national cultures and allegories overwhelmed by the myriad effects of global embedment (*Geopolitical* 3). Although Jameson concentrates on Modernist and postmodern focal points, the terms "geopolitical aesthetic" and "geopolitical unconscious" nicely capture the imperial disavowal and anxieties over sovereignty evinced during the mid-Victorian decades of realism's flourishing. As perceptions of stalwart nationhood succumbed to the worlding effects of capitalism and imperialism, the novels of this and of comparable periods developed diverse aesthetic registers including the *sociological, archeological, phenomenological,* and *international* variants described in this book. Serial publication distended the experience of reading this fiction over long stretches of time and ramified it through public conversation, criticism, and commentary. In this way, Victorian fiction provided an ideal medium for channeling the many ways in

---

[12] See, for example, Rancière for the argument that Agamben's work on sovereignty tends to abandon the emancipatory potential of art and politics in favor of "an immemorial and neverending catastrophe" (*Dissensus* 200); cf. Connolly, *Pluralism* (131–60). See also A. Smith on the "implications of Agamben's failure to address the historically specific and stratified character of the State's targeting in the midst of an emergency" (para. 14). Agamben's earlier work on modern experience, however, resonates nicely with the work of the geopolitical aesthetic (see Ch. 5).

[13] The translator of *Political Theology* defines the "state of exception" as "any kind of severe economic or political disturbance that requires the application of extraordinary measures" (Schmitt 5 n. 1). Agamben's influential adaptation of the state of exception posits "suspension of the law" as the law's "original means of referring to and encompassing *life*" (*State* 1; emphasis added)—in effect, making the sovereign's power to exercise control over biopolitical life the norm rather than the exception. While this study does not offer a sustained discussion of either theorist, I maintain that Schmitt's historically contingent distinction between norm and exception offers the more powerful lens on the exceptional status of Victorian imperialism—including its impact on the management of metropolitan life.

which a period now remembered for its "equipoise" and growing "real" economy, was often experienced as anarchic, vertiginous, precarious, overweening, and surreal.[14]

Many readers will recognize that Jameson's work on the geopolitical aesthetic originates in a book on world cinema. But as I shall be at pains to demonstrate, a Victorian notion of the geopolitical aesthetic—or, more precisely, a notion of nineteenth-century literature as productive of many variations on a recognizably geopolitical aesthetic—is as potentially illuminating of globalization's "landscapes and forces" as of the postmodern condition it was coined to describe. That said, despite a burgeoning interest in realist form, claims for the transnationality and aesthetic vitality of nineteenth-century fiction remain contentious. Jameson, for example, has tended to regard Victorian fiction as the product of a predominantly nation-bound and pre-imperial culture. Following Georg Lukács's influential analyses of literature after the failed European revolutions of 1848, Jameson is one of many scholars who has cast the realist novel as politically stagnant as well as formally antinomistic and circumscribed.[15]

Lukács's germinal ideas about the social provenance of literature are indispensible to this book. *The Historical Novel* famously argues that post-1848 works such as Flaubert's *Madame Bovary* exemplify a paralyzing crisis of bourgeois aesthetics. Yet, as subsequent chapters will show, to apply such a thesis to mid-Victorian literature is to cast the decades leading up to the Royal Titles Act as politically dormant in the face of world events like the annexation of the Punjab, the "18th Brumaire" of Louis Napoleon, the Crimean War, the Second Opium War, the outbreak and suppression of the Indian rebellion, the unification of Italy, the United States Civil War, the Governor Eyre crisis in Jamaica, and the opening of the Suez Canal—all of which occurred as Benjamin Disraeli's Tory party "dished the Whigs" to usher in the age of mass politics. It is hard to imagine a more fecund set of historical contexts for a geopolitically sensitive literature, alive in multiple ways to what Lukács saw as narrative fiction's "essential aim" of capturing "the way society moves" (*Historical* 144).

---

[14] Baucom's fascinating *Specters of the Atlantic,* based partly on Arrighi's economic analyses in *The Long Twentieth Century* (1994), argues that the nineteenth century was "commodito-centric" in contrast to the finance capitalism of the eighteenth and twentieth centuries (9). Yet, the assumption that the Victorian era was not yet a moment in which "capital accumulates ... in the paper, credit, stock, or other speculative forms of finance capital" is contested by prominent mid-Victorian fiction including Dickens's *Dombey and Son, Little Dorrit* and *Our Mutual Friend*; Trollope's *The Prime Minister* and *The Way We Live Now*; and (later) Gissing's *The Whirlpool*. One reason for this odd mischaracterization of the nineteenth century is that Arrighi's "long" twentieth century begins in the 1870s, contemporaneous with Trollope's naturalistic narratives of capitalist globalization (along with economic analyses like Walter Bagehot's *Lombard Street: A Description of the Money Market* [1873] which claimed, "There never was so much borrowed money collected in the world as is now collected in London" [13]). That said, since Dickens's novels were written earlier it seems likely that the spectral qualities Baucom associates with a finance economy are as much to do with the overarching process of globalizing capital as with the predominance of credit in any given economy. For reconsideration of W. L. Burns influential notion of a mid-Victorian "age of equipoise" see Hewitt.

[15] On Jameson's recent book-length elaboration of the topic in *Antinomies of Realism* (2013), see the Coda.

ARC OF THE BOOK

The Victorian Geopolitical Aesthetic begins by setting forth the theoretical challenges that guide this study and considering the current frameworks for transnational Victorianist scholarship from the perspective of an evolving capitalist globalization. Chapter 1 notes the tendency for ethical approaches to literature and culture to isolate themselves from historicism's focus on material conditions and vice versa. Thus, while critical historicism and critical ethics share a common interest in transnational political horizons, they often run aslant of one another: historicists describe geopolitical structures such as imperialism, while ethicists seek to recuperate cosmopolitan standpoints or to restore voices lost to violence and oppression. The result is a persistent disconnect between cultural and structural analysis along with difficulty in characterizing the kind of work which a "geopolitical aesthetic" might do. By contrast, this book aims to bridge the gap between ethics and geopolitics and does so partly by reevaluating the literary materialisms of Erich Auerbach, Walter Benjamin, Lukács, Jameson, and Raymond Williams. Chapter 1 lays out a theory of the Victorian geopolitical aesthetic which integrates artistic expression and geohistorical structure (and, in doing so, calls for openness to the normative aspirations of both poststructuralism and the Enlightenment). At the same time, the book calls for renewed attention to literary form, noting the range and intensity of Victorian fiction's aesthetic engagements with global encounter. In embracing Lukács's notion of form as an index of historical forces, the subsequent chapters do not so much redeem a set of novelistic conventions as prize open the category of realism to appreciate its suppleness, variety, and longevity.

The challenge of the geopolitical aesthetic is to attend to globalization's *longue durée* without neglecting the close-range historical engagements that shape particular fictional milieux. Historicization of this kind is not a suspicious hermeneutics run amok, but a practice of situating the work of literature from multiple long and close-range perspectives. Chapter 2, "Imperial Sovereignty, the Limits of Liberalism, and the Case of Mysore" sets up a number of touchpoints for the literary analyses that follow. On the one hand, the chapter offers a broad-strokes account of the conundrum of imperial sovereignty, from the mid-eighteenth-century trial of Warren Hastings to debates over the controversial Ilbert Bill in 1882. On the other, it offers in-depth analysis of an important (if largely forgotten) mid-Victorian debate over the fate of Mysore—scene of the 1799 battle of Seringapatam with which Collins's *The Moonstone* famously begins.

The liberal discourses of the post-rebellion era offered two incompatible modes of legitimating sovereignty beyond England's borders: a "Greater British" idealization of white settlement and trade which was antithetical to territorial empires like India, and the "civilizing mission" that, since the 1830s, had provided a state-sanctioned justification for rule in densely populated South Asia. In fact, neither discourse provided stable ground for the formalized "New Imperialism" that emerged in the wake of crises like the "mutiny" and the Jamaica insurrection. With Britain's transition to an adult male franchise in the foreground of their thinking, liberal intellectuals like J.S. Mill and John Morley struggled to make sense of Britain's identity as a democracy as well as an empire.

The debate over Mysore, which entailed the efforts of an aging maharajah to preserve his dynasty under "indirect" British rule, illustrates how the lack of a coherent British vision of empire was eventually answered by Tory neo-feudalism. As imagined by charismatic Conservatives such as Disraeli and the Earl of Lytton, the New Imperialism was an aestheticized and romanticized neo-feudal relation between sovereign and subjects which would appeal to Indians as well as the newly enfranchised British working classes. Thus, while the Tories recast India as the proverbial jewel in the empress's crown, so-called liberal imperialism foundered over its numerous contradictions. Liberal intellectuals of the 1870s and 1880s became noticeably anxious, authoritarian, and racist as well as prone to ad hominem demonization of "the Jew premier" (*Church Times* qtd. in Glassman 86).

Perhaps no author was better poised than Trollope to translate these mid-Victorian currents into a richly *sociological* variation on the geopolitical aesthetic. As well as an astute ethnographer of provincial clergymen and London MPs, Trollope was an avid traveler who wrote extensive accounts of his visits to the West Indies, North America, and South Africa. Yet, while Trollope embraced the "Greater British" vision of expanding Anglo-Saxon culture and blood, he was at best ambivalent about territorial empire and stridently critical of Disraeli's Tory vision. Chapter 3, "Trollopian 'Foreign Policy': Rootedness and Cosmopolitanism in the Mid-Victorian Global Imaginary" looks at Trollope's multi-faceted oeuvre to demonstrate the centripetal and centrifugal cross-currents in his writings and the distinct notions of sovereignty they sustain. Taking the present-day interest in "actually existing cosmopolitanism" for its starting point, the chapter shows that in the mid-Victoria era, the word "cosmopolitan" was more likely to evoke the impersonal structures of capitalism and imperialism than an ethos of tolerance, world citizenship, or multiculturalism. Trollope's Barsetshire series eulogized England's rootedness while his travel narratives affirmed a tentacular global expansion—thus creating a two-part "foreign policy." In evoking the asymmetrical play between heirloom "rootedness" and capitalist "cosmopolitanism," Trollope's global imaginary illuminates the difficulties of a genuinely negotiated rooted cosmopolitanism. In the 1870s, on the cusp of the New Imperialism, this tense dialectic between a rooted heirloom sovereignty and cosmopolitan outreach collapsed, ushering in a new Trollopian form: the "naturalistic narrative of capitalist globalization." In vividly dramatizing the experience of breached sovereignty and the trope of the alien insider, novels like *The Eustace Diamonds, The Way We Live Now* (1875), and *The Prime Minister* (1875–6) instance the naturalistic variation on sociological realism which arose prior to the influence of Émile Zola.[16]

---

[16] In thus coining the term *naturalistic narrative of capitalist globalization* to describe a Trollopian genre—in effect, a naturalistic engagement with a metropolitan historical phenomenon sometimes described as "reverse colonization" (e.g., Arata "Occidental") but which might be more comprehensively put as "reverse *globalization*"—I do not suggest that Trollope's novel is the only example that might defensibly be described as a "narrative of capitalist globalization." To the contrary,

Chapter 4, "'India is "a Bore"': Imperial Governmentality in *The Eustace Diamonds*," focuses on one of the best-known examples of the genre as well as Trollope's most sustained meditation on South Asia. In doing so, the chapter complicates Trollope's reputation as a formally dull and politically complacent realist. While most Trollope novels exemplify an engaged sociological realism, *The Eustace Diamonds*—famously influenced by Wilkie Collins's *The Moonstone*—channels the author's growing disdain for the theatrical style of the emerging New Imperialism. As the most formally distinct of the Palliser series, *The Eustace Diamonds* explores the relation between two classic realist characters (Lucy Morris and Lord Fawn) and the Sawab of Mygawb, a "non-character" who marks the novel's geopolitical unconscious. Through a narrative triangulation of *realpolitik* (marital, political, and geopolitical), the novel points to the imperial governmentality consolidating behind an affect of technocratic boredom on the one hand and, on the other, a show of imperial aesthetics. One of the most distinct formal features of this exceptional work is the anti-heroic Lizzie Eustace whose exceptional characterization personifies the Tories' performative arts.

For Trollope, as for many like-minded contemporaries, the New Imperial posture was the handiwork of Benjamin Disraeli, the Tory's leading impresario from the 1860s through to his death in 1881. As Michael Ragussis has shown, the author of the Pallisers regarded Disraeli (who had been baptized at age twelve) as a kind of "secret Jew" whose simulated Christian identity was more pernicious than avowed Jewishness. In a wide variety of late-1860s and 1870s writings, Trollope figures his aversion to Disraeli through a "conjuring" political agency. But in *The Eustace Diamonds*, it is Lizzie rather than the Jewish Emilius who most piquantly embodies the Tories' imperial performativity. A Disraeliesque schemer, Lizzie introduces a stylistic referentiality that is alien to Trollope's customary sociological register. She becomes the sign of a Trollopian power to stretch form beyond the crude villainy of the anti-Semitic scapegoat.

Chapter 5, "'Dark, like me': Archeology and *Erfahrung* in Wilkie Collins," transits from Trollopian naturalism to the Victorian era's most famous sensation novelist. Although Collins shared Trollope's engagement with the transnational currents of mid-Victorian-era experience, the form and tone of his fiction are strikingly different. The perception of breached heirloom sovereignty that dominates Trollope's naturalistic narratives gives way to multi-perspectival narration,

---

almost every work discussed in this book, and many more besides, could be called "narratives of capitalist globalization" in some form. The specifically (pre-Zolaesque) "naturalistic narrative of capitalist globalization" that recurs throughout this book (reappearing in Chapter 6 to characterize Flaubert's *Madame Bovary* and, in Chapter 8, to designate a style of realist television) is a terminological convenience—not an attempt to universalize any one form of engagement with transnational processes and still less to insist that only naturalistic metropolitan forms from the Anglophone heartland can body forth narratives of globalization's *longue durée*. While this is, to be sure, a book primarily *about* the realist formal experiments produced through British experiences of the global, it does not assume that British viewpoints were more valuable or even, in the long run, more determinative than other contemporary viewpoints—including not only the viewpoints of other geopolitically dominant nineteenth-century powers such as France or the United States, but also those of imperial contact zones, as well as non-Western cultures in general.

elaborate plotting, and outlandish events that conduce toward an almost postmodern notion of sovereignty as porous and pluralized. Thus, not anxieties over sovereignty, but the quest for integrated histories of transnational experience is the crux of Collins's experimental narratives. While Trollope's fiction often vilifies racialized figures of otherness like Emilius, Collins's mixed-raced characters migrate to the foreground where their unconventional stories stimulate the rendering of that historically cumulative form of experience which Walter Benjamin called *Erfahrung*.

In his famous essay on Charles Baudelaire, Benjamin described art's task as the filling in of "blank spaces"—a charge anticipated by some of Collins's most ambitious fictions. *Armadale* (1864–6), a novel begun midway through the U.S. Civil War, uses fictive archeology to explore the disavowed history of Britain's participation in Atlantic slavery, while *The Moonstone* (1868), often read as a "mutiny" narrative, traces a multi-authored path to "Discovery of the Truth." The first of two proximate experiments in a Collinsian variation on the geopolitical aesthetic, Ozias Midwinter's story reaches back to early-nineteenth-century Barbados to excavate a submerged Atlantic experience before giving way to conventional abolitionist universalism. In *The Moonstone*'s more sustained experiment, Ezra Jennings, another mixed-race character, provides experimental access to the differently situated history of imperial violence in "the East." A character whose crucial piebald knowledge "is entirely out of the experience of the mass of mankind" (388), Jennings enables a formal shift from detective narrative to utopian romance—a genre we might specify as an *anti-naturalistic* narrative of capitalist globalization.

The next chapter, "The Adulterous Geopolitical Aesthetic: *Romola* contra *Madame Bovary*," turns to George Eliot, the author whose 1876 novel, *Daniel Deronda*, ran concurrently with Trollope's *The Prime Minister*, making Eliot's protagonist the philo-semitic counterpart to Ferdinand Lopez. Like Collins, Eliot experimented with diverse alternatives to naturalistic realism. Yet, in Eliot's case, these formal innovations become especially visible in comparison to a French variation on the narrative of capitalist globalization: Flaubert's landmark novel of adultery, *Madame Bovary* (1856). Whereas Auerbach described Flaubert's naturalism as the "serious imitation of the everyday," Lukács observed the displacement of a "typical character" such as Walter Scott's Waverley or Ivanhoe by a hedonistic consumer and adulteress, signaling bourgeois decadence, annihilated experience, and political stasis.

Recent scholarship on the "literary channel" between Britain and France has called attention to the dialogue of Anglo-French forms, yet *Madame Bovary*'s impact on the transnational marriage plot is as yet under-explored. Although Eliot left behind no recorded commentary on Flaubert's novel (and may possibly never have read it), Flaubert's influence on British domestic fiction is both explicit (as in Mary Elizabeth Braddon's 1864 *The Doctor's Wife* which concludes happily by eschewing consummated adultery) and implicit (as in Trollopian novels like *The Eustace Diamonds, He Knew He Was Right*, and *The Prime Minister*, all of which narrate the pitfalls of marriage beyond the happy endings Trollope winkingly normed at the close of *Barchester Towers*).

A kind of Lukács *avant la lettre*, Eliot turned to historical fiction by way of bypassing the naturalistic tendency to figure broken marriages like that of Lopez or Eliot's own Gwendolen Harleth. Eliot is in fact a significant novelist of adultery, a narrative structure that haunts the stories of Hetty Sorrell, Maggie Tulliver, Mrs. Transome, Dorothea Brooke, Rosamund Vincy, and (as I shall argue) Romola. Written at the height of British enthusiasm for the Risorgimento, Eliot's historical fiction is palpably detached from the kind of "romance of Italy" one finds in Italophiles from George Meredith to G.M. Trevelyan. Instead, Eliot's return to an era and locale famous for its "Machiavellian moment" seeks to resist the naturalistic impulse by imagining Romola as a world-historical Antigone and female typical character modeled partly on the genres made famous by Scott and George Sand. Following Sharon Marcus's suggestion to "just read" (*Between*), one finds Romola replacing the alien Tito as the head of a household, allegorizing a new kind of female subject.

Chapter 7, "Where Liberals Fear to Tread: E. M. Forster's Queer Internationalism," is the first of two chapters to follow the geopolitical aesthetic beyond its mid-Victorian distillations. The *mise-en-scène* for Forster's Edwardian-era fiction is no longer imperial disavowal, but New Liberalism's efforts to curb a fully-fledged empire with a vision of global internationalism. Forster was sympathetic to "new" liberal internationalists such as Trevelyan. In part for that reason, scholars since Lionel Trilling have upheld him as liberalism's literary standard bearer and a precursor to liberal philosophers such as Jürgen Habermas and Richard Rorty. Against such assumptions, this chapter focuses on *Where Angels Fear to Tread* (1905) to argue that the embodied ethics in Forster's first published novel flummox liberalism's ethico-political categories—up to and beyond the New Liberal moment.

As what I call "queer internationalism," the Forsterian geopolitical aesthetic bends toward ethics rather than politics and toward affective rather than procedural alliances. *Where Angels Fear to Tread*, a border-crossing realist romance tinged with tragedy and magic realism, makes the volatile encounter between Europe's North and South the scene of vitalizing bodily experiences that transgress national sovereignties without wishing away the eroticized differences nation-states are seen to cultivate. Yet, while Forster's novels explore embodied relations across borders, they do not, in doing so, anticipate political progress, post-imperial justice, or even stable interpersonal ethics. Instead, Forster's dramatic encounters with "the South" trouble liberal ideals of synthesis, mutual recognition, equality, and universality, even as they aspire toward a reconfigured ethic of care (both like and unlike the work of feminist political theorists). As a queer internationalist— a contextualist who embraces difference for its world-enlarging *frisson*—Forster does not nurture the rejuvenated liberalism Trilling proposed (*Forster* 13).

The final chapter, "The *Mad Men* in the Attic: Seriality and Identity, in the Modern Babylon," considers the reinvention of a mid-Victorian form at the turn of the twenty-first century—a comparable moment in globalization's *longue durée*. Connecting the AMC television series *Mad Men* (2007–present) to Trollope's *The Prime Minister* and Flaubert's *Madame Bovary*, the chapter argues that each of these works is a serialized naturalistic narrative of capitalist globalization in which motifs of exile articulate the experience of breached sovereignty in modern milieux from Trollope's City of London and Flaubert's provincial city to *Mad Men*'s Madison Avenue. Though *Mad Men*'s provenance is clearly the neoliberalism of today (not the early 1960s it so lovingly depicts in its first four seasons), the series extends a long line of naturalistic narratives in which the outsider within, often a Jew or probable Jew, assimilates the myriad impacts of globalizing capital. In doing so, *Mad Men* also follows Eliot's *Romola* in exemplifying the periodic resurgence of historical realism which Lukács predicted in *The Historical Novel*.

Whether on television or in print, serialization synchronizes naturalist representation through a slow temporality that enables audiences and characters to share deferred longing for the social transformations once symbolized by revolutionary eras like 1848 and the 1960s. Although *Mad Men*'s objective situation is millennial neoliberalism, the show's reinterpretation of Judaized otherness is rooted in the centuries-long *durée* of capitalist and imperial unfolding. Don Draper is not a "secret Jew" like Lopez, but a *virtual Jew* in whom the minority subject's aberrant particularity and the majority subject's universalistic status collide. Moreover, cinematographic forms like montage reproduce the synchronies of multi-plot fiction, enabling Don's virtual condition to resonate with the experiences of the show's "mad women." Like Emma Bovary, Don is a "madwoman in the attic": a protagonist for whom aestheticism and adultery become the sole consolations for the experience of singing for one's captors.

The concluding Coda, "The Way We Historicize Now," reflects on the antihermeneuticist critical trends that have emerged in force during the course of this book's production. Influential examples of this diverse body of scholarship include Stephen Best and Sharon Marcus's co-edited 2009 special issue of *Representations* on "surface reading," Rita Felski's ongoing critique of "context" (inspired by Latourian network theory); and Franco Moretti's call for digitalized "distant reading." *The Victorian Geopolitical Aesthetic* intersects with this critical project in cultivating strong attention to literary form which is not reflexively "suspicious." But it also insists on historicism's powerful formalist insights—resisting Felski's tendency to regard contextualization as a fatal distraction from "what is in plain view" ("After" 31). Though their call for attention to critical ethics and aesthetics is salutary overall, Best and Marcus's focus on Jameson's *The Political Unconscious* (1981) misses the work of the geopolitical aesthetic: its potential to work against the critical stalemate that pits a surface-focused ethics of reading against a depth-focused politics of reading.

If some of its discernments are deeply synchronic—most especially the prolonged focus on mid-Victorian-era fiction—*The Victorian Geopolitical Aesthetic* is, nonetheless, about a period of time which we inhabit today. The formal cluster of greatest interest to this study—serialized realism in its nineteenth-century and present-day instantiations—would be invisible to an anti-historicist post-hermeneutics that focused on synchronic assemblage alone. As this book shows, the serialized naturalistic narrative of capitalist globalization is one of several variations on the geopolitical aesthetic to spring from what Fernand

Braudel called the *longue durée*. Such genres capture the unfolding of structures that share fundamental commonalities over decades and centuries while simultaneously elucidating the complex effects of incremental change. Thus, whether by elaborating the features of naturalistic genres or finding worlded alternatives in Collins, Eliot, and Forster, this book is committed to recognizing historicism as a constitutive condition of the critical enterprise. From this favorable vantage point, it urges readers to recognize the dialectic of depth and surface, structure and aesthetics, ethics and geopolitics, close and distant reading, and synchronic and diachronic time frames, as the daunting, humbling, and oh-so-inviting challenge of the way we read now.

1

Toward a Victorian Geopolitical Aesthetic

> [L]iterature has in our day received an impulse and a development which may be described as not less extraordinary nor less revolutionary than the impulse and the development which it derived successively from the creation of an alphabet and from the invention of printing . . . [W]e can point to the concurrence of a vast number of new applications and new arrangements that have tended to diffuse education, and not only to cheapen but also to improve and enrich books in a manner previously unexampled . . . At the same time the railway and the steamship, the telegraph and the penny postage, by daily and hourly bringing near us a vast world beyond our limited circles, and giving us a present interest in the transactions of the most distant regions, have enormously increased the number of readers, have of themselves created a literature, and through that literature have had a mighty influence upon the movement of the time.
>
> E. S. Dallas, The Gay Science (1866)

In "The Ethical Current," the long final chapter of *The Gay Science* (1866), *Times* literary critic, E. S. Dallas, contemplated the relation between contemporary literature and ethics. Although the goal of his ambitious tome was to develop a "critical theory" of art, its "processes," and "its influence in the world" (1:4), the passage I have taken for my epigraph finds Dallas locating literature in the same vortex of modern forces which interests present-day scholars in many disciplines. In a recent essay on British political thought, for example, Duncan Bell describes "the increasing sensitivity to the pervasiveness of global interconnections" which began in the mid-eighteenth century ("Dissolving" 527). And in his 2009 study of the British world-system, John Darwin writes that industrialism "transformed the geographical space within which people in the British Isles could imagine their lives." Informing that momentum was the sheer "velocity with which information and ideas could circulate" (47–8)—the same "new applications and new arrangements" that led Dallas to conclude that the railway, telegraph, and steamship, along with the decreased costs of print and postage, had created a global literature that was "a mighty influence upon the movement of the time" (2:311–12).[1]

---

[1] On the railway, Schivelbusch's classic *The Railway Journal* remains crucial, but see also Daly, "Railway." For a recent study of how the arrival of newspapers "affected a society formerly

Dallas's perception of the growing proximity of the "vast world beyond our limited circles" was augmented by his views on the nineteenth-century novel. "To transport us into new villages which we have never known, to lodge us in strange houses which we have never dreamt of, to make us at home among new circles of our fellow-creatures," he wrote, are among the ways in which writers of fiction expand "the range of our sympathies" (2:286–7). This belief in the close-knit relation of literature and ethics may bring to mind Lionel Trilling's claim—offered in response to a mounting Cold War—that the novel provides the modern world with its "most effective agent of the moral imagination" (*Liberal* 214). In our own day of neoliberal triumphalism, a new generation of literary critics offers comparable perceptions, describing narrative fiction's facility for "creative world-formation" (Schoene). If there is a thread running through these different meditations on "the ethical current," it is the conviction that literature is a vehicle through which greater apprehension of modernity's ever-larger scale can foster hope for intimacy and common endeavor.

It is worth noting, however, that Dallas begins his discussion with a historical concern: "when we attempt to understand or to delineate the age we live in, we are apt to forget that we have no chance of viewing it from a sufficient distance—that we are too much in it to be able to see how it looks on the broad plain of history" (2: 243). Here too he anticipated an enduring modern predicament. In *The Concept of the Political* (1927), Carl Schmitt reminded his readers that it is impossible to "say anything worthwhile about culture and history without first becoming aware of our own cultural and historical situation" (80). Over the course of *The Gay Science*, Dallas struggles valiantly to transcend the constraints of lived time and space. As he diagnoses the decline of public heroism, he sweeps over topics from the flourishing of Plutarch in a decadent Greece, to the invasion of the Goths, and the history of modern Venice. Though we can no longer take seriously the positivistic *telos* of a "gay science" of ethics, we can appreciate Dallas's belief that judging the contemporary world is an inherently historicist endeavor.[2]

Dallas's remarks provide a fitting prelude to *The Victorian Geopolitical Aesthetic* in that it too is concerned with theorizing literature's globality "on the broad plain of history." The current global turn finds humanistic scholars determined to foster ethical responsibility to otherness while negotiating long-term processes and world-scale structures that may be more favorable to macrosociological analysis and "distant reading" than to a literary practice rooted in the close, the nuanced, and the contextual.[3] Dallas's belief that novels transport us to "new villages which

---

accustomed to slower rhythms of publication" (4), see Rubery; and on the telegraph as exemplum of the Victorian era's new "information technologies" (3), see Menke.

[2] On Dallas's "physiological psychology" of the novel, see Dames, *Physiology* 67.

[3] On "distant" as opposed to close reading, defined as a "focus on units that are much smaller or much larger than the text: devices, themes, tropes—or genres and systems," see Moretti "Conjectures."

we have never known" may strike us as an auspicious cosmopolitan impulse; but it may also strike us as a worrisome pretense of knowing those who do not speak for themselves. The task of mediating these different ethical insights requires a critical awareness of the relevant "cultural and historical situations"—the nineteenth century's and our own. This book seeks to theorize and develop that awareness through a formulation of the "geopolitical aesthetic" derived from Victorian-era global contexts that remain relevant to, and often resonant in, our own turn-of-the-millennium culture.

By way of introduction, this chapter explores the ethical focal points of recent scholarship on cosmopolitanism and the new Atlantic studies while elaborating the theoretical commitments that underlie this book. As developed in the chapters that follow, the work of exploring the Victorian geopolitical aesthetic entails considering cultural expressions such as literature to be "methodologically inseparable" from overarching and underlying geohistorical structures (Bourdieu and Wacquant 105). Yet insofar as the globalization of capital has entailed long-evolving structural transformations that elude conscious experience, the challenge of working through the geopolitical aesthetic is to light up this ongoing story without losing sight of the concrete conditions that spurred contemporaries like Dallas to speak of the 1860s as a "revolutionary" era. Fredric Jameson has described a "geopolitical unconscious" that renders history in aesthetic form; but the idea has not yet been tested in nineteenth-century contexts.[4] By contrast, scholars of cosmopolitanism have focused on the Victorian era but without elaborating the relation between nineteenth-century ethics and the structural processes of global expansion. More recently, another breed of literary critic has begun to charge historicism with a fatal inattention to literary form. As against a depth model of hermeneutics, Rita Felski, for instance, has called for the need to "respect . . . what is in plain sight" ("Context" 585).

Can a single critical practice achieve all of these ends, combining ethical critique with a formally nuanced, structurally acute, and synchronic as well as diachronic theory of the Victorian geopolitical aesthetic? The belief that it can is the underlying premise of this book. In this chapter, I explain the critical wish list that developed over the course of writing including: 1) the joining of ethics and geopolitics; 2) a historical materialism that recognizes both the synchronic and diachronic dimensions of nineteenth-century history; 3) a corresponding openness to the normative aspirations of both poststructuralism and the Enlightenment; and, finally, 4) renewed attention to literary form. I begin by explaining how the first three desiderata can shape a critical practice of seeking out "actually existing" forms of transnationality. The remainder of the chapter shows how attention to literary form builds on the latter practice to find the Victorian geopolitical aesthetic at work.

---

[4] Jameson himself has more deeply explored nineteenth-century fiction, albeit with little emphasis on geopolitics, in *The Antinomies of Realism* (2013), a book published just as this study was completed. For my preliminary thoughts see the Coda.

ACTUALLY EXISTING TRANSNATIONALITY

The notions of *cosmopolitanism* circulating among Victorianists and others are part of the broad multidisciplinary interest in the topic which began in the 1990s, a decade that saw the end of the Cold War as well as increasing attention to globalization. The sociologists Steven Vertovec and Robin Cohen have described this cosmopolitan turn as a "new politics of the left" which encompasses visions of global democracy or transnational social movements; the advocacy of a "post-identity politics of overlapping interests and heterogeneous or hybrid publics"; as well as the valorization of "behaviours, values, or dispositions" that manifest "a capacity to engage cultural multiplicity" (1). Notably, it is the last of these desiderata which has been of greatest interest to scholars such as Amanda Anderson, who has led the way in fashioning a literary practice focused on a particular nineteenth-century *ethos*. In *The Powers of Distance* (2001), she defines cosmopolitanism to entail "reflective distance from one's original or primary cultural affiliations, a broad understanding of other cultures and customs, and a belief in universal humanity" (63). Anderson thus conceives cosmopolitanism as an embodied aspect of character rather than, say, the evocation of global democracy, or the description of transnational practices, spheres, or contexts. Her focus on ethos is deliberate. While today's cosmopolitan discourses are alert to global politics as well as cultural diversity, she makes clear, nineteenth-century precursors were geopolitically reactionary or naïve (90).[5]

Anderson's readiness to set aside nineteenth-century geopolitics, the more deftly to explore the era's ethical payload, invites a supplementary line of inquiry. Extending transnational study beyond ethical focal points, this critical practice would engage structural process as well as ethos, exploring the nineteenth century's "awareness of geopolitical conditions" alongside its moral discourse (90). Of course, scholars working under the sign of "transnationalism" often explore material structures. But since scholarship of the latter kind tends to yield descriptive rather than recuperative analysis (if not criticism reflexively skeptical of the norms it unearths), the question remains whether nineteenth-century study can combine a potentially affirmative emphasis on ethics with the in-depth description of an aggressively capitalist and imperial age. In hazarding a tentative answer of "yes" at the outset of this book, I am not proposing to valorize Victorian geopolitics. But I do want to recognize the nineteenth century as the visible precursor of our own globalizing moment: the scene of multifarious world perspectives, democratic projects, heterogeneous publics, and transnational encounters (some recuperable for present-day ethics, a great many more merely worthy of illuminating historicization). The critical practice proposed in this book thus aims to integrate the geohistorical as well as aesthetic dimensions of literature's globality,

---

[5] See also Agathocleous and Rudy, whose special issue on the topic defines *cosmopolitanism* as "an ethos that attempts to encompass all humanity while remaining attentive to the pitfalls of humanism" (390).

exploring the manifold intersections of embodied ethics, embedding structures, and experimental forms.

To put this point another way, the nineteenth century was an era of flourishing *actually existing cosmopolitanisms*. Bruce Robbins uses this phrase in his introduction to *Cosmopolitics: Thinking and Feeling beyond the Nation* (1998) to contrast the cosmopolitan conceptions of the 1990s to their Enlightenment antecedents. Whereas the abstract cosmopolitanism of Kant's day projected an elitist "view from above," the term now seeks to capture a wide range of "transnational experiences that are particular rather than universal and that are unprivileged—indeed, often coerced" (Robbins, "Introduction" 1). Such pluralized cosmopolitanisms are deliberately modest: to admit that "cosmopolitanism is located and embedded" is to situate one's object of study and then "measure such critical, normative power as may remain to it" (2–3). In her contribution to the volume, Anderson describes this critical temper as "casual normativity" ("Cosmopolitanism" 196). Straddling poststructuralism's ethical commitment to alterity as well as the Enlightenment's vision of universal justice, the new cosmopolitanisms are resolutely pluralist but eager, nonetheless, for a normative horizon beyond mere endorsement of multiplicity or hybridity.

Of course, with their largely present-day address, the essays in *Cosmopolitics* do not call on readers to embark on historicist projects or probe cosmopolitanism's nineteenth-century forms. The project of "actually existing cosmopolitanism" they define entails revising eighteenth-century ideals by the light of turn-of-the-millennium materialities. Nonetheless, the Romantic and Victorian eras were periods of noteworthy backlash against Enlightenment abstraction. From a mid-Victorian perspective, the term "cosmopolitanism" was more likely to evoke the structures of capital and colonial expansion than an ethos of tolerance, world citizenship, or multiculturalism (Ch. 3); while for J. A. Hobson in the first decade of the twentieth century, *cosmopolitanism* indexed a worrisome contrast to the more rooted agency of *internationalism* (Ch.7). Exploring the nineteenth century's actually existing transnationality thus presents no antiquarian enterprise, but the chance to historicize a century of dynamic global exchange.[6]

The Victorianist practice I propose can be productively compared to the new Atlantic studies prominent among many Americanist scholars (see also Ch. 5). Indeed, Atlantic studies bears a kind of family relation to cosmopolitan critique through the influence on both of *The Black Atlantic* (1993), Paul Gilroy's groundbreaking effort to reconceive modernity through its "constitutive relationship" with diasporic Africans (17).[7] Gilroy is a pivotal partner for the new

---

[6] Although this book describes several situated instances of "actually existing" cosmopolitanism, by and large I prefer the more neutral term *transnationalism* to denote the work of building non-nation-centric frameworks and practices for critical and historical analysis. For comparable approaches to "internationalism," see, for example, Robbins, *Feeling Global* and Brennan.

[7] Anderson singles out Gilroy to exemplify the kind of cosmopolitanism which blends ethical and geopolitical awareness (*Powers* 90; note 36). Although her reference is to *Against Race: Imagining Political Culture Beyond the Color Line* (2000), a book less central to Atlantic scholarship, Anderson elsewhere aligns her project of recuperating a critical cosmopolitan tradition within Western culture

cosmopolitanisms, not least because his work exemplifies a comparable straddle of poststructuralist ethics and the Enlightenment project of modernity. Thus, while Gilroy argues that black Atlantic experience both "found[ed] and temper[s]" a modernity hitherto distorted by the racializing logics of nationalism and eurocentricism (17), he retains the cosmopolitan idea of modernity as substantively global and universalizable.[8] To be sure, since Gilroy focuses on the Atlantic world, not the world at large, his "transnational and intercultural perspective" is, arguably, provincial and even eurocentric (15). "Blacks might be internal to the West," writes Neil Lazarus, but according to *The Black Atlantic*, "modernity is still a Western, and not a global phenomenon"—one in which the experiences particular to "vast regions of the 'non-West' are conspicuously absent" (62–3).[9] This difficulty notwithstanding, Gilroy's book is significant for its readiness to historicize the black Atlantic as, in effect, a mode of actually existing cosmopolitanism. With New World slavery as the transnational structure in which black Atlantic experience is rooted, Gilroy's case for a vital diasporic culture places ethics and geopolitics in the same historical frame. Black Atlantic poiesis expresses a collective transnational ethos that, borrowing Robbins's terms, derives its "normative or idealizing power" from "actual historical and geographic contexts" ("Introduction 2")—not in spite of them.

Gilroy's historical materialism has, however, been criticized by more recent scholars of the Atlantic. In his account of the "new Atlantic matrix," William Boelhower describes an inventive multidisciplinary practice forged through the assemblage of unconventional archives; detachment from postcolonialism's lingering attachments to the nation-state; and, above all perhaps, assertion of the fundamental differences between land and the "Oceanic order" (91; cf. 94). Noting Gilroy's use of terms like *structure* and *system* to describe the Atlantic, Boelhower objects that such vocabulary tends to "eliminate or downgrade standpoint, individual agency, and the possibility of the appearance of the new and the singular" (91). Thus, whereas Lazarus finds Gilroy's focus on slavery to be too subjectivist—too prone to abstracting the "lived crisis" of remembering slavery from the "systemic crisis" in which such memory is enmeshed (Lazarus 66; cf. Gilroy, *Black* 40)—Boelhower, rejecting structure as an overweening "view from nowhere," regards Gilroy as too deterministic (91).

Elaborating a normative vision that is not so much emancipatory as restitutive, this newer Atlanticism sets out to repay "a debt" to "the submerged and

---

with Gilroy's black Atlantic goal of rethinking modernity through its "constitutive relationships with outsiders" (Gilroy, *Black* 17; qtd. in Anderson, "Cosmopolitanism" 272).

[8] Gilroy describes his "battle to represent a redemptive critique of the present," informed by slavery's "vital memories," as a complement to the "critique of bourgeois ideology and the fulfillment of the Enlightenment project under the banner of working-class emancipation" (71).

[9] Likewise, Gilroy's notion of the Atlantic as a "single, complex unit of analysis" which both constitutes and counters modernity, is subject to an exceptionalism similar to that which prompts his own critique of nationalist paradigms. According to Gikandi, "Gilroy seems to want to write from his own European ... identity and to assume that the 'parochial' obligation to account for the place of the black subject in the new Europe has some kind of universal implication" (597).

the drowned of the slave trade" (94–5). Where Gilroy portrayed black Atlantic experience as integral to a universal modernity, Boelhower claims exceptional epistemological properties for an oceanic "ecology" that he interprets in light of Atlantic contexts (93). The result is a practice caught between commitment to the matrix as a contingent and particularistic formation and an equally strong investment in the Atlantic's enduring exceptionality. Hence, for all the inventiveness and passion of the new Atlantic studies, Boelhower's vision offers no clear alternative to what Paul Rabinow describes as cosmopolitanism's "ethos of macro-interdependencies" (56; qtd. in Robbins, "Introduction" 2). Refusing the straddle of poststructuralist ethics and a global modern project, the new Atlantic matrix articulates compelling restitutive aims only to isolate them from any larger normative horizon.[10]

Nonetheless, Boelhower's subjectivist emphases (the commitment to standpoint, individual agency, and the "new and singular") warrant close attention from Victorianist scholars. Whereas Atlanticists begin with an "absence of documentation," creating novel archives to produce histories "dictated by the conquered" (Boelhower 94–5), Victorianists, almost stifled by the evidentiary mass, wrestle with the footprint of history's self-styled hegemons. As Sharon Marcus notes, the field of Victorian studies, however reconfigured by transnational perspectives, remains resolutely Anglophone. Although recent scholarship addresses "England's traffic with the non-English speaking world," few articles "require knowledge of Scottish dialect, Gaelic, Welsh, Sanskrit, Hindi, Arabic, French, German, Latin, or Greek" ("Same" 679–80). Marcus thus offers two distinct takes on a transnational Victorian studies. In the more auspicious of the two, historicism enables a "truly comparative" criticism that studies "variations and interactions" among and within national literatures, in lieu of pseudo-universal

---

[10] For a critique of this "impulse to redeem the past" on the grounds that the continuity it postulates between present-day ethico-political aspirations and past history is, in fact, ahistorical, see Best (456). Note that Boelhower tries for a more inclusive historical materialism when he occasionally references non-Atlantic locales. At one point, he suggests that the ocean "underpins . . . the modern world-system of capitalism" as well as "the stream of narratives of the African, Jewish, Acadian, Italian, and Armenian diasporas," among others, thus linking the latter narratives with the Atlantic project of assigning retroactive sovereignty to "the drowned peoples of Africa" (95). Here Boelhower reverts to the very language of system which prompted his critique of Gilroy to evoke a patchwork emancipatory project in which some large swath of the world's peoples are configured through overlapping diasporas. This inclusive gesture, no doubt, intends to compensate for the exceptionalism elsewhere claimed for "the Atlantic-world order" (94). But the result would be incoherent even if it did not involve the unexplained embrace of Gilroy's repudiated terms. Boelhower misleadingly characterizes the Atlantic's distinctiveness as primarily *ecological* in nature, even while the history of the slave trade is more self-evidently what "holds all together" in the Atlantic's "common but highly fluid space" (92–3). Thus, when Boelhower writes that "the Atlantic world is made up of many contributing seas, and each of these Atlantic worlds has its own history," positing interconnection between Portuguese, Spanish, French, Dutch, and English variations (99; note 21), one is left to wonder why such a pluralistic vision of the trans-aquatic stops with one major body of water. A glance at Hall's account of Jamaica's history makes clear how events in the Caribbean were bound up with contemporaneous Australasia through the alternately ocean-and land-inflected dynamics of imperialism in its various forms (*Civilising*). With its radically deterritorializing hydroscape and its determination to break down geographic conceptions of "inside" and "outside" (91), Boelhower's practice ought to vigorously seek out any number of transoceanic imperial matrices, not occlude them with an underspecified Atlantic exceptionalism.

categories such as "the Novel" (680). Yet, if this promising historicism tallies with cosmopolitanism's interest in actually existing transnational (or transoceanic) formations—suggesting a comparative practice that explores any number of formal, aesthetic, or ethical keynotes in multiple contexts—Marcus's second reflection casts doubt on such an enterprise. On this more skeptical view, transnational Victorian studies, no matter how sophisticated its geopolitical grasp, "continues to lack . . . linguistic and hence conceptual range." By limiting knowledge of imperialism to Anglophone archives, Victorian studies "reproduces the very dominance of English culture and imperial power such work set out to question" (681–2).

One understands, of course, the scruples that motivate Marcus's oscillation between affirming a geopolitically-informed historiography and asserting the perils of monolingualism. Likewise, one understands the impulse "to make mute or fragmented things speak" which motivates Boelhower's determination to assign retroactive sovereignty to Atlantic subjectivities at precisely the moment when eurocentric formations are stripped of theirs (94). Nonetheless, it is worth thinking about the self-imposed standards that regulate these different critical projects. Whereas Boelhower's Atlanticist is empowered by the avowed gaps in her knowledge, Marcus's Victorianist, no matter how alert to the power relations that condition her archive, is pressed to recall the infinite limitations of her Anglophone practice.[11] Clearly, the same ethical commitment to attending otherness enables, in the one case, generous affirmation of submerged standpoints, and, in the other, unflinching vigilance toward discursive formations that retain their power to dominate and exclude. These differences of context notwithstanding, both kinds of project express deeply felt responsibility to otherness. Moreover, both recognize historicism as that aspect of the critical enterprise which strives to illuminate the concrete conditions from which ethico-political and artistic aspirations spring and in which they either flourish or die on the vine.

My concern, then, is that even insofar as historical materialism is recognized as an indispensable premise for transnational practice, one finds a recurrent tendency to pit cultural expressions such as novel-writing against structural analysis in ways that militate against exploring the actually existing cosmopolitanisms of the past. Expression is disarticulated from structure by the separation of ethics and geopolitics and—more emphatically—by the assumption that desirable standpoints, agencies and singularities are immobilized by structural analysis. These tendencies, moreover, are exacerbated by recent critiques portraying historicization as

---

[11] My point is not, of course, to underrate the benefits of a multilingual criticism able to range across archives (though see Moretti's caution about the limitations of simply reading more ["Conjectures"]). I do, however, wish to compare Marcus's ideal of an extensive Victorianist knowledge to Boelhower's Atlanticist ideal. Boelhower conceives the limitations of Atlanticist expertise as serendipitous opportunities. Quoting the historian Alison Games, he writes that Atlantic history links "several regions, in which no one historian can have the [desired scholarly] competence or expertise," "through multiple perspectives" (Games 750 qtd. in Boelhower 90). "For this very reason," he concludes, "current Atlantic history, at its best, is now . . . methodologically daring . . . as it should be if we consider the ethical and political challenges bequeathed to us by five centuries of modern Western civilization" (Boelhower 90).

the enemy of formal nuance (see Coda). So far from anti- or post-historicist, the geopolitically engaged practice I advocate in this book joins historians such as Manu Goswami in conceiving "categories of self-understanding"—including the category of cosmopolitan ethos—as standing in dialectical relation to "the social contexts of their generation and reproduction" (780). If this critical starting point makes it harder to disentwine ethics from geopolitics, it also makes it necessary to theorize standpoint, agency, singularity, and aesthetic form in light of long-evolving structures and ongoing processes.

Goswami derives her materialist premises from Bourdieu and Wacquant who have described the structural and expressive dimensions of modern social phenomena as "two translations of the same sentence" (Bourdieu and Wacquant 105; qtd. in Goswami 771). Her work exemplifies a recent effort among historians to moderate the impacts of poststructuralist methodology. As against a more purely discursive historiography, such scholarship draws out the sociohistorical—and, I would add, geopolitical—conditions that enable transformations within and across multi-faceted and long-lasting discourses such as nationalism and liberalism.[12] This "axiomatic" connection between structure and cultural expression is, of course, hardly new (Goswami 708), it is, rather, integral to the cultural studies approach of Robbins and Gilroy as well as to the diverse literary criticism of Georg Lukács, Raymond Williams, and Fredric Jameson.

What happens when the focus shifts from culture broadly defined to aesthetic forms of expression such as literature? Up until this point I have argued for a transnational Victorianist practice that attends geopolitics as well as ethos, and structure as well as standpoint. In what follows I specify the added rewards of making the same geopolitical turn a turn also toward literature. Jameson's notion of the *geopolitical aesthetic*—revised in light of nineteenth-century literary perspectives—provides a critical framework for reading actually existing ideals and experience through the prism of evolving world structures.

THE VICTORIAN GEOPOLITICAL AESTHETIC

To call for a literary practice that finds transnational experience embedded in ongoing global structures of possibility is, in effect, to say that topics such as cosmopolitanism can be studied not only as ethos and not only as structure or process, but also as *form*. Comparative theorists of the novel have prepared the ground for this idea in a variety of ways: for example, Margaret Cohen and Carolyn Dever's description of the novel's "inter-national" provenance or Franco

---

[12] Where Goswami shows how discourses of nationalism require deeper structural historicization, Sartori, who builds on her example, makes a comparable case for liberalism ("British"). Both historians use the term "sociohistorical" to distinguish forms of social organization from particular cultural expressions. In this book I substitute "geohistorical" for "sociohistorical" in order to emphasize the decidedly global, transnational, and geopolitical forms of organization which nineteenth-century scholarship must especially attend.

Moretti's notion of "world literature" as a global morphology in which local materialities meet and transfigure novelistic shape ("Conjecture"). Both formulations enable critics to capture literature's worldedness through the interplay of aesthetic expression and geohistorical process—conceiving form as a medium through which transnational processes are encountered, figured, and, to some degree, influenced. Moreover, both formulations, while loosely exemplifying a cultural studies approach to understanding the materiality of discourse, also recognize literary form as—in Lukács's words—literature's most "truly social element" (qtd. in Eagleton, *Marxism* 20).

Lukács's insight has been integral to a long critical tradition in which "specifying the features which uniquely distinguish works of literature from other ideological and cultural forms" is a "matter of prime importance" for Marxist analysis (Tony Bennett qtd. in Wolfson 6). At the same time, however, the Lukácsian tradition, influenced by Jameson's example, has often led to depreciative readings of realism, the Victorian era's dominant fictional form. Thus, if Marxist criticism provides, on the one hand, fecund ground for a Victorianist practice that sees literature's formal plasticity as "chronotopically" marking the movement of actually existing transnationality, on the other hand, influential Marxists like Jameson have, to some degree, hindered that end by diminishing the critical status of realism.[13]

Realism has been subject to two relevant lines of critique: on the one hand a poststructuralist mode of argument which finds realist fiction guilty of naïve referentiality and dubious investment in totality and, on the other, the Lukácsian perspective that tasks literature precisely to apprehend totality, but to do so in a revolutionary and utopian way.[14] If, on the former view, realist fiction naturalizes a bourgeois reality that, in actuality, it helps to construct, on the latter, realism is a genuinely progressive form until it loses momentum after the failed European revolutions of 1848. No longer holist and chronotopic like the fiction of Walter Scott and Honoré de Balzac, post-1848 realism is, for Lukács, a welter of disjointed details that symptomatize and sustain bourgeois stasis.[15]

Lukács's influential account of realism entails three interrelated premises important to Victorianist critics: first, that literature's politico-aesthetic potential should be understood as its ability to capture historical movement; second, that such capture, to be meaningful, requires dynamic political conditions; and, third,

---

[13] Bakhtin's suggestive notion of the *chronotope* as "an optic for reading texts as x-rays of the forces at work in the culture system from which they spring" (426) is another generative concept for historical materialism as well as a significant influence on Gilroy.

[14] For an important counter to such critiques of realism, see Shaw, *Narrating*. I discuss critiques of realism and their impact on scholarship at greater length in the chapters that follow. Note that New Criticism was also dismissive of Victorian aesthetics: as C. Levine writes, many New Critics found Victorian literature undesirably "popular, bulky, and all-too lifelike," in contrast to the "the taut and artful paradoxes of metaphysical lyric and experimental Modernist fiction" ("Formal" 1243).

[15] Nonetheless, as I emphasize in Chapter 8, Lukács regarded the crisis of nineteenth-century realism as a temporary condition that was not intrinsic to realist aesthetics—a position that distinguishes his writings on the topic from Jameson's.

that post-1848 realism is (therefore) doubly defunct since its mode of historicism is fine-tuned toward revolutionary conditions that have failed to materialize. Two further assumptions about realism follow from, though do not originate in, Lukács's analysis. First, the 1848-centric understanding of political history tends to cast British realism, especially compared to French, as the complacent product of a relatively undramatic political culture. Second, the premise of a bankrupt post-1848 realism sets the stage for the interpretation of Modernism as offering a necessary break. Influential Marxist critics such as Jameson thus see Modernism (much as Modernists themselves did), as both artistically and politically superior to realism. Scholars of nineteenth-century literature have often followed suit, preferring the arguably proto-Modernist works of experimental realists to those perceived as classical practitioners of the form. The result is a politico-aesthetic calculus that systematically underrates the vitality of Victorian fiction.[16]

In doing so, such critiques of realism rest partly on the outdated assumption that mid-Victorian Britain was the scene of an insular and quiescent nation-bound culture. Yet, as this book demonstrates at length, the period that saw Wilkie Collins, George Eliot, and Anthony Trollope publishing their major works, were years of intense political self-consciousness and imperial dynamism. Opening in the aftermath of the Indian rebellion and closing with the emergence of the New Imperialism, this supposed age of equipoise was noteworthy for its reinvention of empire at a time when Britain was also reinventing itself as a mass democracy. It is a period to which no criticism focused wholly on the European crises of 1848 can do justice.

In works such as *Postmodernism, or the Cultural Logic of Late Capitalism* (1991), Jameson describes the challenge to art in the Modernist and postmodern eras as one of breaching the cognitive disjunction between localized metropolitan experience and the global conditions that subtend it. Imperialism creates this disjunction by severing the metropole's "fixed-camera view" of itself from the "colonial system" on which it relies ("Cognitive" 349). Imperialism "means that a significant structural segment of the economic system . . . is now located elsewhere, beyond the metropolis, outside of the daily life and existential experience of the home country, in colonies over the water whose own life experience" remains "unimaginable for the subjects of the imperial power" (Jameson, "Modernism" 50–1). As art strives "to invent new and elaborate formal strategies" to represent

---

[16] H. Tucker has argued that Victorian epic poetry, "a genre whose nineteenth-century history Victorian studies have too readily accepted on distorted Modernist terms" (paragraph 3), is comparably under-rated. I discuss the evolution of this Modernist bias, from Henry James to Rancière, in Chapter 6. It is worth emphasizing that the tide has clearly begun to turn. For a compelling study of mid-Victorian "art writing" as the germinal ground for Modernist aesthetics, see Teukolsky. Shaw's *Narrating Reality* (1999) and Beaumont's *Adventures in Realism* (2007) have offered important rebuttals of realist critique. Recent studies that construe British realism more capaciously, in part by exploring its transnational dimensions, include Menke's model of a technologically-inflected telegraphic realism that "translate[s] and reimagine[s] . . . data . . . in a medium that maintained a sense of potential connection to that world" (26) and Agathocleous's wide-ranging work on "cosmopolitanism realism" which argues that, while "realism did not display the self-conscious avant-gardism" of Modernism, "it was no less a response to the new scale and scope of the city" (*Urban* 18).

what would otherwise be absent to metropolitan consciousness, the Modernist "moment" emerges ("Cognitive" 350; cf. "Modernism" 44).

The problem with this compelling formulation is its assumption that the disconnect between metropolitan experience and imperial structure begins (like Modernism), in the late nineteenth century—with the full-blown emergence of the New Imperialism. In actuality, imperialism's spatial disjunction begins much earlier and—as the product of a long-evolving capitalist globalization—is also more multi-faceted than Jameson's focus on territorial empire allows. Thus, as Garrett Stewart notes in his geopolitical reading of Charles Dickens's *Dombey and Son*, "the stylistic fallout from colonialism in British fiction is less exclusively modernist than Jameson claims" (192; cf. 203). To be clear: Jameson is not arguing that Modernism's "new mutation" represents a fresh attempt to grasp modernity's globalizing dynamic; he is arguing that the latter dynamic is a "new and historically original problem" that creates the Modernist geopolitical aesthetic ("Modernism" 44, 51).[17] By contrast, Jameson views most of the nineteenth century as corresponding to "the classical stage of national or market capitalism," a period during which realist representation responded to the intact sovereignty of a fully "immanent" metropolitan life (51). Whereas Modernist and postmodern art face the challenge of spatial disconnection, realism copes with an earlier "logic of the grid" ("Cognitive" 349). The result is a Marxist criticism that has tended to overlook the imperial encounter's aesthetic impact on realism.

Consider, for example, the reading of *Howards End* (1910) which Jameson uses to illustrate the nexus of Modernism and imperialism. Although E. M. Forster was "at best a closet modernist," that is all the more reason, Jameson believes, to note how *Howards End,* a narrative that consciously engages industrial modernity, strikes out new formal terrain through a moment of "spatial perception" ("Modernism" 54, 53). Jameson has in mind the passage in which a hurrying Mrs. Munt speeds northward on a train "under innumerable tunnels." "At times the Great North Road accompanied her, more suggestive of infinity than any railway awakening, after a nap of a hundred years, to such life as is conferred by the stench of motorcars, and to such culture as is implied by the advertisements of antibilious pills" (Forster, *Howards*, Ch. 3; qtd in Jameson, "Modernism" 52).

Notably, it is not the grim reference to cars and advertising which marks the break into "modernist *style*" (54), nor even the denaturalizing trope of the "railway awakening" after a century-long nap. Rather, according to Jameson, it is the evocation of "infinity" which represents the leap into Modernism by combining a spatial representation of "empty endlessness" with a radical indeterminacy of meaning—a formal conjuncture that tackles the allegedly new problem of an

---

[17] See also Cohen who, in writing on sea adventure fiction, has noted the "aesthetic blindspot" of Jamesonian readings that focus on "the postwar critical canon" ("Narratology" 58). Note that R. Williams's *The Country and the City* (1973) articulates something comparable to literature's rendering of a geopolitical unconscious in his discussion of Dickens's use of figurative language and anthropomorphized entities (such as "Shares" in *Our Mutual Friend*) to "dramatise those social institutions and consequences which are not accessible to ordinary physical observation" (156).

absent imperial world.¹⁸ Realist fiction is presumably incapable of this stylistic "hesitation" because, in Jameson's view, it is a "national literature" that depicts a fully bounded lifeworld, with no "missing piece" to provoke any glimpse of a ghostly imperial "outside" ("Modernism" 55, 51). Moreover, as Jameson writes in a more recent essay, realism is an essentially epistemological not aesthetic category, artistically driven "to avoid recognition of deep structural social change . . . and of the deeper currents and contradictory tendencies within the social order" ("A Note" 261, 263). Here the inventor of the geopolitical unconscious claims that realism, by definition, (unconsciously) resists the structures of unconsciousness while (aesthetically) advancing anti-aestheticism. As we shall see in Chapter 6, such views hark back to Henry James's description of the Victorian novel as a genre almost categorically indifferent to the stylistic question of what "composition, distribution, [and] arrangement can do" to "intensify the life of a work of art" (*Notes* 91).¹⁹

While there are productive insights to be gleaned from Jameson's stance on realism, there are also flaws. In building his case for Modernism's allegedly new historical problem, Jameson takes 1884, the year of the Berlin Conference, as emblematic of "the codification of the new imperialist world system" ("Modernism" 44; cf. *Antinomies* 298). Yet, as Chapter 2 shows, a crisis of imperial sovereignty was already in the making in 1788 when Edmund Burke urged the House of Lords to heed calls for "justice" emanating "from all parts of a great disjointed empire" ("Speech" 207). In fact, several forms of global expansion produced the spatial disconnect that Jameson believes was "new" to the late nineteenth century, including: the slaveholding practices that haunt Collins's *Armadale*; the dizzying settler mobility that Trollope's Barsetshire novels strive to offset; the conquest of Seringapatam which shadows *The Moonstone*; and even the transchannel aesthetic exchange in which Eliot fashioned her distinct literary experiments. Contra Lukács and Jameson, realism's formal vitality does not end in 1848 but, in many ways, begins in 1857 with the trauma of the Indian "mutiny" (Herbert, *War*).

We should not be surprised, therefore, to find arresting spatial perceptions analogous to Forster's in the mid-Victorian genre I call the *naturalistic narrative of capitalist globalization*—a form in which motifs of exile push sociological realism beyond thick description to "map" (as Jameson might say) the elusive structures of breached metropolitan sovereignties. Consider Trollope's famous description of the Tenway Junction in *The Prime Minister* (1875–6), scene of the self-obliteration of one of British literature's most disturbing anti-heroes. Significantly, the narrator begins as though enunciating the most homely of Trollopian asides: "It is

---

¹⁸ Compare to Stewart: Jameson renders Modernist style as "a figurative register that can only evoke rather than capture the alienating distances on which metropolitan dominance must ground itself" (188). For an example of Modernist discussion of Jameson's "increasingly influential theory of modernist style," see Moses 47.
¹⁹ See also *Signatures of the Visible* (1992) in which Jameson reiterates the correlation between realism and "an essentially national or local capitalism" and between Modernism and the "stage of imperialism" while further articulating the contradictions of an art form driven by an epistemological quest for "this or that type of truth content" (156–7).

quite unnecessary to describe the Tenway Junction as everybody knows it." But this turns out to be a feint; for in the very next sentence, the narrator proceeds to delineate what "everybody knows" in veritably Balzacian detail.

> From this spot, some six or seven miles distant from London, lines diverge . . . round the metropolis in every direction, and with direct communication with every other line in and out of London. It is a marvellous place, quite unintelligible to the uninitiated, and yet daily used by thousands who only know that when they get there, they are to do what someone tells them. The space occupied by the convergent rails seems to be sufficient for a large farm. And these rails always run one into another with sloping points, and cross passages, and mysterious meandering sidings, till it seems to the thoughtful stranger to be impossible that the best trained engine should know its own line. Here and there and around there is ever a wilderness of wagons, some loaded, some empty . . . and others . . . look as though they had been stranded there by chance, and were never destined to get again into the right path of traffic. Not a minute passes without a train going here or there some rushing by without noticing Tenway in the least, crashing through like flashes of substantial lightning, and others stopping, disgorging and taking up passengers by the hundreds. Men and women . . . look doubtful, uneasy, and bewildered. But they all do get properly placed and unplaced, so that the spectator at last acknowledges that over all this apparent chaos there is presiding a great genius of order. From dusky morn to dark night, and indeed almost throughout the night, the air is loaded with a succession of shrieks. The theory goes that each separate shriek,—if there can be any separation where the sound is so nearly continuous,—is a separate notice to separate ears of the coming or going of a separate train. The stranger, as he speculates on these pandemoniac noises, is able to realize the idea that were they discontinued the excitement necessary for the minds of the pundits might be lowered, and that activity might be lessened, and evil results might follow. But he cannot bring himself to credit that theory of individual notices (517–18).

In Chapter 3, I describe Ferdinand Lopez's "gentle" walk into an oncoming train at the Tenway as the culminating irony for this archetypal stranger in a strange land, a suspected Jew whose radical unknowability marks the collapse of "heirloom" sovereignty. The Tenway Junction, where Lopez is "knocked into bloody atoms" (520) is, thus, a powerful metonym for the spatiotemporal annihilation that ushered in naturalism, one of the most enduring nineteenth-century narrative modes. Moreover, the space of the junction generates its own metonymies, including the "pundits" who guide hapless moderns in their passage through cognitive bewilderment and sensory onslaught. Trollope's idiomatic usage of an Indian word incorporated into English enables him to transform an expounder of Hindu law into a type of metropolitan modernity.[20] The same uncanny doubling haunts "the stranger" who stands in for the modern subject. As the figurative twin of the arch-alien Lopez, "the stranger" discerns that "pandemoniac noises" are

---

[20] According to the *Oxford English Dictionary*, the first English citation of *pundit* occurred in 1661. For supportive studies of realist metonymy, see, for example, Shaw, *Narrating* (which draws inspiration from Auerbach, *Mimesis*) as well as Freedgood, *Idea* which develops the idea that nineteenth-century fiction assembles multifarious "things" in the form of "social hieroglyphics" (25).

crucial to stimulating the pundits' mental activity. His insight anticipates Walter Benjamin's evocation of modern experience as *Erlebnis:* the shattering influx of disjointed stimuli (Ch. 5).

One might be tempted to liken the Tenway Junction to the spatial work of bourgeois fiction which Jameson describes in essays such as "The Realist Floor-Plan." In this well-known piece, Jameson argues that realism after Balzac acclimatizes its nineteenth-century readers to a "new form of space": "the parallel lines of a grid" (374–7).[21] Regarding *The Prime Minister* as the bearer of such a floor plan means assimilating the Tenway's metonymically replete space of global traffic and psychic damage into "an abstract experience of sheer unevenness extending in all directions" (377). Yet, while the experience of uneven multi-directionality is clearly integral to the novel's rendering of metropolitan space ("these rails always run one into another with sloping points, and cross passages, and mysterious meandering sidings"), the *abstraction* of this experience from history, materiality, and lived subjectivity surely is not. Rather, as Chapter 3 shows, *The Prime Minister* neither avoids recognition of the deep structural changes behind the spatio-temporal pressures it depicts, nor fails to generate aesthetic styles through which to depict them. On the contrary, the novel's stylistic play with realist conventions marks the disruptive transition from a realism trained on what "everybody knows" to one refocused on what everybody disavows: the imperial space subtending London's privileged place in the global network.

WORLD LITERATURE

What then if Jameson's formulation were revised so as to recognize the globally-inflected spatialities, textures, and experiences that pervade nineteenth-century literature? To read Victorian fiction as a geopolitical aesthetic would be to view British literature as "world literature" in Moretti's sense while also rejecting the rigid tectonics of core and periphery which shape his assumptions about metropolitan form. According to Moretti, world literature is a "system *of variations*," a long chain of experiments which arises when form migrates from Anglo-French centers to imperial outskirts, creating rich panoplies of aesthetic "compromise between West European patterns and local reality" ("Conjectures" 64). Yet, while Moretti describes such formal mutations as expressive of geopolitics, he portrays English and French form as isolated cases of "autonomous development"—the exceptional germs that precipitate the chain of (literary) history (58). Moretti thus repeats the Jamesonian tic of viewing the classical metropole as an autochthonous structure. By contrast, the notion of a *Victorian* geopolitical aesthetic

---

[21] Jameson's analysis centers on "A Simple Heart" (1877), a tale by Flaubert whose *Madame Bovary* I discuss in Chapters 6 and 8. He argues that only an interpretation focused on Flaubert's retraining of the reader's orientation toward abstract space avoids the error of "symbolic" reading (a hermeneutic more suitable to Balzac's pre-1848 realism), or "stylistic" reading (an approach that "presupposes the modernist aesthetic of a unique personal style") ("Realist" 376).

finds nineteenth-century British fiction inside the "system *of variations*" and, thus, fully subject to global dynamics. Much as black Atlantic poiesis expresses the ongoing repercussions of New World slavery, and just as Modernist literature refracts the spatial disjunctions of high imperialism, so the "Victorian geopolitical aesthetic"—several variations of which this book explores—encompasses the formal metamorphoses that grew from the multiple modes of "worlding" which informed nineteenth-century experience and which, moreover, have continued both to morph and to resonate ever since.[22]

Yet another way of contemplating the critical practice such thinking can inspire is to compare Stewart's predominantly geopolitical reading of *Dombey and Son* and Anderson's predominantly ethical reading of *Little Dorrit*. Stewart, by way of complicating Jameson's formal assumptions, dismisses the latter's classical/national stage, locating Dickens's 1848 novel in a transoceanic matrix—as a "study of mercantile power" (184).[23] Just as Jameson reads Modernism's vision of spatial infinity as an expression of imperial disconnect, so Stewart, borrowing the trope of syllepsis from Michael Riffaterre, notes Dickens's "twin vanishing points of oceanic trade and the intertext of death's 'immortal sea'" (185).[24] Thus, in *Dombey*, as in Modernist fiction, relations of power which cannot yet be experienced as "conscious objects" are rendered as aesthetic "structurings" (193).

---

[22] This book's exploration of *variations* on the "Victorian geopolitical aesthetic," in and beyond the nineteenth century, pushes Jameson's concept—which envisions modernity as a singular totality—toward a more pluralistic conception that emphasizes the myriad effects, aesthetic and otherwise, of modernity's constitutively uneven global development. Casanova's Bourdieuvian conception of literature "as a world," which strives to explain "in both structural and historical terms, how many variables, conflicts or forms of soft violence have remained undetected and unexplained [in literary works] due the invisibility of this world structure," may complement the notion of the geopolitical aesthetic even though its object is not geopolitics as such but, rather, a more circumscribed set of factors specific to a relatively autonomous transnational literary field (79). Like Jameson and Wallerstein, Casanova conceives world-scale historical forces in light of the Braudelian *longue durée*. But like Jameson and Moretti, Casanova persistently locates the origins of world literature in Europe (especially London and Paris)—a tendency that a theory of the geopolitical aesthetic both can and should resist. There is, thus, a difference between, on the one hand, providing specifically "Victorian" perspectives on literature's relation to capitalism's ongoing globalization and, on the other, insisting that Victorian Britain (or Victorian-era France or Europe) is the autochthonous origin for the "world literature" that thereafter emerges. That is, the history of "world literature," like that of capital itself, is likely more rhizomatic than any scholarship fixated on the migration of Anglo-French genres imagines. P. Mukherjee's 2011 special issue, "Victorian World Literatures," has articulated a compatible notion of Victorian literature as "world literature." Like Mukherjee and his contributors, I "take as axiomatic that the 'worlding' of Victorian 'English' literature and that of Victorian empire was an interrelational process" and, like them, I believe this historical process "opens up possibilities of investigating the rise and demise of [literary] forms and styles across a long range of time and space through the analysis of their literary specificities" (2, 14). That said, Mukherjee's idea of a "Victorian 'world literary system'" modeled on Moretti-like distinctions between core and periphery may risk foreclosing these possibilities (16). Another productive case for the "world literary system" is offered in McDonald and Suleiman's introduction to *French Global*.

[23] For supportive readings of *Dombey*, see P. Young, *Globalization* and Nunokawa; for a transnational reading of *Little Dorrit*, Çelikkol Ch. 7. For my own discussion of Dickens's adulterous marriage plot as an expression of the geopolitical aesthetic, see Chapter 6.

[24] Stewart's Rifaterrian definition of syllepsis is "the division from within that overtly sustains two simultaneous strata of apprehensions" (203).

With such formal percipience in mind, Jameson (in his work on postmodern cinema) defines the geopolitical aesthetic as the expression of "an unconscious collective effort" to "figure out" the "landscapes and forces" embedded in global processes that are at once lived and beyond conscious experience (*Geopolitical* 3). Stewart's Jamesonian reading thus makes Victorian literature the scene of powerful geopolitical awareness.

What follows is a question provoked by the new cosmopolitanisms: is such a literature as helpful in cultivating an ethos of macro-interdependencies as it is in illuminating the long-evolving material structures of a fast-globalizing world? Acute in dramatizing the formal capture of geohistorical process, Jameson's criticism is less deft in emphasizing literature's links to the embodied features of lived experience, including those valuable critical stances that Anderson finds in nineteenth-century culture.[25] As Jamesonian chronotope, art illuminates a structural condition that is beyond conscious apprehension, in contradistinction to an art that more decidedly proffers subjective standpoints (such as Boelhower's Atlantic perspectives), or cultural practices that mediate that experience (such as Anderson's cultivated distance).

Is it possible to synthesize these views, understanding literature's engagement with history as both structured and subjective, geopolitical and ethical, formal and embodied? The answer, I think, is yes. Just as history's geohistorical and expressive dimensions are "two translations of the same sentence"—and just as the syleptic capacity to figure two different meanings at once is literature's "sign par excellence" (Rifaterre qtd. in Stewart 185)—so critics need not choose between the entwined critical projects of transnational ethos and transnational form.

Indeed, compared from this perspective, Stewart and Anderson articulate two faces of the same modern problem—the need to negotiate transnational experiences that are structurally embedded but personally embodied. Reading *Dombey and Son* geopolitically, Stewart describes the novel's "whole panoply of equilibrated structural contradictions" as an almost-but-not-quite redemptive achievement: "a formal recompense for totality's absence from every other life sphere" (203). Reading *Little Dorrit* as an ethical text, Anderson reaches a comparable semi-affirmation: Dickens's tendency to align his own critical aesthetic with modern depravity, she shows, eventually compromises his grip on the material world. Thus, while Dickensian ethos turns out to require geopolitical awareness, the geopolitical aesthetic turns out to dream of a redemptive ethics. These critical perspectives complement one another insofar as each recognizes the need to integrate cultural expression and material structures by way of recognizing two normative

---

[25] *The Political Unconscious* famously argues for a Marxism that decenters individual consciousness, avoiding the "mirage" of a utopian moment in which individual subjects "become somehow fully conscious of [their ideological] determination" (273). Although cosmopolitan ethics can be sensitive to collective as well as individual consciousness, Jameson's deep-rooted skepticism toward ethical projects, expressed, for example, in *A Singular Modernity* (2002), stems from unwavering commitment to such decentering. There is, however, a new interest in embodied *affect* if not precisely embodied ethics in *Antinomies* (see Coda).

commitments: the poststructuralist imperative to respect cultural difference and the (as yet unrealized) Enlightenment aspiration to affirming justice for all.

Of course, the critical problem I have so far described is anticipated in many ways by the work of another Marxist critic, Raymond Williams. Although Gilroy, among others, has associated the latter's work with an ethnocentric Marxist tradition, *The Black Atlantic*'s dialectic of structure and poiesis is demonstrably Williams-like.[26] Williams's notion of the *structure of feeling* famously strives to grapple the antinomies of objective embeddedness and subjective embodiment. Moreover, such antinomies are intensified when Victorian literature is no longer conceived as the centripetal product of an impermeable sovereign nation, but, rather, as a "world literature" immersed in a pluralizing global matrix. To be sure, the precise meaning of the structure of feeling oscillates in Williams's corpus, never amounting to a systematic theory of the relation between history's material and expressive dimensions. Still, vis-à-vis Jameson's unconscious geopolitical aesthetic, what is valuable in Williams's (and Gilroy's) approach to tendering material histories is the attention to poiesis and an ethics of the self. The something beyond structured reality that art strives to descry which, for Jameson, is an absent cause that eludes embodied experience is, for Williams, an elusive quality *of* that experience. Mindful of "social forms," Williams nonetheless prizes lived categories such as "consciousness, experience, [and] feeling," conceiving them as bulwarks against structuralist ossification which defy the immobilization of standpoint, agency, and singularity (*Marxism* 128–9).

Then too, Williams is a nuanced critic of form. Long before the recent rapprochement with realism, Williams's 1977 essay, "Forms of English Fiction in 1848," rejected the doctrinaire premise that Europe's failed revolutions ushered in "the moment of the initiation in fiction of a characteristic bourgeois realism" (150–51). Among the several problems Williams finds with that thesis is that 1848 novels such as *Dombey and Son*, Thackeray's *Vanity Fair*, Gaskell's *Mary Barton*, and Emily Brontë's *Wuthering Heights* "can be characterized as bourgeois realism only by an extraordinary flattening" that hides "the complex formation of the real forms." Instead, critics must bear in mind that historical time, unlike a specific date, is perpetually moving: "At any particular point there are complex relations between what can be called dominant, residual, and emergent institutions and practices" (150–51). As he considers various forgotten works of the period almost a quarter century before Moretti's proposal for a project of extra-canonical "distant reading" ("Conjecture" 56), Williams finds multiple residual and emergent forms,

---

[26] For Gilroy's critique of Williams, see *Black* 10–11 and *There Ain't* 49–50. Gilroy rightly claims that the British cultural studies tradition that includes Williams too often lapses "into what can only be called a morbid celebration of England and Englishness" (*Black* 10); yet, there is little in Williams's efforts to integrate the embedded and embodied aspects of history and experience which would preclude a less provincial account. Indeed, Williams at times anticipates the importance of anti-ethnocentrism as when he writes that the "complex process" of historical emergence can never be grasped wholly in "class terms" since "there is always other social being and consciousness which is neglected and excluded: alternative perceptions of others, in immediate relationships; new perceptions and practices of the material world" (*Marxism* 126).

each of which claims sensitive historical explanation. The mainstream ideology of the 1840s, he concludes, did not yield a "major form," and still less a formulaic cultural product ("Forms" 153).

In dismantling the notion of a homogeneous "bourgeois realism," Williams finds two modes of formal experimentation relevant to the "worlded" fiction that this book explores. Brontë novels such as *Jane Eyre*, *The Tenant of Wildfell Hall*, and *Wuthering Heights*, he writes, can be grouped as *subjectivist* fictions that "introduce a new stress on . . . intense personal experience" (156). This diverse category includes multiple techniques for dispersing point of view to enable "very complex seeing" against the stereotype of an overarching bourgeois "point of view" (156, 158).[27] In a second noteworthy discovery, Williams identifies a *subjunctive* mode of narrative in contrast to the straightforward recording associated with classical realism. Through such subjunctivity, novels "introduce a perspective which is not socially or politically available." Thus, while realism "is commonly held to exclude the possibility of an alteration of forces," the presence of the subjunctive in Dickens's novels enables him to "connect [to] things that lay far ahead of him" (161).

As the subsequent chapters will show, variations on a *subjunctive* realism inflect several forms of "world literature" including Collins's sensation novels, Eliot's historical experiments, and Forster's queering international ethics. The naturalistic narrative of capitalist globalization, meanwhile, is a highly *subjectivist* form in providing "intense personal experience"—in Erich Auerbach's words "existential realism" ("Serious" 448)—from the vantage of alienated metropolitan protagonists like Flaubert's Emma Bovary, Trollope's Ferdinand Lopez, Eliot's Gwendolen Harleth, and, more recently, *Mad Men*'s Don Draper. Serial publication accentuates subjectivist and subjunctive dimensions alike insofar as serialization elongates their effects by dispersing them among multiple characters in long-evolving plotlines while simultaneously embedding them in the lived temporality of readers and viewers.

At same time, the geopolitically crucial category of *sovereignty* and the multiple scales over which it holds sway illuminate the contrast between subjectivist and subjunctive forms. Whereas the intense subjectivism of naturalistic narratives focalizes the experience of breached "heirloom" sovereignties (Chs. 3 and 4), the subjunctive fiction of Collins (Ch. 5), Eliot (Ch. 6), and Forster (Ch. 7) moves beyond conventional notions of sovereign autonomy in part through the pluralizing and hybridization of race, gender, nationality, ethnicity, and sexuality which an actually existing transnationality makes possible. Rather than a single mid-Victorian-era form or genre, the "Victorian geopolitical aesthetic" is thus a supple

---

[27] Ermarth's landmark *Realism and Consensus in the English Novel* (1983) has provided an especially influential case for the two-dimensionality of realist perspective. In contrast to the multi-perspectival representation of medieval art," Ermarth writes, "realism represents objects as "incomplete" and "from one vantage point" (16). On this account, realist point of view asserts rational consensus through the production of a "realistic effect" that "homogenizes the medium of experience and . . . objectifies a common world" (x).

framework for studying the narrative experiments that emerged from a process of capitalist globalization which is still ongoing.

That is not to suggest that the pursuit of a multi-faceted and lasting Victorian-era geopolitical aesthetic will magically perfect Williams's long effort to choreograph the tango between structure and feeling.[28] Still less will it harmonize particularity and universality, synchronic and diachronic historical perspectives, or poststructuralism and the Enlightenment, in a single stroke. Then too, some readers may regret that *The Victorian Geopolitical Aesthetic* does not explore the translation and/or circulation of literary works outside Britain where, as Priya Joshi's important work on Indian readers shows, realist fiction was often passed over in favor of romance genres (*Another*). For Joshi, the task of reading Victorian literature as world literature entails combining "methodological insights from history of the book with the sociology of reading" to document "the social life of books" in the context of colonial encounter (*Another* 8–9; cf. "Globalizing"). By contrast, the "worlding" elucidated in *The Victorian Geopolitical Aesthetic* strives to deprovincialize metropolitan forms. As Christopher Prendergast notes, Williams was among those critics to see realist fiction as a genre in which "individual experience and social formation" became "mutually necessary for intelligibility" (18). It follows that "Victorian" literature only becomes more compelling when the actually existing "social formation" it engages is recognized as spatially worlded and temporally world-historical in scope.

---

[28] As Simpson writes, "The degree to which the structure of feeling is *not* articulated to the point of 'theoretical satisfaction,' despite its deployment throughout twenty years of major critical work, suggests a strong resistance to such theorization. It is at once central and vague, an insistence on 'something beyond' the extant debate, without any exact address to the terms of that debate" (43).

2

Imperial Sovereignty
The Limits of Liberalism and the Case of Mysore

> England has taken the lead in solving the problem of constitutional government; of government, that is, with authority, but limited by law, controlled by opinion, and respecting personal right and freedom. This she has done for the world, and herein lies the world's chief interest in her history. She has also had to deal with great problems of her own; among them that of national unity, the long postponement of which is indicated by the present lack of any common name except that of the United Kingdom for the realm, and of any common name for the people. Ultimately she became the centre of a maritime empire, consisting partly of colonies, partly of dependencies, and had imperial problems of both classes with which to deal.
>
> Goldwin Smith, *The United Kingdom: A Political History*, Volume 1 (1899, p. 1)

In this chapter, I describe some of the structures that underlay the Victorian era's "geopolitical unconscious," exploring the landscape of liberal ideas, their limitations in authorizing a stable imperial sovereignty, the consequent crises of liberal imperialism (so-called) which arose in the mid-Victorian decades, and the eventual rise of Tory alternatives. The above-cited passage from Goldwin Smith's 1899 political history is exemplary. Opening on a high note, Smith praises England's constitution as an ideal mixture of law, public opinion, and individual right, only to concede that the more expansive sovereignties of the United Kingdom and British Empire confound this supposed perfection. Like many self-styled liberals, Smith was an avid enthusiast of white settlement "colonies" who regretted the corrupting influence of "dependencies" such as India. The problem of legitimate sovereignty in such territories taxed a long line of thinkers including Edmund Burke, John Stuart Mill, John Morley, Charles Dilke, and J. R. Seeley; and the same problem has attracted modern scholars of empire, including H. V. Bowen, Bernard Cohn, Nicholas Dirks, Karuna Mantena, Mithi Mukherjee, and Sudipta Sen.

In recent years the concept of sovereignty has been central to a cluster of new theorizations including Giorgio Agamben's *Homo Sacer: Sovereign Power and Bare Life* (1998) and Michael Hardt and Antonio Negri's *Empire* (2000). The political theorist Wendy Brown has noted the irony of these interests coinciding with the manifest decline of historically privileged forms of sovereignty, including the sovereign individual of the Enlightenment, the popular sovereignty of democratic political philosophy, and the sovereign nation-state enshrined in the "Westphalian" world order. According to Brown, when theorists like Agamben, Hardt, and Negri try to manage the dilemma of waning sovereignty they end up reviving "a theologically contoured" fantasy of political autonomy in the face of a domain overwhelmed by the economic rationality of neoliberalism ("Sovereignty" 250–51).[1]

Brown's belief that theory's flight into quasi-theology is powerless to combat "capital's historically unprecedented powers of domination" has a special valence for the study of Victorian-era globalization. Implicit in her assertion of capital's hegemony (as in Hardt and Negri's formulation of a globalized "Empire") is the assumption that the nineteenth century's imperial sovereignties have, by and large, completed their work. In other words, the neoliberal governmentality that consolidated at the turn of the twentieth century grew out of imperial formations like those discussed in this chapter—including the "dependencies" that riddled the Victorian constitutional ideals of sovereign citizen, sovereign democracy, and sovereign nation-state.

In admitting "imperial problems" only after first declaring them "solved," Smith exemplified the same kind of disavowal which Seeley immortalized in *The Expansion of England* (1883). There Seeley famously wrote that Britons "seem[ed], as it were, to have conquered and peopled half the world in a fit of absence of mind" (12). According to the historian Bernard Porter, this attitude illustrates the cultural marginality of Victorian imperialism (*Absent-Minded*). But such reasoning overlooks the way that free trade discourse and the popular notion of Britain as a liberal vanguard—"solving the problem of constitutional government . . . for the world"—enabled an aggressive and often violent territorial empire to operate as a geopolitical unconscious. The impact of such mass disavowal became even more blatant after the Indian "mutiny" of 1857–8, particularly for the liberals and radicals who struggled to reconcile an increasingly formal imperial agenda with the nation's professed commitments to advancing freedom. Thus, the mid-Victorian decades discussed in this book, were a period in which long-brewing crises of imperial sovereignty became palpable to metropolitan experience—often articulated through the innovative aesthetics of a diverse body of realist fiction.

---

[1] For Brown, the waning of these once privileged forms of sovereignty is demonstrable even though *sovereignty* "is an unusually amorphous, illusive, and polysemic term of political life," the usage of which varies significantly ("sovereignty is equated for some with the rule and jurisdiction of law and for others with legitimate extralegal action, just as some insist on its inherently absolute and unified nature while others insist that sovereignty can be both partial and visible"). In contrast to Hardt and Negri's notion "that nation-state sovereignty has transformed into global Empire" and to Agamben's claim that "sovereignty has metamorphosed into a worldwide production and sacrifice of bare life," Brown argues that "sovereignty is migrating from the nation-state to the unrelieved domination of capital on the one hand and god-sanctioned political violence on the other" ("Sovereignty" 252, 251).

The story of liberal complicity in empire has been told in a number of recent studies (e.g., Mantena, *Alibi*; U. Mehta; Metcalf; Sartori, "British"). While this chapter revisits the much-discussed pro-imperialism of "advanced" liberals like Mill and Morley, it also highlights the prominent though less-discussed outlook of "Greater British" enthusiasts of white settlement colonies such as Smith, and of Tory imperialists including Benjamin Disraeli. Alongside this broad-strokes account of imperial discourse before and after the Indian rebellion, I offer a case study of what Morley, writing almost a decade later, called "a very remarkable and important episode in the history of English rule in India" (259). This concerned the efforts of Kristna Raj Wodyar, the Rajah of Mysore, to preserve his line through the adoption of an heir—one of several debates over aggrieved Indian royals to reach the ears of the metropolitan public. Although Anthony Trollope's *The Eustace Diamonds* offers the most sustained literary engagement with the topic (Ch. 4), Wilkie Collins's *The Moonstone* opens by depicting the siege in Mysore which culminated in the 1799 treaty and conferred sovereignty on the young Wodyar's heirs for "as long as the sun and moon shall endure" (Morley, "Mysore" 95). Morley's "important episode" concerned the British government's determination to annex Mysore upon the death of the aging Wodyar in lieu of recognizing his adopted heir. In doing so, Britain seemed not only to violate the 1799 treaty, but also to undermine a host of assurances which had been issued to Indian sovereigns after the "mutiny." In fact, the loyalty of these royal allies had been so crucial to restoring order that, in 1858, when the East India Company was abolished and the Crown assumed responsibility for governance of the new Raj, the Queen's Proclamation explicitly assured them that "We shall respect the rights, dignity, and honour of the native princes as our own" ("Proclamation" 233). That these "rights" included the customary right of a childless sovereign to adopt an heir was further clarified in Lord Canning's 1860 despatch on the topic.

As Karl Marx wrote in 1857, a sovereign's right to adoption was "the very corner-stone of Indian society" ("Indian"). Here Marx concurred with Disraeli, a rising Tory M.P., in blaming Lord Dalhousie's aggressive liberal policy of annexing territory under the "doctrine of lapse" for inciting a so-called mutiny.[2] Thus, when six years later, the Queen's government refused to recognize Wodyar's adopted grandson, Morley became one of several public figures to intervene in what looked to be another grievous liberal blunder. As this chapter will argue, the eventual resolution of the controversy in Wodyar's favor foreshadowed the coming of a new imperial dispensation in which liberalism's limitations as a philosophy of

---

[2] Under the *doctrine of lapse*, Britain could refuse to recognize the adopted heir of a childless sovereign and, thus, claim (supposedly) legitimate grounds for annexation (see Qanungo 255 note 8). Annexation entailed ending the contractual relation with a local sovereign and subjecting the seized territory to direct British rule—as part of British India. As the author of "Dangers in India" points out, the ability to adopt an heir was important on religious as well as political grounds to Hindu and Muslim rulers alike. Although Canning's Despatch of April 1860 was intended to assure Indian royals of their rights to adopt, the Rajah of Mysore, for reasons I will explain, was deliberately excluded from receiving notification of the new policy. For Disraeli's July 1857 speech in Parliament, see <http://hansard.millbanksystems.com/commons/1857/jul/27/motion-for-papers>

territorial sovereignty would become ever more salient, indirect rule through local "princes" more central to British imperialism, and, thus, Tory visions of empire would become more prominent in India and Britain alike.

When "mutiny" broke out on May 10, 1857, England's "informal" global dominion already included Ireland, Canada, Australia, the British West Indies, and the South African Cape colony. The Indian army's reach, meanwhile, extended British power to theaters such as Indonesia, China, and Central Asia.[3] Yet, despite such energetic expansion, the Victorian culture of 1857 had yet to develop the coherent image of an imperial state. Thus, the need to explain British imperialism to the British people was—like the need to reform the metropolitan franchise—a preponderant challenge of the post-rebellion decades. It was a task that Tory as well as Liberal luminaries would aspire to meet.

Although narratives of the civilizing mission had circulated among liberal-minded proponents of empire since the early nineteenth century, the more typical tendency before 1857 was to gloss British expansion in light of globalizing commerce—evoking the "free trade imperialism" or "empire of liberty" which historians such as Bernard Semmel and David Armitage have described. Such discourses contrasted the liberal ideal of a commercial empire to the dangers of territorial domination. Whereas an empire on land "must inevitably crush civic life" in both metropole and colony, an empire of trade was seen to facilitate liberty across borders and oceans by proliferating "a common set of interests" (Sartori, "British" 628; cf. Pagden).[4] The comforting notion that British expansion was, at heart, commercial and pacific was the overarching message of metropolitan spectacles like the Great Exhibition in 1851 and the London International Exhibition in 1862. Such events helped to forge the proud conviction that British culture and industry were giving rise to a harmonious global economy.

India's actual condition under British rule—de-industrialized, agrarianized along lines recalling the traditions of British agriculture, and subject to the rule and taxation of the British military and the East India Company—was, from this perspective, as anomalous as it was geopolitically pivotal. On the one hand, the possession of a huge Indian empire had helped to compensate for the loss of American colonies: even a reluctant imperialist like Trollope could describe India as "the most populous and important [dependency] that ever belonged to a nation" (*Australia* 507). On the other hand, rapacious territorial expansion of the kind Collins depicted in *The Moonstone* had created "deep and long-lasting confusion over the question of sovereignty" (Bowen 20). It was one thing for a self-consciously freedom-loving Anglo-Saxon people to spread commerce or

---

[3] As Washbrook notes, the large land-based Indian "war-machine that the British had built up in the course of effecting their conquest" on the subcontinent was kept intact so that it could be "utilized for further conquests and 'police' duties beyond British-Indian borders and around the world" (401).

[4] Beginning in the seventeenth century, politico-economic discourses fostered the notion that since "trade depended on liberty," liberty "could therefore be the foundation" of a certain kind of empire (Armitage 143). The term "empire of liberty" has also been employed to refer specifically to the United States in G. Wood's, *Empire of Liberty* (2009).

promote emigration in the world's temperate zones. It was another to claim sovereignty over conquered "Orientals" in the global south.

So-called liberal imperialism was, thus, neither internally consistent nor reliably expressive of any single liberal logic or philosophy. Liberals could be idealistic about future possibility (as J.S. Mill, a radical, strove to be), consciously pragmatic (Morley), or skeptical and conservative (in the mode of Walter Bagehot, Smith, or Trollope). If "liberal" support for imperialism could mean belief in the globalization of trade, it could also entail a full-blown ideology of rule authorized by the civilizing mission. Self-styled liberals might support white settler colonialism as distinct from imperial rule, or they might fuse these projects, conceiving Britons as destined to settle and spread free trade in the world's temperate zones while civilizing non-whites in the southern hemisphere. In India, liberal ideologies of governance could involve unbending allegiance to anglicizing agendas, or could resemble Tory strategies of "engraftment" which claimed to blend Indian and British traditions. Liberals might thus adhere to Enlightenment universalism by rejecting racial essentialism, or they might embrace the pseudo-scientific category of "race" (as increasingly happened after 1857). And whereas liberal racialists might join Tories in offering racial difference to justify a territorial empire, they might instead shrink from long-term rule over alien peoples. Negotiating such tensions, high-minded liberals might exhort their countrymen to meet the best possible standard of imperial ethics, or urge them to recognize that territorial empires were invariably corrupt and corrupting.

Although discussing liberalism and its limits could, therefore, involve an almost infinite parsing of liberal debates, paradoxes, and anxieties, in this chapter my aim is to historicize the particular liberal dilemmas that coincided with the rich literary fiction of the years between the outbreak of rebellion in 1857 and the Royal Titles Act of 1876. This was a period that saw efforts to formalize and legitimate Britain's empire in a climate distinguished not only by "mutiny" in India, but also brutal repression of the Morant Bay rebellion in Jamaica, Fenian "atrocities" in the metropole, and ongoing debates over parliamentary reform ("Fenianism" 222).[5] These charged mid-Victorian circumstances aggravated tensions that extended back to the eighteenth century, demonstrating the limits of what liberalism of any stripe could contribute to Britain's emerging identity as both a mass (male) democracy and New Imperial power.

"IMPERIAL JUSTICE"

> Your Lordships always had a boundless power and unlimited jurisdiction. You have now a boundless object. It is not from this Country or the other . . .

---

[5] On the 1865 Morant Bay rebellion and the subsequent effort on the part of liberals like John Stuart Mill to prosecute Governor Eyre for unlawful abuse of power, see Chapter 5 below as well as Hall, *Civilising*, Semmel, *Governor*, and, most recently, Kostal. On mid-Victorian Fenianism, see also Newsinger.

that relief is applied for, but from whole tribes of suffering nations, various descriptions of men, differing in language, in manner and in rights, men separated by every means from you. . . . [T]hey are come here to supplicate justice at your Lordships' Bar; and I hope and trust that there will be no rule . . . which will prevent the Imperial justice which you owe to the people that call to you from all parts of a great disjointed empire.

Edmund Burke, "Speech on Opening of Impeachment," February 15, 1788

What do you think would be the probable effect of carrying on the government of India . . . by means of a Secretary of State for India?

I should think it would be the most complete despotism that could possibly exist in a country like this; because there would be no provision for any discussion or deliberation, except that which might take place between the Secretary of State and his subordinates in office, whose advice and opinion he would not be bound to listen to; and who, even if he were, would not be responsible for the advice or opinion that they might give.

J. S. Mill testifying before the Select Committee on the East India Company's Charter, 1852 (*C.W.* 30)

In his 1866 article in *The Fortnightly Review*, Morley, a rising figure in advanced liberal circles, warned that the debate taking place over Mysore was of such consequence that its decision would "mark the turning-point of the career of England in India" (259). A few months later, the anonymous author of "The Dangers in India," published in *Macmillan's Magazine*, was equally grave: "A vague sense of coming evil seems to have taken possession of the minds of very many of our countrymen in India. It resembles the presentiment which was common . . . before the great Mutiny" (412).[6] Like *The Moonstone*, which began running several months after these articles appeared, Morley's story begins with the 1799 siege of Seringapatam, after which Mysore fell "by right of conquest" to the East India Company (Morley 260)—the privately-owned trading company through which Britain ruled its Indian empire until 1858. In the wake of this victory establishing British preeminence on the subcontinent, the Company did not opt for direct rule of Mysore but, instead, signed a treaty conferring sovereignty over the region on the Wodyars, an old Hindu dynasty. The state of Mysore was thus part of the large fraction of Britain's empire in South Asia—about one fourth—which was not governed directly by British officials either before or after 1857.

Indirect rule entailed establishing ongoing relationships with a diverse group of local rulers including *rajahs, nawabs,* and *desais*. Since the so-called princely states were "semi-sovereign political entities whose varying shades of internal sovereignty" depended on existing treaties and customs, their status varied considerably (Sever 37). According to Lord Salisbury, Secretary of State for India during

---

[6] According to the Wellesley Index, the author is probably J. W. Wilson about whom almost nothing is known.

much of the Mysore debate, the sovereignty of Indian states under indirect rule was "nominal" (qtd. in Brumpton 175).[7] But as Salisbury was well aware, the allegiance of these royals, including that of the Rajah of Mysore, was widely believed to have been critical in containing the rebellion. The crisis reported by Morley thus concerned the British government's plans to annex Mysore upon the death of the same loyal rajah who had been installed after Britain's defeat of Tipu Sultan in 1799.

How was it that the misfortunes of a single Indian prince could be seen as a potential turning point in Anglo-Indian relations by an advanced liberal such as Morley in the highbrow pages of *The Fortnightly Review*—providing, as Chapter 4 will argue, a key context for Trollope's most distinctive Palliser novel? The answer requires us to explore the notion of imperial sovereignty which began to develop in the eighteenth century as well as the forms of imperial justification to which it gave rise.

At the time of Warren Hastings' trial in 1788, the East India Company's treaty with the Mughal emperor, promising military protection in exchange for the right to collect revenue, was—and was to remain for another 70 years—the principal foundation for Britain's sovereignty in India. Hastings, who had been Governor-General of India between 1772 and 1785, was charged with a wide range of abuses including violations of the Company's treaties with Indian sovereigns.[8] As Burke's stirring speeches suggest, the trial was driven partly by the metropolitan need to reconcile imperialism with the idea of Britain as a justice-loving nation. "God forbid," Burke exhorted, that "when you try the Cause of Asia in the presence of Europe, there should be the least suspicion that the Cause of Asia is not as good with you, because the abuse is committed by a British subject" ("Speech" 208).

Burke's eloquence notwithstanding, the House of Lords acquitted Hastings in 1795. Paradoxically, the trial's final result was to confirm the reformed East India Company as "the legitimate agent of British interests" and the Company's arrangement with the Mughal emperor as "a sufficient basis on which to predicate imperial occupation" (Dirks 8). Thus, while Uday Singh Mehta and Jennifer Pitts have contrasted Burke's arguments to the views of pro-imperial liberals like J.S. Mill, in the long view the Burkean ideal of "Imperial justice" helped to underwrite the high-minded liberal rule advocated by Mill in the Victorian era ("Speeches" 207). Indeed, during the "mutiny," the Victorian state wrapped itself in Burke's mantle, adopting the rhetoric of imperial justice as an "assurance" to

---

[7] For simplicity's sake I use "Lord Salisbury" throughout this chapter even though the correct title for the Secretary of State, until April 1868, was Viscount Cranborne.

[8] In 1764, the British entered into a contractual relation with the defeated Mughal emperor in lieu of eliminating him so as take advantage of his symbolic authority among Indian people of "almost every state and class" (Lord Wellesley, qtd. in Cohn 170). In the case of so-called princely states such as Mysore the contractual relation was with a local sovereign, sometimes installed by the British, like Mysore's Wodyar. On the impeachment see, for example, Clark, Dirks, U. Mehta, M. Mukherjee, and Suleri.

Indians while reissuing Burke's impeachment speeches to facilitate the British public's understanding of colonial conflict (M. Mukherjee par. 80; note 105).[9]

In the decades after Hastings' acquittal, the East India Company shed its reputation for "fury and avarice" and sought to operate as a punctilious governing body (Burke, "Speech" 215). By the time the Company's charter was renewed in 1833, anglicization, a policy professing to westernize Indians, had entered the official discourse, challenging the more conservative ("orientalist") vision of "engrafting" British ideas onto Indian culture.[10] The civilizing mission so-conceived extended to those numerous states in which the Company had signed treaties with local sovereigns, enjoining them to practice good government under British supervision in exchange for military security.

In his well-known essay, "Representing Authority in Victorian India," Cohn describes this contractarian idiom of fairness and contract as an insufficient foundation for sovereignty in India. Mughal rule on the subcontinent had been predicated on ritual incorporation, including a presentation of gifts through which the emperor and his servants were symbolically unified. Rituals such as the *durbar* were important to constituting a "relationship between the giver and the receiver," while the exchanged gifts, "took on the character of heirlooms" (168–70). As Cohn portrays them, India's pre-1858 British rulers were insensible to these meanings since they failed to distinguish between heirloom rituals and commodified exchange.

The reforms of 1858 thus marked a major turning point. By abolishing the East India Company, deposing the Mughal emperor, and vesting India's sovereignty in Queen Victoria, the British at long last transformed themselves into ritual "insiders" (165). The two decades following the rebellion saw the "completion of the symbolic-cultural constitution of British India" including Disraeli's 1876 crowning of Victoria as empress and the staging of an elaborate assemblage in 1877 (179). This *durbar*-like event ritually enacted the feudal relation between India's princes and their empress through the "presentation of a silk banner" (191). Cohn thus locates Britain's success as an imperial power in its post-1858 transition from a consciously liberal style of rule, predicated on ideals of fairness and contract, to a consciously feudal style of rule, predicated on gratifying an alleged Indian "susceptibility . . . to parade and show" (188).[11]

---

[9] Like the liberal imperialists of the nineteenth century, Burke's position was essentially paternalistic. In his 1783 remarks on the East India Bill, for example, he argued that "political dominion" is "a *trust*," to be exercised for the "benefit" of those over whom it is wielded (Burke qtd. in A. Porter, "Trusteeship" 199).

[10] The Company's decreasing commercial role and increasing governing functions occurred through successive parliamentary reforms: in 1813 the Company lost its commercial monopoly and in 1833 it was divested of all remaining commercial functions, while its administrative functions in India were further centralized and its accountability to the London-based Board of Control was enhanced. On debates between "anglicist" and "orientalist" officials see, for example, Carson, Stokes, Viswanthan, and Zastoupil.

[11] Although Cohn does not specifically discuss the "princely" states, the existence of indigenous royals outside the deposed Mughal dynasty was central to this reconstituted symbolism since, as the Queen's Proclamation made clear, India's sovereigns could now be cast as Victoria's vassals.

Yet, what Cohn's influential analysis ignores are the intractable problems that this "complete" constitution created for British liberals. As Cohn recognizes, the Queen's Proclamation encompassed two "contradictory theories of rule": a feudal order that was believed to appeal to "Oriental" nature, and a modern mode of rule "which would inevitably lead to the destruction of this feudal order" (166). To resolve this contradiction, India's British rulers affirmed the feudal relation while portraying representative institutions as a "distant future" toward which India would gradually develop (167). Yet, to make that point is to demonstrate the increasing need to justify Britain's sovereignty over India at least partly through a liberal logic of tutelage. In the words of the best known spokesman for "liberal" imperialism in the 1860s, J. S. Mill, the rule of the colonized was "the highest moral trust which can devolve upon a nation." Rulers who failed to govern for the (supposed) betterment of the ruled were merely "selfish usurpers, on a par in criminality with any of those whose ambition and rapacity have sported from age to age" (*Considerations* 346). "To a cynic," writes Ian Copland, "the idea of an autocratic power worrying" about the justification of its rule "might seem ludicrous but the fact is that the British Raj . . . was desperately keen to hide its machinations under a cloak of legitimacy" (212).

Thus, while scholars of liberal imperialism seldom notice the fact, it was the Tories' distinctly different governmentality which helped to manufacture the new feudalistic picture of an imperial relation that, in actuality, entailed limited British *sovereignty* (as stipulated by various laws, proclamations, and treaties) and absolute *paramountcy* (what Salisbury privately described as "the nakedness of the sword on which we really rely" [Salisbury to Lytton, qtd. in Knight 50]). Whereas *sovereignty* denoted a juridical concept of rule (defined by Carl Schmitt as the power to decide on exceptions to the rule of law [see Prologue]), *paramountcy* indexed the ability to manage the exception through the exercise of force. Schmitt's theoretical distinction between law and the exception is crucial to articulating liberal norms: yet, imperial discourse necessarily entailed much blurring between the two (as when Morley alludes to Britain's "paramount sovereignty" over India [265]). In this way, the constitution of British India enshrined an imperial sovereignty riddled by the immanence—one might even say the permanence—of a state of exception.

That said, India was not the only space of governmentality in which neo-feudalism mixed with modern liberal theories of rule. In the 1860s, as expansion of the metropolitan franchise became inevitable, the British public was called on to renegotiate what Bagehot called the "dignified" and "efficient" components of the English constitution. Bagehot's account of "the mass of the English people" yielding to the "apparent" rule of "splendid" feudal icons, even as "efficient" ministers undertook the real work of governance (*English* 248–9), suggests that Indians were not alone in their supposed hallowing of non-market social relations, neo-feudal hierarchies, and grandiose spectacle.[12]

---

[12] As Nairn writes, as an "old State-nation" Britain had to adapt itself to the modern world: the popularization of monarchy, which was "a patrician oligarchy's unwilling . . . tribute to the plebeian nature of modernity," enabled the development of "a curious, composite simulacrum" of national sovereignty (10).

To consider Cohn's analysis of British India from the perspective of *The English Constitution* (1867) is, thus, to recognize the synergies between a formalizing empire and an emerging mass democracy—both nominally liberal but fundamentally hierarchical (and, thus, both reliant on the state's capacity to manage the exception) and, as a result, both pulled toward the symbolic compensations of invented traditions.

The years between Victoria's 1858 proclamation and the emergence of a fully-fledged New Imperialism were thus a charged transitional period as well as the crucible for a tense geopolitical unconscious. According to Canning's 1860 despatch, the imperial relation, in bringing the "Crown of England . . . face to face with its [Indian] feudatories," was at long last a "reality." What was the impact of this invented tradition on metropolitan consciousness? Were Anglo-Saxons a people illustrious for free trade and industrious settlement, or a dominative imperial "race"? Was Victorian Britain a liberal democracy and the vanguard of world freedom, or the fulcrum of a recrudescent feudalism? Was the sovereignty that Britain claimed to exercise over India that of a just imperial relation, or the crude dominion of a "paramount" military power? Although the answer to such questions varied considerably across Liberal and Tory party lines, the status of India's "princes" was, as we shall see, important from every angle.

A "VERY IMPORTANT AND REMARKABLE EPISODE"

1. HAS THE BRITISH GOVERNMENT ANY RIGHT TO ANNEX THOSE [MYSORE] TERRITORIES?
2. WOULD THE ANNEXATION BE BENEFICIAL TO THE PEOPLE OF MYSORE?
3. WOULD THE ANNEXATION BE ADVANTAGEOUS TO THE BRITISH EMPIRE?

> I shall endeavour to show that all three questions ought to be met with an absolute negative.
>
> Major [T.] Evans Bell, *The Mysore Reversion. An Exceptional Case,* 2nd edition (1866)

From the Tory standpoint, India's princes were loyal feudatories whose alleged love of romantic display enhanced the stability of an imperial order—much like the comparable propensities of the newly enfranchised British working classes. From the outlook of pro-imperial liberals, by contrast, India's royals were important to reconstituting the civilizing mission in light of the rebellion's apparent reaction against aggressive westernization. From this view, the indirect rule of well-trained local sovereigns could be seen as a moderate device through which to diffuse British principles toward the eventual goal (however distant) of Indian independence.[13]

The post-rebellion years thus saw a backlash against an assertive "liberal" approach to the civilizing mission. Among the various causes alleged to have provoked the uprising, there was the view expressed by Disraeli in 1857 that, under Lord Dalhousie's governorship (1848–1856), Britain had advanced a risky westernizing agenda, undermining "Native authority" through annexation and "disturbance" of property rights (qtd. in Metcalf 45). Whereas annexed territories such as Awadh had been hotbeds of resistance, princely states such as Mysore had remained loyal to the British (see Morley 266; "Dangers in India" 414; [T]. Bell, *Mysore* 149). The foolhardiness of alarming these crucial allies was remarked not only by British pundits but also by the Rajah of Mysore. In an 1861 petition urging his claims to sovereignty, Wodyar warned, "A day will come . . . probably in no remote period—when [India's] princes and chiefs, bound to your Government by the double tie of gratitude and self-interest, will present a bulwark which neither the wave of foreign invasion nor the tide of internal disaffection can throw down" (2). And yet, within just a few years, Mysore became a much debated "test case" as to whether the British intended to honor their assurances to India's sovereigns (D. Williams 217; cf. Brumpton 157–63). The situation was complicated partly because Wodyar's governing authority had been diminished in 1831 after he "allegedly failed to exercise" the satisfactory rule stipulated by the 1799 treaty (D. Williams 218).[14] Moreover, since Wodyar's line had been installed by the British, it was possible to argue—as did both Sir Charles Wood, the Liberal Secretary of State for India, and his Tory successor, Salisbury—that the Rajah's sovereignty should terminate with his life (an argument Morley attacked as disingenuous hairsplitting).[15]

---

[13] Though he is sometimes grouped with more zealous reformers such as his father James, J.S. Mill was, in many ways, the prototype for this tempered post-1857 "civilizing" narrative. Throughout his career at the East India Company, including the long period (1828–1856) during which his work involved policies relating to the "native" states, Mill expressed reluctance toward annexation and sought to maintain procedural rectitude toward "sovereign rights guaranteed . . . by Treaty" (qtd. in R. Moore 165). Although Mill believed that more ambitious westernizing policies should be implemented under direct rule, his official writings on the indirect empire advocated "engraftment"—the policy of fusing British principles with Indian traditions and Indian rulers. In ways that Mill did not yet perceive, this ostensibly hybrid approach to the civilizing mission could, and eventually did, become integral to a New Imperial framework that offered the guise of greater Indian autonomy in part through the mechanism of local sovereigns.

[14] The committee that reviewed Wodyar's case in 1861 admitted that "it was purely bad management of finances" which had provoked Lord Bentinck's intervention in 1831 (D. Williams 219). See also [T.] Bell, *Mysore* for British commentary critical of the 1831 decision.

[15] Yet, J.S. Mill's position on the legality of the case was closer to Wood's than to Morley's. In an 1866 letter discussing the *Fortnightly* article, Mill argued that Mysore was a "state created by conquest" and a British "gift," not a "really native state, with a nationality, & historical traditions & feelings." Mill explained that he had presented a petition to Parliament on behalf of the Rajah only because "it came from people who were entitled to be heard, & on the last day of the session they could not find any other member whom they thought suitable" (Mill to John Morley, 26 September 1866, *CW* 16 1202–3). Note that while Mill insisted that Mysore was "created by [British] gift," Wodyar's 1861 petition, describes Tipu Sultan, the Muslim ruler whom the British defeated, as a

Wodyar's petition urged the restoration of his ruling power in advance of his adopting an heir under the provisions described in Canning's despatch. The request was denied two years later on the grounds that the rajah might not maintain the "high state of prosperity" that Mysore had experienced under British administration ("Draft Report" qtd. in D. Williams 218).[16] At the time of Wodyar's second petition, official opinion was split, with some urging annexation while others argued that "fair dealing and conciliation" were "indispensable" to British "security and supremacy" (Sir George Russell Clerk qtd. in D. Williams 225). Frustrated with the delay, Wodyar renewed his request to adopt and, in 1865, sent a British emissary to represent his case to Parliament, where it met with a "lack of interest" (D. Williams 226). Wodyar then proceeded to adopt his grandson, upon which Wood refused to recognize the child as a legitimate heir. Then in 1866, with the election of Lord Derby's Tory ministry, Salisbury became Secretary of State for India. The same year saw yet another petition from Wodyar; a second issuing of *The Mysore Reversion* by Major [T.] Evans Bell (a 300-page-long attack on the pro-annexation position); and, in September, Morley's warning that a critical "turning-point" in Britain's imperial history was taking place and that "all India" was "watching the case" (Morley 259, 266).[17]

In the end, Salisbury, only a few months into his tenure as Secretary of State, reversed Wood's position. In what may have been the most important political decision in his career as an Indian administrator, the future Foreign Secretary and Prime Minister told Parliament that the government would not annex Mysore but would educate the adopted heir (much as Morley's article had advised) and, thus, prepare him for governing responsibilities. Although Kristna Raj Wodyar died unrestored in 1868, his grandson succeeded him as rajah and, in 1881, Mysore was restored to native rule—subject, of course, to supervision by the "paramount" power.

Clearly, the debate over Mysore was charged and complex. If in one sense it concerned a number of abstruse technical disputes over the correct interpretation of a treaty executed in 1799, in another it entailed broader questions about the supposed merits of British rule and the presumed long-term benefits of westernization. It was also, therefore, a debate about how to achieve these various notions of right: e.g., whether to support annexation, with its claim to providing progressive governance, or to uphold indirect rule, with its presumed respect for Indian sovereignty and the "engraftment" of diverse cultures.[18] Yet, from a metropolitan

---

"usurper" while describing himself as "the rightful heir to the throne of Mysore, and the descendant of a long lines of kings" (52:1–2).

[16] Wood and his allies clearly hoped to stall the restoration in the hopes that Wodyar, born in 1794, would die without an authorized heir (D. Williams 219–20). This goal had already been signaled in 1860 when Wodyar was left off the list of royals who received news of the adoption despatch—another disingenuous move according to Morley.

[17] Bell's two editions of *The Mysore Reversion* are significant since the arguments prepared by this prolific defender of indirect rule were cited in "Dangers in India" and may have influenced Morley's article as well.

[18] Note too how these competing notions of right complicate use of the term "liberal." Although I have attempted to use the term in ways that reflect Victorian usage, historians occasionally introduce more contemporary meanings: for example, D. Williams repeatedly describes the views of the

standpoint, the Mysore debate was also about how Britain's much-proclaimed political institutions functioned to negotiate such matters of right and expediency: about Britain's own sovereign condition on the eve of democratic reform.

The Mysore decision was, thus, a landmark in a number of ways. By preserving the region as an Indian state, led by a sovereign whose "engrafted" Western credentials would be promoted by British tutelage, it offered a compromise between the competing philosophies of imperial rule which had surfaced in earlier debates between liberal anglicists and the mainly conservative enthusiasts of "Oriental" traditions. As such, the policy might appear to offer the needed synthesis between modern liberal and neo-feudal conceptions of empire which Cohn identifies. Yet, despite the noteworthy agreement of Morley and Salisbury, it would be a mistake to conclude that the outcome of the debate—and still less the discernible trend toward the New Imperialism—offered a means of satisfying liberal anxieties over the sovereignty of a territorial empire. Instead, Morley's role in the Mysore decision provides a telling index of the politico-imperial governmentality advanced liberals struggled to countenance as they sought to maintain themselves as the progressive advocates of a just and democratic metropole.

As Ian Copland observes, the professed liberality of British rule consisted in the supposed "commitment to principle and precedent, [and] to administration by regulation rather than whim or expediency" (211–12). Yet, "expediency" was the very keynote of Morley's arguments in favor of retaining Mysore as a princely state (266). As a pragmatist, Morley insisted that concern for "expediency" in imperial affairs was no less urgent a consideration than a sovereign's "right" to adopt an heir (262).[19] Under Wood's leadership, policy had focused too narrowly on "technical rights," Morley charged, "disregarding anything like a sagacious" weighing of British "interests" (262). In fact, he reasoned, the policy arguments against annexing Mysore were even more damning than the flawed legal arguments for the "right" to annex. Quite apart from the danger of Indian backlash, the benefits of annexation were not worth the costs (270).[20]

---

anti-annexationists as "liberal," presumably to designate the concern for procedural fairness and, perhaps, cultural tolerance that such views endorsed. Yet, historically, liberal officials such as James Mill and later Dalhousie had regarded annexation as the most efficient means of delivering the supposed benefits of British rule while many who opposed the policy were conservatives.

[19] A version of this recurring distinction between right and expediency appears in Bell's book on Mysore, suggesting that Morley may have read it prior to writing his article.

[20] Occupation of Mysore would entail a "calamitous . . . drain upon military resources" which would leave Britain in the position of "confront[ing] Europe and the West in the attitude of a man with one arm fast tied up. We have abandoned our legitimate influence in the West," in order to "practice material repression in Asia" (Morley 270–71). Clear here is the extent to which Morley, a journalist who eventually entered politics, had begun to articulate a full-blown, pro-imperial worldview in which England exercised a beneficial Pax Britannica. Morley further assumes that such poor decision-making was the fault of the corrupting "zeal" of Anglo-Indian officials for lucrative "places to give away" (270–71; 268). Contra Morley's theory, the reason may well have been generational. Whereas young liberals such as Morley (not yet 30) and Tories such as Salisbury (not yet 40), could readily appreciate the benefits of an indirect empire under the nominal Indian rule, Wood, a veteran of Lord John Russell's Whig ministry, was steeped in the anglicization agenda of the earlier

Although Salisbury's 1867 speech on Mysore introduces the same distinction between "right" and "expedience," it is employed to notably different effect. In contrast to Morley, Salisbury rejects Wodyar's entitlement to adoption and, on that basis, sets the legal question aside. Salisbury, in other words, was content to justify his decision in purely "political" terms (House of Commons Debates, 22 February 1867 col. 838)—or, as the historian Paul Brumpton puts it, as a matter of "policy" rather than "right" (161).[21] Clearly, Salisbury's position, like the New Imperial stance it adumbrated, was less reliant on procedural rectitude than Morley's alternative;[22] for whereas Salisbury was content to exercise power efficiently, liberals faced a murkier fate. An advanced liberal such as Morley might well wish to regard himself as a practical policymaker; but in doing so he needed to reconcile this pragmatism with his professed commitments to liberal principles.

Indeed, for such "advanced" thinkers—conscious of contemporaneous events including the expanding franchise, the abuse of ruling power in Jamaica, and the outbreak of Fenian resistance in the metropole—the debate over Mysore could not but concern Britain's democracy and its claims to be "liberal" in any meaningful sense.[23] Morley was the very pattern of a generation of young mid-Victorian liberals, inspired by Millean ideals of citizenship: a doctor's son and the recipient of an Oxford scholarship who, at age 29, became editor of the *Fortnightly Review* (and would go on to become Secretary of State for India in 1905). Morley's rendering of the Mysore debate as a specifically parliamentary question thus illustrates Catherine Hall's point about imperialism's role in reconstituting the nation in 1867 in at least two ways ("Nation"). That the governmentality Morley describes on the eve of the Second Reform Act is clearly that of an empire marks not only the difference between Tory and Liberal governmentalities but also between Morley's views on representative democracy and those of his mentor, J. S. Mill.

---

nineteenth century. As we will see in Chapter 5, the drift away from the committed universalism on which the anglicization agenda rested began even before 1857, with disappointment over the outcome of the abolition of slavery in the West Indies.

[21] Salisbury was directly replying to the remarks of Sir Henry Rawlinson, the renowned Assyriologist, whose speech shows signs of Morley's influence (and possibly Bell's): "The question" of the Rajah's right to adopt, Rawlinson argued, "might be considered both in a legal and in a political point of view. Firstly, whether the Rajah really had any right to appoint a successor; and secondly, whether it was expedient on our part to acknowledge that successor" (House of Commons Debates, 22 February 1867, column 829. Salisbury replied that Rawlinson had "established . . . a very convenient division" between "the legal and . . . the political grounds" to which he would adhere "because, though upon the legal ground I may differ from him very considerably, I daresay that when we come to the political question we shall be found not very widely apart" (2/22/1867—column 835).

[22] Salisbury may have had principled as well as political reasons for opposing annexation. As Steele, among others, points out, Salisbury, who appears to have been genuinely disturbed by the devastating effects of famine in Orissa in 1866, pointed out that the response of the British administration had been less effective and humane than that of Indian sovereigns in the region (99).

[23] Anxiety over Fenianism, according to Hall, "reached its peak between 1865 and 1868," coinciding with the Jamaica crisis as well as working-class agitation for reform ("The Nation" 216). Fenianism thus provided an additional context for the increasingly reactionary attitudes of self-styled liberals like Matthew Arnold who, in *Culture and Anarchy*, described the Fenian as "desperate and dangerous, a man of conquered race" (87; qtd. in Hall, "The Nation" 187).

Whereas Salisbury famously described the 1867 Reform Bill as an unparalleled betrayal of Conservative principles,[24] Morley's article in *The Fortnightly Review*, published a few months before the bill's passage, evoked a world-historical moment in which the questions of Mysore and of parliamentary reform were intertwined. As Mill had argued in a chapter from *Considerations on Representative Government* (1861) to which Morley refers, the transfer of Indian rule to the Crown—and, thus, to Parliament—had created a liberal conundrum, enlisting a representative institution to govern a people whom it did not represent. "Let any one consider how the English themselves would be governed if they knew and cared no more about their own affairs than they know and care about the affairs" of Indians (*Considerations* 349–50). The result, Mill concluded, could only be a government that sought "to force English ideas down the throats of the natives" or favored European interests over the "good of the governed" (349–50; cf. 352–3).[25] Mill's proposed solution to the dilemma was to commission a body of experts on Indian affairs to ensure a relatively disinterested paternalism that would help to justify the encroachment on Indian sovereignty. In fact, Mill had fought in 1858 to establish such a body in the Council of India, a committee appointed to advise the Secretary of State.[26]

By contrast, Morley's call for reform was not focused on extra-parliamentary councils but on the improved effectiveness of "public opinion" (257)—the core of a democratic sovereignty. That difference aside, his article confirms the dilemma described in *Considerations on Representative Government*. The Secretary of State, wrote Morley, "is expected to govern in the interests of the people of India," but he is responsible "to the people of England" who, in turn, are in a state of "almost inevitable ignorance" about India (258). The problem, as

---

[24] In March 1867, when Disraeli and Derby introduced the Second Reform Bill, Salisbury resigned as Secretary of State. He described Disraeli's move as "a political betrayal which has no parallel in our Parliamentary annals" (qtd. in Steele 56). Yet with his characteristic pragmatism, Salisbury eventually reconciled himself to working with Disraeli.

[25] Morley quotes from the same paragraph: "One people may keep another as a warren or preserve for its own use, a place to make money in, a human cattle-farm to be worked for the profit of its own inhabitants; but if the good of the governed is the proper business of a government, it is utterly impossible that a people should directly attend to it" (Mill, qtd. in Morley 258; cf. Mill, *Considerations* 349). See also Mill's July 8, 1858 letter (313): "The difficulty of governing India in any tolerable manner, already so much increased by the mutiny and its consequences, will become an impossibility if a body so ignorant and incompetent on Indian (to say nothing of other) subjects as Parliament, comes to make a practice of interfering" (*C.W.* 15 560).

[26] In an 1867 speech in the House of Commons, Mill, as M.P. for Westminster, defended the Council, arguing that the most important work of imperial governance was "deliberative," not "executive." He lamented that the "importance of Councils" had thus far "been undervalued" (*C.W.* 28 233). Mill saw the Council as a substitute for the professional expertise of the East India Company, the abolition of which he had vehemently opposed. His description of an "undervalued" Council may have been an understatement. An 1860 article in *Fraser's* complained that after the Company's abolition, "the few persons who knew India well, and were likely to gain opportunities of instructing the public, have been decoyed in the silence and impotence of the Indian Council" ("Chronicle" 543). Morley's article is nearly silent on the matter; Salisbury, for his part, thought the Council of India "a most anomalous institution" and endeavored to circumvent its minimal check on his authority to the greatest possible extent (qtd. in Brumpton 32).

Morley casts it, is not that the British public are willfully selfish but, rather, that the affairs of India cannot but confuse and repel them. The "details of Indian administration" are so "repulsive . . . from their technicality, the uncouthness of their phraseology, [and] the unfamiliarity of the ideas which underlie them" (258) that there is no viable means of holding the Secretary of State for India democratically accountable. The present system thus "makes a man virtually autocrat over India, not because he knows or cares anything about India, but because he is a good politician" (259). Although Salisbury is "able," "industrious," and assertive, Morley asks, "in the absence of possible criticism in the House, is not the otherwise invaluable virtue of having a strong will almost as bad as any vice?" (259).[27] Nonetheless, he concludes with the hope that "public opinion may even now" work to overturn this double miscarriage of "justice" and "expediency" (271).

To be sure, Salisbury's reversal of Wood's policy, announced just five months after the appearance of Morley's article, might well be viewed as just such a victory for public opinion. One might even surmise that Bell's book on Mysore, cited by the author of "Dangers of India," had helped to spur Morley's 1866 article which, in turn, appears to have influenced Henry Rawlinson's speech in Parliament and Salisbury's landmark decision. On the other hand, Mill continued to criticize the Secretary of State's unchecked power in an 1867 speech, doubtless in part because Salisbury had circumvented the advice of the Council of India. In matters of imperial governance, Mill declared, the country "should not rely solely upon the policy of one man" (*C.W.* 28 233). Thus, while the events that transpired favored the expedient policy Morley had recommended, they did little to reverse the fear that the Secretary of State for India was an "autocrat" whose executive authority was beyond the supervision of ordinary Britons and their elected representatives—much less of Indians. Mill himself might continue to believe that the Council of India, in theory at least, could mitigate the defects of imperial governance. But Morley's article had implied that public opinion could ensure a just imperialism even as it worked to demand "a more democratic shape" for Parliament (257).

Although Morley defines "right" throughout most of the article in light of technical legality, he eventually allows that the pro-annexationists could make alternative claims on the ground of justice: for whereas Mysore was said to have suffered under the rajah, it was now said to flourish under British administration.

---

[27] Note that Bagehot, though blasé on the topic of imperialism, used the example of Salisbury's unchecked authority to illustrate one of the "evils" of changes in ministry. "A little while ago [Salisbury] had no more idea that he would now be Indian Secretary than that he would be a bill broker . . . A perfectly inexperienced man, so far as Indian affairs go, rules all our Indian Empire (*English* 183–34). Interestingly, however, in another chapter Bagehot appears to second Mill's idea about the usefulness of extra-parliamentary authority in checking the "the selfishness of Parliament": he offers the colonial governor—he has in mind white settler colonies rather than India—as an example of a "super-Parliamentary authority" that is able to provide "extrinsic, impartial, and capable" governance (224–5)—so long as the authority in question "is morally and intellectually equal" to the task (223). Elsewhere Bagehot alludes to the Council of India, in non-committal fashion, to illustrate the "unsystematic" arrangements of Britain's public offices, which vary from department to department (210–11).

Morley then offers what he presents as an apposite quotation on India from John Stuart Mill:

> A tyrant or sensualist who has been deprived of the power he had abused, and, instead of punishment, is supported in as great wealth and splendour as he ever enjoyed; a knot of privileged landholders, who demand that the State should relinquish to them its reserved right to a rent from their lands, or who resent as a wrong any attempt to protect the masses from their extortion; these have no difficulty in procuring interested or sentimental advocacy in the British Parliament and press. The silent myriads obtain none (qtd. in Morley 267; cf. Mill, *Considerations* 355).

Morley goes on to argue that if annexation were the only alternative to such imperial injustice, "no honourable Englishman could hesitate" to annex "at whatever ultimate risk" (267–8). Fortunately, however, the option of educating Wodyar's heir and establishing a model of indirect rule, offers expediency as well as "good faith" toward the "'silent myriads'" (268).

What Morley does not consider, however, is that the cited passage from *Considerations on Representative Government* is not intended as a case for annexation, but, rather, as proof of the incompatibility of representative democracy with imperial "despotism" (347). Mill's point is that, in a territorial empire, only Europeans and indigenous elites have "the means" to press their claims "upon the inattentive and uninterested" metropolitan public. Worse still, "when the public mind is invoked" on behalf of "justice and philanthropy," there is a high "probability of its missing the mark, producing sympathy for the "tyrant" and neglect of the "silent myriads" (354–5). In actuality, Mill makes clear, "real good government is not compatible" with imperialism. A delegated body such as the Council of India is merely the least imperfect option in a situation almost certain to "fail" (356). Mill comes close to admitting—though he never does admit—that the so-called civilizing mission cannot but be corrupt under the illiberal conditions he has described. But though he continues to assume, against the force of his own arguments, that imperialism can be executed as a "moral trust"—or, at least, that a non-political body such as the Council has the greatest chance of doing so—Mill offers a biting critique of the current constitution. The "British people can scarcely give [India] a worse" governor "than an English cabinet minister, who is thinking of English, not Indian politics" (346; 356–7).[28]

Whereas Mill's arguments are, thus, cogent in illuminating the defects of a parliamentary "despotism," Morley's deflect imperial contradictions in favor of an ideal expedient, a civilizing project that any liberal could love—the educating of a child. That India itself is positioned as perennially child-like in its relation to the paramount power does not trouble Morley's liberalism, as it often does Mill's.

---

[28] See also Mill's remarks in the *Autobiography* on his retirement from Indian affairs in 1858, at which point "it pleased Parliament, in other words Lord Palmerston, to put an end to the East India Company . . . and convert the administration of that country into a thing to be scrambled for by the second and third class of English parliamentary politicians" (143–4). Writing in 1863, Smith offered an almost identical critique of parliamentary rule of India (*Empire* 285–6).

Mill is visibly haunted by the sovereignty of which India and Indians are largely deprived under the logic of the civilizing mission; Morley rather more carelessly displaces Indian sovereignty with British. It is hard to imagine Mill, ever earnest in his belief that British tutelage will gradually lead to Indian self-rule, arguing that the installation of a "royal puppet" in Mysore would be "a piece of harmless pageantry," gratifying to the native "taste" (Morley 270). Such odor of the emerging New Imperialism, evident also in his passing references to a "dominant race" (270), mark Morley, for all his liberal affiliations, as the contemporary of Salisbury rather than Mill.

GREATER BRITAIN

[T]he incorporation of a vast Empire such as India, which is not governed on free principles, with a free country, is apt to taint the political spirit of the free country, and to impair the vigour of its freedom. . . . [T]he influence is in its very nature impalpable, like a malaria in the air, and its pestilential effects may only become visible on looking back over a long range of history. Thus much, however, may easily be understood, that the principle of liberty can scarcely fail to be less sacred in a nation which holds despotic dominion over others. The despot is no more a freeman than his slaves.

Goldwin Smith, *The Empire: A Series of Letters Published in "The Daily News,"* 1862, 1863 (1863)

[T]he term Empire has been greatly misapplied . . . It applies only to India, the Crown Colonies, and the military stations, which alone are held by a tenure really imperial, and governed with imperial sway. An Asiatic dominion extending over two hundred fifty millions of Hindoos, a group of West Indian islands full of emancipated negro slaves, a Dutch settlement at the southern point of Africa, occupied to secure the old passage to India . . .— what have these in common, or why are they likely to be for all time bound up with groups of self-governing British colonies in North America or Australia?

Goldwin Smith, *Canada and the Canadian Question* (1891)

It is easy in retrospect to spot the predicament of advanced liberals like Mill and Morley as they struggled to reconcile metropolitan democracy with justification for an ever more formalized imperial rule. Mill's resort to extra-parliamentary councils was riddled with difficulty not least because India's parliamentary rulers could bypass such experts at will. Morley's straightforward reliance on Parliament was equally flawed: Indians themselves lacked representation, while the British electorate's "almost inevitable ignorance" about India was predictable given the "repulsive" technicality of an imperial bureaucracy (258). Doubtless both men realized that the British Empire's alienating governmentality would take a toll on the informed citizen participation that each saw as the heart of representative democracy. If neither said so explicitly, their writings suggest that they recognized the spirit of a self-styled anti-imperialist like Smith when he wrote that the "incorporation of a vast Empire," that "is not governed on free principles," is "apt to taint the political spirit of [a] free country, and to impair the vigour of its freedom" (*Empire* 288).

Such misgivings were hardly isolated: rather, Smith's prolific writings exemplified a full-blown ideology of "Greater Britishness" to which (as the next chapter will show) Trollope's travel narratives can also be tied. As Duncan Bell writes, the discourse of "Greater Britain" articulated a mid-to-late nineteenth-century vision of global polity between English-speaking, "Anglo-Saxon" countries—sometimes including the United States—with or without formal federal ties. (*Idea* 7). Unlike the figures Mehta describes in *Liberalism and Empire* (1999), "Greater British" liberals such as Trollope's friend Herman Merivale, the M.P. Charles Dilke, the constitutional scholar Smith, and the historian Seeley, expressed persistent worries about territorial imperialism, a form of global expansion which they repeatedly distinguished from the emigration of Anglo-Saxons to colonies of settlement. In 1842, Merivale, a professor of political economy at Oxford and future colonial administrator, published the first edition of his popular *Lectures on Colonization and Colonies*, extolling the democratic potential of white settlement and anticipating a time when Britain, "the commercial metropolis of the world," will have "scattered thick as stars over the surface of this earth, communities of citizens owning the name of Britons" (2:293). Utopian though such ideas might be, he noted, they were distinct from the "fatal" error of imposing a "subjection enforced by bayonets" and "galling expenditure" (2:293).[29]

Written on the heels of the Jamaica crisis, Dilke's *Greater Britain* (1868) was yet another influential work to insist that "white-inhabited, and self-governed" colonies like Canada were fundamentally unlike imperial "dependencies" in Asia and the Caribbean (2:149). In response, Dilke drew the disturbing image of an alien "England in the East" which, so far from a bastion of "liberty," "becomes [in India] a mysterious Oriental despotism, ruling a sixth of the human race, nominally for the natives' own good," "scheming, annexing, out-maneuvering Russia, and sometimes . . . out-lying Persia herself" (2:374–5). As he meditated the possibility that China might soon become another dependency, Dilke worried that Britain's ruling classes had been "exposed to the corrupting influences of power." If he stopped short of rejecting the supposed benefits to China of having the "blessings of Free Trade" "inflict[ed] . . . at the cannon's mouth," he was clear

---

[29] D. Bell does not discuss Merivale or Trollope in his otherwise definitive book (*Idea*). Trollope's *North America*, discussed in the next chapter, articulates a similar opposition between Imperial "conquest" and the supposedly benign settlement of emigrant Britons (28–9). Needless to say, the reiterated distinction between the non-violence and non-imperialism of white colonies of settlement was predicated on nearly unquestioned acceptance of the ubiquitous extinction discourses that assumed that indigenous people in North America and Australia—unlike colonized people in Ireland, South Asia, and Africa—were doomed to wither away (see Brantlinger, *Dark*). Thus, as Sartori notes, if, in the pre-1857 period, "liberalism had a logically immanent propensity for imperial aggression," it was less toward the South Asians who were positioned as beneficiaries of British tutelage than toward the "native peoples of North America who had failed to appropriate land through labor" (630).

that, for Britain, the "danger of a spread at home of love of absolute authority, and indifference to human happiness and life" was regrettable (2: 391).[30]

By far the most prolific and vehement of the "Greater British" authors was Smith. A constitutional historian, Smith called on Britain to emancipate its settler colonies and eventually emigrated to the United States and, then, Canada. Smith's 1863 series of "letters" on empire, published in the *Daily News*, diagnosed a variety of pernicious side-effects derived from Indian rule including the "luxury" and "corruption" of "Nabobs," the political manipulations of Parliament, and the "fiscal evil" of maintaining a large imperial army (*Empire* 286–7). Like other Greater British enthusiasts, he distinguished "self-governing [settler] colonies" from "really imperial" territories (*Canada* 239). But what warrants particular notice, is Smith's argument that such imperial conquests had spoiled the possibility of a pan-colonial federation. For example, how, Smith queried in *Canada and the Canadian Question* (1891), would subjugated imperial populations be integrated under the sovereignty of a federated white settler empire?

> Are the negroes of the West Indies to be included? Is Quashee to vote on imperial policy? But, above all, what is to be done with India? Is it . . . to be taken into the Federation and enfranchised? If it is, the Hindoo will outvote us by five to one, and what he will do with us only those who have fathomed the Oriental mystery can pretend to say. Is it to remain a dependency? Then to whom is it to belong?
> To a federation of scattered communities scattered over the globe . . .? Or is to belong to England alone? . . . How would the American Confederation work if one State held South America as an empire? Some have suggested that Hindoostan would be represented by the British residents in India alone. If it were, woe to the Hindoos (*Canada* 257–8).

Glaringly clear in Smith's questions is the incompatibility between liberal conventions of formal equality, and the hierarchies and exclusions of imperial rule. Whereas settler colonies could be imagined as emptied of indigenes (who were assumed to be on the verge of extinction), the territorial empire in India presented the problem of myriad non-white subjects who, in principle, could claim rights to representation on the same footing as their enfranchised male peers in the metropole. The alternative to such unthinkable equality was a federation distorted by exceptional power. Smith thus tapped the same antinomies that the reactionary utilitarian James Fitzjames Stephen later stressed in his dissent from the Liberal Party's occasional efforts to liberalize imperial policies. If liberal officials in South Asia wanted to remove "all anomalies" from India's government, Stephen quipped in 1883, they should begin by "remov[ing] themselves" ("Indian" 8).

Smith's pronounced racism is yet another feature of his Greater British imaginary. The invocation of "Quashee" (a favored term in Carlyle's "Occasional Discourse on the Negro Question") and the allusion to "Oriental mystery" suggest that the anti-racialist liberalism Mill epitomized in the 1860s had deteriorated

---

[30] For Merivale's perception that China was *already* subject to Britain's quasi-imperial commercial dominion, see his article, "The Colonial Question in 1870."

well beyond Morley's relatively mild essentialisms. Such foregrounding of race was no accident: in Smith's vision, Anglo-Saxon whiteness provided the glue for transnational polity among otherwise discrete nations. Much like Trollope, whose travel writings conceived Anglo-Saxonness to supply cultural, linguistic, and genealogical bonds for Britain's dispersed cosmopolites (Ch. 3), Smith believed that the "moral unity of our race" could be constituted around ties of "blood, sympathy, and ideas" (qtd. in D. Bell, *Idea* 185). Anglo-Saxon essence thus provided a bulwark against globalization's dizzying heterogeneity—a final stanchion for a notion of sovereignty stretched to its limits.

By contrast, the dominant note of Seeley's *The Expansion of England* (1883), is not secure racial hierarchy, but deep liberal discomfiture. "Nothing great that has ever been done by Englishmen," Seeley wrote in these published lectures, "was done so unintentionally, so accidentally as the conquest of India" (143). Historians, he charged, had failed to perceive that "the eighteenth-century history of England" was "not *in* England but in America and Asia" (13; emphasis added). Forward-thinking Britons ought thus "to beware of putting England alone in the foreground and suffering what we call the English possessions to escape our view" (13). So far from insignificant, England's expansion across the globe was, in fact, all too significant.

From Seeley's liberal standpoint, the proto-Jamesonian insight that England's past and future were to be found largely outside the metropole was cause for deep-seated ambivalence. If one could welcome a "Greater Britain" that in "natural" fashion disseminated "the English race" to "thinly peopled" lands (233), one could simultaneously regret the rise of a dominative machinery in South Asia. Seeley's distaste for imperial conquest led him to sever Britain's relation to India "from any distinct moral project or aim" (Mantena, "Crisis" 126). The result was a picture of Britain's Indian empire as burdensome happenstance: "What is the use of it?" "Why do we take the trouble and involve ourselves in the anxiety and responsibility of governing two hundred millions of people in Asia?" (*Expansion* 147). As we will see in Chapter 4, this very question was anticipated in the most significant Indian novel of mid-Victorian England's premier writer of political fiction.

"PROUD TO BELONG TO AN IMPERIAL COUNTRY"

> [The Government of India] is essentially an absolute Government, founded, not on consent, but on conquest. It does not represent the native principles of life or of government, and it can never do so until it represents heathenism or barbarism.
>
> James Fitzjames Stephen, letter to *The Times*, March 1, 1883

Liberal opinion on territorial imperialism in the years after the "mutiny" took two major forms. Whereas supporters like Mill and Morley held to an ideal of imperial justice which extended back to Burke, "Greater British" liberals such as Dilke, Smith, and Seeley worried that empires of conquest were anomalous, dangerous, and burdensome. That said, the point in making this distinction is not to suggest that the Greater British imaginary, with its idealization of Anglo-Saxon "race" and genocidal outlook toward indigenous people, provided significant impetus for resisting imperialism—in India or anywhere else in the world. Mill's dispiriting experience on the Jamaica Committee diminished his confidence in the possibility of an ethical imperialism. Though he never repudiated the British Empire *tout court*, his later writings detailed the damaging effects of British rule, condemned violence, urged land reforms in Ireland, and called for the decriminalization of Fenian prisoners.[31] Smith, meanwhile, though regarding himself as a staunch anti-imperialist, believed that, whatever its hazards, there was no turning back on British India. Having subjugated the subcontinent and "degrade[ed] all the native Governments," Britons had taken on "duties" that they were "bound for the present to perform." His description of Britons as "wedged in the oak which [they had] rent" is a Victorian precursor of today's "Pottery Barn" rule (*Empire* 257).[32] When, in the early twentieth century, liberal resistance to imperialism finally emerged as a significant force in British politics, it was through New Liberals who reconnected with Mill's anti-racism (Ch. 7).

The point to emphasize, then, is not Greater Britain's anti-imperial tenets, but, rather, the limitations of liberalism in any form as a stable foundation for Britain's emerging New Imperial identity. Whereas liberalism's awkward oscillations between free trade enthusiasm, sanctimonious paternalism, Anglo-Saxon exceptionalism, and anxious disavowal could thrive in a structure of informal empire, it could hardly withstand the visibility of a more systematic imperial project. To be sure, liberal justifications for empire could be appropriated by anyone and for any purpose. Thus, in an 1878 speech defending the deployment of Indian troops in Malta to check Russian ambitions, Disraeli concluded that the mainstay of British "imperial strength" was not "fleets and armies," but "Eastern" "confidence" that the British Empire was an "Empire of liberty, of truth, and of justice" ("Berlin Treaty" 202).

Yet, if liberal rhetorical flourishes of this kind could serve the ends of any party, it remains the case that so-called liberal imperialism was in decline as the nineteenth century came to a close. Mill's failure to win support for Eyre's prosecution, writes Mantena, "portended an important ideological shift in the ways in which empire would be justified and colonized peoples would be governed." The British public's sanction of brutal repression exemplified a "deepening sense of racial and cultural difference" and, thus, a "distancing" from the Enlightenment's "universalist and assimilationist ideals" ("Crisis" 122). From the Indian rebellion forward, "advocates of liberal imperialism found themselves consistently on the

---

[31] For a sample of the vast body of writing on Mill and imperialism, see Zastoupil, and Moir and Zastoupil.
[32] As D. Bell points out (*Idea* 203; note 117), Dilke makes a similar argument in the second volume of *Greater Britain*.

losing side" of imperial debates, not only over the exoneration of Eyre, but also in the rejection of the Ilbert Bill in 1882–3—a liberal measure to permit Indian justices to preside over cases involving European defendants ("Crisis" 121).[33] The same could be said for the Liberal Party's ill-fated support for Home Rule in Ireland which, in 1886, led prominent unionists such as John Bright, to join Conservatives in a ministry led by Salisbury—a split within Liberal ranks which augured the party's eventual demise. "It is not by chance," writes Thomas Metcalf, "that the era of greatest imperial enthusiasm, from 1885 to 1905, was also a period of Conservative predominance in British politics" (65).

Imperialism, moreover, had begun to produce the reactionary political effects that Dilke and Smith had prophesied. We have already seen how Morley's views on representative democracy during the Mysore debate were more complaisant than Mill's. In the 1880s, "liberal" imperialism's mutation into authoritarian anti-liberalism was personified in Stephen. Arguing in *The Times* that the foundation of British India was not consent but conquest, Stephen overturned decades of commercial and contractarian arguments for a "liberal" empire. Likewise, refusing Indian judicial authority over white defendants, he rejected the universalistic premise at the heart of the civilizing mission. Ironically, Mill's passionate arguments for the authority of expert officials had empowered Stephen, a member of the Colonial Council in India between 1869 and 1872—precisely the kind of body Mill had fought to establish. As a supposed expert on India, Stephen upheld racial hierarchism, embraced authoritarian government, and even defended the record of Hastings. How telling that Stephen's first major achievement upon his return from India was to publish *Liberty, Equality, Fraternity* (1873–1874), a strident critique of Mill. This "attack on English Liberalism," according to John Roach, "was primarily inspired" by "Indian experiences" (1).

Liberal imperialism's long decline thus helps to pinpoint the significance of the Mysore debate. Although Salisbury's decision overruled the old-school liberals who had urged annexation, his affirmation of Wodyar's sovereignty saw him siding with Morley and—arguably—bucking the anti-liberal trend that had deprived Jamaicans of justice and would reject the equal status of Indian judges. Nonetheless, if Mysore stands out as an exception of sorts, the reason is clearly that Indian royalty, as Wodyar himself had recognized, had become a lynchpin of British rule. If it was not yet clear to annexationists like Wood, it was evident to their successors that "princely allies" were "precious" resources who could be counted on to provide "support against popular movements," even in directly-ruled British India (R. Moore, "Mill" 107).[34]

---

[33] Metcalf describes the Ilbert controversy as "By far the most momentous clash of ideologies in British India." "At stake," he explains, "were contending views of the nature of the Raj that cut to the core of the British justification for their presence in India. . . . On the one side were ideals dear to the hearts of liberals: equality before the law, and the transformative power of education . . . On the other side stood the bill's opponents, who insisted on the essential difference of race, and argued for a legal system that would accommodate that difference" (204).

[34] As R. Moore explains, there were also financial reasons for favoring indirect rule: pressed for cash as they built an expensive and ever-expanding infrastructure, India's British rulers eventually

Thus, by the turn of the century, it was English-educated Indians, not British intellectuals, who rallied behind liberal discourse, arguing the merits of their "advanced" ideas against the reactionary stance of "feudal 'notables'" (Metcalf 203).[35] In December 1905, with the election of a Liberal government, Morley (by now almost 70) became Secretary of State for India, in which position he helped usher in the Morley-Minto reforms of 1909. Extending Indian participation in governance and expanding the power of local councils, the reforms seemed to anticipate an eventual transition "to full parliamentary self-government for India" (223). Yet, as Metcalf emphasizes, Morley-Minto was implemented through an essentialistic rhetoric that saw Minto, the Liberal viceroy, arguing that representative government was a "Western importation" that "could never" suit "the instincts" of India's "many races," while Morley assured the House of Lords that he had no "intention to prepare India for Parliamentary government" (qtd. in Metcalf 223–4; R. Moore, "Imperial" 439). British rule was once again proffered as the answer to India's heterogeneity, even while Liberal reforms exacerbated divisions to curb rising nationalism (224).[36]

According to Mantena, the "late imperial ideologies" that supplanted the liberalism of the pre-1857 era, articulated "opposition to the liberal project" without "necessarily" producing "a comprehensive alternative imperial vision" (125).[37] Mantena is surely right that Seeley's "Greater British" disavowal, Stephen's reactionary utilitarianism, and the compromised Liberal policy of the Morley-Minto years make it difficult to uphold Tory imperialism as the exclusive motive force behind the New Imperial era. Nonetheless, in the 1870s, a conjuncture of "discourse and political interest" like that which Sartori theorizes for liberalism ("British" 627), crystallized around a neo-feudal style of imperialism whose most prominent impresario was Disraeli—a figure whose Orientalized Jewishness became a lightning rod for anti-imperial sentiments (Ch. 4). If, as Metcalf suggests, India ceased to be "a land to be remade in Britain's image" and became instead "a cherished 'jewel in the crown' of the queen-empress" (65), that was

---

realized that indirect rule was "more economical" than the maintenance of an elaborate British bureaucracy (R. Moore, "Imperial" 431). On the importance of indirect rule in Britain's African empire, see, for example, Mamdani.

[35] Indeed, liberalism as such, was no longer a British or European political doctrine but, rather, a hybrid body of ideas influenced by social movements in South Asia and elsewhere; see, for example, Sartori, *Global* and Bayly, *Recovering*.

[36] As Minto wrote to Morley in 1907, he sought reforms that would "satisfy the legitimate aspirations of the most advanced Indians, whilst at the same time enlisting the support of the conservative element of Native society." This strategy meant calibrating reforms so as provide "the requisite counterpoise" between middle-class professionals and landed elites, Muslims and Hindus, aspiring nationalists and those, like India's royals, who saw their interests vested in British rule (qtd. in Moore, "Imperial" 439).

[37] Mantena argues "the hallmark" of liberal imperialism had been "the implicit belief in the temporary nature of British rule in India" ("Crisis" 127). She shows how the "criteria for future self-government" gradually shifted from "assimilation" to "the question of nationality"—an achievement that could be undercut by "belief in the natural tendency of Indian society to devolve into anarchy and/or communal divisions" (127–8).

because Tories, including Disraeli and Lytton, romanticized and aestheticized the imperial project in ways that liberals like Gladstone condemned as immoral displays of "force and splendour" (Metcalf 64).

At the core of neo-feudal imperialism were the tenets of Disraeli's Tory philosophy more generally: the hallowing of national institutions such as the Crown and the Church, and the orienting of the nation toward a vision of Empire. While Tory leaders believed that "Orientals" attached "enormous value" to the symbolic "distinctions" that a neo-feudal imperialism could confer (Northcote qtd. in Metcalf 61), they were equally convinced that the British people and, especially, the newly enfranchised British working classes were, as Disraeli emphasized in his 1872 Crystal Palace speech, "proud to belong to an Imperial country" ("Conservative" 528–9).[38] Thus, what Cohn defines as a stable "cultural-symbolic constitution" for ruling India equally defined the Tory approach to ruling Britain's newly formed mass electorate. Liberals were fully capable of perceiving the potential power of invented traditions, as Bagehot's canny analysis of the "dignified" elements of England's constitution reveals. So, for that matter could the queen: "Victoria was aware that she was a show or spectacle for her people," despite her lamentations about the constant "pressure to perform" (Homans 60).

In his defense of the Royal Titles Act, Disraeli explained that the purpose of "amplifying" Victoria's sovereignty was to "touch and satisfy the imagination of nations" while ensuring that "the people of India feel . . . a sympathetic chord between us and them" ("Royal" 236; 239). One finds an echo here of Sidonia, the Jewish wise man of Disraeli's Young England fiction, an "empire-builder", who tells the young Harry Coningsby that "Man . . . is never irresistible but when he appeals to the imagination" (Harvie 34; Disraeli, *Coningsby* 262).[39] Such romantic appeals were ostensibly as alien to the logics of contract and commerce as were neo-feudal trappings. Nonetheless, we have seen how Morley could selectively borrow from the Tory idiom, just as Disraeli could celebrate an "Empire of Liberty." By 1897, no less self-identified an anti-imperialist than Smith could proclaim that the "name Empire stirs in the British heart a sentiment of pride" ("Empire" 141). The same man who in 1863 had asserted that territorial empire exerted "pestilential effects" (*Empire* 288), and had been ready to agree that "If we were well quit of India, we should be much stronger," now eulogized British India as "the noblest" empire "the world has seen," assuring his readers that "No moral

---

[38] The persistent contrasts in Disraeli's speech between the Tory ideals of nationalism and imperialism, and the Jacobin and cosmopolitan ideals urged by the "advanced guard of Liberalism" were a direct reply to a speech by Dilke which, according to the prefatory note, had created a stir because of its perceived "attack upon the English monarchy" ("Conservative" 526; 523).

[39] One of the earliest scholars of Disraeli's fiction goes so far as to assert that "the whole policy of British Imperialism as it was born in the mind of Disraeli, and first put into effect by him as . . . Prime Minister, is to be found in its inception in" *Tancred*, the third in the trio of political novels that began with *Coningsby* (1844) (Speare 90).

compunction need be felt in retaining this conquest" (N. Senior qtd. in Smith, *Empire* 257; Smith, "Empire" 144–5).[40]

Hence, while Seeley might tell his fellow Britons in 1883 that their absent-minded imperialism had yet "to affect [their] imaginations or in any degree to change [their] ways of thinking" (12–13), the textual record suggests otherwise. Absent-mindedly or not, Britain was, by the mid-1870s, the British Empire and imperial modes of governmentality were becoming indelible features of the metropolitan landscape. Moreover, since liberals were complicit in many aspects of the New Imperial agenda, their partisan attacks on Tory government increasingly centered on "moral judgments and views concerning the personal attributes of policy makers" (Brumpton 13)—an atmosphere in which ad hominem assaults on Disraeli became the outlet for the troubled geopolitical unconscious that also gave rise to the innovative realist fiction to which I now turn.

---

[40] Smith's borrowings from Tory imperial hagiography developed despite the fact that Smith was a cutting-edge anti-semite who, like Trollope, was exercised by Disraeli's rise to political power. As though to distinguish between his own presumably disinterested pro-imperialism and Disraeli's, Smith wrote of the latter as a "Jewish statesman [who had] got up jingoism much as he would get up a speculative mania for a commercial purpose" (Smith, qtd. in *Jewish* 694).

3

Trollopian "Foreign Policy"
Rootedness and Cosmopolitanism in the Mid-Victorian Global Imaginary

> He isn't of our sort. He's too clever, too cosmopolitan,—a sort of man whitewashed of all prejudices, who wouldn't mind whether he ate horseflesh or beef if horseflesh were as good as beef, and never had an association in his life.
>
> Anthony Trollope, *The Prime Minister* (1875–76)

In this chapter, I resume the exploration of the geopolitical aesthetic as an artifact of "actually existing" transnationality. As we saw in Chapter 1, *cosmopolitanism* has been defined as an "ethos that attempts to encompass all humanity while remaining attentive to the pitfalls of humanism" (Agathocleous and Rudy 390). It is, in other words, an ethico-political project that strives to bring the hard-won regulative ideals of an inclusive and democratic ethics to bear on the multiple kinds of worldedness which centuries of globalizing capital have helped to foster. As the critical focus has shifted from the abstract aspirations of the eighteenth century to the extant materialities of the turn-of-the-millennium, theorists of cosmopolitanism have articulated ground-up approaches to ethical possibility. Philosophers like Kwame Anthony Appiah seek a "rooted cosmopolitanism" that balances the claims of the local and global while acknowledging that the cosmopolitanisms of yore offered "imperial [values] . . . puffed up with universalist pretensions" (*Ethics* 232–3, 214; cf. *Cosmopolitanism*). Yet, as Scott Malcolmson writes, the project's most serious challenges are not "in theory but in practice" (238). When cosmopolitan democracy is put forward as an ethical objective, without serious attention to the systemic structural inequalities that immobilize it, the idea may ignore or even encourage the legacies of imperialism (Gikandi, "Race"). Theories of cosmopolitanism, need at the very least "to approach both cross-cultural relations and the construction of social solidarities with a deeper recognition of the significance of diverse starting points" as well as to articulate greater "commitment to the reduction of material inequality, and more openness to radical change" (Calhoun 108).

In the field of Victorian studies, Amanda Anderson has sought to recuperate aspects of British literature which exemplify "the critique of modernity" within Western "modernity itself" ("Cosmopolitanism" 272; see also *Powers* 63). Whether her topic is fiction or philosophy, Anderson has argued that literary critics shortchange the ethico-political potential of mid-Victorian culture when they reflexively associate it with the "more blinkered aspects" of the Enlightenment ("Victorian" 198). Writing in a similar vein, Christopher M. Keirstead has turned to Robert Browning's poetry to describe the cosmopolitan ideal as a lived "capacity for sorting out competing ideas and offering in return a tolerant, humane understanding" ("Stranded" 423).[1] Both scholars carefully note the tensions between Victorian literature's ethically and artistically compelling engagements with multiplicity and its comparatively inert challenges to—often embrace of— hierarchies of nationality, race, class, and gender. Keirstead, for instance, notes how Browning's cosmopolitan "political ambitions" run up against their origins in "class and gender privilege" (429–30; cf. Anderson, *Powers* 89–90). The limit of such Victorianist scholarship is not, therefore, its political blindspots but its finite expectations. Writing from a postcolonial vantage that recognizes the pervasiveness of nineteenth-century eurocentricism, anglocentricisim, and racism, the literary historian of Victorian cosmopolitan ideals is bound to predict the flummoxing of the ethical aspirations she describes.[2]

In this chapter I propose a different critical endeavor that takes the recent interest in actually existing cosmopolitanisms for its cue. By looking at the multi-faceted oeuvre of Anthony Trollope, one of the most well-traveled authors in the annals of nineteenth-century fiction, I seek a more sustained exploration of global aesthetics. Rather than evaluate nineteenth-century ethics by the light of today's theories, I ask what the Victorian era's global genres can tell us about cosmopolitan ethico-political projects—then as well as now. Here, as throughout this book, I consider the multiple ways that realist fiction operates as an enlivening geopolitical aesthetic—creating memorable formal experiments that do not simply reproduce or reify material realities but, rather, capture their dynamism across time and space.

The Trollopian "foreign policy" that I describe below is especially complex because of the author's unique penchant for dialectics *between* genres. As he pivoted from quotidian provincial novels to far-flung travel writings, Trollope's mid-Victorian *oeuvre* staged productive play between perceptions of England's sovereign rootedness and its colonial cosmopolitanism. But its effect was most unlike the "rooted cosmopolitanism" that Appiah and others have offered for

---

[1] For examples of Romanticist interest in cosmopolitanism see Craciun; for Modernist interest see J. Berman and Walkowitz. For a rich discussion of realist fiction which shares my interest in cosmopolitanism as geopolitical aesthetic, see Agathocleous, *Urban*.

[2] For Keirstead, Browning's poetry does not provide "a blueprint for cosmopolitanism, but rather a warning of its complexity, one that takes on renewed pertinence in a time when crossing borders has supposedly become easier thanks to open markets" and "technologies promising a more 'connected' world" ("Stranded" 430). See also Voskuil, "Robert," which argues that the horticultural cosmopolitanism of the East India Company traveler Robert Fortune is "able to accommodate the full complexity of Britain's imperialist practices" (16); and Gagnier, *Individualism*, Ch.5 on Friedrich Nietzsche and William Morris as exemplars of a late-nineteenth-century cosmopolitan commitment to criticizing inequality.

reflection on contemporary ethics. A pronounced racialist and Anglo-Saxon expansionist, Trollope was not a writer whose cosmopolitan attitude was likely to inspire modes of thinking or feeling beyond the nation; and yet, he was undeniably one of the era's most consummate cosmopolites—"the greatest traveler among mid-Victorian novelists," according to Michael Cotsell (243) and, according to Catherine Hall, the nineteenth-century's archetypal "Imperial Man" ("Going"; *Civilising* 211–13; cf. Brantlinger, *Victorian* 28–9 and passim). Trollope's reputation as the "Chronicler of Barsetshire," the author of English novels such as *The Warden* (1855), has tended to obscure the fact that he was also the writer of travel narratives depicting all but one of the major contact zones of Victorian imperialism: *The West Indies and the Spanish Main* (1859), *North America* (1862), *Australia and New Zealand* (1873), and *South Africa* (1878).[3] His oeuvre thus reminds us that from a nineteenth-century perspective, the word "cosmopolitan" was more likely to evoke the impersonal structures of capitalism and imperialism than an ethos of tolerance, world citizenship, or multiculturalism.[4]

To be sure, Trollope did not claim the term *cosmopolitan* to describe any aspect of his writing. His definition, like that of many Victorians, inclined to the pejorative. The word appears in *The Prime Minister* (1875–6) when an English landowner uses it to describe the dubious deracinated qualities of a man who "isn't of [his] sort"—one Ferdinand Lopez (141). This contemporary usage of cosmopolitan—in which the word stands for the social impact of capitalist mobility and, by extension, for the shadowy attributes of Jews and other perceived arrivistes—is, as I will show, ultimately inseparable from the qualities attributed to the "Colonial Man" of Trollope's travel writings.[5] In this way, Trollope exemplifies a mid-Victorian tendency to regard modernity's cosmopolitan features with ambivalence—as the byproduct of a capitalist and colonial expansion of British sovereignty in tension with England's heirloom roots.

As they imaginatively address the dilemmas of British sovereignty discussed in Chapter 2, Trollope's writings of the 1850s and 1860s capture a mid-Victorian *zeitgeist*. By penning a series of comic-ironic novels that eulogize England's rootedness alongside first-person accounts of colonial travel, Trollope became the arch-exemplar of a two-part foreign policy discourse. As the Chronicler of

---

[3] Trollope's reticence on India is no accident as I will demonstrate in Chapter 4. On Trollope and imperialism, see also Birns, "Empire"; Davidson; Brantlinger, *Rule* 4–8 and *Dark* 111–16. I borrow "Chronicler of Barsetshire" from Super's biography.

[4] The *Oxford English Dictionary* defines *cosmopolitan* as the condition of "belonging to all parts of the world" with the first citation taking capital rather than human personality for its object. The reference is to *The Principles of Political Economy* (1848) in which J. S. Mill alleged that "capital is becoming more and more cosmopolitan" (2:588). Marx and Engels describe the "cosmopolitan character [of] production and consumption" in comparable terms (476). For a compact survey of cosmopolitanism's shift from relatively positive usages to the Victorian era's often pejorative meanings see Goodlad and Wright.

[5] I choose "Colonial Man" over Hall's "Imperial Man" as the most applicable term. As Hall recognizes, Trollope was at odds with the New Imperialism of the 1870s: his enthusiasm for British expansion was focused on white settler colonies, not imperial domination of subject people in Asia or Africa.

Barsetshire, his works are veritable archetypes of "autoethnographic" fiction—exerting "centripetal force" against the imperial dispersion of English identity by offering textual "stand-ins for the boundaries of culture and nation" (Buzard, *Disorienting* 43). Sociologically descriptive in style, Trollope's fiction, wrote R. H. Hutton in 1882, "contain[s] a larger mass of evidence as to the character and aspects of English Society . . . than any other writer of his day has left behind him" (Smalley 505).[6] But, as Colonial Man, Trollope's travel writings thrust beyond the British Isles even as his English novels parry with acts of serial autoethnography. Whereas the Chronicler's insular imaginary focuses on the cultivated class credentials and venerable institutions of a hereditary elite—portraying an "heirloom sovereignty" that bolsters English culture and history in multiple ways—the writer of Colonial Man uses racial discourse to create a transportable mode of proprietary Englishness. Evoking the asymmetrical play between two notions of property—heirloom rootedness and cosmopolitan capital—Trollope's mid-Victorian global imaginary simulates (but does not fulfill) the liberal-humanist ideal of a genuinely "negotiated" rooted cosmopolitanism (Appiah, *Ethics* 232). That said, by the 1870s, coincident with the accelerating pace of capitalist globalization and the emergence of the New Imperialism, this Trollopian dialectic came to a close. As it did so, Trollope innovated a new and more naturalistic variation on the mid-Victorian geopolitical aesthetic.

TROLLOPIAN FOREIGN POLICY

> I . . . fearlessly challenge the verdict which this House, as representing a political, a commercial, a constitutional country, is to give on the question now brought before it; whether the principles on which the foreign policy of Her Majesty's Government has been conducted, and the sense of duty which has led us to think ourselves bound to afford protection to our fellow subjects abroad, are proper and fitting guides for those who are charged with the Government of England; and whether, as the Roman, in days of old, held himself free from indignity, when he could say *Civis Romanus sum*; so also a British subject, in whatever land he may be, shall feel confident that the watchful eye and the strong arm of England, will protect him against injustice and wrong.
>
> Henry John Temple, 3rd Viscount Palmerston
> addressing Parliament, June 1850

In suggesting "foreign policy" as the optic for a globally-situated literary criticism, my aim is not to document a wonkish discourse or to focus on the rarefied activities of the Foreign Office.[7] Rather, my broader usage designates a nationalist

---

[6] On Trollope's autoethnographic features see also Sadleir 398; D. Miller 107–45; Langbauer 85–127; Herbert 265–99; and, for Trollope's own remarks on the topic, *Autobiography* 101.

[7] Although the *OED*'s first citation for "foreign policy" is an 1859 *Saturday Review* article, a more interesting appearance is in Marx's 1853 analysis of Palmerston who, Marx believed, was

discourse on the global which professed to explain Britain's place in the world and in history. Precisely because it reeks of Anglo-Saxon exceptionalism, disavowed imperialism, and reflexive adherence to the self-interested sovereign state, Trollopian "foreign policy" illuminates the structures, both material and conceptual, which today's critics aim to historicize. "Foreign policy" in this sense tended to affirm imperialism as well the more purely economic forms of expansion which are associated with globalization today.[8]

Of course, to speak of British "imperialism" is to condense a heterogeneous English expansion that had begun with Ireland in the sixteenth century and, by the 1850s, had come to include settlement colonies such as Canada and Australia, West Indian colonies for the production of commodities, the aftermath of the slave trade, and a presence on the Indian subcontinent which had mutated from a commercial monopoly into a territorial empire, enlarged by conquest and sustained by the rule and taxation of a vast non-European population. As we saw in Chapter 2, Victorian writers often distinguished between Britain's "colonies" of settlement in the world's temperate zones and its "dependencies" or "possessions" in densely populated South Asia.[9] Colonies of settlement could be differentiated from the imperial rule of subject peoples in part because their indigenous inhabitants were regarded as stagnant "races" on the verge of extinction (see Brantlinger, *Dark*). Thus, according to Trollope, the British emigrants who had settled in the United States were non-imperialists: "driven by no thirst of conquest, by no greed of gold, dreaming of no Western empire such as Cortez had achieved and Raleigh had meditated" (*North* 28–9). In viewing settler colonies as organic extensions of the Anglo-Saxon metropole, Trollope anticipated the "Greater British" imaginary of later thinkers such as Charles Dilke, Goldwin Smith, and J. R. Seeley (Ch. 2).

In this way, Trollope's travel writings naturalized practices of empire, embedding them in a domesticated understanding of Britain's perceived historical role as the world's most economically advanced and politically liberal power. The mid-Victorian outlook he helped to popularize was famously set forth by Palmerston in a speech defending the blockading of Athens during the Don Pacifico controversy in 1850. Palmerston's doctrine that "a British subject, in whatever land he may be, shall feel confident that the watchful eye and the strong arm of England will protect him" was restated throughout the nineteenth century.

Consider, for example, an anonymous 1859 article in *Macmillan's Magazine*, one of a running series on current events titled, "Politics of the Present, Foreign

---

"responsible for the whole foreign policy England ha[d] pursued" since 1830" ("Story" Article 2). See also Trollope, *Lord Palmerston*.

[8] As we saw in Chapter 2, capitalism's growth and expansion are inseparable from the history of imperialism: although capitalism imagines itself to be independent of political and military power and strives to be so, the globalization of capital always relies to some degree on these extra-economic, often imperial forms of domination.

[9] Trollope himself warned against the "drift into the possession of undesirable so-called colonies" in the tropics which, unlike colonies in North America or Australia, do not provide "a fitting domicile for a single working European" (*Tireless* 200; cf. *Australia* 1:1–2).

and Domestic" (1). The author, David Masson, describes Britain as standing "on the fringe" of a precarious "continental state."[10] With the empires of France, Russia, and Austria eager to enhance their power in Europe; with the Ottoman Empire's hold over Eastern Europe in decline; and with the "passion for unity" creating nationalist unrest, "all is glaringly out of equilibrium" (2–3). It is only after portraying Britain as a relatively pacific power, compelled to defend "her shores" against the power struggles of illiberal continental regimes (2), that the article alludes to Britain's territorial interests outside Europe: "Britain must make *herself* safe. That is the first duty. There must be navy sufficient to ride round and round her, to keep the silver seas clear between her and the rest of the world and to maintain guard over her scattered dependencies" (4). Britain's sovereign reach thus includes "scattered dependencies" as well native shores. Yet, while the article alludes to the settler colonies and the difficult "imperial question of India," neither aspect of Britain's "varied and ocean-dislocated Empire" claims prolonged attention (8–10).

Instead, Masson goes to some lengths to establish Britain's world-historical role as a beacon of liberal opinion, morally "bound to extend . . . the spirit of liberty" (6). "A blow at the appendages of our Empire were nothing so fatal as a blow at this liberty of our heart" (5). How such commitment to liberty squares with the maintenance of imperial "appendages" (within recent memory of the Indian rebellion, no less) is never explained. Nor would one realize from reading the article that Britain's special stake in the Crimean War was to guard the shortest routes to India against the threat of Russian interference. In the nineteenth century, Britain repeatedly sought to shore up the Ottoman Empire, despite its reputation as a retrograde "Oriental" power, in order to enhance the security of imperial interests in nearby India. Such motives not only explained the Crimean campaign, but also war with Afghanistan in 1838, the deployment of gunboats against Egypt in 1840, and the annexation of the Cape Colony in 1806 through which Britain secured the long route to India (see Davison, O'Brien).

Mid-Victorian foreign policy discourse naturalized a vision of the globe in which major Western states vied to defend and extend the territories over which they claimed sovereignty. The monadic nation-state arose in conjunction with a propertarian understanding of the individual, a Lockean subject whose self-owned capacity to produce economic value provided ideological justification for the settlement of land outside English borders (Wood 82).[11] According to Masson,

> A man . . . lives not only in the spot which he personally occupies, but in every spot to which he may extend his action, or to which he may conceive it possible that his action should be extended. And so, wherever over the world British influence penetrates, or can conceive itself penetrating, there, and not in the mere islands where we have our footing, Great Britain lives (4).

---

[10] Masson, writing anonymously, was *Macmillan's* first editor, a seasoned journalist and literary critic.

[11] On the confluence between the sovereign nation-state and the "the single-point perspective of the autonomous individual" see Liftin 39.

Here is the Palmerstonian homology between British man and British empire which illustrates how the self-possessed Anglo-Saxon traveler personified in Trollope's travel writings authorizes a sovereignty that extends well beyond "the mere islands" of the British metropole. For in a way that structurally reproduces the relation between English "footing" and global reach, Trollope is famous for "thoroughly English" novels even as his travel writings depict colonial expansion as "central to Englishness, [and] part of what was special about the Anglo-Saxon race" (Trollope, *Autobiography* 95; Hall "Going" 184). For Hall, the relation between the two modes of writing is contiguity: Trollope reveals how "a particular preoccupation with the details" of English culture "can sit alongside a set of assumptions about other societies, 'races' and peoples" ("Going" 184). But Masson's article evokes a more productive relation between Colonial Man and the "spot" from which he launches his expansion. The Great Britain that "lives" coextensively with its "influence" may do so because the space that Britons "personally occupy" provides an exceptional ground, irreducible to geography or geopolitics, for such ambitious reach. This productive play between sovereign rootedness and cosmopolitan expansion, deriving from the geopolitics of an ambitious global power, was brilliantly articulated in a Trollopian foreign policy discourse which lasted through the twelve-year span of the Barsetshire novels (1855–1867)—the peak of the author's popularity and prestige.[12]

Rootedness as Heirloom Sovereignty

Those who examined [the arms at Greshamsbury Park] . . . might see . . . a scroll bearing the Gresham motto. . . . [M]ay such symbols long remain among us . . . They tell us of the true and manly feelings of other times; and to him who can read aright, they explain more fully, more truly than any written history can do, how Englishmen have become what they are. England is not yet a commercial country in the sense in which that epithet is used for her; and let us still hope that she will not soon become so . . . She may excel other nations in commerce, but yet it is not that in which she most prides herself, in which she most excels . . . Merchants as such are not the first men among us . . . Buying and selling is good and necessary . . . but it cannot be the noblest work of man; and let us hope that it may not in our time be esteemed the noblest work of an Englishman

Anthony Trollope, *Doctor Thorne* (1858).

---

[12] As Abigail Green notes in a discussion of Don Pacifico, "Nothing could be more ironic than to find [the] stirring language" of *Civis Romanus sum* applied in defense of this Jewish subject of Greek anti-Semitism "who—had he returned to England and been voted into parliament—would have been unable to take his seat. Yet the Jewishness of Don Pacifico was not entirely accidental. Rather, he typified the symbiosis that so often existed in the Mediterranean and the Levant between British imperialism and the Jewish entrepreneur" (180). Trollope, whose ambivalence toward Jews is discussed below and in the next chapter, cast aspersions on Don Pacifico's character in a chapter on the episode in his 1882 biography of Palmerston (see Trollope, *Lord Palmerston*, Chapter 8).

> The use of the Queen, in a dignified capacity, is incalculable. Without her in England, the present English Government would fail and pass away.
>
> Walter Bagehot, *The English Constitution* (1865–6)

To speak of England's rootedness is implicitly to invoke the Barsetshire novels.[13] Their in-depth portraits of England's provincial interior exert centripetal force against a variety of global effects including London's capitalist metropolis, Europe's geopolitical wrangling, projects of Great and Greater Britain, and the impact of a "varied and ocean-dislocated Empire." If, as Benedict Anderson has argued, the modern nation is constituted as an imagined community, then in its best-known Trollopian formation, the English nation is constituted as Barsetshire, the imagined county of an imagined "Cathedral city"—an auto-ethnographic synecdoche (*Autobiography* 63). Nineteenth-century foreign policy discourse persistently asserted Britain's vanguard status: the Victorian public "believe[d] that Britain held a unique position in the world" and "liked to believe both in British benevolence and British power" (Chamberlain 6, 7). The achievement of Trollope's Barsetshire novels was thus to insist that though England was "a commercial country" its exceptionality was founded on a nobler conception of sovereign property than that to which "buying and selling" gives rise (Trollope, *Doctor* 12).[14]

Trollope's first Barsetshire novel, *The Warden*, is a rumination on property, its plot inspired by debates over the Church of England's management of charitable endowments. But while contemporary newspaper coverage focused on flagrant abuses—negligent clergymen who occupied multiple places and farmed out their duties to low-paid proxies—Trollope's Mr. Harding, a dutiful pastor, is "the moral center of the Barsetshire novels" (Nardin 8). The novel's obvious point is that Harding is not the corrupt caricature of reformist rhetoric. But its more subtle message is to concede the legitimacy of moderate reform even while demonstrating that the law, the supposed moral compass of a secular modernity, is inadequate to provide authoritative judgment on questions of rightful ownership. When Harding asks Sir Abraham Haphazard if he is "legally and distinctly entitled to the proceeds of the property" he oversees, the answer he receives from the "eminent Queen's Counsel" is inconclusive. Since the precise modern meaning of John Hiram's will is debatable, the only relevant legal point is that the suit has been abandoned: "nobody now questions [the] justness" of the warden's income. Harding replies, "I question it myself," an ethical concern that leads him to resign rather than risk appropriating "the property of the poor" (36; 153–4).

---

[13] My reading focuses on the key elements of rootedness in *The Warden* which are sustained throughout the series: *Barchester Towers* (1857), *Doctor Thorne* (1858), *Framley Parsonage* (1860–61), *The Small House at Allington* (1862–4), and *The Last Chronicle of Barset* (1866–7).

[14] As E. Michie observes, Trollope uses the marriage plot in *Doctor Thorne* to create "a symbolic barrier in which commercial wealth is defined as not able to penetrate into what Max Weber defined as the status order" (*Vulgar* 112).

Like the Scottian historical novels on which they look back, Trollope's Barsetshire narratives heal a "world torn apart by historical forces" (Duncan, *Modern* 105) with a vision of the holistic power of a shared heirloom history. *The Warden* in particular is a realist fable in which the problem articulated in *The New Zealander*—the problem of how the English can "make [themselves] an honest people" (12)—is imaginatively resolved.[15] The moral center of the Barsetshire novels is the "sheer Quixotism" of an elderly eccentric (154); its most potent expression is that intuitive ethic, symbolized by Harding's performance on an imaginary cello, which triumphs over Church interests, self-righteous reforms, and the struggle for power to which both are subject. "Whatever men do they should certainly do honestly," wrote Trollope in *North America*, and, yet, "When men have political ends to gain they regard their opponents as adversaries, and . . . the old rule of war is brought to bear" (14). Though Trollope is discussing the politics of a looming civil war in the United States, he might be describing Archdeacon Grantly who, as he prepares to defend "ecclesiastical revenues," "shakes his feathers, and erects his comb" like an "indomitable cock preparing for . . . combat" (*Warden* 36). Although the narrator of *The Warden* is ironic, both works attest to a Hobbesean world in which the law, for all its importance in securing property, is ultimately a weapon to be wielded by powerful factions. As the novel makes clear, neither sovereign legislature nor sovereign electorate warrant a truly ethical ownership since both bodies dissolve into the material interests of the Lockean monads who compose them.[16]

Trollope's early novel thus sets the stage for that quietistic, almost cynical literary realism for which he is often taken as arch-practitioner. For George Levine, Trollope's perception of a "compromised world" is so strong that it frees him "to accept the disenchantment that dispels ideals for reality" (*Realistic* 182, 192). And yet, that common view of Trollope's realism is not adequate to capturing *The Warden*'s evocation of an ethico-culturally embedded sovereignty of the kind readers cherished in Walter Scott's Waverly novels. Political sovereignty was a subject of recurring interest to Trollope, discussed in *The New Zealander* (144–50) and, more than ten years later on the eve of electoral reform, in an 1867 article for *St. Paul's Magazine*. In a way that contrasts with the decidedly instrumental account put forward in Walter Bagehot's *The English Constitution* (the serialization of which began in 1865), Trollope's "On Sovereignty" portrays England's constitutional monarchy as the nation's heirloom—a legacy that U. S. republicans cannot comprehend and French subjects of the Second Empire cannot produce. Indeed, England's constitution is so elusive that it defies representation: "so

---

[15] On Scott's influence on various forms of nineteenth-century fiction, French as well as British, see Ch. 6. Drafted in the 1850s and published in 1971, *The New Zealander* is not a travel account but a series of essays on the condition of England. For a reading that emphasizes Trollope's turn away from such strident critique in favor of the temperate Barsetshire novels see Goodlad, *Victorian*, Ch. 4.

[16] On Trollope's efforts to "define an honest understanding of ownership" in *The Eustace Diamonds*, see A. Miller, *Novels* 163; on Trollopian honesty more generally, see Kucich, *Power* Ch. 1; on Trollope and the law, see Cunningham and Ben-Yishai.

intricate in its arrangements" that it cannot be "produced ready made by any brain"; "a thing so complex that gray-headed statesmen" spend their lives interpreting it and "foreigners" fail to grasp its perfection (85–6). In the end, to conjure such ineffable sovereignty, Trollope invokes a Barset-like analogy, comparing England's constitution to Salisbury Cathedral, with the throne representing its "tower and spire":

> The real work for which [the cathedral] was built is not done within those beautiful but narrow confines. But from the tower comes that peal of bells which calls the people to the worship they love, and the spire was built that it might be seen from afar off, and recognised as the symbol in those parts of the religion of the country (87).[17]

Here is a noteworthy exception to the view of Trollope as the staunchly anti-romantic practitioner of complacent moral compromise. *The Warden* depicts English sovereignty as the product of an organic national history, a cherished legacy, "the beautiful and decorous" parts of which, like the "*theatrical show*" Bagehot more acidly described in *The English Constitution*, provide a crucial symbolic function (248; Bagehot's emphasis). Trollope's depiction of this heirloom sovereignty resists realist disenchantment in pitting the cathedral's "real work" (analogous to prosaic modern governance) against the sublime aesthetic effects of its tower and spire. In *The Warden*, the inspirational institutions that exalt English sovereignty are not mere instrumentalities, as with Bagehot's "decorous" parts or the "use of the Queen" (*English* 82), but a romantic structure through which to imagine the potential capture of Harding's embodied ethic. Trollope's "cathedral sublimities" thus seek to locate the warden's irreducible morality in *The Warden*'s figuration of an enchanted heirloom space and time.[18]

As commentators since Karl Marx's day have noted, capitalist modernity produces the spatio-temporal compression that Walter Benjamin described as "homogeneous, empty time" ("Theses" 264). Locke's possessive individual is a symptom of such modern abstraction—the bearer of supposedly sovereign rights that derive from a disembedded and atomized conception of ownership. Yet, by the late eighteenth century romantics such as Edmund Burke were arguing for the particularity and historicity of ownership—for a holistic notion of property that answered to non-economic criteria such as who possessed what and for how long. This was to attempt to instill in modern property that concrete imbuing of time with space, or place with history that, for Trollope, constitutes the heirloom's

---

[17] For an earlier version of the metaphor, see *New Zealander* 149.

[18] I borrow "cathedral sublimities" from Gilmour's introduction to *The Warden*, xxvi. Compare to Bagehot's more disenchanted discussion of the Monarchy: "The best reason why Monarchy is a strong government is, that it is an intelligible government. The mass of mankind understand it, and they hardly anywhere in the world understand any other" (*English* 82). As Harvie suggests, Trollope's rendering of the cathedral as heirloom emerged from a climate so soured by clerical abuse that even Christian Socialists saw no reason to defend the cathedrals: Charles Kingsley proposed that they be made over into "winter gardens" for the working classes (88). On Trollopian ethics, see also apRoberts on Trollope's "flexible morality" (52), Hawkins on the importance of music in articulating the Warden's transfiguring ethics, and Earle on his "exemplary instance of performative self-determination" (23).

status as non-instrumentality, the cathedral's status as a privileged English location, the status of Britain's sovereignty as the embedded growth of the nation's ongoing historical progress—and, from a formal standpoint—*The Warden*'s status as a realist's fable.

Trollope's notion of the sovereign heirloom thus describes a form of property that accumulates particular ethical and cultural worth in excess of abstract economic value and, in so doing, binds rather than atomizes.[19] *The Warden* thus seems to look back to Burke's *Reflections on the Revolution in France* (1790). Why, asks Burke, should the expenditures of "a great landed property" trouble anyone when it produces "the accumulation of vast libraries," "great collections of antient records, medals, and coins," "paintings and statues," etc.—in a word, heirlooms, or auratic autoethnographic objects. In a rhetorical question that one may imagine earning the endorsement of Archdeacon Grantly, Burke asks, "If, by great permanent establishments, all these objects of expence are better secured from the inconstant sport of personal caprice . . . are they worse than if the same tastes prevailed in scattered individuals?" (272). And, yet, when Trollope poses a similar question in *The Warden*, his irony distinguishes Burke's robust post-Enlightenment conservatism from the realist novelist's mid-Victorian defense against the capitalist modernity he ambivalently embraces.

Determined to take on "the Church's enemies," Grantly has set out to visit his unreliably idealistic father-in-law. The privileged locality of "the hallowed close" thus surfaces through the ironizing frame of his indignation (37). Although the point has not been to demolish Grantly's sincerity—he is nothing if not a zealous believer in his own cause—the narrator's sudden leap toward Burke-like affirmation of "great permanent establishments" comes as a surprise. Calling on readers to relax their suspicion and join the archdeacon's appreciation of hallowed ground, the novel momentarily asserts the holistic power of spatio-temporal enchantment:

> *And who has not felt the same?* We believe that [the most ardent reformers of the day] would relent, were [they] to allow themselves to stroll by moonlight round the towers of some of our ancient churches. Who would not feel charity for a prebendary, when walking the quiet length of that long aisle at Winchester . . . feeling, as one must, the solemn orderly comfort of the spot! . . . Who could lie basking in the cloisters of Salisbury, and gaze on . . . that unequalled spire, without feeling that bishops should sometimes be rich? (37–8; emphasis added).

The passage is remarkable for its subtle recasting of Burke. "The tone of our archdeacon's mind must not astonish us," the narrator continues, "it has been the growth of centuries of Church ascendancy" (*Warden* 38). In other words, though Grantly's belief in his own propaganda may at first give pause, why, on reflection, should the ancient institutions he is fighting to preserve "appear intolerable to

---

[19] For a contrast between Lockean and Burkean notions of property to which I am indebted, see Goh 164–8. Blumberg's articulation of "mutual benefit" tallies with my reading up to a point (520): although she rightly argues that Harding's act exemplifies "collective benefit" rather than conventional self-sacrifice, she does not note *The Warden*'s striving for a non-economistic conception of ownership.

you or to me"? "Who, without remorse can batter down the dead branches of an old oak... without feeling that they sheltered the younger plants?" (*Warden* 38). Reading such passages one almost hears the confirmatory voice of Burke's *Reflections*: "A disposition to preserve, and an ability to improve, taken together, would be my standard... Every thing else is vulgar in the conception, perilous in the execution" (267).

And, yet, though Trollope's writing is saturated with such calls for moderation, the author of *The Warden* is not precisely Burkean. Trollope's reverence for established hierarchies was in tension with the decidedly individualist entrepreneurial ethos with which he identified when, for example, he recalled his own rise from the shabbiest of genteel origins to literary renown (see *Autobiography*). When Burke makes a case for "hereditary possession," he is not merely arguing that the heirs of great family fortunes are culturally superior to the "great masses," he is also endowing such scions with an ethical power to "graft benevolence... upon avarice" (*Reflections* 140–41). Trollope, a self-made man in the literary marketplace, had a more complicated view of individual self-interest which was imaginatively interwoven with England's expansion. "Greed and covetousness are no doubt vices," he wrote in *The West Indies and the Spanish Main*, "but they are vices which have grown from cognate virtues. Without a desire for property, man could make no progress" (62). Such acquisitive "virtue" is of more use to Trollope, the upwardly mobile man of letters, than to Grantly, the defender of established privilege.

Of course, it is not Grantly's militant defense of clerical incomes that makes cathedral sublimity a compelling aesthetic, but his father-in-law's ethical leap away from property and privilege. Trollope's narrator thus affirms the existing social order while casting doubt on the moral purity of those who benefit most from its unequal dispensation. In crafting this compromise, the novel purposely conflates two underlying conceptions of property: the holist heirloom, of presumed benefit to all, and the unabashedly individually-held property that constitutes the Lockean subject. The result in *The Warden* is to align British sovereignty, symbolized by the spires of England's ancient cathedrals, not only with the Crown (as in the *St. Paul's* essay), but also with the less exalted aspects of a conservative ideology that includes the prosaic idea that "bishops should sometimes be rich." This Grantlyan recasting of Burke's response to the French Revolution is deliberately ironic: a kind of mid-Victorian rewriting of tragedy as farce.

Crucially, then, the loyal Bunce, Harding's favorite among the impoverished bedesmen, comes forward to supplement Grantly's self-interested defense of the existing hierarchy. Bunce neutralizes the specter of redistribution, not by mocking equality but by articulating an extra-economic version of it that comports with Burke's view of property. As he rebukes his fellow bedesmen for hankering after Harding's income, asking, "A'n't you all as rich in your ways as he is in his?" (34), Bunce insists on the holist effects of an established governing class. He describes a form of rootedness—at bottom, a classist fantasy of non-individualist ownership with the potential to enchant—which Trollope's cosmopolitan travel writings cannot readily incorporate. Whereas the Barsetshire novels offer a potent class mythology in which England's sovereignty is rooted in an established hierarchy, the travel writings, as we shall see, imagine "race" as the warrant for a very different and, yet, geopolitically necessary project of colonial expansion and class mobility.

The Way We Colonize Now

> When we make mention of 'colonies' we should be understood to signify countries outside our own, which by our energies we have made fit for the occupation of our multiplying race ... India is in no respect a colony [since] we do not hold it for the direct welfare of our own race.
>
> Anthony Trollope, *Australia and New Zealand* (1873)

With their strong emphasis on race as a determinant of human difference, Trollope's travel writings were at the vanguard of the increasing tendency for mid-Victorian liberals to abandon the universalistic views of the Enlightenment. But because Trollope's racialism derives from a cosmopolitan conception of global commerce, his ideas differ from polygenetic theories that viewed racial intermixture as biologically impossible.[20] In his book on the West Indies, Trollope sees racial hybridity as part of "the Creator's scheme," a byproduct of the world's economic progress (63). Decades after the abolition of slavery, and with a mixed race of "coloured people" eager for self-rule (80), Trollope regards the work of British colonialism in the Caribbean as all but complete. Having done the job of spreading "civilization," "commerce," and the presumed racial benefits of Anglo-Saxon "blood," Britons should soon "bid farewell to the West Indies." Rather than "swelter ... in the tropics," Trollope's readers should turn their sights on North America and Australia, temperate lands that await "the foot of the Englishman" (82). Notably, in climates deemed hospitable to Anglo-Saxon settlement, Trollope envisions no role for racial intermixture. His assumption that in settler contexts indigenous people will simply "melt away" upon contact with a "higher race" (*Australia* 2:123–4), is part of the ubiquitous extinction discourse that, as Patrick Brantlinger has shown, anticipated the vanishing of indigenes "wherever and whenever" they encountered Europeans (Brantlinger, *Dark* 1). Whether by touting racial hybridity in the tropics, or lamenting the inevitable "extermination" of "natives" in the settler colonies (*Tireless* 200), Colonial Man cultivates a global outlook premised on racialized hierarchies of civilization and progress.[21]

---

[20] On polygenetic pseudoscience, see Ellingson 248–62 and Stocking 248–54. By contrast, Trollope believed that Anglo-Saxon "race" was itself the product of interethnic mixture and that trade was the modern mechanism through which such providential hybridization would continue. With the coming of Chinese and Indian laborers to the West Indies, he predicted, Asian and African blood will mix "and the necessary compound will, by God's infinite wisdom and power, be formed for these latitudes, as it has been formed for the colder regions in which the Anglo-Saxon preserves his energy" (*West* 75)

[21] Trollope's racialization of Irishness took another form, expressive of colonial paternalism. By contrast, his comparative disinclination toward imperial expansion in Asia and Africa stemmed from an anti-paternalistic but also racialized reluctance to see Britain undertake "extended dominion

Of course, postcolonial critics have noted the inherent instabilities of such overweening imperial identity. Travel writers such as Trollope, writes Simon Gikandi, needed to explore "the extremities of empire" to discover their own self-proclaimed Englishness (*Maps* 89). British imperialism, notes Ian Baucom, entailed an inevitable "loss of cultural certainty," a "scattering" of the "locations of identity" on which the stability of Englishness depended (220). If for Hall, Trollope's jaunty Anglo-Saxon traveler "reassured his readers that all was indeed in place" ("Going" 185), for Baucom, imperialism's jarring dispersal of "privileged spaces" left English identities vulnerable and unlocated (220). The imaginative work of sustaining a far-flung Anglo-Saxon identity is as precarious as Baucom suggests. Nonetheless, the Chronicler of Barsetshire does not simply blunder into colonial projects but, rather, describes himself within a structure of cosmopolitan expansion which explicitly requires them.

According to Ellen Meiksins Wood, England's colonies of settlement were the first "form of imperialism driven by the logic of capitalism," justifying the colonization of land not through a political right to rule, such as that which authorizes a hereditary elite, but through an economic "obligation to produce exchange-value" (73, 99). Settler colonialism advanced the "possessive individual," the self-owned subject of Lockean theory (Macpherson), authorizing the expansion of British sovereignty. But Trollope's works express persistent dissatisfaction with possessive individualism, which they figure as a corrosive modern tendency to unleash Hobbesean selfishness at the expense of the crucial holist restraints that heirloom institutions are alleged to preserve. In works from every stage in his career, across a range of genres, Trollope depicts competitive individualism as a threat to honesty, the moral and aesthetic standard that he is least willing to compromise. And, yet, the "desire for property" is also what makes civilization possible, separating Anglo-Saxons from allegedly non-progressive races such as the Afro-Caribbean "negro" (*West Indies* 62). In Trollope, race thus plays the paradoxical part of affirming the progressiveness of English capitalism *and* providing a necessary escape from its pitfalls. His colonial works mythologize Anglo-Saxon "race" in the effort to root and to moralize expropriative practices that, within Barsetshire's imaginary, require the civilizing legacy of heirloom institutions.

In *North America*, the first of Trollope's travel works to focus on the "Greater British" imaginary, class mobility is the predominant theme. Although Trollope is impressed by the transformative impact of owning property, he is decidedly ambivalent about the possessive individualism thus produced: "The western American has no love for his own soil, or his own house. The matter with him is simply one of dollars. To keep a farm which he could sell at an advantage from any feeling of affection,—from what we should call an association of ideas, would be to him . . . ridiculous" (128). It is hard to imagine a less Barset-like image, one less complementary to the Warden's careful tending of a garden that he holds in

---

over black subjects" (*Tireless* 200). While Trollope consistently imagines a racial hierarchy, the geopolitical specificities of particular foreign policies explain his oscillation between racial intermixture and racial extinction, colonial paternalism and anti-paternalism.

trust for the Church and, by extension, for the benefit of humble bedesmen. Yet, Trollope's purpose is not to impugn the American landowner as a deracinated *homo economicus*.

> [T]his man has his romance . . . and above all his manly dignity. Visit him, and you will find him without coat or waistcoat . . . too often bearing on his lantern jaws the signs of ague and sickness; but he will stand upright before you and speak to you with all the ease of a lettered gentleman in his own library . . . He is his own master, standing on his own threshold . . . He is delighted to see you, and bids you sit down on his battered bench without dreaming of any such apology as an English cottier offers to a Lady Bountiful when she calls (128).

Whereas the "rough fellow" who farms for "dollars" in the American West attains "the ease of a lettered gentleman in his own library," the English laborer's deference hobbles manly dignity. To be sure, Trollope has not lost faith in the ethico-cultural value of English gentlemen. But from the vantage of North America's working proprietors, he finds it impossible to dignify the dependent laboring-class condition on which English gentility partly rests. Trollope goes so far as to extend this invidious contrast in racial terms: "I defy you not to feel that [the North American settler] is superior to the race from whence he has sprung in England or Ireland" (129; cf. *Australia* I 180).

Trollope's complicated views on Irishness originated in a sustained encounter with colonized people who were not, like the indigenes of North America and Australia, expected to "melt away." Sentimental and racialized depictions of Irishness are a recurrent feature of his works.[22] Trollope's decision to close his journey in *North America* with a stop in Ireland is, therefore, no accident. It functions as a necessary restorative to undo the jarring effects of settler mobility, including the stunning transformation of Irish settlers. Neither fully a colonizer, like the Anglo-Saxon settler, nor fully colonized like the "kinsman" of Trollope's "intimacy," the Irishman who "expatriates himself" is a markedly rootless cosmopolitan (*North* 599). This deracinated Irishman:

> loses much of that affectionate, confiding, master-worshipping nature which makes him so good a fellow at home. But he becomes more of man. He assumes a dignity which he never has known before. He learns to regard his labour as his own property. That which he earns he takes without thanks, but he desires to take no more than he earns. To me personally he has become much less pleasant than he was. But to himself—! It seems to me that such a man must feel himself half a god . . . (600).

Clearly, in the Irish case Trollope's ambivalence toward the individualizing effects of the settler condition intensifies. He is torn between affection for the essentialized Irishman—a non-autonomous, non-possessive, subject of imperial conquest

---

[22] On Trollope's residence in Ireland in the 1840s and 1850s, during which he launched his literary career, see *Autobiography*, Ch. 4 which describes the Irish as thrifty and intelligent, but also "perverse, irrational, and but little bound by the love of truth" (46). Trollope opposed Home Rule, a measure that Phineas Finn, the Irish MP of the Palliser novels, says he would no more grant to Ireland than he would "allow a son to ruin himself because he asked [him to]" (*Prime* 104; cf. *Autobiography* 51). Trollope tends to figure the Irish as infantilized objects of a caring paternalism (see, *e.g.*, Corbett Ch 4. and Lonergan). On Trollope's Irish novels, see Bigelow.

(emotional, "master-worshipping," and non-proprietary)—and admiration for colonial conditions of possibility which turn all able-bodied comers into comparable variations on *homo economicus*, with or without Anglo-Saxon bona fides. Whereas the racialized and presumably static Irishman of *An Autobiography* is "little bound by the love of truth" (46) the upwardly mobile Irishman of *North America* "take[s] no more than he earns," but takes his earnings "without thanks." The result is a provoking indeterminacy. Trollope's travel writings attempt to root Englishness in blood and language rather than place, imagining an Anglo-Saxon mastery of space and time independent of British political sovereignty or the cultivation of English institutions on colonial soil. But the vision of an Irish *homo economicus* threatens to dissolve such transportable roots. Trollope declares himself "fond of Irish beggars" but in the United States, "men and women do not beg" (600). The ground of this new-model possessive individual is neither blood nor place but mere ownership of property including ownership of one's own self and labor.

This tendency for settlers to appear as proprietary monads and rootless cosmopolitans counters the comforting notion of an essentialized and portable Anglo-Saxon identity.[23] At such moments, Trollopian cosmopolitanism does not so much spatially scatter as stumble over the patent falseness of the moralized expropriation for which Anglo-Saxonness stands. Thus, for all his enthusiasm for propertarian manhood, the closing paragraphs of *North America*, much like the Barsetshire novels, suggest an author deeply invested in a hierarchical society in which property is a privilege, and proximity to "affectionate" imperial subjects one of its perquisites. What the United States ultimately produces is not the rooted Anglo-Saxon settler of the "Greater British" imaginary, but, rather, Cosmopolitan Man at his most deracinated. *North America*'s halting valorization of *homo economicus* ends with a question mark (601)—as though to admit that Greater Britain may have its limits.

Striking though such ambivalence is, it is the inevitable result of Trollope's two-part foreign policy. As both Chronicler of Barsetshire and Colonial Man, Trollope could, on balance, reassure his middle-class readers. The Trollopian play of rootedness and cosmopolitanism articulates a basic geopolitical relation between Britain and its settler colonies which reproduces England's exceptional global status. Whereas the seemingly limitless resources of the colony enable possessive individuals to propagate, Barsetshire's limited but richly cultivated supply requires venerated establishments to conserve a shared sovereign history. This Trollopian writing of foreign policy underwrites the uneven developments of a global economy, creating productive tension between the rootedness of an "old

---

[23] It is worth noting the scale of this emigration: by "the mid-nineteenth century," writes P. Mukherjee, "more than a million British people were emigrating each decade to settle overseas . . . 1.3 million in the 1850s, 1.5 million in the 1860s, and 1.2 million in the first half of the 1870s alone" (3–4). On "portable roots" in relation to Latina women, see Findlay. On the importance of "tangible objects" in constructing a portable "Englishness abroad," see Plotz, "One-Way" 312 and *Portable*.

country" and the cosmopolitanism of its expanding frontier (*Australia* 745). The prosperous nineteenth-century reader, putting down *Macmillan's* and picking up *Doctor Thorne*, perceives that, as a global vanguard, England's heirloom social hierarchy produces genteel governing classes unique to its soil, even as its settler colonies cultivate more democratic versions of Anglo-Saxon, or even Celtic, virtue. It is an exquisitely flexible construction, yet one that requires a readiness to affirm a Barsetshire-like English gentry, ethico-culturally equipped to carry on the "noblest work."[24]

Trollope's deepening pessimism about England in the 1870s is often explained as the direct effect of his growing admiration for the settler colony with, for example, *The Way We Live Now* described as a "sequel to the glowing" portrayal "of the new settler society arising in the Antipodes" (Davidson 306–7; cf. Sutherland, "Introduction," *Way* vii; Buzard, *Disorienting* 50). But it seems equally important to note that the zealous endorsement of colonialism in *Australia and New Zealand* was written after the last Barsetshire novel in 1867, in which Septimus Harding is buried "in the cathedral which he had loved so well" (*Last* 862).[25] As Elsie Michie notes, by the 1870s Britain's economy had shifted from primarily "manufacturing" to "marketing and banking" ("Buying" 103). Trollope's career thus coincided with Britain's rapid transition "from an economy based on money to one based on credit . . . from unlimited liability, which restricted access to investment, to limited liability, which opened the stock market to anyone with a few pounds to risk" (Crosby 294). The scene of *The Eustace Diamonds* (written prior to the author's departure for Australia in 1871, but published in 1873), *The Way We Live Now* (1875), and *The Prime Minister* is the London metropolis: a growing center of global finance and imperial policy. The 1870s thus saw Trollope ceasing to write about "the dear county" he knew so well and instead writing novels in which the forces of capitalist expansion visibly transmogrify the English metropole (*Autobiography* 101). What does such "reverse colonization" suggest about the play of rootedness and cosmopolitanism that, in the Barsetshire

---

[24] Cf. Davidson on the "unwritten code of Barsetshire . . . In the last analysis a gentleman could be neither imported nor exported" (309). I do not argue that Barsetshire's discourse of class and nation is innocent of the presumption of Anglo-Saxon racial supremacy (see Langbauer's case for "the hidden notions of race that underlie *Framley Parsonage*" [113]). Yet, so long as heirloom sovereignty holds, there is no preponderant need for "race" in England (as there is in the colonies where racial discourse forecasts the extinction of indigenous peoples and provides a fantasy of transportable Anglo-Saxon roots). The distinction is important because where "race" appears in the English novels, it testifies to a devastating breach of sovereignty—an insidious and naturalistically depicted metropolitan cosmopolitanism.

[25] Trollope's failed bid for Parliament in 1868 is another biographical event adduced to explain the pessimism of the later novels (e.g. Halperin 111; McMaster 225, n1). See E. Michie for an account of Barsetshire's end in light of capitalist developments ("Buying"; *Vulgar*, Ch. 3); Franklin for a Bourdieuvian reading of *Last Chronicle*; and Dames for a contrast between Barsetshire's relatively stable conflicts and those of the Palliser novels ("Trollope" 265). As I argue in Chapter 4, Trollope's dissatisfaction with the emerging New Imperialism, including his racist dislike for Benjamin Disraeli, is yet another key context for the breached sovereignty depicted in the later novels.

decades, had sustained far-reaching expansion without compromising England's hallowed domain?[26] As England's heirloom sovereignty melts into air, Trollope's works cease to articulate an intelligible foreign policy discourse, and "cosmopolitanism" emerges as a racialized signifier of non-Englishness.

"A RACE OF GENTLEMEN"

> She knew enough of such people as the Whartons and the Fletchers to be aware that as a class they are more impregnable, more closely guarded by their feelings and prejudices against strangers than any other. None keep their daughters to themselves with greater care . . . And yet this man, half foreigner, half Jew—and as it now appeared,—whole pauper, had stepped in and carried off a prize . . .
>
> Anthony Trollope, *The Prime Minister* (1875–6)

Trollope's Barsetshire novels figure an England imbued with a still palpable ethico-cultural richness in which the heirlooms of the past continue meaningfully to signify "more truly than any written history can do, how Englishmen have become what they are" (*Doctor* 12). By contrast, his naturalistic narratives of capitalist globalization are sites of breached sovereignty and spatio-temporal annihilation; they portray a disenchanted modernity in which Hobbesean combatants struggle to wrest money and power from the all but substanceless flow of capital and commodities, an "apparent chaos" that is metonymically expressed in the Tenway Junction (*Prime* 517). With fraudulent ladies like Lizzie Eustace, cads like Sir Felix Carbury, and would-be leaders like Plantagenet Palliser demoralized by corruption, it is no wonder that England's social hierarchy has ceased to sustain a holistic heirloom sovereignty as it did in *The Warden*. Nor is it surprising to find England's hereditary ruling class borrowing racial discourse from Colonial Man to shore up increasingly feeble claims to ethico-cultural authority. Thus, when "cosmopolitanism" returns to England it does so as a discourse of blood without roots, capitalism's blood—the blood of Jews.

"What's the use of money you can see?" says Lopez to Sexty Parker, the partner he coolly ruins in *The Prime Minister* (401). Like *The Eustace Diamonds* and *The Way We Live Now*, Trollope's fifth Palliser novel pictures a metropolitan culture infected by racialized outsiders. Serialized between November 1875 and June 1876, Trollope's eponymous novel offers a not-so-subtle commentary on the real-life Prime Minister, Benjamin Disraeli, a rival political author whom Trollope had portrayed as an un-English fraud. In his review of *Lothair* (1870), Trollope described a "vulgar" and "ill written" work ("Mr." 555) and in his autobiography, he deplored an oeuvre full of "audacious conjurers." *Lothair*, he contended, was the most "false" of Disraeli's works: a book in which "that flavour of hair oil, that

---

[26] On the "remarkable frequency" of reverse colonization narratives "throughout the last decades of the century" see Arata, "Occidental" 623.

flavour of false jewels, that remembrance of tailors, comes out stronger than in all the others" (*Autobiography* 166).

Here is the unmistakable backdrop for Lopez, whose stealthy efforts "to dress himself well" help him to "conjure" in business, politics, and love (*Prime* 12, 291). As one who is "too cosmopolitan," Lopez not only traffics in surreal commodities such as South American guano, New Zealand Kauri gum, and African "Bios," but does so, as the unhappy Mrs. Parker protests, without any "money to pay for [them]" (141, 399). Such desire to "get rich" without "hard work," she declares, "ain't what [she] call[s] manly" (400, 404). In saying so, she provides a potential antithesis between London's speculative global economy and the settler colony's productive labor. Yet, while Mrs. Parker knows that an ambitious bachelor might "go to the Colonies" much as Trollope's son Frederic went to Australia, *The Prime Minister* is not a novel in which Greater Britain revitalizes an ailing metropole (400). On the contrary, the City is the site of colonial blowback, as though the exportation of acquisitive settlers has returned in the un-English speculation of Lopez and Augustus Melmotte (cf. Cotsell 253). Trollope's novels thus seek to isolate the pernicious effects of capitalist globalization in the figure of the Jew, that archetypal foreigner whose organic relation to the "growing cosmopolitanism of capital" seemed obvious even to a high-minded anti-imperialist such as J. A. Hobson (*Imperialism* 51; cf. 56, 59).[27]

John Fletcher's description of Lopez as "too cosmopolitan," a man "white-washed of all prejudices," who, like a North American settler, "never had an association in his life," is, from this view, a sally against the capitalist disruptions the novel aims imaginatively to redress.[28] John's brother Arthur is not merely a gentleman on the model of Grantly, Harding, or Josiah Crawley, but also "the very pearl of the Fletcher tribe" (125), his fair Anglo-Saxon features repeatedly contrasted to those of Lopez, a "swarthy son of Judah" (35). As Audrey Jaffe notes, "Trollope makes it the business of his novels to delineate the distinctions in feeling that separate the gentleman from the non-gentleman" (49). Yet, it is not enough that Lopez be a rootless, disaffected *homo economicus*. In *The Prime Minister*, Lopez's non-gentility must somehow go all the way down, beyond cosmopolitan lack. The novel thus affirms racial essence even as the author who narrates it shows his continuing awareness that race is often an alibi for the deceits of capitalist modernity.[29]

---

[27] I discuss Hobson in Chapter 7. For illuminating discussions of "the Jew" in Trollope, see Amarnick; Baumgarten; Cheyette, *Constructing* 23–42; Dellamora Ch. 4; Freedman Ch. 2; Litvak; and Ragussis 238–60. On Lopez, see also Carter and Gagnier, "Conclusion." As Litvak writes, what scares Trollope most "is less the prospect of any . . . overtly Faginesque cultural presence than the possibility that an assimilated, dissimulated Jewishness, once having entered the bloodstream of English culture, will begin . . . congealing within it" (129).

[28] For a comparable usage, see Ch. 30 of *The Way We Live Now*, which describes Melmotte's bogus North American railway, ironically, as "a great cosmopolitan fact" (1:277).

[29] Cf. Langbauer: Jewish questionability "does not indict capitalism (or imperialism, or racism), but provides them all with a convenient scapegoat to blame and punish" (111).

Lopez's constitutive ambiguity—is he a born scoundrel or just a garden-variety louse, and is either characterization determined by Jewish blood?—enables a novel that operates as both critique of and pretext for capitalist globalization. It is notable, then, that the world at large is less prone to demonize Lopez than are the members of "the Wharton and Fletcher families," that tightly-knit "tribe," more exclusive in many ways than the highly public Pallisers, who have insisted on his racial otherness from the start (531). For all Trollope's belief that Englishness is a "race," the narrator distances himself from the novel's racists, leaving the impression of an author who knows that racial pride is no match for Harding's ethics or even Grantly's zealous partisanship. Ironically, the closer Trollope comes to visualizing England's social structure in terms of blood rather than place—the language of transportable rather than heirloom roots—the more he seems to realize that capitalism's contradictions are untenable and require the production of scapegoats.

As we saw in Chapter 1, this contradiction is built into the novel's most powerful metonym, the Tenway Junction, scene of Lopez's suicide. Moreover, in introducing this haunting locale from the perspective of a "stranger," Trollope momentarily transposes Lopez's status as presumed alien, "half foreigner, half Jew," into an archetypal modern condition (*Prime* 518, 662).[30] Thus, while *The Prime Minister* hews to the piquant mid-Victorian register of a naturalistic narrative of capitalist globalization, the Tenway's unforgettable collapse of hell and capitalist modernity exemplifies the kind of "spatial perception" which Fredric Jameson associates with Modernism ("Modernism" 53). Like E. M. Forster's Great Northern Road (see Ch. 1), Trollope's junction is an aestheticized window onto a global condition that metropolitan consciousness tends to occlude. At the Tenway Junction, "some six or seven miles distant from London,"

> lines diverge . . . in every direction . . . Men and women . . . look doubtful, uneasy, and bewildered. But they all do get properly placed and unplaced, so that the spectator at last acknowledges that over all this apparent chaos there is presiding a great genius of order. From dusky morn to dark night, and indeed almost throughout the night, the air is loaded with a succession of shrieks. The theory goes that each separate shriek,—if there can be any separation where the sound is so nearly continuous,—is a separate notice to separate ears of the coming or going of a separate train. The stranger, as he speculates on these pandemoniac noises, is able to realize the idea that were they discontinued the excitement necessary for the minds of the pundits might be lowered, and that activity might be lessened, and evil results might follow. But he cannot bring himself to credit that theory of individual notices (517–18).

Trollope's description of the Tenway Junction places the British metropole in a global matrix that can be keenly felt but only partially seen. This ominous connectivity resonates through spatialization (the "lines" that "diverge . . . in every direction"), sensorialization ("the air . . . loaded with a succession of shrieks"),

---

[30] For a discussion of this figure in relation to Flaubert and Eliot, see Ch. 6. In Chapter 8, I discuss an intensified, latter-day neoliberal variation on this transposition through the figure of the "virtual Jew."

and personification (the "great genius of order" that presides over the "apparent chaos"). At first glance, the "genius" may appear to invoke the invisible hand—capitalism's niftiest tool for performing the rhetorical work of political economy (see Courtemanche). But the narrator's next observation makes clear that this passing note of providentialism merely glosses the stranger's efforts to parse a mind-boggling web that strains his powers of comprehension. The bizarrely dystopian "theory" of "separate shrieks" posits nightmarish reciprocity between unique sounds and the isolated individuals who descry them. It is a theory the stranger rejects after reaching the (Benjamin-like) insight that "pandemoniac noises" are necessary for habituating the "pundits" to their task of shepherding bewildered passengers through the entropic space of a worlded London. In this way, "all do get properly placed and unplaced": a fitting pronouncement for the self-annihilating violence to come.[31]

Thus, while Trollope's play of rootedness and cosmopolitanism fails utterly as moral or political imaginary, its aesthetic rendering of mid-Victorian-era globality articulates structural processes and ethical concerns that resonate in our own day. As a picture of the nineteenth century's actually existing cosmopolitanism which produces palpable unease, Trollopian foreign policy elucidates the multifaceted transformations of capitalist globalization's *longue durée*. To be sure, much has changed since the origins of naturalistic fiction in Flaubert and Trollope. Yet, racial and other essentialisms, as well as the structural contradictions they mask, are as fundamental to today's anti-immigration and terror discourses as to Colonial Man's fantasies of limitless sovereignty. Thus, while "the Jew" is no longer the most salient marker of "the universalized state of homelessness" which haunts neoliberal postmodernity (Cheyette, "Ineffable" 295), Lopez's condition as the archetypal stranger of naturalistic narrative recurs with uncanny power in present-day serial media (Ch. 8).

According to Timothy Brennan, latter-day cosmopolitan scholarship would thus do well to focus more on equitable "material conditions" than on juridical conceits (42). That task, I propose, is as much one of understanding literary histories as of politics narrowly construed (42). As Bonnie Honig has cautioned, those who rely on the accelerated mobility and tempo of late modernity "to produce a postnational politics wrongly rely on a mere fact to do the work of politics" (*Democracy* 128; note 23). Thus, as Bruce Robbins notes, an "internationalist ethic or culture" is necessary to spurring transnational political movements to coalesce beyond the monadic actors ("separate shrieks") first perceived in the 1870s (Robbins, *Feeling* 17).

Debates over cosmopolitan theory will likely continue: Can the idea be redeemed from its Enlightenment-era exclusivity or is the very premise of an inclusive, emancipatory humanism itself an engine of hierarchy and exclusion? Since the heterogeneity of transnational experience does not in itself ensure justice or democracy, today's global rhetorics are as susceptible to "foreign policy" as in

---

[31] On Benjamin's notion of *Erlebnis*—experience in the form of modern sensory stimulus—see Chapter 5.

the days when patriotic Britons imagined themselves to be the beacons of world progress and liberty. It is a debate that the mid-Victorian perception of "cosmopolitanism" as a structured effect of globalizing capital can enrich.

Lopez's fate is to be "knocked into bloody atoms" in a "marvellous place" created "for certain purposes of traffic." To this grim fate he descends with "gentle, and apparently unhurried steps," as if the novel, having imagined Lopez's racialized non-gentility as an alibi, is eager to vindicate his manners after all (Trollope, *Prime* 519, 517, 520). Race, for all its provoking indeterminacy, has come to pervade the metropolitan imaginary as it seldom did Barsetshire's. England's sovereignty is ineradicably breached by the unanticipated triumph of "routes" over "roots" (Gilroy, *Black*), colonial cosmopolitan over heirloom "footing," and the end of a two-part Trollopian foreign policy. As the next chapter shows, in confronting this dilemma, *The Eustace Diamonds* provides the author's most sustained meditation on territorial empire in South Asia as well as his most naturalistic novel.

4

"India is 'a Bore'"
Imperial Governmentality in *The Eustace Diamonds*

Why is it that Anthony Trollope, "the greatest traveler among mid-Victorian novelists" (Cotsell 243)—the era's archetypal "Imperial Man" (Hall, "Going")—neither visited nor wrote about Britain's empire in India? In 1860, the year after he published *The West Indies and the Spanish Main*, Trollope was offered £3,000 for a series of travel writings on India: more than twice what he earned for *North America* (1862) and *Australia and New Zealand* (1873), and almost four times as much as for *South Africa* (1878).[1] According to Michael Cotsell, Trollope "took no interest in India" (249) and the author himself wrote that though it might suit him "professionally," traveling on the subcontinent would be "a bore" (Booth 61). In his book on Australia, Trollope opined that while India was "the most populous and important [dependency] that ever belonged to a nation," "no Englishman at home can be got to interest himself in the slightest degree" (507). While oblique references to South Asia crop up in his writing, Trollope seemed as reluctant to figure India or Indians in his imaginative works as he was to encounter them in his travels.

As the last two chapters have shown, Trollope's racial views were shaped by a "Greater British" imaginary that distinguished white settlement colonies from territorial empires. Enthusiastic about British emigration to the world's temperate climates, he was at best ambivalent about the project of "extended dominion over black subjects" in the global south (*Tireless* 200). Thus, while Trollope believed that Anglo-Saxons were a "dominant race" (*New Zealander* 11), he rejected liberal as well as conservative arguments for extensive empire-building. In 1875, just a year before the Tories made Victoria empress of India, Trollope wrote that India was not "a colony . . . in any proper sense, as the English who live there are very few, and are confined to those who rule the real people of the land" (*Tireless* 93). As J. H. Davidson has remarked, Trollope seems to have regarded India as an "alien" locale: to claim India as an imperial "keystone" was "preposterous" (320).

In this chapter, I argue that *The Eustace Diamonds* (1871–3) is an important exception to Trollope's reticence on India. Yet, in making this case I do not suggest that Trollope wrote his third Palliser novel explicitly to weigh in on Indian policies or the emerging New Imperialism. Rather, Trollope's meditation on India

---

[1] On the offer from George Smith, see Super 125.

almost certainly sprang from a literary response to a contemporary novel: Wilkie Collins's, *The Moonstone* (1868). As I will demonstrate, both of these novels engaged recent debates over the governance of India that have received surprisingly little critical attention. While Collins is the subject of Chapter 5, the present chapter argues that *The Eustace Diamonds*, the most naturalistic of the Palliser novels, captures the governmentality of "liberal" imperialism in crisis alongside the emergence of a new mode of Tory imperialism.

In making this case, I aim to complicate the caricature of Trollope as a formally unimaginative novelist. Though Henry James was probably the first to identify Trollope with a stolid philistinism that holds it "rather dangerous to be definitely or consciously an artist," he was not the last ("Anthony" 385). According to George Levine, Trollope's fiction "resists the very radical questioning that some of its elements may seem to provoke"; thus, unlike the more experimental fiction of Dickens or George Eliot, Trollope's "sheer plod" justifies the complaint that realism "confirms things as they are" (*Realism* 202–3 cf. Eagleton, *English* 128). The sheer quantity of Trollope's realism, Christina Crosby writes in a similar vein, "ensures that nothing will change" (304). Patrick Brantlinger elaborates: *The Eustace Diamonds*, he notes, produces "a poetry of money and commodities" which "reduces characters' motives to money" and then "reduces the characters themselves to monetary forms" (*Reading* 137). This is the kind of critique which many scholars have wagered on since Georg Lukács argued that realism after Balzac subordinated "human values" to "the commodity structure of capitalism" (*Studies* 63).

As we saw in Chapter 1, scholars of the Victorian novel have begun to rethink the adequacy of these assumptions. Yet, to some degree, Trollope remains the exception that proves the rule. In his contribution to *Adventures in Realism* (2007), Levine describes the constitutive paradox of an art form that shows how "money is essential for success" while also making "the quest" for wealth "a mark of shame, corruption, evil." But, he persists in singling out Trollope as the one notable author whose fiction fails to confront these "ethical (and formal) problems" ("Literary" 25). Should we conclude that *The Eustace Diamonds* merely naturalizes the corrupt politico-imperial order it depicts? That repellent anti-Semitism is Trollope's only alternative to "sheer plod"?

In this chapter, I take a different tack. As what I have called "sociological" realism, Trollope's mature works stand out for density of description; a refusal to figure consolatory private realms; the skillful interlacing of political and domestic plots; and, most distinctive in the Palliser period, the tendency to make globalized social worlds rather than characters alone the predominant focus of a multi-plot fiction.[2] Published between 1864 and 1880, Trollope's six-part Palliser series began in the aftermath of the Indian rebellion of 1857–8 and culminated with the arrival of the New Imperialism in the 1870s. Thus, far from instancing the

---

[2] On this point, see also Herbert: Trollope "conceives of the social order not as the backdrop for the adventures of his characters, and not as a system of confining strictures against which individual personality asserts itself, but as the primary subject of his 'fiction'" (*Culture* 267).

complacency of realism after Balzac, Trollope is arguably the most Balzacian of British novelists—an author famous for creating imaginary worlds whose repeat characters recur in multiple works. As R. H. Hutton put it, Trollope "picture[d] the society of our day with a fidelity with which society has never been pictured before in the history of the world" (Smalley 508). This was not mechanical mirroring, but a "serious fidelity" that the American novelist William Dean Howells readily equated with artistry (181).[3]

Then too, though critics seldom notice the fact, the Palliser novels are remarkably diverse. The sequence neither develops a continuous narrative like, say, *The Forsyte Saga* (1906–21), nor adheres to a single genre.[4] *Can You Forgive Her?* (1864–5), the first installment, appeared while Trollope's Barsetshire chronicles were still in progress. The tale primarily of Alice Vavasour's long-delayed marriage, it carries the quasi-comic courtship plots and Shakespearean doublings of Barsetshire into the milieu of metropolitan politics. But the subsequent novels are discernibly more bleak as Trollope moves from the firm unity of place (Barsetshire as the salt of England) to the more tenuous anchor of personality (the ups-and-downs of the Pallisers and their set). Thus, despite the sustained nobility of Plantagenet Palliser, the shift from clerical squabbles to partisan parliaments, from provincial Barsetshire to the London metropolis, and from courtship plots to dense cosmopolitan networks, makes the later series less comically compensatory than the Barsetshire fictions.

Phineas Finn (1867–8) and *Phineas Redux* (1873–4), the second and fourth Palliser installments, are political *Bildungsromane* that place a sympathetic hero in a situation of almost inevitable compromise (Harvie 92–3). By contrast, *The Eustace Diamonds* and *The Prime Minister* (1875–6), along with the contemporaneous *The Way We Live Now,* reject the *Bildungsroman,* not least to cancel the expectation of progress which that genre invites. Instead, these naturalistic narratives of capitalist globalization render the impact of modern forces on whole social worlds, portraying a "traditional British enclosure" invaded by "golddiggers, speculators, and Jews" (Kendrick 136–7). The central struggle of *The Eustace*

---

[3] Howells, who was himself an accomplished naturalist, called Trollope "the greatest English novelist" after Jane Austen, pointing to the want of humor as simultaneously a flaw and the key, perhaps, to a truthful representation of "the British life and character . . . in the whole length and breadth of its expansive commonplaceness" (181). For the argument that Trollope's penchant for recurring characters owes less to Balzac than to the author's own boyhood practice of "dwell[ing] on a work created by my own imagination" to escape from unhappy circumstances, see Wall (Trollope, *Autobiography* qtd. in Wall 130). On Trollope's toasting Balzac as the inventor of the series novel, see Super 224. For comparison of James and Trollope which contests the view that Trollope's realism lacks "formal reflexivity or metaliterary self-consciousness", see Rowe 60 and, for a more recent comparison, E. Michie, "Odd." For the argument that Trollope's fiction is formally mixed and open—offsetting traditional realist conventions with sophisticated irony and parody, see Kincaid. More recently, Langbauer has depicted Trollope's serial fiction as a narrative mode of proto-deconstruction (Ch. 2). For a recent survey of Trollope's reputation, which further supports my rebuttal, see the introduction to Morse, Markwick, and Gagnier. Capacious studies of Trollope that have emerged since this chapter was written include Morse, *Reforming* and van Dam.

[4] However, for a worthwhile effort to read the Palliser series as a "political epic" and metahistory capturing the contradictions of Victorian liberalism, see Felber (424).

Diamonds, writes Andrew H. Miller, is "to define an honest understanding of ownership" in the face of pervasive capitalist—and imperialist—contradictions (*Novels* 163).

Perhaps unique in Trollope's oeuvre, *The Eustace Diamonds* does not take persons or places for its centerpiece but, rather, objects: specifically, a set of family jewels around whose ambiguous legal status much of the drama evolves. Are the jewels family heirlooms—a form of ethico-cultural property entitled to exceptional legal protection—or are they mere commodities that, like any other repositories of exchange value, may be sold on the market at the discretion of any owner? This question has invited a number of excellent analyses from feminist, Marxist, and psychoanalytic perspectives and has begun to be considered in light of imperial contexts.[5]

In what follows, I describe the novel's sensitive geopolitical capture of an emerging politico-imperial governmentality. The first part of the chapter explores the surprising complexity of two "liberal" characters—Lucy Morris and Lord Fawn—and their relation to the novel's conspicuously voiceless Indian royal, the Sawab of Mygawb. The second part describes the flagrant expropriative persona of Lizzie Eustace, an anti-heroine who symbolizes key performative features of the New Imperialism. Through such devices, Trollope's novel glimpses the governmentality that arose when a romanticized Tory conception of empire displaced the no longer credible story of "free trade" in South Asia. Neither naïve nor self-naturalizing, *The Eustace Diamonds* aspires to that "objective" historical grasp that, for Lukács, vivifies an otherwise random play of objects and psychological effects and, for Jameson, maps the spatial disjunction that confounds lived experience (Lukács, *Historical* 275, cf. Jameson, "Cognitive").

HONEST OWNERSHIP

> The system of heirlooms . . . was devised with the . . . picturesque idea of maintaining chivalric associations. Heirlooms have become so, not that the future owners of them may be assured of so much wealth . . . but that the . . . descendant may enjoy the satisfaction which is derived from saying, . . . my ancestor . . . was graced by wearing on his breast that very ornament which you now see lying beneath the glass. Crown jewels are heirlooms in the same way, as representing not the possession of the sovereign, but the time-honored dignity of the Crown. The Law . . . has in this matter bowed gracefully to the spirit of chivalry and has lent its aid to romance;—but it certainly did not do so to enable the discordant heirs of a rich man to settle a simple dirty question of money.
>
> Anthony Trollope, *The Eustace Diamonds*, 1:258–9

---

[5] Noteworthy readings in addition to those I have already cited include Ben-Yishai, Briefel; W. Cohen; Lindner Ch. 4; Plotz, *Portable*, Ch. 1; and Psomiades.

Looking back on *The Eustace Diamonds* in his autobiography, Trollope offers an oblique account of its relation to *The Moonstone*. Whereas Wilkie Collins would have devoted "infinite labour" to the crafting of such a tale, writes Trollope, his own "plot of the diamond necklace . . . produced itself without any forethought" (*Autobiography* 218). Trollope thus offers an apolitical telling of his interest in *The Moonstone*, portraying himself as a character-centered realist whose tale of purloined jewels "produces itself" without the presumed focus on plotting of the sensation writer. Of course, *The Moonstone*—the only canonical mid-Victorian novel to begin and end with events in India—has become a staple of postcolonial criticism. The famous Prologue opens with the theft of a sacred Hindu diamond, a primal scene that Collins deliberately embeds in an actual historical event, the 1799 storming of Seringapatam. Yet, while the influence of Collins's novel on Trollope's has long been recognized, *The Eustace Diamonds* has only recently been read in light of imperialism.[6]

To be sure, Trollope's engagement with imperial themes is comparatively subtle. Whereas the looting of the fictional Moonstone is set amidst the fourth (and last) Anglo-Mysore War, the Eustace diamonds "formed a part of a set of most valuable ornaments settled in the family . . . in 1799" (1:150)—thus making the Eustace family's quiet acquisition of family jewels contemporaneous with the battle of Seringapatam. The only Indian in the novel is the Sawab of Mygawb, a voiceless figure whom most critics have ignored or dismissed. But as W. J. McCormack argues, the Sawab's appearance as "a non-character" is deceptive. In fact, his claim of having "been robbed" is analogous to the theft of the diamonds and, thus, an important engagement with imperial ethics (xxiv). Although the sensational burglary attempt on the diamonds was a last-minute addition to Volume 2 (*Autobiography* 218), the debate over the Sawab's property is almost certainly part of the novel's original conception. In fact, the prince's predicament is recounted even before Lizzie's claim on the diamonds becomes the novel's focal point.

Significantly, the Sawab's first appearance occurs in a chapter devoted to introducing Lucy Morris, governess to the sisters of Lord Fawn, who is Under-Secretary of State for India:

> There was forward just then [in Parliament] a question as to whether the Sawab of Mygawb should have twenty millions of rupees paid to him and placed upon a throne, or whether he should be kept in prison all his life. The British world generally could not be made to interest itself about the Sawab, but Lucy positively mastered the subject . . . (1:25).

Trollope's narrator thus emphasizes the Sawab's grave situation only to subordinate it to the exceptional qualities of the Fawn family governess. This displacement from an aggrieved Indian sovereign and indifferent public to the novel's most obvious foil for Lizzie Eustace is no accident. Although Lucy is sometimes read as the closest approximation to a heroine in a novel that is explicitly said to

---

[6] Milley, whose 1939 article makes the first connection between the two works did not register the significance of imperialism in either.

lack one, the governess's close tie to the novel's only Indian character demands careful reading.[7]

Let us begin by considering *The Eustace Diamonds*'s account of social relations within Britain's borders; its effort to conceive honest ownership in a post-Barsetshire world. Although the diamonds are said to have originated in Golconda (the famous mine in which the real-life Koh-i-Noor was found), Trollope's jewels do not point directly to any Indian claim or event. Rather, the main fascination of the Eustace diamonds is their ambiguous legal status: the question of whether they are family heirlooms—a form of property entitled to special legal protection—or mere commodities that may be sold on the market at the discretion of any owner. Although the Eustace family solicitor has assumed that the diamonds are heirlooms and, thus, bearers of the extra-economic value that Kathy Psomiades has called "Eustaceness" (103), the law turns out to pronounce a very different view.[8] Mr. Camperdown's mistaken belief recalls the "heirloom" ideal of property which Barsetshire novels like *The Warden* had amply privileged (Ch.3). As though purposely to distinguish the Eustace diamonds from an ethico-culturally valuable form of property, the law regards them as mere "trinkets," reducible to a "dirty question of money" (1:258). In fact, according to Turtle Dove's expert opinion, diamonds are the ultimate *non*-heirlooms, incapable of signifying extra-economic value in any concrete or permanent way.[9] The novel thus creates a homology between the non-heirloom condition of the diamonds (reduced to a commodity form) and Lizzie, the non-heirloom woman ("too much the mushroom" [1:190]) who trades on the residue of heirloom wealth, status, and title.

If anyone in this novel-without-a-hero harks back to Barsetshire it is Lucy Morris. But on closer inspection, even she lacks the lived moral relation to an heirloom social order which Septimus Harding embodied in the Barsetshire novels. Repeatedly likened to a litter of objects the authenticity of which depends on the contrast to Lizzie's false counterparts, Lucy is "good as gold" (1:263), a bona fide "treasure" (1:22, 1:265), and "real stone" compared to Lizzie's "paste" (2:230). Having recognized their governess as a gem, yet one too poor to attract a suitable husband, Lady Fawn and her daughter, Mrs. Hittaway, intend that Lucy be "made over to the Hittaways" like one of the loyal servants whom Lizzie is "too much of the mushroom" to cultivate (1:24, cf. 1:22; 1:190). This is a loss of personal sovereignty that Lucy actively resists.

The novel thus suggests two ways that Lucy's exemplary non-Lizzieness might resolve the problem of honest ownership, neither of which is ultimately sustained.

---

[7] Lucy is the "Una" to Lizzie's "Duessa" in McMaster's Spenserian interpretation. Halperin, though explicitly interested in politics, concludes that the Sawab's claim initiates a "silly debate," an example of the "ersatz issues of the day" (151, 157, 156). For trenchant disagreement, see Langbauer (111) and Daly (75).

[8] For a reading that focuses on the diamonds as a classic imperial trope, see Daly. I discuss the importance of Koh-i-Noor for Collins's Moonstone, in Ch. 5.

[9] Portraying diamonds as pure commodities, Trollope's novel registers the very qualities—"homogeneity," "clarity," "historylessness"—which account for the diamond's becoming, in the

In the more familiar of the two, Lucy is figured as an independent, sovereign proprietor:

> What she had was her own, whether it was the old grey silk dress which she had bought with the money she had earned, or the wit which nature had given her. She coveted no man's possessions;—and no woman's; but she was minded to hold by her own (1:26).

In this fantasy of guilt-free possession, Lucy affirms the liberal individual by erasing its troubling acquisitive desire. As one who possesses without expropriating or even "coveting," Lucy neutralizes an array of ethico-cultural dangers associated with possessive individualism in the mode of John Locke.[10] In the second idealization of the governess, Lucy figures a more sophisticated mode of liberal ethics. On this view, she is not only honest and non-expropriative but also dialogical and intersubjective: the bearer of rare communicative capacities. Lucy is "open to familiar intercourse" (1:23), able to convoke a "community of interest" (1:24), and "the very best" of "listeners" (1:25)—the very qualities that enable her to "take up" a subject like the Sawab's case and "make it her own" (1:25). "[N]o man or woman was ever more anxious to be effective, to persuade, to obtain belief, sympathy, and co-operation" than Lucy (1:26), the narrator avers. Trollope's governess thus adumbrates a communicative alternative to Locke's sovereign monad—perhaps even an anti-imperial ethics.[11]

Significantly, however, this evocation of Lucy as a potential liberal exemplar is deeply gendered. Every one of her exceptional qualities—heirloomesque invaluability, non-expropriativeness, and intersubjective ethics—is expressed through the prism of an idealized femininity that, in this novel, she uniquely (if unstably) represents. Lucy's morality is likewise filtered through the gendered economy of upper-middle-class marriage. By the time the narrator introduces the Sawab, her gloomy marital prospects have been fully disclosed: she is a penniless governess who is in love with Frank Greystock, an ambitious politician who needs a rich wife. In the post-heirloom world of this novel, all characters acknowledge more or less openly that Frank's marriage to a governess would spell death for his professional ambitions. Lucy's honesty and Lizzie's cash value are thus rendered as incommensurable goods: one moral and the other economic. As against the corrupt materialism that enables Lizzie's "filthy lucre" to challenge Lucy's moral worth (1:22), the narrator only occasionally insists on a tenuous idealism—a view from which Lucy's extra-economic goodness would, perforce, earn the reward of a faithful fiancé. This naturalistic shift toward depicting a "degenerate age" marks a break with earlier Trollope works in which "mercenary marriage" was portrayed

---

later nineteenth century, a new social currency (Proctor 398). My thanks to Jenni Lieberman for this reference.

[10] For the classic critique of possessive individualism, see C. B. Macpherson. As A. Miller sees it, Lucy is an exception of sorts: "her virtue represented as the proper attitude towards and behavior with possessions" (*Novels* 171); see also Psomiades (95). Plotz, however, notes that Lucy's "shifting interest in the Sawab is a predictable articulation of a well-lubricated system" (*Portable* 35).

[11] Compare these aspects of Lucy to the Habermasian ethics D. Thomas finds in Steel's *On the Face of the Waters*.

as egregious (1:219, 1:273).¹² But, for now, my point is that Lucy, the novel's closest approximation to a liberal ideal, is inescapably embedded in the "real" situation of the marriage economy. Hence, while Trollope's governess "covet[s] no man's possessions," she most certainly covets marriage to Frank.

Over the course of the novel, as Lizzie aggressively competes with Lucy, tempting Frank to break his engagement, the governess tenaciously struggles to avoid the fate of a Fawn family "treasure." In *North America*, Trollope quipped that the "best right a woman has is the right to a husband" (262). In *The Eustace Diamonds*, Lady Fawn encourages Lucy to disown that very right and to regard herself as too poor to marry. It is a view that Lucy—at once humble family retainer and Lockean proprietor—both accepts and rejects. Although "Lady Fawn could have no right to tell her governess not to be in love," Lucy knew "well enough" that she "was not entitled to have a lover" (1:59). At various points she contemplates releasing Frank from his burdensome promise (in the manner of several Trollope heroines). In not doing so she reinforces her Lockean tendency "to hold by her own."¹³

Like many other Trollope novels, *The Eustace Diamonds* demonstrates the injury to middle-class women who lack satisfactory economic alternatives to marriage, including Miss Macnulty, Augusta Fawn, and the tragic Lucinda Roanoke. Lucy's case stands apart, however, in linking female adversity to a test of liberal-imperial morality. Thus, Lucy's dismal prospects concerning Frank, which are likened to the physical "loss of a leg or an arm," are explicitly tied to "the injured prince," with her maimed condition corresponding to the Sawab's jeopardized throne (1:25–6). Yet, while Lucy is therefore a potential double for the victimized Indian royal, she is instead depicted as his advocate. The governess not only "masters" the Sawab's case but also urges Fawn to "stand up against his chief," the Secretary of State for India, on the prince's behalf (1:25).

Yet, Lucy's arguments in favor of the prince are never described; instead, her advocacy materializes in the form of fantasies about her fiancé's heroism. Thus, in a detail that cannot be accidental, Lucy is contemplating her lamentable marriage prospects when "Lord Fawn suddenly put into her hands a cruelly long printed document respecting the Sawab," the reading of which prompts her to think, "*how wonderfully Frank Greystock would plead the cause of the Indian prince*" (1:26–7; emphasis added).

And that is only the beginning. In a chapter entitled "Mr. Burke's Speeches," Lucy's fantasy, after a fashion, comes true. For unspecified reasons, Fawn's chief finds it politically necessary to oppose the Sawab's claim, providing Frank, a Tory, with an opportunity to attack him and Fawn, two Liberals, in Parliament:

> We all know the meaning of such speeches. Had not Frank belonged to the party that was out, and had not the resistance to the Sawab's claim come from the party

---

¹² In *Doctor Thorne* (1858), for example, Frank Gresham never wavers toward his impecunious beloved while the title hero of *Phineas Finn* (1867) ultimately remains true to his Irish sweetheart (whose early death enables the professionally advantageous match with Madame Max).

¹³ As McMaster notes, Lucy differs from "self-abnegating" Barsetshire heroines like Mary Thorne and Grace Crawley (83).

that was in, Frank would not probably have cared much about the prince . . . It is thus the war is waged. Frank Greystock took up the Sawab's case, and would have drawn mingled tears and indignation from his hearers, had not his hearers all known the conditions of the contest. *On neither side did the hearers care much for the Sawab's claims.* (1:61; emphasis added).

Thus, while Frank is motivated purely by the desire to get "his lance within the joints of his enemies' harness," and while Fawn, in fact, is more desirous than his attacker "to favour the ill-used chieftain," Lucy's amorous fantasy of Frank's pleading the Sawab's cause is actuated (1:61–2).

The plot thickens when Fawn takes Greystock's political tactics personally and accuses him, in Lucy's hearing, of ungentlemanly behavior. Now it is Lucy's turn to engage in *realpolitik*: "it seemed to her that she could rush into the battle, giving a side blow at his lordship on behalf of his absent antagonist, *but appearing to fight for the Sawab*" (1:64; emphasis added). When Lucy reveals her actual motive, calling Frank's speech "the very best" she has ever read, the thin-skinned Fawn quizzes her on parliamentary oratory. This amusing scuffle between pompous Under-Secretary and feisty governess explains the title of the chapter since, in flaunting his superior knowledge of Parliament, Fawn alludes to Edmund Burke's "opening address on the trial of Warren Hastings" (1:66). A few chapters later, Lucy, now Frank's fiancée, quarrels again with Fawn. When Fawn accuses Frank of bearing a personal grudge "because he was so ridiculously wrong about the Sawab," Lucy declares that Frank is incapable of "bearing malice *about a thing like that wild Indian*" (1:245–6; emphasis added). It is in this way that the voiceless Sawab exposes Lucy's ethical limitations: "English blood is thicker than Indian justice," McCormack rightly observes (xxv). Yet, it is also in this way that Lucy increases her odds in the uphill battle for "the right to a husband." Her argument with Fawn enables her to remove herself from Fawn family patronage while tenaciously clinging to her "property" in Frank's tendered proposal of marriage (1:132).

Fawn's allusion to Hastings, the infamous Governor-General of India charged with crimes and misdemeanors in a 1787 impeachment proceeding, is, as McCormack avers, an "integral part" of the "larger pattern" that ties Trollope's tale of stolen jewels to *The Moonstone's* more explicit imperial narrative (xxiv). I propose that such connections are even more resonant than McCormack's excellent reading suggests. "Ever since Burke's famous prosecution of Hastings," writes Karuna Mantena, the "question of the legitimacy of British rule in India" has been "intimately tied to one's position *vis-à-vis* this originary moment" ("Crisis" 126). In fact when Trollope began writing *The Eustace Diamonds* in the late 1860s, the subject of Indian sovereigns was very far from the "ersatz" issue discerned by an earlier generation of scholars (Halperin 156). To the contrary, as we saw in Chapter 2, John Morley's warning in 1866 of a "very remarkable . . . episode in the history of English rule in India" directly concerned the importance of Indian royals in the post-rebellion era. It is therefore no accident that Trollope, the inveterate traveler, pronounced India "a bore," even as he wove "Mr. Burke's Speeches" and a dispossessed Indian prince into his stark tale of metropolitan politics.

THE GREAT PARLIAMENTARY BORE

> A year or two ago a correspondent writing about Mysore would have had to begin by telling the British public in what quarter of the globe Mysore happened to be, and what claim to a place so little known to ears polite could have upon the attention of a civilized community. But Parliamentary debates and leading articles compel people to rub up their geography, and I may, perhaps, venture to assume that even Macaulay's average Briton, though he may have yet to learn "whether Holkar was a Hindoo or a Mussulman," knows that Mysore is somewhere in India, and that the House of Commons a few months ago magnanimously resolved not to annex it on the death of the present Rajah, but to hand it over, in due time, to his adopted son.
>
> "Durbar at Mysore," *The Times of London*, October 4, 1867[14]

If hardly as sensational as *The Moonstone*'s tableau of John Herncastle despoiling an Indian sanctum, the debate over Mysore opened a real-life window onto the conduct of high-ranking Britons in the post-rebellion imperial theater. An 1865 article in the *Examiner,* for example, expressed "mortification" at Lord Canning's apparent reversal on the important matter of "annexation"—that is, the termination of an Indian sovereign's indirect rule in favor of direct incorporation into British India (a transition achieved by denying childless royals their customary right to adopt an heir). Such aggressive annexations under Dalhousie's governance had been singled out as a principle cause for rebellion by commentators including Benjamin Disraeli, Lord Salisbury, and Karl Marx. Thus, in 1860, Canning had exercised his newly-minted authority as Queen Victoria's viceroy by issuing a special despatch to assure India's royals that their rights to adoption would be duly recognized. The *Examiner* was one of a chorus of media to express consternation upon finding that the very same man who had urged close alliance with India's "princes" was reverting to Dalhousie's "rapacity" and preparing to commit "a most flagrant breach of good faith" ("Indian" 194–6):

> We are utterly dismayed at finding [Viceroy Canning] at the very moment of writing sentiments [in favor of Indian sovereigns], actually contemplating the overthrow of the kingdom of Mysore, and the repudiation of a solemn treaty . . . Wonderful is it to see an English gentleman of high integrity . . . when transmuted into an Indian politician, fancying figments and adducing reasons which would damage the reputation of a village attorney (195).

This almost Trollopian quip appeared alongside grave premonitions of imperial debacle: Britons in India, warned *Macmillan*'s were experiencing a "presentiment" of "coming evil" like that reported "before the great [Indian] Mutiny" ("Dangers" 412). Both articles cited *The Mysore Reversion* (1865), T. Evans Bell's weighty defense of indirect rule, a second edition of which appeared in 1866. As Bell argued forcefully, the plan to annex Mysore was not only a violation of

---

[14] The article, signed "From an Occasional Contributor" in Madras, is dated August 25, 1867. The author is citing Macaulay's 1840 essay, "Lord Clive" (184).

contract, but also a grievous misstep that could rock the stability of empire. Yet, by 1867, the tide had turned and the *Times* reported on a durbar celebrating recognition of the adopted young heir to Mysore's throne ("Durbar"). Kristna Raj Wodyar, the maharajah whom the British had installed after defeating Tipu Sultan, had at long last won his battle to uphold the 1799 treaty that had promised to honor the Wodyars' sovereignty "for as long as the sun and moon shall endure" (qtd. in Morley, 95).

As we saw in Chapter 2, the Mysore controversy culminated in a major shift in British policy: a turn toward a quasi-feudal form of rule more conducive to Tory romanticizations of empire than to the modernizing aims of liberal imperialists. Although the debate concerned abstruse disputes over a treaty which few contemporaries could parse, it bore on larger questions of imperial legitimacy at a time when heated discussions of Governor Eyre's conduct in Jamaica were still ongoing. At the same time, the Mysore debate marked a period during which even "Macaulay's average Briton" could find Indian royals, such as Trollope's fictional Sawab, a topic of continuous metropolitan discussion.

In the 1860s, after Prince Gholam Mohammed (the son of Tipu) traveled to London twice to increase his family's stipend, direct "princely appeals" to Parliament and the press became commonplace—much to the chagrin of Secretaries of State for India such as Sir Charles Wood and Salisbury (Knight 503). In some ways the Sawab's predicament—either to "have twenty millions of rupees paid to him and placed upon a throne," or to "be kept in prison all his life"—though deliberately facetious, is reminiscent of the situation of Prince Azeem Jah. Described at length in *The Great Parliamentary Bore* (1869), another book by Bell, Jah sought to succeed his nephew as titular sovereign of the Carnatic.[15] The limp reaction to Jah's claim prompted Bell to allege that India was, "by common consent of all political parties," "a great Parliamentary bore" (*Great* iii).

If Trollope read Bell's book in 1869, he knew that yet another deposed prince, the heir of the Rajah of Sattara, a territory annexed in 1848, "is, or was lately, a state prisoner" near Bombay, suspected of treason during the rebellion (158). Bell's book may have inspired Trollope's vision of an Indian royal teetering between enthronement and incarceration. What is certain is that in the 1860s the Indian "prince" became a familiar metropolitan type: a signifier of feudal loyalty and an occasional rallying cry for imperial justice. In 1863, Duleep Singh, titular Maharaja of the Punjab and friend of the Queen, purchased Elveden Hall in Norfolk. As the infant Maharaja, Singh had not yet begun to govern when, in 1849, he was forced to renounce his rule and to hand over the famous Koh-i-noor diamond as a "gift" to Queen Victoria (Ch. 5).[16] In April 1870, as Trollope resumed

---

[15] Jah's case was brought before the Commons six times between 1860 and 1865, but without any result. I use the term "titular" to refer to the wholly nominal mode of sovereignty which was sometimes preserved after annexation. When the Carnatic was annexed in 1801, a royal stipend was conferred by treaty on the deposed Nawab and his heirs. Jah was thus attempting to be recognized as the heir to the title under these terms. For more on Bell, a writer whose "inspiration was an ardent belief in the material and moral importance of indirect imperialism," see Knight (503).

[16] Nicknamed the "Black Prince," Singh could name the Prince of Wales among his hunting guests (Visram 71–3).

writing *The Eustace Diamonds* after a brief pause spent on a non-fictional project, *Vanity Fair* published a sympathetic account of Syud Munsoor Ullee, the Nawab Nazim of Bengal. Ullee had traveled to London to protest a series of reductions in the stipend promised to his family according to the eighteenth-century treaty in which they surrendered their rule to British authority. The caption described Ullee, a merely titular sovereign, as "A living monument of English injustice" ("Sovereigns") (see Fig. 4.1).

Though Bell popularized the idea of Parliament's apathy toward India, he did not invent it. Macaulay himself had suggested it in 1840 when he observed that "the great actions of our countrymen in the East . . . excite little interest" ("Lord Clive" 184). Twenty years later (and just a few years after the "mutiny"), an article in *Fraser's* began, "India, which is forgotten when Parliament is sitting, rises into importance when the vacation gives us time to think how we are to govern a hundred millions of Orientals" ("Chronicle" 543). And in his famous series of essays, *The English Constitution* (1865–7), Bagehot wrote that "the greatest defect of the House of Commons" was the "distracting routine" of governing the empire (135). Salisbury, the real-life Secretary of State for India, enhanced the impression of a boring India, describing Indian administration in an 1867 speech as "routine," "listless," and "elaborate" (qtd. in D. Williams 235). Hence, when Trollope wrote in *Australia and New Zealand* that "no Englishman . . . can be got to interest himself in [India] in the slightest degree" (507), he was reiterating a widespread sentiment that his fiction further pronounced. According to the narrator of *Phineas Redux*, "any allusion to our Eastern Empire will certainly empty" the House of Commons (322); and when the narrator of *The Prime Minister* describes the intense political interest in Lady Glencora, he notes wryly that if "the welfare of the Indian Empire [had] occupied the House, the House would have been empty" (492).

Herman Merivale, the Permanent Under-Secretary of State for India during the Mysore debate, and an old friend of Trollope's, declared himself positively flummoxed by Indian matters. A lawyer and political economist who had spent 13 years in the Colonial Office before transferring to Indian administration in 1860, Merivale "admitted to his friends"—including Trollope, perhaps—that "the more detailed questions of Indian affairs amused him in their randomness and sometimes impenetrability" (Beasley 40).[17] Like Trollope, whose views on the topic Merivale had influenced, the Under-Secretary of State for India was an enthusiast of white settler colonies which, by 1860, were semi-autonomous and did not require "minute" supervision from London. A respected authority on settler colonialism, and the author of *Lectures on Colonization and Colonies*, Merivale,

---

[17] Merivale's civil service position as Permanent Under-Secretary of State for India is distinct from the politically appointed position of Parliamentary Under-Secretary—the position that Fawn holds in *The Eustace Diamonds*. D. Williams describes the increasing importance of the permanent position relative to the parliamentary position during the 1860s when the latter office was held by ten different occupants between 1858 and 1869 (120). On Trollope's longstanding friendship with the Merivale family, see *An Autobiography* (40).

Fig. 4.1. "A living monument of English injustice." Cartoon from *Vanity Fair*, April 16, 1870. Artist: Alfred Thomspon ("ATn").

like Trollope, identified himself with "the great general thrust forward of . . . English-speaking civilization" (Beasley 38–9; cf. Hall, *Civilising* 212–13). Just as the transfer from Colonial to India Office left Merivale feeling like "a fish out of water" (Beasley 38), so the idea of "extended dominion" over non-Europeans seemed both to worry and alienate Trollope (*Tireless* 200).

As a novelist neither eager for a liberal civilizing mission nor for a conservative romanticization of neo-feudal ties, Trollope was not so much strongly opposed to the Indian Empire as uninspired by the vision of Britain's future to which it gave rise. At various moments his suspicion of imperial dishonesty is unmistakable. Moreover, as a writer transitioning from Barsetshire to the Palliser series, Trollope doubtless heeded the political discussions generated by the Mysore debate as well as the claims of sundry titular royals. The most resonant imperial focus for *The Eustace Diamonds* is, thus, not India itself or the character of the Sawab, but the Parliament that decides his case: a metropolitan institution enmeshed in the moral fog of a territorial empire.

As late as 1864, the narrator of *Can You Forgive Her?* had eulogized Parliament, describing "that more than royal staircase" that leads to "those passages and halls which require the hallowing breath of centuries to give them the glory in British eyes which they shall one day possess" (2:44). Trollope here renders the House of Commons, physically rebuilt in 1834, as an heirloom establishment whose historical legacy is as yet ongoing—a political institution from which "flow[s] . . . the world's progress" and an "advancing civilization" (2:45). Throughout the series, Plantagenet Palliser, even when cast as an ineffective leader, maintains his reputation as a dignified "legislator who served his country with the utmost assiduity" (*Can* 1:191; cf. *Autobiography* 118). *The Eustace Diamonds* thus stands out as the Palliser novel in which earnest political struggle is least in evidence and parliamentary affairs almost wholly reduced to the kind of party politics occasioned by the Sawab's case. It is a novel in which, to echo the *Examiner*, one finds British gentlemen "fancying figments and adducing reasons which would damage the reputation of a village attorney."

We have seen how the Sawab enters the novel as an adjunct to Lucy's marriage plot. The governess's readiness to make use of the "injured prince" in the "game" of husband-hunting (2:28) tarnishes the sterling morality that Lucy would otherwise exemplify. We can by now appreciate that the "cruelly long printed document" that Lucy "masters" (2:27, 25) concerns the technical legalities of the Sawab's claim. Lucy's interpretation of the case—that the prince is being "kept out of his rights" and "used very ill" (2:65)—is one that Fawn initially finds persuasive; but, like the real-life Merivale, who served under Wood in the early stages of the Mysore debate, Fawn feels obligated to bow to the needs of his chief. According to Donovan Williams, Merivale probably took the annexationist position on Mysore not from conviction but "from a sense of duty towards" Wood who "was perpetually anxious about Indian affairs being aired in Parliament" (220, 126). Yet if Merivale was quietly ambivalent about the Rajah of Mysore, he felt strongly enough about Jah, future subject of *The Great Parliamentary Bore*, to pen a private memorandum. A close look at the relevant documents, Merivale wrote, had "left . . . the strongest impressions" that Jah is "entitled to what he asks for, that great wrong has been done him by withholding it." "It may seem easy, in theory to separate the question of right from that of expediency," he added, but "in practice it would be found extremely difficult indeed" (qtd. in D. Williams 126).

Did Merivale discuss such ethical quandaries with his old friend Trollope? Did Trollope notice how the same tensions between "right" and "expediency" recurred in the parliamentary debates over Mysore? Although it is entirely possible, the point is not so much to identify Trollope's sources as to capture the liberal-imperial governmentality his novel evokes. I suggest that the absence of concrete details about the Sawab's case is integral to a novel that is precisely *not* concerned to parse the fine points of any single imperial dispute. What *The Eustace Diamonds* renders is not a particular disagreement about a claim or treaty, but an entire category of debate over right and expediency—a full-blown governmentality— which a so-called liberal imperialism has introduced into public life. There is, as a defensive Fawn tells Lucy, "a great deal to be said on both sides" about the Sawab's case (1:65). If the "British world could not be made to interest itself" in such affairs (1:25), it was because the "details of Indian administration" were, as Morley wrote, "repulsive . . . from their technicality;" "random" and "impenetrable" according to Merivale; "routine" and "elaborate" according to Salisbury; and "very dull and long" according to *The Eustace Diamonds* (1:61). Yet what the novel thereby shows is that India's position as the "great Parliamentary bore" is no isolated or even purely imperial feature of the metropolitan political condition. As Bagehot opined in *The English Constitution*, "the dull . . . habit of mankind" is what, in actuality, "guides most men's actions" (64). Rather less sanguine and certainly less cynical, *The Eustace Diamonds* makes boredom the signpost of a governmental malaise quite unlike the glorious parliamentary future limned in *Can You Forgive Her?* It is the sign of a pervasive conflation between right and expediency, a technocratization of ethics so abstruse it produces boredom as the answer to what would otherwise stand out as dishonest ownership and illegitimate sovereignty.

Lord Fawn, a respectable man made interesting according to *The Times* and *The Spectator*,[18] is the novel's chief embodiment of this lifeworld: a thoroughly conventional man "gifted with but little of that insight into things which teaches men to know what is right and what is wrong" (2:139). Personifying the technocratic governmentality that came to prevail in an era of expedient policy and mass politics, Fawn, according to Lizzie, is "a load of Government waste-paper" whose very marriage proposals are spun out "like an Act of Parliament" (2:253–4). Yet, if the ultra-realist Fawn is, on one reading of the novel, a likely example of Trollopian "plod," the Under-Secretary's interrelation with the Sawab points to a mutation of sociological realism which marks a vivid geopolitical aesthetic at work. Less "character" than figural marker, the Sawab of Mygawb recurs uncannily in

---

[18] According to the *Times*'s reviewer, "Lord Fawn is interesting in spite of his small ideas, his slow perceptions, and, above all, his eminent respectability" (Smalley 375).

narratives about marriage, party politics, empire, the nation's coinage, and, of course, the Eustace diamonds.

First introduced in light of Lucy's marital cares, the Sawab's later appearances haunt the amatory trials of her employer. The disappointed suitor of Madame Max and Violet Effingham, Fawn is accepted by Lizzie early on but then insists that she return the Eustace diamonds. Pressured by Frank to renew his pledge, Fawn bemoans his bad luck in love at the India Office: *"As he read some special letter in which instructions were conveyed as to the insufficiency of the Sawab's claims,* he thought of Frank Greystock's attack upon him, and of Frank Greystock's cousin" (1:103; emphasis added). As in the earlier link between Lucy and the Sawab, Fawn's reflections on the case are displaced by romantic misfortune, occluding the reader's familiarity with claims that the Under-Secretary had initially found compelling.

As the Conservatives transform from defenders of the Sawab to avowed "Lizzieites," exposing Fawn to gossip and ridicule, the Under-Secretary is "hardly as true to the affairs of India as he . . . wished" (1:143). A "whipped dog" on account of Lizzie's Tory champions (1:147), Fawn is soon assailed in his own party by Glencora who, in quasi-feminist admiration of Lizzie's pluck, takes the young widow's part. A Liberal social event at which ministers gather to advise Palliser on his five-farthing bill includes Fawn so that Glencora may "flatter" him *"as to the manner in which he had finally arranged the affair of the Sawab"* (2:141; emphasis added). In this oblique fashion, wedged between Planty's penny and Glencora's marital maneuvers, Trollope reveals that the prince's case has been decided. When we next hear of the Sawab, the beleaguered Fawn is explaining to his brother-in-law that there is no support to be had from Camperdown, who was mistaken about heirlooms and has withdrawn his bill in Chancery. "As far as I can see," Fawn moans to Hittaway, "lawyers always are wrong": the Eustace family solicitor, as wrong about heirlooms as the government's lawyer, Finlay, had been wrong about *"those nine lacs of rupees for the Sawab"* (2:149; emphasis added). The precise fate of the Indian royal—enthronement? incarceration? some Fawnian compromise between the two?—is never divulged.

To be sure, such rendering of a South Asian sovereign as a voiceless subaltern on one level simply extends the racial binarisms of Trollope's colonial writings. Throughout his massive oeuvre, Trollope's vision of encounter between "races," though always premised on the presumed superiority of Anglo-Saxons, varies according to the relevant geopolitical aim. As we saw in Chapter 3, Trollope describes racial intermixture as a progressive outcome in the West Indies, only to anticipate the extinction of indigenes in climates like New Zealand's which are suitable to British settlement. Then again, in Ireland, where Trollope spent the early part of his career, he advocates paternalistic kinship between colonizer and colonized—precisely the relation he rejects in non-European locales such as India. Clearly, Trollope was enough of a racial absolutist to disdain the idea of a "liberal" civilizing mission bent on anglicizing Indians, but enough of a liberal to dislike the premise of territorial domination without justifiable cause. Thus, the Sawab of Mygawb is a non-raced figure—a blank screen who marks the novel's geopolitical unconscious—not because Trollope resisted the notion of "Oriental" essence, but because the novel captures a guise of imperial justice that takes "Oriental" essence for its alibi. As the Sawab who does not speak, the prince figures an entire discourse over Indian sovereigns: from the loyal feudatories of the Queen's Proclamation, to the Rajah of Mysore, to *Vanity Fair*'s "living monument to English injustice."[19]

Thus, in *The Eustace Diamonds*, "the great Parliamentary bore" extends beyond the claim of a single Indian royal (a more stimulating topic, as it happens, than the hours-long Palliser penny speech that leaves Mr. Gresham "fast asleep" [2:133]). Nor is boredom limited to the "repulsive" technicalities that a so-called liberal imperialism invents to obscure what Salisbury described as "the nakedness of the sword on which [the British empire] really relies" (qtd. in Knight 500). The bore the novel captures is the politico-imperial governmentality that prompted Merivale to observe that questions of "right" and "expediency" were, in practice, inseparable. It is the cover for an imperial theft more demoralizing even than the mercenary culture that prompts "an honest" aristocrat to propose to a wealthy widow "he knew nothing about" (1:76, 78). Both sociological in the mode of a sophisticated mid-Victorian realism, and formally inventive in the ways I have described, *The Eustace Diamonds* is among those naturalistic works of the 1870s to capture the world historical processes of imperial expansion and their uncanny metropolitan returns. Realism of this kind, neither naïve nor transparent, aspires to that historical grasp that defines the geopolitical aesthetic at work.

DIZZY BEN LIZZIE

There is a large class of Englishmen, and it includes most of what would be called genuine Englishmen, who have a feeling that Mr. Disraeli is something of a charlatan. He seems to act a part, to like melodrama in public affairs, while the English race does not like it, and is very suspicious of it in politics. Mr. Disraeli's success in his political career is one of the surprises in English history.

"Editor's Easy Chair," *Harper's Magazine*, vol. 53 (1876)

A man who entertains in his mind any political doctrine, except as a means of improving the condition of his fellows, I regard as a political intriguer, a charlatan, and a conjurer.

Anthony Trollope, *An Autobiography*

According to the *Spectator*'s review of *The Eustace Diamonds*, the "picture of Lord Fawn's official and personal weakness, and upright moral cowardice," is "one of the most striking of Mr. Trollope's innumerable striking studies of modern life"

---

[19] Space does not permit me to describe the comparable way that *The Way We Live Now* figures the Emperor of China (whose visit includes a fictional peek at the Secretary of State of for India himself).

(Smalley 373). Yet, while Fawn clearly provides a memorable portrait of vapid parliamentarianism and dejected liberal morale, Trollope's most outstanding Palliser novel simultaneously points to dilemmas beyond the bureaucratic governmentality that Nicholas Dames nicely captures as "nothing more or less than a career" ("Trollope" 268). The novel's most noteworthy twist on the Lukácsian "typical character" is one whose expropriative persona not only performs the New Imperial determination to *invent* heirlooms but, also challenges the formal conventions of Trollopian characterization as it is usually conceived.

Consider Trollope's oft-cited defense of his realistic characters in *An Autobiography*. Far from cynical, Trollope claims a didactic function for his fiction: if readers recognize his characters as "like to themselves," then his novels "might succeed in impregnating" their "mind[s] . . . with a feeling that honesty is the best policy, that truth prevails while falsehood fails" (96). Trollope's aim is less to inculcate sympathetic understanding (in the mode, say, of Eliot) than to seize fiction's potential to illuminate actually existing moralities. Trollopian realism is thus premised on the belief that a sociologically acute fiction can positively reproduce—and not simply invent—normative differences between fair and foul, true and false.

Trollope's doctrine of mixed human nature is borne out almost throughout his career. If its famous debut is *The Warden*'s satire on the characterological extremism of Dickens and Thomas Carlyle, it remains visibly intact even in the dark, naturalistic landscape of *The Way We Live Now* in which the narrator writes of Lady Carbury, "The woman was false from head to foot, but there was much of good in her, false though she was" (1:17). Later Palliser novels such as *Phineas Redux* and *The Prime Minister* ennoble and, at times even heroize exemplary characters. The thoroughgoing corruption these novels depict does not neutralize human virtue so much as portray public life as a grueling duty (Palliser) or exacting challenge (Finn) to which ethical exemplars must submit. When Trollope diverges from such mixed characterization, it is usually to depict racialized stock figures like the chronically "greasy" Joseph Emilius (2: 241)—a point to which I'll return.

In *Phineas Redux*, the sequel to *The Eustace Diamonds*, the title character, though as ambitious and needy as Frank Greystock, incarnates an ideal of "political honesty" which is unknown to the story of Lizzie's diamonds (1:320). In contrast to Greystock's cynically partisan defense of the Sawab, Finn's speech calls out Conservative opportunism and checks his own party's machine in a single stroke. He is both the anti-Greystock, a man who refuses to play politics for self-advancement, and the anti-Fawn, a career politician who averts lackeydom. Finn's political victory, small though it is, provides a clear normative contrast to the unprincipled politics for which the Disraeliesque Mr. Daubeny stands.

How, then, does *The Eustace Diamonds* compare to its sequel? As contemporary reviewers observed, Trollope's third Palliser lacks any significant counterweight to the "sordidness" that is its most "powerful effect" (Smalley 373). Perhaps the most Balzacian of Trollope's works, the novel's milieu is so palpably suffused with dishonesty that the morality of many characters merely emblematizes prevailing material forces. Whereas, in the Finn novels, the conflict between ideals and ambition creates the moral tension for political *Bildungsroman*, in *The Eustace Diamonds*, Greystock and Fawn are the all-but-determined products of a social environment. *The Eustace Diamonds* thus evinces a sociology so deterministic it snuffs out idealism, divorcing its thick account of the world-as-it-is from the presumption that what-it-ought-to-be, is, in some sense, immanent if not generally prominent in existing social structures.

Nonetheless, if *The Eustace Diamonds* stands out for the extent of its anti-idealism, it also offers an anti-realism distinct from, and even antithetical to, the mode of naturalistic unmasking. As contemporary critics were the first to observe, Lizzie Eustace is not a mixed character. So far from the credible "human being" that Trollope prescribed, Lizzie is, according to the *Spectator,* a "living and breathing pretence of dissimulation" (Smalley 372)—the trope of "paste" diamonds in human shape (*Eustace* 2:230). This formal mutation springs from the novel's intensified geopolitical aesthetic: a world-historical character in the Lukácsian sense, Lizzie figures an emerging fusion between imperial expropriation and hyper-romantic aesthetics.

Indeed, when Bagehot wrote that "the dull, traditional habit of mankind" is "the steady frame" in which "each new artist must set the picture he paints" (*English* 64), he captured the way in which aestheticized arts of government could supplement the reign of "boring" parliamentarianism. While one might turn to Bagehot himself for the argument that feudal theatrics usefully depoliticize the masses, or to Tory imperialists such as Salisbury for their role in creating a "show" of Indian sovereignty, for an example of neo-feudal invention conceived as aesthetic performativity, one must finally turn to Disraeli—the only British prime minister to become the subject of a scholarly volume devoted to "self-fashioning."[20]

When the Second Reform Act doubled the size of the British electorate in 1867, the confluence of mass politics and formalizing empire created an ideal opening for the theatrical style of the man Salisbury referred to as a "political gamester" (qtd. in Halperin 169). Although Tories like Salisbury came, by and large, to accept their leader, the period of Disraeli's rise to power is remarkable for growing anti-Semitism among Liberals. Fueled by Tory policies perceived to favor geopolitical interests at the expense of vulnerable Christians in "the East," this strident Liberal critique of Disraeli was the backdrop for Trollope's rendering of a "conjuring" political agency that could master the theaters of popular democracy and imperial expansion. W. E. Gladstone's Midlothian campaign stoked the English antipathy for a plutocratic class of "hybrid or bastard men of business" bound to one another "by the bond of gain" and driven by an amoral "pursuit of material enjoyment" ("Lord Rector's" 237–8).[21] By 1879, when Gladstone delivered this speech, the

---

[20] On the depoliticizing effects of feudal iconography see Bagehot, *English* 248–9. The 1874 letter in which Salisbury speaks of the "show" of Indian sovereignty is quoted in Brumpton 176. On Disraeli's performative persona see, for example, Richmond and Smith's edited collection as well as Voskuil, *Acting* Chapter 4.

[21] According to Cain, this often anti-semitic mode of mid-to-late-Victorian liberal discourse was the effect of Disraeli's "re-activation" of a popular radicalism "not seen since Cobden's day" (216).

association of political opportunism, showy performativity, and Judaized caricature had become almost a staple feature of Trollope's writings.[22]

As Michael Ragussis has argued, Trollope's *The Prime Minister*, which appeared midway through Disraeli's second ministry, stages an imaginative reversal. Ferdinand Lopez, a secretive foreigner who "fails to win a seat in Parliament, is the epitome" of "moral bankruptcy," while Palliser, Trollope's fictional prime minister, is "a paragon of virtue and "the truest nobleman in England" (234; 258). Still, as we saw in the last chapter, Lopez is neither a stock character like Emilius nor, for that matter, a confirmed Jew. A figure whose story in many ways tells against British prejudice, Lopez is as much victim as villain, as well as the prototype for the deracinated neoliberal subject that haunts the naturalistic narratives of our own day (Ch. 8).

Thus, while Lopez is the most compelling of Trollope's Judaized characters, it is Lizzie's story, I contend, which most vividly fuses Trollope's distaste for the New Imperialism with his antipathy for the "conjuring" Disraeli. Sensitive to the waning of England's heirloom sovereignty, Trollope was one of many Britons to regard Disraeli as a political imposter, eager to turn once dignified institutions into fodder for grandiose personal designs. "As the 'Jew premier' with an 'Asiatic mind,'" writes Lynn M. Voskuil, Disraeli was "represented as an exotically alien, manipulative mountebank who had bargained away the nation's authentic English identity and had imperialized England almost beyond recognition" (*Acting* 142). Thus, when the Royal Titles Act reinvented the monarchy as, in Ian Baucom's words, "the place where England and India became one" (*Out* 44), Disraeli readily became the man behind the curtain. The well-known 1876 image from *Punch* titled "New Crowns for Old," depicts him as the power-seeking wizard Abanazar (from the Aladdin story), exchanging Victoria's hallowed crown for a pretentious imperial substitute (Fig. 4.2).

As exemplified by Emilius, the cartoon villain of *The Eustace Diamonds* and *Phineas Redux*, Trollope's anti-Jewish sentiments express an obvious wish to localize the disruptive spatio-temporal effects of capitalist and imperial expansion. Such all-too-familiar caricature is hardly dynamic in literary terms. It is, thus, through Lizzie, the "female swindler" whom fans of the novel loved to hate (1: 229), that Trollope creatively figured the anti-realist aesthetics he discerned in Disraeli's fiction and politics. Phrases such as "sly mendacity," "cynic solitude," and "paint and unreality" apply to either Dizzy or Lizzie and Trollope used the trope of "paste diamonds" to describe both.[23] The daughter of a presumably Anglo-Saxon

---

[22] Trollope repeatedly associated Disraeli with "conjuring." In *An Autobiography*, he described the typical hero of Disraeli's fiction as an "audacious conjurer" (166). In *The Duke's Children*, the Disraeliesque (though not Judaized) Sir Timothy Beeswax is said to have "invented a pseudo-patriotic conjuring phraseology which no one understood but which many admired" (164). Running for a parliamentary seat in 1868, Trollope described Disraeli's politics as "hocus pocus" and "conjuring tricks" (qtd. in Halperin 274). His campaign speech thus fused disdain for opportunistic politics with a mode of rhetoric that, as Teal has noted, portrays "the Jew as wizard" (59). On Liberal anti-Semitism see also Wohl; on Disraeli's imperial policy, see Feuchtwanger.

[23] For "sly mendacity", see the *Spectator*'s review (Smalley 372); for "cynic solitude" see Trollope's 1869 article, "Mr. Disraeli and the Mint" 448; for "paint and unreality" and "paste diamonds,"

Fig. 4.2. "New crowns for old ones." Cartoon from *Punch,* April 15, 1876. Artist: John Tenniel.

family, Lizzie is not directly associated with "Asian blood"; but she is Orientalized and described as a guilty "blackamoor" in need of "washing white" (1:321).[24] Stylistically, Lizzie's cultivation of a Byron-adulating, hyper-romantic persona parallels the portrait of Disraeli as one whose "quest for empire" was the product of a "'mind infected'" with grand Jewish "'ideas'" (Wohl 394; qtd. in Wohl 394). Whereas the novelist Disraeli, according to Trollope, astonished readers with the "uncommon" and "grand" (*Autobiography* 166), the character of Lizzie is driven by a "passion for romance and poetry," even a "grand idea" (1:99, 1:43).

At a structural level, Lizzie's hyper-romantic acquisitiveness parodies imperialism run amok. Urged to return the diamonds, Lizzie declares that she will "never give them up" for they are her "very own" (2:105). The diamonds have "scorched [her] horribly" and "nearly killed" her, "like the white elephant which the Eastern king gives to his subject when he means to ruin him" (2:123). There is a telling parallel, a geopolitical insight at work, between Lizzie's determination to retain burdensome

both references to Disraeli's novels, see *Autobiography* 166–7. In *The Eustace Diamonds* Trollope describe Lucy Morris as "real stone" in contrast to Lizzie's "paste" (2:230).

[24] For "Asian blood," an anonymous reference to Disraeli, see Wohl 396. On Trollope's use of the "blackamoor" phrase in various works, see Langbauer who suggests that Trollope takes part in a "familiar Victorian equation in which foreign equals Jewish equals black" (123).

booty and the imperial onus that J. R. Seeley, another liberal enthusiast of white settler colonies, would describe in his lectures, *The Expansion of England* (1883). While the advantages of maintaining a vast Indian dominion are "doubtful," he wrote, the empire "involves us in enormous responsibilities and confuses our minds with problems of hopeless difficulty." "May we not feel tempted to exclaim that it was an evil hour for England when the daring genius of Clive turned a trading company into a political Power?" (153). Such harrowed liberal puzzlement illuminates how Lizzie's ruinous "filching" typifies imperial avidity, anticipating a liberal self-critique that would not fully emerge until the end of the century (*Eustace* 1:40).

As an instance of the geopolitical aesthetic at work, however, Lizzie does more than figure increasing liberal crisis. The embodiment of a performative New Imperial aesthetic—hyper-romantic, grandiose, and acquisitive—Lizzie also represents an attendant break with the conventions that govern Trollope's realism, thus making *The Eustace Diamonds* the most formally idiosyncratic of the Palliser novels. According to Kendrick, Lizzie is Trollope's "attempt to represent realistically the opposite of realism, to appropriate and condemn a way of using language which is inimical to that of the Trollopian novel" (137). Such anti-realism, he suggests, is a sally on poetry—Lizzie's favorite genre; but this depoliticized interpretation overlooks the novel's sustained engagement with imperialism. If Lucy instances would-be ethical intersubjectivity undone by imperial *realpolitik*, Lizzie, her Tory supplement, marks the bottom of that slippery slope: not just the failure of communicative ethics, but the practice of communication as non-ethics. Hence, Lizzie's pernicious performativity does not indict romantic ideals and poetic genres so much as indict them in the specific form of New Imperial trappings.

As a Disraeli-like schemer, pursuing her interests through intrigue and self-invention, Lizzie introduces a stylistic referentiality that is alien to Trollope's "pellucid" linguistic ideal (*Autobiography* 151). Her characterization troubles the ideal of transparent communication not merely because she lies, but because the "truths" she dissimulates are so plausible. Thus, if the future Mrs. Emilius is at her most glaringly Disraeliesque when she produces self-aggrandizing falsehoods such as her alleged ownership of Eustace property, in formal terms, she is even more radical as the performer of homelier mimicries. Seeking to seduce Frank, Lizzie's "dress was such as a woman would wear to receive her brother, and yet it had been studied. She had no gems about her but what she might well wear in her ordinary life, and yet the very rings on her fingers had not been put on without reference to her cousin" (1:212). The Lizzie of this scene denaturalizes the ordinary, exposing it as but another posture through which to pursue one's interests. Such stage props should, according to *An Autobiography*, "prick the conscience" (166); yet Frank is an all-too-willing participant in Lizzie's theater of the ordinary. As Frank threatens to adopt Lizzie's self-inventing worldview, the presumed normative opposition between Lucy and Lizzie or his own "true" and "false" impulses loses its foundation. There is, he tells Lizzie,

> a cringing and almost contemptible littleness about honesty, *which hardly allows it to assert itself.* The really honest man can never say a word to make those who don't know of his honesty believe that it is there . . . Let two unknown men be competitors

for any place . . . and who can doubt but the dishonest man would be chosen rather than the honest? Honesty goes about with a hang-dog look about him, as though knowing that he cannot be trusted till he be proved. Dishonesty carries his eyes high, and assumes that any question respecting him must be considered to be unnecessary (2:124–5; emphasis added).

As he considers "honesty" from this instrumental calculus, Frank describes a self-effacing habitus that is vastly inferior to aesthetic self-fashioning. His demoralizing "philosophy" (2:125) contradicts the key moment in *Phineas Redux*, in which Finn's political honesty punches through the party system that normalizes cynical interests and unprincipled rhetoric. As against the author whose core belief is that "honesty is the best policy," Frank taps a fear that swaggering *realpolitik* may not be the contemptible byproduct of imperial modernity but modernity's very mode.[25]

To be sure, Trollope's conflict between ethical idealism and unflinching naturalism is traceable partly to the political conservatism of an author opposed to any but the most gradualist "liberal" change. In more formal terms, Trollope's narrator struggles to control the novel's experiment in anti-realist characterization. "The world is so false, so material, so worldly!" the narrator wants to say again and again—as though unaware that Lizzie utters this very pronouncement while she urges Lucy to accept a bribe (1:139). Like the invention of pseudo-heirlooms to ground a New Imperial aesthetic, Lizzie's hyper-romantic performative style co-opts normative assertions, transforming them into the rhetorical tools of her self-fashioning arsenal.

Far from a moribund or predictable literary aesthetics, Trollope's Palliser novels are thus formally versatile and geopolitically acute. Whether captured through political *Bildungsromane* like *Phineas Finn* or darker narratives like *The Way We Live Now*, the cardinal feature of Trollope's sociological realism is the rendering of complex material conditions. It should come as no surprise that *The Eustace Diamonds* is both the most formally experimental of Trollope's naturalistic narratives of capitalist globalization and the work that most visibly engages territorial empire. If, as I have also suggested, Lizzie Eustace marks the representational limits of sociological realism—its wishful normative tenets as powerless to control her aesthetic play as Lucy's "liberal" ethics are to justify the imperial governmentality with which she is complicit—she is, simultaneously, the sign of a Trollopian power to stretch sociological form beyond the crude anti-realism of the anti-Semitic scapegoat. What is more, Disraeli himself seems to have agreed: when the two men met for the first time in 1871, Disraeli was "quick to compliment Trollope on the main character of *The Eustace Diamonds*" (Teal 66). Trollope's reply appears to have been silence.

---

[25] Notably in *The Way We Live Now*, it is the dubious Mrs. Hurtle who articulates a comparable relation between modern ambition and "small scruples": describing Melmotte, the novel's Judaized fraud, she avers that "such a man rises above honesty . . . as a great general rises above humanity when he sacrifices an army to conquer a nation" (1: 245). In thus aligning Melmotte's persona with the questionable Hurtle, *The Way We Live Now*, often regarded as Trollope's bleakest indictment of modern life, hews to a conventional morality that *The Eustace Diamonds* more thoroughly flummoxes.

5

"Dark, Like Me"

Archeology and *Erfahrung* in Wilkie Collins's *Armadale* and *The Moonstone*

> Men make their own history, but they do not make it as they please; they do not make it under circumstances chosen by themselves, but under circumstances directly found, given and transmitted from the past.
>
> Karl Marx, *The Eighteenth Brumaire of Louis Bonaparte* (1852)

> More and more often there is embarrassment all around when the wish to hear a story is expressed. It is as if something that seemed inalienable to us, the securest among our possessions, were taken from us: the ability to exchange experiences.
>
> Walter Benjamin, "The Storyteller: Reflections on the Works of Nikolai Leskov" (1936)

So far this book has focused on the geopolitical aesthetic familiar from Anthony Trollope's fiction, with its strong bent toward sociological realism and naturalist unmasking. Trollope's most powerful genre is the *naturalistic narrative of capitalist globalization,* a form that encapsulates the experience of "heirloom" sovereignties under siege from the impacts of capitalism and imperialism. Novels like *The Eustace Diamonds, The Way We Live Now,* and *The Prime Minister* famously depict insidious foreigners who personify the corrosive impact of modern forces on metropolitan life. But these narratives simultaneously evince a geopolitical unconscious that haunts this scapegoating, asserting a countervailing sense of shared ethical and political crisis.

As this chapter will demonstrate, Wilkie Collins is another mid-Victorian author whose geopolitical engagements assume a strong ethico-political cast. Yet, while *The Moonstone* directly influenced *The Eustace Diamonds,* Collins is a very different novelist in several respects. Whereas Trollope ran for Parliament and was the best-known political novelist of his day, Collins, a comparatively bohemian figure, preferred the art and theater worlds to the domain of politics proper. And while Trollope prided himself on writing character-driven realist fiction, Collins, an author who could not "draw character" according to one contemporary review (Page 159), is arguably not a realist at all. Famous as a pioneer of sensation fiction, a genre that transports Gothic devices to modern-day settings, Collins was a master of elaborate plots, extraordinary locations, arcane events, and inventive alternatives to narrative omniscience. Thus, while Trollope's mature fiction tends toward naturalism, Collins's tends toward the marvelous, romantic, and uncanny.[1]

In at least one sense, however, Collins is Trollope's close counterpart: both writers were keen travelers who crafted vibrantly transnational fiction that illustrates mid-Victorian culture's global textures at multiple levels.[2] Different from Trollope in mode and mood, Collins's geopolitical aesthetic takes the form of a series of narrative experiments in writing transnational experience. Moreover, Collins renders such experience as sensitive to circumstances "directly found, given and transmitted from the past"—to borrow Marx's well-known formulation (*Eighteenth* 437). As Beth Palmer suggests, "sensation fiction's most significant legacy is its self-consciousness about how print culture . . . mediates the past" (86). Though *Armadale* (1864–6) and *The Moonstone* (1868) are not historical romances like Eliot's *Romola* (1862–3) or Collins's own *Antonina* (1850), their contemporary settings are saturated by the semi-repressed histories of England's global expansion. Collins's works thus render modern experience as the experience of suppressed world histories.

As they articulate variations on a geopolitical aesthetic that pulls disavowed histories to the fore, *Armadale* and *The Moonstone* negotiate a crisis of experience often associated with Modernism. Indeed, sensation fiction, a genre that flouts the conventions of classic realism, is sometimes read as a Modernist precursor. Christopher GoGwilt, for example, reads *The Moonstone* as prefiguring the "afterimage" of a universalistic notion of culture associated with Matthew Arnold (85). But, as GoGwilt's locution suggests, in *pre*figuring an *after*image, Collins's novel captures salient features of its contemporary condition, situating mid-Victorian modernity as the inception of a "destruction of experience" which Giorgio Agamben describes by invoking Walter Benjamin (Agamben, *Infancy* 13ff.).[3] In essays such as "On Some Motifs in Baudelaire" and "The Storyteller" Benjamin describes "the increasing atrophy of experience" ("On" 159). Just as Baudelaire's determination "to parry the shocks" of urban life offered Benjamin a template for this modern condition ("On" 163), so Baudelaire's British contemporary Collins helped to inaugurate a genre that critics from H. L. Mansel to D. A. Miller have associated with the stimulation of "adrenalin effects" (D. Miller 146; cf. Mansel 482).

---

[1] The two authors were friendly but not closely acquainted: Trollope's *An Autobiography* singles out Collins's oeuvre to describe a "branch" of literary "art" "which I have not myself at all cultivated" (129); Collins described Trollope (in a letter) as a formidable "workman" whose "immeasurable energies" produced a remarkably consistent fiction, never "in any marked degree either above or below his own level" (Collins qtd. in Peters 392). According to Wellek, realist fiction "implies . . . a rejection of the improbable, of pure chance, of extraordinary events" (10)—precisely what Collins's art does not reject.

[2] On Collins's travel in Europe and the United States as well as the international success of his writings see Law and Maunder, Ch. 9.

[3] GoGwilt's incisive analysis of mid-Victorian imperial sovereignty is, to my mind, hampered by the unsubstantiated assumption that mid-Victorian fiction like Collins's is beholden to Arnoldian universalism. The organization of "geopolitics" around the belief that mid-Victorian culture overwhelmingly affirms a *pre*-geopolitical confidence in human universality makes GoGwilt's often fascinating book tangential to my very different theorization of geopolitics (cf. Goodlad, "Victorian Geopolitics").

Should Collins be read, like Baudelaire, as a Modernist *avant la lettre?* Nicholas Daly's answer to this question is finally negative. In *The Woman in White* (1859–60), he argues, Walter Hartright's chance encounter with a ghostly female instances precisely the kind of "shock" Benjamin identified with the modern city ("Railway" 462). In this way, the mid-Victorian sensation novel trained modern bodies by steeling them for the dizzying impacts of new technologies like the railway and telegraph. Collins's fiction thus provided a temporary fix for a crisis of experience which (according to Daly) the aesthetics of Walter Pater and Oscar Wilde more fully resolved. Whereas the sensation novel merely contained the crisis by offering "temporal readjustment," Aestheticism and, eventually, Modernism solved it by defining modernity as "a potent source of experience" to be seized through revivifying *dandysme* (473, 477; see also Daly, *Literature*).

Daly's contrast between "declining Victorianism" and *fin-de-siècle* renewal entails considerable modification of Benjamin's thesis (479). Like Benjamin, Daly believes that "low-level anxiety" is a heightened form of consciousness that helps modern subjects to defend against urban shock (465). But Daly is "less convinced" by what is usually taken as the crux of Benjamin's analysis: the idea that such defensive "hyper-consciousness" coincides with "a declining capacity for true historical experience, or *Erfahrung*" (481, n17). Daly thus sets aside a distinction between two modes of experience which has been important to modern thinkers from Kant through Agamben: the opposition between *Erfahrung* (experience in the form of cumulative, historical engagement) and *Erlebnis* (experience in its most individualized, intense, and ephemeral form). By reading Collins's fiction as though it were consumed by the dilemma of sensory shocks, Daly leaves out the plangently Benjaminian quest for *Erfahrung*—for the integrated experience of repressed global histories.[4]

As Martin Jay has shown, Benjamin rejected the association of *Erlebnis* with lived authenticity, regarding it instead as "the prereflexively registered influx of stimuli." He used *Erfahrung*, by contrast, to signify a "more complexly mediated, historically integrated, and culturally filtered totalization of those stimuli into a meaningful pattern" (44). For Benjamin, modernity's production of the "immediate, passive, fragmented, isolated, and unintegrated inner experience of *Erlebnis*" stood in opposition to "the cumulative, totalizing accretion of transmittable wisdom, of epic truth, which was *Erfahrung*" (49). Daly's reading thus restores the privilege of *Erlebnis* which Benjamin denied; for once Aestheticism's embrace of modern stimuli is understood to redress the crisis of experience, Benjamin's worry

---

[4] Daly's take on sensation fiction resembles the "canonical" critical perspective on science fiction which Jameson evaluates in the 1982 essay that anticipates his *Archaeologies of the Future* (2005): "in a moment in which technological change has reached a dizzying tempo," science fiction narratives are understood to "have the social function of accustoming their readers to rapid innovation, of preparing our consciousness and our habits for the otherwise demoralizing impact of change itself." My reading of sensation fiction thus aligns with Jameson's claim that science fiction entails more than "an elaborate shock-absorbing mechanism" for denizens of the modern city ("Progress" 286). For a different comparison of Collins and Benjamin, see Trodd.

about the loss of coherent *Erfahrung* recedes—as though it, like the sensation novel, were a species of outdated Victorian earnest.⁵

It is worth remarking, then, that *The Woman in White,* for all its vivacious staging of an "age of sensation"—"the sense of continuous and rapid change, of shocks, thrills, intensity, excitement" (*Secret* J. Taylor 3)—is also a novel about evacuated historical experience. Consider the depiction of Welmingham, the small town to which Walter travels in search of documents to reestablish Laura's identity. The location prompts Walter to pause from detective flânerie to describe "the civilised desolation" and "depressing influence" of a new-minted "English country town" (*Woman* 503). Surveying the abandoned spot that the new Welmingham has replaced, he observes that the "dreary scene ... in the worst aspect of its ruin," was "not *so* dreary as the *modern* town" (515; emphasis added). Earlier in the narrative we find Blackwater, the Glyde estate, "situated on a dead flat," "almost suffocated by trees" (220). Such scenes dramatize the modern devastation of space, old as well as new.

The human counterpart to this spatial deracination is Count Fosco—a prototypical *Übermensch* who invents a morality beyond good and evil. As a self-styled "citizen of the world," Fosco taunts Marian Halcombe with his ethical relativism: "Here, in England, there is one virtue," he declares, while "there, in China, there is another" (257). The implication, of course, is that neither English nor Chinese morality—and, by implication, no morality—transcends its particular context. The reference to China reminds us that *The Woman in White* was serialized in 1859–60 while Britain, still in the recent aftermath of rebellion in India, waged the second Opium War against the Qing Dynasty (1856–60). More fundamentally, Fosco's aside on cosmopolitan ethics confirms the novel's global *mise en scène*. Exploring modern quandaries beyond individual consciousness and the fantasy of a sovereign England, Collins's fiction evokes a distinct mid-Victorian-era geopolitical aesthetic: an imaginative effort to grasp the "landscapes and forces" shaping experience on a transnational scale (Jameson, *Geopolitical* 3).

When Marian attempts to oppose England's "unquestionable" liberality to China's repressiveness, Fosco replies: "John Bull is the quickest old gentleman at finding out faults that are his neighbours', and the slowest ... at finding out the faults that are his own ... Is he so very much better in his way than the people whom he condemns?" Challenging Marian's ethnocentric perception of British virtue, he adds: "English Society ... is as often the accomplice as it is the enemy of crime" (258). *The Woman in White* thus suggests that *Erfahrung*—that historically engaged experience that enriches lived consciousness—must be wrested from a more complex and contingent geopolitical terrain. Although Collins's early novel arguably concludes in rapprochement with the status quo, it nonetheless

---

⁵ In aligning sensation fiction with Victorian "earnest," in contrast to Wildean satire, Daly exemplifies the common critical tendency to view mid-Victorian literature either as foil for or, at best, precursor to the Modernist innovations of the *fin de siècle*. Such reading occludes the fact that aesthetic pioneers like Pater and Baudelaire were the contemporaries of novelists like Collins; and that these aesthetes, like Collins, were responding to mid-Victorian-era conditions of possibility which Agamben is among those to trace back to the nineteenth century (*Infancy* 14).

anticipates the author's emergence in the 1860s as the premier novelist of a global aesthetic bent on describing transnational experience as part of an ongoing stream of history. Like the poetry Benjamin describes in "On Some Motifs on Baudelaire," Collins's novels "assign a mission" to art: the task of filling in "blank spaces" with poiesis (Benjamin, "Some Motifs" 162).[6]

In this chapter, I focus on *Armadale* and *The Moonstone*, which fill in the "blank spaces" of experience and, thus, restore a cumulative *Erfahrung*. Both novels, in doing so, extend the sensation novel's global ambit, structuring their plotlines around the guilty and semi-repressed histories of Atlantic slavery (*Armadale*) and British conquest on the Indian subcontinent (*The Moonstone*). Both figure this lost experience in part through racially-mixed characters: Ozias Midwinter, the scion of slaves and slaveholders in the West Indies, and Ezra Jennings, the son of an English colonial and his "Eastern" paramour. Both novels experiment with multi-perspectival voice—Collins's alternative, on the one hand, to Fosco's troubling relativism and, on the other, to narrative omniscience. Both novels thus illustrate the case I laid out in Chapter 1 for the formal and political dynamism of post-1848 British fiction and, especially, the heightened global consciousness of literature in the years after the Indian rebellion.

Yet, these proximate sensation novels are also quite different, for while both offer richly worlded perspectives, each represents a distinct formal approach to the mid-Victorian geopolitical aesthetic. Whereas *Armadale*, a novel criss-crossed by bodies of water, renders transnational experience spatially—through a fictive archeology that evokes recent study of the Atlantic matrix—*The Moonstone* offers a phenomenological approach to what is deliberately cast as an epistemological quest: "The Discovery of the Truth." As if Collins had attempted two successive experiments in writing the geopolitical aesthetic, Ozias Midwinter's story excavates the submerged legacy of Atlantic slavery, while the story of the Moonstone takes up imperial violence in the "contact zone" (Pratt 4). If *Armadale* is, however, a less successful experiment than *The Moonstone*, the reason is not that archeology must fail where phenomenology thrives. Rather, given the uneven history of global expansion, Collins connects more readily with the imaginative tools for writing "dark *Erfahrung*" in the situation of the Indian Empire—a geopolitical space that inspires his most powerful multi-genre work.

ARMADALE, THE ATLANTIC, AND THE ARCHEOLOGICAL AESTHETIC

[A]lthough he thinks Count Fosco is his best creation, Mr. Collins does not consider *The Woman in White* to be his best book. It is to *Armadale* that he

---

[6] On the novel's conclusion, in which Walter steels his manhood in the "wilds of Central America" (*Woman* 474) while Marian's vigorous femininity is tamed, see Nayder, "Agents". However, see Knoepflmacher for a reading that emphasizes Fosco's embodiment of a stirring Victorian counterworld.

gives the palm.... "It is by far the best thing I have ever written, and, in my opinion, no other book of mine can compare with it."
>> "A Novelist on Writing: An Interview with Mr. Wilkie Collins" (1887)

British historians wrote almost as if Britain had introduced Negro slavery solely for the satisfaction of abolishing it.
>> Eric Williams, *British Historians and the West Indies* (1964)

[D]enial has a long, ingenious, and endemic tradition within English culture when it comes to Atlantic slavery.
>> Marcus Wood, *Slavery, Empathy, and Pornography* (2002)

Armadale has long been remembered as the novel that marked Collins's rise to the ranks of England's best-paid authors. Famous after publishing *The Woman in White*, Collins was offered £5,000 to write a new novel for the *Cornhill*, prompting him to boast to his mother that "nobody but Dickens has made as much" (qtd. in Peters 236). Scholars have speculated that the stress of living up to such expectations precipitated an attack of "rheumatic gout" (Peters 257). More relevant to my reading, the research for *Armadale* entailed a flurry of travel. Whereas Collins prepared for *The Moonstone* by reading Indian history in the Athenaeum library, his groundwork for *Armadale* included trips to Italy and Germany as well as research on the topography of Norfolk and the Isle of Man. As John Sutherland notes, *Armadale*'s "extraordinarily far-flung narrative" begins "in the Black Forest, jumps parenthetically to the Caribbean, returns to the English West Country, makes a gloomy excursion to the Isle of Man, plays out ... among the flat waters of the Norfolk Broads, and climaxes bloodily in Naples and London's newest suburb, Hampstead" (xi). These spatial traverses, along with recurring shipwrecks, sea voyages, and watery locales shape the novel's uncanny Atlantic imaginary.

In his landmark study, *The Black Atlantic* (1993), Paul Gilroy argues that the "image of ships in motion between Europe, America, Africa, and the Caribbean" serves a chronotopic function. Since ships represent "a living, micro-cultural, micro-political system in motion," they offer resonant figures for the Atlantic milieu (4). *Armadale* anticipates this thought by making a guilty ship the stage for the novel's primal act of violence. Indeed, Collins's narrative is quite literally haunted by *La Grace de Dieu*, a French timber ship that founders in an Atlantic squall while sailing from Madeira to Lisbon—two ports associated with the triangle trade.[7] In a crime echoing the fate of drowned slaves in the Middle Passage, a man is left to die when a "murderous hand" locks him in his cabin on the flooding ship (*Armadale* 42). The killer, who confesses his crime in the novel's opening pages, is the owner of the largest estate in Barbados; his victim is the dispossessed cousin whose name and slave-owning property the dying man inherited. Both men are called Allan Armadale. Thus, begins a novel in which Britain's

---

[7] On Madeira as a resonant Atlantic locale in Charlotte Bronte's *Jane Eyre*, see Freedgood, *Ideas* 40–42.

Atlantic history is allegorized through an elaborate plot that features two lines of inheritance—the Armadale estate in Barbados, which is overtly implicated in the sugar plantation complex, and the Blanchard estate in Norfolk, which is superficially free of moral taint.[8]

Chronotopic ships appear throughout the pages of *Armadale* not least during the surreal moment when *La Grace de Dieu* resurfaces to "imprison" the second generation of Allans (135). Yet, though *Armadale* is quite possibly the most powerful black Atlantic narrative to come from the pen of a white Victorian, it is not precisely Gilroyesque. Gilroy's black Atlantic articulates a kind of poiesis: "the stereophonic . . . cultural forms originated by, but no longer the exclusive property of, blacks dispersed within" diasporic "structures of feeling" (3). New World slavery is, thus, the bearer of lived experiences that continue into the present day. Gilroy's formulation recalls the "particular kind of consciousness" which, in his keyword entry on experience, Raymond Williams describes as "full and active awareness" (*Keywords* 126). Indeed, black Atlantic experience is comparable to that historically engaged *Erfahrung* which, according to Benjamin, has the potential to integrate and resist the atomizing shocks of modern life.

If Collins's novel figured such dark *Erfahrung* it would likely be through Ozias Midwinter, the only one of the novel's five Allan Armadales who is of mixed racial descent. The son of Allan Wrentmore (who takes the name Armadale when he inherits the Barbadian property), Ozias's "dusky" phenotype is the legacy of his mother, a Trinidadian "Creole" (60; 397). When she marries the Scotsman who witnessed her first husband's confession of murder, the couple mistreat the young son whom they associate with his father's guilt. Eventually the boy runs away and, after a string of abuses, takes up with a "half-bred gipsy" from whom he borrows the name Ozias Midwinter (91). The stage is set for a test of Wrentmore's ominous prophecy: "Never let the two Allan Armadales meet in this world" (100).

As so often in Collins's fiction, racial hybridity is a resounding feature of *Armadale*'s geopolitical aesthetic. Ozias's "superstitious nature" is figured, on the one hand, as a racialized attribute of African descent and, on the other, as the expression of a complicated transatlantic past (136). Hence, while the "hot Creole blood" of his Trinidadian mother is tied to a variety of un-English characteristics, Ozias's "hereditary superstition" is explicitly the legacy of his guilty white father (131, 396). The anthropologist Paul Rabinow has described the modern-day cosmopolitan condition as "an acute consciousness . . . of the inescapabilities and particularities of places, characters, historical trajectories and fates" (56)—precisely the kind of transnationality which *Armadale* meditates. Yet, though Ozias bears the genealogical marks of both master and slave, he never develops a "full and active awareness" of the historical experience that haunts him. Rather, at his most compelling, Ozias is an archeological subject: one defined (in the terms used

---

[8] On the "sugar plantation complex" that, in the sixteenth century, migrated to Brazil, then Barbados, and "diffused to the rest of the Caribbean and ultimately the wider world," see Drayton 102.

by William Boelhower to describe Olaudah Equiano) "by a series of positions, encounters, kinds of discourse, and entangling trajectories" (93).[9]

In contrast to Gilroy's historical materialism, Boelhower's approach to the Atlantic is *archeological*: he urges study of the ocean's "ecology" to enable history's "scattered shards [to] say what they do not say of their own accord" (93–4). As Marcus Wood observes, the experience of African slaves "is, in a very real sense, lost" to conventional historiography since the available evidence is mainly secondhand white accounts (*Slavery* 9; cf. "Significant"). Archeology strives to overcome this deficit by recovering "a critical space of experience"; an imaginative means of voicing "mute or fragmented things" (Boelhower 93–4). In a comparable way, *Armadale*'s watery locales suggest an archeological effort to excavate slavery's impacts on a culture that has disavowed its own history—an ambitious project for an author seeking to write his "masterpiece" (Sutherland xi).[10]

In fact, *Armadale* was probably too ambitious a project to hazard in the charged climate of the years between the outbreak of the US civil war in 1861 and 1865, the year of the Jamaica rebellion. As Ozias struggles to liberate himself from a racial burden his white namesake is never made to bear, *Armadale* wavers between the impulse to recuperate lost experience and to liberate the mixed-race subject from further suffering. While this tension, to be sure, is built into the history of racism and slavery, it is one Collins's narrative is unevenly equipped to mediate. Insofar as *Armadale* seeks to fill in "the blank spaces" of Atlantic history, it produces a wonderfully evocative series of archeological disturbances which are quite possibly unique in mid-Victorian fiction. By contrast, the task of rescuing Ozias from intensified racial prejudice leads to a sterile (if prescient) return to the abolitionist worldview. *Armadale* thus presents a flawed but fascinating experiment in the geopolitical aesthetic.

In making early-nineteenth-century Barbados his point of origin, Collins singled out Britain's oldest colony in the Americas during a high point in slavery's influence on European modernity. The sugar plantations of this period were "at the cutting edge of capitalist civilization" in helping to inculcate "task specialization," "time discipline," "economies of scale," and "dependence on long-distance trade" (Drayton 104). But the story of capitalism's entwinement with New World slavery was vigorously suppressed. Britain did not simply forget its complicity, but actively recast it as the moral triumph of abolitionism. As Eric Williams observes,

---

[9] Compare to J. Taylor's identification of Ozias as the "sensitive subject who indirectly transmits the tensions and mysteries of the story" (*Secret* 151); her description of the novel as a "palimpsest of traces of the past" nicely complements my archeological interpretation (173).

[10] M. Wood calls the post-abolition attitude toward slavery "denial" (*Slavery* 21); but, to my mind, "disavowal" offers a more precise description of British attitudes toward the nation's involvement in slavery (and imperialism). Whereas *denial* implies refusal of reality, *disavowal*—the defense mechanism that Freud tied to fetishistic behavior, entails a condition both of accepting and refusing reality, with the fetishistic object or practice enabling this contradiction by standing in for reality. Although my theorization of the geopolitical aesthetic does not rest on psychoanalysis, it is worth noting that fetishistic tendencies accompanied geopolitical disavowal throughout the nineteenth century; for example, the intense fetishization of Anglo-Saxon racial superiority along with other exceptionalistic notions.

British historians "wrote almost as if Britain had introduced Negro slavery solely for the satisfaction of abolishing it" (233).[11] To understand *Armadale*'s archeological aesthetic, one must therefore consider the fate of abolitionist universalism during a period of increasing racism and formalizing empire.

THE CONTEST IN AMERICA

> The South are in rebellion not for simple slavery, they are in rebellion for the right of burning human creatures alive.
>
> John Stuart Mill, "The Contest in America" 1862

As we saw in Chapter 2, imperial practices in India were distinct from contemporaneous developments in the Atlantic. The East India Company bureaucrats responsible for governing this important "dependency" were professionally invested in a sustained civilizing mission. Although the Company's reforms were contemporaneous with the abolitionist movement, "anglicization" of Indians was never a popular or well-publicized cause. Notwithstanding this relative obscurity, imperial officials like Thomas Babington Macaulay forecast a gradual transition to Indian rule as an educated class of Indians, "English in tastes, in opinions, [and] in morals," became self-governing ("Minute" 729). Though a universalistic outlook was its necessary predicate, the project of training this anglicized Indian governing elite was understood to require imperial tutelage and the passage of time (cf. Stokes; Viswanathan, *Masks*).

By contrast, abolitionists often believed that self-acting market forces, along with the civilizing powers of Christianity, would ensure speedy transition from slavery to disciplined wage labor. Such advocates for anti-slavery were, therefore, disappointed when liberated Afro-Caribbeans sought alternatives to grueling subsistence labor on the plantation (Holt 278–309). Whereas the British state's interests in India increased throughout the nineteenth century, its commitment to humanitarian goals in the West Indies was and remained minimal. In 1854, less than twenty years after the end of apprenticeship, Parliament removed the duties that protected British sugar from slave-grown competitors.

Economic decline in the Caribbean conduced toward racism and political reaction in the metropole, amplified by settler hostility toward indigenes in Australia and New Zealand (Lester); cultural exchange with the American South, and, of course, "mutiny" in India. In July 1857, shortly after the outbreak of violence in South Asia, *The Times* pronounced abolition of slavery to have been an undeniable "failure" that had "destroyed an immense property," while "degrad[ing] the negroes still lower than they were" ("Nineteenth"). By 1860 Britain's antislavery

---

[11] According to Peterson, this self-affirming tendency was still at play during the recent bicentennial commemorations of the 1807 Slave Trade Act, abolishing the slave trade (6–7). In addition to the 1807 Act, the relevant legislation included the Abolition of Slavery Act of 1833, the culmination of which was the end of forced apprenticeships in 1838.

and humanitarian societies had lost the "political weight of . . . a popular movement" (A. Porter "Trusteeship" 214). On the eve of the Morant Bay rebellion, racist ideology had become a major obstacle to recognizing the structural problems undermining Jamaica's economy: as Thomas Holt writes, when "ex-slaves chose to define the content of their freedom in apparent opposition to market forces," they were redefined as "a different kind of human being" (279; 309).[12]

Yet, though abolitionism no longer inspired popular confidence in human universality, it continued to flourish as an emblem of British superiority. As a "marker of Britain's status as the most progressive Western nation" (Midgley 173), abolition of slavery provided justification for an array of imperial practices, demonstrating a "'free' nation's capacity to govern transnational commerce 'morally'" (C. Berman 190). By the time Collins turned to *Armadale* in the 1860s, the British state had become habituated to wielding its authority as a moral police while simultaneously strengthening its geopolitical standing in regions such as Brazil—the locale for the shady business dealings of Lydia Gwilt's second husband in *Armadale*.[13]

It is tempting to read *Armadale* in light of the landmark debates over the Jamaica insurrection, which pitted liberal-minded defenders of the rule of law (e.g., Charles Buxton, the son of the abolitionist Thomas Buxton; J. S. Mill; John Bright; and Herbert Spencer) against defenders of Governor Edward Eyre's unstinting use of force (e.g., Thomas Carlyle, Charles Dickens, Charles Kingsley, and John Ruskin). As Gilroy points out, Morant Bay marks an important "instance of metropolitan, internal conflict that emanates directly from an external colonial experience" (*Black* 11; cf. Gikandi, *Maps* 52–3). That said, *Armadale* was conceived, plotted, and at least half-written before news of rebellion in Jamaica reached the metropole at the end of 1865. While it is true, as Lillian Nayder writes, that the novel engages a preoccupation with "colonial and race relations" which was pervasive in the 1860s, the leap to concluding that *Armadale*'s "representations of racial conflict . . . reflect . . . the Jamaica Insurrection of 1865" is questionable (*Wilkie* 105). Since Collins finished writing *Armadale* before the standoff between Eyre's defenders and detractors became the object of public controversy, the case for reading the novel as a mediation between polarized pro- and anti-Eyre forces is tenuous at best.[14]

The Morant Bay rebellion was one of an intense cluster of events which marked a crisis for the liberal justification of imperial sovereignty (Ch. 2). Heated divisions over Jamaica thus coincided with the suspension of the Habeas Corpus Acts in Ireland (in reaction to Fenianism) as well as debates over the sovereignty of the

---

[12] British ideological investment in English-style agrarian capitalism meant that colonial policy favored large sugar plantations worked by proletarianized wage laborers even though Afro-Jamaicans (as well as many white missionaries) sought to implement a diversified agriculture organized through peasant proprietorship. On the ongoing wars with the Maoris in New Zealand, which provided yet another cause of the decline of the universalistic outlook, see Lester as well as A. Porter, "Trusteeship" 213.

[13] On the "symbiotic relationship" between humanitarianism and imperialism, see A. Porter, "Trusteeship" 204 as well as R. Law; on Brazil, see Forman.

[14] Nayder concedes that the connection to Morant Bay is indirect—a response to "cultural anxieties" about empire rather than a particular set of events—but suggests nevertheless that *Armadale*

Rajah of Mysore in the "indirect" Indian Empire.[15] These multiple crises of imperial sovereignty overlapped with demands to extend the franchise, including the Hyde Park riots of July 1866. While this makes the period from late 1865 through the end of the decade a charged context for *The Moonstone,* it also helps us to see that *Armadale,* by contrast, is not fundamentally *about* a crisis of sovereignty but about historical amnesia in the years leading up to that crisis.

Instead, *Armadale*'s archeological take on black experience likely responded to the U.S. Civil War which, from its inception in April 1861, illustrated how far British opinion had drifted from commitment to emancipating Africans, much less from remembering Britain's history in enslaving them. Attitudes toward the war were complicated by the common perception that the South was an invincible foe and the North, an aggressive power more determined to preserve the union than to end slavery. Thus, in the first of two December 1861 articles in *All the Year Round,* readers learned that the most heinous aspect of the American conflict was the North's "unnatural and unavailing struggle" to maintain the union ("American Disunion" 295–6). The article closed by recommending the work of James Spence, described by a recent historian as the "chief spokesmen of English pro-Confederate sympathy" (Campbell 67).[16]

Members of Parliament who openly sympathized with the South outnumbered pro-Northern counterparts and included William Gladstone (whose public speeches supported the Confederacy), John Arthur Roebuck (who disliked

---

"draws on the views of both camps" in the Eyre debate to represent "the conflict in a typically mixed way" (*Wilkie* 105–6). The time frame of *Armadale*'s composition makes this seem unlikely. Collins intended to begin submitting his new novel in December 1862, but was delayed by illness. Nonetheless, his travel during this hiatus provided important locations for *Armadale*: he spent the early months of 1863 in Wildbad, scene of the novel's opening chapters, and knew by that point that his new book required a research trip to the Isle of Man. According to Peters, Collins laid the groundwork for *Armadale* a year later in Naples (the location for Ozias's journalism) and began writing in April 1864 (266–7). Delivering the first part of *Armadale* in June, Collins traveled to the Norfolk Broads in August 1864 and serialization began in November. Throughout serialization, Collins stayed approximately three months ahead of the publication schedule (Peters 270). On October 5, 1865—six days before the outbreak of violence in Morant Bay—he wrote that he knew the "main events which are to lead to the end [of *Armadale*] as plainly as [he could see] the pen in [his] hand." The same letter adds that the characters themselves had been fleshed out two years before in Italy (qtd. in Peters 270). Scattered news of an insurrection in Jamaica began to reach England in November 1865 but "extensive coverage" of the affair did not begin until early 1866 (Hall, *Civilising* 275). "Between the summers of 1866 and 1867," writes Hall, "public opinion swung away from the Jamaica Committee to the supporters of Eyre. By June 1868, when a third attempt to prosecute Eyre failed, it was clear that defense of "black Jamaican rights was no longer a popular cause" (275; 25). If Peters' account of Collins's schedule is correct, he finished writing *Armadale* in February or March of 1866—late enough to have been aware of the controversy as he wrote the closing chapters, but far too early in the sequence of events for the novel to be read as a synthetic commentary on Morant Bay and its aftermath. Notably, in a recent chapter ("Collins and Empire"), Nayder does not reassert the connection between *Armadale* and the Eyre debates.

[15] Yet another topic claiming public attention at this time was the rise of a unified Germany under Otto von Bismarck with Prussia's victory over the Austrian Empire in 1866.

[16] The second article argues that protective tariffs, advantageous to Northern industry but injurious to Southern agriculture, were the heart of the dispute, making Dickens's journal one of a "minority" of English papers to regard tariffs as a principal *casus belli* (Campbell 45; cf. "Morrill").

Northern aggression), Lord John Russell (who equated the Southern cause with "independence"), and Sir Charles Wood (Secretary of State for India, who likened the cause of the American South to Italy's Risorgimento—despite Garibaldi's firm support for the North). Notably these spokesmen for the Confederacy all favored some measure of expanding the male franchise in Britain.[17]

In "The Contest in America," an anguished February 1862 article in *Fraser's*, written during the heightened criticism of the North which followed the *Trent* affair,[18] John Stuart Mill confronted this tendency for relatively progressive Britons to take up the Confederate cause as a liberal stand against Northern tyranny. Mill warned that Britain's abolitionism would be squandered were the nation to support the South: "Every reader of a newspaper to the furthest ends of the earth, would" remember "that at the critical juncture which was to decide whether slavery should blaze up afresh . . . or be trodden out," "England stepped in, and . . . made Satan victorious" (128). Writing a year before the Emancipation Proclamation, Mill sought to convince his readers that "extinction of slavery" was the real issue at stake (134). Even if there is some uncertainty as to the North's intentions, he wrote, there is "no question as to those of the South" who loudly preach the doctrine "that slavery . . . is a good" (135).

> "Heaven knows," Mill continued, there are vicious and tyrannical institutions in ample abundance on the earth. But this institution is the only one of them all which requires . . . that human beings should be burnt alive. . . . [T]here has not been a single year, for many years past, in which this horror is not known to have been perpetrated in some part or other of the South. . . . What must American slavery be, if deeds like these are necessary under it? . . . The South are in rebellion not for simple slavery, they are in rebellion for the right of burning human creatures alive . . . I am not frightened at the word rebellion. I do not scruple to say that I have sympathized more or less ardently with most of the rebellions . . . which have taken place in my time. But I certainly never conceived that there was a sufficient title to my sympathy in the mere fact of being a rebel . . . It seems to me a strange doctrine that . . . those who rebel for the power of oppressing others, exercise as sacred a right as those who do the same thing to resist oppression practiced upon themselves . . . Secession may be laudable . . . but it may also be an enormous crime. It is the one

---

The author of both pieces was probably Henry Forster Morley (see Storey 330), a regular writer for Dickens and future English professor. As Law and Maunder observe, Collins himself, whose personal politics are often difficult to pin down, seems to have shared Dickens's view that the North was motivated by selfish interests alone: "Slavery has in reality nothing on earth to do with" the Civil War; "the North hates the Negro" and merely found it "convenient to make a pretence that sympathy with him was the cause of the War" (Dickens qtd. in Law and Maunder 153).

[17] On Gladstone, Roebuck, Russell, and Wood, respectively, see Campbell 10, 168–76, 55, 157. Two Tory advocates for the South would eventually become central to the emerging neo-feudal view of India: Robert Cecil, the future Lord Salisbury (Secretary of State for India during the Mysore controversy) and Lord Bulwer-Lytton (future Viceroy of India).

[18] This concerned the North's boarding of the *Trent*, a British mail ship, and the removal of two Southern diplomats on their way to urge British recognition of the Confederacy, actions that constituted, as Mill conceded, "an insult to [Britain's] flag" ("Contest" 128). Eventually the diplomats were released but not before fears were raised that Britain might recognize the South or even declare war on the North.

or the other, according to the object and the provocation. And if there ever was an object which, by its bare announcement, stamped rebels against a particular community as enemies of mankind, it is the one professed by the South (136–7).

Mill thus attempted to restore the moral urgency that had made abolition politically viable in the 1830s. Insofar as the Confederacy was fighting to perpetuate a "Satanic" institution, support for the South was support for the "right to burn human creatures alive." Any other line of reasoning amounted to forfeiting the moral mantle of antislavery.

But while Mill's commitment to human universality was unbending, the public he addressed was now growing accustomed to racial discourse even while regarding antislavery as a confirmed British virtue. When Mill visited his old friend George Grote, the erstwhile philosophical radical described him as "violent against the South in this American struggle; embracing heartily the extreme Abolitionist views, and thinking about little else in regard to the general question" (Grote qtd. in Capaldi 306–7). In place of the Enlightenment creeds that had fueled abolition when Grote was in Parliament, an alleged science of "race" now attacked human universality as an old-fashioned dogma. Books by American racialists such as John H. Van Evrie's *Negroes and Negro 'Slavery'; The First an Inferior Race; the Latter Its Normal Condition* (1861), argued that British "philanthropy" had propagated a "'negro' movement" predicated on a fallacious "theory of a single race" (11).

Van Evrie's writings found an avid British disciple in James Hunt, who, in 1863, founded the Anthropological Society of London, an organization committed to propagating racial pseudo-science. Mill soon became a target of their attacks, described as a figure who illustrated the "absurdities" to which "the greatest minds may be driven" when "afflicted" by the pernicious doctrine of "[h]uman equality" (Hunt qtd. in Ellingson 250). Although Hunt's racist invectives represented a rhetorical extreme, the racial hierarchies he endorsed were becoming commonplace. Two years later, the *Morning Herald* encapsulated the zeitgeist. Observing how great a change had occurred since abolition, the article reflected that "the world-renowned question, once thought so convincing, of 'Am I not a man and brother?' would nowadays be answered with some hesitation by many—with a flat negative to its latter half by those who regard the blacks as an inferior race" (qtd. in Lorimer 198–9).

When this article appeared in November 1865, *Armadale*'s serialization had been in progress for a year, the Civil War was over, and the Morant Bay rebellion was just beginning to dominate the news. Conservative newspapers like *The Times*, with no details in hand of the actual events, hastened to accuse Afro-Jamaicans of perpetrating "a wanton insurrection against a Government from which they had received nothing but benefits." The cause of the turmoil, *The Times* did not hesitate to speculate, was an incorrigible dislike of work particular to Negroes and the Irish ("A most unpleasant"). In actuality, the same Afro-Jamaicans whom *The Times* was certain had "no grievance whatever . . . to afford [even] a colourable pretext for insurrection," had for years been suffering in a depressed economy aggravated by the inflationary effects of the Civil War. Poverty was so severe that many could not survive on wages manipulated to keep them at a bare subsistence. The inevitability of unrest was anticipated more than a year before the event (Lorimer 182).[19]

In hindsight, it is clear that the failure of the Jamaica Committee to bring Eyre to justice was the result of racism that had been on the rise for twenty years. This was a time, after all, when Matthew Arnold (writing in the *Cornhill* in 1868) could commend "the old Roman way of dealing" with working-class protest as a route to cultural progress: "flog the rank and file, and fling the ringleaders from the Tarpeian Rock!" ("Anarchy" 250).[20] The combination of refurbished Tory politics and a reactionary Liberal political culture, riddled by imperial contradictions, would soon provide fertile soil for a New Imperial outlook that romanticized hierarchies of race and class in a Disraeliesque idiom. Nonetheless, from the perspective of *Armadale,* what stands out is the transformation of abolitionist universalism from a mainstream political philosophy to the cant of "extremists." To an age that had come to doubt whether blacks were "brothers" as well as men, *Armadale* proffered a novel archeology.

THE ATLANTIC UNCANNY

> If it were the object of art to make one's audience uncomfortable without letting them know why, Mr. Wilkie Collins would be beyond all doubt a consummate artist.
> Unsigned review of *Armadale,* the *Saturday Review,* June 16, 1866

Armadale provokes the discomfiture described in the above quotation from the *Saturday Review* because it rejects the moral triumphalism of the post-abolition era, depicting a mid-century Britain haunted by uncanny ecologies and peopled by characters whose stories evoke the "submerged and the drowned" (Boelhower 95). That is not to allege that Collins felt moral outrage and political fervor like Mill's, but, rather, that his ingrained distaste for British racism, ethnocentrism, and hypocrisy was mobilized at the level of form. Whereas classic sensation novels like *The Woman in White* resemble *Bildungsromane* in enabling male protagonists to prove themselves through heroic masculinity (Garrett, "Sensations"), archeological texts do not produce the "synthetic knowing subject" (Boelhower 93). Rather, the archeological story is assembled from semi-forgotten trajectories, objects, and

---

[19] When the newly appointed Eyre was warned by a leading missionary that black workers were driven to thievery because they were "starving, ragged," overtaxed, "refused just tribunals," and "denied political rights," the governor's outraged reply was that "such ministers . . . stimulate resistance to the laws and constituted authorities" (Eyre qtd. in Hall, *Civilising* 252–3).

[20] Many modern reprints of *Culture and Anarchy* excise the line since Arnold deleted it from the second and third editions of the work.

spaces. *Armadale* develops this aesthetic by making strange watery topographies, as much as characters themselves, express the disruptive presence of the past.

To be sure, the opening chapters of *Armadale* extend the depredations of slave ownership beyond particular locales. The elder Armadale has "never seen" the vast West Indian property that he leaves to his young cousin Wrentmore (28). The son he disinherits grows up in England where his youthful "disgrace" has no direct link to the Caribbean (28). By contrast, Wrentmore's upbringing in Barbados is marred by the slave-owning milieu: "My boyhood and youth were passed in idleness and self-indulgence, among people—slaves and half-castes mostly—to whom my will was law" (27–8). Britain's ties to plantation slavery are, thus, multifarious and deep with the moral damage visiting metropolitan and colonial subjects alike.[21]

This situation changes once the narrative moves forward in time and away from the Caribbean, focusing on the third generation of Armadales more than a decade after the 1833–8 abolition of slavery. While the fair-skinned Allan seems unaware that his grandfather was the wealthiest slave-owner in Barbados, his mixed-race double, Ozias, is haunted by the past. An "ill-conditioned brat, with [his] mother's negro blood in [his] face," his "first recollection" is of his stepfather "beating [him] with a horsewhip" (89). Ozias's youth is spent in a series of marginal positions: "vagabond," "blackguard," "street-tumbler," "tramp," "gipsy's boy," "common sailors' cook," and "starving fisherman's Jack-of-all-trades" (132). At one point, having lost his temper under provocation, he sails, slave-like, "to the port of Bristol in irons" (94). Clearly, the dark-skinned Armadale's position is overdetermined by the racial legacies of slavery while his fair "brother" appears untouched by Atlantic history.

Collins's emphasis on this racial double standard both inspires and sets limits on his archeological aesthetic. When we first meet Ozias, he is a "startling object to contemplate," his "haggard" body a contrast to the "healthy, muscular" Englishmen of the neighborhood (64, 66). According to the affable Allan, such otherness is "a perfect godsend" (67); yet, as a brotherly intimacy develops between them, Ozias's distinctiveness increasingly centers on the "heathen" fatalism he hopes to escape (103). In the novel's most bizarre chapter, "The Shadow of the Past," the two young Armadales end up "imprisoned" on the decades-old wreck of *La Grace de Dieu* (135). Whereas Allan, unaware that he is visiting the scene of his father's murder, boards the ship blithely, Ozias, "shaking and shivering," spies the ghosts of the elder Armadales and swoons (131). When Ozias bids Allan to "shake hands, while we are brothers still"—recalling the abolitionist slogan remarked by the *Morning Herald*—the "careless" Allan responds by proposing

---

[21] Although there is no evidence of Collins's having researched the writings of Caribbean slaveholders, there are interesting parallels between this aspect of *Armadale*'s plot and the life of Simon Taylor, a wealthy Jamaican planter, who died in 1813. Taylor (whose only direct descendants were the illegitimate children he fathered with a quadroon servant) left the bulk of his wealth to a "profligate" nephew whose premature death meant the transfer of the property to an English niece and her husband who, like the elder Allan, were entirely unfamiliar with the West Indies (Watson 29).

a stiff drink (126–7). Allan's ignorance thus amplifies the already stark opposition between Ozias's archeological embedding and his own disencumbrance. The novel thereby creates a troubling tension between Ozias's appearance as an archeological subject—one whose "fate" signifies an Atlantic history that will *not* be submerged—and his desire to join his "brother" in an ostensibly post-racial future.[22]

In resurrecting a guilty ship from the pre-abolition era and transporting it to the Isle of Man, Collins's archeological aesthetic waxes uncanny. The *uncanny*, writes Tzvetan Todorov, is a form of allegory in which "events are related which may be readily accounted for by the laws of reason, but which are, in one way or another, incredible, extraordinary, shocking, singular, disturbing or unexpected" (46). *Armadale*'s uncanny works through the strange coincidences that peculiar ecologies enable, scattering the evidence of Atlantic history across conventional boundaries of space and time. Thus, when Allan and Ozias, "eager for adventure in unknown regions" (84), set out for the Isle of Man, their chosen destination is a quasi-sovereign domain in the Irish Sea which is home to a unique Manx topography, language, and culture. Collins's well-researched rendering of this thick ecology transforms the "dark and dangerous" Manx coastline into a liminal space for a fateful rendezvous that oscillates between *heimlich* and *unheimlich*, near and far, past and present, real and surreal (120). A few chapters later, the Norfolk Broads, renowned for its "low-lying labyrinth of waters," provides a comparable location for Ozias's prefigured encounter with Lydia. As the stage is set for this dreamlike event, the narrator describes the "startling anomalies" of an "inland agricultural district" surrounded by "networks of pools and streams" (244–5). Aquatic ecology thus underwrites what the *Saturday Review* described as a "lurid labyrinth of improbabilities" (Page 151), spatializing the Atlantic past through recurrent watery webs.

Yet, while this powerful uncanny dominates *Armadale*'s most memorable pages, the narrative is shot through with a countervailing desire to liberate Ozias from the burdens of a condition depicted as alternately socio-historical (the legacy of particular Atlantic contexts) and psycho-biological (the effects of "hereditary superstition"). Consider, for example, Allan's dream which occurs on the wrecked *La Grace de Dieu*. Unsurprisingly, Ozias sees the dream as confirmation of his father's prophecy: he believes that he is destined to harm Allan in some future connection with Lydia Gwilt, the mysterious *femme fatale* who, as a young maid, aided Jane Blanchard's elopement. When the sober-minded Dr. Hawbury dismisses such fears, Collins plays with his readers' expectation of a "natural explanation" while prolonging their fascination with fatalism (144).[23] But Ozias

---

[22] Sutherland's footnote also makes the connection between Ozias's invocation of brotherhood and the famous abolitionist slogan, "Am I not a man and a brother?" (n. 1 688). In an earlier passage, Ozias assures Brock that he would not have disobeyed his father's warning had he "not loved Allan Armadale with all that [he had in him] of a brother's love" (102–3).

[23] By pitting Hawbury's explanation against what might appear to be Ozias's superstition, Collins maintains the "hesitation" that Todorov aligns with fantastic narratives that require readers

eventually rejects Hawbury's "rational" account (151)—not (or not only) because he is "superstitious" but because, as readers can see for themselves, the doctor cannot explain how Allan can have dreamed of a drowning like his father's without knowing the circumstances of that event (136). Significantly, then, *Armadale*'s narrator embraces the very fatalism Ozias strives to overcome: "the fatal parallel between past and present was complete," the narrator pronounces, "What the cabin had been in the time of the fathers . . . the cabin was now in the time of the sons" (125). Ozias's "heathen" fatalism thus becomes the archeological sign of the novel's deep roots in New World slavery even as Ozias himself yearns to free himself of its "horror" (101; 104).[24]

At its most experimental, *Armadale* moves beyond this impasse by diffusing the legacy of slavery. Waterborne subjectivities abound, from Ozias's early "life at sea" to the young Wrentmore's ability to don a "sailor's coat" and impersonate a crew member with ease (130; 36). And while Allan's "thoroughly English love of the sea" is recognizable as a normative Anglo-Saxon trait (55), it is also an instance of how the Armadale name, even when embodied in its white ("Blanchard") form, multiplies Atlantic tropes. As Atlantic subjectivity becomes a lived experience of haunted memory augmented by uncanny space, *Armadale* transcends the dilemmas of disavowed history, a compromised archive, and the Victorian tendency to racialize and marginalize Atlantic experience. It offers a Victorian prefigurement of the diasporic structure of feeling Gilroy describes in *The Black Atlantic*.

From this view, the most potentially powerful "Atlantic" subject is Lydia. That is so even though many readers regarded this charismatic *femme fatale* as a distraction from the male storyline. In an 1887 interview, Collins himself noted that *Armadale* was well-received "until Miss Gwilt came on the scene" ("A Novelist"). By refusing passively to channel male desire, Lydia undermines the heteronormative triangle that cements male bonding—her drive for agency, revenge, and (eventually) Ozias's love, surpassing that of any man. Thus, while Lydia's "gwilt-y" tale of female wrongs is potentially feminist, scholars have argued that her upstaging of the male Armadale drama serves reactionary ends.[25] Nonetheless, it is worth pausing to recognize Lydia's potential for amplifying Atlantic archeology. The only character whose story spans two generations of Armadales, it is Lydia whose "suicide-leap" from the deck of a ship brings about the "succession

---

and characters "to hesitate between a natural or supernatural explanation" of events (33). Collins's Appendix, which defends the novel's realism, attempts to restore such gothic hesitation, inviting readers "to interpret [the dream] by the natural *or* the supernatural theory as the bent of their own minds may incline them" (678; emphasis added).

[24] On fatalism in Collins, see also Brantlinger, "What?"; J. Taylor calls *Armadale* a narrative about how "the present and present identity are over-determined by the forces of the past" (172). Sutherland's introduction notes that "*Armadale* is . . . obsessed with fate, congenital doom and inherited blight" but speculates that the reason was Collins's fear of inherited venereal disease (xii). According to Reitz, *Armadale* asks, "Will England's guilty past become a guilty future?" (92). For Dever, central to *Armadale* is the question of whether "individual men and women [are] bound to a predetermined fate, or . . . free to create their own futures" ("Marriage" 116).

[25] For example, Nayder argues that Lydia's "sexual differences" obscure Ozias's racial differences (*Wilkie* 113). I borrow "Gwilt-y" from Young-Zook.

of deaths" which enables Allan to inherit the Blanchard property (*Armadale* 79–80, 105). With her vilified red hair a kind of substitute for skin color, Lydia begins life as a friendless child who is "beaten," "half starved," and "exhibited" in the "market-place" before being turned into Jane Blanchard's "plaything" (521, 520, 522). Later, she is "shut up" in a convent and—in a scenario that recalls Rochester's Creole wife in *Jane Eyre*—confined "in a lonely old house" in the Yorkshire moors (525). When Lydia's first husband strikes her with his "whip," she poisons him (546). Her next spouse, the unsavory Captain Manuel, is "a native of Cuba" with business interests in "the Brazils"—two infamous holdovers of New World slavery (527, 212). And while Lydia is not fatalistic, she shares Ozias's longing to "break the chain that binds" her to a "horrible" past (433). In all of these ways Lydia's slave-like positionality anticipates her attraction to the novel's principal mixed-race subject. Dismissing "Allan the Fair" as a "noisy, rosy, light-haired" "young fool," she describes her future husband as "little and lean, and active and dark, with bright black eyes which say to me plainly, 'We belong to a man with brains in his head and a will of his own'" (425, 284, 287).

That Lydia's attraction to Ozias resonates with the archeological project she eventually disrupts points to the flaw in *Armadale*'s execution. In purely technical terms, the strong first person voice that Lydia develops through letters and diaries drowns out the comparatively voiceless Ozias. Nonetheless, the root of this problem is the novel's symbolic investment in the abolitionist construct of *brotherhood* as a vehicle of anti-racism. As Catherine Peters notes, neither Allan nor Ozias "exists fully without the complementary qualities of his other self" (276)—a homosocial glue borne of the double standard. As Collins relentlessly contrasts Ozias's "dark" burdens to Allan's "fair" disencumbrance (425), the desire to redress this injustice snuffs out the archeological diffusion of Atlantic subjectivities. *Armadale* ends up caught up in the imaginary restitution of abolitionist "brotherhood."[26]

That is not to say that *Armadale* simply abandons the archeological aesthetic. To the contrary, Atlantic tropes proliferate in the final chapters but are overwhelmed by Lydia's vigorous self-writing. With her narrative consumed by the plan to impersonate Allan's widow, Italy—the location for Ozias's work as an "industrious journalist" (547)—becomes a mere background for sensation, its Risorgimento-era politics and geography emptied of substance. When Atlantic tropes appear, like the message in the bottle that creates the false impression of Allan's drowning (580), or Lydia's off-hand allusion to Ozias's employers as "slave-owners" (552), they instance the kind of "décor" Lukács describes in his critique of bourgeois fiction (*Historical* 290). Filtered through Lydia's presentist

---

[26] According to Dever, no "heterosexual attraction in the novel" is as "authentic" as the bond between Allan and Ozias (117). Her point complements my own sense that the "Atlantic" bond between Lydia and Ozias fails in part because Ozias is locked into a dyadic relation to his white "brother." For a reading that emphasizes a homoerotic bond between Allan and Ozias, see Salih who posits an "affirmation of same-sex interracial affect" which also "puts paid to the novel's unconventional but nonetheless overdetermined and doomed interracial marriage" (151).

outlook, such details are mere contrivances for a hypermodern landscape dominated by *Erlebnis*—powerless to constitute Italy as an "Atlantic" locale or even connect it to the stream of ongoing history of which the Risorgimento was actually a part.

In a noteworthy diary passage, Lydia renews her "resolution to look forward only" as she names the date: December 1—"The last month of the worn-out old year, eighteen hundred and fifty-one!" (599). The omniscient narrator repeats the gesture, making Bashwood's stake-out at the South Eastern Railway commence on "the night of the second of December" (615). Intentionally or not, Collins makes the climax of *Armadale* coincide with the December 2, 1851 coup memorialized in the *Eighteenth Brumaire of Louis Bonaparte* in which Marx famously declares history's repetition "the first time as tragedy, the second as farce" (594).[27] As the narrative builds toward its prefigured climax, Lydia and Ozias cross the Channel in a Paris-bound "tidal train," while Allan's yacht sails midway between "Land's End" and "Finisterre" (541). Like the names of these ports, which signify extra-territoriality in English and French, the channel is a potentially powerful figure for the submerged histories that archeology renders for modern experience. But the final chapters of *Armadale* suspend the archeological aesthetic: Atlantic allegory mutates into sensation as fatal history becomes *femme fatale*.

To be sure, the conclusion of *Armadale* fascinates in instancing the "'sensation novel' with a vengeance" (*Athenaeum* qtd. in Page 147). As the *mise-en-scène* changes from uncanny ecologies to claustrophobic interiors, the novel glimpses Victorian biopower in a London sanatorium equipped with high-tech treatments for the "nervous" (640).[28] But such self-conscious hypermodernity—the reign, in effect, of pervasive *Erlebnis*—is at odds with the temporal challenge of remembering the past. Thus, while Lydia's sacrifice confirms her devotion to Ozias, the substitution that sees her breaking *his* chain to New World slavery confutes archeology. Consigning Lydia to a nearly unmarked grave, *Armadale* concludes by pulling Ozias free from Atlantic embedding: creating a bland vision of experience beyond consciousness of color and history. The last few pages banish fatalism, reconcile the two Armadales, and declare that "the darkness has passed." In language that blends disencumbered futurity with the bleaching effects of sunlight, Ozias's once "tawny" face becomes a canvas for the "first light of the new day" (64, 677).

Hence, in a stunning turn away from history, Ozias vows to silence the past: not only will Allan never know "the secret of the two names," he will never learn of his mother's elopement, his father's death, and his family's deep connections to the West Indies. When the carefree Allan sanctions this silence, declaring that

---

[27] As the epigraph to this chapter shows, Marx's text provides a fitting commentary on *Armadale*'s shift from buried racial history to blithe racial transcendence even if the choice of 1851 (also the year of the Great Exhibition) was not deliberate.

[28] It is tempting to compare the *Athenaeum*'s review to the self-conscious hypermodernity of Harker's narrative in *Dracula* (1897) when he aligns his own practices with "the nineteenth century up-to-date with a vengeance" (Ch.3). Conversely, Dr. Seward's technologically sophisticated asylum may owe something to *Armadale*'s depiction of Dr. Downward's sanitarium. For a comparison of *Dracula* and *The Woman in White*, see Case.

he "has heard all [he] ever want[s] to know about the past," Ozias responds with lines lifted from Decimus Brock, invoking an "all-wise" and "all-merciful" God against the contingencies of past and present alike (677). The novel that began with the cumulative temporality of an archeological aesthetic concludes with a complaisant and dehistoricizing providentialism, anticipating the post-raciality of neoliberalism today.

ABOLITIONIST UNIVERSALISM AND POST-RACIALITY

> The general tone of thought [of the American people during the Civil War] . . . may be fairly imagined by taking [the example] of the average Englishmen, who . . . condemned the war heartily; thought it was nonsense to fight to force men into brotherly kindness; [and] considered the Abolitionists to be humbugs . . . Such a man, transplanted for a sufficient time, would . . . adopt . . . a different set of national commonplaces. He would insensibly substitute a fanatical belief in an idol called the Union for a belief in old England, he would hate humbugs and agitators . . . and unreasonable philanthropy more heartily still. The hatred which Englishmen felt for "red tape" in the Crimean war, and the contempt which they (some of them at least) have expressed for niggerworshippers during the Jamaica troubles, may represent the feelings of the genuine Yankee population towards . . . shoddy aristocracies on the one hand, and the irrepressible negro on the other. We who wished honestly to see the nigger free, hated him as the cause of the troubles, and as our English or "Anglo-Saxon" breed always hates an inferior race."
>
> [Leslie Stephen], "American Humour" (1866)

For an apolitical novelist like Collins, writing in a period that saw "race" become a fixture of modern discourse, the challenge of sustaining the Atlantic aesthetic was to imagine dark *Erfahrung* as distinct from the assimilative universalism of the abolitionist era. Whereas abolitionists had made interracial brotherhood the emblem of their moral intervention, in the years following the Indian rebellion, the U.S. Civil War, and the Governor Eyre controversy, the idea became the butt of crude satire even in high-minded journals like the *Cornhill*. Indeed, the final chapters of *Armadale* were published in the same volume that included "American Humour," an article that casually derided the abolitionist cause of "forc[ing] men into brotherly kindness." In this jocose spirit, the author mused that Britons and "Yankees" could at least find common cause in their mutual contempt for negroes and "negrophilites." In a sentence that epitomized the shift from abolition's high moral ground to the begrudging and racist antislavery of the 1860s, the author wrote, "We who wished honestly to see the nigger free, hated him as the cause of the troubles, and as our English or "Anglo-Saxon" breed always hates an inferior race" ("American" 37). The starkness of this reaction is even more pronounced when we consider that the author was Leslie Stephen, the scion of a famous abolitionist family and a strong supporter of the North throughout the war. In this way, *Armadale*, a novel invested in the structure of brotherhood, reached the end of its serial run in a climate as hostile to the family of man as to the aesthetic project of remembering the past. We might even surmise that this intense antipathy spurred Collins to push universalism to the fore: producing the closing image of a whitened Ozias reclaimed from the trials of "race" and its history.

One understands why some critics take *Armadale*'s neutralizing conclusion at its word, arguing, as Nathan Hensley does, that *"Armadale* teaches the (liberal) lesson that . . . every subject can break free from his family history through the magic agency of individual virtue" (*"Armadale"* 619). By "liberal," Hensley has in mind the Reform era's "domestic project of abstraction," including "the liberal state's" production of "modern citizens [who are] formally free, able to conclude contracts, and implicitly male"; a project that *Armadale* "ironizes"— until it does not (609–10). The implication is that *Armadale*'s colorblind conclusion is ideologically overdetermined. Indeed, Collins's fiction becomes, on this view, indistinguishable from the worldview that Uday Singh Mehta describes in *Liberalism and Empire* (1999): a form of Enlightenment discourse that, in committing to pseudo-universalizing abstraction, regards "everything [as] an instance of something general" (96).[29]

If *Armadale* offers a spokesperson for such pro-imperial liberalism it is Brock, the avuncular rector who seeks to cure Ozias's "paralysing fatalism." Brock's appeal to Ozias's "higher nature" asks him to mobilize Christian identity in affirmation of God's omniscience—achieving something like the rapid transition to *homo economicus* which abolitionists had anticipated for liberated Afro-Caribbeans. By this logic, one simply believes that providence explains the "mystery of Evil" or one "lowers [oneself] to the level of the brutes" (513). Brock's Christian dogma thus contradicts the Atlantic uncanny that connected Ozias's fatalism to his slave-owning white father. Moreover, Brock's Christian universalism, like the imperial civilizing mission it resembles, is haunted by a reflexive fear of racial difference. When we first meet him, "the rector's healthy Anglo-Saxon flesh [creeps] responsively" at the sight of Ozias's "brown fingers" and "yellow face" (512, 64).

Armadale's conclusion thus requires careful consideration of the novel's account of "race." When Ozias describes his early life, he explains that "a written character" was useless in combating racial prejudice: "I produced a disagreeable impression at first sight" (97). Reflexive racism is once again on view when one of

---

[29] As Hensley rightly notes, this is but part of the novel's "ambivalent historicism" (*"Armadale"* 625). Of course, the mid-Victorian state's production of "modern citizens" was quite explicitly male—as well as explicitly propertied and middle-class. In common with the roughly 80% of adult males who remained disenfranchised after 1832, women did not become citizens until the reforms of 1918 and 1928. There was, moreover, nothing abstract about the dominant discourses that justified the exclusion of women and working-class men (including those rural working-class men who remained disenfranchised until 1882). Even less abstract were the racial discourses that claimed to justify undemocratic rule over Indians and other imperial subjects. On the sensation novel as a form that expresses "a fear of a general loss of social identity as a result of the merging of the classes" see Loesberg, "Ideology" 117.

Allan's servants regards Ozias's "face" with "distrustful consideration" (190). And it subtends the tortured emotion of Ozias's mother when she asks if Wrentmore's first love was "dark, like me" (31). Like the colorblind ideology of today, Brock's racist recoil is but the flipside of his determination to subject Atlantic experience to a sanitizing civilizing mission that undermines "dark *Erfahrung*." This supposed solution to the problem of racial prejudice, even when ostensibly vindicated by the pat ending, derives from the same abolitionist assimilationism that enables Stephen casually to pronounce the "Anglo-Saxon's" "hatred" for the "inferior race" he wishes to see "free."[30]

In the months after *Armadale*'s appearance, acrimonious racism intensified as the Jamaica Committee's tireless efforts to prosecute Eyre alienated a public that had, at best, become weary of the debate. In October 1866, a year after the outbreak of violence in Morant Bay, the *Saturday Review* asked its readers, "What have the English people done that the irrepressible negro should make an interruption into their daily press, disport himself at their dessert, chill their turtle, spoil their wine, and sour their pineapple and their temper? . . . Are we henceforth to be separated, as a nation, into negrophiles and anti-negroites?" ("Negro" 446). Yet, despite such aversion, Collins went on to create his most famous mixed-race character in *The Moonstone* and to feature the mixed-race descendants of African slavery in *Black and White* (a play he co-wrote in 1869), *Miss or Mrs?* (1871), and *The Guilty River* (1886) (see Fisch). In *Poor Miss Finch* (1872), he contemplated racial difference through the bizarre device of a protagonist whose medical condition turns him dark blue, complicating his attachment to a heroine who (though blind) has a horror of dark skin. Such persistent efforts to render racialized experience in multiple forms suggest that Collins could no more rest content with an ideology of universalizing abstraction then he could ignore the intensifying racism of his contemporary moment.

As scholars of post-raciality often note, colorblind perspectives disavow the systemic features of racial inequality through a "rhetoric of racial transcendence" (Wise 64). While *Armadale*'s conclusion exemplifies this disavowal, the longest part of the narrative resists the move. Readers know, for example, that the Blanchard estate is a lucrative property, while the Armadale estate, "ruined" by "emancipation of the slaves," was sold for what it "would fetch" (99). Lydia's declaration that the Armadale names "haunt" her thus indexes more than a sensational plot to substitute one Armadale scion for another (424). As Jane's "plaything," Lydia has witnessed the Blanchards' eagerness to marry their daughter into the sugar plantation complex. Indeed, Thorpe-Ambrose—described as the "product . . . of the commercial English mind," a "conventional country-house,"

---

[30] That is not to say that all abolitionists were necessarily invested in the belief that blacks were an "inferior race" but only that the universalistic framework underwriting abolition could readily accommodate such beliefs for at least two reasons. First, the supposed *cultural* inferiority of certain groups could be perceived as so entrenched that the difference between "cultural" racism and "biological" racism becomes effectively slight. Moreover, as we have seen, the perceived failure of emancipated Afro-Caribbeans to assimilate to Anglo-Saxon norms resulted in rapid skepticism among abolitionists and their allies about presumed racial equality.

"barely fifty years old"—is a species of Atlantic artifact (170). Built just prior to the abolition of the slave trade, the house derives from a period when Britain's sugar-producing colonies were fueling the global economy (Heuman 471).[31]

According to Jenny Bourne Taylor, Allan Armadale becomes "a name without an identity"; "a blank space standing for a property that has no real owner" (152). This linguistic analysis nicely captures the dizzying profusion of Armadales while anticipating its geopolitical supplement. As Hensley notes, *Armadale* "helps us to appreciate that in the 1860s, it was not just unsavory opinions on race . . . but also a modern financial system that furthered British hegemony and masked its expansion under the sign of peace" ("*Armadale*" 610). In this sense, the novel never forgets that its title names a wealthy slaveholder as one such agent of globalization's *longue durée*. When Collins has Wrentmore urge his mixed-race son to "[m]ark how the fatalities gathered" (46), the move down the chain of Armadales constitutes a haunting geopolitical aesthetic. *Armadale*, despite its foreshortened archeology, enables "mute or fragmented things" to speak. Although Collins's closing retreat from history and toward "post-racial" erasure marks a false step in an ambitious author's experimentation, it is a pitfall he avoids in *The Moonstone* when he makes racial hybridity the direct phenomenological channel for an invaluable *Erfahrung*.

THE MOONSTONE'S STORY OF EXPERIENCE

To move from *Armadale* to *The Moonstone* is to transit from a comparatively marginal work to one of the most discussed novels in British literature, not least since the advent of postcolonial studies. Scholarly readings of *The Moonstone* and empire began in 1973 with John Reed's claim that Collins's anti-imperial novel revealed "the representatives of Western Culture" to be "plunderers" (283). In the 1990s, Nayder argued that *The Moonstone* loosened the grip of the "imperial ideal" ("Robinson" 215; cf. J. Mehta), while Ashish Roy insisted that the novel's "mythos" is "entirely consonant with arguments for empire" (657). The crux of this debate, I suggest, should not turn on whether *The Moonstone* conforms to the paradigm Edward Said described in *Orientalism* (1979)—which, in certain respects, it does—but, instead, on what *kind* of orientalism it displays, why, and with what effect. From this perspective, the most important avenues for exploration are the unsettled question of *The Moonstone*'s form and the impact of that form in fashioning transnational experience.

We have seen how *Armadale* attempts to render the experience of racial injustice archeologically—replacing damaged archives and conventional identities

---

[31] On the practice of "large Caribbean landowners" trading "wealth in the West Indies for an estate and social standing in England" see Watson (29); cf. Hensley: *Armadale* shows "the moment when the money issuing from [West Indian] sugar plantations has been forgotten, laundered, 'Blanched'—arriving through Liverpool but transformed into cleaner, more respectable English money in countryside manors like Thorpe-Ambrose" (625).

with subjectivities wrested from estranged spaces and positionalities. In *The Moonstone*, Collins gestures toward an archeological aesthetic when he makes the Shivering Sand the setting for the novel's most dramatic disclosures. Described as "the most horrible quicksand on the shores of Yorkshire," this occult space emits a weird "shivering and trembling" caused by "something" in "the unknown deeps below" (35).[32] Then too, Collins's titular gemstone recalls the "strangely anomalous objects" that haunt the pages of *Armadale* (248). John Plotz calls the Moonstone "a portable metonym for India" (*Portable* 40; cf. J. Mehta 613), while Paul Young stresses the explicit connection between Collins's stone and the legendary Koh-i-Noor ("'Carbon'"). Made over as a "gift" to Queen Victoria upon the conquest and annexation of the Punjab, this renowned diamond became "the single object in the [Great Exhibition] that most intensely represented India" (Kriegel, "Narrating"166).

Chronotopic objects and resonant "things" such as diamonds are central to *The Moonstone*'s story of disavowed imperialism. Yet, as I will show, the chief revelations of this novel are phenomenological rather than archeological—centering on what subjects experience and how that experience can be articulated and shared. Although *The Moonstone* features a parade of colorful experts, their specialized knowledge provides a merely partial epistemology, an incomplete phenomenology, and nothing like a comprehensive basis for modern sovereignty. Collins's novel approaches this experiential gap though a series of formal innovations: *The Moonstone* begins with imperial history, proceeds to detective fiction, mutates into a multi-voiced story of experience, and ends in a kind of utopian romance. By the end of the text, the Benjaminian task of filling in "blank spaces" has evoked forms of knowledge "entirely out of the experience of the mass of mankind" (*Moonstone* 388).

ROMANCING THE STONE

> The history of [the Koh-i-Noor] is one long romance . . . but it is well authenticated at every step, as history seems never to have lost sight of this stone of fate from the days when Ala-ud-deen took it from the Rajahs of Malwa, five centuries and a half ago, to the day when it became a crown jewel of England.
>
> Professor [Nevil Story] Maskeleyne, qtd. in Charles William King,
> *The Natural History, Ancient and Modern, of Precious Stones and Gems, and of Precious Metals*, 2nd ed. (1867)

> Diamonds triumphed . . . because they are 'stones without qualities'; they dazzle and sparkle, but at the end of the day they all look pretty much alike. They are, in fact, the world's most homogeneous stones; pure elemental

---

[32] On the Sand as a "central image" for the oppressed see Heller, *Dead* 149; as a physical space that "absorbs" knowledge of the past, see J. Taylor 198; cf. J. Mehta 625–6; Sabin 90.

> carbon, of course, with an inflexible crystal structure, but also consistently small, unpatterned... and inoffensively neutral... with virtually no marks of origins or histories, distinguished only by weight and by cut, qualities imposed by the cutter.
>
> Robert N. Proctor, "Anti-Agate: The Great Diamond Hoax and the Semiprecious Stone Scam" (2001)

In recent years, Victorianist scholarship has grown ever more attentive to *things*, not least in the two proximate novels whose titular stones mark the diamond as a mid-Victorian object of choice. According to Plotz, *The Moonstone* and *The Eustace Diamonds* illustrate "portable property," showing how Victorian fiction "was defined" through its "obsession with objects represented as problematically endowed with sentimental and fiscal value simultaneously" (*Portable* 4). Whereas "portable property" posits jewels as archetypal "things" irrespective of form, Stefanie Markovitz delineates the interrelation of the two ("Form" 592). In her ingenious take, diamonds are "generic touchstones" whose recurrence across a range of literary forms signals "moments... of extreme generic self-consciousness." In contrast to lyric poetry, she contends, novels use diamonds to "focus and trouble sub-generic distinctions between plot- and character-based fiction" (608). Thus, whereas Collins's Preface proclaims *The Moonstone*'s exceptional interest in "the influence of character" (3), Trollope's shift from *Bildung* to bijou enables "a productive dalliance with sensation" (Markovitz, "Form" 609). In the end, however, these distinctions matter less than the idea that the diamonds of mid-Victorian fiction anticipate "the more obvious formal fractures of modernism" (615).

"Portable property" and "form-thing" analysis thus enable scintillating survey; but neither notes the impact of geopolitics in shaping forms and things over long and short *durées*. For Plotz, diamonds are "at their most distinctive" when they are "manifestly *riven*" between sentiment and cash (*Portable* 31). But from a geopolitical standpoint it is novelistic form that cleaves into two as *The Moonstone* glimpses a resilient sovereignty that *The Eustace Diamonds* devastates. With its chronotopic capacity to body forth spatio-temporal difference, Collins's stone metonymizes India's *resistance* to portability. A thing whose constitutive form is romance, this "unfathomable" gem eludes the status of property (whether Herncastle's, Rachel's, or Queen Victoria's)—a Western construction that extends only so far as the makeshift sovereignty of empire (*Moonstone* 74). The particularity of the Moonstone as a formative thing thus stands in marked contrast to Trollope's fungible necklace.[33]

Significantly, both novels appeared during a transitional period that saw diamonds evolve from rarefied symbols of royalty and romance to singular fixtures

---

[33] Compare to Hennelly (33 and passim), as well as P. Young: "The English characters" in *The Moonstone* "are never fully in control of [the stone]; just as the diamond goes beyond their conceptual grasp, so too their physical hold over the jewel is weak" ("Carbon" 347). Duncan even more emphatically associates the diamond with an "alien force that breaks in and out of the [English] domestic order, effortlessly eluding a circumscribed agency of detection" (302). For Park, the Moonstone stands "metonymically for Indian national and Hindu religious sovereignty" (94).

of bourgeois modernity: "the luxury good that is also a mass-market item" (Proctor 384).[34] As Robert N. Proctor explains, the 1859 discovery of diamonds in South Africa soon produced a glut in world supply, generating new and more democratic kinds of diamond narrative. Thus, while the on again/off again couples of *The Eustace Diamonds* were suggesting the uncertainties of Victorian betrothment, diamonds in real life were on their way to becoming a new "social currency" to replace the "hoary rituals" of dowry or bride-price (396). That diamonds in general and the diamond engagement ring in particular would, by the end of the nineteenth century, become "one of the greatest triumphs of mass consumer marketing" was not, however, the inevitable outcome of increased supply (390). Rather, the diamond's intrinsic features—homogeneity, clarity, and historylessness—made it an ideal modern bullion: a gem that could replicate the durability and portability of a paper currency while proffering a "precious" store of value which could be circulated with ease (398).

Written in the late 1860s, *The Eustace Diamonds* preceded the ritual of the diamond engagement ring by more than twenty years, but it is prescient in recognizing the modern diamond as a commodified signifier of luxury.[35] Trollope's naturalistic narrative of capitalist globalization thus substitutes a necklace with little connection to an Indian past for the "sacred gem" at the heart of the novel that helped to inspire it (*Moonstone* 51). Penned by an author who regarded Britain's political constitution as an heirloom, *The Eustace Diamonds* captures the growing power of the commodity form to infiltrate venerable establishments like Parliament, exposing them to the corrosive "cosmopolitan" circuits of capital and empire. In such a world, valuable objects such as diamonds cannot but be fallen: the disenchanting glitter Marx implied when he wrote that the *"increasing value* of the world of things proceeds in direct proportion to *devaluation* of the world of men" (*Economic* 107).[36]

From this perspective, Collins—though an equally prescient novelist who recognized the diamond's modern telos—stages what might be termed the auratic

---

[34] According to Slade, before the nineteenth century, "diamonds were so rare in England that even Shakespeare ... probably learned about [them] from reference works" (171). King's first edition cites Pliny: the diamond "was long known to none but kings, and to but a very few of *them*;" diamonds became known to Europe through "direct intercourse with the nations of Southern India" (19). For a more recent addition to this ongoing history see Popper, "Diamonds as a Commodity," http://www.nytimes.com/2012/04/14/business/turning-diamonds-into-a-must-have-commodity.html?pagewanted=all&module=Search&mabReward=relbias%3As%2C%7B%221%22%3A%22RI%3A6%22%7D&_r=0. This is an April 2012 article on a proposal "to create the first diamond-backed exchange-traded fund ... It would buy one-carat diamonds and store them in a vault in Antwerp, Belgium, providing daily values with an as-yet-unnamed index."

[35] Fittingly, the only "property" Lucy obtains upon Frank's marriage proposal, is the letter that enunciates his offer (*Eustace* 1:132). Yet, while diamonds had yet to become signifiers of betrothal, their market value had already, in 1823, been "standardized" and "reduced to formulae" (Proctor 384 n.11).

[36] Compare to B. Brown, "The story of objects asserting themselves as things ... is the story of a changed relation to the human subject and thus the story of how the thing really names less an object than a particular subject-object relation" ("Thing" 4). In the Trollopian narrative of capitalist globalization this is always a story of fallenness.

diamond's last stand. The only character to describe the Moonstone as "mere carbon," fittingly enough, is the crypto-malefactor Godfrey Ablewhite (74). But with that telling exception, Collins's "thing," so far from a homogeneous vendible, stands out as a resilient chronotope whose extra-economic value radiates not through the British traditions dear to Trollope, but through their correlatives in Indian history, religion, and ethos. Of course, auratic booty would soon become a cliché of the imperial adventure fiction that Collins anticipates. But as a narrative depicting a "romantic region" outside Europe's purview (470), *The Moonstone* (and the Moonstone) resist reduction to orientalist cliché while instancing a unique geopolitical aesthetic at work.

In arguing that the Moonstone stands for an intact heirloom sovereignty distinct from Trollope's Barsetshire variation, I do not suggest that Collins portrays a non-coeval India that lags behind Britain on some normative path to modernity. Rather, *The Moonstone* depicts India's difference as an ontological fact, while tracing the outlines of an alternative (post-imperial) future (a point to which I will return). Although the novel undeniably essentializes Indianness, (if often from the perspective of "John Bulls" like Betteredge and Bruff), one need not conclude that it is resolutely imperialist. As Said writes, orientalism depends on a "*positional* superiority, which puts the Westerner in a whole series of possible relationships with the Orient without ever losing him the relative upper hand" (*Orientalism* 7). In *The Moonstone*, by contrast, Westerners have, at best, a tenuous hold on this privileged positionality.[37] Indeed, nothing shows this precarity more than the Moonstone itself which metonymizes India's sovereignty while refracting Britain's contingent imperial power.

To see how the novel conveys these meanings, we must consider what diamonds like the Koh-i-Noor signified in the years between 1848–50—*The Moonstone*'s main timeframe—and January 1868, when the novel's serialization began in *All the Year Round*. Though Collins is known to have consulted C. W. King's *The Natural History of Precious Stones and Gems* (published in 1865 and expanded in 1867), the Koh-i-Noor had in fact been widely discussed for decades in copious articles and books. A "stone of fate" whose story usually begins with the thirteenth-century rajahs of Malwa, the Koh-i-Noor (literally, "Mountain of Light") became part of the Peacock Throne, a famed emblem of Mughal power, before passing to Persian hands when Nadir Shah conquered Delhi in 1739 (Maskeleyne qtd. in King 2nd ed. 70). There it "emitt[ed] its sardonic gleams over the vicissitudes" of another declining dynasty until the exiled Shah Shuja was forced to surrender it to Ranjit Singh, Sikh maharaja of the Punjab ("Koh-i-Noor," *Chambers* 51). Then, in 1849, after two Anglo-Sikh wars for control of the Punjab, the Koh-i-Noor was presented to Queen Victoria at a ceremony marking the 250th anniversary of the East India Company. As one commentator put it, "After symbolizing the

---

[37] That is not to dismiss the merits of nuanced discussion of *The Moonstone*'s essentialism; for example, Manavalli's discussion of how Collins's "ethnographic fascination with the institution of caste" constitutes Brahminical traditions such as the caste system as "the 'essence' of Indian social formation" at the expense "of other ethnic and religious communities" (67).

revolutions of ten generations by its passage from one conqueror to another," the "great diamond of the East, comes now" to England "as the forfeit of oriental faithlessness and the prize of Saxon valour" ("Koh-I-Noor" *Leader* 342).

Such bluster notwithstanding, much nineteenth-century writing on the Koh-i-Noor's history was more tentative on the subject of British supremacy. Consider, for example, the Koh-i-Noor's connection to Ranjit Singh, whose military prowess and "decision of character" had curbed British ambitions until after his death in 1839 ("Punjab" 166). As *Chambers Edinburgh Journal* explained in 1846, "The British government, perceiving how strongly [Singh] had seated himself," opted "to negotiate a treaty" even though possession of the Punjab was by some accounts, "a question of life and death for [British] power in India" ("Punjab" 166–7). Thus, in 1799, while the British were storming Seringapatam in Mysore, their young Sikh ally, fearless in the "heat of contest," was consolidating his own dominion in Northern India ("Punjab" 166). There is an interesting parallel between Singh, the famed Lion of the Punjab, whose 40-year reign was too formidable to challenge, and Tipu, the Tiger of Mysore who withstood British assault in 1766, 1779, and 1791. While Collins's Prologue makes "Tippoo, Sultan of Seringapatam" the real-life possessor of his fictional gem, it was Ranjit who owned the legendary diamond that, like Collins's Moonstone, had once been in the hands of "Aurungzebe, Emperor of the Moguls" (*Moonstone* 12–13). The *Moonstone*'s artful troping on the Koh-i-Noor's story thus layers the 1848–9 conquest of the Punjab (contemporaneous with the novel's main events) over the conquest of Mysore (consummated at Seringapatam, but revisited in the 1860s controversy that anticipated Collins's work on his new novel).[38]

As we saw in Chapter 2, the Mysore controversy concerned the efforts of the aging Kristna Raj Wodyar—the rajah installed after Tipu's defeat—to adopt an heir and extend his line under indirect British rule for "as long as the sun and moon shall endure." The debate thus highlighted the importance of Indian royalty in reshaping the imperial project after the "mutiny." In contrast to Trollope's more mimetic narrative, *The Moonstone* distances its story from this backdrop of princely appeals and partisan politics. Instead, Collins's Prologue turns the contemporary moment of Wodyar's legal dispute back into the scandal of British rapaciousness at Seringapatam in 1799.[39] The result is to constitute the Moonstone as an Indian heirloom whose sovereignty does not rest on the temporal claims of a Tipu, Ranjit, or Wodyar, but is, rather, embodied in a religious shrine watched over for centuries by devoted acolytes—faithful Brahmins unlike the fraudulent

---

[38] As J. Mehta notes, the "handing over of the Koh-i-noor occupied an entire item of the five-item Treaty of Lahore" (614).

[39] As GoGwilt notes, "What made the storming of Seringapatam so famous for the first half of the nineteenth century was the scandal of looting and plunder that marked the success of the campaign" (58). Thus, as J. Mehta suggests, Collins's substitution of "Seringapatam for the Mutiny ... chooses the event most sensationalized before the 1857 revolt, yet an event more distant, more equivocal, and hence more susceptible to revisionism"; he is thus "able to show the Mutiny's resistance to British rule while deflecting the hysteria surrounding it" (620). See also Roy, Manavalli, and, on imperial scandal more generally, Dirks.

French priest reputed to have stolen the Orloff diamond from the eye of a Hindu idol (King, 1st ed. 35; cf. Collins, *Moonstone*, 3). This sacral economy not only heightens the stone's romance, but heightens it on grounds that, unlike the "passage from one conqueror to another," constitute the jewel's proper ownership as Hindu. The fictional narrative of the Moonstone thus plays off of historical trophies like the Koh-i-Noor without compromising the allegorical power of Collins's decidedly unconquerable gem.

According to Young, when the Koh-i-Noor made its first public appearance at the Crystal Palace it undermined the effort to legitimize empire under the banner of trade ("Carbon"). The problem was the stone's old-fashioned rose-cut, which in maximizing size rather than brilliance, disappointed the visitors who expected a jewel befitting the Koh-i-Noor's name. The so-called Mountain of Light, lamented one observer, was "nothing more than an egg-shaped lump of glass" (qtd. in Young 346). The "sundry specimens of sham jewels" on view at the exhibition, opined another, "sparkle infinitely more brilliantly than the Koh-i-noor" ("Hurry-graphs" 508). When the organizers countered this deflationary press, they contradicted themselves. The exhibition sought to uphold India as a source of raw materials whose native industry was progressing under British influence. But by glamorizing the Koh-i-Noor as an object "shrouded [in] Eastern history," which "defied objective analysis," the Exhibition portrayed India's essence as unassimilable to Western norms (P. Young, "Carbon" 346).

Then, as though to stamp British sovereignty directly onto this Indian thing, Prince Albert engaged state-of-the-art technology to recut the Koh-i-Noor. As the *London Journal* reported in 1852, "Steps have been taken to bring forth the beauties of this celebrated diamond" by removing the "defects" of "Oriental cutting." No less a national hero than the Duke of Wellington, "having manifested great interest in the precious gem—so associated with the land of the East, where his first . . . glorious laurels were won—attended several times during the progress of the preparations, to personally assist in the commence of the delicate operation" ("Cutting" *London Journal* 407). On the afternoon of July 17, *The Times* reported, this veteran of multiple Indian campaigns, arrived at the Queen's jewelers: "His Grace placed the gem upon the *scaife*, an horizontal wheel revolving with almost incalculable velocity, whereby . . . the first facet of the new cutting was effected" ("Cutting" *Times* 8).

More than ten years later, the Koh-i-Noor's recutting remained a topic of discussion in widely-reviewed books such as King's *Natural History of Precious Gems* and Harry Emanuel's *Diamonds and Precious Stones; their History, Value, and Distinguishing Characteristics* (1865). According to the latter, the Koh-i-Noor's cutting had been supervised by the "the first scientific men of the day." Although "of less weight than before," the famous gem now "possesses nearly the same size, and instead of being a lustreless mass, scarcely better than rock-crystal," "has become a brilliant, matchless for purity" (79). So formidable was this coup that the author of an 1867 article mused that a visit to the Koh-i-Noor's cutters "would exceed one of [William] Beverley's transformation-scenes"—a reference to a stage effect entailing the seemingly magical transmutation of one object into another—"and be a reality into the bargain" ("Diamond-Cutting" 689). Far from deromanticizing the legendary jewel, such accounts suggested that Britain had cured the Koh-i-Noor of its Oriental "defects" while elevating it into a genuine treasure whose splendor confirmed the improving powers of the West.

But as with most imperial narratives, there is another side to the story. Whereas Emanuel's book rehearsed the benign accounts of 1852, King's description of the recutting—the one text Collins is known to have consulted—told a rather different tale. A "most ill-advised proceeding," the Crown's recutting of the Koh-i-Noor, according to King, "has deprived [it] of all its historical and mineralogical value" and reduced it from the largest diamond in Europe to "a bad-shaped, shallow brilliant, of but inferior water, and only 102 ½ carats weight" (1st ed. 36).[40] King's second edition repeated this criticism before adding a twist on the stone's reputed curse: "The Brahmin sage who studies the Book of Fate is probably not dispossessed of his hereditary superstition touching the malign powers of this stone when he thinks upon the . . . [Crimean] war, that completely annihilated the prestige of the British army . . . and upon the events of the Sepoy mutiny, three years later" (King 2nd ed. 74). Though there is no certainty of Collins having seen them, King's Brahmin referents and direct allusion to the rebellion anticipate *The Moonstone*'s status as a complicated species of "mutiny" narrative.

"OUR JEW, OUR JEWEL"

The Koh-i-noor, new cut, became
More worthy of its Eastern name.
Our Asian chief has learnt new views
And shines with iridescent hues.
To every gem, the more to grace it,
We give, by turning, a new facet;
But then, to keep it steady, we imbed,
Our Jew, our Jewel, in a mass of lead.

W.J. "Tories Re-Cut a Crown Jewel" (1852)

King's second edition points to yet another diamond narrative constellating in the years between the young Duleep Singh's surrender of "the largest and most precious [diamond] in the world" and the publication of *The Moonstone* ("Our" 1299). If, on the one hand, diamonds were the ideal global commodity—"with virtually no marks of origins or histories"—on the other hand, that condition of sovereign lack could stoke antipathy toward globalization's perceived impresarios: not only the "cosmopolitan" financiers whom J. A. Hobson later portrayed as the powerbrokers of imperialism, but also dealers in and fashioners of

---

[40] By contrast, *The Times* had reported that the recutting would not "diminish by any material degree" the pre-cut weight of 186 carats ("Cutting" 8). According to modern sources the post-cut weight is 105.6 carats.

diamonds. As *Chambers Edinburgh Journal* reported in 1852, "In England, the art of diamond-cutting has ceased to exist, but in Holland it still maintains its ancient pre-eminence; and from thence the cutters of the Koh-i-noor have been brought" ("Diamond-Cutting" 199). It is to Holland that Ablewhite flees in the hopes of dividing the Moonstone into saleable parts. But there is another feature of this milieu which Collins's novel does not foreground and which was not made explicit in the original press on the Koh-i-Noor's refashioning. The nineteenth-century art of diamond-cutting, a "business almost confined to the city of Amsterdam", was also "entirely carried on by Jews" (King, 2nd ed. 110). Absent from *The Times*'s catalogue of high technology, "scientific gentleman," royal outfitters, and national heroes like Wellington was the fact that "the two Dutch artists" whom the Crown had engaged to beautify Britain's imperial prize were Jews ("Cutting" 8).

Discerning contemporaries were, nonetheless, in the know. Indeed, the occasion was seized to liken the Koh-i-Noor's refashioning to the political career of Disraeli, who, at the time, was Chancellor of the Exchequer. In September 1852, *The Examiner* published "Tories Re-Cutting a Crown-Jewel," an anonymous poem that appears to liken Disraeli's surprising aptitude for budgetary work to the technique for turning ancient stones into "iridescent" brilliants—thus highlighting "a new facet" of his abilities as a rising Tory. In line with the orientalized status of European Jewry, Disraeli, "Our Asian chief" as well as "Our Jew," is compared both to an Indian diamond ("our Jewel") and to the Jewish cutters who achieved its transformation. The poem thus anticipates the self-fashioning wizardry attributed to him at the height of his power (Ch. 4).[41]

Throughout the nineteenth century, Jews such as the Gibraltarian, Don Pacifico, were integral to the advance of Britain's geopolitical interests. As "key intermediaries" in the "zones of 'informal' influence" necessary to a growing commercial empire, diasporic Jews provided "local partners for British merchants" as well as "employees of the growing consular corps" (A. Green 177–8). This association with far-flung empire provides yet another context for the anti-Jewish animus that grew alongside the heightened capitalist globalization of the mid-Victorian era. An early sign of the trend is "Diamonds," an 1862 article in the *London Review and Weekly Journal of Politics, Society, Literature and Art*, which folds anti-Semitism into a critical discussion of the jewels on display at the International Exhibition. The author laments that if a visiting Arab were to "scrutinize the gaudy and pretentious tabernacles in which Messrs. Emmanuel and other jewelers

---

[41] As Wohl notes, "The setting of the budget transformed [Disraeli's] standing in the world of politics" with the revelation of a "practical side" endowing him with "new brilliance" akin to the Koh-i-Noor's. More speculatively Wohl adds, "'new views' may refer to his fiscal maneuvering and his playing down of the Tory protectionist tradition" with which he had been associated. The "mass of lead" (a reference to the process of embedding the diamond in lead in order to stabilize it during the cutting process) might even stand for "the mass of schedules and fiscal minutiae that were an inevitable part of the budget and the interminable debates surround it" (Wohl, e-mails to Lauren Goodlad, August 6, 2011). My thanks also to Michel Pharand and Martin Weiner for their thoughts on this poem.

have exposed their wares," the experience might "lower [his] opinion of the civilization of the great nations who place themselves in the van of the world." This interesting variation on orientalist discourse trains an imaginary Arab gaze on Anglo-Jewry in the metropole. The author then brings up the Koh-i-Noor to show that Britons, not Asians, "are the barbarians" in making "a great diamond [a] symbol of power" only to "submit it to the hands of an artizan Hebrew to give it a conventional form" (337).

> [T]he Koh-i-noor shows a huge face of diamond, but in order to attain this vulgar attribute of size . . . it has been cut so thin, that it is not a brilliant in the true sense of the word; it is a thin slab of a diamond with facettes [*sic*] cut on it in imitation of those of a brilliant. . . . [T]o reduce it to this form 185 carats were reduced to 103, and the second diamond in Europe in point of size . . . and the first in quality, became a broad but ineffective jewel, and fell to the rank of fifth or sixth among the Crown diamonds in the Western world (337–78).

On this account, if modern diamonds are homogeneous, it is the "artizan Hebrew" who makes them so—a picture in which Europe's Jews play an integral part in the ruinous commodification of heirlooms.[42] "Diamonds" thus depicts a diffuse Jewish influence that emanates from global capitals like London and Amsterdam, foreshadowing a pattern in which Jews provide a conduit for anxieties concerning capitalism and empire. In doing so, the article anticipates the affective logic of the naturalistic narrative of capitalist globalization: a form in which alien figures who occupy the boundary of inside and outside signal the unnerving condition of ethical unmooring, injured sovereignty, and homogenizing universalism.

What is remarkable about *The Moonstone*, therefore, is its *refusal* of this structure of feeling. That is not to ignore the orientalist stereotypes shaping the novel's portrayal of Hindu priests. Such depictions evoke the post-1857 discourses that singled out Brahmins "as the principal agency of the rebellion" (Rand 18 n. 47). Structurally, however, *The Moonstone*'s Hindus are not internalized outsiders like Emilius, Lopez, or the real-life Disraeli but, rather, temporary visitors, like knights on a quest, who have voyaged to England for a sacred purpose. This sympathetic mission was clear, for example, to Geraldine Jewsbury whose review in the *Athenaeum* declared, "Few will read the final destiny of *The Moonstone* without feeling the tears rise in their eyes as they catch a glimpse of the three men, who have sacrificed their cast[e] in the service of their God" (Page 170). Such ennobling readiness to sacrifice caste could not but resonate for contemporary readers who believed that loss of caste had been at stake in the practice often said to have incited the Sepoys: the use of cartridges greased with prohibited animal fats. Jewsbury's review thus illustrates *The Moonstone*'s success in humanizing a

---

[42] The article does not specify the ethnicity of "Messrs. Emmanuel" but in the context of sundry references to "Hebrews," the name Emmanuel and the Hebrew-derived word "tabernacle" seem to make the point implicit. The piece may also recall us to Messrs. Harter and Benjamin, the shady jewelers of *The Eustace Diamonds* who entangle Lizzie in debt and secret the stolen diamonds in their strong box "in the City" (2: 117).

much-demonized segment of Indian society while identifying "as their rightful property a valuable diamond looted by British forces" (Nayder, "Collins" 139; cf. Lonoff 42–55 and J. Mehta 648). Moreover, insofar as *The Moonstone* incorporates a proto-Lopezian imposter whose deception fuels the main storyline, that figure is not a "mahogany-coloured" Indian or Jew (*Moonstone* 29), but the "able white" who is Lady Verinder's nephew. The novel's "blackguard" is a "flaxen"-haired Anglo-Saxon whose final appearance is the *disguise* of "swarthy complexion" and "bushy black beard" (445, 67, 447, 434). It is as though Collins invented him to subvert the device of racialized villainy.[43]

I have suggested the importance of recognizing a number of timely diamond narratives that *The Moonstone* takes up for its artful bricolage as it envisions the condition of sovereignty in a post-heirloom metropole. If the Indian chronotope at the heart of this work were the whole of Collins's experimental form, *The Moonstone* would be remembered (if remembered at all) as a romance of Hindu otherness. But as I have already suggested, *The Moonstone*'s form is hybrid and polymorphous. According to Alexander Welsh, it is a "story of experience," which shows "that there may be still more sides to the truth than can fairly be represented" (*Strong* 198–9). Experience, the topic to which I now turn, is the focal point of Collins's phenomenological variation on the geopolitical aesthetic. *The Moonstone*, I will argue, is not only the tale of a mystery solved, an heirloom returned to its proper place, and an English country house restored to order. It also about the sovereignties forged through imperial encounter—a "story of experience" enabled by the merger of groundbreaking detective narrative and utopian romance.

"OUR OWN TRUMPERY EXPERIENCE"

> Modern man makes his way home in the evening wearied by a jumble of events, but however entertaining or tedious, unusual or commonplace, harrowing or pleasurable they are, none of them will have become experience.
>
> Giorgio Agamben, *Infancy and History: On The Destruction of Experience* (1978; trans. 1993)

> Nothing in this world . . . is probable unless it appeals to our own trumpery experience; and we only believe in a romance when we see it in a newspaper.
>
> Franklin Blake, *The Moonstone*

One formal feature of the detective genre that *The Moonstone* shares with most mystery stories is dispersal of the appearance of guilt. At various points, the

---

[43] *The Moonstone* includes Septimus Luker, a character who fits the Judaized pattern to some degree but as I shall argue below, Luker's partial Judaization is framed by a particular perspective. Likewise, Ezra Jennings, a prominent mixed-race character occupies the distinct role that I describe below. Collins's anti-Judaizing strategy can be compared to the resistant anti-naturalism of Eliot's *Romola* (Ch. 6).

shadow of culpability is cast over a "devilish" English black sheep (45), a set of "heathenish" Indians (60), an "impudent" housemaid (69), a "self-willed" heiress (173), her "cosmopolitan" suitor (368), a two-faced "man of pleasure" (452), and a "wretched" collector of Oriental gems (286). This multiplication of suspicious parties parallels the eyewitness accounts that provide the raw material for *The Moonstone*'s multi-voiced structure. According to D. A. Miller, however, the detective plot consolidates what only appears to be a plurality of voices: "an apparent lack of center at the level of *agency* secures a total mastery at the level of *effect*" (56; Miller's emphasis). Underlying this insistence on monologue is the untested assumption that *The Moonstone* fixates on detection—as though the novel itself were the product of the "detective-fever" it wryly describes (133). Though *The Moonstone* has long been regarded, in T. S. Eliot's words, as "the first and greatest of English detective novels" (525–6), it is worth standing back from this *donnée* to ask if Collins's multi-genre work upholds detection as an end in itself. From a formal and phenomenological perspective, I suggest, "common detection" is but the pretext for translating experience into legible narrative (D. Miller 54).[44]

Over the course of *The Moonstone*, readers encounter thirteen discreet reports including eleven different narrators and "various subnarrators." As Donald J. Greiner observes, this "complicated narrative technique" far exceeds the plural viewpoints found in epistolary novels such as *Clarissa* (4).[45] Collins thus calls on his readers to compare and calibrate a diverse assemblage of situated experience. Presented with a text in which the manner of telling is at times more significant than the tale that is told, readers must heed multiple claims, remark their provenance, and judge their legitimacy. Scholars of the novel often note Franklin Blake's instructions to his narrators to record their stories only "as far as their own personal experience extends, and no farther" (21–2). Less noticed, however, are his remarks on the limitations of "personal" experience: "Nothing in this world . . . is probable," he tells Betteredge, "unless it appeals to our own trumpery experience" (49). In offering this comment, Blake tries to distinguish his own "cosmopolitan" outlook from the "common sense" that had led his father to dismiss John Herncastle as an opium addict obsessed with a "wretched crystal" (368, 48). Given the novel's emphasis on "The Discovery of the Truth," what does it mean for the architect of the *The Moonstone*'s "vertical narration" to declare that

---

[44] As Duncan writes, Miller's analysis is "strategically blind to the novel's most conspicuous signifier of historical power" (302). Likewise, for Heller, the "model of a master voice" is "less useful for understanding" *The Moonstone* than "the theory of the double voice that feminist critics have used to describe the subversive undercurrent, conveyed by irony and indirection . . . in nineteenth-century women's writing" ("Blank" 256). For a reading of *The Moonstone* and the *Woman in White* as dialogical, see Wills. GoGwilt sees a different kind of singularity in Collins's "economy of plotting," which turns "a 'public' and 'private' disgrace into a single plot, organized around . . . compromised feminine virtue" (62).

[45] In its original serial form, these segmentations were further broken down into 32 weekly installments in *All the Year Round*. For discussion of the added dimension of "visually arresting . . . high-quality letter-press with exceptional woodcuts" which the novel's original U.S. readers found in the serialization in *Harper's*, see Leighton and Surridge (209). On Collins and serialization, see also Wynne.

personal experience is *trumpery*: at best, overrated and limiting; at worst, downright fraudulent?[46] To ask this question is to place *The Moonstone* in the thick of ongoing discussion about the crisis of modern experience which it will be helpful to explore.

As we have seen, Benjamin's formulation of the crisis makes lost historical awareness the constitutive lack in modern consciousness. Taking up this legacy in *Infancy and History* (1978; trans. 1993), Agamben articulates it in absolute form: one of "the few self-certainties to which" today's subjects "can lay claim," he writes, is the "incapacity to have and communicate experiences" (15). Whereas Benjamin tied the destruction of *Erfahrung* to catastrophic events like the First World War, Agamben contends that, in the late twentieth century, everyday life itself has ceased to sustain experience: hence, "no one now seems to wield sufficient authority to guarantee the truth of experience" (14).

From a longer and wider perspective, however, the crisis of historical experience points to an evolving modern condition. The globalization of capital entails the advancement of transnational structures and processes such as empire-building which "have direct experiential effects but are not directly objects of experience" (LaCapra, *History* 48). The modern condition thus fuses "a specificity of historical experience and place" to a structure of "worldwide macro-interdependency" (Rabinow 56). The result is that even those who recognize that their outmoded ideals of sovereignty are subject to unseen contingencies must contend with an experience of history which constellates in partial and culturally specific ways.

When Raymond Williams describes the potential for experience to entail "the fullest, most open, most active kind of consciousness"—a "full and active 'awareness'" that involves "an appeal to the whole consciousness . . . as against reliance on the more specialized or limited states or faculties" (*Keywords* 127)—he sets forth the kind of subjective basis necessary for negotiating modernity's structural predicament. "Experience" on this utopian view involves the wherewithal not only to weather the onslaught of new-fashioned shocks and specialized knowledges, but also to mediate the disjunction between history's movement across space and time and the ordinary human capacity for grasping scale, complexity, and duration. Williams carefully distinguishes between this ideal of active consciousness and the more passive experience produced by "social conditions" or "systems of belief" (*Keywords*). His definition thus helps to explain the precarity of fully-fledged historical awareness (*Erfahrung*), as against the pervasiveness of an incoherent *Erlebnis*.[47]

---

[46] The roots of "trumpery" are in the French *tromper* (to fool or deceive), suggesting that experience may beguile or even defraud. The word's more commonplace meanings—the *OED* cites *Johnson's Dictionary*'s "'Something of less value than it seems'; hence, 'something of no value; trifles'"—recall those sparkling "sham jewels" at the Crystal Palace. I borrow "vertical narration" from Greiner who defines it as the device of one narrator's compiling information from subnarrators and passing it on to an "editor" (2, 20 n. 11).

[47] Williams's *Keywords* entry on experience does not invoke Benjamin or stipulate the importance of historical awareness; but given the emphasis on holism, it seems certain that his definition

Writing from a feminist standpoint, the historian Joan Scott has argued that "experience" often functions as an essentialistic category, positing subjects as the bearers of a prediscursive experiential reality without questioning the impact of (for example) gender or race. When historiographic work appeals to the authority of an experience that is simply assumed to exist, the "evidence of experience" becomes "evidence for the fact of difference, rather than a way of exploring how difference is established" (777).[48] The challenge, then, is to avoid this damaging essentialism without reducing experience to a mere play of linguistic signs, with no potential to perform the integrative work of *Erfahrung*. Rabinow explores a crucial dimension of this quest when he articulates a normative "ethos of macro-interdependencies" which "attempts to be highly attentive to (and respectful of) difference, but is also wary of the tendency to essentialize difference." Such an ethos, he stipulates, must be "suspicious of sovereign powers, universal truths, overly relativized preciousness, local authenticity, [and] moralisms high and low" (56). Ella Shohat puts forward a comparable project in her call for "a relational understanding of feminism." A "multicultural/transnational feminist project," she argues, must define *experience* and *knowledge* as "dialogical concepts" ("Area" 68 70). "What kind of relational maps of knowledge," she asks, "would help illuminate the negotiation of gender and sexuality as understood in diverse contexts, but with an emphasis on the linked historical experiences and discursive networks across borders?" (70)

According to Linda Zerilli, building on the thought of Hannah Arendt, theorists who approach this multicultural challenge often err in seeking *epistemological* solutions to problems that are fundamentally *political* in nature.[49] The task of judging plural cultures, she insists, is concretely historical and practical, not abstractly epistemic. The point is not that "no claims to knowledge and truth are at stake in politics," but rather that the struggles through which these debates will be settled cannot be decided by epistemological rules (307). Arendt's *Lectures on Kant's Political Philosophy* (1982) teaches us that if political judgments do not rest on "objective" proofs, "neither are they merely subjective," or "matters of individual cultural preference" (Zerilli 309). Thus, "the real problem of judgment in the context of widespread value pluralism is not relativism," but, rather, "the failure to take genuine account of the strangeness of what we are judging" (315).

> Finding solace in our own norms cannot possibly count as critical judging—and yet the threat of relativism leaves us with little other choice. . . . I have therefore suggested that we rethink political judgments as fundamentally anticipatory rather than . . . justificatory in structure. When I judge political things I say more than how it appears to me (as subjectivism would have it), for (as Arendt and Kant argue) I have

---

requires awareness of the *history* that, in another entry, he defines as that which teaches and shows us "most kinds of knowable past and almost every kind of imaginable future" (148).

[48] Scott includes Williams among her examples of essentialistic treatments of experience. However, as Ganguly notes, Scott overlooks the constructivist dimensions of Williams's historical materialism which is rigorously attentive to concrete circumstances—not abstract identities.

[49] Zerilli's main example of this epistemological focus is Martha Nussbaum.

taken the standpoints of others into account. My judgment anticipates your agreement but it cannot compel it with proofs (as objectivism would hold). There simply is no extrapolitical guarantee (e.g., epistemic privilege) that my judgment is valid or that it will be accepted by others or even ought to be (315).

A universalism understood *politically*, Zerilli argues, is, to be sure, a "fragile" achievement that depends on "practical context" to survive (315). But, rather "than see this fragility as a failure," Zerilli urges openness to the opportunity it presents to rethink "apparently settled and stark differences of value" across cultural boundaries. In this way she moves beyond the terms of crisis to make the case for an avowedly political practice of judging across cultures.

I have described these various meditations on modern experience in part to demonstrate the recurrent appeals to particular instantiations of a capacious ethico-political subject: e.g., Scott's historian who highlights the construction of difference; Rabinow's critical cosmopolitan who cultivates a vigilant "ethos of macro-interdependencies"; or Zerilli's Arendtian subject whose political commitments compel her to judge from the "standpoints of others." Although Williams's "full and active 'awareness'" also gives rise to a critical subject, his writings simultaneously look beyond the individual's ethos. His core notion of the "structure of feeling" also points to the material conditions that subtend individuality—a turn to history as a vehicle of "collective unity" (Jameson, *Political* 274) which, in Jameson's thought, underwrites the geopolitical aesthetic. Collins's phenomenological variation on that aesthetic in *The Moonstone* envisions a tentative route to holist materiality through a formal enactment of experiences that are individually perceived but collectively wrought.

The reading I propose stands in contrast to the idea of *The Moonstone* as a fictional byproduct of the increasing authority of professional science. Thus, according to Ronald R. Thomas, the novel illustrates the "techniques of the emerging nineteenth-century science of forensic criminology and the practices of criminal investigation it inspired." On this reading, Sergeant Cuff's failure to solve the mystery single-handedly paves the way for the supplementary authority of "forensic medicine" (*"Moonstone"* 66). As detective mastery shifts from police to medical experts, what "begin[s] as the most political of Collins's novels (investigating the criminal implications of a plundering colonial policy in British India and the vengeance of the Empire), ends by being the most scientific (shifting the focus of the investigation from international politics to a laboratory experiment)." "Science," concludes Thomas, is *The Moonstone*'s "sanctioning authority," "superseding and eventually collaborating with that of the law to reveal the truth" (71).

In concentrating authoritative experience in the novel's professionals, Thomas asks us to recognize a set of characters including Bruff (a solicitor), Cuff (a detective), and Jennings (a doctor and scientist) as if they were a seamless class, "uniquely empowered" to "authenticate the documents that record this history" (60). By definition, this group of truth-making authorities excludes four narrators (Betteredge, Clack, Blake, and Murthwaite) as well as three other principal characters (Rachel, Lady Verinder, and Rosanna). Moreover, by proposing that *The*

Moonstone's fictional professionals are the beneficiaries of the ascendant power enjoyed by the mid-Victorian era's "lawyers, solicitors, physicians, and other such officials" (60), Thomas affords little significance to the work of narrative art: for example, to the question of how a character's authority to pronounce the truth is shaped by features such as the narrative voice that introduces her or him and the dialogue and situations that ensue. This essentially reflective hypothesis (regarding *The Moonstone* as a device for documenting ascendant forms of power) assumes that the novel does not (or cannot) creatively situate power through aesthetic perception. In fact, according to Thomas, *The Moonstone* does frame such a story ("the criminal implications of a plundering colonial policy") only to abandon it, for unspecified reasons, for the task of documenting the growing authority of "science."[50] The question remains: Does *The Moonstone* convey this sense of a modern experience warranted by the growing clout of professional and scientific experts?

To answer we need go no further than the climactic exchange between Cuff and Lady Verinder near the end of Betteredge's narrative. As Thomas's reading predicts, the "celebrated" Cuff accrues extraordinary authority over the course of the "First Period," in direct contrast to the bumbling Seegrave (107). With his forensic finesse established by the mystery of the paint smear, he takes Betteredge for his sidekick and the game is afoot. As narrated by Lady Verinder's steward—part skeptic, part enthusiast—the taciturn Cuff soon assumes an almost oracular voice: *"Nobody has stolen the Diamond"* (115), he confides to Betteredge; "The whole experience of my life is at fault if Rosanna Spearman has the Diamond" (139); and finally, "I don't suspect . . . *I know*" (143; emphasis added). We begin to see how detective fiction provides an innovative approach to that need "for some version of the Sacred" which, according to Peter Brooks, explained the arrival of the Gothic in the late eighteenth century (*Melodramatic* 16). For Jameson, detective fiction's mythologies derive from "a story of knowing" which secures "some common world shared by the knower and the doer" (*Geopolitical* 36). The world in this case is the upper-class English sanctum undone by inexplicable events: "nothing is like what it used to be" (*Moonstone* 146). To this scene of derangement Cuff is summoned as a virtuosic "knower" to put things to rights. Yet, as every reader learns, Cuff is at the very peak of his authority when he spectacularly fails.

Cuff fails, moreover, because his much-ballyhooed experience, if never quite "trumpery," is thoroughly inadequate to the case at hand. It is no accident, therefore, that in preparation for meeting the policeman who suspects her daughter of fraud, Lady Verinder recovers that "grace and voice of manner" which have been

---

[50] My point is not that Thomas's in-depth research on forensic science could not provide the basis for a persuasive interpretation of *The Moonstone*; in fact, a similar discussion of professionalism works well with reference to *The Woman in White* in Thomas's *Detective*, Ch. 4. For a reading of *The Moonstone*'s scientific experiment as a means of compelling "even the most conventional, resistant audiences to suspend judgment" see C. Levine, *Pleasures* 51. For Dames, who argues that Collins anticipates scientific understanding of amnesia, Jennings is the prescient spokesman of a scientific discourse that would eventually "become normative psychological practice" (200).

as much a part of Betteredge's theology as *Robinson Crusoe* (170). Here is her case for the defense:

> "Now, before you begin, I have to tell you, as Miss Verinder's mother, that she is *absolutely incapable* of doing what you suppose her to have done. Your knowledge of her character dates from a day or two since. My knowledge of her character dates from the beginning of her life. State your suspicion of her as strongly as you please . . . I am sure, beforehand, that (with all your experience) the circumstances have fatally misled you in this case. Mind! . . . I am as absolutely shut out of my daughter's confidence as you are. My one reason for speaking positively is the reason you have heard already. I know my child" (171–2).

A sympathetic figure despite his dour certainty of a "miserable world," Cuff responds by dismissing Lady Verinder as a fond parent (130). The crucial judge, of course, is the reader who, up to this point, has no reason to anticipate that the famous detective will go off on the wrong scent. The reader thus finds herself refereeing a contest between two appeals to truth based on two different kinds of experience. Lady Verinder's "positive" knowledge of her daughter's honesty is predicated on long and proximate knowledge of "her character." But as scholars like Thomas make clear, such appeals to old-fashioned *Gemeinschaft* are precisely what the nineteenth century's scientific discourses had begun to displace.

Cuff's reply must therefore solidify his prestige as modern "knower"; an impartial expert whose grasp of the facts catapults him over the shortfalls of ordinary experience. As one who has spent twenty years "employed in cases of family scandal," he explains,

> "It is well within my experience, that young ladies of rank and position do occasionally have private debts which they dare not acknowledge to their nearest relatives and friends . . . [E]vents in this house have forced me back on my own experience . . . (172).

Recounting Rachel's unwillingness to cooperate, he continues:

> "[A] young lady . . . has lost a valuable jewel . . . She betrays an incomprehensible resentment against . . . [the people who have] been trying to help her recover her lost jewel . . . I begin to look back into my own mind for my own experience . . . [which] explains Miss Verinder's otherwise incomprehensible conduct. It associates her with those other young ladies that I know. It tells me she has debts she daren't acknowledge, that must be paid . . . That is the conclusion which my experience draws from the plain facts. What does your ladyship's experience say against it?" (173).

Unsurprisingly, Lady Verinder's "experience" refuses Cuff's conclusions entirely. Although Betteredge heightens the drama, describing Cuff's "piling up proof against proof," the reader can see that these so-called proofs are no more than theories, while Cuff's implacable "reason" merely tenders an unsubstantiated hypothesis (174). That hypothesis, moreover, is built on a generalization: Cuff is arguing, in effect, that because many "cases of family scandal" turn out to expose young ladies in debt, the Verinder case must be such a scandal and Rachel must be such a lady. Yet, Cuff cannot show that Rachel has incurred any debts, much less that she has colluded with moneylenders to pay them. As the celebrated detective fails to consider (in Zerilli's terms) the "strangeness" of what he is judging, one is reminded of Franklin's prophesy that nothing in the world "is probable unless it appeals to our own trumpery experience."

Looked at this way, Cuff offers the kind of self-affirming generalization which Uday Mehta has tied to imperialism. The "long history of liberalism's support of the British Empire," Mehta contends, is traceable to its "impoverished conception of experience" (192). Indeed, the so-called crisis of experience, he suggests, is "the culmination" of this very history—"a process in which experience becomes provisional on the telos attached to a particular experiment and in which any 'present' can be understood only from the . . . anticipations [which] that teleology and those experiments make possible" (209). In other words, when the British see "India" they recognize only the kinds of evidence which confirm their preexisting assumptions. Thus, when Cuff claims to "know" that Rachel is guilty of "a deeply planned fraud," his supposedly scientific methodology rests on a faulty universalizing of particulars which is much like the logic of the civilizing mission (*Moonstone* 143, 176).

That said, *The Moonstone* does not demolish Cuff's authority: it merely cuts it down to an appropriate size. After confronting her daughter with news of Rosanna's suicide, Lady Verinder insists once again that "circumstances have fatally misled" the sergeant (183). While Cuff persists in believing she is duped, readers are likely to concur with Lady Verinder that the "mystery which baffles" her "baffles him too" (187–8). On the other hand, Cuff gains some credibility by predicting the importance of Rosanna's letter, the return of the Indians, and the surfacing of the moneylender Septimus Luker. Only in retrospect do we realize how clearly these very predictions point outside the purview of a domestic affair as *The Moonstone* follows the "devil's dance of the Indian Diamond" to London and beyond (197).

By the end of the first period, the great Sergeant Cuff, already discussing retirement and gardening, no longer stands forth as a modern answer to "the Sacred." Indeed, as readers of the next period pursue "The Discovery of the Truth," they quickly realize that the novel's resolution will not arrive through the ingenuity of any single "knower." Thus, while the mystery continues to the very last page, in one important sense "the first and greatest of English detective novels" ends with the close of Betteredge's narrative. For at this point, *The Moonstone* abandons the fledgling detective genre and becomes a multi-sited "story of experience."

PLURALIZING SOVEREIGNTY

> What is the use of my experience, what is the use of any person's experience, in such a case as that? It baffles me; it baffles you, it baffles everybody.
>
> Matthew Bruff, *The Moonstone*

> Sovereign is *that* which decides an exception exists and how to decide it, with the *that* composed of a plurality of forces circulating through and under the positional sovereignty of the official arbitrating body. Such a result may discourage those who seek a tight explanation of the economic and political causes of legal action . . . a closed model of legal process . . . or a tight model of legal paradox . . . But it illuminates the complexity of sovereignty.
>
> William E. Connolly, *Pluralism* (2005)

In his well-known study of *Madame Bovary*, Dominick LaCapra writes that Flaubert's controversial novel departed from the narrative convention of "a reliable center of value and judgment which integrated various aspects of experience in an intelligible and secure manner" (*"Madame"* 56). In Chapter 6, I will make the case for the importance of comparing Flaubert to Victorian literature's most accomplished realist, George Eliot. Here I am less concerned to argue that *Madame Bovary* helped to instigate sensation fiction (though it may well have done) than to show how *The Moonstone* also departs from "a reliable center of value and judgment," albeit with the decided purpose of integrating "various aspects of experience" through an alternative structure of narrative intelligibility. We have seen how Collins's variations on the geopolitical aesthetic spotlight the temporally long and spatially wide embedment of modern experience. Beginning with the twinned invasions of Tipu's palace and an English country house, *The Moonstone* eclipses the sovereign nation and empire, opening onto the worlded space that capitalism and imperialism bring into being. In a formal complement to this imperial *mise-en-scène*, *The Moonstone* replaces singular omniscience with a multi-perspectival series of narratives which pressures the abstraction of the sovereign individual—the kind of subject whose concrete literary form is the *Bildungsroman*.

In making that claim, I do not deny that the *Bildungsroman*'s hero is usually the socially immersed creature of a dialogical form.[51] Rather, in exaggerating the degree of sovereign autonomy granted to characters such as Dickens's David Copperfield or Eliot's Dorothea Brooke, my point is to emphasize how their accrued moral and social experience presupposes something akin to the critical subject that Rabinow envisions when he puts forward a scrupulous "ethos of macro-interdependency." Although Collins values ethos—not least the spirited "conduct" that enables Rachel to illustrate the "influence of character on circumstances" (*Moonstone* 3)—his multi-sited novel does not focalize the conditions for cultivating it through individuals. On the contrary, *The Moonstone* tends to ironize or satirize characters who believe that their experience qualifies them for apprehending the truth. Hence, while Cuff's failed attempt to universalize his experience concludes the novel's first period, Miss Clack's risible example is the object of broad satire at the start of the second. Repeatedly drawing on her "large

---

[51] This is the kind of reading of *Bildung* which Robbins rightly emphasizes in *Upward*. On disruptions in the female *Bildungsroman* see Fraiman and on the stunted *Bildungsroman* in Modernist contexts, see Esty, *Unseasonable*. On Eliot's interest in female *Bildung* see also Ch. 6.

experience," Clack determines, for example, that the Verinder home is in dire need of her instruction and that the doctor tending her aunt is the "infidel" purveyor of a "blinded materialism" (223, 232).[52]

It is therefore no surprise that, beginning with Bruff's narrative (the second in the eight-part sequence comprising "The Discovery of the Truth"), the preference for a porous and pluralistic alternative to the model of the sovereign subject becomes the implicit core of *The Moonstone*'s story of experience. Discreet to a fault, knowledgeable in his domain, and affectionate toward the clients whose material interests he serves, Bruff is in many ways an exemplary blend of professional and personal ethos.[53] Yet, in contrast to Cuff, he is almost *too* ready to admit the limitations of his experience: a man whose preferred comfort zone is the small world of his family and upper-class clients. Describing his encounter with Murthwaite, Bruff confesses a lack of interest in politics and declares, "The Indian plot is a mystery to me" (288). His earlier conversation with Clack evokes the impotence of the solitary subject: "What is the use of my experience, what is the use of any person's experience, in such a case as [this]?" (230). Yet, Bruff actively prefers such impotence to a deeper engagement of the "strangeness" that confounds him. In contrast to his generally affable demeanor, he is the most prejudiced of *The Moonstone*'s characters (more so than Betteredge, in his being the more urbane of the two). Of the Indian who visits his office, Bruff says: "this Oriental gentleman would have murdered me" to gain the Moonstone, but at least he "respected my time" (284). Regarding Septimus Luker, his strident antipathy is unleavened by humor. Whereas Luker is described neutrally up to this point as a collector of oriental gems and "money-lender" (186), Bruff's first impression is of a "sickening servility." He was "such an inferior creature to the Indian," he adds, "so vulgar, so ugly, so cringing, [and] so prosy . . . that he is quite unworthy of being reported" (285). Like the author of the 1862 "Diamonds" article, Bruff contrasts an "Oriental" from abroad to a probable Anglo-Jew. His revulsion momentarily evokes the strident affect of the naturalistic narrative of capitalist globalization—its characteristic aversion to metropolitan others.[54]

Bruff's limited ability to contend with otherness surfaces in his dialogue with Murthwaite, the famous world traveler, whom he meets at a dinner party. As the same lawyer who expertly protected Rachel from Ablewhite becomes a foil to Murthwaite's "superior knowledge of . . . Indian character" (293), the

---

[52] For a more recuperative reading of Clack, which posits her as one who understands the precarity of "the modern English self," see Carens 120.

[53] Bruff enjoins a solicitor who is indebted to him to divulge the name of the client interested in Lady Verinder's will: a "breach of professional" ethics which he readily undertakes for the sake of exposing Ablewhite's "mercenary" interest in marrying Rachel (275–6). He is also a far more discerning judge of Rachel's character than the myopic Cuff, defending her "self-dependence" despite its manifest difficulties (278). With such difference in mind Welsh writes, "*The Moonstone* is largely a case of Bruff versus Cuff: faith in personal acquaintance rather than chains of circumstance" (228).

[54] While Luker is never identified as a Jew and no one besides Bruff describes him at length, Milley, writing on Collins and Trollope in 1939, unhesitatingly grouped him with the "unscrupulous Jews" of *The Eustace Diamonds* (652).

scene confirms Bruff's provinciality while demonstrating the traveler's ability to move beyond the domestic focus that had stymied Cuff. Coaxing the wary solicitor into applying his "experience" to the task of fathoming Indian affairs, Murthwaite lays claim to the mantle of a professional authority whose expertise is the borderless world of geopolitics (289). "Lawyer as I was," writes Bruff, "I began to feel that I might trust Mr. Murthwaite to lead me blindfold through the last windings of the labyrinth" (294). But the point is neither that Murthwaite has become a new master agency, nor that Bruff's limited experience can be trained for the task. As the traveler announces his scheduled return to India, questions such as the identity of the thief, the meaning of Rosanna's suicide, and the mystery of Rachel's silence await the expertise of other characters. Bruff's narrative thus initiates the pattern of collective knowledge-seeking across multiple sites. "The Discovery of the Truth" is not a classic detective tale of a single "knower" but a multi-voiced assemblage akin to Shohat's project of building "relational maps of knowledge" which draw on "linked historical experiences and discursive networks."

Crucial to this pluralistic enterprise is Franklin, the novel's vertical narrator, a character whose object in penetrating the mystery is, of course, deeply personal. It is important, therefore, not to overstate Blake's cosmopolitan competence or his resemblance to Walter Hartright in *The Woman in White*. Whereas Hartright's sojourn in "the wilds of Central America" prepares him to assume the role of hero, Blake's "wandering in the East" thickens *The Moonstone*'s transnational web without constituting him as the master of his destiny (*Woman* 474; *Moonstone* 296). At the start of the novel, Franklin is an immature protagonist who holds forth on "the patience of Oriental races" while regarding himself as "an imaginative" alternative to Britons like his father (51–2, 48). It is only once he confronts the "impenetrable puzzle" of his guilt that he begins to evince the self-awareness that makes him a compelling narrator. His response to his predicament is not "sovereign will" but a turn to multi-authored mapping and collective *Bildung*: "I resolved—as a means of enriching the deficient resources of my own memory—to appeal to the memory of the rest" (264, 361–2).[55]

The Moonstone is thus designed to unsettle Blake's cosmopolitan self-assurance (in contrast, for example, to the free pass enjoyed by Allan Armadale in the earlier novel). Addressing contemporary readers just a decade after the Indian rebellion, in recent memory of the Jamaica crisis, and on the heels of the Mysore controversy, the novel deliberately evokes the looting of Seringapatam, the conquest of the Punjab, and the cutting of the Koh-i-Noor. We have seen how mid-century Britain's deep-seated culture of disavowal saw commentators such as Harriet Martineau

---

[55] The phrase "sovereign will and pleasure" is used by Godfrey's father to rebuke Rachel by implying (mistakenly) that she has jilted his son without cause (264). Wills's dialogical reading goes too far in arguing that Betteredge's aversion to Franklin's difference establishes the latter as a "European Other" whose position resembles that of the Brahmins (94). Although Blake's "adoption of foreign ideas, and an awareness of other cultural positions" is indeed "a source of understanding" (95–6), it does not follow that Betteredge's comic antipathy to the Continent positions Blake as a bona fide outsider.

resort to denial upon the outbreak of violence in India. Britain's "footing in India," Martineau wrote, "began and extended without the national cognizance"; thus, the question of whether India "*shall* be ruled by the British Government" is a "tremendous problem" that has yet to be considered (*Suggestions* 178). This remarkable pronouncement appeared 70 years after the Hastings impeachment became the first imperial scandal to penetrate metropolitan consciousness. Such repeated denials in the face of one's own history provide the geopolitical impulse behind Blake's amazed discovery of his name on the paint-smeared nightgown— the smoking gun in a novel that captures "absent-minded" imperialism in the act. "My heart's darling, you are a Thief," Rachel says as Franklin tries to assure her that they are both victims "of some monstrous delusion which has worn the mask of truth" (352, 348). The "monstrous delusion" is the disavowal of a long imperial history; the figure of the somnambulant hero committing a crime he does not remember is the geopolitical aesthetic at work.[56]

As the organizer of a collective *Bildung*, Franklin must outgrow his trite Continental eccentricities, even as the novel denies him the role of a singular hero. In this way, *The Moonstone* reinvents the "subjective" fictional form (R. Williams, "Forms" 156)—its structure committed to relating experience through multiple viewpoints, composite histories, and subjectivities articulated in and through this relational web. The consequent revision of sovereign experience is comparable to the pluralistic nation-state sovereignty that the political theorist William Connolly has described. Sovereignty, writes Connolly, "*circulates uncertainly between authoritative sites of enunciation and irresistible forces of power.*" This indeterminate state is "not a *confusion* in the idea of sovereignty," but, "rather, the *zone of instability* that sovereignty inhabits" (*Pluralism* 141; emphases in original). This is the kind of multi-sited sovereignty which *The Moonstone* projects when it portrays knowledge-making as a collective project of assembling the plural formations of transnational experience.

In doing so, *The Moonstone* makes clear that the path from innocence to experience (in a character doubtless named "Blake" for a reason) requires maps of knowledge which push outside Europe's borders. Even more fundamentally, *The Moonstone* itself requires knowledge-making resources from outside the anglocentric telos Uday Mehta identifies with the crisis of experience. This glimpse outside the extant framework of the realist imaginary emerges toward the end of the second period, in the uncanny form of a character whose obscure origins cross East and West and whose unconventional theories are "entirely out of the experience of mankind" (388). The full import of this shift in character is a shift in genre. With the appearance of Ezra Jennings, *The Moonstone* moves from a story of experience to a story of experiment; from a subjective to a subjunctive narrative; and from an erstwhile detective narrative to a prototypical utopian romance.

---

[56] See also J. Mehta, especially 645–6, and Sabin who calls "the novel's depiction of oblivion . . . the Victorian remedy for colonial as well as other kinds of ethical distress" (90). Both scholars note the prescient relevance to Seeley.

DARK *ERFAHRUNG*

> My father was an Englishman; but my mother—
>
> Ezra Jennings, *The Moonstone*

> I am reckoned to have got as pretty a knowledge and experience of the world as most men. And what does it all end in? It ends, Mr. Ezra Jennings, in a conjuring trick . . .
>
> Gabriel Betteredge, *The Moonstone*

> He envisioned blank spaces which he filled in with his poems.
>
> Walter Benjamin, "On Some Motifs in Baudelaire" (1939)

We have seen how *Armadale* projects experience onto spatial motifs with partial success. If Midwinter's "dark *Erfahrung*" anticipates black Atlantic consciousness in some fashion, that achievement relies on an uncanny ecology that the novel does not sustain. *The Moonstone*'s phenomenological alternative, I have suggested, turns truth-seeking from the specialized turf of a master-detective into a composite project that entails striking formal departures from omniscient narration, the *Bildungsroman*, and the still-emerging conventions of the detective genre. Moreover, these formal innovations facilitate a revision of sovereignty which stresses the deep and multi-sited embedding of history and experience. Such achievements notwithstanding, the task of addressing a crisis that is transnational in scope requires even more from this shape-shifting narrative. Thus, when "dark *Erfahrung*" makes its entrance it comes from a source so obscure that it would be a case of *deus ex machina* were not the point so clearly to introduce "something entirely new" (438).

At the start of *The Moonstone*, the Prologue's primal scene of loss and violence sets the stage for a romanticized India inaccessible to British experience: in Jamesonian terms the ability to create a "common world" that links knowing and doing is impeded by the geopolitical constraints on metropolitan consciousness. Although Murthwaite provides some necessary translation, his advice to "destroy the identity" of the Moonstone reveals his allegiance to the imperial status quo (292). The integration of Indian perspectives into the novel's story of experience is, thus, foreclosed by a geopolitical divide that pits a Britain mired in crisis against a region that is romanticized but never encountered. India's appearance in the main body of the text takes the form of tropes: the "unfathomable" gem, the wily Brahmins, and the "tawny naked arm" that takes the villains by surprise (74, 208). But these romantic figures—not unlike Trollope's more fundamentally silenced Sawab—do not contribute to the novel's *Erfahrung*. That is not because a "prehistoric" India has nothing to say to modern British experience, but because India's "irresistible positivity" eludes the instrumental compass of an imperial power (Duncan, "*The Moonstone*" 303, 301).[57]

---

[57] I quote from Duncan's excellent reading of *The Moonstone* even though I do not agree that Collins's India is depicted as "prehistoric" (303)—a difference to which I will return.

This is the phenomenological impasse that summons Ezra Jennings, a character whose "dark" difference offers a more sustained prefiguration of Gilroy's diasporic *Erfahrung* (albeit rooted in a Eurasian rather than an Atlantic matrix). Jennings's difference does not stand for *Indianness*, but, rather, for a less determinate *uncanniness*. "I was born, and partly brought up, in one of our colonies," he says (371), with the use of "colonies" a sign, perhaps, that his "Eastern" descent is not Indian.[58] What matters less than how we construe these scant clues is our absolute uncertainty: in Zerilli's terms, Jennings cues us to a problem of cross-cultural judgment that offers us no simple epistemological solution. Indeed, indeterminacy is Jennings's primary condition: from the details of the "horrible accusation" that haunts him, to the "incurable internal complaint" that kills him, to the ellipsis (and suggestion of illegitimacy) which follow the single allusion to his non-English parent: "but my mother—" (379, 380, 371). In all of these ways, Jennings's "story is a blank" (460).

That "blank," moreover, distinguishes Ezra from Ozias Midwinter, a character whose more knowable difference yields too readily to assimilationist erasure. Whereas *Armadale* ties Ozias to uncanny spatial effects that eventually ebb, *The Moonstone*'s uncanny is inscribed in Ezra's most salient features: his physical appearance and his research. The "most remarkable-looking man" Blake has ever seen (326), Ezra claims a "female constitution" (373), "looks old and young both together" (369), and sports a piebald hairline that, in "preserv[ing] no sort of regularity" (326) epitomizes the zone of instability which the novel's porous idea of sovereignty evokes. In this way, Jennings points to the "experience of limits" which Todorov cites to describe how uncanny genres merge the deeply familiar and the radically strange (48).

Jennings's uncanniness is, thus, key to recognizing *The Moonstone*'s formally rich conclusion, from the final chapters of Franklin's narrative through Jennings's diary entries and the multi-part Epilogue. Yet both Jennings and this last quarter of the novel are surprisingly underread.[59] Welsh perceptively argues that *The Moonstone*, in the end, is an "antidetective novel" (229), but he also believes that Collins's "story of experience" is eventually "compromised" by "routine

---

[58] Critics occasionally identify Jennings as being "part Indian" but there is no evidence for this conclusion (R. Thomas, *"Moonstone"* 71; cf. Welsh 227 n.28). Apart from his avowal of a colonial upbringing and mother (*Moonstone* 371), the only signs of Jennings's geographic origin are his "gipsy darkness" and his nose which "presented the fine shape and modeling so often found among the ancient people in the East" (326). Jennings's mother might perhaps have been the Indian (or "Eastern") mistress of an Englishman who transported her to "one of our colonies," or the "colony" in question may have been "Eastern" (at the time of Collins's writing, Borneo, Ceylon, and Singapore had all been under control of the Colonial Office for decades, while the Government of India held several "dependencies" in the Malay Peninsula), or Jennings may be referring to some part of the Indian subcontinent under direct or indirect British rule as a "colony."

[59] D. Miller groups Ezra with other "detective figures" like Blake and Bruff, while identifying him (anachronistically) as a "psychologist" (48). R. Thomas calls him "the forerunner . . . of the practice of medical science as a form of surveillance and discipline" (*"Moonstone"* 77). By contrast, Heller singles out Ezra's hairline as a marker that "draws attention to issues of race and power" and provides an apt "symbol of the new directions in Collins studies" ("Afterword" 361); see also Heller, *Dead* 156–63 and Sabin 105–10.

submission" to the "highly conventional" marriage plot (200, 228). Stephen Arata similarly discerns a domestic conclusion in which Ezra's sympathetic qualities are eclipsed by a mystery that centers on "Rachel's compromised virtue" (*Fictions* 136). Thus, Herncastle's plunder of the Moonstone is not an indictment of imperialism but the act of a "bad man"; and the novel's "most pressing concerns" are "those of the High Realist novel" (137).[60]

This is a very long way from the actual content of a novel that, as it draws to a conclusion, focuses on elaborating and testing an experimental "theory" (388). The case for reading *The Moonstone* as (finally) domestic realism rests presumably on Franklin's description of his "reconciliation" with Rachel, as well as Betteredge's parting words on their marriage and expectation of a child (431). But these brief accounts are folded into a patchwork of texts that oscillate between detective novel, adventure fiction, elegy, and imperial romance (431).[61] If, as Ian Duncan suggests, the restored domestic order near the close of *The Moonstone* "appears reduced, artificial, bright but fragile" ("*The Moonstone*" 300), that is partly because, at the level of form, domestic realism has been crowded out by the demands of other genres. Yet, even more significant than the heterogeneous components is Ezra's influence in pushing the gestalt toward utopian romance. In Williams's terms, the introduction of Jennings finds the novel not only working *subjectively* (by dispersing multiple points of view), but also *subjunctively* (by introducing perspectives that are not yet "socially or politically available" ["Forms" 161]).

Ezra's feat is not detection but an expansion of consciousness, the literal content of which is his method for filling in the "blank spaces" of Candy's blighted utterance. After putting his "broken sentences together," Ezra explains, "I found the superior faculty of thinking going on, more or less connectedly, in my patient's mind, while the inferior faculty of expression was in a state of almost complete incapacity and confusion" (375). That incapable state is the fragmented and incommunicable experience of *Erlebnis*, figured by the "large spaces between . . . broken phrases" that Jennings records (375). Jennings's method, therefore, is a restoration of integrated meaning, historical awareness, and narratable experience.

---

[60] Arata contrasts *The Moonstone* to Conan Doyle's *Sign of Four*, which, he argues, "constitute[s] an extended if usually clandestine indictment of the domestic ideology purveyed by Victorian realism" (139). By contrast, J. Mehta regards Doyle's fiction as the more likely of the two works to counterpose mystery "to the increasingly encompassing . . . forms of imperial knowledge" (612; cf. 643). According to GoGwilt, *The Moonstone* retells "the world-historical defeat of Tipu Sultan," in order to "set [its] family plot in counterpoint to [the] history of British imperial conquests" (68). See also Brantlinger for the argument that sensation fiction's ostensibly risqué content is formally tame in importing Gothic "romantic elements into realism" only to reduce them to "Biedermeir frames" ("What" 4).

[61] Franklin's few sentences on the reconciliation are followed by a lengthy description of the hunt for Ablewhite in which the star of the show is Gooseberry (a model for Conan Doyle's Baker Street Irregulars as Kemp's edition notes). It is followed by Cuff's official report (which unpacks the details of the Ablewhite plot and the Indians' flight with the Moonstone) and Candy's letter (announcing Ezra Jennings's death and burial). Betteredge's short narrative concludes the second period after which comes the Epilogue: two statements detailing the Indians' escape along with Murthwaite's closing account of the Moonstone's restoration in Somnauth.

Above all, it is that crucial act of the imagination which Benjamin assigned to art: the task of envisioning blank spaces to be filled in with poiesis.

Jennings's "dark *Erfahrung*" marks the introduction of a utopian imaginary that transcends the crisis of experience by overcoming the inability to imagine a future of "otherness and radical difference" (Jameson, "Progress" 288). In "Progress versus Utopia," Jameson argues that the decline of the historical novel after Scott and Balzac coincided with the emergence of science fiction in the novels of Jules Verne (286). The significance of science fiction's "realistic" depiction of fictional futures, he explains, is to "defamiliarize and restructure our experience of our own present" (286). Such defamiliarization is precisely the task of sensation fiction's transposition of Gothic conventions to contemporary milieux. But in contrast to most other sensation novels, including Collins's own, *The Moonstone* is unique in having a genuinely utopian dimension in Ezra and his work: a glimpse of a radically different future.

Indeed, Ezra enters *The Moonstone*'s phenomenological impasse as though he were *from* the future. This is the final meaning of his "blank" story: the unknown origins, the premature death, the buried manuscripts. "Let my grave be forgotten . . . Let me sleep, nameless. Let me rest, unknown," he writes in preparation for exiting the narrative that his presence has transformed. Jennings was "a great man," writes Candy, "though the world never knew him" (461). In contrast to the Hindus, notes Robert Crooks, "Jennings's actions are fully explained though no description of the circumstances that would account for their difference is available" (222). Crooks thus identifies the sign of Jennings's utopian provenance: the circumstances that would account for his difference are (as yet) unknowable because they are futuristic. Jennings is a kind of brother from another planet: a character whose absolute exile from the world-as-it-is creates the condition of his radicalizing *Erfahrung*.

In this way, Jennings not only represents a utopian alternative to the essentialized Hindus, but also to the demonized boundary figures who are his counterparts in naturalistic fiction. As Collins's most fully realized type of the mixed-race subject, Ezra provokes the aversion of an Emilius, Lopez, or Collins's own Ozias: "My personal appearance (as usual) told against me," he writes upon observing Bruff's reflexive "distrust" (414). Yet, unlike the irreclaimable Emilius, the self-annihilating Lopez, or the whitened Ozias, Ezra evokes a path to dialogue beyond paralyzing racial anxieties. Not coincidentally, the same watchwords used to vilify otherness in Trollope's imaginary—"trickery," "conjuring," "hocus-pocus"—are used by Jennings's detractors to impugn his experiment (402, 403, 416). As the sympathetic Rachel tells him, "They seem to be in a conspiracy to persecute you . . . What does it mean?" Ezra's reply marks the burdens of utopian thinking: "Only the protest of the world . . . against anything that is new" (417).

These futuristic qualities are significant too in that utopian fiction is a perversely riven genre. Examples such as H.G. Wells's *A Modern Utopia* (1905) and *In the Days of the Comet* (1906) border on the dystopic.[62] One of the best-known

---

[62] See Goodlad, *Victorian*, 218–28.

Victorian utopias, William Morris's *New from Nowhere* (1890) is, as Tanya Agathocleous notes, an "ahistorical depiction of a timeless rural order" in which "the local transcends the global, place and race become fixed, and cultural and ethnic diversity are precluded" (161, 159). This is the kind of ethnocentrism which *The Moonstone*, written decades before these works by Morris and Wells, teaches readers to associate with Betteredge's eccentricity or Bruff's insularity and to contrast with Jennings's "unsought *self-possession*" and fervor for knowledge (376).

It is this enlarged consciousness—this capacity to imagine "radical difference"— through which *The Moonstone*'s Epilogue should be read. Though its setting is a "romantic region" beyond metropolitan experience, the elegiac tone and solitary exile of the Brahmins recall us to Ezra's embodiment of the future. In this way, Ezra's utopian imaginary inflects the reader's witness of a sacred stone restored intact after its centuries-long odyssey: the apotheosis of a Hindu sovereignty resilient in the face of conquest and the civilizing mission.

To be sure, other ways of reading proliferate. For Roy, the romance form serves the imperial agenda by infusing "the thrilling global space of Preface, Prologue, and Epilogue" (669). This seems to me to describe how *The Moonstone* would look if its sole narrator were Murthwaite and its implied reader a philistine like Bruff taking a rare break from the Law. [63] In a more nuanced interpretation of *The Moonstone*'s romance, Jaya Mehta diagnoses ambivalence. Collins, she notes, pushes his contemporary readers to experience imperial violence from the standpoint of British rapacity. Yet, "the project of detection depends for its success" on obscuring this violence anew in the interest of "romantic closure" and "domestic tranquility" (648).[64] Once again, we find *The Moonstone* cast as a detective project—this time by a scholar who notes the diamond's return to India "long after the official detective has given up the case" (647). Yet, in fact, Cuff has not given up. His final report describes an energetic project of metropolitan detection— albeit one that fails utterly to track the Indians and recover the Moonstone (459). It is as though Cuff reappears to demonstrate anew the curbs on his prowess. As Murthwaite predicts, "You have lost sight of [the Moonstone] in England, and (if I know anything of these people) you have lost sight of it forever" (472).

"These people," moreover, transcend the orientalist voice in a text that finally renders them "sublime and tragic" (J. Mehta 648). Duncan recognizes this sublimity as well in a powerful reading that places Collins's novel in "the tradition founded by [Walter] Scott, in which romance represents an allegory of historical and cultural formation" (300). The strength of this reading is its grasp of India's

---

[63] As Sabin notes, such a critique reserves "knowingness for itself, leaving Victorian authors blindly enclosed in their culture's dynamic of denial, repression, and repudiation of responsibility" (90–91).

[64] This is the same misgiving that troubles Arata with the difference that Mehta sees the problem as endemic to detective romance, Arata to domestic realism. Mehta's somewhat skeptical reading of *The Moonstone*'s conclusion derives partly from her view of Blake as a "romantic hero" and "master narrator" (646) and of Jennings's death as marginalizing—interpretations that differ from my own arguments for a shift in genre.

irreducible sovereignty: "the positive alterity" to which I have already alluded. But at moments the Scott analogy goes too far, transposing the historical relation of Scotland and England to that between India and Britain. With Scott's inevitable British syntheses in mind, Duncan too readily characterizes India's otherness from the imperial standpoint, as "an archaic, sacral, and fatalistic world where priestly devotion fulfills destiny" (303). This notion of a "prehistoric" India overlooks the lessons of the novel's first period: the expert who cannot consider the strangeness of what he is judging is doomed to fail.

Duncan is closer to capturing the India of *The Moonstone* when he describes "a space more vast and perilous than a 'margin'—[with] its own fatal center and dark origins" ("*The Moonstone*" 303). Yet, even here he seems to overstate the demonizing effects of the Epilogue's picture of untamable difference. The point of this wild and romantic India is structural, not anathematizing: it says that in positing India as a knowable object of domination, the imperial relation has made India more inaccessible than ever. As many critics have pointed out, Collins's post-1857 "A Sermon for the Sepoys" is almost unique in recommending Indian ethical culture to India's rebels (e.g., J. Mehta 618). What the novel seems to wish for the future, if not exactly to anticipate, is the kind of fragile multicultural dialogue that Zarilli describes and Jennings foreshadows.

The Moonstone's parting glimpse is, thus, not a space we should see (as Murthwaite sometimes authorizes us to do, in a novel that does not always authorize Murthwaite) as "a devilish India . . . triumphant in its darkness" (Duncan, "*The Moonstone*" 305). The term "devilish" is, in fact, Betteredge's descriptor—used to characterize Herncastle, Rachel, and Sergeant Cuff, as well as the Indian diamond).[65] In considering this parting India we need, therefore, to distinguish between Murthwaite himself and the scene that he narrates.

> A new strain of music, loud and jubilant, rose from the hidden shrine . . . There, raised high on a throne . . . with his four arms stretching toward the four corners of the earth—there, soared above us, dark and awful in the mystic light of heaven . . . the god of the Moon. And there, in the forehead of the deity, gleamed the yellow Diamond, whose splendour had last shone on me in England, from the bosom of a woman's dress! (472).

This is no more an evocation of a "devilish" India than the sign of a heroic Blake "extending" his unseen editorial control over India (J. Mehta 647). Indeed, given this novel's emphasis on the future, it is not too much to suggest that what Murthwaite reports in *The Moonstone*'s closing pages is the eruption of the world-historical process that we today call decolonization—(transformed from the "mutiny" to a romanticized scene of sovereign restoration which Collins's readers could applaud).

This is not to forget that decolonization is itself an ongoing project. Not for nothing, Jennings's dying words, before returning to the future, are "Peace! peace! peace!" (461). Jennings prompts us to resist the invitation to regard the temporality

---

[65] See 45, 46, 65, 151.

of *The Moonstone*'s conclusion as cyclical or repetitious—history looping between tragedy and farce. His *Erfahrung* points us toward the forward-looking temporality of the desire called utopia, signaled in the text by the shift to the future tense. "What *will* be the next adventures of the Moonstone?" The answer, "Who can tell!," is a question we have yet fully to answer (472; emphasis added).

6

The Adulterous Geopolitical Aesthetic
Romola contra *Madame Bovary*

> It was only the other day that M. Sainte Beuve devoted a long article in the *Moniteur* to one of the most revolting productions that ever issued from a French novelist's brain . . . *Madame Bovary* of M. Gustave Flaubert has become the *beaux success* of the season, and its author is decorated with the title of a "chef de file" of the rising literati of France. It was satisfactory to find the *Journal des Débats* refusing to swell the chorus of M. Flaubert's admirers, and proving that the coarseness of his so-called *realism* was, if possible, aggravated by the most flagrant breaches of taste in point of style. And yet such is the garbage of which we are invited to partake by the reviewer of the official journal of the French empire.
>
> "French Literature," *Saturday Review*, June 6, 1857

> [*Madame Bovary*] contains not a few passages which would of themselves justify very strong language if there were any danger that M. Flaubert's example would be followed in this country, or that his book would become popular amongst English readers. We do not, however, feel ourselves called upon to make use of any very indignant expressions. There is no fear that our novelists will outrage public decency. Their weaknesses forbid such dangerous eccentricity quite as much as their virtues.
>
> [James Fitzjames Stephen], "Madame Bovary," *Saturday Review*, July 11, 1857

On July 11, 1857—two weeks after the first reports of "mutiny" in India reached English shores—*The Saturday Review* published the second of two articles on a literary rebellion taking place in France. The anonymous reviewer, James Fitzjames Stephen, assured his readers that "considerable hesitation" had preceded the decision to review *Madame Bovary* despite the book's having been "hailed with much applause, as a specimen of 'realism' in fiction, by very eminent French critics" (40). *Madame Bovary* had appeared serially in *La Revue de Paris* between October and December of 1856, but the book's notoriety swelled when Flaubert was put on trial in January 1857 for endangering public morals—a landmark event that culminated in vindication of the author, his work, and (from a historical standpoint) art and artists everywhere. Nonetheless, the prosecution's claim that the female readers of such scandalous fiction were, like Emma herself, susceptible to corruption, remained a topic of concern for moralists on both sides of the channel. As the anonymous author of "French Literature" made clear, the continuing debate over the Matrimonial Causes Act meant that Flaubert's novel entered the scene at a time when the condition of marriage was "undergoing discussion in England" (525). When the act became law a few weeks later, it widened access to a legal proceeding that had long been prohibitive for all but the rich while enabling married women to sue for divorce in cases of adultery compounded by physical cruelty, bigamy, incest, or bestiality. As marriage assumed the characteristically modern form of a contract, a wife's adultery stood forth as the most fundamental form of breach.[1]

For critics of *Madame Bovary*, Flaubert's "deleterious trash" epitomized the contrast between French and British morality ("French" 525). Stephen's nuanced review, however, saw no occasion for self-congratulation: "Our statistical returns, the nightly appearance of our streets, and [the] verbatim reports of trials . . . surely teach us that we are not so very immaculate" ("Madame" 41). In fact, the new divorce courts would soon amplify the contrast between newspaper reports of scandalous marital breakdown and a censored fictional culture that insisted "that no novels should be written except those which are fit for young ladies to read" (41). Stephen's review was, thus, less a critique of Flaubert than a meditation on the "weaknesses" of British literature. "Surely," he opined, "it is very questionable" to desire that novel-writing alone be "calculated for girlish ignorance" when works in theology, philosophy, science, and law are subject to no such proscription. "If Shakespeare had never written a line which women in the present day could not read, he would never have been the greatest of poets" (41).

Concern for the "emasculation" of British fiction also surfaced in the most positive review of *Madame Bovary* to appear at this time ([Stephen] 41). Part of a recurring series of anonymous essays in the *Westminster Review*, George Meredith's "Belles Lettres" for October 1857 praised the recently published *Barchester Towers*: in Anthony Trollope, it affirmed, "we have a caustic and vigorous writer, who can draw men and women, and tell a story that men and women can read." By contrast, Margaret Oliphant's *The Athelings* (1857), is "altogether

---

[1] Prior to the 1857 act the common law doctrine of *couverture* subsumed the legal personality of a married woman into that of her husband, effectively reducing her to his property. Despite its built-in double standard, which entitled husbands to sue for divorce on grounds of (mere) adultery, the act made divorce accessible to those neither wealthy nor influential enough to pursue divorce by "private Act of Parliament, an extraordinarily complex and expensive procedure" (Shanley 9). Yet, as Chase and Levinson note, the act was hardly revolutionary: by setting aside the demands to reform married women's property laws, "by continuing to make it difficult for those of modest means to pursue a divorce (by restricting the proceedings to a London court), and by refusing to grant women equal grounds to petition, the act stands as the cautious outcome to long public brooding" (191).

feminine" (596). This emphasis on gender prepared the ground for commendation of Flaubert: "A great change is coming over French works of fiction":

> In "Madame Bovary" . . . [t]he old blandishing graces of Dumas, Sand, and De Balzac, are quite excluded . . . All is severe matter of fact painfully elaborated . . . The Author is right: if an adultery is to be treated of at all . . . it should be laid bare—not tricked out in meretricious allurements . . . No harm can come from reading Madame Bovary; but it is physic for adults, as the doctors say . . . M. Gustave Flaubert is a singularly powerful writer (600–1).

Thus, while Stephen rejected the naturalistic unmasking that Meredith cautiously embraced, both critics upheld Flaubert as a novelist who wrote for adults, especially men. At a time when divorce had become a public concern and extra-marital sex a fixture of the daily news, *Madame Bovary* subjected a wife's adultery to "stern analysis" instead of the "mere toys" that a bowdlerized literary culture proffered to British readers ([Stephen], "Madame" 41).

In the years following Flaubert's debut in the space of transcultural exchange which Margaret Cohen and Carolyn Dever have called the "literary channel," the discussion of Britain's literary "emasculation" continued. In 1858, Augustus Egg offered a painterly complement by making wifely adultery the subject of his famous triptych, *Past and Present* (1858)—in which two young daughters unknowingly build a house of cards atop a Balzac novel. The *Saturday Review* praised Meredith's novel, *The Ordeal of Richard Feverel* (1859), for boldly depicting "the temptations to which men are exposed." There should be books explicitly identified as "men's novels" to avoid the "great danger" of giving male readers the "impression that all the representations of life given in fiction are hypocritical and superficial" (48).[2] In effect the review called for a gender-segregated literature to match the double standard that the Matrimonial Causes Act had enshrined when it made it a wife's adultery—but not a husband's—sufficient grounds for divorce.

Such critiques of an allegedly feminized British literature overlapped with an ongoing discourse on "lady novelists." In 1852, an anonymous essay in the *Westminster Review* affirmed "the right of Woman to citizenship" in the transnational "Republic of Letters." A "female literature" drawn from "woman's experience," declared the author—George Henry Lewes—might provide a stirring "new element" ("Lady Novelists" 141, 131). Less optimistically, W. R. Greg's anonymous essay for the *National Review* in 1859 addressed "The False Morality of Lady Novelists." The essay included Elizabeth Gaskell's *Ruth* (1853) under that rubric, not because her tale of a young girl's seduction was immoral, but because, according to Greg, the author lacked the courage of her convictions: if Gaskell's point was "to awaken . . . compassion for the ordinary class of betrayed . . . Magdalenes," Greg wrote, "the circumstances of Ruth's error should not have been made so innocent, nor should Ruth herself have been painted as so perfect" (167). But by far the best-known essay on "lady" novelists came from the

---

[2] Ironically, the theme of adultery in Meredith's "men's novel" derived from the actions of a woman—Meredith's wife who left the author for another man in 1858.

reviewer who had preceded Meredith as the writer of the *Westminster Review*'s "Belles Lettres" series. Describing several species of "feminine fatuity," including the kind that spares "no expense . . . to get up as exciting a story as you will find in the most immoral novels," the essay implies that the real problem is sexism: "No sooner does a woman show that she has genius or effective talent, than she receives the tribute of being moderately praised and severely criticized" ("Silly" 301, 296, 318). Little surprise that by the time she issued this sally in 1856, the author of "Silly Novels by Lady Novelists" was embarking on her own fictional career under a male pseudonym.

George Eliot is hardly remembered as a novelist of adultery; yet, the topic in some form shadows all of her works, beginning with *Adam Bede* (1859). Indeed, like Flaubert and Meredith, Eliot rose to fame as the author of a first novel acclaimed for its pronounced realist style and centered partly on illicit sex. As Nina Auerbach writes, if "Hetty Sorrel is presented to us as fallen from her first lush and sensuous appearance in the novel" it is because she "wills to possess the social glamour and power Arthur embodies" (40, 44–5). The most vain and ambitious of the mid-Victorian era's "fallen" women, Hetty stands apart from such sympathetic heroines as Frances Trollope's Jessie Phillips, Hawthorne's Hester, Gaskell's Ruth, and even Hardy's Tess.[3] In *The Way of the World* (1987), Franco Moretti singles out Eliot as a rare British novelist in negotiating "the issues characteristic" of Continental fiction. But he maintains nonetheless that England's is the only narrative tradition never to have "dealt with the theme of adultery" (214, 188).

In this chapter I wish to complicate a number of critical commonplaces about mid-Victorian fiction by reading George Eliot's works—and, in particular, *Romola* (1862–3)—as an expression of an *adulterous geopolitical aesthetic*. Among the several interventions this reading entails is the importance of understanding Eliot from a worlded perspective along with the need to reconsider the misleading assumption that while the "great narrative tradition[s]" of France, Germany, Russia, and the United States, have perforce "dealt with the theme of adultery," in "England" the result has been "nothing—absolutely nothing" (Moretti, *Way* 188). *Madame Bovary*, I will argue, is not only "a novel of adultery" (a term this chapter will complicate), but also an important precursor for the naturalistic narratives discussed in previous chapters and in Chapter 8. This reconsideration resists the binary of French "realism" and British "idealism" to connect Eliot's formal experiments to the comparable mid-century conditions that produced Flaubert's naturalism.

Of course, literary critics often reserve the term *naturalism* for the quasi-scientific creed that Émile Zola set forth in "The Experimental Novel" (1879). Zola called for a systematic authorship that first reports "the facts" and then sets "characters going in a certain story so as to" confirm "the determinants of the phenomena under examination" (8). The naturalist movement he helped to

---

[3] Just as Hetty's name may echo that of Hester, so her upbringing on the Poyser farm may recall Emma Bovary's origins as a farmer's daughter—though Eliot's less bourgeois character has never read a novel.

ignite influenced Americans such as Theodore Dreiser and Frank Norris, Britons such as George Gissing and George Moore, as well as the Norwegian playwright Henrik Ibsen. That said, the Zolaesque focus on the environmental determinants of working-class life is tangential to my exploration of Flaubert's earlier naturalism.[4]

In the 1940s, Georg Lukács associated Flaubert with a lamentable transition from a realism that captured the "essential features of social reality"—exemplified by Walter Scott's historical novels and Honoré de Balzac's social fiction—to a post-1848 literature consumed by "details" (*Studies* 143–4). In his 1857 review of *Madame Bovary*, Charles Augustin Saint-Beuve had prepared the ground for this view: Flaubert's "relentless detail," he wrote, was a case of "overreach" ("*Madame*" 401). Henry James echoed this kind of charge when he described Eliot's *Middlemarch* (1871-2) as a "treasure-house of detail" ("Review" 425).[5] From this standpoint, Roland Barthes's *The Reality Effect* (1968), was the climax of a century-long tradition of casting detail as realism's singular defect. Whereas Lukács diagnosed a post-Balzac crisis signaled by a new naturalistic fixation on superficial detail, Barthes discerned a "referential plenitude" that signified "the category" but not "the contents" of "'the real'" ("Reality" 455; cf. Schor, "Details," 28–9). This two-pronged indictment was just a step away from Catherine Belsey's poststructuralist account of realism in 1980 as "the presentation of an intelligible history which effaces its own status as discourse" and "does the work of ideology in suppressing the relationship between language and subjectivity" (*Critical* 60).

Yet, there is, of course, another and strikingly different story to tell about Flaubert's legacy. Although James was an early critic of realist detail, he eventually became an important spokesman for Flaubert's distinct impact on novelistic art.[6] By the 1890s, *Madame Bovary*'s renown in Britain had soared, thanks in part to Eleanor Marx's 1888 translation. Paul Bourget's Oxford lecture in 1897 contrasted Flaubert's artistry to a naturalist movement that had begun to view aesthetics as a distraction from unvarnished social determinants.[7] James's preface to a new edition of *Madame Bovary* in 1902 reflected these changes, expressing a

---

[4] While Flaubert and Zola were on cordial terms, the former "did not hide [his] disdain for Zola's formulas." According to Baguley, Zola's codification of naturalism paradoxically attempted "to arrive at a more scientific type of realism" while also vindicating the author's "deep-seated Romantic belief in individual genius" (21, 57). Zola included Flaubert in a genealogy of naturalism which began with the positivism of Diderot and included Stendhal and Balzac (12).

[5] Criticism of realist detail extended back to Balzac, whose tendency to amass detailed particulars had been likened to the work of an auctioneer preparing inventories (qtd. in Weinberg 39). See also R.L. Stevenson's 1883 essay criticizing the "merely technical and decorative stage" to which the Balzacian use of detail has "recently" fallen in France and singling out Zola especially for this alleged abuse (279).

[6] In 1876, James praised *Madame Bovary* as a "masterpiece," but was still ready to discuss its author under the heading, "The Minor French Novelists." "Realism," he declared, "seems to me with 'Madame Bovary' to have said its last word. ("Minor" 226).

[7] Bourget described *Madame Bovary* as the "starting-point" for a "School of Realism" which was the offspring of the "French Romantic School of 1830" including Victor Hugo and Saint-Beuve as well as Balzac (158, 155). For an account of American naturalism which stresses the masculinist focus on science over art in male novelists such as Frank Norris, see M. Bell.

"more sophisticated sense of how style can *create* value" and "not simply express it" (Seed 314). The charm of *Madame Bovary*, he wrote, was its "unsurpassable form": "The work is a classic because the thing, such as it is, is ideally *done,* and because it shows that in such doing eternal beauty may dwell" ("Gustave" 80). Although James tempered this praise—Emma Bovary, he wrote, "is really too small an affair" (81)—he nonetheless articulated the kind of aestheticism which complemented his own Flaubert-influenced literary experiments.

In *The Art of George Eliot* (1961), W. J. Harvey lamented this Jamesean influence, arguing that the Flaubert-inflected preference for "form" over "life"—encapsulating a tension that James himself never wholly reconciled—had been taken up by later critics as though it were an absolute *doxa*. James's misgivings over Flaubert's ability to sustain the "human mind" or inhabit "the moral world" were ignored while his admiration for *Madame Bovary*'s formal achievements became the basis of an aesthetic creed ("Flaubert's" 366; "Anthony" 124). Through such selective reading, James became the best-known progenitor of a "concept of form" which excluded the great majority of narrative fiction: pertinent to *Madame Bovary, The Ambassadors*, and *Mrs Dalloway*, but not to *War and Peace* or *Middlemarch*. The result, Harvey believed, was "a fundamental distortion" of Eliot's "novels of 'life'" (30–31).[8] Gender, moreover, played a prominent part in this judgment: according to James, British fiction had been "preponderantly cultivated" by women, "a sex ever gracefully, comfortably, enviably unconscious . . . of the requirements of form" ("Gustave" 91). But since Eliot's works feature multiple "centres of interest," Harvey countered, their distinct formal achievement is in the relationships and tensions *between* these parts." To read Eliot's form correctly, we must "think of a network of relations rather than of a single governing character" (27).[9]

Thus, while Marxist and poststructuralist literary theory conduced toward rigorous critiques of realist detail, the aestheticist tradition beginning with James, valorized select formal principles in opposition to fictional styles more "at home in the moral world." This is the backstory for New Criticism's "thoroughgoing neglect" of mid-Victorian fiction (C. Levine, "Formal" 1242) as well as those symptomatic readings determined to expose realism's work on behalf of ideology and disciplinary power. The result, I contend, has been to marginalize the kind of perspective which could recognize novels such as *Madame Bovary, Romola, Daniel Deronda* (1876), Trollope's *The Prime Minister* (1875–6), and James's *Portrait of Lady* (1880-81), as the co-negotiators of comparable conditions of possibility. But just as James need not be reduced to those aspects of his *oeuvre* which oppose him to Eliot, so *Madame Bovary* can be read against its dual reputation as a timeless

---

[8] Writing almost fifty years later, Claybaugh renders Hardy's concern in a nutshell: "Rather than acknowledging that Eliot adheres to formal principles different from his own . . . James instead implies that Eliot's novels have no form at all" (116).
[9] Hardy's contemporaneous work on Eliot reaches a similar conclusion: "The largeness and comprehensiveness of [Eliot's] novels have meant that she has not been admired as a great formal artist" (*Novels* 1). On this point, see also Garrett's classic study of the multiplot novel's dialogic structure (*Victorian*). On James's gendered assumption on form, see also Claybaugh 166, W. Harvey 28–30, and C. Levine "Formal" 1243.

manifesto for the autonomy of art and a power-saturated device for reifying the status quo. Indeed, precedents for such "worlding" critical practices already exist. Decades before the good work of *The Literary Channel*, comparatists such as Christopher Heywood were arguing for "the mixed origins of Victorian literary thought and expression." Victorian "realism," he wrote in 1979, developed in a succession of waves . . . in sympathy with the literature of France, New England, and, later, of Russia" and one such wave was "the shock of recognition which followed the appearance of *Madame Bovary*" ("French" 107, 121).

As a study of realist representation across time, space, and genre, Erich Auerbach's *Mimesis* (1946) is an important starting point for such a "mixed" genealogy. For Auerbach, *Madame Bovary* is an exemplary nineteenth-century novel not despite but because of its formal innovations. Too banal to qualify as tragedy, Flaubert's "existential realism" expresses the "gravity of being caught up in history's workings" ("Serious" 448; cf. *Mimesis* 482–91). The name Auerbach coins for this naturalistic mimesis is "the serious imitation of the everyday" (433). In this chapter I will suggest that Flaubert's "strange" mixing of "tragic pity and critical disdain with an everyday character" (433) provided a crucial French prototype of the *naturalistic narrative of capitalist globalization*—a genre I have so far discussed in light of Trollope's later works. While the conditions particular to Britain's New Imperial era were distinct from those of the French Second Empire, both Trollope and Flaubert crafted naturalistic styles to express the worlded state of heirloom collapse.[10] Adultery, I will show, was both a catalyst for and frequent trope of this existential condition.

That said, adultery is not exclusively wed to naturalistic representation. Indeed, precisely in *resisting* the naturalist's fusion of pity and disdain, Eliot's experiments in writing "novels of adultery" produced realist genres devoted to that fuller mode of life which, according to James, Flaubert had stifled in making Emma "too small an affair." To illustrate this case, I will first explore the adulterous geopolitical aesthetic as it had begun to emerge in Britain prior to Eliot's appearance as novelist. My goal is to break open the so-called novel of adultery so as to recognize its generic overlap with narratives that share Flaubert's focus on exile, alienation, and damaged sovereignty. The remainder of the chapter describes Eliot's transition from early works such as *The Mill on the Floss* (1860) to *Romola* (the author's best known attempt to rework the genre made famous by Scott), and then briefly to *Daniel Deronda* which (despite being Eliot's most naturalistic novel) offers an alternative to naturalistic treatment of the exilic Jew—that veritable archetype of capitalist deracination.

Although *Romola* has had a mixed critical reception, it is persistently described as a major turning point: "[a]fter *Romola*," writes Andrew Sanders, in a sentence

---

[10] For the argument that the television series *Mad Men* is a neoliberal version of the genre, see Chapter 8. On the "heirloom sovereignty" that Victorian versions of the genre show to be violated, see Chapter 3's discussion of Trollope's Barsetshire fiction (in which heirloom institutions like the Church of England are portrayed as repositories of a robust ethical culture) as well as Chapter 4 on the loss of such rootedness in *The Eustace Diamonds*.

that encapsulates the worlded quality of Eliot's later fiction, "there is a new feeling for history ... with the life of the fictional community related outwards to political events of more than parochial significance" (169). Indeed, as I will argue, Eliot strove to write what Lukács later described as the "historical novel of our time"—a genre designed to turn the matter of the past into forms fit to augur the future (*Historical* 350). In doing so, Eliot and Lukács share a largely eurocentric notion of "world-history" which tends to assimilate the material impacts of imperial expansion to the frame of a cosmopolitan Europe. Yet, as David Kurnick argues, Eliot's reputation as a "*sanguine* cosmopolitan" overlooks her persistent formal restlessness ("Unspeakable" 490). As a result, Eliot's variations on the novel of adultery provide an ideal optic for illustrating the kind of comparativism which the geopolitical aesthetic helps to inspire.

THE ADULTEROUS GEOPOLITICAL AESTHETIC

What is the tritest theme of all, worn out by repetition, by being played over and over again like a tired barrel organ?
Adultery.
Charles Baudelaire, "*Madame Bovary* by Gustave Flaubert"
October 18 (1857)

It is such an obvious and legible phenomenon that many of those nineteenth-century novels that have been canonized as "great" ... center on adultery ...
Tony Tanner, *Adultery and the Novel* (1979)

In Chapter 5, we saw how sensation novels such as *Armadale* (1864–6) and *The Moonstone* (1868) resist naturalistic structures and affects, articulating plural sovereignties at multiple scales. My discussion of Collins thus had little occasion to explore how different versions of the geopolitical aesthetic transfigure the marriage plot—one of realist fiction's most resilient devices. In the decades since feminist scholars brought domesticity to the fore, attention to how novels negotiate "marriage's evolving relationship to the state, civil society, and private life, to friends and kin, to consent, contract, and pleasure" has become a staple of literary criticism as we know it (Marcus, *Between* 193). By enabling "relationships within marriages and within families" to "describe other kinds of relationships" (Loesberg "Deconstruction" 441), the marriage plot proffers limitless stock for a metonymic form. Thus, according to Tony Tanner, "marriage is *the* central subject for the bourgeois novel" for it provides "the all-subsuming, all organizing, all-containing contract for bourgeois society" (*Adultery* 15).[11]

---

[11] On political fiction's diversion of class conflict into the "reassuringly static" cul-de-sac of the courtship plot, see Yeazell (127). On use of "courtship and marriage" to cultivate middle-class

From this perspective, Trollope's *Barchester Towers*, praised by Meredith as a novel for grown-ups, is notable for its feint of giving the game away. In a plot that threatens to pair the widowed Eleanor with the odious Mr. Slope, la Signora Madeline Vesey Neroni, a Barsetshirian siren estranged from a dubious Italian spouse, opines, "There is no happiness in love, except at the end of an English novel" (245). As la Signora entices Eleanor's intended, Trollope teases his audience with the prospect of this Italianate temptress rocking the foundations of the genre she helps him to ironize. By contrast, in *The Prime Minister*, Emily Wharton's marriage to a "stranger and foreigner" is no laughing matter (185). Middle-class wedlock in what Helena Michie calls a "dysphoric marriage plot," is nearly as devastated a scene of breach as the Tenway Junction, site of Lopez's suicide. Terrible in its description of courtship betrayed, this naturalistic narrative makes Lopez's unknowable origins a source of "epistemological emergency" (*Victorian* 185). Thus, while adulterous sex is technically irrelevant to Emily's conjugal leap in the dark, and merely toyed with in Barchester, Trollope's novels illustrate the diverse ways that British realism could stretch courtship and marriage plots to their limits. As marriage supplied an "all-subsuming" figure for bourgeois society, so "unhappy wedlock" indexed an array of modern ills (Boone, *Tradition* 330).

In consecrating the family as the chief institution through which property is organized, bourgeois marriage seeks to consecrate itself as a form of heirloom sovereignty, irreducible to mere civil statute or common law convention. In this ideal state—as a God-given bond that no man should put asunder—marriage promises a bulwark of extra-economic and extra-juridical value which claims to redeem modern society from atomized self-ownership, commodification, and the "cash nexus." Moreover, as Emily Wharton's marriage to a "stranger and foreigner" suggests, the potential ambit for this exceptional institution is the globalizing world.[12] Adultery implies the unraveling of all that marriage holds dear, portending "the possible breakdown of all the mediations on which society . . . depends" (Tanner, *Adultery* 17).

In its most familiar usage, adultery denotes a "violation of the marriage vows" as well as the "sin or crime" entailed by this breach, and the "state or condition of having committed" this sin or crime (*OED*). Adultery in this primary sense enfolds a sexual act and a religious and civil offense as well as a metaphysical

---

"fantasies of political power," proffering domesticity as a seemingly neutral means of consolidating bourgeois cultural authority, see N. Armstrong (29). On industrial fiction as a means of constituting the family as "society's primary reforming institution," see Gallagher, *Industrial* 115. On a counter-tradition in the marriage plot which "translat[es] the unresolved tensions of conjugal warfare into principles of narrative structure," see Boone, *Tradition* 215; Boone, "Modernist"; as well as (germinally) Heilbrun. More recently, Psomiades has discussed the relation between the marriage plot, social contract theory and nineteenth-century anthropology ("Marriage") while E. Michie has argued that Victorian marriage plots create structures "that . . . allow us to dig up the latent aesthetic value . . . hidden by the more manifest material values . . . [of] commercial culture" (*Vulgar* 181).

[12] Consider not only Lopez's eventual trafficking in African and New Zealand commodities but also the many works that find Trollope's heroines emigrating to Australia (e.g., *The Three Clerks*), growing up in fictional tropical islands (e.g., *He Knew He Was Right*), or in actual colonies such as Jamaica (e.g., "Miss Sarah Jack of Spanish Town").

condition. In its secondary usages adultery operates through a logic of extension. Hence, in a well-known verse from Matthew, "Whosoever looketh on a woman to lust after her, hath committed adulterie with her already in his heart" (5:28, qtd. in *OED*), the category expands to include the contemplation of acts that may never be consummated. In yet another extension, the violation of vows widens to encompass any illegitimate sexual activity, including sex between unmarried partners or even adultery *within* marriage.[13] Finally, the Latin *adulterium*, from which the English "adultery" derives, denotes not only "conjugal infidelity" but also the "blending or mixing of different strains or ingredients," thus expanding adultery through a homology that likens broken vows and profligate acts to the "debasement" or "corruption" of religious doctrines or material essences (*OED*). Yet, despite such marked proliferation of meaning, adultery consistently signals violation or breach: of a legal contract or sacred vow; of one's mental or physical condition of purity, chastity, fidelity, or innocence; of material or spiritual essence.

In *Adultery in the Novel: Contract and Transgression* (1979), Tanner focuses on three novels, of which only one, *Madame Bovary*, centers on adultery in its most blatant form.[14] The backstory for this wide-ranging account of adultery in the novel is a Western literature rooted in mythic events like the Trojan War, which represent "a violation of boundaries" which civilization strives to defuse by transforming "the *stranger* into a *guest*" (24). While Tanner's cross-temporal analysis is well worth exploring, the drift into timeless truisms obscures the historicity of his subject.[15] For from the perspective of capitalism's *longue durée*, the stage for "the *stranger-enemy*" is global rather than western and the relevant contexts include the geopolitical projects of trade, settlement, and conquest which pervade the nineteenth-century's fictional imaginary. Thus, if marriage is, as Tanner suggests, "the structure that maintains the Structure" (25, 15), the point for scholars of the novel is that "the Structure" in question is not (or not only) the French or British nation-state or "the West," but, rather, the ongoing globalization of capital in all its persistent unevenness and myriad material effects.

---

[13] Chaucer's "Parson's Tale" thus details the kind of adultery which takes place when "a man and his wyf . . . take no reward in hire assemblynge but oonly to hire fleshly delit" (qtd. in *OED*). In modern English the complete quotation is rendered, "The third kind of adultery is sometimes between a man and his wife. That's when they regard sexual union as just for their fleshly delight, as Saint Jerome says, and care for nothing but their coupling; but because they are married, they think everything's all right. But in such people the devil has power" (see lines 904–6).

[14] The other two examples, Rousseau's *Julie, or the New Heloise* (1761) and Goethe's *Elective Affinities* (1806) concern, respectively, a sexual romance between unmarried partners and a husband and wife who contemplate but do not consummate adulterous affairs. The Protestant reformation aggressively expanded the Old Testament's proscription against adultery to include pre-marital as well as extra-marital sex. See, for example, the 1854 translation of Calvin's commentary on the seventh commandment: "[I]t is sufficiently plain, from the principle laid down, that believers are generally exhorted to chastity; for, if the Law be a perfect rule of holy living, it would be more than absurd to give a license for fornication, adultery alone being excepted" (68). The *OED* cites usages of adultery to denote "any illicit sexual intercourse or activity; lust, debauchery, fornication" as far back as the sixteenth century.

[15] On Tanner's tendency to interpret "the transgressions of adultery as existing in an ahistorical time warp" see Matlock (342) as well as Leckie (368).

To "world" such a literature is not, however, to reduce it to the product of a homogeneous global history.[16] The preceding chapters of this book have shown the embedding of mid-Victorian fiction in a series of crises over sovereignty as well as the New Imperialism that arose to address them. A comparative history of France might emphasize how conquest in North Africa bolstered the July Monarchy (1830–1848), or might note the relative insignificance of settler colonies in an agricultural economy sustained by a well-ensconced peasantry and an industrial economy regulated by the state.[17] Historians have considered the various ways in which the large-scale emigration of British workers conduced toward a comparatively deradicalized metropolitan political culture. Moreover, in nineteenth-century France, as Balzac's novels attest, "state office, not capitalist accumulation was the most highly prized bourgeois career" (E. Wood, 121). These differences helped to shape a distinct novelistic culture: whereas British authors tended to mute or encode adultery, in France the topic was "worn out by repetition" as Baudelaire observed in his review of *Madame Bovary* (406). Under the same regime that perpetuated a 17-year-long war of conquest in Algeria to shore up its authority, adultery "became a powerful way of indicting" the government. Plots centering on adultery, illegitimacy, and divorce, writes Jann Matlock, provided "tools for political protest hitherto unimaginable as wielding such power" (345). This was the provenance for the fiction of Balzac, whom Collins described as "the deepest and truest observer of human nature whom France has produced since the time of Moliére" ("Portrait" 153).

As a naturalistic narrative of capitalist globalization which diverges from Balzac's *Bildungsromane*, *Madame Bovary* evokes the failed revolution of 1848 and the regime that followed when Louis Napoleon declared himself France's emperor.[18] The French Second Empire combined reactionary politics with expansionary policies that included "a vast program of infrastructural investment both at home and abroad." Modernizing French financial institutions in order to raise credit, Napoleon III helped to launch imperial projects such as the Suez Canal, while rebuilding the capital and creating "a whole new urban way of life" (D. Harvey, 7–8). The France of this period, according to Jacques Rancière, was "an unrelenting turmoil of thoughts and desires, appetites and frustrations"; its "social body" dissolved into the "hustle and bustle of free and equal individuals that were dragged together into a ceaseless whirl in search of . . . excitement" ("Why" 235). This was the "universe of commodities" which Walter Benjamin described in "Paris, Capital of the Nineteenth Century" (153)—a world of

---

[16] As Ward notes, the practitioners of so-called world history, though less beholden to nation-centric frameworks, are subject to the foibles of macro-analytic scale and economistic focal points (51).

[17] By contrast, the institution of agrarian capitalism in Britain helped to produce a surplus population of dispossessed and proletarianized workers which fueled industrialization on the one hand and colonial settlement on the other (see, for example, E. Wood, 92, 120–22).

[18] Although Flaubert excised the dates from his finished manuscript and omitted any reference to national politics, it is nonetheless clear that Emma's suicide coincides with the 1848 revolution (LaCapra, *Madame* 201).

speculative finance and fetishized objects which enters *Madame Bovary* through Monsieur Lheureux, the protean moneylender, salesman, and fashion maven. "No one knew what he had been formerly," Flaubert's narrator intones; "some said he was a peddler, others that he was a banker" (*Madame* 86). Although such remarks intimate that Lheureux may be a secret Jew, like Trollope's Lopez, in the end, this consummate figure of a post-heirloom social order is as much Emma's mentor as her nemesis: "We are no Jews," he tells her (87). A parody of what Benjamin called the *flâneur*, if not of the emperor himself, Emma purchases the latest goods on credit through financing she cannot reckon. To lay hold of hard cash, she "bargain[s] rapaciously" and borrows from her own maid. When she tries to calculate her finances, the results are so "staggering" she does not "believe they [are] possible" (226–7). By the end of the novel, her husband is ruined and her daughter is a proletarianized factory worker.

The "stranger-enemy" motifs and "violation of boundaries" in *Madame Bovary* thus speak directly to invented traditions and economic innovations on a transnational scale. Although Flaubert makes Emma herself the primary figure of exile, Zola (like Balzac before him) was more prone to rendering unassimilable otherness in Judaized form. As anti-Semitism and imperialism were depicted as "codependent orders in a single world system," writes Emily Apter ("Speculation" 401), the Judaized speculator became a naturalistic archetype on both sides of the channel. Real-life icons of Jewish power such as the Rothschilds incarnated "the dangerous cosmopolitanism of modern global capitalism," while Jews in general served as "lightning rods for critiques of France's incipient economic modernization" (Samuels 404–5). From this standpoint, the inscrutability of Emma's affairs (both financial and amorous), the "hermeneutic wormhole" that opens around Melmotte's speculation (Apter, "Speculation" 400), and the "epistemological emergency" created by Emily's marriage, mark unstable flux as the sign of a trans-channel geopolitical aesthetic in naturalistic form. Describing the British literature of this period, Raymond Williams points to the "country-house novel" which in Eliot's *Daniel Deronda* and in novels by Meredith and James becomes "the country-house not of land but of capital." In such fiction, "houses, parks and furniture are explicitly objects of consumption and exchange. People bargain, exploit and use each other ... Money from elsewhere is an explicit and dominant theme" (Williams, *Country* 249). This devastating penetration "from elsewhere" invades sovereignty at multiple levels, informing the signal motifs of the adulterous geopolitical aesthetic: commodified marriage, eroticized consumption, the collapse or cooptation of the heirloom's extra-economic value, and, not least, adulterous sex infused with the affects of racial contamination and existential exile.

Madame Bovary thus provides an illuminating comparison for British variations on the "dysphoric marriage plot"—including Trollope's naturalistic meditations on globality under Tory imperialism. Indeed, when Auerbach writes that the characters in Flaubert's fiction are isolated from a common community "so that no one can understand the other" and "no one can help the other to understanding" ("Serious" 430), he might be describing *The Eustace Diamonds* (1871-3) or *The Way We Live Now* (1874–5). The central theme of the latter novel is "the radical isolation or separateness of most of the characters" (Tanner, "Trollope's" 267). Hence, when Apter likens *Madame Bovary* to a species of business novel in lending "itself to being read as '*Kapital*, the novel'" ("Speculation" 388), she makes the kind of comparison between Marx and nineteenth-century fiction which has interested many Trollope scholars.[19] Like *The Way We Live Now*, *Madame Bovary* was part of a "literary world system of financial novels" which recorded "tectonic shifts in the identity of capitalism" (Apter, "Speculation" 399, 389).

That said, in Britain the business novel-*cum*-novel of adultery predated the advent of literary naturalism. In addition to the Indian rebellion, the Matrimonial Causes Act, and the arrival of *Madame Bovary*, the year 1857 brought the first financial crisis to follow the Limited Liability Act of 1855, a watershed that enabled speculators to gamble with borrowed capital and culminated in what historians have called "the first world-wide commercial crisis in the history of modern capitalism" (J. Hughes 194). But the speculative booms and busts that followed had been anticipated in the 1840s, when systematic loosening of trade restrictions sparked what Marx described as the "first great railway swindle" (qtd. in Bryer 441; cf. Poovey, *Making*, Ch. 8).[20] Thus, the first British literary expression of the emerging world system of financial novels was *Dombey and Son* (1846–8), a work that marks "Dickens's creation of a new kind of novel" (Williams, *Country* 154). To be sure, Edith Dombey's flight to a French hotel, where she joins her husband's business manager, stops short of consummated adultery.[21] Nonetheless, several features invite us to consider *Dealings with the Firm of Dombey and Son: Wholesale, Retail, and for Exportation* not only as a geopolitically acute business novel in which far-flung mercantile power provides "a structuring of consciousness" which informs the picture of metropolitan "upheaval" (Stewart 193), but also as a work that makes broken marriage intrinsic to its addled landscapes, alienated social relations, and stultified familial bonds. From this perspective, Edith's simulated adultery with Carker foreshadows Emily's disastrous misalliance, making Carker's "distressing" smile and superficial good looks the antecedents of Lopez's more emphatic cosmopolitan lack. Like Trollope's Judaized *homo economicus*, the feline Carker is carefully "buttoned up" and "dressed," his performative falseness concealed by a manner that is "deeply conceived and perfectly expressed" (*Dombey* 195). Although Carker stumbles to his death, while Lopez takes his own

---

[19] See, for example, Franklin; Hensley, "Mister"; and E. Michie, *Vulgar*, Ch. 3.

[20] J. Hughes argues that speculation was an even greater factor in the 1840s than it had been in 1857 but that the iconic status of the later crisis was the result of the "unprecedented" speed at which the catastrophe had spread thanks to the rapid communications facilitated by steam navigation and the telegraph. Within weeks a crisis that originated in New York had "paralysed" the "major industrial and commercial centres of the world" including London, Paris, "and other Continental centres . . . from Vienna to Stockholm" (194).

[21] Scholars have described this submission to "middle-class moral sensibilities" as a lamentable misstep in an otherwise cogent design. H. Stone attributes Dickens's last-minute detour from consummated adultery to the influence of John Forster (9). Notably, in *The Doctor's Wife* (1864), Braddon's homage to *Madame Bovary*, Isabel Gilbert not only reads novels "and dream[s] her dreams" like Flaubert's Emma, but also acts the part of "Edith Dombey before her looking glass" (156). For a recent study of Dickens in the context of divorce, see Hager.

life, both perish in scenes that portray the human body crushed by the railway—that modern "type of the triumphant monster, Death" (*Dombey* 311). As he falls into the path of an oncoming train, Carker is "beaten down, whirled away, and caught up on a jagged mill, that spun him round and round, and struck him limb from limb . . . and cast his mutilated fragments in the air" (842).

Thus, if Emily's marriage in *The Prime Minister* evokes the dramatic affects of an adulterous liaison, it is not because she is not lawfully wedded to the "nasty foreigner" who insinuated himself into her social circle (*Prime* 110), but because the law does not protect virtuous Anglo-Saxon maidens from the strangers adulterating the nation at large. Although Trollope's novel is the grimmer of the two, his clear debts to *Dombey and Son* illuminate how very far Dickens's tale of speculative commerce and marital breach is from what Moretti describes as "children's literature" (*Way* 185). We are reminded that Esther, the heroine of *Bleak House* (1852–3), is Lady Dedlock's illegitimate daughter; that *Hard Times* (1854) centers on the miserable marriage of Stephen Blackpool while staging Louisa's flight from another unbearable marriage to a businessman; that *Little Dorrit* (1855–7) pairs financial chicanery with illegitimate birth; that even *David Copperfield* (1849–50) includes Little Emily's ruin at the hands of Steerforth. If these novels do not wax naturalistic like Flaubert's or Trollope's it is not because they are hostage to English morals but because their often harrowing domestic realism is offset by alternative realms like the Wooden Midshipman's shop and the circus—"subjunctive" spaces rendered in a non-realist mode that purposely interrupts a more concerted focus on the "serious imitation of the everyday."[22]

The "development of the British novel between 1820 and 1880," Cohen writes suggestively, hinges on [the] paradox" that "international influences were formative" even in "the most nationalistic of eras" ("International" 409). Nonetheless, the internationalism advanced in *The Literary Channel* says little about the expanding capitalist and imperial matrix in which Anglo-French cultural encounters were immersed. The result is a critical practice that embellishes a nation-centric comparatism but, by and large, does not challenge it with the more thoroughgoing "worlding" of geopolitical analysis.[23] Cohen's chapter reprises a familiar binary, opposing Victorian realism (in which "characters retreat into their private spheres to practice their ethically sanctioned negative freedoms") to French realism which, in refusing to parse virtue, sustains tragic conflict and renders a "contemporary society utterly devoid of ethical force" ("Sentimental" 108, 123). From "the first-generation novels of Dickens and Thackeray to the second-generation

---

[22] As Duncan puts it, the elements of fairy-tale in British fiction (not only Dickens's but also that of Eliot, Hardy, and Scott) do not represent some "pupal shell the creature has failed to outgrow, but its living tissue of ethical, spiritual and ideological contention" (*Modern* 5). On R. Williams and the "subjunctive" novel, see Chapter 1.

[23] Apter's afterword describes the literary channel as "a zone of mutual refraction where Britain defines itself through its incongruent reflection of Frenchness, and vice versa." She imagines a "transnational sequel" that would also "take account of how colonialism and postcolonial theory have altered the shape of European studies" by asking questions that challenge the disciplinary assumptions "that grew out of national traditions" (286–87). My chapter offers one such sequel.

novels of Eliot and Anthony Trollope," she writes, "the need to follow the way of the world in principled fashion, adapting to manners without sacrificing morals, was," for British novelists, "a constant throughout" ("International" 415). Her analysis follows Moretti's in opposing the presumed closure of the "English 'family romance'" to transformative French narratives in which "meaning is not the result of a fulfilled teleology but of the total rejection of such a solution" (*Way* 7).

Of course, few nineteenth-century scholars would deny the impact of Victorian morality on the literature emanating from the English side of the channel. One finds the young Lewes, for example, upholding Balzac as a "One-eyed king" whose "great and peculiar talents" produce "masterpieces" sapped by the defects of "French spiritual existence at this present time" ("Continental" 463–4, 466). But does it follow that Victorian fiction is adequately grasped by comparative standpoints that hastily pronounce it to be juvenile, beholden to social convention, and silent on adultery? This question is especially salient for George Eliot, the mid-nineteenth century's most accomplished British realist. Paradoxically, despite and perhaps even because of her oft-asserted maturity, Eliot is the British author who suffers most from comparison to French contemporaries. That is true despite the fact that, as John Rignall argues in *George Eliot, European Novelist* (2011), Eliot was steeped in a "common intellectual culture" encompassing the Continent as well as Britain (11).[24] Then too from a biographical standpoint, the invention of "George Eliot" at a time when British critics had begun to express misgivings about self-censorship in an age of divorce, coincided with a union that censorious contemporaries did not hesitate to denounce as adultery.

The tendency to regard Eliot as a "Victorian" novelist—rather than, say, the co-creator of an adulterous geopolitical aesthetic that crossed the channel—is, thus, the result of longstanding habits of reading British fiction through invidious contrasts that date back to the late nineteenth century. In 1888, for example, Moore wrote that Balzac's "criticism of life" was "as profound as Thackeray's is trivial and insignificant, and as beautifully sincere and virile as Eliot's is canting and pedantic" (492).[25] Such contrasts were compounded when influential twentieth-century comparatists passed over Eliot entirely. The brief allusions in Auerbach's *Mimesis* to Dickens, Meredith, and Thackeray—though not Eliot—like its references to Henry Fielding but not Jane Austen—may signal a bias against nineteenth-century women writers. But according to Sharon Marcus it was the Victorian novel's "allegiance to moral norms" and the "fail[ure] to be

---

[24] As editor of *Westminster Review*, Eliot contributed to a publication that "kept up to date with the latest developments in art and literature, philosophy and history in France and Germany, Italy and Austria, and the smaller countries of Europe" (Rignall 11). This international outlook was crucial to Eliot's geopolitical imaginary even if Rignall at times overstates her refusal to "separate" British from Continental cultures (11). Virginia Woolf famously wrote that *Middlemarch* was "one of the few English novels written for grown-up people" (qtd. in Haight, *Century* 277); yet as Newton notes, Woolf's "admiration for Eliot as an artist was very qualified" (1).

[25] See also James's "The Art of Fiction" (1884), which argues that the "English novel" has "no air" of "a theory, a conviction, a consciousness of itself . . . of being the expression of an artistic faith" (502).

fully and consistently realist" which led Auerbach to omit it from his "history of literary realism" ("Comparative" 32). Of course, in the years since Harvey and Barbara Hardy helped to revitalize Eliot studies, Victorianists have often praised her works precisely for diverging from realist conventions which, by then, had become the target of poststructuralist critique. Hence, for my purposes, the question of whether British fiction qualifies as "realism" is largely terminological; the more pressing goal is an open-minded comparatism less invested in nation-centric generalizations and more attentive to the worlding of mid-nineteenth-century fiction of many kinds. For in isolating Eliot's works from substantive comparison to novels like *Madame Bovary*, scholars miss the experiments she undertook to shape her own (primarily non-naturalistic) variations on the adulterous geopolitical aesthetic.

THE HISTORICAL NOVEL OF OUR TIME

> [The] historical novel of our time . . . will by no means take the form of a simple renaissance, a simple affirmation of [the] classical traditions [of the past], but, if one will allow me this phrase from Hegel's terminology, a renewal in the form of a negation of a negation.
>
> George Lukács, *The Historical Novel* (1947)

> The finest [literary] effort to reanimate the past is of course only approximative—is always more or less an infusion of the modern spirit into the ancient form . . .
>
> George Eliot, "Silly Novels by Lady Novelists" (1856)

The genealogical starting point for my approach to Eliot "contra" *Madame Bovary* is Walter Scott, whose historical novels galvanized the early nineteenth century's fictional imaginary. According to Cohen, Scott is the "common forbear" from which "realism on both sides of the Channel developed" ("Internationalism" 417). Hence, while Ian Duncan makes Scott the crucial mediator between the Gothic and Dickens (*Modern*), Cohen stresses his importance as a precursor for Balzac. In his introduction to *La Comédie Humaine*, Balzac praised Scott as the first writer to make a drama about an entire society "interesting" (n.p.). Whereas Duncan highlights the persistence of romance forms, and Cohen stresses the realisms that emerged "independently" in France and Britain ("Internationalism" 417), both scholars agree that Scott's seminal fiction helped to usher in national consciousness. In Duncan's words, Scott rendered Scottishness "as the local and ancient archetype of a distinctive modern condition of being British: the subject of an imperial commercial nation state" (*Modern* 54–5).[26]

---

[26] Cultural nationalism is also the focal point for Trumpener's reading of Scott as one of several Romantic-era authors who merged bardic poetics with the national tale to create English-Celtic dialogue. Scott's impact was also transatlantic: Arac, e.g., points to James Fenimore Cooper as the "American Scott" (97).

That said, for Lukács, the energizing force of realist fiction is not nation-building per se, but historicity. Moreover, what Lukács means by historicity requires intact social structures comparable to the holistic ontology of the heirloom: that is to say, conditions conducive to rendering history as a transformative force to which all are subject. Lukács would doubtless confirm Duncan's belief that novels such as *Waverley* (1814) heal a "world torn apart by historical forces" through the restoration of an "extended patriarchal family" (*Modern* 105). But for Lukács, it is not so much the British nation that Scott's novels thereby rescue, as *the typicality of the characters* through whom history is expressed. *The Historical Novel* thus describes a border-crossing fiction whose geographical ambit ranges from the regional and national to the international and European.[27]

Moreover, Lukács's study is no simple elegy for Scott: it is a forward-looking account of literary innovation which anticipates "the historical novel of our time" (350). Balzac could inherit Scott's mantle, according to Lukács, because his richly sociological fiction illuminated an ongoing history. As an urbane realist with the heart of a *romancière,* Balzac recognized that "the problem of his own transition period" required a new genre to articulate "the emergence of modern France" by exchanging Scott's narratives of "*past history*" for narratives depicting "*the present as history*" (*Historical* 82–3). Yet, in describing this crucial engagement, Lukács privileged familiar terrain: "whole cultures which lay outside [his] personal interests and background" are simply absent from the book (Jameson, "Introduction" 3–4).

The Victorian Geopolitical Aesthetic has sought to redress this gap by exploring a number of correlatives for Scott and Balzac. Trollope's Barsetshire chronicles, I have argued, enlist comic irony and autoethnographic description to convey the Church of England's modest power to uphold a waning heirloom history through a clerical web that supports quotidian heroes such as Septimus Harding. In *Framley Parsonage* (1860–61), the fourth of the series, we find a hint of the would-be Rastignac in Mark Robarts's brush with a social-climbing set of "gamblers and adulterers" (82). A few years later, *Phineas Finn* (1867–8), the second of the Palliser novels, places a handsome Irishman at the center of a parliamentary *Bildungsroman* to express the changing complexion of the metropole. At about this time, Collins was experimenting with hybrid sensation genres that spoke to the forgotten histories behind the decade's recurring imperial crises (Ch. 5). Yet, according to Lukács, British literature after Scott lacked this vitalizing connection to history. Thackeray's nostalgic realism, he wrote, signaled "a deep and bitter disillusionment" with the present (*Historical* 201–2). *A Tale of Two Cities* (1859), a historical novel that culminates in "escape into bourgeois private life," exacerbated Dickens's "petty bourgeois humanism and idealism." Although Lukács recognized that Dickens's finest works were social novels in which ideals are offset "by reality," he nonetheless insisted that even this "great" artist

---

[27] Scott's synthetic "'middle way,'" writes Sanders, allows for a broad view which stretches panoramically from Scotland, through England, to Europe beyond" (9).

succumbed to the ahistoricism of a post-revolutionary epoch (*Historical* 243–4). Caught up in his own romance of 1848 as an epic fall whose tragic protagonist is Europe, Lukács could no more discern the notes of alterity in Dickens's "subjunctive," than recognize the 1840s as a mere starting point for Victorian fiction's keen "use of the historical imagination" to consider "the crises of [its] own immediate time" (Williams, *English* 13).

Lukács's neglect of Trollope and Collins can hardly surprise but his passing over Eliot is more noteworthy, as well as damaging to his account of European fiction. Like Collins's fascination with mixed-race characters, Trollope's globality emerged from an imperial imaginary that Lukács tends to overlook. But as Victorian Britain's premiere "European" author, Eliot's outlook was forged in the same republic of letters which concerns *The Historical Novel*. As a young woman, Marian Evans translated the works of David Strauss, Baruch Spinoza, and Ludwig Feuerbach. The detailed letters she wrote during her first trip to the Continent were like the preparation for writing "a Balzac novel" (Ashton, *Life* 70). In "The Natural History of German Life" (1856), she wrote that "a vital connection with the past is much more vividly felt on the Continent than in England, where . . . Protestantism and commerce have modernized the face of the land." Thus, in W. H. von Riehl's social ethnography and John Ruskin's study of the picturesque, Eliot perceived the "conception of European society as incarnate history" (283–4).

As a budding novelist, Eliot looked to Scott, Goethe, Sand, Balzac, and Stendhal for literary models.[28] Sand had been a favorite novelist since her twenties: "I should never dream of going to her writings as a moral code," she wrote to a disapproving friend, but "it is sufficient for me as a reason for bowing before her in eternal gratitude . . . that I cannot read six pages of hers without feeling that it is given to her to delineate human passion and its results" and even "some of the moral tendencies" with "such truthfulness" and "tragic power" that "one might live a century with nothing but one's own dull faculties and not know so much as those six pages will suggest" (qtd. in Haight, *George* 60).[29] And while both Eliot and Lewes expressed misgivings about Balzac's morality, they were enthusiastic readers: Lewes collaborated on translations and adaptations of Balzac's works and

---

[28] "By her own admission," notes Raleigh, "it was Scott who first unsettled" Eliot's "orthodoxy and started her on the way to agnosticism"—an author who provided the Victorians with a fictional world that intermingled public and private life as well as the insight that "history was . . . process, change, and metamorphosis" (27). Lewes's gift to Eliot in 1860, the year in which she began researching *Romola*, was a 48-volume set of the Waverley novels. He wrote on the fly-leaf, "To Marian Evans Lewes, The best of Novelists, and Wives, These works of her longest-venerated and best-loved Romanticist are given by her grateful Husband 1 January 1860" (Haight, *George* 319). In an 1871 letter to Alexander Main in which she lamented the misunderstanding of *Romola*'s historicity, Eliot likened her predicament to Scott's adding that "her worship for Scott" was "peculiar" since she began reading him as a 7-year-old child and, as a young adult, spent several years reading Scott's novels to her ailing father: "No other writer would serve as a substitute for Scott, and my life at that time would have been much more difficult without him" (Cross 111).

[29] Lewes also admired Sand whom, he wrote, "surpasses everything France has yet produced" in "the matter of eloquence" ("Lady Novelists" 136).

sent copies of *Illusions Perdues* (1837) and *Modeste Mignon* (1846) to Charlotte Brontë (Kendrick, "Balzac"). His 1847 review of *Le Cousin Pons* described Balzac as a "Dutch painter in prose"—foreshadowing the famous digression on "Dutch paintings" in *Adam Bede* ("Recent Novels" 695; Eliot, *Adam* 195). The Marian Evans who launched her literary career in 1856 was thus prepared in multiple ways to provide a "European" voice in British fiction—responsive to the same trans-channel conditions of possibility which gave rise to *Madame Bovary* in the very same year.

That Eliot should be drawn to the subject of adultery seems, in retrospect, all but inevitable. Her strong "opinions about marriage and divorce," writes Nancy Henry, long anticipated her career as a woman of letters (*Life* 95). According to Rosemary Bodenheimer, Evans's "rebirth" in Germany, where she and Lewes traveled in 1854 before disclosing their relationship, coincided with a newfound desire "to redefine 'woman' in more generous terms than Victorian England allowed" (*Real* 88). In one of the most telling essays from this period, "Woman in France," Evans describes the powerful impact of what she euphemistically calls "gallantry" on female character. In "France alone," she writes, "if the writings of women were swept away, a serious gap would be made in the national history" (41, 38). The seventeenth-century Frenchwoman endured marriages of convenience at age fifteen, followed by "a career of gallantry from twenty to eight-and-thirty" (41). Of course, the 34-year-old author of this account was nearing the close of her own "career" which had included the rejection of a marriage offer in her 20s, a close and possibly amorous relationship with John Chapman (publisher of the *Westminster Review*), an unrequited attraction to Herbert Spencer, and, finally, the "elopement" with Lewes (Bodenheimer, *Real* 86)—a man who could not divorce his wife without an embarrassing trial.[30]

In *The Woman and the Demon* (1982), Nina Auerbach suggests that the "role of the fallen woman" provided Evans with the "crucible in which" her "unpromising beginnings were forged into unprecedented triumphs" (183–4). Yet, as Bodenheimer counters, Eliot "felt she was not a fallen woman, and she knew that her culture defined her as one" (*Real* 86). Indeed, one may wonder if the melodramatic rhetoric of fallenness accurately captures Evans's social milieu after her introduction to Caroline and Charles Bray in 1841. A freethinking manufacturer, whose home served as a meeting place for "radical and liberal intellectuals and reformers," Bray and his family provided the young Evans with the educated dialogue she craved. As their intimate friend, Evans doubtless knew that Charles "kept a mistress and brought his illegitimate daughter home to be raised by his wife and his sister-in-law (Bodenheimer, "Woman" 24, 26). A decade later, when she became too close to Chapman ("a notorious philanderer" according to

---

[30] Eliot's trip to Germany with Lewes in 1854 was "an experiment in living together, and the couple did not call their union a marriage until much later." Many scholars cite the theory that Lewes could not divorce his wife because he had condoned her adultery with Thornton Leigh Hunt but, as Henry argues, what is certain is that none of the involved parties "wished to be dragged through the courts and into the public limelight" (*Life* 96, 101).

Haight), Evans found herself ejected from his domestic circle by the combined efforts of his wife and mistress, the family "governess" (Haight, *George* 86, 81). Lewes, meanwhile, was the legal father of his wife's children with Thornton Leigh Hunt and was himself the son of the "illegitimate second family of a father who disappeared from the scene after his birth" (Bodenheimer, "Woman" 27).[31] If, as Stephen put it, the same British public that scorned to read French fiction was, in actuality, "not so very immaculate," few young women were in a position to inhabit that reality as fully as Marian Evans.

In "The Morality of *Wilhelm Meister*" (1855), Evans argues that if Goethe's classic *Bildungsroman* "appears immoral to some minds," it is "because its morality has a grander orbit than any which can be measured by the calculations of the pulpit and of ordinary literature." In fact, Goethe's subtle handling of conduct exerts a more effective influence than would any explicit "intention to moralize" (129–30). By contrast, Balzac is "perhaps the most wonderful writer of fiction the world has ever seen," albeit one prone to excess: "He drags us by his magic force through scene after scene of unmitigated vice, till the effect of walking among this human carrion is a moral nausea" (131). While such remarks may seem to affirm Victorian prudery, the distinction between Goethe and Balzac is, in fact, highly nuanced. In a letter to Caroline Bray, Evans defended her adulterous union: "That any unworldly, unsuperstitious person who is sufficiently acquainted with the realities of life can pronounce my relation to Mr. Lewes immoral," she wrote (cognizant, perhaps, of addressing a woman who was raising her husband's illegitimate daughter), "I can only understand by remembering how subtle and complex are the influences that mould opinion." "Light and easily broken ties," she continued, "are what I neither desire theoretically nor could live for practically. Women who are satisfied with such ties do *not* act as I have done—they obtain what they desire and are still invited to dinner" (qtd. in Haight, *George* 190). In other words, if Evans had sought the kind of casual affair of which one might read in Balzac, she could have conducted it discreetly and eluded public censure. Instead she was paying the price for a very different order of relationship. At stake in the letter was the distinction between the "unmitigated vice" of Balzac's characters and a principled decision to enter a union, the morality of which could not be "measured by the calculations of the pulpit and of ordinary literature."

But if a literature depicting such "realities" could not be "ordinary," there should be such a literature, nevertheless. In an 1853 essay that is "probably" Evans's according to Haight, the reviewer calls on the young Collins to consult *The Scarlet Letter* in order "to learn how adultery may be treated so that 'the most pure need not turn away'" (qtd. in Stang 956). Such remarks index a desire to make novels of adultery an object of writerly care. Hence, according to Richard Stang, Eliot rejected "the idea that only certain subjects were fit for art" (956).

---

[31] Questions had been raised in 1853 about Eliot's brief "emotional intimacy" with Dr. Robert Brabant, resulting in her "early departure" from her "long visit" with this older married man. Bodenheimer describes the relationship with Chapman as a "brief encounter—quite possibly a sexual affair" ("Woman" 27).

Asked by her publisher to provide a sketch of *Adam Bede*, she refused "on the ground that I would not have it judged apart from my *treatment,* which alone determines the moral quality of art" (qtd. in Stang 956). This is the kind of argument which had exonerated Flaubert during the trial of *Madame Bovary*.

"Woman in France" thus bears a palpable biographical and aesthetic freight. It is, Evans writes, "undeniable"

> that unions formed in the maturity of thought and feeling, and grounded only on inherent fitness and mutual attraction, tended to bring women into more intelligent sympathy with men, and to heighten and complicate their share in the political drama. The quiescence and security of the conjugal relation, are doubtless favourable to the manifestation of the highest qualities by persons who have already attained a high standard of culture, but rarely foster a passion sufficient to rouse all the faculties to aid in winning or retaining its beloved object—to convert indolence into activity, indifference into ardent partisanship, dullness into perspicuity. Gallantry and intrigue are sorry enough things in themselves, but they certainly serve better to arouse the dormant faculties of woman than embroidery and domestic drudgery (41).

English domesticity, Evans seems to say, stifles wifely culture: "The quiescence and security of the conjugal relation" not only fail "to rouse all the faculties," they also fail to bring most "women into . . . intelligent sympathy with men" or to "heighten" their share of "political drama." In contrast to *The Saturday Review*'s advocacy of a literature for men, Evans thus proffers extra-marital "unions" as an alternative to female torpor and literary stagnation.

Yet, according to Cohen, Eliot ultimately typifies capitulation to British norms. Early works such as *The Mill on the Floss* demonstrate the impact of French sentimentalism: Maggie Tulliver in particular fits the Sandian "type of unconventional, passionate, dark-haired women destined for romantic tragedy." By pitting "private happiness against social duty" such works evoke the tragic double-bind of Sophocles' *Antigone* (Cohen, "Internationalism"414, 412–13; cf. "Flaubert" 751). Yet, by the time she wrote *Middlemarch* and *Daniel Deronda*, Cohen contends, Eliot's once agonistic fiction conformed to characteristically British forms of "compromise"—aligning "emotional and spiritual maturation" with "adaptation [to] the norms and expectations of society" ("Internationalism" 415). Notably, Cohen ignores *Romola*, a work that seeks to renovate Scott's genre through a heroine explicitly likened to Antigone.[32] Moreover, though Cohen is one of the foremost scholars of Flaubert, she never mentions him in her discussion of the Anglo-French literary channel.

By contrast, Rignall devotes an entire chapter to comparing *Madame Bovary* and *Middlemarch*—two works that center at least partly on "The Doctor's Wife" (to borrow the title of Mary Elizabeth Braddon's bowdlerized knock-off of

---

[32] Antigone, "one of the chief images" in *Romola* according to Bonaparte, was "a figure Eliot had long admired . . . Eliot knew no Greek playwright better" than Sophocles and was "moved most deeply by *Antigone*, which she had first read in December 1855"—a few months before her 1856 essay on the topic for the *Leader* (74–5).

Flaubert's novel from 1864).[33] As near contemporaries, he notes, Flaubert and Eliot "achieved fame in the late 1850s with novels of provincial life" (*Madame Bovary* and *Adam Bede*), "devoted themselves to laborious reconstructions of the distant past in exactly contemporaneous historical novels" (*Salammbô* [1862] and *Romola*), and "turned to very different versions of the Bildungsroman in their final novels" (*L'Education sentimentale* [1869] and *Daniel Deronda*) (86).

Although scholars agree that Flaubert probably never read Eliot, the latter's familiarity with Flaubert is less certain. Copies of *Madame Bovary* and *Salammbô* were listed on the inventory of books drawn up by Lewes's granddaughter (Rignall 86). And while there are references to Lewes's buying *Salammbô* in 1869 and to the couple's reading *L'Education sentimentale* while Eliot was working on *Daniel Deronda*, neither Lewes nor Eliot made any reference to *Madame Bovary*. Is it likely, however, that Eliot never looked at the controversial work by a "singularly powerful writer" which Meredith recommended when he took over her position as the "Belles Lettres" reviewer? And would she and Lewes have looked at Flaubert's later works without reading the novel that had brought him fame and notoriety?

Whereas Flaubert depicted modernity as a "disabling loss of boundaries," notes Rignall, Eliot saw boundary-crossings as opportunities to generate "fellow-feeling and beneficent human solidarity" (87, 91) Rignall thus highlights the difference between rooted cosmopolitanism and deracinated flux, demonstrating how Flaubert's naturalistic innovations erode the deep social connectivity that courses through Lukácsian genres such as epic and historical romance. But Rignall also refuses a reductive antithesis between realism and idealism, atomism and holism, French and British fiction. He notes, for example, how variations on Emma's quixotic imaginary infect multiple characters in *Middlemarch*: Dorothea's experience in Rome evokes an overwhelming "sublime" (94; cf. Hertz 34–41) and Lydgate's excitement in "playing billiards for money," "a kind of *bovarysme*" (97).

Like Rignall, I do not insist that *Madame Bovary* directly influenced Eliot; but I do contend that she was alert to the strengths and limitations of naturalism—a realist modality already latent in Balzac. The "moral nausea" she sought to mitigate was no simple aversion to adultery; rather, Eliot's investment in the "moral quality of art" was as much to do with art as morality. Deeply influenced by the same German materialism from which Lukács's Marxism derives, Eliot deemed the quality of art to be inextricable from its capacity to capture social movement. The historical conditions she engaged brought forth variations on the adulterous geopolitical aesthetic from Dickens, Flaubert, Meredith, Trollope and, later, James, Tolstoy, and Hardy. But in negotiating this terrain, Eliot anticipated *The Historical Novel* to a greater extent than any other Victorian-era novelist.

---

[33] Rignall rightly describes Heywood's early effort to link Eliot to Flaubert through Braddon's novel ("A Source") as "far fetched" (86). But as Smalley notes in her book-length study of Flaubert and Eliot, both authors "focus on the intimate patterns of the inner life of their characters with an emphasis unknown in the novelists that preceded them." Moreover, the subtitle of *Madame Bovary*—"*Moeurs de Province*"—adumbrates that of Eliot's *Middlemarch*, "Study of Provincial Life" (1, 3). Smalley's oscillation between chapters on Flaubert and on Eliot diminishes its comparative

By comparison, Dickens takes the condition of England for his ambit, Flaubert explores the isolated subject's desire for art, and Trollope records the devastation of an heirloom sovereignty invaded by empire and global capital. Only Eliot anticipates Lukács's determination to mediate all of these conditions from the standpoint of a realist literature emanating from Europe's republic of letters. As Eliot herself put it, the historical novel should entail "an infusion of the modern spirit" and, in doing so, bear out Goethe's insight into (what Lukács called) the typical character: "What you call the spirit of the age is at bottom the gentlemen's own spirit, in which the age is mirrored" (qtd. in Eliot, "Silly" 316–17).[34]

Eliot's early novels exemplify this historicism through pastoral evocations of the past.[35] Although *The Mill on the Floss* is often "taken to mark the end of the bildungsroman's 'classic' phase" (Esty, *Unseasonable* 26), Book IV opens with an excursus in which the narrator transplants her story outside the "classic" alignment of individual and nation. As she invites her readers to "journey down the Rhône" and contemplate the "ruins on the castled Rhine" (*Mill* 361), Eliot's narrator enacts the "effort of memory and reflection" necessary to recall the "conception of European society as incarnate history" to the English mind ("Natural" 283–4). The novel thus creates a historicizing standpoint in which aesthetics and genre play decisive roles. Unlike the "commonplace" relics of a "vulgar" modernity, the ruins of the Rhine evoke a Scott tableau: "a time of colour," "adventure," and "fierce struggle." Whereas the crumbling castle forms part of "the grand historic life of humanity," the "dead-tinted ... angular skeletons of villages on the Rhône oppress [us] with the feeling" that much of "human life" is a "narrow" existence that "even calamity does not elevate." Heirloom ruins thus retain their power to signify, while "dead-tinted" villages are the inchoate stuff of a naturalistic world. The paragraph closes with the "cruel" possibility that this cast-down modernity is irrecoverably exiled from history (361–2).

But instead Eliot upholds new novelistic forms to rescue latter-day lifeworlds from "oblivion." "It is a sordid life, you say, this of the Tullivers and Dodsons, irradiated by no sublime principles." The reader may, thus, be "irritated" with "these dull men and women" who seem "out of keeping with the earth on which they live." *But*—the narrator protests—it is "*necessary that we should feel*" this "*oppressive narrowness,*" "*if we care to understand how it acted on the lives of Tom and Maggie,—how it has acted on young natures in many generations*" (emphasis added). "[W]e need not shrink from" the "comparison of small things with great," since there is "nothing petty to the mind that has a large vision of relations" (362–3).

---

standpoint. Leckie, who focuses on adultery and sensation fiction, regards *Madame Bovary* as everything "the English novel is not" (34).

[34] I use the translation of this quotation from Part I of Goethe's *Faust* given in the notes to Eliot, *Selected Critical Writings* 379; the actual quotation is "Was irh den Geist der Zeiten heist,/Das ist im Grund der Herren eigner Geist,/In dem die Zeiten sich bespiegeln."

[35] See also Coundouriotis who argues that *Adam Bede* complicates the dominant historiographic mode of Macaulay's *History of England* (1848), "fractur[ing]" his "narrative of progress" and "pit[ting] contradictory historical explanations against each other" (286).

As Cohen avers, *The Mill on the Floss* ends in the tragic mode of sentimental fiction: "I desire no future that will break the ties of the past," says Maggie to Philip, the friend who shares her passion for Scott and de Staël (*Mill* 564). Reproducing the fateful split between public and private duties, Eliot depicts a figurative adultery in which Maggie "carries away" her cousin's lover like the "dark woman" of a romance (433). The modern genre she adumbrates does not seek a compromise with "oppressive narrowness" but, rather, a gauge of its historicity. Hence, according to John McGowan, Eliot turned to historical fiction after *The Mill on the Floss* to explore the social processes through which the "cultural contents" of a realist literature come into being (182–3, cf. Carroll, *Conflict*, Ch. 4). Such fiction communicates the particulars of a "humanly constructed" reality "so [that] a community might act upon" them (McGowan 183). Realism of this kind substitutes "the logic and texture" a moving process for static "pictures of a persisting form" (Shaw, *Narrating* 99–100).

In taking up *Romola*, Eliot turned from the "prosaic" life of rural England to a "time of colour" in Florentine history (*Mill* 361–2). In doing so, she drew on genres familiar to the readers of Scott and Sand. With its strong female protagonist and tacit address to Italy's Risorgimento, *Romola* infuses "the modern spirit into the ancient form" in order to craft a historical novel of its time. Yet, as the editors of a recent collection observe, *Romola* was "a problem text for its nineteenth-century readers" which "has encountered difficulties in the twentieth century for a rather different set of reasons" (C. Levine and Turner 2). At the same time, *Romola* is the least naturalistic of Eliot's novels and may, thus, seem remote from "adulterous" narratives that combine speculative commerce and broken domesticity with serious imitation. Nonetheless, we should not hasten to juxtapose an Eliot (allegedly) invested in compromise to a Flaubert so consummately devoted to art that he eclipsed history entirely. In fact, Flaubert turned to historical fiction for much the same reasons Eliot did: because of his keen "sensitivity to the relativity of historical truth and his awareness of its contribution to a fuller understanding of the present" (A. Green 16). Despite the formal differences that clearly distinguish them, both authors set out to write the "historical novel of our time"; and both offered versions of that project using temporally proximate and distant settings. In describing *Romola* "contra" *Madame Bovary*, my goal is to explore two distinct variations on an adulterous geopolitical aesthetic that crossed the literary channel and beyond.

ROMOLA *CONTRA* MADAME BOVARY

> What strikes me as beautiful, what I would like to write, would be a book about nothing, a book without any external connection, which would be held together by the external strength of its style, just as the earth, suspended in the void, depends on nothing external for its support . . .
>
> Gustave Flaubert, Letter to Louise Colet, January 16, 1852

> For those who come upon Flaubert's book, Emma Bovary is the frightening incarnation of [the democratization of] desire . . . She constantly negotiates

between material and ideal sources of excitement . . . A critic [from 1859] sums it up as follows: "Madame Bovary, this means the pathological overexcitement of senses and imagination in dissatisfied democracy"

Jacques Rancière "Why Emma Bovary Had to Be Killed" (2008)

What has become alien to men is the human component of culture, its closest part, which upholds them against the world. They make common cause with the world against themselves, and the most alienated condition of all, the omnipresence of commodities, their own conversion into appendages of machinery, is for them a mirage of closeness.

Theodor Adorno, *Minima Moralia* (1951)

Like Scott, Sand is a crucial reference point for the formal experiments of Eliot and Flaubert. Consider the role that Sand plays in Cohen's nuanced discussion of "Flaubert's bid for literary prestige" ("Flaubert" 749) in an analysis informed partly by Pierre Bourdieu's *The Rules of Art* (1996). In France, Cohen explains, the fictional imaginary of the early nineteenth century had been dominated by the female sentimental novelists who were Scott's contemporaries and Sand's precursors. When male realists such as Balzac and Stendhal came to the fore after 1830, they disparaged "the sentimental fantasies of lady readers" in an "aggressive" bid to "masculinize the novel." *Madame Bovary* built on this masculinist "attack" by tying Emma's escapism to her "unwholesome" consumption of feminine literature (Cohen, "Flaubert" 750; cf. *Sentimental*). Yet, in describing the latter, Flaubert omitted the sentimental novels of adultery which had anticipated Balzac's fiction and his own. This determination to "kill even the memory of the sentimental legacy," Cohen argues, was motivated by Flaubert's need to distinguish his work from realism (755)—to create an anti-sentimental stance that helped him transcend the "morality of compromise" and enunciate a new "aesthetic of undecidability" (757).[36]

I will return to the question of gender but, for the moment, I want to emphasize how Cohen's reading of *Madame Bovary* elevates the proto-Modernist masterpiece over the realist text embedded in the Second Empire. Although such treatments of Flaubert as an "epochal" "hero of modernity, modernism, or postmodernism" are widespread (Amann 215), they reinforce the problematic tendency to postulate Modernism as a radical break from the aestheticisms of the past. Such Modernist exceptionalism (as Raymond Williams argued in the 1980s) promulgates "a highly selective version of the modern which then offers to appropriate the whole of modernity," as though Modernism alone articulated a fitting aesthetic response to the modern condition (*Politics* 33).[37]

---

[36] Flaubert admired Sand, but, according to Cohen, he identified her works with male forms of realism instead of portraying her as the creator of a new "genre of sentimental social fiction" ("Flaubert" 755).

[37] Bourdieu argues that this tendency derives from the Modernist's bid for aesthetic "autonomy"—an invented form of cultural power which strives to transform economic powerlessness into voluntary "renunciation" through a cult of artistic disinterestedness (*Rules* 28).

In "Why Emma Bovary Had to Be Killed" (2008), Jacques Rancière sets out to solve this problem by affirming art's potential to constitute equalitarian political effects.[38] But his theory never fully explains how art sustains its tenuous autonomy, or even how it circumvents the kind of bourgeois-sanctioned cultural capital described by Bourdieu. To be sure, Rancière describes Flaubert's milieu at length. Atomized and leveled by revolution, industrialization, and new modes of consumption, the French Second Empire was a scene of "anarchic excitement" (235) comparable to the incoherent "*Erlebnis*" discussed in Chapter 5. Thus, while Napoleon III could stamp out political unrest, his regime was powerless to curb "the multitude of aspirations and desires" which "modern society" engendered. This was not merely desire for "all the things that gold can buy, but also" and, indeed, worse, for "all that gold cannot buy—passions, values, ideals, art, and literature" (236). Rancière here discerns an emancipated multitude whose most ardent yearning is for the extra-economic forms of value which democracy destroyed when it mowed down the hierarchies of the *ancien régime*. Flaubert's novel speaks to this dilemma by depicting a condition of "pathological overexcitement" which, like Emma Bovary, cannot distinguish between "the material enjoyment of material goods and the spiritual enjoyment of art, literature, and ideals" (235).

Although Rancière is not especially interested in adultery, his analysis nonetheless shows how in a world in which "anybody can exchange any desire for any other desire" (236), extra-marital sex becomes symptomatic of a larger problem for bourgeois morality. This is not the exposure of marriage as a bankrupt institution that requires the compensations of adulterous love (a task that Sand and Balzac had already achieved), but the more *bovaryesque* revelation that the satisfactions of adulterous love are not especially different than those of purchasing a chic riding habit or new set of curtains. Rancière's concern is how such leveling of desire threatens art. In contrast to the art regimes of the past, he writes, the "new art of writing" which *Madame Bovary* exemplifies "blurs the distinction between the realm of poetry and the realm of prosaic life" by making *any* subject matter equal to any other from the standpoint of art (237).

It is important to recognize that while Rancière singles out Flaubert, the democratization of literature's subject matter was an important feature of realist fiction in general. Balzac persistently blurred the boundaries of high and low; and when the narrator of *The Mill on the Floss* insists that readers encounter "oppressive

---

[38] This effort to enlist art and literature on behalf of progressive politics has been especially welcome at a time when the limitations of a rigid critical suspicion have become clear. For a concise introduction to Rancière's project, see *The Politics of Aesthetics* (2006) which elaborates how an "aesthetic regime of art" which dissolved older artistic hierarchies, bears the potential to achieve comparable equalizing effects in the political realm. According to Rancière, "Man is a political animal because he is a literary animal who lets himself be diverted from his 'natural' purpose by the power of words." Such "*literarity*" has the power to "introduce lines of fracture and disincorporation into imaginary collective bodies." Those in power thus rightly fear the potential of literature to modify "the sensory perception of what is common to the community"; to help form "political subjects that challenge the given distribution of the sensible" (*Politics* 39–40).

narrowness" so as to grasp its impact, she too makes the case for a "new art of writing." Indeed, Rancière's analysis illuminates Eliot's *oeuvre* in noting that the old aesthetic regimes had divided society into an artistic realm of "action" and a prosaic realm of "life" occupied by "people—mostly women—who were satisfied with living, reproducing life, and looking after their living" ("Why" 237). Such deep-seated gendering enabled novelists like Eliot to transform masculinist genres by introducing female characters into conventionally male roles. Hence, in *Romola*, Eliot invents a female variation on the typical character—the kind of role Scott assigned to male every-men such as Waverley and Ivanhoe.

None of this, however, is discernible in Rancière's account of nineteenth-century fiction. When Balzac confronted the problem of democracy, Rancière notes, he "was above all concerned with the social aspect of the question" ("Why" 238). But because Rancière's subject is Flaubert, and because Flaubert, in his view, cares only for art, Rancière insists that literature after *Madame Bovary* must dispense with "the social aspect." The central post-Flaubertian concern, he contends, is to restore the distinction between "Art" and "nonartistic life" (238). That is, since Emma conflates "Art" with everything from the tropes of hackneyed fiction and the pleasures of extra-marital sex to the possession of a new blotting pad, Flaubert must distinguish between the powerful aestheticism articulated in his novel and the failed aestheticism of Emma's *bovarysme*. Flaubert achieves this end, according to Rancière, by confining "Art" to the words on the page—not in the poststructuralist sense that insists on the priority of language but in a particular Modernist sense that insists that what is artistic in literature is primarily a question of *style* (241). What Flaubert's art categorically is *not*, on this view, is "an aestheticization of life" ("Why" 240).

Of course, Rancière is hardly the first to name style as the crux of Flaubert's achievement—a view the author himself encouraged in his letters to Louise Colet. Interpretations of *Madame Bovary* as an "autotelic structure almost without subject" have flourished ever since the judge's ruling affirmed the defense of Flaubert's novel as an autonomous work of art (Culler 685 cf. Ferguson 100). That said, the exceptionality Rancière claims for Flaubert is highly selective. Whereas Cohen merely regards him as the first to reject realism's "compromise" with the world in favor of a malleable "aesthetic of undecidability" (thus pointing both to Modernist and postmodern aestheticisms), Rancière makes Flaubert the arbiter of a particular artistic vision that distinguishes itself from "Aestheticism." The "war of Art versus Aestheticism," he postulates, seeks to protect art from the decadence that threatens artistic autonomy ("Why" 239; cf. Bourdieu, *Rules*).[39]

---

[39] As Foucault argued in "What is Enlightenment?" (1984), Baudelaire's dandy is the model for a capacious aesthetics of the self: an ironic "will to 'heroize' the present" premised on a cultivated determination to "make of [one's] body, [one's] behavior, [one's] feelings and passions, [one's] very existence, a work of art" (40, 41–2). On Rancière's reading, such *dandysme* either is, or risks becoming, *bovarysme*—a promiscuous pursuit of art outside of the "enclosed" artwork ("What" 241). Hence, Art's "war" against Aestheticism is "not only a question of preserving Art from vulgar people" such as Emma, but also "of preserving it from refined people" such as Des Esseintes (Rancière, "Why" 240), the aesthete at the center of Joris-Karl Huysmans's *À Rebours* (1884).

In doing so, I contend, Rancière grants a victory to "the pure artist" which is profoundly pyrrhic ("Why" 239). For it entails an absolute break not only with the aesthetics of the self (in the trajectory leading from Baudelaire, Nietzsche, and Wilde onto Foucault), but also with any literature that foregrounds the "social aspect of the question"—the very aspect that, from Balzac's moment to the present, becomes ever more perceptibly global in scale. In contrast to social fiction, Rancière argues, *Madame Bovary* "deals with what" Adorno "will spell out as the problem of kitsch." "Kitsch" writes Rancière, "means art incorporated into anybody's life, art become part of the scenery and the furnishings of everyday life" ("Why" 240).

But this is a mischaracterization of Adorno, whose definition of kitsch does not support the exclusion of realist literature from an account of art after Flaubert. So far from kitsch entailing art's entry into "the furnishings of everyday life"—as though an "Art" carefully insulated against this seepage could lay claim to the status of "antikitsch manifesto" ("Why" 240)—kitsch, for Adorno, stands for something integral to art which haunts it most keenly precisely when "Art" seeks to disavow it. "In the end," writes Adorno, "indignation over kitsch is anger at its shameless reveling in the joy of imitation" even while art's "power . . . continues to be secretly nourished by imitation." Kitsch "incurs hostility because it blurts out the secret of art" (*Minima* 225–6). Such writings on kitsch, which turn on the irreducible dialectic of the beautiful and the ugly (Adorno, *Aesthetic* 47–8), contest Rancière's vision of an impersonal style that enables the author to inoculate his art against the "shameless reveling" of his character. Indeed, far truer to Adorno's idea than a Flaubert who kills his character to save his art, is the Flaubert who famously (if, perhaps, apocryphally) asserts, "*Madame Bovary c'est moi.*"

Whereas Rancière gives us a Flaubert who proclaims his antikitsch manifesto at the expense of Emma's vulgarity, Adorno suggests a *Madame Bovary* that is "secretly nourished" by Emma's blotting pads (and Rodolphe's clichéd love notes, Binet's wooden replicas, and so on). Flaubert himself seemed to recognize that his dream of stylistic transcendence could not alter the fact of an art reliant on imitation any more than Emma's fantasies of adultery could elude "the platitudes of marriage" (*Madame* 231). The fullest expression of this irony is the "cracked cauldron" of language which condemns humanity to "beat out tunes to set a bear dancing when we would make the stars weep with our melodies" (154). As Naomi Schor writes, this famous passage encapsulates the fundamental paradox of the literary artist: "how does one give an individual charge to words used by all?" (*Breaking* 11). Clearly, Flaubert could no more "kill" the problem of the artwork's relation to everyday life than he could kill the "human tongue" on which his novel depends (*Madame* 154).

In emphasizing the mimesis that "nourishes" art, I am, of course, returning to Auerbach's "serious imitation of the everyday"—a standpoint that does not pit *Madame Bovary*'s style against its naturalism or historicity. That is not to deny Flaubert's influence as a stylist who inspired Modernist and postmodern alternatives to the realist novel. It is merely to recall that *Madame Bovary* is the product of nineteenth-century conditions of possibility and—as I contend—a powerful expression of the adulterous geopolitical aesthetic. As a naturalistic narrative of capitalist globalization which takes adulterous breach for its motive and "impersonality" for its mode, *Madame Bovary* is, thus, simultaneously "the indisputable realist novel" of Peter Brooks's reading (*Realist* 69) and the harbinger of a crisis of realism which arguably persists today. Notably, then, though Lukács (rightly) designates Flaubert as a naturalist, he persistently depicts him as the author of *Salammbô*, not *Madame Bovary*—a failed historical novelist, rather than an author who strove to illuminate "the *present as history*."

In *Importing "Madame Bovary"* (2006), Elizabeth Amann reclaims the nineteenth-century textures of Flaubert's novel with a sophisticated focus on genre. Like Marx's opposition of tragedy and farce in *The Eighteenth Brumaire of Louis Napoleon* (1852), the two-part structure of Emma's affairs, she writes, contrasts the "revolutionary vision of 1789 to its degradation in 1848"; that is, a sentimental narrative of the romance with Rodolphe versus a bourgeois novel of adultery emphasizing Emma's death and Léon's maturation (236–7). According to Schor, realism is "that paradoxical moment in Western literature when representation can neither accommodate the Otherness of Woman nor exist without it" (*Breaking* xi). And while Brooks acknowledges that the "preoccupation with language" may cast doubt on Flaubert's realism, he concludes that the claim is "ratified" by the novel's "investment in the things of the world" (*Realist* 69). Flaubert's realism is thus confirmed by such concrete manifestations of historicity as genre-bending, gender-bending, and immersion in "the things of the world."[40]

It is worth remarking, that Shaw, whose *Narrating Reality* (1999) makes a powerful case for the historicity of British realism, holds to a quintessentially Lukácsian judgment on Flaubert. Working closely to Auerbach, Shaw defines realism as a form that engages the structures that "confer reality" on the contingent particulars of history. Though realism comes in many varieties, its singular strength is the "dynamic metonymy" that, without ever representing "the world 'directly,'" conveys some sense of what it is "really like" (94–5). Hence, while Modernism's refuge is autotelic style, realism's is the world-disclosing potential of metonymy: by "forg[ing] connections between the disparate elements of a reality seen as radically historical," the realist novel strives "to place the reader in a fruitful relationship with the tentative totalities it creates" (98). Yet, like Jameson and Lukács, Shaw identifies Flaubert as a problematic case. The "grave limitations" of Flaubert's fiction include "the lack of any narrative issue to the lives of the characters, the lack of any 'common world' of intelligence that they might share, [and] the lack of clear connections between characters and the historical stream" (96). In *The Political Unconscious*, Jameson describes "*bovarysme*" as a "congealment

---

[40] Compare to E. Auerbach: Flaubert's "change in the imitative practice of art" would not have been possible "if the objects treated by him were not to be encountered in the world of his time" (Auerbach, "Serious" 435). Flaubert's commitment to the fidelity of language facilitated an "impartial, impersonal, and objective" style in contrast to the Balzacian realism that injected the author's "fiery" temperament into the narrator's personality (Auerbach, *Mimesis* 482). Such innovation was the "imprint" of a particular naturalistic condition: the "extenuation" of an "unrelenting" historical situation "whose motion . . . is almost imperceptible" (Auerbach, "Serious" 435, 448).

of language, fantasy and desire" which "transmutes Balzacian longing" into "cliché" and "tawdriness" (159). Jameson thus returns us to the "cracked cauldron" of language and finds vulgar reification in place of either "serious" metonymy or autotelic style. In doing so, he reproduces Lukács's tendency to conflate the ironic and aestheticized naturalism of *Madame Bovary* with scientistic "mirroring" (*Essays* 93).

Yet, there are moments when even Lukács seems to acknowledge that Flaubert, like Balzac before him, created a new realist genre. Describing the anachronistic Salammbô, Lukács contrasts her to Emma, whose plight as a "stranger" to "provincial life" corresponds "to the real, social-historical character of emotion and desire" (*Historical* 189–90). Emma, in other words, speaks both to the Otherness of Woman and the position of exile in a transforming world. The "hero" of epic form, according to Lukács, is "life itself" and, in Scott's romances, events "over-shadow human personality" (*Historical* 35). From this Lukacsian vantage, Flaubert's Emma might perhaps be the very *ne plus ultra* of the modern subject overshadowed by "life itself."[41]

Why is it, then, that the prospect of Emma as typical character strikes so many readers as the sign of a literature adrift? For an answer we might return to Henry James's demurrals. The "dignity" of *Madame Bovary*'s "substance," James wrote in his preface, cannot be separated from the diminished "dignity of [Emma] herself as a vessel of experience"; yet, the "triumph of the book" is that Emma interests readers not for her "consciousness," but for "the reality and beauty" of its depiction—a depiction that not only "represent[s] *her* state," but also "the state, actual or potential, of all persons like her" ("Gustave" 413–14). Paradoxically, Emma's greatness inheres in the typicality that her "small" character commands. For Auerbach, such "lack of tragic dignity" was inseparable from the "gravity of being caught up in history's workings" ("Serious" 448). More "Victorian" than he liked to admit, James, by contrast, pondered whether Flaubert's style was not fatally lacking in that quality of being "at home in the moral world" which he appreciated in a lesser artist such as Trollope ("Anthony" 124; cf. "Flaubert's" 366). James's concluding series of questions thus suggests genuine perplexity: Why did Flaubert choose such "abject human specimens?" Why did he imagine "nothing better for his purpose than such . . . limited reflectors and registers?" (415).

In the century of literary criticism since James's questions, scholars have often focused on narrative technique. Culler, for example, argues that critics must resist the temptation to interpret Flaubert's ambiguous narration as though it were mediated by a "perceiving character" in the mode of James (690–91). James's intense focus on particular characters projects a heightened significance onto their experience—a "new plenitude" to replace the absent center in Flaubert (Brooks, *Melodramatic* 200). By contrast, Flaubert obscures the question of "who sees or who speaks" and manipulates temporality so as to produce a "surreal, hallucinatory

---

[41] Flaubert's excision of dates from his novel thus marks a style of historicity which enhances the existential temporality that has prompted scholars to claim that Emma "suffers from the quintessential malady of modernity, the inability to incorporate time into experience" (Marder 131).

effect" (Culler 694–5). Flaubert thus actualizes his dream of a novel about "nothing" through self-effacing narration, hypertrophied objects, and characters whose flat typicality is the very opposite of James's auratic "reflectors."

While such form may seem too stifling to compass a moving history, this very risk intensifies the naturalistic effect. As we have seen, Flaubert mutes the tendency of contemporaneous financial narratives to Judaize the threat of lost sovereignty and "money from elsewhere," instead making Emma herself the focal point of modern exile. The leveled spirituality Rancière describes marks the absolute collapse of the heirloom; yet, "pathological overexcitement" does not produce indiscriminate desire so much as discriminate desire for *adultery*—for experience beyond the sanctioned pleasures of bourgeois domesticity. Madame Bovary's iconic position as woman and wife is, thus, crucial: for while the adulterous geopolitical aesthetic recognizes sovereign breach as a universal condition, nineteenth-century morality constructed the sin of adultery as archetypally female. Novels of female adultery thus figure the comeuppance of a modernity that only claimed to constitute "free and equal individuals" while, in actuality, propagating naturalized differences such as the bourgeois woman's supposed care for "life" (Rancière, "Why" 235).

The aberrant gender that Baudelaire called "bizarre and androgynous" facilitates a corrupting relation to the commodity which is prior to—and, indeed, productive of—illicit sex ("*Madame*" 407). Thus, as the focal character in a narrative that fuses business and seduction, Emma commits adultery not only when she falls into the grass with Rodolphe, or rides off in the carriage with Léon, but also with each and every purchase she makes. The commodities that tempt her derived from an industrial revolution that crossed the channel which, in turn, grew out of capital amassed from the sugar-plantation complex. Some of these wares were imported from "France's growing colonial empire and trade networks" (Paskow 326). This worlding consumer culture subtends the adulterous geopolitical aesthetic.

As Adorno notes, kitsch originates in the exploitation of an age-old "fissure" between human beings and their culture. As capitalist modernity develops the potential for freedom alongside the reality of oppression, it produces a condition in which people can no longer recognize "the human component in culture." The result is a society of modern subjects who "make common cause with the world against themselves" so that "the most alienated condition of all, the omnipresence of commodities," becomes "for them a mirage of closeness" (146–7). Although Adorno wrote these words to describe the culture industry that helped to usher in fascism, they are stunningly anticipated by Flaubert's novel, in which Emma repeatedly mistakes commodified objects for "closeness." Indeed, the more keenly Emma thirsts for this human component, the more this very desire becomes the engine of a thoroughgoing corruption.

By making adultery a repetition of marriage, moreover, *Madame Bovary* makes clear that, in fact, it is adultery, not marriage, which provides the "structure that maintains the Structure." "What is so profoundly disturbing and depressing" about Flaubert's novel, writes Slavoj Žižek, "is that by depicting adultery "as a false escape," it turns a presumed "last refuge" into "an inherent moment of the dull and grey bourgeois universe" (11). This *cul de sac* is not a reified *bovarysme*, but the mark of the geopolitical aesthetic at work. For while *Madame Bovary* is an antikitsch manifesto, it does not jettison the social in the interest of hermetic stylistic enclosure; instead, it transplants the social aspect to the terrain of the new genre that Flaubert's style helps to innovate. The first naturalistic narrative of capitalist globalization, *Madame Bovary* is a historicist novel for its time: a "tentative totality" in telling its tale of the radically attenuated sovereignty of modern subjects caught in the grips of an eroticized, aestheticized, and consumerized mirage of closeness.

In Chapter 8, I will return to *Madame Bovary* in light of seriality: a forgotten dimension of the novel which helps to illuminate the recurrence of naturalistic realism in recent television. Serialization has the potential to mediate the existential temporality of naturalistic narrative by slowing down and collectivizing modernity's hyperactive pace. As we shall see, even James embeds his first encounter with Flaubert in a memory of chancing upon a number of the *Revue de Paris* as a youth. Although the various problems that the novel raises for James, Lukács, Jameson, and Shaw diverge from my own sense of it as a surprisingly Lukácsian work, they provide a useful window on Eliot—another nineteenth-century author "at home in the moral world." For while Eliot clearly sought to create alternatives to naturalistic realism, she did so as an artist called upon to meet the challenges of the adulterous geopolitical aesthetic.

By way of considering those challenges, let us take one last look at "Woman in France":

> The dreamy and fantastic girl of this period was awakened to reality by the experience of wifehood and maternity, and became capable of loving, not a mere phantom of her own imagination, but a living man, struggling with the hatreds and rivalries of the political arena; she espoused his quarrels, she made herself, her fortune, and her influence, the stepping-stones of his ambition; and the languid beauty, who had formerly seemed ready to 'die of a rose', was seen to become the heroine of an insurrection. The vivid interest in affairs which was thus excited in a woman, must obviously have tended to quicken her intellect, and give it a practical application; and the very sorrows—the heart-pangs and regrets which are inseparable from a life of passion—deepened her nature by the questioning of self and destiny which they occasioned, and by the energy demanded to surmount them and live on (41).

Evans here imagines "wifehood and maternity" as but the first stage of the Frenchwoman's life. The ingénue who falls in love with a "phantom" goes on to become the protagonist of a second narrative focused less on romance for its own sake than on the indirect access romance provides to the "political arena." Adultery thus enables a mature woman to take an active part in her lover's cause. It seems to go without saying for Evans, that this "vivid interest" in public affairs—even if, in actuality, the affairs of one's lover—is so intellectually enlivening that it outweighs the "sorrows" of "a life of passion." What is more, the "sorrows" themselves are worthwhile in spurring "the energy to surmount" private troubles. Thus, while "[n]o wise person . . . wishes" to make adultery the "ideal programme of woman's life" (41), such conditions enabled Frenchwomen to participate in the republic of letters.

While Eliot never wrote a novel that hews to the Frenchwoman's narrative, *Middlemarch* enacts a variation by making Dorothea's girlish marriage to a "phantom" give way to a mature second marriage (shadowed by the faint aspersion of infidelity cast by Casaubon's will). Nor do we find precisely this narrative in Sand, in whose works the conflict between happiness and duty predetermines a tragic conclusion. We have seen how Eliot's first two novels enact variations on this sentimental arc. But, by the time Eliot turned to *Romola*, realism had become the most prestigious form of fiction on both sides of the channel.[42]

Of course, the rise of sensation fiction provided fascinating *femmes fatales* such as Lydia Gwilt and Lady Audley; bowdlerized Emmas such as Braddon's Isabel Gilbert; and errant wives including the long-suffering Isabel of *East Lynne* (1861).[43] Eliot's lack of explicit interest in these genres may explain why, in *Culture and Adultery* (1999), Barbara Leckie barely mentions her except to note that "even George Eliot" read the same newspapers that provided inspiration for sensation fiction (104). The so-called great novels of adultery—*Madame Bovary*; Tolstoy's *Anna Karenina* (1873–7), and Theodor Fontane's *Effi Briest* (1894–5)—are all realist novels; yet like sentimental fiction, all conclude tragically. Although the heroines of these works are characters of consequence, none offers a template for the sustainable female *Bildung* that Evans contemplates in "Woman in France." Thus, as Susan Winnett argues, the author of *Romola* saw that European literature needed "new legends to rescue female experience from the margins of narrative and to render it intelligible in its own right" (515).

According to Raymond Williams, *Romola* is but a "fanciful" prelude to the more proximate historicism of *Middlemarch* (*English* 13). Yet, the "deficiencies" of Eliot's most explicit historical romance are easily overstated (Levine and Turner 2). One learns quickly that Eliot felt the pressure of writing it had turned her into "an old woman" (Cross 253) and that detractors like James judged *Romola* to be a "splendid mausoleum" that "smells of the lamp" (qtd. in Carroll, *Critical* 18, 500).[44] One learns less quickly, if at all, that R. H. Hutton, the exacting critic for the *Spectator*, reversed his initially tepid reviews of the novel's serial run: "'Romola' improves as it advances," he wrote in February 1863 before deeming the finished book to be "one of the greatest works of modern fiction" (qtd. in Carroll, *Critical* 198). Decades later, the American novelist William Dean Howells named *Romola* alongside *Middlemarch*, *Daniel Deronda*, Zola's *L'Assomoir*, and *Anna Karenina*,

---

[42] On the displacement of sentimental fiction in France and the canonization of masculinist realism, see Cohen, *Sentimental* and Schor, *George*.

[43] See also Humpherys on the impact of divorce on "the conventional marriage plot" in making the "novel more multi-voiced, more diffuse, [and] more open-ended" (42).

[44] Not to be outdone by James, Leslie Stephen wrote that *Romola* "suggests the professor's chair" (136). James, it should be noted, was of two minds about *Romola* which, he wrote, "is on the whole the finest thing she wrote," though "its defects are almost on the scale of its beauties" (Carroll, *Critical* 500). See also the review of *Middlemarch* which calls the earlier novel a "rare masterpiece" (James, "Review" 424).

to illustrate how fiction had become "the chief intellectual stimulus of our time" (qtd. in Arac 94). Thus, while *Romola* has never been a general favorite, it is only in retrospect that it has come to be regarded as a failure.

In *The Forms of Historical Fiction* (1983), Shaw describes *Romola* as the "attempt by a great moralist to examine certain ethical and cultural concerns by projecting them onto the past" (109)—a critique much like that which Lukács levels against *Salammbô*. Shaw's refinement of Lukács's overblown criteria for historical fiction is astute. But his effort to insist that *Romola* is anachronistic and that Lukács cares too little about "depiction of the past as an object in its own right" obscures the extent to which *Romola* works precisely in the terms suggested by *The Historical Novel*—that is, as a fiction that depicts the Florentine republic as the forerunner of the mid-nineteenth century's adulterous geopolitical aesthetic.[45]

ROMOLA'S *ANTIGONEAN MOMENT*

> We said that the dramatic motive of the *Antigone* was foreign to modern sympathies, but it is only superficially so . . . The turning point of the tragedy is not . . . "reverence for the dead and the importance of the sacred rites of burial," but the *conflict* between these and obedience to the State. Here lies the dramatic collision: the impulse of sisterly piety which allies itself with reverence for the Gods, clashes with the duties of citizenship; two principles, both having their validity, are at war with each.
>
> [George Eliot], "The *Antigone* and Its Moral" (1856)

When Eliot left home for her first-ever trip to Italy in March 1860, the condition of Britain had begun to reflect the relative quiescence that historians associate with the emergence of a staid Liberal Party. With leaders such as Palmerston and Gladstone at the helm, this was a liberalism shorn of radical ambition and more determined to extend "free trade" and reduce taxes than to enfranchise working-class men or women of any class.[46] As we saw in Chapter 2, liberals of this ilk

---

[45] Lukács does not, to my mind, overlook the importance of the "past as the past" when he argues (in Shaw's paraphrase) that historical novels should depict a "historical process which promotes the discovery of the present as history" (*Forms* 45). Rather, Lukács holds that historical novels should depict the past as part of an (ongoing) "historical process"—a depiction that promotes "the discovery of the present as history." The relation between the (synchronic) history of a *particular* past and the ongoing (diachronic) history that includes the contemporary world of the reader is dialectical and it is this aspect of "the way society moves" which enables novels *about* the past to awaken awareness of present-day historicity (*Historical* 144). That Lukács recognized the importance of depicting the past in its own right is demonstrable in his discussion of Flaubert: the problem with *Salammbô*, he wrote, was the complete lack of "connection between the outside world and the psychology of the principal characters" (*Historical* 189). For more affirmative discussions of *Romola* as historical novel see Sanders and Fleishman. On Lukács and historicity in light of Jameson see the Coda.

[46] Emigration to a "Greater Britain" of white settlement colonies was another feature of this worldview—a significant difference from France as we have seen. Between 1841 and 1880 almost 6 million Britons emigrated to North America, Australia, or New Zealand (Darwin 42). On the emigration of Lewes's sons, see Henry, *British Empire*.

were also prone to disavowing Britain's expanding territorial dominion. Although imperialism was harder to ignore after the Indian rebellion (1857–8), in May 1860, when the Leweses visited Florence, it was the unification of Italy which had captured the British imagination.

The British public exuberantly welcomed Italy's "resurgence" under a constitutional monarchy modeled on England's (though in reality Palmerston's government had done less to promote this liberal "miracle" than the French Empire).[47] Upper-class Britons cheered the establishment of a new kingdom while radicals applauded the partnership of Garibaldi and the republican Giuseppe Mazzini whose failed revolution in 1848 was the subject of Meredith's *Vittoria* (1867). As we shall see in Chapter 7, belief in the kinship of Britons and Italians during the Risorgimento became the inspiration for a flourishing internationalism among turn-of-the-century New Liberals such as the Italophile historian G. M. Trevelyan, a friend of E. M. Forster's. Support for Italy's emancipation took republican shape in the poetry of Elizabeth Barrett Browning, Arthur Hugh Clough, and Algernon Charles Swinburne, among others.[48] Hence, while neither Eliot nor Lewes was an avid Italian nationalist, Eliot's enthusiasm for Lewes's suggestion that Savonarola's "life and times afforded fine material for an historical romance" expressed the zeitgeist (qtd. in Ashton, *George* 243). Savonarola was a dominant figure in the Risorgimento mythos that had helped to "make Italians conscious of their past." Set between 1492 and 1498, *Romola* depicts his leadership of a republic that had come to be seen as a high point in Italy's "epic journey" to nationhood (Thompson 7, 69). Like Robespierre, whose biography Lewes had written in 1849, Savonarola eventually fell victim to his own fanaticism. To write about the Florentine republic was, thus, to engage the challenges of modern history.[49]

Britain's social condition at this time was both like and unlike the "excited" French public of Rancière's account. Far from a remote event, Italy's emancipation seemed to confirm an unfolding liberal order with Britain at its vanguard, perhaps even a "United States of Europe," (Mazzini qtd. in D. Smith 220). The conflation of spirituality and materiality which Rancière names as the "fatal disease" that galvanized Flaubert's writing is, thus, distinct from (but comparable to) the seeds of *Romola*. According to Daniel S. Malachuk, *Romola* was part of a Victorian "conversation about the role of virtue in polities otherwise dedicated to the fullest realization of individual autonomy"—a "liberty problem" that extends back to the republican thought of Machiavelli (84). In our own day, these tensions come to the fore in debates between liberals and communitarians; but for Eliot, writing at a time when women and working men did not stand on equal

---

[47] In a November 1860 letter, Palmerston described the unification as "miraculous" since "no one in his senses or in his dreams could have anticipated such continuous success" (qtd. in Thompson 196; note 7). Eliot's Italian trip overlapped with Garibaldi's famous Expedition of the Thousand. The Kingdom of Italy was established in March 1861—just a few weeks before Eliot returned to do additional research for *Romola*.
[48] On this topic see, e.g., M. Reynolds; Saville; and S. Weiner.
[49] See also O'Connor: for the British people, she writes, Italy's past "contained lessons to be learned" while the Risorgimento offered them the "chance to help in the rebuilding of a new Rome" (4).

footing with the male ruling class, the question was how to expand popular sovereignty without exacerbating those deracinating tendencies that she had already described as impediments to collectivity and historicity. Informed by intensive study of the Florentine past, including the works of Machiavelli, *Romola* explores the epic clash between private desire and the public good.

Yet, *Romola* is simultaneously the stage for a new kind of typical character—a female protagonist who relocates Antigone's dilemma from the sentimental terrain of marriage and adultery to the civic terrain of republican life.[50] By placing Romola at the center of a romance of Europe's past, Eliot turns a "dreamy" girl into a "heroine" without making her the adulterous lover of a powerful man. To do so, she challenges the rift between action and life which, according to Rancière, had dominated the old regime of art. Crossing boundaries of gender and genre through a fusion of Scottian and Sandian forms, *Romola* explores a host of unresolved tensions which continued to plague nineteenth-century modernity including action versus life, masculine versus feminine, public versus private, universality versus particularity, spirituality versus materiality, and justice versus care.

Significantly, the opening chapters of *Romola* introduce Florence from the perspective of Tito, the "Shipwrecked Stranger" of Chapter 1's title. Handsome and secretive, this "selfish smiler" with "a double identity," is the kind of Lopezian figure who creates "epistemological emergency" in naturalistic fiction (335, 337). "That pretty Greek," says Romola's godfather Bernardo, "has a lithe sleekness about him that seems marvellously fitted for slipping easily into any nest he fixes his mind on" (74). Fatefully, Romola's father Bardo ignores this warning: he is already hoping that Romola's marriage will provide him with the male scion he lost when his son Dino became a religious zealot. Though affectionate, Bardo fails to recognize his daughter as a "rare gem" (74). Imputing feminine weakness to her intellect, he treats her as an object to be exchanged for a son-in-law rather than an end in herself or, still less, a scholar.[51] At the same time, Dino's apostasy—abandoning the "liberal" life of learning to "lash himself" with "besotted friars" (53)—points to the classical and Christian poles that Renaissance humanism strove to synthesize. According to Gary S. Wihl, *Romola* depicts a period in which "humanist rhetoric, classical constitutional theory, and Christian and secular notions of fortune and virtue were refined, argued, and synthesized" (248). As J. G. A. Pocock has shown in *The Machiavellian Moment* (1975), the republican focus on civic participation in "secular time" is at odds with the "Christian insistence" on asceticism and eschatology (7–8). Thus, in a way that reveals her to be

---

[50] The idea of sentimental fiction's tragic split between public duty and private happiness, it should be noted, is founded on a Hegelian interpretation of *Antigone* which holds that a pious care for the dead is confined to the private realm (for a very different reading, see Honig, "Antigone's"). However, regardless of whether one accepts or rejects Hegel's interpretation, one must recognize that 1) Romola's concerns never explicitly bear on religious piety and 2) her embrace of civic republicanism confutes any assumption that—as a woman—her affairs must perforce be purely ethical and/or private.

[51] "With classical stoicism, energy, pride, and misogyny," writes Carroll, Bardo "has cut himself off from the world in order to pursue this self-imposed and exclusive mission" (*Conflict* 174).

Bardo's true scion, Romola repeatedly rejects religious dogma as the answer to any emergency.

Chapter 36, "Ariadne Discrowns Herself," marks a defining moment for Romola, not least since Tito's "treachery" has plunged her into a fugue (316). In selling off Bardo's library, Tito transforms the legacy of a life of scholarship into a store of disposable cash. Devastated, Romola experiences "dreamy disbelief in the reality" of her position and a sense that "the world was barren to her" (315). Of course, Tito is also involved in an extra-marital coupling as yet unknown to Romola; but the betrayal that prompts her to flee, significantly, is an injury to filial duty, not the commonplace transgression of male adultery. No longer an Ariadne wed to Bacchus, Romola dresses herself as a nun in order to escape a "hateful" husband and the "ignobility" of either Bovaryesque decline or religious asceticism (316, 322). As she changes her garments, her self-fashioning evokes Foucault's observation that modern man must "face the task of producing himself" ("What" 42). "[T]hrust[ing] her soft white arms into the harsh sleeves" of a nun's mantle, Romola does what no "Florentine woman had ever done." Like Foucault's modern subject, she "invent[s] a lot for herself"; she will become the female scholar her father never recognized (*Romola* 318, 320, 322).

But this aesthetics of the self is cut short when Romola encounters the Dominican friar whose scorching sermons have ignited popular desire for a new Jerusalem. Savonarola envisioned Florence as the epicenter of a "divine mission" of "spiritual renewal" through "restoration of republican citizenship"; he combined "Aristotelian, civic, and apocalyptic language in a single synthesis" (Pocock 105). Thus, when Savonarola hails Romola on the road from Florence, she encounters his version of the world-historic reconciliation between Hellenism's life in the public sphere and Christianity's emphasis on the next world. As Max Weber noted at the turn of the century, a Christianity focused on worldly deeds eventually took shape in the Protestant embrace of capitalism. This Anglo-American tradition was anticipated by Florentine early-moderns such as Machiavelli whose writings explore how republican virtue might withstand corruption (Pocock). Romola's encounter with Savonarola is, thus, a species of Machiavellian moment, albeit one that must accommodate female experience.

It is therefore no accident that just as Romola begins to experience the liberty of a self-inventing subject, Savonarola accosts her and issues his "command from God": "You are not permitted to flee," he tells her. At first this injunction provokes secular resistance, "I acknowledge no right of priests and monks to interfere with my actions," she says. But Romola soon perceives the appeal of "strength" in "submission" to "some valid law." To leave Florence, says Savonarola, would be to commit "one of the greatest wrongs a woman and a citizen can be guilty of" (355–7).

As the novel's typical character, Romola thus illustrates the appeal of the Frate's religio-political synthesis at a crucial juncture in Europe's history. But overall, *Romola* is less interested in Savonarola's vision than in capturing the multiple factors that undermine it. By the time he wins Romola to his cause, readers have already witnessed the Rucellai Gardens, where influential Miceans plot to pay lip-service to the dream of "popular government . . . for the general good." There "are but two sorts of government," says Ridolfi, "one where men show their teeth . . . and one where men show their tongues." When they approach Tito to serve their cause because the young Greek has a knack for "dissimulation" (343), the door opens wide to the realpolitik of men ready to show their tongues when their actual object is "snarling" (344).

Romola thus becomes the exemplary citizen of a millenarian republic, while her husband, a triple agent, plays a "tempting game" without "care for the result" (347). Tito himself stresses the gendered dimensions of this split between virtue and realpolitik: "You fair creatures live in the clouds," he tells Romola (406). As David Wayne Thomas writes, Eliot's "marital stalemate [is] a collision between Tito's repressiveness and Romola's cooperative sensibility." For Thomas, working from the neo-Kantian standpoint of communicative ethics, Tito's "coercive authority "is emblematic of the "premodern political order," while Romola's consensuality characterizes "modernity" (135). But as Romola's transformative status as a female typical character suggests, the historical conditions of early-modern Florence (and Victorian Britain) confute the opposition of premodern/modern. Among the various binaries that nineteenth-century modernity had only partly unloosed from "coercive authority," was the gendered division between public and private spheres.[52] Savonarola's republicanism thus appeals to Romola by offering public duties to "citizens" who are excluded from politics. Embracing the "inspiring consciousness" of "marching with a great army" (468), she innovates heroic practices of care which bridge "action" and "life." But while Romola herself rises to this millenarian occasion, *Romola* dramatizes the male conspirators who undermine republican stability.

On one side of this genre fusion, Eliot enables the female *Bildung* she anticipated in "Woman in France," suggesting that Romola's true double is Antigone, not Ariadne.[53] In her essay on *Antigone*, Evans identified Sophocles' focus as the contest between "the impulse of sisterly piety" and "the duties of citizenship"—a conflict that sentimental fiction sublimates into romance narrative. By taking a world-historical republic for its context, *Romola* restores the gravitas of Antigone's double-bind, in effect overlaying an Antigonean moment on the Machiavellian one for which the period is known. As a devoted citizen, Romola continues to regard the Frate as a model of "public virtue" (457) even as she observes the rigidity and corruption to which the godly republic is vulnerable. When Tessa is ordered to turn over her necklace during the Pyramid of the Vanities, Romola intercedes: "That is not what Fra Girolamo approves," she tells the young zealots who do his bidding, "he would have such things *given up freely*" (431; emphasis

---

[52] A division that persists today despite the achievement of formal equality, as the feminist theory I discuss in the next chapter makes clear.

[53] Tito commissions a painting of himself and Romola as Ariadne and Bacchus; but as Piero di Cosimo tells him, he plans to ask Bardo and Romola to sit for "Oedipus and Antigone at Colonos" (185). Subsequently he takes to calling her "Madonna Antigone" (e.g., 257); see also Bonaparte on Romola's likeness to the Antigone of *Oedipus Coloneus* (75).

added). Befitting a character who is already called "Madonna Antigone" (257), Romola begins to generate her own interpretations of "valid law."

The novel's most striking Antigonean moment occurs when Romola realizes that Tito is the father of Tessa's children. Less pained by his infidelity than disappointed to find that the fraudulent wedlock with Tessa does not nullify her own conjugal bond, Romola reconsiders the case for duty:

> The law was sacred. Yes, but rebellion might be sacred too. It flashed upon her mind that the problem before her was essentially the same as that which had lain before Savonarola—the problem where the sacredness of obedience ended, and where the sacredness of rebellion began. To her, as to him, there had come one of those moments in life when the soul must dare to act on its own warrant, not only without external law to appeal to, but in the face of a law which is not unarmed with divine lightnings—lightnings that may yet fall if the warrant has been false (469).

Notably, Romola's conflict does not involve the sacrifice of personal happiness (as in sentimental fiction) but, rather, an inner conviction of right that compels defiance of "external law" (as in *Antigone*).[54] In conceiving her desire to separate from Tito as a duty to rebel, Romola likens her readiness "to act on [her soul's] own warrant" to the enterprise of a world-historic leader. This is a very different character than the woman who accepted the idea that her duty to Florence required her return to a faithless husband. Drawing a principled distinction between duty to one's marriage and duty to one's city, Romola decides, in effect, that one's justified rebellion against the former does not jeopardize one's fulfillment of the latter.

But these thoughts are soon overshadowed by the crisis brought on when Tito falsely implicates Romola's godfather Bernardo in a conspiracy against Savonarola. Thus, in yet another Antigonean moment, Romola attempts to persuade the Frate to spare the life of an innocent man. Like Antigone, she speaks as a conscientious advocate for a kinsman, urging Savonarola to ensure Bernardo's legal right to appeal. But Savonarola has made up his mind to placate public opinion by affecting neutrality. When Romola presses him, he tells her that Bernardo has "lost the right to appeal" and that the "common good . . . demands severity" (488–9). Aware of Tito's treachery, Romola replies by making her own republican case: "what safety can there be for Florence when the worst man can always escape?" Moreover, as Romola knows, the Frate has "*not*. . . been neutral" (489); "It is not . . . as a Medicean that my godfather is to die," she protests, "it is as a man you have no love for" (490).

Romola here taps into Savonarola's peccant core: his is "a power-loving and powerful nature" in tandem with "a mind possessed by a never-silent hunger after purity and simplicity, yet caught in a tangle of egoistic demands, false ideas and difficult outward conditions that made simplicity impossible" (490). Savonarola must finally show his hand: "*You* see one ground of action in this matter," he tells her, whereas, "I see many . . . The death of five men—were they less guilty than

---

[54] One might argue that the risks involved in rebellion entail potential sacrifice of happiness—but this is not a concern that *Romola* makes paramount.

these—is a light matter weighed against the withstanding of the vicious tyrannies which stifle the life of Italy." When Romola rejects this argument as "sophistry and doubleness," the result is a climactic break. Savanarola declares that the cause of his party is "the cause of God's kingdom," to which Romola retorts, "I do not believe it!" "God's kingdom is something wider—else, let me stand outside it with the beings that I love" (492).

Reading this exchange from a Machiavellian standpoint, Wihl observes a conflict between "civic necessity" and "liberal values" which Romola helps to synthesize. Yet he also recognizes that when Savonarola "retreats" into sophistry, he fails according to Machiavelli's terms as well as Romola's (257). As Eliot's Machiavelli says of the Frate: "It is a pity his falsehoods were not all of a wise sort" (*Romola* 537). Savonarola thus instances flawed "political management" (Wihl 257) while Machiavelli speaks for statecraft that is more wise if not more true. It seems unlikely, therefore, that Romola would embrace the republicanism of either man, no matter how tempered by "liberal values." To be sure, *Romola*'s moment is "Machiavellian" in harnessing the Christian's yearning for salvation to a temporal project of civic good. But the Antigonean conflict that comes to a climax in this passage is less about the limits of secular ideals than about the failure of male characters to realize them. Whereas *Antigone* turns on the conflict between "reverence for the Gods" and "the duties of citizenship," in *Romola*, Savonarola appoints himself the arbiter of *both* of these principles. Hence, Romola's ground is not religion but, rather, her hard-won qualification to judge when to rebel or obey.

As the political theorist Bonnie Honig notes, Antigone's multi-faceted actions have generated centuries of debate. In a reading inspired partly by Rancière, Honig argues that Antigone's third and final lamentation—a dirge for herself—"makes a new kind of sense." "She suffers for this, but she is not defined by her suffering" ("Antigone's" 22). Although Romola's story culminates in marriage rather than death, Eliot's rendering of an Antigonean typical character also strives to "make a new kind of sense"—reducible neither to the ordinary heroism of male counterparts in Scott, nor to the tragedies that befall the female rebels of sentimental fiction. Then too, while the conflict between Antigone and Creon concerns two valid principles, they are clearly unequal. As Felicia Bonaparte notes, "Creon represents . . . the right of the world as it is," while Antigone speaks for a visionary right "that has yet to be achieved" (75; cf. 211). Eliot's reworking of Antigone's narrative thus points to a utopian dimension that is important to understanding *Romola*'s conclusion. The friar who calls Romola back to Florence speaks for the future; but by the time he claims God's Kingdom for his party, the Frate is a fallen Machiavel and arrogant priest. Thus, in the final chapters, Romola takes Savonarola's place as the exponent of a visionary outlook. In anointing a female heroine who is excluded from politics as the type of Europe's future, *Romola*'s "Antigonean moment" comes to a close. From this point on, this "genuinely experimental work" must complete its narrative of female experience through other means (G. Levine, "Romola" 81).

DRIFTING AWAY

> There is no compensation for the woman who feels that the chief relation of her life has been no more than a mistake.
>
> "Drifting Away," *Romola,* Chapter 61

> Romola in her boat passed from dreaming into long deep sleep, and then again from deep sleep into busy dreaming . . .
>
> "Romola's Waking," *Romola,* Chapter 68

> "You admit now we couldn't have done anything better?"
> "No—I see nothing better. I think we shall go on always, like the Flying Dutchman," said Gwendolen, wildly.
>
> *Daniel Deronda* (1876)

As Winnett powerfully shows, Eliot's efforts to insert Romola's experience into European history are curtailed by the patriarchal structures that render male characters such as Tito and Savonarola as the preeminent types of world struggle. From this view, the change of genres with which *Romola* concludes is testimony to the limits of the Scottian romance to accommodate a female typical character—even one modeled on Antigone. Yet, this is a difficulty Eliot seems to have anticipated: her letters indicate that *Romola*'s much-discussed "drifting away" scene and the encounter with the plague-stricken village "belonged to [her] earliest vision of the story" (qtd. in G. Levine, "Romola" 83). Critics ever since have singled out these features doubtless because they surprise the reader's expectations of the (masculine) historical genre. Hutton described the epilogue as "feeble and womanish" while the *Westminster Review* called it *Romola*'s "weakest part, because here, if anywhere, there was need of action" (Carroll, *Critical* 205, 219). More recently, Alexander Welsh has noted that in comparison to the end of a Scott novel, in *Romola* "the heroine's sense of identity is . . . uncertain" and the "resolution" has little "to do with any concrete historical event" (*George* 193–4).

As we have seen, Eliot was in a position to draw on three distinct genres in addition to historical romance. The first is the French sentimental novel of adultery which pits happiness against duty and ends tragically—the model for Maggie Tulliver's story. More embryonic is the cluster I have organized under the rubric of the adulterous geopolitical aesthetic: novels such as *Dombey and Son* and *Madame Bovary* which depict the impacts of capitalist globalization by making adultery the sign of heirloom collapse, commodified marriage, existential exile, and the threat of contamination "from elsewhere." But Eliot herself imagined a third genre of adultery narrative. Modeled on "Woman in France," this genre is a female *Bildungsroman* in which a young girl marries and is soon disabused of her "phantom" love, but goes on to engage in mature "unions" that enable her to participate vicariously in public affairs.

As one of Eliot's most experimental novels, *Romola* fuses elements from all of these genres. After the crushing realization of Tito's duplicity, she cultivates two mature unions. The first is a discipleship under Savonarola (structurally analogous to an adulterous affair) which she outgrows when she matures into a full-blown Antigone who outstrips her mentor. The second—which takes place after the "drifting away" and plague sequences—is a marriage to Tessa which entails her becoming the head of Tito's illegitimate family. In calling this union a "marriage" I am inspired by Sharon Marcus's notion of "just reading"—accounting for what is most visible on the surface (*Between* 75). From this perspective, *Romola* includes multiple foreshadowings of the heroine's taking her husband's place in a marriage that is not (and has never been) legally sanctioned. For example, Romola saves Tessa's necklace (a gift from Tito) from the bonfire; and when Tessa shows her a lock of hair which Romola recognizes as her husband's, she responds by giving Tessa a lock of her own hair.[55]

Less obviously, *Romola* includes anticipatory features of the naturalistic narrative of capitalist globalization. This is especially evident in the depiction of Tito as a cosmopolitan exile—a dark-haired Greek reared by an Italian stepfather. Tito's alien condition subtends his role as an arch-Machiavel with no firm allegiances to any people, party, or creed. According to Bernardo, he is "one of the *demoni*, who are of no particular country"—his "mind . . . too nimble to be weighted with all the stuff . . . men carry about in [their] hearts" (191).[56] Like Flaubert in *Madame Bovary*, Eliot adopts tropes from an emerging discourse of anti-Semitism without attaching them to any strongly Judaized character. Rather, in depicting Tito as an example of a larger exilic condition, she makes it possible to connect his "demonic" rootlessness to the more sympathetic "Otherness of Woman" and to embed both kinds of otherness in Europe's ongoing history. Thus, in the wake of Bardo's death, Tito's deceit, Bernardo's execution, and Savonarola's fall, Romola herself becomes an exile: a woman with no firm anchor or calling. This is the meaning of "Drifting Away"—the title of Chapter 61 and a status that is literalized when Romola disappears over a period of seven chapters.[57]

---

[55] As with many of the female marriages Marcus describes, Eliot's contemporaries took the union in stride and even commended it. According to a review that is probably by John Morley, nothing in Romola's "behavior seems to us more admirably conceived than her conduct to Tessa . . . She is very kind . . . and learns to love the children, and in fact, after [Tito's] death, has Tessa and the children to live with her. There is, perhaps, a little exaggeration of romance in this, but her general treatment of Tessa gives us her measure" (Carroll, *Critical* 211–12). See also Corner's recent analysis: "By fostering his children, Romola overrides all previous alienation and makes good Tito's redeeming qualities" (85). I discuss the theoretical implications of pitting "just reading" against Jamesonian materialism briefly in the Coda and, at greater length, in Goodlad and Sartori. See also the Coda for commentary on Jameson's discussion of *Romola* in his recent *Antinomies of Realism*, which includes a chapter on *Romola*.

[56] Evocative of the Jewish jewelers discussed in previous chapters, Tito carries gems to Florence which include a "Jew's stone" (80). See also Henry on Eliot's recoding of Florentine homosociality and male same-sex desire in the depiction of Tito ("*Romola*").

[57] As Corner notes, the readers of *Romola*'s serialization in the *Cornhill* waited two months before learning of the heroine's fate (76).

In "Romola's Waking" (Chapter 68), the heroine disembarks to find a population of marooned Jews, forced by the Inquisition "to abandon their homes" and stricken with plague. This surreal episode, described by Eliot as "romantic and symbolical," repurposes narrative elements that are familiar from the comparatively realist Antigone plot. Thus, at a time when readers know that Tito is dead, his rootlessness recurs in the form of Jewish exiles in need of rescue. This enables Romola's heroized civic practices of care to return in the herculean form of her nursing an entire village of the sick and dying. Steeled by her long "experience in the haunts of death and disease" Romola's "thought and action" are so prompt and efficacious, her care so larger-than-life, that she is soon taken for "the Holy Mother" (*Romola* 552, 554). The scenario suggests a miraculous curative power—perhaps even a millennial conversion of the Jews.

When Romola parts from this dream-like space, she returns to a Florence purged of overbearing men. Able to forgive Savonarola for his failings and adopt Tito's family, Romola's *Bildungsroman* concludes with the second marriage to Tessa. In the Epilogue we find her happily immersed in realist fiction's favored domains of family and community. As Geraldine Jewsbury wrote, "Romola is left in the possession of a far better life than if all her early hopes had been fulfilled" (Carroll, *Critical* 198).[58] The concluding tableau of Romola's instructing Nello is no sentimental throwaway: when "Romola chooses not to tell the version of her husband's life that *Romola* has just told," writes Winnett, she challenges us to read her narrative in "the way she has chosen to teach it" (515). Like Nello, readers of *Romola* are asked to reinterpret the world with a legend of female experience at their disposal.

Yet, as Eliot turned from *Romola* to the realism that dominates her later fiction, she recognized that modern female experience required more than the new mythologies romance genres could offer. In Mrs. Transome, whose adultery results in the illegitimate parentage of one of the two male radicals in *Felix Holt* (1866), she created a character that readers might find in any Balzac or James novel. In doing so, she anticipated the groundbreaking novel that "opens on a cosmopolitan world of pure exchange and immediately introduces the major representatives of that sphere: the beautiful but sinister and reckless woman and the Jewish pawnbroker" (Gallagher, "George"; cf. Gallagher, *Body*, Ch. 5). What may be less obvious is how Romola's "Drifting Away" already adumbrates the exilic interiorities of *Daniel Deronda*. As the figure of an existential estrangement without reprieve, the drifting Romola of Chapter 61 is a kind of Bovary: a woman whose "impulse to set herself free" rises up "with overmastering force" (*Romola* 500). With the bonds of "strong affection . . . snapped," Romola's decision to "glid[e] away" toward freedom from "the burden of choice" is part suicide attempt and part self-erasure (500, 503). It "is an attempt at extinction, a desperate act of negation and isolation" (Sanders 191).[59]

---

[58] Fryckstedt (55) identifies Jewsbury as the author of the anonymous *Athenaeum* review in Carroll's volume.

[59] Cf. Corner: "Romola's "drifting away expresses the aimlessness which results when one's environment ceases to maintain its hold" (74). Kurnick notes that Romola experiences many turning

This latent *bovarysme* shadows a character whose spectacular heroics overlay the threat of futile existence, "without bonds, without motive; sinking in mere egoistic complaining that life could bring . . . no content" (*Romola* 560). In the 1870s, the conditions conducing toward such British variations on naturalism would dramatically increase: the result partly of an ever-more pronounced collapse of the sovereign heirloom as metropolitan society was increasingly penetrated by imperial crisis, unknowable strangers, and "money from elsewhere." Thus, by the time Eliot began to write *Daniel Deronda*, she was reading Flaubert's *Sentimental Education* and Trollope's *The Way We Live Now* (Henry, *Life* 210). Daniel's story of unknown Jewish origins appeared almost concurrently with that of Ferdinand Lopez.[60] But it is also worth noting that the dislocated subject of "drifting away" recurs throughout Eliot's fiction. In *Middlemarch*, a comparable disorientation marks the bedazzled grief described at the start of Dorothea's marital ordeal: "in certain states of dull forlornness," the narrator says, "Dorothea all her life continued to see the vastness of St. Peters . . . and the red drapery which was being hung for Christmas spreading itself everywhere like a disease of the retina" (194). In *Adultery and the Novel*, Tanner discusses the fateful boating trip of *The Mill on the Floss*: as it carries Maggie and Stephen into irreversible transgression, "the gliding water induces a loss of volition and . . . above all a temporary disinclination to participate in language and thought" (68).[61] These states of decentering fugue and evacuated volition rub against the classic device of an embedded narrative personality, albeit one whose authoritative pronouncements sometimes nicely punctuate these effects: "There is no compensation for the woman who feels that the chief relation of her life has been no more than a mistake" says the narrator of *Romola* as the heroine sets off into the unknown (500). Such episodes of dislocation resemble states that, in *Madame Bovary*, are triggered by adulterous sex.[62]

"Drifting away" is, thus, part of the genetic code that we find powerfully at work in Eliot's most naturalistic novel, *Daniel Deronda*, which is simultaneously the most utopian of her romance narratives and a work (in Barbara Hardy's words) that "touches the limits of Victorian fiction" (*Collected* 110). Daniel's restoration of Gwendolen's necklace echoes Romola's saving of Tessa's, while also indicating how the recurrent trope of heirloom jewels reduced to fungible objects connects these works to contemporaneous narratives of capitalist

---

points in the novel "in a kind of fugue state," a "drifting lassitude" that he reads as expressive of the reader's condition ("Abstraction" 493–4). For my purposes, the readerly lassitude that he observes is the sign of a lingering *bovarysme*.

[60] See also Henry, *British*, Ch. 4 for a reading that details the various ways in which the plot of *Daniel Deronda* is embedded in global capitalism and imperialism—for example, Gwendolen's family ties to Barbados (a plot point that recalls Collins's *Armadale*).

[61] At the close of the novel, "Maggie felt nothing, thought of nothing"—a "dreamlike" state of unconsciousness and numbness which Ablow likens to the world "before the subject becomes conscious of itself as a self" (Eliot, *Mill* 650; Ablow 89).

[62] For example, as Emma "abandon[s] herself to" Rodolphe for the first time, "the horizontal sun passing between the branches dazzled the eyes . . ."; traveling to Rouen for her weekly tryst with Léon, the city "spreads out before [Emma] like . . . a Babylon," a "mass of human lives that left her dizzy" (130, 207).

globalization as different as *The Moonstone* and *The Eustace Diamonds*. Daniel's exodus is further anticipated in *The Spanish Gypsy* (1868): though it is Eliot's only major work of poetry, it depicts victims of the Spanish Inquisition (like those in *Romola*), while concluding with an ethnically alien protagonist who leaves Europe to found a new homeland on another continent.[63] Then too, throughout Eliot's *oeuvre*, Italy provides the southern other of Britain's northern European imaginary. In *Romola*, Florentine character provides a middling essence suitable to typifying Europe's history—between "the heavy sottishness" of "thicker northern blood" and "the stealthy fierceness" that characterizes "the more southern regions of the peninsula" (192). In the more realistic *Middlemarch*, Roman otherness and decay enhance a sensory overload that stands in for the details of conjugal dysphoria. And in the naturalistic *Deronda*, details of Genoa are minimized to create an aloof backdrop that throws direful cosmopolitan experience into proper relief.

In such a novel, Lydia Glasher's gothic imprecation cannot but reverberate ironically as it turns lawful wedlock into fatal transgression: "I am the grave in which your chance of happiness is buried as well as mine" (*Daniel* 349).[64] Yet, as Hardy reminds us, *Daniel Deronda* is also the story of "a man in love with two women" (*Collected* 109) and, in this sense, adultery of a very specific kind facilitates the novel's experimental form. What else is the novel's famous opening tableau—"Was she beautiful . . .?" (*Daniel* 7)—if not a confirmation of Matthew: "Whosoever looketh on a woman . . . hath committed adulterie with her already in his heart?" Daniel's fascination with Gwendolen's "face" and "figure" is all the more dramatic in contrast to the "uniform negativeness of expression" of the gamblers who have occupied his attention hitherto—their collective daze the sign of a modernity well past the early throes of capitalist consumption (*Daniel* 8–9). If "pathological overexcitement" is the state of Flaubert's Second Empire, then pathological non-excitement has become the uniform condition of *Deronda*'s more jaded cosmopolitans.

Gwendolen's hold on Daniel bespeaks the pull of naturalistic modernity itself: he longs to rescue her from the "gravity of being caught up in history's workings" or at least to make her journey less rudderless and pained. The stronger current that pulls him in a different direction is imbued with proto-Zionist nationalism (as though Eliot were once again saving the victims of the Inquisition). But its underlying motive is a more general wish to join what the narrator of *The Mill on the Floss* called "the grand historic life of humanity." That is to say, Eliot is not so much keen to deliver the Jews from their diasporic condition as she is to redeem society as a whole from a modernity that threatens to turn the delusive dream of atomized liberal autonomy into a nightmare of universal alienation. To this

---

[63] See Kurnick, "Unspeakable" for a reading of the "unsettling formal texture" of *The Spanish Gypsy* which in highlighting the "striking resemblance" to *Deronda* nicely aligns with the arguments in this chapter.

[64] On the intensifying gothic elements of *Deronda*, see, for instance, Dever Ch. 5 and Garrett, *Gothic*, Ch. 8.

extent, *Deronda* is haunted by a prevision of the neoliberal era's virtualization of the Jewish condition (Ch. 8).

In a recent essay, Bruce Robbins has shown the ease with which *Deronda*'s vision of rootedness slips into an essentialistic nativism ("Cosmopolitanism" 404). Eliot's fascination with Jewish identity, as Aamir Mufti shows, is inseparable from the historical "problematic" of Jewish particularity "in a Europe of nations" (94). As a symbolic motif, the notion of a Jewish homeland in "the East" provides the novel with a moralizing mission and a space of unfigured (indeed, unfigurable) open-endedness which evokes the futural temporality of utopian romance. But there is no question that Deronda's choosing this mission, open-ended though it is, would be symbolically inert were it not for the surprise of Jewish ancestry.[65] Daniel's discovery "leaves Gwendolen . . . to stand for the modern or cosmopolitan norm, a norm which is also a malaise" (Robbins, "Cosmopolitanism" 405). If that is an uncontrovertibly accurate assessment of Eliot's qualified cosmopolitan outlook, it is also, in formal terms, the mark of the geopolitical aesthetic. As Brooks writes, *Daniel Deronda* is "a novel that first sums up a certain Victorian tradition of the novel, [and] then leaps beyond or explodes it" (*Realist* 97). In other words, the story in which Daniel falls in love with a woman caught up in history's workings pushes Eliot to a new naturalistic gravity; but the story in which he falls in love with "the grand historic life of humanity" pushes her beyond "serious imitation"—toward some unknowable grasp on history which may one day be realized in the future Daniel and Mirah set out to create. This is why *Deronda* ends with Mordecai's death and Daniel's departure.

That Gwendolen's fate is quite possibly an incurable *bovarysme* is surely the message of her own fateful passage of drifting away, midway through the seventh of the novel's eight books (Chapter 54). Who knows better than Gwendolen Grandcourt that, "There is no compensation for the woman who feels that the chief relation of her life has been no more than a mistake." Spoken by the narrator in *Romola*, the observation is plangent; in reference to *Deronda* it resonates with "unbearable tension." Where Romola is motivated by a desire for disburdenment; Gwendolen hopes merely to drown: "She was afraid of her own hatred, which under the cold iron touch that had compelled her to-day had gathered a fierce intensity" (681). The irony, of course, is that the lurid sexual violence these words connote is not what the world calls adultery. When Gwendolen "wildly" says that she and Grandcourt should "go on always, like the Flying Dutchman" (682), she depicts drifting as a kind of Sartrean exitlessness. Unlike anything Emma could feel (or that Romola deserves to feel), Gwendolen's desperation is intensified by remorse. The reprieve that comes after Grandcourt determines to "put about" spares her the fate of murdering her husband, like a Braddon femme fatale, or of taking her own life like Emma (682).

---

[65] For Kurnick, *The Spanish Gypsy* is "agonizingly aware . . . that minorities will continue to exist, that the nation as telos for all of them is unfeasible"—an awareness, he suggests, which may illuminate the "counter-nationalist" aspects of *Deronda* ("Unspeakable").

In the same chapter, Eliot introduces a reference to Madonna Pia, who "makes a pathetic figure in Dante's Purgatory, among the sinners who repented at the last and desire to be remembered compassionately" (668). By the end of the novel we realize that Gwendolen is Pia: though she will spend her life in the grip of historical forces she can only aspire to fathom, her saving grace may be her desire to be remembered compassionately. *"It is better,"* she writes to Daniel, *"it shall be better with me because I have known you"* (810). So concludes her part of the novel that consummates British realism and then "explodes it."

To be sure, for some readers, Eliot's attempt to braid the threads of utopian romance into the borders of a naturalistic fabric fails stylistically. And for some it fails because it is too tainted by the footprint of nineteenth-century nationalism and imperialism to work as utopian romance. Whether judged to succeed or to fail—a debate I would not shut down if I could (despite my own sense of this novel's peculiar power)—*Daniel Deronda* is the last of several efforts of the most proto-Lukácsian of British novelists to imagine the "negation of a negation" through which to narrate the present as history.

7

Where Liberals Fear to Tread
E. M. Forster's Queer Internationalism and the Ethics of Care

> I hate the idea of causes, and if I had to choose between betraying my country and betraying my friend I hope I should have the guts to betray my country.
>
> E. M. Forster, "What I Believe" (1939)

In an oft-cited remark from 1946, E. M. Forster described himself as belonging "to the fag-end of Victorian liberalism" ("Challenge" 71), a quip that expressed his growing unease with the bureaucracy of the postwar welfare state. At the launch of his literary career, Forster had supported the political innovations of contemporaries such as G. M. Trevelyan and C. F. G. Masterman. These self-styled New Liberals advocated "sanity in imperialism and foreign affairs, and a policy of constructive reform at home," thus proffering modest alternatives to the outmoded individualism and laissez faire of the Victorian age (Nathaniel Wedd qtd. in Furbank 1, 108). In works such as *The Heart of Empire: Discussion of Problems of Modern City Life in England* (1901), Masterman perceptively argued that the condition of the English metropole and the "great Empire lying beyond the sea" were ultimately inseparable (viii).[1]

Ever since Lionel Trilling's *E.M. Forster* (1943) linked the author of *Howards End* to "The Liberal Imagination," perhaps no novelist has been more consistently upheld as liberalism's literary standard bearer. Forster has been described as an "archetypal" liberal humanist and the precursor to contemporary liberal lights such as Richard Rorty and Jürgen Habermas. Yet, as this chapter will show, liberalism is a misleading rubric for Forster, a novelist whose focus on embodiment flummoxes liberal categories up to and beyond the New Liberalism of the Edwardian years.[2]

---

[1] On New Liberalism see, for example, Collini, "Political"; Fraser; Freeden.

[2] For "archetypal" liberal humanist, see Parry "Politics" 136; for a survey of Forster's reputation in this vein, see Davies's "Introduction." Forster's alleged liberalism has been recast along Rortyan lines by P. Armstrong, Born, and May: I discuss the Habermasian elements of Armstrong's reading below. It is worth emphasizing that Trilling cast Forster as one who challenged "the liberal imagination" from within (*Forster* 13). Subsequent criticism has thus tended to mute what Trilling saw as Forster's agonistic if ultimately revivifying stance on liberalism. Baucom, writing on *A Passage to*

Central to the reading I propose is a closer look at Forster's first-published novel, *Where Angels Fear to Tread* (1905). A tale of border-crossing encounter between northern and southern Europe, Forster's early "Italian" work makes the itinerant body the register of ethically vitalizing experiences that reconfigure the sovereign subject. Yet, in so doing, *Where Angels Fear to Tread* simultaneously constitutes a world of nation-states as its underlying condition. According to Perry Anderson, *internationalism* is an "outlook, or practice, that tends to transcend the nation towards a wider community, of which nations continue to form the principal units" (6). This definition helps to explain Forster's depiction of national difference—the pull of foreign parts—as a metaphor for queer sexual desire and, by extension, ethics in a heterogeneous world of diverse bodies, cultures, and geographies. The result is a distinct Edwardian-era geopolitical aesthetic: the "queer internationalism" explored in this chapter.

Although Trilling devoted ample space to *Where Angels Fear to Tread*, his designation of *Howards End* (1910) as "Forster's masterpiece"—the novel that most fully develops "the themes and attitudes of the early books and throws back upon them a new and enhancing light" (*Forster* 114–15)—helps to explain the comparative inattention to Forster's first book by many scholars of liberalism. Likewise, while postcolonial scholars have focused on *A Passage to India* (1924), few critics have read the "southern" qualities attributed to Italy in the first-completed novel as anticipating the orientalist South Asia depicted in the last. Instead, *Where Angels Fear to Tread* is typically read alongside *A Room with a View* (1908), a comparatively sunny work, as well as short stories set in Italy such as "The Story of a Panic."³ Nonetheless, as a border-crossing tragicomedy alight with prescient flashes of magic realism, *Where Angels Fear to Tread* offers a disruptive counterpoint to *A Room with a View*, a contrast to anglocentric novels like *The Longest Journey* (1907) and *Howards End*, as well as an important antecedent for *A Passage to India*. As this chapter will demonstrate, what Trilling described as Forster's "war with the liberal imagination" (*Forster* 13) was no mere "fag-end," but, rather, an ethic of queer internationalism propelled by a geopolitical imaginary organized along Europe's latitudinal axis.⁴

India, helpfully suggests that "not liberalism but friendship" provides a suitable way of characterizing what Forster offers in opposition to violence (*Out* 117).

³ For an interesting exception, see Bakshi and, briefly, Siegel 201. According to G. E. Moore, next to *A Passage to India*, "the most enjoyable of Forster's novels was the first" (qtd. in Rosenbaum 196)—an unusual opinion.

⁴ Forster's border-crossing imaginary is "international" rather than "cosmopolitan" because the transformative effects his novels describe require the concrete and embodied differences that nations are seen to constitute. In addition, Forster (like Trollope) internalized the pejorative meanings circulating around "cosmopolitan"—a point to which I will return. At the same time, Forster's fiction figures modes of sovereignty which can be compared to the porous, pluralistic, and multi-sited sovereignty described in Chapter 5 in light of Collins's archeological and phenomenological focal points.

PROLEGOMENON: LIBERAL INTERNATIONALISM AT THE TURN OF THE CENTURY

> Eurocentrism blocks . . . [the prospect of "humanistic practice as an integral aspect and functioning part of the world"] because . . . its misleadingly skewed historiography, the parochiality of its universalism, its unexamined assumptions about Western civilization, its Orientalism, and its attempts to impose a uniformly directed theory of progress all end up reducing . . . the possibility of catholic inclusiveness, of genuinely cosmopolitan or internationalist perspective, of intellectual curiosity.
>
> Edward W. Said, *Humanism and Democratic Criticism* (2004)

When Jeremy Bentham coined the term "internationalism" in *An Introduction to the Principles of Morals and Legislation* (1780) his focus was interstate jurisprudence. The potential for a more fluid internationalism, evoking contingent spaces of interaction between non-state as well as state actors, gradually arose during the course of the nineteenth century and since.[5] Although an internationalism so conceived de-centers the nation by stressing movement across borders rather than consolidation within them, it is neither *post-national* nor necessarily *anti-national*. That is, while nation-states may rely on regional, transnational, translocal, and imperial conditions of possibility, such contingency neither does, nor should, obliterate the nation-state's materiality or potential efficacy as one political structure among many.[6]

To be sure, whereas "transnationalism" as defined by Inderpal Grewal and Caren Kaplan emphasizes "the asymmetries of the globalization process" (664), internationalism of the kind celebrated by many Victorians took British superiority for its starting point. An unsigned 1862 essay in *Blackwood's*, for example, describes the International Exhibition of that year as a scene of "friendly rivalry" as well as a sign of Britain's continuing "supremacy" ("International" 472–3, 479). And while Matthew Arnold's *England and the Italian Question* (1859) supported the Italian struggle for nationhood, it argued that other stateless Europeans—the Hungarians, Irish, and Poles for example—lacked sufficient "greatness" to warrant political sovereignty (13, cf. 17). To study the internationalist writings of this period is, thus, more often than not, to confront a variety of hierarchical discourses on the global.

But that is not to say that the nineteenth century's actually existing internationalisms offer no critical or aesthetic purchase for scholarship. As we saw

---

[5] See Barkawi and Laffey for a recent articulation of this standpoint and Cheah for discussion of the transition between eighteenth- and nineteenth-century conceptions of nationhood.

[6] For an example of a post-national understanding of modernity see Appadurai and, for an account of a postcolonial and deterritorialized "Empire," see Hardt and Negri. For defenses of the nation-state's ongoing importance within globalized contexts see, for example, Brennan; Jameson, "Globalization"; Robbins, *Feeling*; and E. Wood.

in Chapter 6, Margaret Cohen and Carolyn Dever use "inter-national" to designate the novel's origins in a "cross-Channel literary zone," a space of transcultural exchange between Britain and France, which "both vindicate[s] and challenge[s] the imagined contours of the nation-state" (2–3). The same term can accommodate the more "worlded" and geopolitical internationalism that embeds George Eliot's *Romola* (1862–3) and *Daniel Deronda* (1876). Bruce Robbins has offered "internationalism" as a supplement or alternative to cosmopolitan ethics (*Feeling*); and Timothy Brennan upholds it in contradistinction to any global movement that ignores the importance of nations in securing "respect for weaker societies and peoples" (42). Clearly, *internationalism* is a complicated but valuable concept for scholarship: a term that may arguably transcend, but can never erase, its historical connections to the nineteenth century's imperial world order.[7] Evaluating Forster's "queer internationalism" thus requires contrasting the worlds of his fiction to the self-consciously progressive liberal internationalisms of his contemporaries.[8]

Probably the best-remembered of the New Liberals is J. A. Hobson, whose 1906 essay, "The Ethics of Internationalism," described "internationality" as a predominant feature of modernity. Indeed, it was no longer possible, Hobson believed, for any "great task of modern social reform" to be adequately addressed within a merely national context (19–20). As a liberal internationalist, Hobson promoted a sustained analogy between individuals and nations: "The instinct for internationalism is just the same within the nation," he wrote, "as the instinct for society within the individual" (27).[9] Though nations are born of shared history, geography, and culture, Hobson noted in *Imperialism: a Study* (1902), they are organic entities with the potential to develop "collective reason" and to exercise "deliberate conscious choice" in favor of cooperation and consensus (182). Indeed, were it not for the perverting influence of imperialism, he argued, nationalism would be "a plain highway to internationalism" (11). "Let international government put down wars and establish Free Trade," and "the truly vital struggles of national expression will begin" (186).[10]

Hobson here showed his ostensible debts to John Stuart Mill, who, in formulating a humanistic utilitarian ethic, had argued that true progress was not narrowly material but must also encompass the moral and intellectual gains of civilization

---

[7] Chandler distinguishes between the postwar era's "juridical" sovereignty and the nineteenth century's "empirical" notion. Unlike the formal sovereign equality that the United Nations charter—in theory though not in practice—grants to all member nations, the "rights of sovereignty" in the pre-charter past "were effectively restricted to the major powers and there was no explicit framework of an international community which could formally limit their exercise" (28).

[8] This prolegomenon explores the examples of J.A. Hobson and G. M. Trevelyan, both self-styled "New Liberals": I discuss the homophile and Fabian-influenced internationalism of Edward Carpenter below.

[9] Hobson's organic view of the social world led him to reject the notion of atomized, self-interested nations much as New Liberals rejected the self-interested individual of classical political economy. Those who insisted that "the social feelings . . . cannot pass the limits of nationality," he argued, were mired in Hobbesean dogma and "hide-bound individualism" (26).

[10] On Hobson and "Little Englandism," see Esty, *Shrinking* 25–8.

writ large. Thus, whereas imperialism was the product of crude bourgeois selfishness, internationalism, according to Hobson, stood for the cooperative sensibilities that Mill had identified with "an improving state of the human mind" (Mill, *Utilitarianism* 305). Hobson's "freedom of nationality" would be "fed and ripened by the establishment of international relations on a just basis" ("Ethics" 28) in much the same way as Mill's individuality stipulated "society between equals" (*Subjection* 159). But there are important differences as well. Mill's anti-racialist belief in the universality of human creation came under pressure in the wake of economic decline in the West Indies and a host of crises over imperial sovereignty (Chs. 2 and 5). To counter such pessimism, New Liberal intellectuals turned to social science in order to ground "their progressive political convictions" (Collini, "Political" 226–7). The organic conception of society they theorized posited evolution as an underlying foundation beneficent social forces. On this basis, Hobson blended a liberal emphasis on free will and human agency with a New Liberal emphasis on collectivism, statist intervention, and federated world governance.[11] These were the intellectual grounds for *Imperialism: A Study*, described by Robert J. C. Young as "an unsurpassed economic and ethical critique of the ideology of imperialism" (98).

In *Imperialism* clearly distinguished *internationalism* from *cosmopolitanism*. He used the latter term signifying phenomena external to the holistic ontology of unique but interdependent nation-states. In the past, Hobson explained, cosmopolitanism had an historic role to play in ushering in a defining premise of modernity. The French Revolution was "human and cosmopolitan," rather than purely national, because its soldiers were fighting for a "body of Right" which was "dimly perceived to be the cause of general mankind" (10–11). In the present, however, world progress depended on a rooted international order, purged of imperialism's perverting influence. *Cosmopolitanism*, by contrast, described either a naively impracticable idea—as in the "holy aspiration" for a world socialist brotherhood—or, more ominously, an actually existing tendency toward the "anarchic" and "individual." By way of illustrating such a worrisome decay of "national life," Hobson pointed to the "cosmopolitan organization" of Jewish-led financiers whose alleged control over capital enabled them to misdirect the "policy of nations" (*Imperialism* 10–11; 59; cf. 57). At such moments, his vision of metropolitan sovereignties breached by "cosmopolitan" outsiders borders on anti-semitic conspiracy theory (cf. Long 92–3). In proffering "the Jew" to stand for "particularist forces" that impeded "a progressive, universalist liberalism or socialism" (Cheyette 57), Hobson injected a personified racial agency into what purported to be a structural analysis of the world economy.[12]

---

[11] Yet, Hobson was neither an evolutionary determinist nor a positivist like Comte or Herbert Spencer. Rather, Hobson placed "the creative power of the human will" at the center of his social theory while arguing that such agency was not reducible to immutable laws, physical causes, or narrow scientific explanation (qtd. in Long 11).

[12] See also Hobson's 1900 polemic against the Boer War which calls the war "a 'Jew-Imperialist design' because 'Jews are par excellence the international financiers'" (qtd. in Cheyette 57).

In fact, Hobson's "impartial universal standard of humanity" was laced with racial assumptions (*Imperialism* 186). As he repeatedly cast the future in terms of "higher kinds of competition" and "struggle," his outlook was less a Millean picture of ongoing diversity than a Darwinian vision of evolving consensus over standards of "human excellence" (186–7). In chapters such as "Imperialism and the Lower Races," the inconsistent use of quotation marks around charged terms such as "backward," "civilized," "progress," and "lower races," suggested a wavering attitude toward imperial discourse. While Hobson was clearly reluctant to take this language on board, he was equally unready to dispense with it. The "mission of civilization," he admitted, was a pretense for economic exploitation. Yet, he went on to describe a more "justifiable" practice (228)—in effect producing a version of the civilizing mission which required no quotation marks.[13]

Were European governments simply to renounce their colonial projects, Hobson explained, the result would be to "abandon the backward races to [the] perils" of private plunder (231). Moreover, there is "no inherent natural right in a people to refuse that measure of compulsory education which shall raise it from childhood to manhood in the order of nationalities." This analogy between subject peoples and children (another echo of Mill) is not, he wrote, "invalidated by the dangerous abuses to which it is exposed in practice" (*Imperialism* 229). Thus, while Hobson realized that imperialism legitimates exploitation under the guise of "care and education" (243; cf. 281–2), he responded by urging what he believed (but also doubted) would be a more authentic form of the civilizing mission. Like the expert councils that Mill recommended in the 1860s (Ch. 2), Hobson's "enlightened policy of civilized assistance" enjoined careful study of indigenous cultures and capacities. Such "friendly" tutelage, like that of a benevolent teacher, should aim to "place" unprogressive peoples "in the natural history of man" (243). In the end, Hobson's trenchant critique of imperialism fomented anti-Semitism while installing the kind of paternalistic European paragon which David Lloyd has called the "Subject without properties"—a subject whose allegedly universal credentials qualifies him as "the perfect, disinterested" civilizer (256).[14]

---

[13] For examples of Hobson's use of quotation marks around these terms, see, for example, *Imperialism* 223, 224, 229; see page 231 and *passim* for the use of "backward races" and "civilized" without any quotation marks. Although such racially charged vocabulary was commonplace during this period (appearing in Carpenter's critique of imperialism, discussed below), Gooch's "Imperialism" (1901), another example of New Liberal writing, minimizes its usage. Though Gooch also ends up describing the prerequisites for an ethically tolerable imperialism, he is more specific than Hobson about the role of racism in perpetuating indefensible practices. For example, Gooch objects that "native" races (a term he uses in place of "backward" and "lower" races) are "denied the personal rights recognized at least in theory as the privilege of the white man" (328). He protests against "the unworthy colour-prejudice which everywhere poisons [Britons'] social relations" with native peoples (341; cf. 354).

[14] That said, Hobson's European civilizer is also a developing subject insofar as the disinterested tutelage he urges explicitly requires the further internationalization of the West. The authority to govern "a lower race," he makes clear, cannot be entrusted to individual nations but must proceed from and remain subject to the scrutiny of "some organized representation of civilized humanity" (*Imperialism* 232)—some as yet unrealized framework for global justice (279, 243).

Although Hobson used "cosmopolitanism" in *Imperialism* to signify the threat of rootless actors, the term could also express more benign features of the modern world. In "The Ethics of Internationalism," the phrase "modes of cosmopolitanism" denoted the technological transformations of a shrinking globe: for example, transoceanic travel, wire transfer, and transnational print cultures that enable "direct communication with the thoughts and feelings of distant peoples" (21). In this way, Hobson foreshadowed the structurally interdependent economies, polities, and cultures that Etienne Balibar, almost a century later, called "real universality" (51). As Duncan Bell has remarked, technological innovations like the submarine telegraph and ocean-traversing steamship "impacted not only on the material structures of social and political life but also on the cognitive apprehension of the world" ("Dissolving" 526). Given Hobson's confidence in progressive evolutionary forces, such palpable globality reinforced his belief in the power of social science to "alter the scale of human values and desires" (*Social* 264).

But what of those who lacked Hobson's confidence in the progressive synergy of nature, science, and human will and eschewed his tendency to racialize and Judaize the exploitative dimensions of capitalist globalization? For them, such world-scale modernity could portend the extinction of particular modes of living in favor of those very standards of "human excellence" which Hobson welcomed. The expectation that all societies were heading toward convergence (a teleology that reached its peak in the modernization theories of the 1950s) was already germinal in the works of Karl Marx, Emile Durkheim, and Max Weber (Eisenstadt; cf. Taylor, "Two"). *Howards End* conveys a gloomy meditation on this theme when it depicts "cosmopolitanism" as a near total surrender to the deracinating effects of capitalism and imperialism—a dissolution of the "binding force" of place, and, thus, a profound alteration of human nature. Should such cosmopolitanism ever come, "[t]rees and meadows and mountains will be only a spectacle," and "personal relations" will become the last bulwark of the human (*Howards* 272–3). As Fredric Jameson notes, Forster's situating of this "single historical tendency" as "the bad opposite of place" is not mere nostalgia ("Modernism" 57) but, rather, a protest against a dominatory "type" that, in aiming to "inherit the earth," advances a "grey" cosmopolitanism (Forster, *Howards* 338–9).

Whereas *Howards End* depicts nature's ominous proclivity to favor "the Imperial" (338), for Hobson, the lesson of "biological evolution" was the superiority of "social and cooperative power" over "individual fitness and force" and, thus, the gradual "tendency to equalization of the [world's] material, intellectual and moral resources" ("Ethics" 26, 20). It is as though Hobson expected the cooperative civilizing missions of the future to restrain the competitive urges of Wilcoxian man (or perhaps some Jewish equivalent) through an evolutionarily privileged assertion of Schlegelian ethics. Forster's plea for connection is thus a defense against modernity, while Hobson's social-scientific confidence is an embrace. It is a belief that the modern world is, at least potentially, more national and international than it is "cosmopolitan" and, as a result, more various, more emplaced, and less dominatory than Forster fears.

As the title suggests, *Howards End* is among the least international of Forster's works. A story about the role of a family "heirloom" in resisting the devastation of the modern, it can, in some ways, be likened to Trollope's Barsetshire fiction or to Eliot's *Adam Bede*: a kind of Edwardian-era autoethnography. By contrast, *Where Angels Fear to Tread* takes Italy for its setting without investing in "heirloom sovereignty" or the anchoring ontological properties of place.[15] Instead, what Forster called his "Gino" novel, focuses on people rather than place; and the resort "to Love alone"—a prospect contemplated with alarm in *Howards End*—is already the focus of the earlier novel (*Howards* 273).

While Forster seems to have had no personal contact with Hobson, a man twenty years his senior, he was the contemporary of another New Liberal supporter and outspoken internationalist, the historian G. M. Trevelyan.[16] In 1903, Trevelyan helped to launch the *Independent Review*, a progressive monthly that Forster, a contributor, later described as "decency touched with poetry" (qtd. in Furbank 108). But the most interesting connection between Trevelyan and Forster was their mutual affection for Italy. Trevelyan was the author of a well-known trilogy on the Risorgimento (1907–1911) and related works such as *English Songs of Italian Freedom* (1911), and *Englishmen and Italians* (1919), derived from a lecture delivered to the British Academy and printed that year. Although the "priggish" Trevelyan (Cannadine 65) at times suggests a Wilcox, it seems likely that he helped to inspire the character of Philip Herriton in *Where Angels Fear to Tread*. When Trevelyan's middle-aged aunt married an Italian doctor to the "great disapproval of her family" the future historian of the Risorgimento was the only relative "to pay her friendly visits in Sicily" (Furbank 109, note 1).[17]

Trevelyan's international theory provides an illuminating perspective on Forster's fiction as well as a contrast to Hobson's more scientific approach. In *Englishmen and Italians*, Trevelyan argued that English affection for Italy was the key to international relations during the Risorgimento: Britain's Italian policy was uniquely "wise" because the Victorian public "had an intimate and personal knowledge of Italy" (3). Gladstone's knowledge of Italian culture, for instance, was "an essential part of his being" (16), while novels like George Meredith's

---

[15] On heirloom sovereignty in relation to Trollope's Barsetshire novels see Chaps. 3 and 4 and for brief discussion of Jameson on the spatial perception of *Howards Ends* see Chap. 1.

[16] As an avowed New Liberal supporter, it seems likely that Forster was familiar with works such as *Imperialism*. In addition to age difference, Hobson, was "born and bred in the middle stratum of the middle class of a middle-sized industrial town of the Midlands" (Hobson, qtd. in Siegelman vi), while Forster emerged from a privileged upper-middle-class background. Like Forster, Trevelyan, the grandson of Thomas Babington Macaulay, had family roots in the elite Clapham Sect and close ties to the Cambridge Apostles. Forster, however, was closer to Trevelyan's younger brother, R. C. Trevelyan, a minor Bloomsbury poet and playwright with whom the novelist traveled to India in 1912.

[17] The character of Philip is, however, typically associated with Forster himself as well as with E. J. Dent, whom Forster named as his model (see Rosenbaum 182). For Forster's own account of his inspiration for writing the novel, see "Three" 291. In what might be a scene from one of Forster's novels, Furbank recounts how the young Forster first met Trevelyan at the urging of his aunt, only to find "his mind wandering" to a mysterious Brussels sprout while his host "thundered" on about politics (1:70).

Vittoria (1867) provided "insight such as the writers of one country seldom have shown for the affairs of another" (8). Institutions such as the League of Nations were, thus, doomed without the "mutual understanding" that derives from "personal ties" (20, 19). Britons must cultivate "a great variety of connexions of all sorts with all of the nations of the world" (12).

There are, to be sure, telling affinities between Trevelyan's stress on "connexions" and Forster's fiction. When the historian worries that modern British travelers "more and more consort in cosmopolitan hotels with those of their own speech rather than . . . with the inhabitants of the country visited" (18), he could be describing *A Room with a View* (1908). Arriving in Florence to find a hotel full of "English people" and portraits of the Queen, Lucy Honeychurch protests that, "It might be London" (*Room* 3).[18] For Forster as for Trevelyan, the tendency to limit one's experience to a "Baedeker Italy" of tourist attractions is a troubling sign of British insularity (qtd. in W. Stone 165)—the symptom of a nationality without a view. Nonetheless, *Where Angels Fear to Tread* does not affirm the historian's contention that the willing traveler has but to claim an "intimate and personal knowledge of Italy" in order to steer international progress (Trevelyan, "Englishmen" 18). Though Forster's novels explore embodied relations across borders, they do not portray them as a path to epistemological transparency, utopian ethics, or world-historical progress. Indeed, when Philip Herriton tells his sister-in-law Lilia that "it is only by going off the track that you get to know the country" (Forster, *Where* 3), his Trevelyanesque advice precipitates a series of tragic ironies.

The problem for Philip and, thus, potentially for Trevelyan, is that when the former urges Lilia to "[l]ove and understand the Italians," he has "never contemplated having one as a relative" (4, 18). As James Buzard notes, Philip believes that he is superior to "the run-of-the-mill tourist" (*Beaten* 310), just as Cecil Vyse, the pretentious aesthete of *A Room with a View*, regards himself as an "Inglese Italianato" (91). The truth, however, is that Philip's supposed rapport with Italy amounts to little more than a timorous rebellion against English propriety. Though Forster might have welcomed the idea of "international" Britons, his novel suggests that the world citizenship Trevelyan idealizes is a self-delusion, if not an outright guise for British power. Returning to Italy in a belated attempt to prevent Lilia's misalliance with the déclassé Gino, Philip is a "bewildered tourist," foundering in "the enemy's country" (20, 22). When bourgeois pride compels Mrs. Herriton to remove Lilia's "wretched baby" from its Italian father, she dispatches her children to acquire the infant by whatever means necessary: "There is nothing like personal influence," she advises them (*Where* 93, 70). The Herritons' kidnapping thus becomes a powerful metaphor for the imperial civilizing mission.

---

[18] Trevelyan's disdain for the "cosmopolitan" tourism that precludes such authentic engagement, exemplifies what Frow identifies as a familiar contrast between the inauthentic "*faux voyageur*" and "the heroic figure of the traveler" (127). Forster himself struck a similar chord when he described his first trip to Italy as a "timid outing" during which he made no "Italian friends" and never once "entered an Italian home" (qtd. in Furbank, 96).

As Matthew Reynolds notes, the typical British "tourist experience" positioned Italy "as an object of observation" (78). Roberto Dainotto has shown how the idea of a universalistic Europe rests on a latitudinal split between North and South which is comparable to the orientalist division between East and West. From the reign of Charlemagne forward, writes Dainotto, "Europe" came to signify "a northern *difference* from a South that was European in theory only" and "increasingly abhorred as the site of corruption, decadence, and decay" (25; cf. Reynolds 81). On this view, Europe's "South" is anachronistic: its backward condition equivalent to the past history of "the North." Historicist perspectives of this sort are fundamentally objectifying; their methodology incapable of recognizing that the observer "himself or herself" is "also the figure he or she is investigating" (Chakrabarty 239).[19]

Of course, the Italians Trevelyan portrays are not objects of British tutelage, but potential partners in an evolving international world order. Trevelyan's precursors were those mid-Victorian liberals who cheered Italian unification as an affirmation of universal progress that would gradually migrate from northern to southern Europe and then to the global south. Yet, as Forster's fiction helps us to see, Trevelyan's internationalism instances a characteristically British myopia. It is not that his writing exemplifies the "undeveloped heart" that Forster later described as the foremost limitation of English character: for he is not "afraid to feel" ("Notes" 5). It is rather that, having identified human affect as the medium of international relations, Trevelyan assumes that the emotive body can be harnessed to moral prescription. While he is not as heartless or parochial as Mrs. Herriton— or rather, because he sets out to be the very reverse—what Trevelyan shares with the Britishness she represents is the certainty of a world designed to conform to (his view of) what is right.

Forster's fiction thus captures the British tendency to internalize a self-universalizing anglocentrism. But it also portrays the paradoxical reliance on un-English locales to supply desirable spaces of enchantment. As Edward Said has observed, "skewed" historiography, parochial "universalism," and "unexamined assumptions" about its own "civilization" drain an ethnocentric humanism of its vigor (*Humanism* 53). As though to compensate for that lack, the upholding of Italy as Europe's "South," like its global analogue in "the East," supplements an impoverished knowledge of self and other. "There is something potent in the south that speaks to you like a friend, or rouses you like a party," wrote the French novelist, Madame de Staël, in 1805 (qtd. in O'Connor 28). While "the South" often stands for decline and decay, it can also stand for a living relation to the past: here, personifying indolent or irrational nature; there, embodying artistic sensitivity, intact emotion, or carnal vitality. Whereas bourgeois modernity dulls the senses, Italy revives them and, in *Where Angels Fear to Tread*, prizes open the portals to ethical reflection. "Queer internationalism" mobilizes this encounter as

---

[19] See also Fabian, Gunder Frank, Lloyd, Escobar and, for an example bearing specifically on homosexual discourse, Hoad.

it wages its "war with the liberal imagination." Challenging liberal norms where liberalism least expects that challenge, Forster's novel glimpses an ethic of care in the act of breaking loose from its customary precincts in femininity, domesticity, and "Southernness."

A PHILOSOPHY WITHOUT A VIEW

> I didn't go [to India] to govern it or to make money or to improve people. I went there to see a friend.
>
> E. M. Forster, "Three Countries" (1959)

If Trilling's legacy gives us Forster as liberal archetype, the author's posthumous publications have produced the somewhat different commonplace of a closeted writer whose preferred code for queer sexual desire was the allure of the transnational. By making "foreignness" include "the tabooed 'Otherness' of homosexuality," that is, Forster displaced onto "nationality" themes that he tackled more directly in posthumous works such as *Maurice* (Goscilo 193). In the remainder of this chapter, I explore these twinned legacies, describing the tensions between Forster as "queer internationalist" and as liberal, and locating them in a variation on the geopolitical aesthetic which points to the blindspots of turn-of-the-century New Liberalism. Although Forsterian internationalism is, thus, an experiment in post-Victorian realist form, I am especially keen to demonstrate the implications of its intense meditation on ethics.

Reading Forster from the vantage of feminist political theory one finds that his post-Trilling reputation as a "tolerant humanist . . . whose forms look back to the nineteenth century" (J. Levine 87) understates the complexity of novels such as *Where Angels Fear to Tread*. Yet, quite apart from Trilling's influence, there is a difficulty in illuminating what is most powerful in such works. Although Forster's criticisms of Edwardian society are often astute, they lacks the coherence of a full-fledged political analysis. Formally, *Where Angels Fear to Tread* diverges from the "sociological" register of serialized three-decker novels such as *Bleak House* (1852–3), *Middlemarch* (1871–2), and *The Way We Live Now* (1874–5). Its ironic concision is better suited to exploring the geopolitical unconscious as an embodied effect. As a novelist of politics, Forster comes up against a visible impasse; but as a novelist of eros and ethics he is prescient and original—recalling Raymond Williams's notion of literature's "subjunctive" capacity to anticipate forms of consciousness which are not yet socially available (Ch. 1). In this way Forster's war with the liberal imagination, though deeply embedded in turn-of-the-century contexts, illuminates the transnational critical projects of our own day.

In *Liberalism and Empire* (1999), Uday Singh Mehta shows how liberal thought, played a key role in justifying British imperialism despite its ostensible commitments to liberty and equality. Discounting human emotion (as opposed to reason), the local and particular (as opposed to the general), and concrete experience (as opposed to abstract human nature), liberalism so conceived lacks the ability to encounter difference without lapsing into judgment, exclusion and, the will to dominate. Liberalism, on this account, is so deeply teleological and unflinchingly totalistic that it reflexively relegates particularity to the undifferentiated status of that which merely precedes its own professed endpoint: "civilization."[20]

Mehta's postcolonial critique intersects with a view of liberal modernity which feminists have propounded for decades. As Seyla Benhabib has argued, the liberalism of the Enlightenment inserted a rift between male and female domains, masculinizing a public world of civilization and feminizing a private world of nurture and reproduction. Moral and political theorists since that time have adopted the standpoint of the *generalized* other (a universalized abstraction of the rational and rights-bearing individual) at the expense of the *concrete* other (a particularized understanding of the individual based on life history, personal views, and emotional constitution). Seen from this feminist vantage, the history of liberalism and empire can be seen as the story of how an ideology of incommensurable sexual difference, predicated on a capitalist division of labor, helped to produce what readers of Forster might call a philosophy without a view.

Scholars of Trilling will recognize that the emphasis on affect, locality, and experience is also part of the challenge Forster is seen to pose to the unimaginative liberalism of the 1940s. Thus, though Benhabib, Mehta, and Trilling respond to disparate historical challenges, all seem to agree that "in struggling to implement "its active and positive ends," liberalism "unconsciously limits its view of the world to what it can deal with" (Trilling, *Liberal* 9).[21] Following Trilling, each of these critics might regard Forster as a novelist who, in warring with the liberal imagination, seeks to correct its faulty perceptions. By foregrounding the embodied features of care—the "vital mess" noticed by Trilling (*Forster* 173)—Forster provides the affect and attention to difference so conspicuously lacking in masculinist ethics. That said, Forster's works ultimately flummox the reconfigured liberalism they are often taken to exemplify. As this chapter will demonstrate, his fiction helps to show how a still ongoing revision of Enlightenment ethics continues to rely on undertheorized notions of care.

---

[20] See also Chap. 5 for further discussion of Mehta in light of *The Moonstone*.

[21] The nineteenth-century civilizing mission Mehta describes was rooted in a laissez-faire liberalism that, for all its universalistic rhetoric, explicitly limited the rights of full citizenship to British men of a certain class. Benhabib's project is to illustrate the persistent distortions of gender in a variety of advanced liberal theories including the communicative ethics of Jürgen Habermas. Liberalism of this neo-Kantian stripe does not produce explicit hierarchies of the civilized, but, rather, portrays itself as an impartial set of principles and procedures. Such liberal ethics purport to enshrine what I. Young has called "a transcendental 'view from nowhere' that carries the perspective, attributes, character, and interests of no particular subject" (*Justice* 100). Benhabib and Young have demonstrated how this supposedly impartial construction privileges dominant groups (see also W. Brown, *States*, Ch. 6). Trilling, in contrast, is interested in the normalizing effects of a broadly conceived twentieth-century collectivist liberalism as institutionalized in the bureaucratic state, with its technocratic determination to maximize good (and fend off communism) on behalf of a universal citizenry.

In its original articulation, in the feminist psychology of Carol Gilligan, the *ethic of care* described a marginalized feminine moral disposition, distinct from the dominant masculine perspective inscribed in the *ethic of justice*. Whereas "care" is a contextual ethics, situating morality in terms of concrete relationships, "justice" is allegedly universal, centering on the formulation of abstract rights and principles. Thus, as Joan C. Tronto has explained, care is an ethical "activity," rooted in "the daily experiences and moral problems of real people" ("Beyond" 648; cf. 663). The problem for feminists (and for critical theory more generally) is how to retain such needful attention to concrete experience—not only that of gender but also that of race, ethnicity, class, sexuality, and so on—while avoiding the essentialisms of a distinctly female morality.[22]

Thus, while "care" has been discredited as the essential foundation of a feminist ethics, the term continues to stand for the embodied features that are abstracted and excluded by masculinist moral theorists, from Immanuel Kant and Jean-Jacques Rousseau to Jürgen Habermas and John Rawls. Whereas Benhabib cautiously embraces a language of care that Iris Marion Young eschews, both feminists see "context and affiliation" as the twin correctives to two Enlightenment deficiencies: intolerance toward difference and emotional disavowal (Young, *Justice* 97).[23] Moreover, in emphasizing "context" to speak to the embeddedness and embodiment of lived social relations, both specify what are, in actuality, two overlapping requirements: *epistemological adequacy* (the ability to perceive difference) and *normative response* (the responsibility to attend difference in an ethical way). Finally, both fully recognize the deficiency of any purely contextualist ethics: each seeks a reconciliation between the ethical claims of particularity and what Benhabib describes as "the justificatory constraints" of overarching principles such as equality (188–9). It is this emphasis on universalizable norms which links both theorists to a "liberal" project of modernity, loosely defined.[24]

---

[22] As Tronto argues, the essentialist tendency to present the ethic of care as "intrinsically female" ensures that it will be dismissed as "secondary and irrelevant to broader moral and political concerns" ("Beyond" 649, 655). Likewise, Gilligan attributes exclusively to gender characteristics that may also derive from patterns of class-, race-, and nationality-based social and geopolitical subordination (see also Moody-Adams).

[23] For Benhabib, care is part of the normative fabric for an "interactive universalism" that would acknowledge generalized as well as concrete standpoints (165; c.f. 153, 159). Although Young rejects "care" as a self-defeating reification, she calls for post-Enlightenment theorizations of "moral reasoning" which attend the "particularities of context and affiliation" (*Justice* 97).

[24] For other useful critical discussions of care, see Okin and White. Note that in designating as "liberal" the work of Young, a post-Habermasian feminist who draws on a wide variety of Marxist and poststructuralist thinkers, I deliberately move beyond a narrow definition in which liberalism stands either for a static legacy of the Enlightenment, for the Victorian meanings discussed in earlier chapters, or for *neoliberalism*—that is, the idealization of market forces which has become the dominant justification for deregulation and capitalist expansion since the late 1980s. One need go no further than Hobson to remember that self-identified liberals—as well as Marxists and poststructuralists—have offered worthwhile criticisms of atomized individualism, laissez-faire, "free" markets, and other neoliberal shibboleths. Discussing Forster in light of the left-leaning, social democratic tradition within liberalism—the "large tendency" of Trilling's description (*Liberal* 5)—enables me to offer a more nuanced assessment of his relation to "liberalism" in the broadest possible sense of that term.

Forster's works complement these feminist and transnational projects by upholding a broad-minded but sensitively particularizing *view*—an ethically attentive relation to otherness. Yet, though Forsterian view is formally acute, epistemologically rich, geopolitically alert, and normatively auspicious, it is, nonetheless, an elusive and wholly contingent ethical warrant: the novels do not endorse the Benhabibian aim of seeking "to take the standpoint of the other" (Benhabib 168). Instead, in *Where Angels Fear to Tread*, Forster's multi-faceted crossings—between Northern and Southern, male and female, Protestant and Catholic, heteronormative and queer, upper-class and déclassé—expose the troubling disjunctions between affective expressions of care (affiliation) and the ethical relations to which they only sometimes give rise (epistemological adequacy and normative response). As in *A Passage to India*, the emotive and sexual charge of difference ignites the experience of crossing borders; but Forster's formal investment in transnational phenomenology is not, like Collins's in *The Moonstone*, or Eliot's in *Daniel Deronda*, an effort to envision utopian and futural ends. Instead, Forster's realist aesthetic renders international encounters that are as volatile and unpredictable as they are ethically enlivening.

A WELL-ORDERED MACHINE

Pride was the only solid element in her disposition.
E. M. Forster, *Where Angels Fear to Tread*

Forster can exert such critical pressure in part because, as a "queer" novelist who seeks "to disrupt the economy of the normal" (Martin and Piggford 4), he is acutely aware that care has historically been yoked to an instrumentalizing civilizing mission.[25] With its scathing exposure of Herriton family values, *Where Angels Fear to Tread* reveals that, as the space of nurture, the domestic sphere is not only a mechanism for exclusion, but also, and simultaneously, a prolific site for the production of bourgeois-imperial norms. In the hands of Mrs. Herriton, a "well-ordered . . . machine" (86), parenting is exercised as managerial control. Philip's sister Harriet, a frigid xenophobe and fanatic Protestant, is so unmaternal that she is disgusted by the thought of bathing a baby. In one of the novel's most powerful scenes, her inept attempt to dandle the child she has stolen leads

---

[25] To adopt a "queer self-understanding," Warner has argued, is to know that one's "stigmatization is connected with" deep cultural norms such as gender, the family, and the state (xiii). "Queer theory," writes Dean, "is a theory . . . of how identitarianism serves normalizing power by investing our subjective and social sense of ourselves in taxonomic hierarchies" ("Response"). In *Where Angels Fear to Tread*, British middle-class identity is represented as the primary mode of such normalizing identitarianism, investing subjects in the taxonomic hierarchies of the civilizing mission. See also Dellamora: "Forster's critique of the heterosexual contract radically qualifies his investment in patrician liberal ideals of high culture, individual sensibility, and personal relationship" ("Textual" 163). For other readings that describe or illuminate a "queer" Forster see Aldrich 302–28; Bristow; Buckton 206–18; Caserio 305–7; Lane, "Forster"; Markley; Martin and Piggford; Rahman.

her brother to "wince" in dismay (158). Philip himself is the docile tool of this matriarchal regime: although he knows that he is his mother's "puppet" (85), he does not realize until too late that the "business" for which he has been dispatched to Italy concerns a vulnerable human life (138). As he eventually learns, in a world caught up in the storm of progress, even the best-intentioned nurture may be harnessed to instrumentalist ends, haunted by asymmetrical relations of power, or plagued by desires to eradicate difference.

Care, in this view, is the Edwardian foundation for turning middle-class children into tools of family aggrandizement, working-class Britons into bourgeois aspirants, and non-Western people into "children" requiring the tutelage of the civilized. Thus, the practice of district visiting, in which women like Caroline Abbott entered working-class homes to impart moral guidance, was thought to provide a more caring source of poor relief than the state (see Goodlad, *Victorian*). Caroline's domestic project found its global counterpart in the imperial civilizing mission. Britain's expansion was fueled by developmental hierarchies in which so-called backward peoples were figured as children—in need of care.[26] It is therefore no accident, that in *Where Angels Fear to Tread*, a child's fate is at the center of a story about the impact of Italian *mores* on uptight Britons. When a misalliance between the Herritons' widowed daughter-in-law, Lilia, and, Gino, a young Italian, ends with her death in childbirth, bourgeois pride compels the Herritons to adopt the baby to spare it the presumed injury of an Italian upbringing. To their immense surprise, Gino loves his child and wants to parent him. The stage is thus set for a transformative "interview between the South pole and the North"— albeit one that culminates in tragedy (157).

As Rita Felski has argued, the domestic sphere, though "often portrayed as a domain where natural and timeless emotions hold sway," has been "radically implicated in patterns of modernization and processes of social change" (*Gender* 3). Forsterian matriarchs such as Mrs. Herriton and Mrs. Honeychurch are, in this sense, exemplary: ruling the roost in the interests of their nation and class. Yet, in *Where Angels Fear to Tread*, it is not only the stalwart materfamilias who attests to ethical dysfunction, but also the younger, more congenial women to whom she is contrasted. Such unsparing censure points to the blindspots of Forster's fiction as it faults women for their role in symbolizing and sustaining the ideological work of global capital.[27] But in *Where Angels Fear to Tread*, this misogynistic tendency is also, as we shall see, the sign of Forster's ambivalent investment in Edwardian ideals of male friendship. There are thus two distinct anti-heteronormative narratives in the novel and each one is tied to a young Englishwoman's attempt to negotiate bourgeois norms. The first is a stalled narrative of male friendship involving Lilia Herriton—a fantasy of homosocial care which depends on women's exclusion.

---

[26] On the connections between domestic and colonial versions of the civilizing mission, see, e.g., Thorne, Stoler, Hollis, and Hall.

[27] See Freedgood for a trenchant critique of Forster's misogyny in *A Passage to India* ("E. M." 124); for a discussion of his tendency to build his modernist credentials against the "feminine," see Cucullu.

The second is a more propitious narrative of queer kinship in which Caroline, the novel's most sympathetic character, plays a central role.

DEMOCRATIC AFFECTION

> It would be tempting to make an intelligent man feel towards an intelligent man of the lower class what I feel . . . My motive should be democratic *affection*, and I'm not sure whether that has any strength.
>
> E. M. Forster, "Desire for a book" (1910)

> Eros is a great leveler.
>
> Edward Carpenter, *The Intermediate Sex* (1906)

In one of the best-known passages from *Where Angels Fear to Tread*, the narrator describes Italy as "a delightful place to live if you happen to be a man":

> There one may enjoy . . . that true Socialism which is based not on equality of income or character, but on the equality of manners. In the democracy of the *caffè* . . . the brotherhood of man is a reality. But it is accomplished at the expense of the sisterhood of women (46).

This picture of Italian society, which punctuates the narration of Gino and Lilia's unhappy marriage, makes clear that Forster's novel—notwithstanding its tendency to romanticize "the southern knack of friendship"—is alive to the ethical failings of the Italian masculinity it depicts (172). Indeed, critics who have argued that the Italians in the novel never treat people as "business items" (Beer 68), seem to forget that Gino repeatedly turns marriage into an economic transaction, marrying Lilia for her money, and a second well-off wife because "she is what [he] require[s]" for his son's maintenance (*Where* 135). Nonetheless, it is important to recognize that the narrator's remarks on *Italian* misogyny, which haunt the relation between Gino and Philip, are part of an attempt to negotiate a *British* ideal of homosocial friendship which sought male utopia "at the direct expense of women" (Cole 29).

As critics such as Sarah Cole, Richard Dellamora, and Robert K. Martin, have demonstrated, Forster's works were in dialogue with an influential body of homophile discourses. In the writings of John Addington Symonds and Edward Carpenter, friendship between men was upheld as a liberating alternative to the status quo. Symonds envisioned male friendship as a democratic and equalitarian relation. Yet, as Martin has argued, the Platonic bonds described in his writings encouraged elitism and misogyny ("Edward Carpenter" 105).[28] By contrast, Carpenter's Whitmanesque poem, *Towards Democracy* (1883–1902), depicted

---

[28] Note that the meanings attached to "democracy" and "democratic" in homophile discourses of friendship, as in Forster's "democracy of the *caffè*," emphasize caring relations between men of different classes—not formal rights or the achievement of substantive political equality.

"an ecstasy of loving male community" (Cole 26). In prose works such as *The Intermediate Sex* (1906), Carpenter described "Love" as a "binding and directing force" that could harmonize bonds of sex, nurture, brotherhood, and citizenship (114). Somewhat like Hobson's international theories, his groundbreaking homophile writings offered optimistic solutions to the dilemmas of an embodied ethics—a vision of social democracy in which desire and ethics, justice and care would be mutually sustaining.

In the future, Carpenter believed, working-class men, women, and colonized people would be gradually raised and empowered. But in the here and now, inequality provided a "democratic" spark for mutually uplifting desire. Hence, though Carpenter saw himself as an earnest socialist, feminist advocate, and antiracist, his writings are saturated with developmental tropes in which working-class men, women, "savages," "barbarian races"—as well as ruling-class Englishmen— are likened to children.[29] Moreover, by envisioning homosexuality as an innate moral competence—a built-in ethics of care—Carpenter saw the "Uranian spirit" as prefiguring evolved social relations in which erotic, nurturing and civic affects would harmoniously commingle (107–9).[30]

Of course, Forster could no more share Carpenter's optimism than Hobson's or Trevelyan's, because, as Cole has argued, he "refused to concede that the physical body can be controlled within a transformative or idealizing narrative" (23).[31] Nonetheless, Forster's more tenuous effort to translate homoerotic feeling into "democratic" social practice combined a male friendship ideal like Symonds' with an idealization of inequality like Carpenter's. In this way, Carpenter's description

---

[29] In *Love's Coming of Age* (1911), Carpenter laments that "the world" is dominated by an incompetent Anglo-Saxon male ruling-class, "fatuous" men "to whom it seems quite natural that our marriage and social institutions should lumber along over the bodies of women, as our commercial institutions grind over the bodies of the poor, and our 'imperial' enterprise over the bodies of barbarian races" (37). Carpenter describes women as "the more primitive, the more intuitive, [and] the more emotional" of the two sexes, "in a way . . . nearer the child herself, and nearer to the savage" (46). Yet, ruling-class Englishmen are the victims of lopsided modern development which, though "advanced in mechanical and intellectual invention," is "ungrown . . . on its more human and affectional side" (34). The same man who masters "the world with his pluck, skill, [and] enterprise," is "in matters of Love for the most part a child" (31). Like Hobson, Carpenter believes that Jews exert an undesirable influence: the rule of white middle-class men is corrupted by "the Jew and the Speculator" (36). On the racialist developmental logic in which Carpenter's evolutionary theory is implicated, see Somerville and Hoad. For a more in-depth discussion of Carpenter's wide-ranging and often complex thought, see Geoghegan, and, for a worthwhile exploration of its queer potential, see Bredbeck and Buckton 161–204.

[30] Both nature and environment contribute to the production of Uranians' exceptional pastoral qualities: Carpenter adduces a scientific theory of embryonic "sex-inversion" (*Intermediate* 62) in which biological difference is enhanced by the domestic situation of people who, unlike married heterosexuals, are not absorbed by "the care of their [own] children" (68). As Mosse notes, Havelock Ellis similarly "believed that homosexuality, by directing men's energies toward public rather than private concerns . . . made human civilization possible" (38).

[31] Like Young, Forster values "context and affiliation" (*Justice* 97) but he also emphasizes the tensions between them: affective relations do not reliably yield either adequate perception of or respectful attention to otherness. Since the components of "care" are themselves so fraught, the quest for an embodied liberal ethics that blends particularizing attention with just standards becomes, from a Forsterian perspective, dubious and even counterproductive.

of a "true Democracy" that rests on the leveling powers of "Eros"—that "sentiment which easily passes the bounds of class and caste" (*Intermediate* 107)—recalls "the true Socialism" which, in Forster's Italy, flourishes between men of different classes and nationalities. Indeed, Gino is a discernibly Carpenterian figure: the embodiment of an affective, even nurturing masculinity, and one in whom the enticements of class difference are magnified by the supplementary eroticism of southernness.

But whereas Carpenter's Uranian utopia intends to be gloriously inclusive, Forster's explicitly does not. The novel's depiction of Italy as a homosocial paradise—but one constituted by women's exclusion—is thus a revealing sign of ambivalence toward the homophile friendship ideal. For through it, Philip and Gino's budding intimacy is directly tied to Lilia's failed rebellion against the Herriton regime. Galled by her mother-in-law's tutelage, Forster's wayward widow believes that marriage to an obscure Italian will enable her to wield Herritonian power on her own terms. Her effort to install a British social hierarchy on southern soil, though doomed by ineptitude, seeks to replicate the Victorian pattern through which women's social rituals consolidated middle-class gentility. As Nancy Armstrong and Elizabeth Langland have shown, bourgeois Englishwomen played a crucial role in depoliticizing and stratifying the public sphere: making social calls, visiting working-class homes in the manner of Caroline, and identifying the "principal people" as Lilia hopes to do with her "real English tea-parties" (*Where* 44). Such habits were part of the "portable imperial culture" that, as John Plotz has argued, underwrote a far-flung English expansion ("One-Way" 309).

The "democracy of the *caffè*" thus concludes with a telling aside to the (presumptively male) reader. When in Italy, the narrator opines,

> Why should you not make friends with your neighbour at the theatre or in the train, when you know and he knows that feminine criticism and feminine insight and feminine prejudice will never come between you? Though you become as David and Jonathan, you need never enter his home, nor he yours. All your lives you will meet under the open air, the only roof-tree of the South, under which he will spit and swear, and you will drop your h's, and nobody will think the worse of either (*Where* 46).

In this remarkable passage Forster's narrator suggests that "true Socialism" thrives in Italy because the female social project Lilia hopes to import does not—the project, that is, of policing class hierarchies under the sanction of "feminine" domestic authority. Hence, in Forster's imagined south, male community flourishes across lines of class and nationality because female institutions and the women who supervise them are deprived of social authority.[32]

Lilia's hope of wielding the authority of the British gentlewoman captures a social practice that feminist political theory does not always observe. In *Justice and*

---

[32] In *A Passage to India*, it is the objectionable Major Callendar who declares "it's [British] women who make everything more difficult out here" (214). But Forster appears to have agreed; in a 1959 lecture he wrote that "the manners of" British "womenfolk" in India "could be ghastly" ("Three" 297). See also Freedgood ("E. M." 124).

the Politics of Difference (1990), Young describes the domestic sphere as the space of particularity against which the illusion of universality is maintained: "The public realm of citizens achieves unity and universality only by defining the civil individual in opposition to *the disorder of womanly nature, which embraces feeling, sexuality, birth and death, the attributes that concretely distinguish persons from one another*" (110; emphasis added). By imagining the Italian public sphere as an "open air" space of relaxed homosociality, free of the ordering femininity that Italy is shown to repress, Forster's novel nearly reverses this formulation. In Young's analysis "womanly nature" operates as an enclosure for particularity, authorizing an abstract liberal subject who is, in actuality, a privileged male. But for Forster, "feminine criticism" is an all-too-public engine of stratification, instrumentalizing the embodied features that Young seeks carefully to attend. Thus, whereas Young describes a domestic sphere in which difference is relegated to an excluded space, Forster portrays an assertive feminine regime whose hierarchization of difference transplants the logic of British geopolitics to British life. The "democracy of the *caffè*" is thus a fantasy of beating back the female domestic order to create a zone of liberated male heterogeneity. It is a glimpse of masculine sociality and care that, in Carpentarian fashion, enables affect, eros, citizenship, and nurture to thrive.

Unsurprisingly, toward the end of the novel, the reader is recalled to the "democracy of the *caffè*" in the novel's most homoerotic (and arguably most misogynistic) scene. Gino and Philip meet in the open-air setting of the Caffè Garibaldi. As they cordially agree that not they, but "the ladies," are exercised about the baby's upbringing, Gino lays "a sympathetic hand on Philip's knee" just as Philip sees Harriet "watching them" (*Where* 151). As the uptight spinster interrupts the affectionate male couple, it becomes momentarily possible to believe in the fantasy of a homosocial democracy; possible, in other words, to forget that Philip, an elitist aesthete, has all along supplied more than his share of "criticism" and "prejudice." The reader is asked to see how the man who once "shuddered all over" at the thought of dining with a dentist's son has become indifferent to spitting and swearing (26)—or, at any rate, sufficiently indifferent to distinguish *his* democratic affect from the unrelenting snobbery of his female relatives.[33]

Writing in his journal in 1910, Forster contemplated a new novel that would depict the attraction between a man like himself and "an intelligent man of lower class" (qtd. in Heine xiv). "My motive should be democratic *affection*," he wrote only to add, "I'm not sure whether that has any strength" (qtd. in Heine xiv). In thus attaching "democratic" motives to a bond of "affection," Forster clearly sought to describe an erotically charged friendship between men of different social

---

[33] In the novel's most misogynistic moment, Philip ceases, at last, to be a tourist and is enabled to "live more graciously" through the medium of the Italian language, "the very phrases of which entice one to be happy and kind." This fantasy of a fully internationalized or even post-national male habitus is facilitated by invidious contrast to Harriet's hidebound Englishness: "It was horrible to think of the English of Harriet, whose every word would be as hard, as distinct, and as unfinished as a lump of coal" (152).

standing—precisely the relation that develops between Philip and Gino in *Where Angels Fear to Tread* (cf. Lane, "Forster"). His uncertainty, with its foreshadowing of dwindling productivity in the years after 1910, illuminates the tensions that structure *Where Angels Fear to Tread*, a novel in which "democratic" relations between men are ultimately unsustainable.

Nonetheless, if the homosocial "south" turns out to be an illusion, that is not only because the author was a sheepish misogynist and skeptical Carpentarian. It is also because he was an incisive novelist of care. The narrator's awareness that male friendship flourishes at women's expense presages the tragic violence to otherness which soon follows. In the end, *Where Angels Fear to Tread* foregrounds another and more auspicious anti-heteronormative narrative of international encounter. Although this queerer narrative is very much centered on the geopolitically overdetermined question of violence to otherness, it affords no significant part to misogyny.

QUEER FORSTER

And this was the machine on which she and Mrs. Herriton and Philip and Harriet had for the last month been exercising their various ideas—had determined that in time it should move this way or that way, should accomplish this and not that . . . Yet now that she saw this baby, lying asleep on a dirty rug, she had a great disposition not to dictate one of them, and to exert no more influence than there may be in a kiss or the vaguest of the heartfelt prayers.

E. M. Forster, *Where Angels Fear to Tread*

Critics have often associated Forster with a tentative liberal fiction characterized by failed synthesis between feminized aesthetes and heroic male foils.[34] In June Perry Levine's account of this dialectic, "The Tame in Pursuit of the Savage," Britain's "auntish" ruling-class males seek out the heroic qualities of their foreign and working-class social inferiors in a quest for "completion" and humanist tolerance (72). Joseph Bristow's nuanced variation on this theme argues that Forster aims to "synthesize" the effete aesthete and the brute athlete (57). But since the figure of the "wilting aesthete" derives from Matthew Arnold's effeminate ideal of culture, Forster's homoerotic fusions are impeded by Aestheticism's disabling relation to the feminine (61). As the desired connections between tame and savage are undermined by female intermediaries, it is "as if [the] wished-for homoerotic coupling were itself structured by the assumptions of the dominant heterosexual ideology of the day" (67).

---

[34] Forster himself provided support for the latter view when he explained that in "Arctic Summer," an unfinished novel begun after *Howards End*, he could not see beyond "the antithesis between the civilized man" and his "heroic" counterpart (qtd. in Heine xi).

What Bristow thus reads as normative capitulation, however, Martin interprets as a process of queering. In novels such as *Where Angels Fear to Tread* and *Howards End*, he argues, a distinct mode of relationality, "the formation of a circle of desire around a child," symbolically displaces the antitheses that preoccupy many critics ("Umbrella," 257). Circular patterns involving children articulate "alternative genealog[ies]" to contest the heteronormative logic that privileges marriage over friendship and biological and legal definitions of kinship over elective relations "based on affection or passion" (257, 265). Such fiction is queer both in rejecting binary stalemates and in exploring modes of relationality and "begetting" for those who neither marry nor biologically reproduce (272). One of the most important effects of Martin's reading is that, by directing attention away from the tame/savage antithesis, it enables a focus on feminized traits that are extraneous to that tension. Thus, whereas conventional "feminine" proclivities such as desire for and care of children are lacking in self-involved aesthetes, such as Philip Herriton and Cecil Vyse, they are prominent in an "athletic" character such as Gino Carella.[35]

In fact, in "The Feminine Note in Literature," a lecture he delivered in 1910, Forster developed a notion of gender difference quite unlike that suggested by the tame/savage split and, at the same time, unlike the gender binary articulated in the "democracy of the *caffè*." The key distinction between masculine and feminine writing, Forster's lecture explains, concerns "ethical standards": "Men have an unembodied ideal," whereas women "embody their ideal in some human being." Female authors such as George Eliot prescribe standards of "personal worthiness," while male authors such as Joseph Conrad hew to "some shadowy ideal of conduct beyond the grave" (32–3). One must hasten to add that though Forster thus offers debatable literary assessments based on sexist clichés, his address was written not long after *Howards End* had been lauded as a novel written with "a feminine brilliance of perception" (Monkhouse 123; cf. Piggford, "Introduction" 9; Leavis 35). Through his reading of Carpenter, moreover, Forster knew that "Urning" men, could be described as "feminine soul[s]" enclosed in "male bod[ies]" (*Intermediate* 19).[36] Hence, though Forster's lecture straightforwardly aligns gender with

---

[35] Forster may have chosen "Carella" as Gino's surname because it is a diminutive of *cara*, which is both the feminine form of *caro* or "dear," and the Spanish and Portuguese word for "face" and thus, according to *Dictionary of American Family Names*, a possible "nickname for someone with a beautiful or otherwise distinctive face." Carella may also suggest cognate Italian words such as *cari*, the plural of *caro*, which means either "loved ones" or "family members." Whereas recent critics like Bristow have tended to focus on Gino's strong masculine features, contemporaries noticed his parental affect. According to the *Manchester Guardian*'s 1905 review, Gino's "half-womanly tenderness . . . towards his child" is suggestive of "a real Italian type" (qtd. in Gardner 49). Cucullu's way of reading the male antitheses captures Gino's "femininity" more successfully: she argues that Forster projects feminine emotional credentials onto "the bodies of Eastern men and native sons whose virility will liberate the inchoate desires of English gentlemen" (25).

[36] Carpenter is paraphrasing the views of K. H. Ulrichs. Forster would have been able to read Carpenter's "The Intermediate Sex" when the essay was included in the 1906 edition of *Love's Coming-of-Age*. On Carpenter's influence, especially in *A Room with a View*, see T. Brown.

anatomical sex, the author of *Howards End* had various reasons for contrasting his own perceptions to the "unembodied" masculinism of Conrad or Rudyard Kipling.

Forster's views on sex/gender thus exceed the antithesis of tame and savage masculinity even as they complicate the bourgeois "femininity" derided in *Where Angels Fear to Tread*. His observations on gender and ethics turn on a very different opposition between generalization and particularity. In a way that anticipates feminist and postcolonial critiques of liberalism, Forster's lecture associates a disembodied, decontextualized, and allegedly universal standpoint with masculinity, while characterizing femininity in terms of concrete differences and affective relations. As the gendered marker of an attention to embodiment and particularity, the "feminine note" becomes a potential ethical corrective to British viewlessness.

Forster's aesthetes, despite their conspicuous refinement and effeteness, lack precisely those aspects of so-called femininity which inform the novelist's embodied ethics. Thus, while Bristow rightly associates the Forsterian aesthete with Arnold's ideal of culture (and rightly shows how such "feminine" views were disparaged by later critics), it does not follow that Forster would have rested content with the Arnoldian ideal had there only been "brute strength" to spare (Bristow 57). On the contrary, Arnold's Platonic fixation on the "best that has been thought and said" is, in Forster's terms, a demonstrably masculinist and eurocentric cultural ideology. Likewise, Arnold's famous dictum, "to see the object as in itself it really is" ("Function" 178), can be seen to legitimize the dispassionate posture that dooms Philip to "look on life as a spectacle" rather than to "enter it" (*Where* 178).

As against the limitations of such overweening male spectacularity, Forster portrays Caroline Abbott, a woman able to perceive that ethical decision-making is profoundly contextual—that it invariably emerges from "the muddle" (*Where* 146). Although Caroline has internalized anglocentric middle-class norms, she is a consistently sympathetic character as well as the key female figure in either a reading like Bristow's (in which she impedes male homosexuality) or like Martin's (in which she completes the queer "circle of desire" around Gino's child). Significantly, the focal point of her dreary life in the London suburbs is her "dull acts of charity" (82). Allusions to charity work occur at various charged moments, as when Philip is amused by the notion of Caroline's urging Gino to give up his baby "in the spirit of a district visitor" (109). Caroline's involvement in district visiting, with its deep ties to "feminine" disciplinarity and imperialism, has visibly molded her experience of care, predetermining her reflex to regard such relations from the standpoint of the civilizing mission.

Yet, Caroline's encounter with Italy results in repeated lapses from that ingrained anglocentrism. In what is narrated as a vicarious "fling" (21), the upstanding Miss Abbott abets Lilia's marriage to Gino. When the handsome, young Italian turns out to be an unfaithful husband and the broken-down Lilia dies in childbirth, Caroline seeks to atone for her neglect by retrieving the baby. Her return to Italy is ironically described as a deluded quixotism: "She was here to champion morality and purity, and the holy life of an English home" (122). In a crucial scene, Caroline's missionary zeal is undone by her Italian encounter. As she braces herself for a principled "battle" with the "evil" south, she instead discovers Gino affectionately babbling to his infant son and surrounded by domestic clutter (128)—"the vital mess . . . that nourishes a life" (Trilling, *Forster* 173). Recognizing the baby as "so much flesh and blood," not the disembodied object of Herritonian propriety, Caroline wavers. Though she tries "to imagine that she was in her district," her impulse is to abandon the civilizer's standpoint entirely—"to exert no more influence than there may be in a kiss" (128). Europe's emissary from "the North" thus drops the guise of "the Subject without properties"—recognizing herself as "also the figure . . . she is investigating" (Lloyd 256; Chakrabarty 239). As Caroline and Gino bathe the infant together, she yields to a hopeless, life-altering passion.

Yet, in the end, Caroline leaves Philip to decide between leaving the baby with a loving father "who will bring him up badly," and bringing him to Britain, "where no one loves him, but where he will be brought up well" (147). As Bristow's thesis helps us to predict, the floundering aesthete vacillates: it is not Philip, but his fanatical sister Harriet who acts decisively by kidnapping the infant. The accidental death that follows is deeply tragic but also a prelude to rapprochement between Philip and Gino. Their homoerotic bond, as Bristow remarks, requires the "love, nourishment, and intimacy" that Caroline figures (67). Yet it is important to remember that the Italian man, not the British woman, is the first to embody care in this aspect. Thus, the circle of desire that forms around Lilia's infant is more resiliently anti-heteronormative than any couples-focused reading allows; for it is not only Philip, but also Caroline who is queered by her Italian experience. Both northerners are drawn to Gino because of a physical and emotional spontaneity that they desire but cannot express. Both therefore realize that, as Mr. Emerson says in *A Room with a View*, "love is of the body" (189). Yet, "John Bull to the backbone," each returns from Italy in this much darker novel to a life of almost certain sterility (*Where* 21). Though the international encounter no more gives rise to a full-bodied homosexual love than to a happy Anglo-Italian marriage, it disabuses Caroline and Philip of their bourgeois complacency and—in doing so—renders them unable to couple and propagate Herriton family values. The novel leaves Caroline to return to her "district" (175); but it makes clear, nonetheless, that her faith in the civilizing mission is irreparably shaken.

THE NOVEL WITH A VIEW

> "The Signora had no business to do it," said Miss Bartlett, "no business at all. She promised us south rooms with a view, close together, instead of which here are north rooms."
>
> E. M. Forster, *A Room with a View*

Forster's queer internationalist exploration of the ethics of care is, thus, an exacting and powerful manifestation of an Edwardian-era geopolitical aesthetic. As an expression of what Young calls "affiliation," Forsterian care may entail a father's passion for his son, a yielding to forgiveness for a violent wrong, a British man's yearning for an Italian man's affection—or, as he later wrote—a decision to betray one's country rather than one's friend ("What" 82). Such articulations of care, as Emerson says in Forster's most Carpenterian novel, are "of the body" (*Room* 189). Yet, in contrast to Carpenter's works, *Where Angels Fear to Tread* also suggests that a morality embedded in affective relations will often be narrow, undemocratic, reactionary, violent, sexist, or simply selfish. Although ethics are, for Forster, about the relation to otherness, and though no disaffected relation can be ethical, his novel suggests that for care to be ethical it must also be informed by *view*.

Forsterian view articulates the possibility of a broad-minded but carefully particularizing attention to otherness: a glimpse of how embodied affect and enlarged perception may stimulate one another, sparking ethical revision. Although, historically speaking, view can be deeply implicated in imperious fantasies ("I am the monarch of all I survey") and delusions of universality (the transcendental "view from nowhere"), in Forster's novels view is never monological or abstract, but always situated and concrete.[37] As depicted in the Italian novels, view stands for an openness to difference which is lacking not only in hardcore xenophobes (Mrs. Honeychurch, Harriet Herriton), but also in the self-proclaimed travelers who unwittingly reduce difference to objectified knowledge (Cecil Vyse, Philip Herriton, and the real-life G. M. Trevelyan). Thus, in *Where Angels Fear to Tread*, the "view from the Rocca" unsettles the standpoint of the tourist or civilizer, heightening Philip's sensitivity to Caroline and to Caroline's own heightened "consciousness of wider things" (110–111). Though one's view on this account is invariably perspectival, it is not purely visual; rather, as an embodied and lived situation—a view *from* somewhere—view is multi-sensory, dialogical, performative, and lived. In thus signifying an attentive and deeply felt relation to otherness, an ethos in which context and affiliation are mutually sustaining, view represents a formal confluence of subjective and subjunctive possibility which produces Forster's most optimistic conception of the potential for a caring ethics.

Of course, "view" also references a specific narrative feature of Forster's variation on the realist geopolitical aesthetic—the Forsterian point of view that, as Trilling suggests, enacts a "double turn," simultaneously affirming and contesting norms in its "respect for two facts co-existing" (*Forster* 17). As an innovation in realist form, the novel-with-a-view not only portrays the ethically desirable stance of favored characters, but also actively promotes it through a narrative technique that is not so much omniscient as multi-perspectival (without recourse to the multiple narrators of Collins's fiction). Although the Forsterian narrator puts several viewpoints into play, subjecting each to varying modes of irony and assessment, such irreducibly different perspectives cannot, finally, be synthesized, balanced, or otherwise reconciled. Forster's novels thus enable readers to understand and

---

[37] Pratt adopts the phrase "I am the monarch of all I survey" to describe the unironical perspective found in many nineteenth-century travel writings, the "solemnity and self-congratulatory tone" of which (201, 208) resonates with the anglocentric and eurocentric perspectives critiqued by Chakrabarty, Dainotto, U. Mehta, and Said. On the "view from nowhere" which underwrites the allged impartiality of masculinist and eurocentric ethics, see I. Young (*Justice* 100).

connect "worlds which are opaque to each other" (P. Armstrong 375). In so doing, they express skepticism toward a key aspect of Benhabib's feminist ethics: the "reversibility of perspectives" which, she believes, is integral to cultivating a universalizable "moral point of view" (164). Instead, Forster's novels affirm the more modest ethical practice of "moral humility" described by Iris Marion Young ("Asymmetrical" 49). From such a stance "one starts with the assumption that one *cannot* see things from the other person's perspective and waits to learn." To cultivate such a view, the Forsterian subject must learn to listen and communicate "across distance" ("Asymmetrical" 49, emphasis added; 168n).[38]

Young's description of moral humility precisely captures Caroline's "abashed" response when, during her encounter with Gino and the baby, she abandons the civilizer's standpoint and wishes "to exert no more influence than there may be in a kiss or in the vaguest of the heartfelt prayers" (134, 128). Yet, while Young helps to elucidate the kind of ethical relation which Forster's novels valorize, there are powerful tensions in *Where Angels Fear to Tread* which neither she nor Benhabib fully explores. Caroline's impulse to suspend judgment and withhold influence represents care in its most ethical aspect: "She was in the presence of something greater than right or wrong" (134). But even as Gino's passion for his baby enables this ethical encounter, it is itself a quaintly narcissistic affect. So far from grounding ethics, parental love exemplifies care in its most asymmetrical form: the "wonderful physical tie" that binds parents to children is, according to Forster, rarely reciprocated (136).[39] Similarly, Caroline and Philip's passion for Gino springs from their openness to his "strange refinements." Yet, for all its affective power, their encounter with otherness does not neutralize their ingrained reflex to equate middle-class British morality with civilization, nor erase the underlying perception of Gino as a "cruel, vicious fellow" (134).

As is so often the case in Forster's fiction, the emotions that stir us the most are the most precarious—the least reliably ethical. One may valorize moral humility and openness to difference, cultivating one's view by way of surpassing rigid standards of "right or wrong," but, in the end, one's perspective remains attached to, if not absolutely predicated on, those very standards. Precisely because of its ethical value, Forsterian view is all but impossible to sustain. Though one can and, indeed, should feel moved to recognize its normative power, such emotive

[38] Central to Benhabib's feminist theorization of post-Habermasian communicative ethics is the cultivation of an "enlarged" judgment predicated partly on the "reversibility of perspectives" or the "ability to take the standpoint of the other" (164, 168). According to Young, such reversibility is impossible and the presumption of its possibility tends counterproductively "to collapse the difference between subjects" ("Asymmetrical" 58). Young's notion of cultivating enlarged thought through a stance of moral humility thus more closely approximates Forster's skeptical and limited affirmation of view.

[39] As Rosenbaum notes, Santa Deodata, the patron saint of the Italian town where Gino resides is an important symbol "in a novel that is as much about the relations of parents and children as about England and Italy"; the saint was "so holy" that "she would not help her mother after the devil had thrown her downstairs" (183). The saint, in contrast to Forster's wish, betrays her "friend" for her "country."

and fully enlarged attention to otherness is not, and can never be, the foundation of a stable universal creed.

One finds a comparable sense of the limitations of view in *A Passage to India*, Forster's most complex narrative of "Southern" encounter. As Paul B. Armstrong has argued, Forster's last novel recognizes "the impossibility of reconciling different ways of seeing" (365). Armstrong goes on to argue that Forster is a "liberal ironist" in the mode of Richard Rorty. Thus, *A Passage to India*

> invokes the ideal of non-reified, reciprocal knowledge of other people and cultures only to suggest that interpretation invariably requires distancing, objectifying prejudgments. The novel insists that truth and justice can be determined unequivocally—Aziz is innocent, and India must be liberated from the yoke of British oppression—but its manipulation of point of view demonstrates the difficulty (perhaps impossibility) of attaining a lasting consensus about any matter or of discovering a final, uncontestable meaning to any state of affairs (367).

Although Armstrong deftly dispels the cliché of a naïve Forster, subject to the "fallacies of liberal humanism," his reading projects a novelist who is entirely comfortable with the Rortyan split between the infinite contestability of norms, on the one hand, and, on the other, the imperative to uphold "a defensible faith in ideals of justice and community as necessary guides for social change" (Armstrong 365, 367; cf. Rorty, *Contingency*). But this Rortyan commitment to abstract justice, no matter how tempered by postmodern skepticism, jars with Forster's emphasis on concrete and embodied relationships.[40]

Recounting his first visit to India in a 1959 lecture, Forster describes his "connection" to "that strange country" as "peculiar and personal."

> I didn't go [to India] to govern it or to make money or to improve people. I went there to see a friend . . . The tension between the Indians and the British was increasing . . . The sense of racial tension, of incompatibility, never left me. It was not a tourist's outing, and the impression it left was deep ("Three" 296–7).

In this remarkable quotation Forster concisely rehearses the critical themes of his internationalist aesthetic—the capitalist and imperialist aims of the civilizing mission and the complicities of tourism. In opposing a purely personal motive ("to see a friend") to the instrumentalizing goals of bourgeois travel, the novelist illustrates his own inclination toward an affiliative and contextual ethics. By contrast, Armstrong aligns Forster with an "unembodied ideal" that is largely alien to his writing (Forster, "Feminine" 33). Fielding's refusal to succumb to Anglo-Indian prejudice in *A Passage to India* is thus said to "resolutely endorse" the Habermasian "ideal of justice based on consensus" (P. Armstrong 376)—this, despite the fact that Fielding's resistance to prejudice springs from prior intimacy with Aziz: not

---

[40] One imagines that the imputation of a Rortyan Forster, ready to agree "with Habermas that positive norms are necessary to provide goals for social change" (381), would also give Trilling pause. For additional Rortyan readings of Forster, see May and Born. For a discussion of Rorty's "casual" stance, which confirms my sense that Rorty's sensibility is quite unlike Forster's, see A. Anderson, *Way*, Chapter 5. For a critique of Rorty's tendency to romanticize the nation, a most un-Forsterian project, see Honig, *Democracy* 115–22.

the distant pursuit of a just consensus, but the felt demands of a caring relation. Thus, while Aziz "sometimes dreams" of "universal brotherhood," he dreams of it feeling—as Habermas surely would not—that "as soon as it was put into prose it became untrue" (*Passage* 145). Forster, on this reading, is a postmodern ethicist who faces down skepticism, above all, by refusing to betray his friend.

Although Forster urges moral humility and openness to difference, it is, therefore, by no means clear that *A Passage to India* insists "unequivocally" that "India must be liberated from the yoke of British oppression" (Armstrong 367).[41] The politics of decolonization haunt Fielding and Aziz, driving a wedge between them; but, from the vantage of the "peculiar and personal," anti-imperialist manifestos are the "prose" of a different aesthetic register. As Christopher Lane has argued, "far from resolving political distance into personal connection," Forster's narratives of interracial desire culminate in "sexual indeterminacy and colonial ambivalence" (*Ruling* 146). Queer internationalism is predicated on an embodied pull toward otherness which is innocent of the intention to dominate, improve, or instrumentalize—indicative of what Trilling, in a phrase borrowed from *A Room With a View*, calls Forster's "relaxed will" (*Forster* 11; Forster, *Room* 123). But though "relaxed will" encourages respect toward otherness its very resistance to rigor makes it a wobbly foundation for procedural rectitude or radical politics.

There is a comparable indeterminacy in *Where Angels Fear to Tread*—one that shadows the queering effects of the circle of desire around Gino's child, anticipating tragic violence. Although Caroline's enlarged view has subdued the will-to-civilize, her reflexive presumption of British moral superiority remains surprisingly intact. At various points the novel suggests that a British middle-class upbringing entails superior education, better grooming, and a higher "standard" of conducting extra-marital affairs than Gino, as a representative Italian male, exhibits (64). These meager advantages are hardly extolled; indeed, their ethical and emotional costs are presented as all but devastating. Yet, the novel never seriously rejects the assumption that the baby's upbringing will somehow go "well" in Britain and "badly" in Italy (147). Caroline's ethnocentric attachment to British norms is allowed to stand, not because it is admirable, but because the attachment is real; its force so ingrained that it visibly permeates the narrative.[42] *Where Angels*

---

[41] A more accurate suggestion might be that the novel makes clear that India's liberation is inevitable, that Indians such as Aziz will resist the British yoke—though undoubtedly at the expense, at least temporarily, of the cross-racial and cross-cultural intimacies that it is the novel's immediate concern to romanticize and aestheticize. On Forster's investments in imperialism, see, for example, Baucom, *Out*; Lane, *Ruling*; J. Marx; Parry, "Politics" and "Materiality"; Said, *Culture*; and Suleri.

[42] Forster's early narrative of encounter with Italy thus prefigures the more vexed imperial encounter; in *A Passage to India*, "the advance into new and profoundly astonishing perceptions is accompanied by retreats into the confines of known sterilities" (Parry, "Politics" 138). It is during one such retreat that Italy, often figured as the object of dubious British tutelage in *Where Angels Fear to Tread*, is said in the later novel to exemplify a mode of "civilization that has escaped the muddle" (*Passage* 282).

Fear to Tread thus concludes with a limited affirmation of the ethical impact of a queering international encounter, which curbs the civilizing mission but does not profess to dismantle it. Inhabiting the "view from the Rocca" has, to be sure, altered Forster's erstwhile tourists irreparably but, having left "the South" it is clear, as Caroline says, that "all the wonderful things had happened" (180). Lest one understate the tragic seriousness of this concluding note of indeterminacy, it is crucial to remember that it is not only "wonderful things" that Caroline and Philip leave in their wake, but also a dead child.

INFINITE RESPONSIBILITY

The face is not constituted by the I but emanates from the Other, putting the Same in question.
Emmanuel Levinas, *Totality and Infinity*

Philip had seen that face in Italy a hundred times—seen it and loved it, for it was not merely beautiful, but had the charm which is the rightful heritage of all who are born on that soil. But he did not want to see it opposite him at dinner. It was not the face of a gentleman.
E. M. Forster, *Where Angels Fear to Tread*

Harriet poised the umbrella rightly, and for a full quarter minute they contemplated the face that trembled in the light of the trembling flame.
E. M. Forster, *Where Angels Fear to Tread*

As a comedy turned tragic, and a realist narrative turned surreal, magical, and allegorical, *Where Angels Fear to Tread* helps to elucidate unresolved problems in feminist efforts to theorize an embodied liberal ethics. As articulated by Benhabib, feminist ethics seek to "acknowledge the centrality of justice as well as care in human lives," expanding the "moral domain" to attend embodied particularity "without giving up the justificatory constraints" of overarching principles (188–9). "Interactive universality" is described as an ongoing project that "aims at developing moral attitudes and encouraging political transformations that can yield a point of view acceptable to all" (153). Yet, this universal point of view is simultaneously invoked—as though it were a *fait accompli*—to place "justificatory constraints" on particular notions of the good.

Young's feminist ethics, by contrast, are more radically attentive to the claims of difference, but she too seeks to reconstruct liberal norms: "some standard of equality is ultimately necessary for theorizing justice" ("Asymmetrical" 50; C.f. *Justice* 106 and *Inclusion* 57–62). Young thus aligns her work with the ethics of Emmanuel Levinas which posit the existential priority of the encounter with otherness, enjoining infinite responsibility for the other's care. As Young interprets it,

Levinas's constitutive ethical encounter enables subsequent appeal to measures of "comparability"—in effect, positing irreducible difference as the prior ground for equalitarian justice. This creative appropriation of Levinas underwrites Young's efforts both to deconstruct and relegitimate equalitarian norms.[43]

As a novelist for whom the encounter with otherness is primary, Forster is quite possibly Levinas's most astute literary precursor. But, whereas Young seeks to build a bridge from irreducible difference to asymmetrical reciprocity, reconstituting the liberal ideal of mutual recognition between equals, Forster casts doubt on any such normative project. Forster looks askance not only because, as a Levinasian might argue, notions of equality reduce difference to sameness, but also because the very hope of an equalitarian social order threatens to eradicate the compelling strangeness on which encounters wrested from geopolitics depend for their efficacy. Instead, Forster's stress on the affective power of bodily encounter evokes Luce Irigaray's notion of *wonder*, yet another influence for Young. Like Irigaray, Forster portrays wonder as "openness to the newness and mystery of the other person" (Young, "Asymmetrical" 56).

To be sure, wonder invites the exoticizing and fetishizing of otherness, a pitfall to which Forster's fiction is arguably subject.[44] Forsterian desire thrives on the heady mixture of nurturing and erotic affects, as when Caroline's southern encounter combines the baby's "glorious, unquestionable Fact" with proximity to his full-grown father, a "born artist's model" (*Where* 180; 128–9). Moreover, such potent affiliation does not, as it would for Young, culminate in calls for justice. Instead, Forster's tendency to romanticize "democratic" social relations blunts his sensitivity to inequality as a problem requiring an active political response.

That said, Forster's variation on the geopolitical aesthetic registers these limitations through a formal break with the quotidian conventions of the "novel with a view." In the most surreal scene, Philip confronts the baby in an allegory of ethical failure. The shift from comic irony to something like magic realism is first articulated through Philip's recoil from "a ghastly creature"—the "poor idiot" whom Harriet has commissioned to deliver instructions to her brother (155).[45] Unaware

---

[43] Space does not permit me to provide a full discussion of Young's inventive adoption of Levinas's seminal reversal of ontology and ethics. For Levinas, a philosophical stress on ontology totalizes the other by positing him or her as a knowable phenomenon (recalling the problems of "Western" methodology described by Chakrabarty). By insisting on the priority of ethics, Levinas seeks instead to recognize that the other's difference is irreducible, that one's ethical relation to the other confers obligation, and that this encounter is constitutive of one's moral being. For an elucidation of these ideas as they are articulated in *Totality and Infinity* and other works, see Critchley, "Introduction" and *Ethics*; Ahmed; and Peperzak.

[44] Puar articulates a comparable concern with respect to the fetishized 'Third World" of today's queer tourists: "A culturally defined and driven homophobia does not, after all, deflect the lure of an exotic (queer) paradise; instead, it encourages a continuity of colonial constructions of tourism as a travel adventure into uncharted territory laden with the possibility of taboo sexual encounters, illicit seductions, and dangerous liaisons" (113). Masterman's review of *Where Angels Fear to Tread*, which describes Gino as possessing "something mysterious and terrible, congruous with the hot night and magic of the hills and valleys, and all the enchantment of a land where the intellect is paralysed by the emotions" (53–4), suggests the kind of quasi-Orientalist exoticization that Forster's novel could evoke.

[45] Although Forster is not generally recognized as a magic realist, the moments in his fiction which have promoted critics to describe a "mystical strain" (J. Levine 87) are illuminated by provisional use of this term. The narrative innovations of magical realism respond to the fragmented histories and hybridized cultures of postcolonial experience. Forster's effort to resist the bogus ethics

that she has resorted to kidnapping, Philip believes that Gino has relinquished his son in a final confrontation between "the South pole and the North" (157). As they descend toward the train station in a dark carriage, the stolen baby bundled in Harriet's "bony" embrace, Philip has a deep sense of foreboding:

> He had last seen the baby sprawling on the knees of Miss Abbott, shining and naked, with twenty miles of view behind him, and his father kneeling by his feet. And that remembrance, together with Harriet, and the darkness, and the poor idiot, and the silent rain, filled him with sorrow and with the expectation of sorrow to come (157).

Striking a match to view the baby's face, Philip finds it "all wrong"—"puckered queerly," with soundless tears "well[ing] inexhaustibly from the little eyes" (157–9).[46] Anxiously lighting another match, Philip sees the baby's face "that trembled in the light of the trembling flame" (160). The crash of the overturning carriage follows immediately, killing the helpless being that has languished in their care. When we next see the baby, the "face was already chilly, but thanks to Philip it was no longer wet" (161). Philip has, at last, encountered otherness, recognizing his infinite responsibility for another's suffering—only such ethical awakening has occurred too late.

QUEER INTERNATIONALISM

> For even if I kill the other or chase the other away in order to be safe from the intrusion, nothing will ever be the same as before.
> Adriaan Theodoor Peperzak, *To the Other: An Introduction to the Philosophy of Emanuel Levinas* (1993)

The author of *Where Angels Fear to Tread* is both more and less than a humanistic liberal. If he is, as critics have often noted, morally complex where other liberals are rigid, and "relaxed" where others are hortatory and sanctimonious, that is not because of any programmatic allegiance to liberal individualism or the internationalisms of New Liberals like Hobson or Trevelyan. Neither is it because, as some readers of *Howards End* might imagine, he is committed to seeking out dialectical solutions to political conflict. Rather, what is consistently distinctive

---

of the civilizing mission by means of international encounter strive after comparable breaks with realistic conventions. As Simpkins has argued, magic realism offers a defamiliarizing "supplement" that "may enhance, through its own theatricality, the force of an otherwise commonplace development, boosting its significative show in the process through a transcendent power" (145). Forster uses the "poor idiot," a figure whose embodied difference would be radically suppressed ("shut up") in a northern culture (*Where* 155), to signal this defamiliarizing shift—in effect, mobilizing British repression of disability as a paradigmatic instance of what Ahmed calls "violence against the otherness of 'the other'" (138).

[46] This noiseless crying is foreshadowed earlier when Caroline, concerned about Gino's rough but tender handling of the child, exclaims, "Oh, do take care!" Gino replies, "It is nothing. If he cries silently then you may be frightened" (135). This exchange sets up a direct contrast between Gino's loving, masculine care and Harriet's "harsh crooning," presaging the baby's death in British hands.

in this author's outlook is his unswerving attention to embodiment including the kinds of encounter—both ethical and not—to which embodied relations give rise.

Ironically, it is Forster's reputation as a liberal, albeit an iconoclastic liberal, which tends to obscure the salience of his embodied standpoint. As many theorists have argued, the privileging of concrete and affective relations tends to engender illiberal effects, skewing one's perspective "with a centripetal emotional intensity that threatens public interactions with communal suffocation" (White 109). One expects a morality committed to preserving particular relations to cling to tradition, resist change, or malign or exclude outsiders. Indeed, theorists such as Benhabib and Young seek out the introduction of universal norms precisely to offset such contextualist excesses. Here is what makes Forsterian ethics so difficult to categorize. While the novelist is too "relaxed," personal, and anti-normative to count as a serious liberal—though his works are committed to a web of lived relations rather than a set of abstract ideals—he is unlikely to be mistaken for a conservative or communitarian. The reason, however, is simple. Forster is not primarily an exponent of British liberalism or traditionalism because he is, first and foremost, a queer internationalist. The author of *Where Angels Fear to Tread* is a contextualist attracted to the *frisson* of difference; a relationalist who asserts the power of affective ties to disclose the world rather than either perfect or preserve it.

Once again, Rorty's liberalism provides an ideal backdrop against which to illuminate Forster's idiosyncrasies. Writing on the subject of internationalism, Rorty argues that "justice" (by which he means ethical obligations to outsiders) can be conceived as an enlargement of one's primary loyalties to one's closest kin. "To behave morally," Rorty alleges, "is to do what comes naturally in your dealings with parents and children, or your fellow clan members." As families and clans have confederated into tribes and nations, the scope of such "naturally" moral behavior has expanded in recognizably modern ways ("Justice" 47–8). Rorty thus seeks to collapse the conceptual difference between justice and care by recasting overarching principles as mere extensions of narrower loyalties to family and clan. By contrast, Forster denaturalizes precisely such loyalties: his novels contrast the heteronormative, anglocentric, and imperial morality of the Herritons to the queer circles of desire which form, however fitfully, across boundaries of class, nation, geography, and race. Indeed, for Forster, the "natural" morality of the British family is deeply implicated in domination and exclusion.

Thus, whereas Rorty presumes that the sole ground for ethical relations is the possibility of seeing that others are "like us" ("Justice" 55), Forster makes the opposite perception the central insight of the queering international encounter. For him, what is ethically bracing in the notion of care is not to do with close ties to those "like us" but, rather, with epistemological revision: with the transfiguring view that an engaged attention to otherness can, at least momentarily, spark. True to his embodied ethics, Forster strives to preserve a fragile web of relationships, only the queer kinships he values (Gino, Caroline, Philip and the baby; the Schlegel sisters and their Bast child; Fielding and Aziz) are those "elective human relations based on affection or passion" which a heteronormative and propertarian society refuses to legitimate (Martin, "Umbrella" 265). Forster thus invites a

Levinasian perception of infinite responsibility to otherness—an ethical conception that Rorty dismisses as a "stumbling-block" and "nuisance" (*Achieving* 97).

Of course, the so-called ethical turn in recent criticism has had a mixed reception.[47] Certainly, the inadequacies of friendship as a strategy for overturning imperialism in *A Passage to India* make clear that ethics alone are unlikely to deliver just conditions. Feminists and other proponents of "equality and non-domination" may thus find Forster's investments in asymmetrical relations of care unhelpful or, as Young herself might propose, might view such investments as useful in articulating a "level of ethics and ontology" which is supplementary to "the level of politics" at which justice is pursued (*Inclusion* 59).[48] There is, it seems, clear justification for both assessments. *A Passage to India* will continue to be read—rightly—as a text complicit with imperial power, and—also rightly—as one that contests imperialism by refusing to privilege "one kind of certainty," leaving "gaps in representation for 'otherness' to show through" (Malik 224). Which Forster one chooses to emphasize at any given moment ought perhaps to depend—in a mode of reading that might itself be called Forsterian—on context.

As a "Levinasian" novel, *Where Angels Fear to Tread* complicates the mid-Victorian-era modes of sovereignty described in previous chapters. Whereas autoethnographic works like Trollope's Barsetshire series perceive the ethico-culturally intact nation as the repository for an "heirloom" sovereignty that evolves over time, naturalism makes the collapse of the heirloom social order simultaneous with the violation of the sovereign nation and sovereign individual. Wilkie Collins's alternative mode of worldedness anticipates a postmodern understanding of sovereignty as ontologically pluralized, circulatory, and multi-sited. In contrast to either, Forster—in making ethical embodiment the focus of geopolitical insight—figures the deeply situated flesh-and-blood body as both sovereign and non-sovereign. That is to say, breaching the body's sovereignty becomes the condition of that infinite responsibility to otherness which queer internationalism takes for its ethical horizon.

What, then, can queer internationalism contribute to the more emphatically globalized and postcolonial contexts of today? Young's work on cosmopolitan democracy offers a useful starting point for reflection. As Young doubtless realized, her call for transnational "obligations of justice" is subject to the temporal paradoxes of an ongoing project (*Inclusion* 242)—one that aims to realize an inclusive, democratic ideal that derives from shared norms of justice which have yet to emerge. U. S. aggression in the wake of September 11 has made clearer than ever that the very notions of democracy which theorists invoke to equalize world politics can be appropriated on behalf of neo-imperial projects. It is worth noting,

---

[47] See, for example, Jameson (*Singular*), which favorably cites Badiou's strong critique of ethics, including the writings of Levinas and Irigaray.

[48] Young views Levinas's account of the encounter as a supplement, expressed at the level of ethics, to a political "theory of communicative democracy" (*Inclusion* 59). She aims thereby to reconstruct universalism by privileging norms of reciprocity and respect which are, she argues, embedded within practices of communicative exchange.

then, how little Rorty's demotion of Western values—from universal truths to "local" concepts ("Justice" 50)—offers to restrain neo-imperialism. Rorty believes that it is simply natural for "loyal Westerner[s]" to wish other nations to adopt their own notions of justice. His advice is that "we Westerners" adopt a "more frankly ethnocentric and less professedly universalist" strategy toward promoting Westernization (56). To be more persuasive, the West should present itself as having "an instructive story to tell" (57).[49] Rorty thus abstracts his account from geopolitics (the impression he conveys is that the West's only interest in non-Western affairs stems from the "natural" desire to promote its own vision). The effects of power are as irrelevant to his analysis as is the possibility that the Western "story" might itself gain something from the encounter with difference. Thus, though Young is the theorist who insists on shared standards of justice, it is the more relativistic Rorty who urges a liberalism without a view.

Nonetheless, one imagines that Forster would welcome the recognition of a "densely interdependent world" more than the insistence that "political institutions" "lay down procedures" for "negotiating relationships" in a world so conceived (*Inclusion* 260). Forster's fiction seems not only to doubt the viability of such institutional edifices but also the perfectionist impulse that underlies them.[50] Though he believes in the existence of an "aristocracy of the sensitive, the considerate, and the plucky . . . in all nations and classes," he describes them as an "invincible" minority ("What" 87). Ethically and politically desirable though such prized attributes are, they are emphatically embodied and contingent; thus, the effort to codify or institutionalize them is invariably misguided. It is in this way that Forster wars with the liberal imagination of Trilling's era—and of our own.

But that is not to conclude that Forster's works afford us nothing beyond an illustration of liberal humanism in conflict. To the contrary, as a queer internationalist, the author of *Where Angels Fear to Tread* may well be a most timely novelist. Though it is true that the politics of anti-fascism and decolonization required a "language which [Forster] could not speak" (Parry, "Politics" 147) in our own world of simultaneously deepening interdependence and schism, the merits of a "relaxed will" cannot be dismissed. Thus, in her study of Islamist women's movements in Egypt, Saba Mahmood urges critics to recognize the ways in which theories of political subjectivity which were crafted to resist normativization inadvertently limit what counts as agency or resistance to Western preconceptions. "Critique," writes Mahmood, "is most powerful when it leaves open the possibility that we might also be remade in the process of engaging

---

[49] By contrast, Young suggests that "[s]elf-determining peoples" should ideally "govern themselves democratically. They cannot be said to be self-determining, however, if democracy, or particular interpretations of democracy, is imposed on them" (*Inclusion* 264).

[50] It should be added, however, that Forster, who knew that "[t]olerance, good temper and sympathy" are not enough in a world "rent by religious and racial persecution" might well have applauded Young's efforts to inject moral humility into progressive politics (Forster, "What" 81). Likewise, one wonders if Forster might have been persuaded by A. Anderson's argument that a liberal commitment to procedures such as the rule of law need not be disembodied, disaffected, or lacking in ethos (*Way*, esp. Ch.6).

another's worldview . . . This requires that we occasionally turn the critical gaze upon ourselves, to leave open the possibility that we may be remade through an encounter with the other" (37). Mahmood thus captures the core insight of queer internationalism. To inhabit the "view from the Rocca" is not only to open oneself to multifarious disclosure but also to recognize oneself as "the figure [one] is investigating" (Chakrabarty 239).

Given the variable impacts of a still-globalizing capitalism plagued by war, inequality, and climate crisis, Forster's strengths as a novelist of moral humility and queering encounter can no more provide a comprehensive guide for today's projects of justice than they did for the anti-imperialism of his own day. But in offering a richer, queerer, and more international exploration of care than critical theory has yet to articulate, Forster's fiction contributes a vital resource. The world of the twenty-first century will often need to do a great deal more—but cannot afford to do less—than to cultivate a criticism with a view.

8

The *Mad Men* in the Attic
Seriality and Identity in the Modern Babylon

> It is certainly of service to a man to know who were his grandfathers and who were his grandmothers if he entertain an ambition to move in the upper circles of society . . .
>
> He had no father or mother, no uncle, aunt, brother or sister, no cousin even whom he could mention in a cursory way to his dearest friend . . . [T]he fact remained that though a great many men and not a few women knew [him] very well, none of them knew whence he had come, or what was his family.
>
> He was certainly a handsome man,—his beauty being of a sort which men are apt to deny and women to admit lavishly.
>
> Anthony Trollope, *The Prime Minister* (1875–6)

This and much more greets the reader in the opening pages of *The Prime Minister*, the fifth in Anthony Trollope's six-part series of Palliser novels, which appeared in eight monthly parts between November 1875 and June 1876 and then in a three-volume edition.[1] The subject of this description, as we saw in Chapter 3, is Ferdinand Lopez, one of Victorian literature's most famous frauds. As the narrator goes on to say, though few "believed that Ferdinand Lopez was well born," "he was," nevertheless, "a gentleman" (11). If this sounds like a simple statement of fact, appearances can deceive. For Lopez is not only not a gentleman but is "one of the author's most obviously blatant cads."[2]

There are at least two reasons to conclude this book by comparing the AMC television show *Mad Men* (2007–) to a mid-Victorian work such as *The Prime Minister*. The first has to do with Trollope's mastery of a mode of realist narrative which, like today's "quality" television, won its first and most devoted audience in serial form. In the mid-Victorian decades that saw Britain's transition into a formal empire and mass male democracy, realism and seriality were inextricably linked in classic works

---

[1] The three quotations above are from Trollope, *Prime* 9, 10, 11.
[2] See the quotation from Asa Briggs in the Trollope Society's edition of *The Prime Minister*: http://www.trollopesociety.org/palliser.php#thepm

by Trollope, Collins, Eliot, and others, which appeared in weekly or monthly installments before being published as multi-volume novels that could be purchased or borrowed from circulating libraries. An interesting parallel finds the most acclaimed television dramas of our own day—including *The Sopranos* (1999–2007), *The Wire* (2002–8), *Deadwood* (2004–6), and *Mad Men*—broadcast serially and then packaged in DVD boxed sets that can be purchased, rented, or downloaded in digital form.

Of course, Lopez is also suspected of being a Jew: "a swarthy son of Judah" in the words of the English "man of ancestry" who reluctantly becomes his father-in-law (*Prime* 35, 10). That is the second reason why *The Prime Minister* illuminates *Mad Men*. Both texts represent a long line of naturalistic narratives in which figures of the outsider within—always parvenus, and often Jews or probable Jews—help to assimilate the myriad impacts of capitalist globalization. These "strangers in a strange land" are vilified others. But in a more complicated way, these figurative Jews represent a condition of exile which resonates for insiders and outsiders alike. Expressive at once of capitalism's *longue durée*, and the recurring power of serialized realism, these often racialized aliens inhabit modern lifeworlds from Trollope's City of London to *Mad Men*'s Madison Avenue.

At various points, this book has identified the geopolitical aesthetic particular to the *naturalistic narrative of capitalist globalization*.[3] If one recurrent marker of this genre is the Jewish or Judaized subject, two additional features I shall emphasize in this chapter are the temporality of serial delivery and the trope of Babylon: a space of modernity haunted by an existential condition, "singing the Lord's song in a strange land."

SERIALITY, "QUALITY" TELEVISION, AND REALISM

> [T]here are only two roads leading out of the monotonous commonplace of naturalism, which results from the direct, mechanical mirroring of the humdrum reality of capitalism. Either the writer succeeds in revealing the human and social significance of the struggle for life and lifting it to a higher plane by artistic means . . . or else he has to overstress the mere outward scenery of life, rhetorically and picturesquely, and quite independently of the human import of the events depicted.
>
> Georg Lukács, *Studies in European Realism* (1950)

Unsurprisingly, television scholars have begun to remark on how seriality connects early twenty-first century media to nineteenth-century antecedents. As

---

[3] As noted previously, my use of this term is not intended to be exclusive. Many nineteenth-century and present-day genres could legitimately be described as "narratives of capitalist globalization" but, for the sake of concision, I am using the term to describe naturalistic and serialized works that evoke the experience of breached sovereignties. See also Chapter 4 on *The Eustace Diamonds* and Chapter 6 on *Madame Bovary*.

Jason Mittell writes, the advent of "quality" television shows packaged in boxed sets has conferred the prestige of publication on a medium once characterized by ephemerality. DVD viewers can "immerse" themselves in the spectator experience: "binging" on multiple episodes and reviewing particular scenes and episodes at will (Mittell para. 16, 34). The DVD boxed set thus aligns television with classic multi-plot fiction, even while providing a physical object that can be displayed on a shelf like the works of Eliot or Trollope. Just as today's viewers discuss recent episodes of their favorite shows at the workplace, on blogs, and on new social networks, so Victorian enthusiasts of serial fiction published reviews, commentaries, and letters in the press (see Hughes and Lund).

This communal effect is enhanced by the regular intervals of waiting between serialized installments, which encourage a "daily routine" of reflection and anticipation (Mittell para. 30). Indeed, according to Robyn Warhol, serial narratives are "devices for structuring what bodies do in time and space," their resistance to closure a means of prolonging the relation between audience and text (*Having* 72). Whether by reading a novel published in monthly parts, or viewing a television narrative that airs weekly, audiences of serial media cultivate rituals of enjoying new installments followed by interludes of contemplation, discussion and expectation—developing a kind of serial *habitus*. The most striking effect of the serial temporality, according to Warhol, is the generation of feelings, at once more "familiar" and more "intense" than those elicited by non-serial media (72).

Although both Mittell and Warhol compare today's serial media to Victorian precursors, neither insists that realism, the dominant form of the nineteenth-century canon, is central to seriality per se.[4] In *The Victorian Serial* (1991), Linda K. Hughes and Michael Lund argued that serial fiction's interruptive temporality encouraged authors to adopt realist form: "Reading one installment, then pausing in that story, the Victorian audience turned to their own world with much the same set of critical faculties they had used to understand the literature" (11). But subsequent work on non-canonical genres such as the "penny dreadful" shows that Victorian seriality was diverse and often non-realist (Law). One might make comparable observations about today's "quality" television. The game-changing prestige of *The Sopranos* rests partly on the vivid character development associated with realist narrative. But *The Sopranos* is actually a postmodern hybrid that tends toward narrative dispersion, logical discontinuity, and formal experimentation.[5] Serial television since *The Sopranos* has taken a variety of non-realist forms including

---

[4] Mittell (paras 11-12) describes the "forensic" spectatorship provoked by the non-realist *Lost* (2004-10). Warhol, writing before the dramatic surge of "quality" television, discusses a variety of serial forms, from Victorian novels and Patrick O'Brien's naval adventure series, to television soap operas. Given my interest in realist narratives that evolve over time, the reading of any long novel is, to some degree, "serial" in requiring more than one sitting. Yet, outside of pedagogy and scholarship, the reading of older fiction is unlikely to facilitate the ongoing discussion and community-building that surrounds today's serialized television. But see Bernstein's account of online projects devoted to re-serializing and discussing Victorian texts.

[5] As Polan's *The Sopranos* argues, the show challenges the narrative coherence particular to Victorian fiction (32).

HBO's *Deadwood,* a kind of national romance; Showtime's *Dexter* (2006–), a cross between black comedy and crime drama; Showtime's *The Tudors* (2007–10), a mix of biopic and blue movie; and FX's *Damages* (2007–10), a blend of courtroom drama and postmodern thriller.

Still, it is no surprise to find two of the most critically acclaimed serial dramas standing out for their resonance with nineteenth-century realism. The first is HBO's *The Wire,* a show so self-consciously engaged with Victorian social forms, that the title of one of its Season 5 episodes is "The Dickensian Aspect."[6] The second is *Mad Men,* the Victorianesque quality of which is captured in its famously measured pace. The "Victorians valued slow, steady development in installments over time," in contrast to the "fast-forward" temporality that dominates more recent literature and thought (Hughes and Lund 275). *Mad Men*'s distinctive style works partly by rejecting this hyper-modern tempo: the show is "glacially slow"—a "masterpiece" precisely because "[a]lmost nothing happens in any single episode."[7] Contrary to appearances, then, *Mad Men*'s distinct aesthetic is not merely the effect of its celebrated focus on the early 1960s, but also of its reinvention of a naturalistic aesthetic like that of Trollope and his French precursor, Gustave Flaubert.

As the previous chapters of this book will have suggested, television's reinvention of realist form has coincided with a reconsideration of Victorian-era realism. To quote Ulka Anjaria's recent study of the Indian novel, critical suspicion of realism's formal effort to represent "reality" extends back "to high modernism in Europe" and "has been successively reinforced by structuralist and poststructuralist" theorists who perceive it as "anything from a misguided materialism to a more dangerous, hidden ideological project" (3). As we saw in Chapter 1, Marxist critiques tend to center on Georg Lukács's analysis of the crisis of bourgeois realism after the failed European upheavals of 1848. Whereas Lukács believed that naturalistic fiction such as Flaubert's symptomatizes bourgeois decadence, Fredric Jameson has contended that realist fiction reproduces a "fixed-camera view" of the nation-bound metropole ("Cognitive" 349; cf. Jameson, "Modernism"). This tendency to dismiss realism as a depoliticized form, disarticulated from global process and historical consciousness, has extended beyond the nineteenth-century examples that Lukács and Virginia Woolf had in mind. When Terry Eagleton wrote in 1976 that Trollope's works are bathed in a "blandly undifferentiated ideological space" (*Criticism* 191), he anticipated the kind of critique some critics today level against *Mad Men.* Thus, for Mark Greif, the show exemplifies a smug historical pastiche that arises when realist depiction "of the past is used to congratulate the present" (para. 10).

We have seen how nineteenth-century realism at its most powerful is characterized by dense social description, the metonymic interweaving of political and domestic plots, and—as a result—the vivid capture of world-historical processes

---

[6] For discussion of this deliberately but not wholly ironic reference to Dickens, see Goodlad, "Afterword."

[7] This quotation comes from the British newspaper *The Guardian,* which, in 2010, voted *Mad Men* fourth in a list of the 50 best television dramas of all time (see Dempster).

of capitalist globalization including the reign of speculative finance, the "blowback" of imperial expansion, and the commoditization of modern lifeworlds. Lukács and Jameson regard literary form as a sensitive index of such change, but maintain that realism's capacity to perform this function declined in the mid-nineteenth century—when Flaubert innovated the literary techniques that Émile Zola later codified as "naturalism."[8] Novels like *Madame Bovary* (1856) and *The Prime Minister* subject principal characters to devastating modern forces while maintaining a cool narrative distance from the wreckage. For Lukács, fiction of this sort marks the post-revolutionary acceptance of "human values" overcome by "the commodity structure of capitalism" (*Studies* 63). The resulting crisis in bourgeois aesthetics isolates characters, fetishizes detail, reduces the author to "a mere spectator and chronicler of public life," and divorces art from "the real, dramatic and epic movement of social happening" (*Studies* 89, 43; cf. Schor, "Details" 28).

In our own day, the contrast between a realism that connects human experience to "social happening," and one that dramatizes atomization, deracination, and the quashing of *Bildung*, recurs in *The Wire* and *Mad Men*. Like the Dickensian fiction it explicitly invokes, *The Wire*'s multi-plot structure, "privileges the social network over the representative character" (C. Levine, "Historicism"; cf. Polan, "Invisible"). Nevertheless, just as Esther's narration in *Bleak House* (1852–3) tempers and subjectivizes the world of Chesney Wold and Tom-all-Alone's, so characters such as the heroized Omar and the honorable Cedric Daniels, inject human purpose into *The Wire*'s urban Baltimore. By contrast, *Mad Men*'s *mise-en-scène* is dominated by a central character who is neither virtuous nor able to sustain moral growth.[9]

Yet another aspect of *The Wire*'s Dickensian slant is its autoethnographic structure; for all the intricacy of the show's multiple webs (drug dealing, law enforcement, labor unions et al.), its focus is consistently Baltimore: an archetype of the United States city. If such a "Baltimore" metonymizes urban America—figuring municipal space in competing matrices of state, federal, and multinational power—it nonetheless sustains the city as imagined community.[10] *The Wire*'s centripetal pull thus stands in marked contrast to *Mad Men*'s early-1960s New York City, which is less an urban infrastructure ("New York" is depicted through a small number of sets) than a hub for the marketing of global commodities. In all these ways, *Mad Men*'s story world is, in Lukács's terms, more Flaubertian than *The Wire*'s; the "mad" experience it portrays is that of captured human values. Although such fictions are often called naturalistic, they can also be described as narratives of capitalist globalization in which conventional

---

[8] See, for example, Zola's 1880 essay, "*Le Roman Experimental.*" However, Flaubert does not share Zola's scientism or his signature focus on working-class life and hereditary determinism (see also ch. 6)—it is this pre-Zolaesque naturalism that *Mad Men* evokes.

[9] On the apparent shift in character at the end of Season 6 see Goodlad, "The Only." This chapter primarily focuses on the show's acclaimed first three seasons.

[10] *The Wire*'s Baltimore can thus be compared to the British nation that *Bleak House* upholds, according to Buzard, against the specious free trade universalism of the Great Exhibition era ("Anywhere's"). See also Jameson "Realism" on *The Wire* as a "sociological mystery" (362) that, at one level, is "very much about Baltimore" (359).

modes of sovereignty are breached by conspicuous outsiders including speculators, parvenus, people of color, and (most especially) Jews.

Of course, *Mad Men* is also historical fiction—the genre Lukács singles out for attention in *The Historical Novel*. For Lukács, such genres offer the best possible expression of the "life sentiments that [grow] out of concrete, social, historical situations" ("Hegel's" 106). And in Europe after the French Revolution and Napoleonic wars, that situation is the experience of history itself: history understood as "the bearer . . . of human progress" (*Historical* 27). Touched by these transnational events, Europe's peoples came to regard history, for the first time, as "something which deeply affects their daily lives." This transformation of consciousness became the crucible for works like Walter Scott's *Ivanhoe* (1819), which figure ongoing class struggle through the typical character. Precisely because he is an "average" man, Ivanhoe embodies contemporary struggles rather than individual greatness—rendering epic history in popular form (*Historical* 24, 33).

Lukács's analysis in *The Historical Novel* might seem to bode ill for *Mad Men*: a show celebrated for gorgeous surfaces, meticulous attention to period details, and a male protagonist whose potential to transcend ordinary manhood is at times almost Nietzschean.[11] Yet, for a number of reasons, that appearance is misleading. As we have seen in previous chapters, Lukács's fixation on the revolutions of 1848 imposes a Eurocentric prism that obscures the Victorian engagement with multicultural nationhood, an extensive commercial empire, and an expanding Raj in South Asia. Then too, Lukács holds that aesthetic forms such as the historical novel are destined to rise, fall, and, potentially, rise again—in accordance with the movement of history. As genres respond to what Hegel called the *Weltzustand* (state of the world), their shape is determined by "their capacity to bring to expression" the signal features of their socio-historical moment ("Hegel's" 98–9). Hence, as Jameson notes, Lukács's book "calls for a revitalization of the historical novel in radically new social and political configurations": for Lukács, the Stalinist era and "for us," "a new moment of multinational capitalism" ("Introduction" 4). This is a noteworthy claim from a critic who tends to regard realism as a nation-bound aesthetic that is, at best, split between art and epistemology (*Signatures* 156–7) and, at worst, "driven to avoid recognition of deep structural social change" ("Notes" 261). When Jameson looks for dialectically engaged genres, he generally seeks them in Modernism, postmodern film, or science fiction.

That said, Jameson's 1995 book on cinema describes a conspiratorial genre that is primarily realist. U.S. films such as Alan J. Pakula's *All the President's Men* (1976) and Oliver Stone's *Salvador* (1986) illustrate a vital geopolitical aesthetic at work, bending realist form in the effort "to grasp . . . the social totality as a whole." As Jameson defines it, the "geopolitical aesthetic" entails art's mediation in articulating "landscapes and forces" beyond the grasp of individual experience

---

[11] Though it is worth recalling that Lukács specified that typicality was not a question of rendering the "lifeless average"—a sign of the naturalism he deplored. Rather, "what makes it a type is that in it all the humanly and socially essential determinants are present on their highest level of development, in the ultimate unfolding of the possibilities latent in them, in extreme presentation of their extremes" (*Studies* 6).

(*Geopolitical* 36, 3). In films like *Salvador*, rebellious characters become the instigators of crises situated among "the anachronistic traces . . . of a recent historical past"—"the waning of the 1960s" (77).[12] In thus marking the 1960s as the subversive back story that haunts the postmodern moment, Jameson references what Terry Anderson calls a decade of "social activism and cultural change" (v); what Todd Gitlin names as "Years of Hope, Days of Rage"; and what the editors of a recently launched journal on the topic describe as an era of "transformative longing" for, and belief in, "the possibility of dramatic change and the mobilization of this hope" (Varon et al. 2).

Needless to say, this is not the 1960s depicted in the first three seasons of *Mad Men*. By taking the years between March 1960 and December 1963 for its *mise-en-scène*, the show's first seasons elongate the opening years of a decade that has been remembered for its dynamic close. To watch *Mad Men* is, thus, to sublimate and defer that "transformative longing": to wait endlessly (and communally) for the radical '60s whose "waning" signifies the fallen condition of the present. If *Mad Men* invites its audience to believe in anything, it is not in social movements but in isolated feats of self-invention. Protean self-fashioning—a mode of self-advertisement—enables Don Draper to maintain his limited mastery over office politics, geopolitics, domestic and sexual politics. That is the secret to his having nine lives.

Indeed, *Mad Men*'s objective situation is not the 1960s at all, early or late, but, rather, today's neoliberal condition: a *Weltzustand* in which the radical '60s are not so much "waning" as mythologized, derided, and repressed—if never quite forgotten. The show might even seem less historical fiction than nostalgic pastiche, a form that is "beyond history" in representing a "pathological" inability to deal with time (Jameson, "Postmodernism" 117). However, likeness to the nineteenth century's serial novels illuminates *Mad Men* as a deliberately non-pastiche aesthetic that responds to current neoliberal contexts. Distinct from non-serial media like movies, as well as postmodern serial television like *The Sopranos*, *Mad Men*'s naturalistic neo-realism recreates the tempo of mid-Victorian-era serial fiction in making the lived experiences of its characters stretch slowly *over* time and, thus, *in* it. A serialized successor to the conspiratorial films of the 1980s and 1990s, *Mad Men* embeds its aberrant protagonist in a "process of historical obsolescence" (Jameson, *Geopolitical* 77): a world of broadsheet newspapers, electric typewriters, middle-class prosperity, glamorous air travel, and overt sexism and racism that defamiliarize present-day experience while remaining palpable to it. Aiding *Mad Men* in evoking this realist geopolitical aesthetic are a set of formal structures which work through the motifs of Judaized otherness and virtualized Jewishness.[13]

---

[12] Unsurprisingly, Jameson regards *The Wire*'s incipient utopianism in similar terms: the series' "increasingly socialized and collective historical space" eventually shows "that genuine revolt and resistance must take the form of a conspiratorial group" ("Realism" 363). But for the fact that the rebellious hero is multiplied, *The Wire*, on this reading, is recognizably heir to the conspiratorial films of the 1980s and 1990s (though, in this form, the show represents a merely virtual "Utopian impulse" [364]).

[13] On the later seasons of *Mad Men* which diverge from naturalism as the show moves into the later 1960s, see, for example, Goodlad "The Only" and Goodlad "Let's."

VIRTUALIZED JEWISHNESS AS GEOPOLITICAL AESTHETIC

> I have been a stranger in a strange land.
>
> Moses, *Exodus* 2:22

In a vivid account of mid-Victorian London, art historian Lynda Nead cites an 1862 article that declares: "In forming our idea of the great capital of the British Empire and of the nineteenth century . . . we naturally . . . call her 'the Modern Babylon'" (qtd. in Nead 3). As Nead explains, the image of London as Victorian Babylon—"the centre of a global commerce that was subjugating the rest of the world"—was double-edged. Then as now, Babylon conjured destructive "worship of the commodity," as well as the awe of modern progress (3). But Babylon is also the setting for the haunting Psalm 137, "By the waters/river of Babylon," which, along with comparable passages from the Old Testament Book of Exodus, figures the experience of exile, captivity, and estrangement. Ordered by their Babylonian captors to "Sing us one of the songs of Zion," the exiled Jews of Psalm 137 ask, "How shall we sing the Lord's song in a strange land?" (ll.3–4).

The mid-Victorian era was a period of rising anti-Semitism as Benjamin Disraeli's political ascent saw the biblical narrative of Moses in Egypt used to "underscore the idea of the secret Jew who subverts and eventually destroys the dominant culture in which he lives" (Ragussis 236).[14] As the gaslit emporium became an ambivalent sign of modern commerce, firms like Moses and Son, a well-known outfitter of men's ready-to-wear, became the "butt of mid-Victorian anti-Semitism" (Nead 89). Although the best-known literary example of Victorian-era Mosaism is George Eliot's philo-Semitic *Daniel Deronda*, whose story of emergent Jewish nationalism began to appear in February 1876, Trollope's Lopez presents an earlier and less sympathetic instance of the "secret Jew." Lopez explicitly identifies himself with Moses, describing his father-in-law as "an Egyptian" whom he "will despoil" just as "the Israelites despoiled the Egyptians" (*Prime* 456; cf. Exodus 3.22). Of course, Lopez's secret is ambiguous: his Jewish descent alleged, but never confirmed. Trollope's narrative thus indicts ambiguity as much as Jewishness itself; as Ragussis writes, "Jewish ancestry" becomes "almost synonymous" with "unknown ancestry" (249).

Mad Men's Don is another self-made man with mysterious origins. Draper's hidden identity is the show's central motif: "He could be Batman," says Harry Crane, the budding television account man ("Marriage"). "Who's in there?" Betty whispers to her sleeping husband at the end of the second episode. For while she knows that Don "doesn't like to talk about himself," she also suspects that the husband whose family she has never met has more than infidelity to hide

---

[14] On Disraeli and anti-Semitism, see also Wohl, "Dizzi"; Arendt 68–79 and, with regard to Trollope's *The Eustace Diamonds*, Chapter 5.

("Ladies'"). As her father reminds her, "He's got no people. You can't trust a man like that" ("Color"). When Roger Sterling prods Don about his childhood, Don replies: "Think of me as Moses. I was a baby in a basket" ("Ladies'").

It may, nonetheless, seem perverse to compare Trollope's largely pejorative depiction of the secret Jew to *Mad Men*—a turn-of-the-millennium narrative about America's postwar past in which the Jew often stands for the assimilative pressures of the American Century, so-called. Yet, as Aamir Mufti has argued, Europe's nineteenth-century "Jewish Question" provides an illuminating paradigm for minority subjects in our postcolonial moment (cf. Kalmar and Penslar). Then too, as we saw in Chapter 4, Trollope's anti-Semitism is not straightforward. While Emilius, the perfidious crypto-Jew of *The Eustace Diamonds* (1871–3) is an anti-Semitic caricature, sympathetic Jewish characters like Ezekiel Breghert, the honest banker of *The Way We Live Now* (1874–5), suggest a different attitude entirely. If Lopez's penetration of a guarded social stratum heightens the perception of ruptured heirloom sovereignty, it is also true that this arch-figure of the stranger is as clearly the victim of prejudice, as the embodiment of Judaized depredation.[15] The most consistent feature of the Jewishness depicted in British writing, according to Bryan Cheyette, is its "protean instability." Nineteenth-century literature does not "draw on eternal myths of 'the Jew'" so much as illustrate the dialectic between constructions of Jewishness and of Britain's own national, ethnic, and—I would add—global identities (8, 268).

What is true for British literature is true also for *Mad Men*, which depicts American experience through the prism of Madison Avenue's golden age, in dialogue with Jewishness in various forms. Indeed, *Mad Men* indulges in an unapologetic Jewish exceptionalism. Peppered with Jewish characters and reference points, the show includes few African Americans or other minorities. By contrast, *Mad Men* makes anti-Semitism endemic to a postwar New York City in which Jews are both ubiquitous and excluded. "Have we ever hired any Jews?" asks Roger in the pilot, hoping to impress a Jewish client. "Not on my watch," Don replies ("Smoke").

Such remarks would not surprise Rachel Menken, the Jewish department store heiress and client with whom Don has a passionate affair. Rachel turns out to be the first of several Judaized love interests for Don in a pattern that finds him married to the Nordic-Teutonic Betty—a Bryn Mawr graduate and "Main Line brat" ("Shut")—while having affairs with women whose social situation and unconventional femininity more closely resemble his own invented persona. More interesting than this familiar split in male desire are the subject positions of secret and virtual Jewishness it enacts. Although Rachel is the primary example of explicit Jewish identity, *Mad Men* features many characters who in various ways, appear to be Jewish. Indeed, showrunner Matthew Weiner has said he "hope[s] people can tell" or "know at some level," that certain assimilated characters are Jews (Itzkoff).

---

[15] Nuanced readings of Lopez include those by Carter, Dellamora, and Gagnier, "Conclusion."

Thus, according to Weiner, Jimmy Barrett and his wife Bobbie (with whom Don has an affair in Season 2) are "transparently Jewish," while Dr. Faye Miller (Don's lover throughout much of Season 4) is someone whom Weiner "hopes people can tell" is Jewish (Itzkoff).

Hopes people can tell. If so, why not give Faye an unmistakably Jewish name, or a father named Yankel or Solly? And if Bobbie is "transparently" Jewish why not have her use Yiddish words, as does Don's accountant, or the Hebrew phrase *"l'chaim"* for a toast, as does Roy, the young playwright who eventually comes between Don and his beatnik mistress Midge? Why, in other words, does Weiner confirm the Jewish identity of certain characters in interviews, while *Mad Men* itself merely suggests that these and many other characters *might* be Jewish?[16]

The answer, I believe, is that these characters are secret Jews: the kind whose ultimate referent, like Lopez's, is not Jewishness per se, but ambiguous identity. That *Mad Men* is thick with characters who may be Jews means that Weiner's "story about . . . assimilation" demonstrates neither the erasure of Jewish difference, nor a tolerant multiculturalism in which self-proclaimed Jews claim the same respect as social insiders like Betty or Peter Campbell (Itzkoff). Rather, *Mad Men* depicts Jewishness as at once legible (inviting viewers to detect Jewish signs) and ambiguous (denying the certainty granted to Rachel). Historically, "secret Jew" was one of the names given to Spanish or Portuguese Jews who, though forced to convert during the Inquisition, maintained stealthy allegiance to Jewish faith. This early-modern notion of subterranean Jewry was exacerbated by the later nineteenth century's tendency to racialize ethnic difference—suggesting the impossibility of authentic Jewish conversion. The upshot in Trollope's imaginary is to make unconverted Jews like Breghert more sympathetic than self-proclaimed Christians like Emilius, Lopez, and the real-life Disraeli. But rather than egregious prejudice, Trollope's ambivalence exemplifies how anti-Semitism thrives within liberal modernity's universalistic premise. As the world's self-proclaimed liberal vanguard, Victorian Britain offers a salient example of the nation-state's tendency to suppress "alternative collectivities, local and diasporic loyalties" in the effort to modernize and unify a diverse population (Cheyette and Valman 2; cf. Bauman). Considered from this perspective, it is no surprise to find Jewish immutability as central to Eliot's philo-Semitic imaginary as to Trollope's Lopez: both novels adopt an Exodus narrative in which departure for the Promised Land—through Zionism or death—is the only escape from troubled identity.

---

[16] Faye uses the Yiddish word *punim* (face) which may explain why Weiner hopes viewers will "know at some level" that he intends for her to be Jewish ("Chinese"). On the other hand, Harry Crane, who does not appear to be Jewish, also uses a Yiddish word, *gonifs* (thieves) ("Rejected"). Use of Yiddish thus ambiguously stands either for Jewish identity or simply for the currency of Yiddish vocabulary in a city with a large Jewish population. Weiner appears to assume that non-Jewish viewers will be able to interpret these and other signs of potential Jewishness.

In Chapter 3 we saw how Lopez's radical ambiguity enables Trollope to indict Victorian Babylon while proposing a scapegoat for its ills. An exemplary naturalistic narrative of capitalist globalization, *The Prime Minister* portrays modernity as the disenchanted site of breached sovereignty and substanceless exchange. *Mad Men*'s neoliberal variation on this narrative secularizes the motif of the secret Jew, shifting the stakes of ethnic immutability from nineteenth-century conversion to twentieth-century assimilation. Rachel aside, the show's first three seasons figure metropolitan Jewishness as the paradoxical state of both revealing and hiding one's "true" identity. In doing so, *Mad Men* instances the kind of double bind which Eve Sedgwick called the regime of the "open secret" (*Epistemology* 67).

Yet, *Mad Men* goes further still by universalizing the condition of secret Jewry. Whereas *The Prime Minister* and *Daniel Deronda* are famous for narrative splitting—the Lopez plot versus the Palliser plot, and the "Jewish" Deronda plot versus the "English" Gwendolen plot—*Mad Men* articulates today's metropolitan imaginary by making Don a "virtual" Jew in whom the minority subject's aberrant particularity and the majority subject's universalist status collide. If this is a demonstrably late-capitalist phenomenon, enabled by the ever more contingent and hybrid status of "identity" under neoliberalism, it is also a message that has been legible in Exodus and Psalm 137 for centuries.

Don's virtual Jewishness is the heart of *Mad Men*'s geopolitical aesthetic, enabling the show's reinvention of a mid-Victorian motif: precarious identity amplified through the form of the serialized naturalism. But crucial to that premise is the viewer's awareness that Don is not, in actuality, a secret Jew—or for that matter, a closeted gay or passing black man. Rather, as viewers learn in the first season, Don is actually Dick Whitman—a Midwestern farm boy who, like a latter-day Jay Gatsby, took the opportunity offered by the fog of war to recreate himself. An enlisted soldier who deserts after stealing the identity of his dead commanding officer, Don, or rather, Dick was born dirt poor. He is the product of an illicit union between a prostitute who dies giving birth, and a crusty farmer who is killed by his horse, leaving his bastard son to be reared by step-parents. These details emerge through flashbacks spread across multiple episodes, providing a fragmentary back story that inflects Don's efforts to maintain his invented persona. *Mad Men* thus makes sustaining Don's unknowability the core of its storyline: its open secret.[17]

While this narrative is potentially melodramatic and sensational, the slow pace (36 episodes for a wife to look inside her husband's desk drawer!), the strong emphasis on character, and the structure of synchronic episodes in a diachronic storyline endow the first three seasons of *Mad Men* with the novelistic cast of

---

[17] When Jimmy Barrett tells Don "I loved you in *Gentleman's Agreement*" ("Benefactor"), he links *Mad Men*'s protagonist to a 1947 film about a character who impersonates a Jew for the purpose of exploring Jewish positionality. Don's status as virtual Jew does not preclude but, rather, predicts his ability to inhabit other virtual positions: e.g., passing black man, closeted gay, or (as we shall see) madwoman in the attic. For comparable arguments regarding *Mad Men* see Szalay and Doty; on the topic of Trollope, Litvak argues, "*Not* unlike . . . homosexuality, [assimilating] Jewishness in Trollope . . . is by definition mysterious" (127; Litvak's emphasis).

historical realism and naturalist aesthetics. Through the serial form's gradual unfolding, these multi-plot and layered but thematically unified installments can stand alone artistically, even while contributing to an overarching trajectory. Richest of all, and indicative of *Mad Men*'s neo-Lukácsian form, is the careful emplotment of Don's story in early-60s history. Thus, Season 1 aligns the troubled Draper marriage with Kennedy's win over Nixon, auguring change. Season 2 pairs Betty's pregnancy and the couple's reconciliation with the Cuban missile crisis; and Season 3 finds Betty leaving Don for the staid Henry Francis amid the turmoil of the Kennedy and Oswald assassinations. Don's virtual Jewishness is thus a slow-burning realist effect, sustained over years and, like its Victorian precursors, meditated and discussed by viewers from episode to episode, season to season.

THE MODERN BABYLON

It's a long road to Canaan.

Paul Simon, "Bleecker Street" (1964)

While *Mad Men*'s interplay of secret and virtual Jewishness is dispersed throughout the series, one particular episode in the first season—"Babylon"—encapsulates the show's distinct geopolitical aesthetic. Laden with biblical referents, the episode begins with Genesis as Don, falling on the stairs, flashes back to a "fall" after the birth of his half-brother, Adam. "Babylon" then moves to Exodus courtesy of a visit from the Israeli Ministry of Tourism which, encouraged by the popularity of Leon Uris's 1958 novel, seeks the help of Madison Avenue. While reading *Exodus*, Don learns that Betty's first kiss was from a Jewish boy at a dance organized to help "Those poor skinny people in the boats"—in other words, European refugees from the Holocaust like those on the real-life *SS Exodus*, the inspiration for Uris's novel and the 1960 movie to come.

"Babylon" thus combines Psalm 137's meditations on exile and captivity with the Old Testament's most powerful deliverance story. As George Bornstein writes, "For centuries the narrative of Moses leading the enslaved children of Israel out of bondage in Egypt into freedom in Canaan has represented liberation of the spirit from things of this world" (374). Exodus has been invoked by English Puritans, African Americans, Irish republicans, Rastafarians, and Mormons among others. Psalm 137's haunting rendering of Babylon also resonates across time and space.[18] Fredrick Douglass made the psalm's opening lines the centerpiece of his 1852 speech, "The Meaning of July Fourth for the Negro"; Swinburne enlisted it

---

[18] As Boyarin notes, citing Shavit, "the Return to Zion" anticipated in Psalm 137 "was an indisputable historical event (unlike the Exodus from Egypt)," as well as "an outstanding messianic event" (Shavit qtd. in Boyarin 60). Although the two exiles are often conflated, what is important for *Mad Men* is that the Babylon of Psalm 137 offers a resonant trope of modern alienation—distinct from redemptive return.

for the Italian Risorgimento ("Super Flumina Babylonis" 1871); and Benjamin Zephaniah gave it a dub spin in his 1996 poem, "City River Blues." The psalm has inspired musical arrangements from Byron's 1814 collaboration with Isaac Nathan to "Babylon," a track on Don McLean's 1970 *American Pie* album–the arrangement used in *Mad Men*.

Of course, Exodus has also been a focal point for Middle East politics, including the debate between Edward W. Said and Michael Walzer.[19] Exodus motifs were central to England's colonial imaginary, supplying a vision of Anglo-Saxon settlement as Promised Land which became a founding myth of the United States. But according to Jonathan Boyarin, it was not until the 1940s—the period of Betty Draper's refugees—that Exodus was harnessed to a project of Jewish nationhood. The travails of ships like the *SS Exodus,* which carried Jewish refugees to Palestine in the face of British hostility, fostered pro-Zionist analogies between liberation from Egypt and the founding of a Jewish homeland. The use of "Exodus" to denote a continuum of Jewish experience—in Egypt, in Europe under the Nazis, in transit to Palestine, and, finally, in Israel fighting for nationhood—was "popularized immensely" through Leon Uris's novel and Otto Preminger's film (Boyarin 59). In this way, *Exodus* helped to affirm a "special relationship" between Israel and the U.S. at around the same time that the term "Holocaust" came to signify the Nazis' genocidal assault on Europe's Jews.

Central both to novel and film was the construction of the "new Jew" as product of post-diasporic nationhood. Critics have noted the remarkable casting of the fair-haired, blue-eyed Paul Newman (of Jewish descent on his father's side) in the role of Ari Ben Canaan—literally "Lion, child of Canaan"—alongside actors like the Italian-American Sal Mineo, and the Greek-American George Maharis (the latter a sex symbol after his starring role in the macho television series *Route 66*).[20] These Hollywood stars portrayed Jewish manhood as classically handsome, action-oriented, and aggressive, thus overturning anti-Semitic caricature and the status of victimhood (Fig. 8.1). Yet another noteworthy choice was the casting of the British Jill Haworth to play Karen, a blonde Holocaust survivor befriended by Kitty Fremont, an American Christian portrayed by Eva Marie Saint. Over the course of the narrative, Kitty transits from American spectator to Karen's substitute mother and Ari's lover. As Ella Shohat writes, "The same Waspish-looking woman" who confides to a British officer that she "feel[s] strange among" Jews "becomes an enthusiastic supporter of Zionism" (*Israeli* 66). *Exodus*'s cultural work thus included translating Zionism into US-friendly form, neutralizing Arabs (through the figure of Ari's Palestinian "brother," Taha), and burying the *Shoah* (through Karen's death). In all of these ways, the text depicts a post-Holocaust Jewry redeemed through nationhood and a "new Israeli identity free of the burden of Jewish diaspora" (Loshitzky 125).

---

[19] See Walzer's *Exodus and Revolution* and Said's reply, "Michael Walzer's."
[20] On the "new Jew" in *Exodus* see, for example, Boyarin 60; Shohat, *Israeli*; Weissbrod; and Loshitzy, On Uris's attraction to Israel's "fighting" Jews, see Kaplan.

Fig. 8.1. Paul Newman as Ari Ben Canaan and George Maharis as Yoav. Scene from *Exodus*. Dir. Otto Preminger. United Artists, 1960.

If *Mad Men*'s engagement of this terrain hardly illuminates the Palestinian plight, neither does it hew to the Zionist narrative found in *Exodus*. Perusing photographs of Holocaust victims and a boat like the *Exodus*, Don opines, "I can see why they want the guns." But during most of the episode he is less moved by Jewish suffering, or stirred by Jewish heroism, than stumped by the task of making Israel a tourist destination. "So," he quips, "we have a quasi-communist state where women have guns. And it's filled with Jews. Well, not completely filled; let's not forget there are also Arabs."

As we have seen, *Exodus*'s "new Jew" squares the circle of liberal universalism, elevating Jews from diaspora into the family of nations: Newman's Westernized, masculine Ari Ben Canaan stably occupies the double position of idealized *sabra* and universal paragon, just as Israel stands for Jewish homeland as well as Promised Land.[21] By contrast, *Mad Men*—to borrow a line from a Paul Simon song used in Season 4—depicts a "long road to Canaan" with no end in sight. Whereas *Exodus* proffers Israeli identity "free from the burden of the Jewish diaspora," *Mad Men* makes diaspora the archetypal condition of global modernity, and makes New York City the new Modern Babylon.

This revision is announced by the hyper-Judaized form of the visiting Israelis, Lily Meyer and Yoram Ben Shulhai (Fig. 8.2). In contrast to Rachel, an icon of diasporic glamour, or assimilated secret Jews like the Barretts, Lily's heavy accent, wrinkled mien, and dowdy dress mark her as an "old Jew" and probable Holocaust survivor. If her name recalls Golda Meir, the future Iron Lady of Israeli politics, Lily's demeanor evokes Frau Blücher, the dour housekeeper of Mel Brooks's *Young Frankenstein* (1974), played for laughs by Cloris Leachman. Her younger male colleague, Yoram (mispronounced as "Urine" by a clueless Roger) is a swarthy *sabra* in contrast to the dashing Hollywood alternatives portrayed by Newman

---

[21] On Preminger's enlistment of Dalton Trumbo to write the screenplay for *Exodus*, with the effect of enhancing its vision of universality, see Weissbrod.

Fig. 8.2. Lily Meyer and Yoram Ben Shulhai. Scene from "Babylon" *Mad Men* (Season 1, Episode 6) AMC, August 23, 2007.

and Maharis. Thus, the same patriotism that heroizes the *Exodus* characters, enabling them to transcend Jewish particularity, makes Lily and Yoram look out of place—their earnestness alien to a deracinated world of hedonism and stylish self-fashioning. "This is America," says Bobbie in a line that defines her as secret Jew as well as neoliberal subject, "Pick a job and then become the person that does it" ("For Those"). Such protean invention is precisely the aspect of a commodity culture which the Israelis seek for the economic wellbeing of their fledgling nation, but which they—saturated with Jewish history—cannot perform. Their exchange with Don is, thus, ironic as *Mad Men*'s viewers, trained to applaud self-invention, confront a robust identity, morally superior to Madison Avenue, but stripped of the glamour of the new Modern Babylon.

Still, Don is visibly discomfited by the Israelis whose embodied Jewishness troubles his cool Manhattan façade. Though their wish to parlay the popularity of *Exodus* into tourism is business as usual, Don protests too much—repeatedly reminding them they are outsiders. As Roger explains, the task at hand is to portray Israel as "a land of exotic luxury" and position Haifa as the Rome of the Middle East. "Of course," Don objects, "Rome has the Coliseum." "And Tel Aviv is about to have a Hilton," returns Roger. His remark anticipates Season 3, in which the eccentric Conrad Hilton takes a shine to Don, whom he imagines as a self-made maverick like himself. In a crucial line that he attributes to Don, Hilton captures the hubris of global hegemony: "America is wherever we look, wherever we're going to be" ("Wee"). *Mad Men* thus reprises the mentality of the British Empire of Trollope's day: "[W]herever over the world British influence penetrates," wrote the *Macmillan*'s commentator discussed in Chapter 3, "there, and not in the mere islands where we have our footing, Great Britain lives" ([Masson] 4).

Like the Hilton storyline, the Israeli plan to partner with Olympic Cruise Lines indexes an epoch in capitalism's history when success in the global market meant seducing America's consumers. Don's Hilton campaign plays to American hubris, promising familiarity "wherever over the world" American "influence penetrates." "How do you say 'fresh towels' in Farsi?" Don's tagline reads, prompting the answer, "Hilton" ("Wee"). The "Babylon" episode thus finds Don resisting his own game, reluctant to accept Israel as a global commodity Americans will buy. Brandishing *Exodus*, Lily insists, "This book has been on the best-seller list for two years in the States . . . America has a love affair with Israel and we'd like to bring the two parties together." The scene closes with Don asking the Israelis to describe their "ideal tourist. What's their yearly salary?" Lily replies: "Whatever *you* make."

In Season 3, Don and Betty travel to Rome, rekindling their romance in a setting that invites comparison with the courtship of Kitty Fremont and Ari Ben Canaan in *Exodus* (Figs. 8.3 and 8.4). The analogy explains Don's reluctance to pursue "America's love affair with Israel." Whereas the *Exodus* scenario aligns him with the American Kitty, Don is what passes for *Mad Men*'s hero. As a closeted outsider and virtual Jew, he can no more incarnate Kitty's Midwestern wonder than Ari's devotion to the Promised Land. Thus, in "Babylon," when Sal Romano, holds up the image of a dark-haired Jewess to suggest a potential selling point for Israel—"the people are good-looking"—Don recalls his passion for Rachel, who warily agrees to meet him for lunch.

Rachel's stable diasporic Jewishness stands for a feminized power that, for all its glamour, is more substance than show. During her first meeting with Don, their awkward exchange anticipates the tension with the Israelis. When Pete suggests that "there are a dozen agencies better suited to [Rachel's] needs," she retorts that if she wanted an ad man "from the same village as [her] father," she would not be meeting with Sterling Cooper ("Smoke"). Rachel thus defines herself as one who does not hide Jewish identity, but will not be defined by it either. Her family business is a luxury department store adjacent to Tiffany's: not a *Jewish* department store. Frustrated by her resistance, Don asks her the same question he puts

Fig. 8.3. Ari Ben Canaan and Kitty Fremont dining in the "Rome of the Middle East." Scene from *Exodus*. Dir. Otto Preminger. United Artists, 1960.

Fig. 8.4. Don and Betty Draper dining in Rome. Scene from "Souvenir" *Mad Men* (Season 3, Episode 9) AMC, October 4, 2009.

to Lily and Yoram, "So, what kind of people do you want?" "I want *your* kind of people Mr. Draper," she replies, identifying Don (just as the Israelis do) as the American ideal.

Don's anxieties in the pilot ostensibly stem from his having nothing to pitch to Lucky Strike, the firm's biggest account. The entire episode is framed by a marketing problem: how does one advertise an addictive and lethal product when bogus health claims are no longer permissible? Soon after the encounter with Rachel, Don meets with market researcher Greta Guttman, another heavily-accented and austere middle-aged woman who, like Lily Meyer, appears to be an "old Jew" and possible Holocaust survivor. "Before the war, when I studied with Adler in Vienna," she says apropos of Lucky Strike, "we postulated that what Freud called 'the Death Wish' is as powerful a drive as those for sexual reproduction and physical sustenance." Don's aversion is palpable: "Dr. Guttman, psychology is terrific at a cocktail party," but "people were buying cigarettes before Freud was born."[22] When he tosses her report into the trash, viewers know that her findings are partly correct: she offers "conclusive proof" that neither low-tar nor filtered cigarettes reduce the incidence of lung cancer. Still, Don is also correct: the issue for advertisers is not "*why* should people smoke," but "why should people smoke *Lucky Strike*." Though he does not realize it, Don's sparring with this probable Jew inspires the insight that later wows the Lucky Strike executives: while everybody else's "tobacco is poisonous," he tells them, "Lucky Strike is *toasted*." Don's strategy extracts a desirable particular from a universal negation. Advertising, he explains, is "freedom from fear. It's a billboard on the side of the road that screams

---

[22] In fact, Don is mistaken: Schudson cites the 1881 invention of the cigarette machine as the birth date of the commercial cigarette (more than 20 years after Freud's birth in 1856). Cigarettes did not overtake the more masculine pipe and cigar until the 1920s (178–208).

with reassurance that whatever you're doing is okay." The irony is that the fear that prompted this winning insight isn't Don's fear of death, but the fear of unmasking which Greta's ambiguous difference provokes.

When Don meets Rachel to seek her advice, he tells her that the Israelis ("those people") were "definitely Zionists." "Zion just means Israel," she answers, "It's a very old name." "I'm American," she says, "I'm really not very Jewish"—though she is Jewish enough to point out the significance of Adolf Eichmann's recent arrest. A "country for 'those people' as you call us," she says, (with "us" linking her with the Israelis), "seems very important." "My life is here," she goes on, "I'll visit but I don't need to live there. It just has to *be*." Rachel thus articulates a common Jewish-American standpoint: both identified and non-identified with Israel, she professes to balance Jewish and American identities as though they were seamless. She endorses Jewish nationhood, but neither regards herself as an Israeli, nor acknowledges Zionism as a political construction. Still less does she consider the Palestinian people. Like the popularity of *Exodus,* such reflexive pro-Zionism among Jewish-Americans who regard themselves as "not very Jewish," has been integral to forging the "special relationship" between Israel and the United States.

But in *Mad Men*'s layered symbolic imaginary, Rachel's support for a Jewish homeland is less salient than the Babylon she helps to evoke. Neither wholly assimilated like a secret Jew, nor affixed to Israel like a committed Zionist, she is the only character to exemplify diaspora as a kind of rooted cosmopolitanism. As such, Rachel sees beneath Don's façade: "I know what it feels like to be out of place," she tells him, "To be disconnected . . . And there is something about you that tells me you know it too" ("Smoke"). If these words announce her as the one woman who can help Don face up to his secrets, the moment is fleeting. A married man, he cannot pledge himself to this diasporic goddess, or find Canaan in her embrace.

Mad Men, in this sense, reads Psalm 137 against a narrative of redemptive return. In *Exodus,* Kitty tells Ari that there "are no differences" between Jews and Christians, cementing the love affair between Israel and America. But in "Babylon," when Don asks Rachel to explain "the difference," she points to the condition of exiles singing for their captors. "Look," she says, "Jews have lived in exile for a long time. First in Babylon. Then all over the world . . . and we've managed to make a go of it. It might have something to do with the fact that we thrive at doing business with people who hate us" ("Babylon"). Whereas Kitty's reply universalizes the Promised Land, Rachel's anticipates Babylon as global condition, and the exilic Jew as its paradigmatic subject.

Later in the season, spurred by the shock of Roger's heart attack, Don shows up at Rachel's door. Consummating his long-simmering desire, he tells her he is the bastard son of a drunk and a prostitute. But though Rachel has anticipated this mélange of passion and confession, she knows their coupling has "no future" ("Babylon"). When Pete discovers Don's fraudulent identity, Don asks Rachel to start a new life in California. "What kind of man *are* you?" she asks, stunned by his readiness to uproot their lives. "This was a dalliance, a cheap affair. You don't want to run away with me; you just want to run away" ("Indian"). This finale is foreshadowed in "Babylon"'s allusion to utopia, which, as Rachel tells Don, etymologically combines "good place" and "no place." In a coded exchange as much about their romance as Zionism, Rachel intimates that the Promised Land is "the place that cannot be." "Babylon" concludes with Don's visit to Midge, his Greenwich Village mistress, where their tryst is interrupted by a visit from the jealous Roy. With the three assembled at a nightclub to hear the live performance of a friend, the episode ends with their male rivalry shut down by a musical version of Psalm 137.

SINGING THE LORD'S SONG: BABYLON AND BOVARY

> By the rivers of Babylon, there we sat down, yeah, we wept, when we remembered Zion.
> ... For there they that carried us away captive required of us a song; and they that wasted us required of us mirth, saying, Sing us one of the songs of Zion. How shall we sing the LORD's song in a strange land?
>
> Psalm 137, ll. 1, 3–4

The sixth of thirteen episodes, "Babylon" is the center of Season 1's arc, proffering a rich illustration of how *Mad Men*'s "chapters" reinvent the synchronicity of the nineteenth century's serialized realism. As a virtual subject in a multi-plot web, Don's narrative intersects with the storylines of four female characters, each of whom exerts her own center of gravity while refracting his. Whereas classic multi-plot fictions use techniques such as free indirect style to enmesh secret Jews in the lives of others, *Mad Men* uses televisual forms like music and montage to articulate synchronous experience. Thus, "Babylon" discloses Joan's affair with Roger who has bought her a caged bird (Fig. 8.5a)—an age-old symbol of female captivity at least as far back as Walter Deverell's 1853 "A Pet" (Fig. 8.5b). Likewise, "Babylon" highlights a new dimension of Betty's dependence. Frequently likened to a child, she is also sexually hungry, thinking about her husband "all day." "It's all in a kind of fog because . . . I want you so badly," she tells Don, intensifying the "secret" of his infidelity. Finally, with the introduction of Belle Jolie's lipstick account, "Babylon" features Peggy Olson's chance remark about a "basket of kisses," revealing to her male superiors that Don's young secretary is a creative force—a display of female skill that copywriter Freddy Rumsen likens to "watching a dog play piano."

The visual montage that accompanies the performance of Psalm 137 synchronizes Don's response with the contemporaneous experiences of the show's "mad women." As a trio of musicians begins, literally, to sing the Lord's song, the camera closes in on Don's expression. The scene then fades to a wistful Rachel, arranging men's ties; and then to Betty playing dress-up with Sally, teaching her how to apply lipstick. The latter image not only figures Betty's

Fig. 8.5a. Joan looks at a caged bird. Scene from "Babylon" *Mad Men* (Season 1, Episode 6) AMC, August 23, 2007.

own dress-up—the dependent marriage that infantilizes her—but also evokes Peggy's earlier moment during the Belle Jolie focus group. While the other "chickens" play compliantly with lipsticks, Peggy refuses to be "one of a hundred colors in a box." When the camera fades back to Don he is immersed in mournful reflection (Fig. 8.6). The scene then cuts to Roger and Joan departing from their tryst, the caged bird in her hands. Finally, as the music reaches an end, Joan and Roger stand on opposite sides of the hotel entrance, pretending to be strangers.

The white, middle-class patriarchy of *Mad Men* divides wives from husbands, and deforms the ambitions of working women. Yet Don's emotional world is dominated by the "[i]mages of enclosure and escape," "maddened doubles," and "metaphors of physical discomfort" (Fig. 8.7) familiar to nineteenth-century women's writing (Gilbert and Gubar xi). That Don is himself a "Mad Man in the Attic" is occasionally literalized, as in Season 4's allusion to Dorian Gray.[23] But at a figurative level, Don's virtuality opens him to a range of alienated identifications whose common thread is exile, captivity, and the necessity of singing. From this perspective Don is not only a closeted male like Lopez or Dorian, but also a madwoman in his own right, like Flaubert's Emma Bovary.

I have so far suggested that *Mad Men* and *The Prime Minister* are serialized narratives of capitalist globalization, exemplifying a naturalistic engagement of global forces beyond mere "mechanical mirroring." Yet, while Trollope's ambivalence toward the secret Jew anticipates *Mad Men*'s troping on neoliberal identity, the

---

[23] In the Season 4 premiere, a reporter writes, "One imagines somewhere in an attic, there's a painting of [Don] that's rapidly aging." The same episode features a commercial in which a boy is imprisoned while his mother does housework ("Public"). These doubles for Don enable us to see, as Kaganovsky writes, that "somewhere in an attic, there's not simply a portrait that's rapidly aging, but a mad man, screaming to get out."

Fig. 8.5b. Walter Deverell's "A Pet" (1853). Licensed by Tate Images.

Fig. 8.6. Don, fading in, listens to "Babylon" as Sally and Betty, playing dress-up, fade out. Scene from "Babylon" *Mad Men* (Season 1, Episode 6) AMC, August 23, 2007.

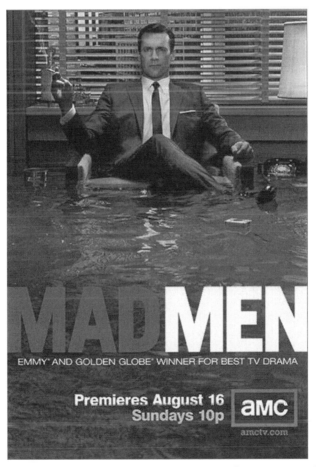

Fig. 8.7. Metaphors of physical discomfort. Publicity for Season 3 of *Mad Men* AMC 2009.

show is famous for a conscious aestheticism that Trollope, by and large, eschews. In this respect, Flaubert is *Mad Men*'s most salient precursor. For while Flaubert's rendering of the Modern Babylon abjures the racial animus that would Judaize an insidious figure like Lheureux in a Trollope novel (see Ch. 6), *Madame Bovary* anticipates *Mad Men*'s stake in the stylized surfaces and sensuous textures that punctuate lives lived through commodities.[24]

"This is all there is," Don insists as he embraces Rachel, persuading her for a time that adulterous passion is better than no passion at all ("Long"). *Mad Men*'s three-season narrative arc has something of *Madame Bovary*'s finitude: although Don does not end his life at the close of Season 3, there is a sense in which *Mad Men* is a three-decker novel whose denouement is Betty's discovery of Don's "Jewishness" and the subsequent collapse of their marriage. Formally, *Mad Men* cultivates Bovaryesque pace, a Flaubertian eye for detail, as well as what Caroline Levine calls "the shock of the banal" ("Shock"). While *Madame Bovary* is not a multi-plot narrative, it produces careful synchronies, as when the blind beggar's song shatters Emma's fantasy of a magical "Babylon" that nurtures the passions of a "hundred and twenty thousand souls" (207). Like Don's hearing Psalm 137 in the company of his mistress, the beggar's voice pierces Emma's escapist pleasure, revealing a well of melancholy. This is the beggar whose song spurs the "desperate laugh" that is literally her last (257). As Don might say, she lived her "life like there's no tomorrow" ("Smoke").

Yet, while Emma and Don are hedonists, neither is wholly cynical; each believes in illusions at least some of the time. Both, to borrow Henry James's line about Emma, remain "absorbed in romantic intention and vision while fairly rolling in the dust" (*Notes* 80). Their intense yearning for the realization of what is only imaginary paradoxically humanizes as well as corrupts them. If Don fares better it is because his male privilege includes the modern vocation Flaubert's novel foreshadows. While both live their lives as "one long tissue of lies" (*Madame* 213), Don alone is a paid storyteller—saved, though never redeemed, by his work in advertising. Emma, by contrast, is an ad man *avant la lettre*. Though highly skilled in "readaptations" of life (Ferguson 11)—her every move intended to "scream with reassurance that whatever she's doing is okay"—Emma invents herself through buying. This is how she sings for her captors, personified by the perfidious Lheureux.[25]

While *Mad Men* glamorizes Madison Avenue, the point of this aestheticism, as in Flaubert, is hardly to express complacency toward the Modern Babylon. As Michael Schudson has shown, advertising's mode is *capitalist realism*: a form antithetical to historical engagement (209-33). In contrast to Lukács's call for

---

[24] Cohen's introduction elaborates Flaubert's connection to the rise of Napoleon III, calling it "a historical novel with a subterranean connection to the destruction of revolutionary ideals" (xv); see also my discussion of Rancière's reading of *Madame Bovary* in Chapter 6. As is well known, Flaubert's travels to the Middle East catalyzed his ideas for a novel of provincial French life.

[25] According to Ferguson, Emma is a "social engineer," convinced, like many *Mad Men* characters, that "there is nothing genuinely bad or sad" in life, only actions calling "out for a different context" (110–11). Notably Don, unlike Emma, is seldom seen purchasing anything, his fabulous

a literary realism of concrete social situations, advertising offers dematerialized abstractions (the same fantasmatic mode that enables Lopez to hawk faux commodities like "Bios"). To be sure, advertising's trick is its appeal to the emotions: as Don tells Peggy, "*You* are the product. *You* feeling something. *That's* what sells" ("For Those"). Advertising produces this fantasmatic effect in the effort to fill the gap between human needs and the consumer habits that leave them unsated. As Raymond Williams writes, "The system of organised magic which is modern advertising" is first and foremost a means of obscuring political alternatives ("Magic" 27). In such a world, adultery is to needy subjects what advertising is to capitalism; for, as Schudson puts it, "Advertising is capitalism's way of saying I love you to itself" (232). Thus, when Don tells Rachel that "guys like me" invented love to sell nylons ("Smokes") he explains why he gives his best hours to the task of mystifying commodities. Along with the latest seduction, creating new ways for capitalism to say "I love you" to itself is the only channel he knows for poiesis and self-love alike.

Were *Mad Men*'s achievement merely to ironize the advertising world it aestheticizes, the show might risk the kind of naturalist impasse that Lukács calls "mirroring . . . the humdrum reality of capitalism" (*Studies* 93). But the show's reinvention of serialized realism does considerably more. By cultivating the viewer's belief that Don is better than the world that made him—as when it synchronizes his experience with that of compelling female characters—*Mad Men* intensifies the habits of watching his (and their) stories unfold over time, inducing private reflection, communal discussion, and waiting (waiting for the next season, waiting for the 60s to come at last, waiting for what Frank Kermode called "the sense of an ending").[26]

Studies of advertising and literature which have not considered the impact of seriality thus neglect a remarkable feature of realist narrative. In her memorable study, *Advertising Fictions: Literature, Advertisement, and Social Reading* (1988), Jennifer Wicke writes that advertising is, for the foreseeable future, "interminable . . . because there will be a plethora of stories to tell" (175). Likewise, Bill Brown argues that advertising is interesting to Henry James because it intuits how artistic forms assert the imaginative "subject over the object" (20)—that same elusive object that Williams seeks in the name of unanswered human needs. To consider advertising from this aesthetic perspective is thus to confront the fact that all forms of realism, like all forms of art, rely on imaginative subjectivities of some kind.

Notably, then, when James writes on *Madame Bovary*, he sets aside *l'art pour l'art* to emphasize a moment in time. "The author of these remarks," he writes, "remembers

> that when a very young person in Paris he took up from the parental table the latest number of the periodical in which Flaubert's then duly unrecognized masterpiece

---

wardrobe notwithstanding. An interesting exception finds Don buying a new Cadillac in which Betty, learning of his affair with Bobbie, promptly vomits ("Golden"). Conversely, when Emma tries to sell the only thing she can—offering her body to Rodolphe in exchange for a loan—he rebuffs her.

[26] On this serialized temporality, see also the Coda.

was in course of publication. The moment is not historic, but it was to become in the light of history ... so unforgettable that every small feature of it yet again lives for him: it rests there like the backward end of the span. The cover of the old *Revue de Paris* was yellow ... and *Madame Bovary: Moeurs de Province* ... was already ... as a title, mysteriously arresting, inscrutably charged. I was ignorant of what had preceded and was not to know till much later what followed; but present to me still is the act of standing there before the fire ... and taking in what I might of that installment, taking it in with so surprised an interest, and perhaps as well such a stir of faint foreknowledge, that the sunny little salon, the autumn day, the window ajar and the cheerful outside clatter of the Rue Montaigne are all now for me more or less in the story and the story more or less in them (*Notes* 77–8).

As James makes clear, his adequate appreciation of *Madame Bovary* requires him to consider Flaubert's story as an experience in seriality which takes place in time. That experience, moreover, inhabits James's memory indistinguishably from certain histories that only later become accessible to his cognition: Emma's full narrative arc, *Madame Bovary*'s evolution from scandalous text to literary masterpiece, and James's own development from "very young person" into the famous "author of these remarks." Finally, James's experience—what Don might call "*James* feeling something"—is no less an experience of seriality for its entering *in medias res*, temporarily isolated from the beginnings and endings that structure realist form. So far from decadent and detail-oriented, James's *Madame Bovary* lives in its rescue of an otherwise fragmentary moment, its vivid affects (the "inscrutable charge," the "surprised" interest, and the "stir" of foreknowledge) now woven inseparably into the histories of Emma, *Madame Bovary*, and James himself. James's account of *Madame Bovary* thus differs from any imaginable account of an advertisement: no matter how charged, surprised, or stirred. For while advertising artfully produces feeling in *medias res*, its fragments are absolute; not histories but abstractions of histories which cannot "rest there like the backward end of the span."

It is therefore crucial to recognize that *Mad Men*, however playfully coy, knows the difference between advertising and its own naturalistic realism. Indeed, in one of its most famous scenes, Don pitches the Kodak "carousel" by way of illustrating this very point. "Nostalgia," he explains, "literally means 'the pain from an old wound.' It's a twinge in your heart far more powerful than memory alone." Using Kodak's new device to screen happy scenes from a marriage he is inexorably destroying, Don tells us (and his clients) that we are looking at a "time machine." "It goes backwards, and forwards," taking us "to a place where we ache to go again. . . . It lets us travel the way a child travels—around and around, and back home again" ("The Wheel").

Don's winning pitch takes precisely the form that Schudson identifies as capitalist realism: isolating a series of attractive moments, it disarticulates them from concrete histories, and elevates the sentimentality to an abstract ideal—eliciting desire for the sentiment and, presumably, for the product. By the end of Season 1, *Mad Men*'s savvy viewers can see that Don has exploited his own reservoir of despair to produce this affective "story" for advertising. But "The

Wheel" is not advertising, but, rather, the concluding episode in a long season arc at the heart of which is the lingering aperçu of Don in Babylon, singing for his captors. Thus, Don's description of the "time machine," its backward and forward motion taking us "around and around, and back home again," is, at another level, a metaphor for the experience of serial viewers. His painful wound, aching for any number of objects he has lost while spinning a long tissue of lies in the first volume of *Mad Men*'s three-decker novel, is not (or not only) a brilliant pitch. It is also a structure of feeling that lives for the viewer, resting there like the backward span of time.

Coda: The Way We Historicize Now

In his 1996 book, *On Television*, Pierre Bourdieu, the leading critical sociologist of the postwar era, provides a lengthy account of why television has become a force for "depoliticization" and "disenchantment with politics." On television news shows, Bourdieu explains, history is reduced to entertaining recital:

> The result is a litany of events with no beginning and no real end, thrown together only because they occurred at the same time. So an earthquake in Turkey turns up next to proposed budget cuts, and a championship sports team is featured alongside a big murder trial. These events are reduced to the level of the absurd because we see only those elements that can be shown on television at a given moment, cut off from their antecedents and consequences. There is a patent lack of interest in subtle, nuanced changes, or in processes that, like the continental drift, remain unperceived and imperceptible in the moment, revealing their effects only in the long term. This inattention to nuance both repeats and reinforces the structural amnesia induced by day-to-day thinking and by the competition that equates what's important with what's new—the scoop (6–7).

Bourdieu's case for the importance of "long term" history complements the study of the Victorian geopolitical aesthetic. As television news assembles simultaneous events that are disarticulated from each other and from their own "antecedents and consequences," it engenders a "structural amnesia" that reduces contemporary life to the visible, synchronic, ephemeral, and "new." What such television fails to do—what underlies its "patent lack of interest" in subtle or long-evolving change—is to historicize.

When Bourdieu wrote these words in the mid-1990s, the New Historicism, so-called, had been a dominant influence on scholarship for at least a decade. Marxist theory provided yet another incitement for a critical practice committed to "subtle, nuanced changes" and long-term "processes." In the preface to *The Political Unconscious: Narrative as a Socially Symbolic Act* (1981), Fredric Jameson wrote that the call to "Always historicize!" was the "absolute imperative of all dialectical thought" (9). Yet, recently, the tide has turned as literature scholars have begun looking to form or to newer practices such as "surface reading," "distant reading," and "description," to combat a perceived overemphasis on historical context or ideological content. In doing so, scholars such as Rita Felski and Heather Love are inspired by the sociologist Bruno Latour who has written copiously on the pitfalls of a "suspicious" mentality in polemics such as "Why Has Critique Run out of Steam?" (2004). Other critics hark to Eve Kosofsky Sedgwick's concerns about "paranoia," another oft-cited resource for surface reading.

In the introduction to one of the best-known iterations of this conversation, a special issue of *Representations* called *The Way We Read Now* (2009), Stephen Best and Sharon Marcus write that in "the last decade or so," critics "have been drawn to modes of reading that attend to the surfaces of texts rather than plumb their depths" (1–2). A surface reading approach attends to "what is evident, perceptible, apprehensible in texts; what is neither hidden nor hiding; what, in the geometrical sense, has length and breadth but no thickness, and therefore covers no depth" (8). In concert with Latour's assertion of an exhausted critique, such methods proposed "to move past the impasses" created by "an excessive emphasis on ideological mystification" (Best and Marcus 17–18). But according to John Kucich, one of several scholars so far to respond, this critical project is worrisome insofar as arguments against critical suspicion drift into arguments against historicism ("Unfinished").

This Coda opens up a dialogue between these conversations and the preceding chapters of *The Victorian Geopolitical Aesthetic*. At the outset of this book, I called for a critical practice that combined ethical critique with a formally nuanced, structurally acute, and synchronic as well as diachronic theory of the geopolitical aesthetic, attempting to show in subsequent chapters how that practice might look in relation to the realist fictional experiments of Anthony Trollope, Wilkie Collins, George Eliot, Gustave Flaubert, E. M. Forster and the AMC television series *Mad Men* (2007–present). As a scholar thus profoundly immersed in historicizing, I believe that the attention to surface which organizes *The Way We Read Now* accommodates a variety of historicist methods.[1] It is, I will argue, more explicitly Latourian arguments against context which cast historicism as a focal concern. Nonetheless, the critique of critique which underlies such calls for methodological change, poses difficulties for scholars who seek out "subtle, nuanced changes" and processes that "remain unperceived and imperceptible in the moment." Indeed, when the embrace of surface is defined as an ethical stance that critical suspicion subverts, the argument for attentive reading, I contend, entangles itself in an anti-hermeneutic, neo-positivist turn to ontology, which is under-explicated and counter in many ways to the promised rewards of an anti-suspicious criticism. Such a critique thus exacerbates a habit of defining "historicism" narrowly and in terms of what we already know.[2]

I conclude my book with these debates over "reading" in part to contrast the picture of Jameson's legacy which has emerged from these discussions with the Jamesonian insights developed in *The Victorian Geopolitical Aesthetic*. In making *The Political Unconscious* ground zero for the "symptomatic reading" that holds meaning to be "hidden, repressed, deep, and in need of detection," Best and Marcus pin their discussion of the way "we" have been reading until quite recently, to the way that Jameson wrote in this early landmark (1). Felski

---

[1] The essays by Cheng, Cohen, and Price are self-evidently historicist; Nealon historicizes critique by way of articulating its condition; even Crane, in grounding her case for cognitive theory, explodes "the historical conditions that produced a theory of symptomatic reading" (83)—in other words, historicizes.

[2] For discussion of the tendency among some critics to regard "historicism" as invariably synchronic and ideologically driven, see Goodlad and Sartori.

is even more emphatic about the lasting power of the 1980s when she holds up Catherine Belsey's *Critical Practice* (1980) and D. A. Miller's *The Novel and the Police* (1989) to exemplify a "suspicious" hermeneutic that "assumes the worst about its object" ("Suspicious" 220). Influential though these classic studies from the 1980s have been, it is worth questioning the extent to which they exemplify the current state of the art. Do scholars of literature today inhabit a mindset that ties them unreflectively to critical standpoints that were groundbreaking thirty years ago?[3]

According to Kucich, historicism is still very much with us but has gradually gravitated toward "methodological hybridity." While the first wave of New Historicists "used deconstructive techniques to turn the whole social text into an object of formalist analysis," today's scholarship "pragmatically amalgamates empirical and theoretical methods" to explore "literary and social intersections" ("Praise" 62). A complete abandonment of critical suspicion, Kucich cautions, would amount to the "rejection of [a] political orientation" that still has much work to do (71). Crystal Bartolovich agrees: the surface reader's appeal "to the 'text itself,'" she writes, "marks a pointed withdrawal from politics and theory" (cf. Hack, Lesjak, Rooney). Kucich advises historicists to ground their political aspirations by integrating synchronic and diachronic methods of reading; showing how past inflects present and vice versa.

It is worth comparing his account of recent historicism to Felski's nearly contemporaneous essay, "Suspicious Minds" (2011). Whereas Kucich sees pragmatic amalgamation, Felski perceives a need to rescue scholars from "entrapment within a suspicious sensibility"—a "mentality" she traces to the "medieval heresy trial" and the biological mandate to look out for "predators" (218–20). And whereas Kucich recommends historicism as an enlivening "foundation for humanistic study" ("Praise" 64), Felski associates it with interpretive modes "tightly bound to exposure, demystification, and the lure of the negative" ("Suspicious" 232). With no recent examples to illustrate this allegedly (still) dominant critical mindset, it is difficult to guess what she has in mind. Although Felski describes Sedgwick's "Paranoid Reading and Reparative Reading" (1997) as a "virtuoso meditation" on the advent of suspicion (218), she deliberately distinguishes it from her own critique to avoid diagnosing the mental condition of scholars. Yet, by harnessing Latour's agenda, Felski implicates her work in the very pathologization she seeks to avoid. To put this another way, literary criticism has become caught up in a *Methodenstreit*, the origins of which are in the social sciences; and yet some of its principal literary interlocutors seem unaware of the stakes of the battle they are helping to wage.

---

[3] While Felski's articles and the Best and Marcus special issue offer comparable interventions, they also differ. Felski foregrounds the hermeneutics of suspicion, while Best and Marcus question a hermeneutics of "depth" which includes suspicion but is defined instead by "symptomatic" unmasking. Whereas Felski perceives a still "ubiquitous" investment in suspicion, Best and Marcus discern a multi-faceted turn to surface which is gaining ground. For two related special issues, both published in *New Literary History*, see *New Sociologies of Literature* (2010), edited by English and Felski, as well as "*Context?*" (2011), edited by Felski and H. Tucker.

MARXISM, HISTORICISM, AND THE GEOPOLITICAL AESTHETIC

In questioning "the present-day ubiquity" of a suspicious mentality (Felski, "Suspicious" 215), I do not suggest that no such mentality ever existed. While working on *Victorian Literature and the Victorian State* (2003), I noticed a tendency for scholars to favor Foucault's genealogical insights into nineteenth-century disciplinary power even when Victorian writings seemed to require a more flexible analysis.[4] In the decade since, I have been struck by the capaciousness and variety of scholarship on the nineteenth century. In researching nineteenth-century literature and geopolitics, I consulted a vibrant body of secondary writing which includes Emily Apter on the business novel, Carolyn Vellenga Berman on the Creole, Nicholas Birns on white settlement in Australia ("Receptacle"), Roberto Dainotto on the idea of Europe, Elaine Freedgood and Harry Shaw on realist metonymy, Sharon Marcus on Victorian marriage (*Between*), Helena Michie on Victorian honeymoons, and John Plotz on portable property. While each of these scholars is in some sense motivated by the precept to "always historicize," none of these studies was written in the grip of high suspicion. Moreover, none is committed to "symptomatic" reading of any stripe—the presumption that "a text's truest meaning lies in what it does *not* say" (Best and Marcus 1; emphasis added).

In fact, the book I am now concluding, while deliberately eclectic, is demonstrably more Jamesonian than any of the examples cited above. *The Victorian Geopolitical Aesthetic* comes together at the intersection of several critical innovations including the "new imperial history" with its use of networks and matrices to reformulate the space of empire; the transnational and global turn in theories of postcoloniality and the nation-state; the interest in politics and ethics as partners for literary criticism (including key terms such as sovereignty); the openness to the normative aspirations of both poststructuralism and the Enlightenment; and the rejuvenated focus on literary form. Nonetheless, the outlines of the "geopolitical aesthetic" developed in Jameson's 1995 book on cinema, inform this study throughout. *The Victorian Geopolitical Aesthetic* has thus looked to form and aesthetics to explore their engagements with global situations that are at once lived and beyond the scope of individual experience.

Such a Jamesonian stance is hardly suspicious. To the contrary, it endows literature and art with a crucial capacity to articulate structures that elude ordinary cognition. Thus, whereas Felski writes that suspicious reading "pivots on a fealty to the clarifying power of historical contexts" that shape literature—but which literary texts themselves do "not see" ("Context" 574)—Jameson urges historicization to elucidate what texts *do* see. Nor does the geopolitical aesthetic insist that a "strong" criticism "must rewrite narrative in terms of master codes" to disclose the

---

[4] In fact, the theoretical resources for that flexibility could be found in Foucault's own later work on governmentality (see Goodlad, *Victorian*, Ch. 1 and *passim*).

text's "status as ideology" (Best and Marcus 4). Rather, as Carolyn Lesjak notes, the task of critical "unmasking" is but one half of Jameson's two-fold dialectical practice, "the other half of which" is his "articulation of the positive Utopian impulses that lie along negative critique" (18; cf. Bartolovich 117–18).[5]

Of course, as a scholar primarily of the twentieth century, Jameson has never been the leading light of the New Historicism familiar to most Victorianists.[6] Moreover, the relation between Marxism and New Historicism has often been contentious. In *Practicing New Historicism* (2000), Gallagher and Stephen Greenblatt described the approach that the journal *Representations* had helped to forge as a "history of possibilities" best defined by the "lack of a given set of objects" (6). Beckoning scholars to "push beyond" unified histories so as to render a multiplistic "social imaginary" (57), the leading theorists for this practice were Foucault and the anthropologist Clifford Geertz whose notion that "cultural fragments" such as the anecdote could "'widen out' into larger social worlds" fueled a project of "counterhistory" which was inimical to *grands récits* such as Marxism (26, 52). Gallagher tied New Historicism to the Left's disenchantment with Marxism: the "American radicalism of the sixties and early seventies," she explained, "bred just those preoccupations that have tended to separate new historicist from Marxist critics" (38; cf. Greenblatt "Towards" 2). With Foucault's works to inspire them, New Historicists rejected Marxism's "meta-narrative of class conflict" and insisted "that power cannot be equated with economic or state power, that its sites of activity" are "also in the micro-politics of daily life" (Gallagher, "Marxism" 43).

One of the problems implicit in such critiques is that Marxist theory, in espousing its dream of a classless future, hews to a *responsibility to act* that, at least in its original formation, is relatively unintegrated with a countervailing *responsibility to otherness*.[7] In Chapter 7, we saw how Forster's "queer internationalism" upheld the ethical enlivenment of encountering otherness as distinct from an activist commitment to universal justice. By contrast, Marx's Hegelian conception of a revolutionary subject never prompted him (despite his clear sympathy for the victims of racism) to work out "the strategies of a politics that would combat racial hostility and division" (R. Peterson 240). Marx thus set aside the practical question of how of to negotiate the fissiparous investments in the politics of difference which capitalist social relations help to foster—a "fateful gap in Marxist thought," writes Richard K. Peterson, given the reactionary effects of racism, nationalism, and sexism, as well as the democratic potential of the identitarian freedom movements that emerged in the 1960s (248).

---

[5] For a recent example, see Jameson's discussion of the utopian dimensions of Walmart in *Valences*, Ch. 16.

[6] Influential studies such as Miller's *The Novel and the Police*, and Gallagher's *The Industrial Reformation of English Fiction* do not mention Jameson while N. Armstrong's *Desire and Domestic Fiction* and Poovey's *Uneven Developments* give him a passing nod before crafting practices more influenced by Foucault. As LaCapra noted in 1982, Jameson's effort to update Marxism "accorded surprisingly little explicit treatment" to Foucault ("Review" 88).

[7] These useful terms appear in Stephen K. White's *Political Theory and Postmodernism* (1991).

In the wake of Stalinism and the failure of revolutionary student movements, the closing decades of the twentieth century saw a wave of radical theorizations of otherness, including Foucault's archeology of madness; Levinas's infinite responsibility to the Other; Derrida's *différance*; Irigiray's feminism; Said's "Orientalism"; and the rise of postcolonial, queer, and disability studies. In speaking for an ethical responsibility to attend the object of one's critique, proponents of surface reading are clear bearers of this poststructuralist mantle. There is, thus, no necessary disconnect between the new ethos of attentiveness to one's object and a historicism keen "to trace the connections among texts, discourses, power, and the constitution of subjectivity" (Gallagher, "Marxism" 40). By contrast, it should come as no surprise that such an ethos finds fault with a Marxism that, even in Jameson's modulated form, seems to *defer* its responsibility to otherness by locating the fulfillment of that ethical relation in the radically alternative future to which its unchastened politics aspires. As Marx himself put it, the point is not to interpret the world, but to change it ("Theses" 145). This arguably makes him one of the world's most suspicious readers.

Post-Marxist theorists such as Ernesto Laclau and Chantal Mouffe have sought to substitute radical democratic politics for the residue in Marxist theory of stagism, inevitabilism, and naïve faith in a revolutionary subject.[8] Jameson shares with these latter-day theorists a determination to view *culture* openly, considering its "active role in defining social relations and resisting political domination" (Nelson and Grossberg, "Introduction" 3). But Jameson is also an unrepentant Hegelian whose dialectical materialism owes more to Georg Lukács than Antonio Gramsci. Famously, Jameson tries to renovate Hegelian dialectics through an innovative use of Althusser's notion of "absent cause" which Jameson defines as the nonrepresentability of "history itself" in a landscape of materialities so large in scale, complex in effect, and long in duration that it is not readily accessible to individual consciousness (*Political* 146).

Whatever one thinks of history as "absent cause," I believe we can affirm Jameson's conviction that the long and ongoing process of capitalist globalization is empirically real and, yet, fundamentally absent to individual perception *as the totality of that process*. This is not because of any ideological ruse that critics must demystify. It is, rather, because certain historical phenomena, however materially consequential, are (like Bourdieu's continental drift) not cognizable in the form of objects "in plain view" (Felski, "After" 31)—not only globalization but also commodification, the turn to neoliberalism, the financialization of the world economy, the entrenchment of racism and sexism, the reduction of biodiversity, and climate change. Closer to the arguments of this book, we might think of the looming crisis over imperial sovereignty which "absent-minded" Britons disavowed for more than a century. The conviction that literature and art have the potential to pronounce on such "absent" realities thus offers a compelling critical optic. By placing artistic form in dialogue with processes that are both real and

---

[8] See Laclau and Mouffe, *Hegemony and Social Strategy* (1985).

spatio-temporally complex, the notion of a geopolitical aesthetic posits a "surface" that is inextricable from its "depth."

Victorianists seeking to adapt Jameson's ideas will not find themselves mired in doctrinaire symptomatism; but they will encounter the reflexive privileging of Modernist forms.[9] As we saw in Chapter 6, the tendency to uphold Modernist innovation at the expense of realism dates back to the nineteenth century. Since that time, Victorian-era realism has been criticized (or simply ignored), by Modernist authors such as Virginia Woolf as well as literary scholars working under the sign of the New Criticism, Marxism, structuralism, and poststructuralism. Jameson's specific contributions to this outlook have been a tendency to assume that realist fiction emerges from nation-bound and pre-imperial conditions as well as a related tendency to eternalize the crisis of realist aesthetics which Lukács envisioned as the temporary effect of the failed revolutions of 1848. *The Victorian Geopolitical Aesthetic* has challenged the faulty assumption that nineteenth-century literature was autarkic. To uphold mid-Victorian fiction as the flavorless vintage of an insular culture, I have argued, is to overlook the intense global dynamism of a period that saw major structural transformations in industrialization, finance, and telecommunications; continuous use of military force; and challenges to British power in Afghanistan, Canada, China, Egypt, India, Ireland, Jamaica, New Zealand, and South Africa.

As Marx put it in an 1853 article on India, "bourgeois industry and commerce" were creating the "material conditions of a new world" in the same way that "geological revolutions have created the surface of the earth." The "market of the world and the modern powers of production" advance an exploitative form of "human progress" which "drinks" its "nectar . . . from the skulls of the slain" ("Future"). The consequent yearning for a holism that could be mourned as the communal past—or sought as its future—was channeled by romance forms that, as Jameson writes, figure "a transition moment in which two distinct modes of production, or two moments of socioeconomic development, coexist." What was significant about such forms was less their accurate depiction of history than the work they did in cathecting the sense of "an organic social order in the process of penetration and subversion, reorganization and rationalization" (*Political* 148). For Jameson, as for Lukács, Walter Scott's historical romances were the bearers of this elegiac historicity, while Balzac's realism achieved a comparable effect by depicting "the *present as history*" (Lukács, *Historical* 82–3). Working both with and against this legacy, *The Victorian Geopolitical Aesthetic* has placed the mid-century fiction of Flaubert, Trollope, Collins, and Eliot at the heart of the "new world" evoked by Marx: an evolving world-system intertwined with a "literary

---

[9] Scholars who have in various ways resisted the widespread tendency to project exceptional ethico-political powers and exemptions onto Modernism which are not typically granted to Victorian-era or realist literature include Kaye, David Kurnick (*Empty*), Joyce, Teukolsky, H. Tucker, and Potolsky, among others. For the rethinking of realism in the context of postcolonial literature, see also *Peripheral Realisms*, a special issue of *MLQ* edited by Esty and Lye. For a complementary study of realism in the Indian novel, see Anjaria and, on African fiction, see Andrade.

system" that was equally determined to cross "the surface of the earth" (e.g., Kinoshita 18).

Trollope's variation on Scott's historicism (as we saw in Chapter 3), was the "heirloom sovereignty" eulogized in *The Warden* (1855), while George Eliot (as we saw in Chapter 6), drew on Scott as well as George Sand in writing *Romola* (1862–3), a romance of Florentine republicanism with a female typical character at its center. While such novels take part in the overarching conjuncture of literature and geohistory, they also speak eloquently to spatio-temporal particularities of many kinds: e.g., the fallen ideals of the French Second Empire in Flaubert's *Madame Bovary* (1856); the trans-channel engagement of the novel of adultery for George Eliot; the forgotten history of Atlantic slavery in Collins's *Armadale* (1864–6); and the estranging effects of Disraeliesque imperialism in Trollope's *The Prime Minister* (1875–6).[10] As we saw in Chapter 5, Collins brought an almost Baudelairean sensibility to the task of innovating "sensational" styles to express the transnational experience of the racialized alien. If this phenomenological aesthetic invites symptomatic searching for history's forgotten traces, it simultaneously calls for meticulous attention to surface, from the "broad brown face" of the Shivering Sands (*Moonstone* 39) to *La Grace de Dieu*, the wrecked ship whose return to the surface stirs up guilty memories in *Armadale*.

Chapter 6 put forward Eliot as a proleptic Lukácsian who struggled to reinvent the kind of Scott novel which Balzac admired and Flaubert put on Emma Bovary's reading list. The writing of *Romola* entailed a formal merger of the historical romance, the sentimental novel of adultery, and the female *Bildungsroman*. As a narrative that concludes with the heroine taking her husband's place as the head of his mistress's family, *Romola* cries out for the "just reading" described in Marcus's *Between Women* (2007). Yet, from a geopolitical standpoint, Eliot's female alternative to heterosexual marriage is also a formal alternative to Flaubertian naturalism. Indeed, Eliot's apprehension of a naturalistic impasse was strong enough to split *Daniel Deronda* between the decadence of the "country-house novel" (Williams, *Country* 249) and a veritable Victorian Exodus narrative.

In *The Political Unconscious*, Jameson affirmed Lukács's diagnosis of naturalism as the post-Flaubertian product of an "age of reification." He took Theodore Dreiser's *Sister Carrie* (1900) to exemplify "the congealment of language, fantasy and desire" in the wake of "*bovarysme*" (139–40). But just as Europe's failed revolutions are too narrow in scope to compass the worldedness of nineteenth-century literature, so the reduction of naturalism to decadent private despair obscures the

---

[10] Readers may ask why this book never ventures into non-realist genres such as the late-Victorian imperial adventure fiction of Ouida, Rider Haggard, Conan Doyle, Bram Stoker, and Kipling—or even into poetry or drama. The answer is largely to do with concision. Although Collins's fiction is arguably no more realist than many adventure narratives, his contemporaneity with Flaubert, Eliot, and Trollope, and his comparable focus on the globalized metropole enabled me to focus on mid-Victorian conditions of possibility and their resonance in later decades. That said, the move to a geopolitical exploration of late-Victorian genre fiction and to poetry and drama should provide compelling terrain for future scholarship.

genre's recurrent tropes of exile.[11] Naturalistic narratives such as *Madame Bovary* and *The Prime Minister* do not congeal language but compress it, producing strains of global anti-romance. Whereas romance genres imagine freedom from ordinary spatio-temporal constraints, naturalism inhabits its small, sociologically thick, and often catastrophically broken quixotism. Paradoxically, then, naturalism's utopian impulse is its uncompromising vision of a modernity without progress, egress, or salvation—a powerful solvent to chasten imperial (or neoliberal) grandiosity. There is no promised land in these works because the stranger-in-exile is already home. Thus, like the science fiction genres of Jules Verne and H.G. Wells whose emergence they anticipate, naturalistic narratives of capitalist globalization "defamiliarize and restructure our experience of [the] present" (Jameson, "Progress" 286).[12] While a more dialectical fiction would, to be sure, add the subjunctive vision of a future beyond homogeneous, empty time (much as Eliot concludes her most naturalistic novel with an Exodus narrative), naturalism of this kind underscores its task of narrating the present as history.

THE ANTINOMIES OF REALISM

As *The Victorian Geopolitical Aesthetic* will have made clear, Jameson's vibrant legacy of meditation on literary form provides invaluable resources for scholars of nineteenth-century literature despite the stubborn tendency to wedge "realism" between the Scylla of an obsolescent structure of "national or local capitalism" and the Charybdis of an "epistemological category" fettered by an alleged "need to avoid" social contradiction (*Signatures* 156; "A Note" 261; 263). Keen to elucidate the *longue durée* of nineteenth-century geopolitics, this book has insisted that the "stage of imperialism" long pre-dated the advent of Modernist aesthetics (*Signatures* 156). But there is also much to say about the distinctly Jamesonian notion (absent in Lukács) that realism marks the paradoxical condition of an art form trapped in the antithetical grasp of an epistemological function. That is not to deny that, as Harry Shaw writes, "[n]ineteenth-century realism responds to a historical and ideological situation of which ... philosophy can no longer give an

---

[11] In *Antinomies of Realism*, Jameson hews to the convention of reserving "naturalism" for a post-Zola genre centered on the deterministic milieu of the "lower depths" (148). Hence, he never addresses the signal fact that Flaubert's "*bovarysme*"—with its focus on embourgeoisement—represents a strain of mid-nineteenth-century fiction which is less readily cordoned off from realism at large. In contrast to the recurrent naturalistic aesthetic described in this book, with its deliberate counter to Lukács's critique of naturalistic realism after 1848, *Antinomies* defines naturalism as a short-lived, late-Victorian-era "sub-genre" that anticipates "the various emergent modernisms" (149–50).

[12] Jameson reiterates the importance of science fiction in *Antinomies* while rehearsing the questionable claim that "the emergence of imperialism on a world scale" begins with the Berlin Conference of 1884–5 (289). Notably, Verne's first major work, *Le tour du monde en quatre-vingts jours* (1873), is a comic meditation on the same globetrotting Briton who recurs in works such as Trollope's *The Way We Live Now* (written in 1873). See also Chapter 5 on the science fiction and utopian dimensions of *The Moonstone*.

adequate account" (*Narrating* x). But it is one thing to define realism as a form that animates existing conditions of possibility and another to conclude that, *precisely for that reason*, it is "peculiarly unstable ... owing to its simultaneous, yet incompatible, aesthetic and epistemological claims" (Jameson, *Signatures* 158). In *Signatures of the Visible* (1992), Jameson goes on to say that

> ... the [realist] emphasis on this or that type of truth content will clearly be undermined by any intensified awareness of the technical means or representational artifice of the work itself. Meanwhile, the attempt to reinforce and to shore up the epistemological vocation of the work generally involves the suppression of the formal properties of the realistic 'text' and promotes an increasingly naïve and unmediated or reflective conception of aesthetic construction and reception. Thus, where the epistemological claim succeeds it fails; and if realism validates its claims to being a correct or true representation of the world, it thereby ceases to be an *aesthetic* mode of representation and falls out of art altogether. If, on the other hand, the artistic devices and technological equipment whereby it captures that truth of the world are explored and stressed and foregrounded, 'realism' will stand unmasked as a mere reality-or realism-*effect*, the reality it purported to deconceal falling at once into the sheerest representation and illusion (158).

Here Jameson avers that the only way realist art can "validate its claims" to "true representation" is to deny its status *as* representation and perpetuate the illusion of its reality. Yet, there is simply no evidence that authors or readers in the nineteenth century or since, have taken up realist novels to convince themselves of fiction's "reality." Nor is there much to support the proposition that realist novels "suppress" their "formal properties" to "promote" naïve conceptions of aesthetics.[13]

In fact, one of the leading Victorian enthusiasts of realist fiction made the opposite point. Writing in the *Westminster Review* in 1858, George Henry Lewes described a lamentable tendency to associate great literature with an 'ideal element.' "A distinction is drawn," he wrote, "between Art and Reality, and an antithesis established between Realism and Idealism which would never have gained acceptance had not men ... lost sight of the fact that Art is a Representation of Reality—a Representation which, inasmuch as it is not the thing itself, but only represents it, must necessarily be limited by the nature of its medium; the canvas of the painter, the marble of the sculptor, the chords of the musician, and the language of the writer" ("Realism"). Here Lewes argues that the successful alignment of "Art and Reality"—as distinct from flattering idealizations of the world—requires authors who recognize that literature is "an *art*" (490). Moreover, no less self-conscious an aesthete than Henry James agreed. James's wish in "The Art of Fiction" (1884) is to liberate the novel from its reputation as a didactic tool. Although his criticism is often remembered for its effort to distinguish his

---

[13] The most thoroughgoing analysis of the faulty premises of such critiques is Shaw's *Narrating* which persuasively argues that Ian Watt's *The Rise of the Novel* (1957) laid the groundwork for this misconception: "Watt's 'formal realism' can easily become a 'material realism,' in which the mere presence of discrete objects will serve to indicate ... epistemological priorities. It's a short step from 'formal realism' to 'transparent representation'" and then to "Barthes's 'reality effect'" (45).

own aesthetic conviction from that of realist precursors, the overall message of the essay is, nonetheless, that the novel's purpose is to "compete with life" (503). While such a fiction does indeed proffer "true representation of the world," it by no means encourages "naïve and unmediated" conceptions of aesthetics. To the contrary, to "compete with life," for James, is to practice the Art of Fiction as a "search for *form*" (505; emphasis added).

These concerns notwithstanding, Victorianist scholars should welcome the arrival of *The Antinomies of Realism* (2013), the capstone of Jameson's thinking on nineteenth-century fiction after decades of provocative writing. With a new interest in affect as a constitutive component of realist form, alongside incisive readings of authors including Eliot, the book warrants closer consideration than this parting glance will afford. Still, for the purposes of this Coda, it is important to emphasize that, while *The Antinomies of Realism* is a not-to-be-missed elaboration of Jameson's long-cultivated views on realism, it is by no means a reversal and, still less, an occasion for upholding nineteenth-century literature as a realist *geopolitical aesthetic*. Rather, as the title suggests, Jameson's focal point is realism's antinomistic condition: the sense in which any attempt to seize it will invariably find realism morphing into something else: "not the thing itself," but its "emergence," or "degeneration," or "dissolution" into other forms including, of course, Modernism (*Antinomies* 1).

In making this case for an antinomistic realism, Jameson distinguishes himself from those influential "apologists"—Lukács, Bakhtin, and Auerbach—who take the formal resilience of realist fiction as their *donnée* (4). By contrast, his book sets out to explore the dilemma already set forth in *Signatures of the Visible*. Realism, he reminds us,

> is a hybrid concept, in which an epistemological claim (for knowledge or truth) masquerades as an aesthetic ideal, with fatal consequences for both of these incommensurable dimensions. If it is social truth or knowledge we want from realism, we will soon find that what we get is ideology; if it is beauty or aesthetic satisfaction we are looking for, we will quickly find that we have to do with outdated styles or mere decoration (if not distraction). And if it is history we are looking for—either social history or the history of literary forms—then we are at once confronted with questions about the uses of the past and even the access to it which, as unanswerable as they may be, take us well beyond literature and theory and seem to demand an engagement with our own present (*Antinomies* 6).

It is the last (somewhat Delphic) claim that I hope especially to address in this Coda on historicization; but, before doing so, I want to compare this rather devastating assessment of realism's predicament to some words from a contemporaneous essay, "Antinomies of the Realism-Modernism Debate" (2012). Written as the afterword to *Peripheral Realisms,* a special issue on realist fiction from outside Europe and North America, Jameson's essay pauses to clarify Lukács's relation between realism and totality. He writes, "I believe that for Lukács totality was history" and that

> his conception of realism had to do with an art whereby the narrative of individuals was somehow made to approach historical dynamics as such, was organized so as to reveal its relationship with a history in movement and a future on the point of

emergence. Realism would thus have to do with the revelation of tendencies rather than with the portrayal of a state of affairs ("Antinomies" 479).

In these few words, Jameson captures several ideas that have been central to *The Victorian Geopolitical Aesthetic*. First, he illustrates one of Lukács's most generative suggestions—the insistence on *form* as the one "category of literature that is both social and aesthetic" (Lukács qtd. in J. Bernstein 77). In addition, he shows why the most salient Lukácsian feature of *realist* form is not nationhood (as Jameson himself tends to allege) but *historicity* (which only sometimes concerns national histories). At the same time, Jameson demonstrates that literary historicity so conceived is a synchronic formation (a particular "narrative of individuals") that deliberately opens out onto a diachronic, ongoing, and encompassing horizon (part of "a history in movement and a future on the point of emergence"). Finally, he shows why Lukács is central to his own theory of the geopolitical aesthetic which, as we have seen, posits art's turn to formal experiment for the "revelation of tendencies" which everyday experience occludes. Yet, in all of these ways, this brief gloss on Lukács also demonstrates how *Antinomies of Realism* forecloses the very possibility of what the present study has put forward as a richly variegated, but still identifiably realist and Victorian-era geopolitical aesthetic that neither "degenerates" into the kind of naturalism Lukács deplored nor "dissolves" into the Modernist experiments Jameson prizes.

This is not to say that *Antinomies of Realism* lacks éclat as it "come[s] at realism dialectically" by taking up its "failure" as a kind of "success" (6).[14] In his *Romola* chapter, Jameson's Eliot anticipates Sartre in proffering bad faith as a successor to moral absolutes; her "moralizing project" is, paradoxically, "her intent to persuade us that there are no villains and that evil does not exist." Behind this Sartrean impulse is a "solution" to the "form-problem of the villain": a dilemma created when realism, which is committed to "inwardness," can no longer incorporate the melodramatic type of the stage villain (122, 116). Thus, the true protagonist of Eliot's experiment with Scott's form is not "the eponymous heroine"—who is "for the most part a witness rather than an actor"—but her husband, Tito. The latter's "psychological complexity" constitutes him as "a new type" that answers modernity's democratizing impulses by introducing minor characters as protagonists (124, 126). Merely embryonic in *Romola*, this formal strategy comes to fruition in *Middlemarch* (1871–2) with the creation of virtuoso minor characters such as Casaubon and Bulstrode. Eliot thus mobilizes the dramatic potential of evil while discrediting "the metaphysical and moral ideologies" that underlie it (137). Yet, despite its efficacy, bad faith as narrative formation does not perdure; "examples of its later use are infrequent" (135). This historical failure is not so much demonstrated as it is foreordained by realism's antinomistic condition. That is to say,

---

[14] One of the most intriguing perceptions to emerge from this enterprise is the notion that realism's symbiosis of storytelling, description, and affective investment develops "towards a scenic present which in reality, but secretly, abhors the other temporalities which constitute the force of the tale" (11). I will return to this particular observation in future work.

Jameson has already made clear that a formal "battle" against "the dominance of point of view" will "exhaust and destroy" realism, leaving behind "an odd assortment of random tools and techniques to its shriveled posterity, who still carry its name on into an era of mass culture and rival media" (11).

Jameson's seizing on "representations of villainy . . . 'from the inside'" cannot but interest scholars of geopolitics insofar as his reading of Tito evokes the same stranger-in-exile that has haunted naturalistic narratives since Flaubert, producing the distinct affective structure of breached sovereignty through the mode of mimesis which Auerbach called "existential realism" ("Serious" 448). The reader of these chapters will also recognize Trollope's Lopez as a remarkable variation on the type.[15] Yet, Jameson's demotion of Romola from typical character to the passive witness of her husband's apotheosis obscures how Eliot's response to "the Otherness of Woman" simultaneously switches the valences of Scott's masculinist genre, emphasizing Antigone's (not Machiavelli's) challenge to the reign of bad faith (Ch. 6).[16]

These remarks may, perhaps, establish that Eliot's realist experiment fails neither as truth content nor aesthetic. But the question remains whether *any* art form can surmount the "unanswerable" questions about the past ("which take us well beyond literature and theory") which Jameson puts to realism. By contrast, Lukács's less esoteric understanding of literature's historicity was (in Jameson's own words) "the revelation of tendencies." The question in that case becomes whether realism today is so "shriveled" that such revelations collapse into ideology or decoration.[17] Notably, when Jameson discusses Modernist, science fiction, and fantasy genres in his powerful closing chapter on the future of historical fiction, he discerns a more active role for literature and a more auspicious account of its historicity. Setting aside imponderable questions, he asks how "the content of a given historical moment enables or limits its representational form" and "narrative possibilities." He writes,

---

[15] In *The Eustace Diamonds* (1871–3), the cartoonish Emilius instances the classic type of the stage villain even while anticipating a Judaized villain "beyond good and evil" in Lopez. Yet, for Jameson, Trollope functions only as a passing example of how realism after Scott loses the capacity to represent capacious standpoints on history as politics devolves into the "specialized" subject matter of "those institutionalized genres which deal with" Parliament (*Antinomies* 272; cf. 217). Of course, since Jameson continues to hold that the "stage of imperialism" was not launched for another decade, he is unable to discern Trollope's profound engagement with the rise of a theatrical Tory mode of empire-building.

[16] As Jameson writes in a later chapter, "the famous 'average hero' whose presence Lukács posits as a necessary meditation between everyday life and the great historical events is precisely the theatrical spectator" (268). He thus begs the question why Romola's "witness" should preclude the character's working as a gender-crossing variation on Scott. The compelling dialectical idea of switching valences derives from Jameson's *Valences of the Dialectic* (2010).

[17] Certainly in his afterword to *Peripheral Realisms*, Jameson seems to cast the case for a more resilient realism as tarnished by the "miniaturization" of its political stakes: "Not the teeming masses fighting on de Gaulle's side for his promise of independence," but, "rather the schools and departments, the theoretico-political tendencies which will secure recognition for their student and intellectual constituencies" ("Antinomies" 484).

The tension, in Marxism and elsewhere in social thought generally, between sociology and history, or better still, between structure and the event, between everyday life and its cultural continuities and the cataclysm of a genuinely historical turning point or paradigm shift—this tension . . . also makes possible moments in which *the two kinds of realities overlap, and in which therefore complex or dual possibilities are momentarily available* (*Antinomies* 264; emphasis added).

Here, I contend, while harking back to a comparable passage in *The Political Unconscious* (148), Jameson makes clear that the antinomies actually at stake in his book are not reducible to a formal mismatch between epistemology and aesthetics and—in fact—not reducible to realism at all. Rather, what might more properly be described as the antinomies of *any* historical literature concern persistent tensions "between sociology and history," "between structure and the event," between "cultural continuities" and the emergence of the new—and, from a formal standpoint, between "a narrative of individuals" and "historical dynamics as such."[18] Scott's fiction could overlap these riddling tensions because, as Jameson goes on to say, "his focus on a specific kind of historical catastrophe" enabled him "to write a kind of social description of the past as well as to single out a historical event" (*Antinomies* 264).

Of course, in the centuries between the Waverley novels and our own turn-of-the millennium, the "catastrophes" that beset literature's historicity have dramatically deepened. In ways that recall us to the "structural amnesia" that television news exacerbates in an ever more presentist age, Jameson describes the recourse to a historiography so averse to animating "cultural collectives" or dramatizing "historical events" that the historical novel, to the extent one can even imagine it, veers toward "sheer anthropological description" (282)—or perhaps toward the macrosociological analytics that world-systems theory has long encouraged and "distant" reading now prescribes (Ch. 1). "Still, the problem of what to do with the future in the historical novel," Jameson assures us, "is scarcely an unrewarding one" (297). And, indeed, when he tells us that "historicity today . . . demands a temporal span far exceeding the biological limits of the individual human organism: so that the life of a single character—world-historical or not—can scarcely accommodate it, nor even the meager variety of our own chronological experiences of a limited national time and place" (302–3), he articulates a consciousness of history's *durée* that would not have surprised many readers of Collins, Eliot, Flaubert, and Trollope. Can it really be true, then, that a realist form of historicity is no longer possible: that realism can no longer figure the clash of realities in transition or reveal "tendencies" that have yet to harden into a "state of affairs"?

The question is one that *Antinomies* declines to revisit, inasmuch as realist literature after Scott, Balzac, and Tolstoy does not enter the concluding discussion

---

[18] One might compare this formulation to Raymond Williams's efforts, discussed in Chapter 1, to theorize the "structure of feeling" as that which opens a space of encounter between history and literature by articulating concrete conditions of possibility from both "objective" and subjective standpoints.

of the historical novel. Among the many hurdles Jameson explores, historical fiction today must find a "dimension of collectivity" to take the place of Scott's typical characters and Balzac's engagement of a history still in progress (267). As he ranges across diverse examples—including *The Wasteland,* Proust, *Ragtime,* Hilary Mantel, *Cloud Atlas,* and Christopher Nolan's film, *Inception*—Jameson makes clear that Modernist aesthetics continue to resonate because they uphold the "overweening autonomy" of "an autoreferentiality of the aesthetic" (292). By contrast, postmodern science fiction and fantasy genres derive their strength from the rejection of realism's spatio-temporal constraints: since "the original no longer exists," there "can no longer be any question either of the accuracy or truth of representation, or of any aesthetic of mimesis" (293).[19] Thus, as Nolan's *Inception* (2010) shows us, the "historical novel today" is "as an immense elevator that moves us up and down in time, its sickening lifts and dips corresponding to the euphoric or dystopian mood in which we wait for the doors to open" (301).

It is worth adding, however, that in a recent essay on the HBO television series, *The Wire* (2000–08), Jameson is decidedly less certain of realism's fatal shrinkage. Since the "ultimate structure" of reality in *The Wire* eludes the police in remaining "too abstract for any single observer to experience," he writes, the show "opens up a space for realism: for seeing things, finding out things, that have not been registered before" ("Realism" 361–2). To put this another way, *The Wire*'s variation on realism's epistemological project invites the perceptions of a geopolitical aesthetic. Thus, so far from moribund, realism in *The Wire* gives rise to "a virtual Utopianism, a Utopian impulse" and—eventually—a "utopian project or program" (364).[20]

Most pertinent to this Coda, however, are the salient likenesses between Jameson's discussions of *The Wire*'s "raw material" (366) and of Eliot's *mauvaise foi*. As the "spread of a new kind of reason" psychologizes a wide range of aberrations, writes Jameson, "what used to be thought of as pathology" is now "human, in such a way that the very category of evil" has "drastically been reduced" ("Realism" 367). *The Wire* thus faces a form-problem much like that which challenged Eliot: "the melodramatic plot . . . becomes increasingly unsustainable" and "villains," with the exception of serial killers and terrorists, "become impossible too" (376). Although I am not sure that Jameson is right about the waning of villains or melodrama—reality television seems to generate no end of either, much as penny dreadfuls and their ilk did in Eliot's time—what is no less remarkable is

---

[19] Modernism escapes this obsolescence because its "commitment to mimesis" does not constitute "a belief that the representation can somehow fully reproduce its original. Rather, the point is to demonstrate its failure, its structural incapacity to represent reality, to designate its grandiose project of doing so as 'mere' art and artifice" (*Antinomies* 292). Such remarks imply that realism's commitment to mimesis *does* constitute a "belief that the representation can somehow fully reproduce its original" as well as a denial that its project is art. Although realist fiction however defined, is indeed unlikely to designate its project as "*mere*" art, Victorian exponents of realist literature, as we have already seen, recognized the limits of literary representation, while embracing its aesthetic dimensions.

[20] In this sense, *The Wire*, which is often compared to Dickens's macrosociological realism, can be compared as well to the multi-perspectival narration of *The Moonstone*, which also begins as detective mystery and concludes as utopian romance (Ch. 5).

the strain of recurrent realist experimentation he identifies across a span of more than a century.

It is worth emphasizing, then, that Jameson overlooks a crucial formal dimension of realism both then and now. Among the many differences that distinguish *Middlemarch* from *Romola* is the interesting fact that the serialization of the later novel was a great success while that of *Romola* was a disappointment: Eliot's detailed historical romance, as most commentators agreed, was much more enjoyable in its three-volume form than as a monthly feature in the *Cornhill*.[21] With his minimal interest in seriality, Jameson obscures what is arguably the most compelling feature of a "quality" television series like *The Wire*. For on his reading, the "unique temporality" of a weekly serial (and, later, a DVD rental) exemplifies the "pleasures of repetition" (360, 366). "Repetition enhances the function of the television set as a consolation and security; you are not alone when it is on in the house with you, and you are not lonely or isolated when your space is peopled by so many familiar faces and characters" (360). To this extent, *The Wire* is no different than episodic television genres (including game shows, situation comedies, home improvement shows or, to recall Bourdieu, the nightly news) which proffer repetitive pleasure in the absence of unfolding storylines that span multiple seasons. By contrast, as we saw in Chapter 8, serial television dramas—especially those "quality" series that cultivate the writerly aspects of nineteenth-century realism—recreate an experience that has been almost dormant since the serials of the mid-Victorian era. This entails something beyond the introduction of repeat characters into otherwise lonely parlors and bedrooms; it also about the more tantalizing perception that the modern reader or viewer is least alone when he or she joins the audience for a serial narrative that everyone is talking about.

PEOPLE FIGURE OUT HOW TO TALK ABOUT IT

Indeed, if *The Victorian Geopolitical Aesthetic* has stressed the importance of naturalistic narratives of capitalist globalization—in Flaubert, Trollope, Eliot's *Daniel Deronda* and the television series *Mad Men*—that is partly to make the case that this haunting expression of the mid-Victorian-era geopolitical aesthetic is timely in articulating a slow temporality, punctuated by dramatic rupture, which, so far from "shriveled," speaks volumes to our neoliberal world. The preceding chapters have argued that historicizing globalization requires a theory of networked space woven through an elongated stream of time—a temporal dimension that Fernand Braudel, the Annales school historian, called the *longue durée*.[22] In Chapter 7,

---

[21] See C. Martin's excellent discussion of this topic in her Chapter 4.

[22] In a 2007 collection of interviews, Jameson described Braudel as the repressed theoretical germ of *The Political Unconscious:* "I must have thought it was so obvious I didn't have to mention it" (*Jameson* 3). I am grateful to Marshall Brown for pointing this out to me in his response to an early draft of this Coda at the January 2012 MLA.

I appealed to Braudel's idea to follow the story of realist innovation into the turn-of-the-century advent of New Liberalism. Whereas the years between Trollope and Forster saw realist fiction morph from the triple-decker series novel to the svelte quasi-Modernism of *Where Angels Fear to Tread* (1905), the new millennium has exploded with televisual arts that remake nineteenth-century forms. Clearly, serial formats are responding to recent cable and internet technologies, much as their precursors did to the dynamic print media of the nineteenth-century. But it is also true that serialized realism, in ways Jameson does not quite capture, proffers an apt formal structure for tapping the submerged historicity of any lifeworld that blends continuous transformation with the simultaneous perception of having reached an epochal if, nonetheless, crisis-prone "end of history."[23]

Consider the contrast between neoliberalism's blend of market fundamentalism, endemic uncertainty, and self-conscious postmodernism on the one hand and, on the other hand, the morally and economically *dirigiste* Cold War-era liberalism that drove Lionel Trilling to seek an antidote in Forster's "relaxed will." In a well-known book from the Cold War years, Frank Kermode had Forster's works partly in mind when he undertook to explain how narrative fiction "makes sense of the world" (29). Fiction, he wrote, provides a vehicle for "humanizing time by giving it a form": "the sense of an ending" (45). Notably, then, while serialized fiction also gives humanizing form to time, it does not pivot on the sense of an ending. Instead, seriality's special illusion is never ending at all. Serial narratives foster dialectical movement between a slowly unfolding diachronic arc and the internal momentum of synchronic episodes or installments. In this way, serial narratives recognize that audiences lead serial lives pitched between what has already happened and what cannot yet be foreseen. Such narratives oscillate between the event-based temporality of the newspaper—Braudel's *"l'histoire événementielle"* (*On History* 3)—and a *longue durée* that individuals cannot compass but in which they nonetheless feel themselves palpably immersed. Thus, more than a mimetic picture of "real life," what serialized realism conveys is the real-life experience of inhabiting long-evolving structures that challenge our limited capacities to grasp ongoing histories.

Trollope's *The Prime Minister* and *Mad Men*, I have argued, share a slow-burning pace that enables audiences to experience this condition vicariously (through characters) and communally (with fellow enthusiasts). Although part of what propels the comparison is a recurrent formal response to a lost "dimension of collectivity" (Jameson, *Antinomies* 267), it is also manifestly to do with a morphing material culture—that "whole spectrum of social practices for which" individual books (and, by analogy, individual television series), provide merely a "prompt" (Price, "From" 120). Thus, when Dickens chose a line from Shakespeare's *Othello* to help brand the new weekly he launched in 1859—"The story of our lives, from year to year"—he was demonstrating more than keen business instincts. At a time when

---

[23] The recurrent fascination with serialized realism is noteworthy even though present-day neoliberalism is, in many respects, quite unlike the mid-Victorian era's blend of liberal individualism, civic republicanism, and rising Toryism (see also Goodlad, "Afterword").

All the Year Round was competing for sales and prestige in a burgeoning field of periodicals, Dickens drew on Shakespeare to express seriality's power to portray and create collective experience through a material structure that reassembled the audience for live drama on a scale both more "micro" (the individual parlor, kitchen, bedroom, club, or reading room) and more "macro" (the multiplication of these sites, in Britain and beyond, and the ensuing discussion and debate). AMC did something similar when the station chose "Story Matters Here" to signal its transformation from a vehicle for movie reruns to an acclaimed destination for "quality" television.

The 1860s were the crest of the boom for serial publication which the "unanticipated runaway success" of *The Pickwick Papers* had triggered in 1836 (G. Law 15). Not only *All the Year Round*, but also the *Cornhill, Macmillan's, Temple Bar, Argosy,* the *Fortnightly Review, Belgravia, Tinsley's* and *St Paul's Magazine* joined established periodicals, such as *Blackwood's*, in featuring long-running narrative fictions whose commercial success depended partly on "enormous length." Rising literacy, cheaper paper, and tax reform were among the circumstances that turned serialized novels into high-octane fuel for "a publishing machine" that enabled profit-making at several stages: first serialization; then "triple-deckers" sold to circulating libraries such as Mudies; and, finally, the "cheaper reprints published at a later date" (Crawford n.p.). Readers on the Continent, in the United States, and throughout the imperial network provided a global audience.[24] Given the high economic stakes of a work's debut, no publisher was too dignified, and no author too much the artist, to spurn the chance to manipulate serial delivery to maximal advantage. We thus find John Blackwood writing in 1875 that he was considering "an interval of two months" between the parts of the forthcoming *Daniel Deronda* because the experience of *Middlemarch* had taught him that "it takes the public a long time to digest and fully appreciate the value of such food" as George Eliot offers, and to "talk to their neighbours about it" (qtd. in C. Martin 216).

In February 2013, Netflix, the online DVD rental and streaming service, became a serial innovator by trying a rather different experiment. The company's first venture into producing its own serial content used digital streaming in lieu of broadcasting or cable technology and, in so doing, invited viewers to "binge" by watching an entire season of episodes at their own pace, without waiting for a prior serialization to conclude. Asked if he was concerned that Netflix's delivery model loses "the weekly suspense and water cooler chatter" that emerges when "people discuss the episodes one-by-one," the spokesman for Netflix replied that the new model empowered viewers to make their own decisions about the pace of consumption. While some might speculate that the company was angling for a more atomized viewer, willing to trade the pleasures of serial community for the greater autonomy of asynchronous viewing, Netflix took a different view: "People figure out how to talk about it," said their spokesman. "It's a different style of

---

[24] Though see Priya Joshi, *Another*, for the impact of Indian readers in creating a market for non-realist fiction in English.

water cooler. If you are on episode eight and I am on four, I know not to talk about five" (Farber).

As a paradigmatically neoliberal narrative, *Mad Men*, I suggested in Chapter 8, universalizes the condition of unassimilable otherness. Whereas Trollope's *The Prime Minister* (like Eliot's *Daniel Deronda*) splits between "Jewish" and "English" plots, *Mad Men* makes Don Draper a "virtual" Jew in whom exilic particularity becomes generalized. But there are also differences. As the creation of a largely unsung writer for *The Sopranos*, which aired on a low-prestige cable station with a cast of unknown actors, the show's fusion of mid-twentieth century aestheticism and Flaubert-like naturalism—not unlike *Madame Bovary* in 1856—took critics as well as admirers by surprise. *The Prime Minister*, by contrast, was the twenty-seventh novel from an author who, as the *Examiner* put it in 1876, was always "interesting" but "never very brilliant" ("Mr. Trollope's" 825). Trollope's forté was repeat characters so beloved by his readers that the *Spectator* did not hesitate to describe them as "*people* who have become a possession of the reading world" ("Prime" 922; my emphasis).

Contemporary commentators thus expressed keen ambivalence toward *The Prime Minister*. Though pleasurable in reviving characters "more real to us than half of the people we shall meet to-morrow," Trollope's novel was disturbing in subjecting these beloved figures to "degrading" naturalistic effects ("Prime" 922–3). Thus, according to *The Times*, the "capacity for making your characters so life-like that your readers grow into their intimacy" is a mixed blessing, inviting praise as well as "resentful criticism" ("Recent" 4).[25] By means of the commonplace device of the double plot, *The Prime Minister* foregrounded the troubling proximity of Plantagenet's "public" story of political failure to the "private" tale of Lopez's failure to sustain his bid for insider status ("Prime" 922). More disturbingly still, the novel made this insidious stranger the protégé of "our old friend Lady Glencora"—to borrow a term of endearment from Richard F. Littledale's write-up in the Guernsey *Star* (n.p.). According to *The Spectator*, Lopez was "a mere rogue" who makes the reader "glad when he is dead." Would that Trollope could focus on much-loved "people" rather than vulgarize them with the preposterous conceit that such a "coarsely-conceived" cad (and a suspected Jew no less) could manage to penetrate "good society" ("Prime" 922).

Yet, according to *The Examiner*, Lopez was "an extremely well-drawn character" whose insinuation into the Wharton family instanced "marvelous adroitness." For this reader, the problem was not Lopez's ability to secure Emily Wharton's hand without providing "a particle of information as to" his "fortune" and "respectability." Rather, the problem was that it was so "difficult to know whether one ought to sympathise with [Lopez] or not" ("Mr. Trollope's" 826). To sympathize or not to sympathize? The same provoking question repelled many readers of *Madame Bovary*. As Auerbach put it, Flaubert's "existential realism" was the peculiar effect

---

[25] Indeed, *The Prime Minister* seemed to touch a nerve that even *The Eustace Diamonds* and *The Way We Live Now* did not—no doubt because the latter was a stand-alone novel and the former was not generally regarded as one of the Palliser novels by contemporaries.

of Emma's prosaic stature which, in lacking ennobling features, elicited conflicting emotions of "tragic pity" and "critical disdain" ("Serious" 432–3). The same kind of dilemma has spawned a sea of *Mad Men* commentary debating whether Don Draper's lack of a virtuous center makes him (merely) a reprehensible cad, or a cad who is also a resounding anti-hero for our times.

Naturalistic characters provoke this discomfiture while dramatizing the terrible pathos of their otherness. "Mr. Lopez's wits" turn out to be "his whole fortune," *The Examiner* wrote, and in the end he must avail himself of "the last resort of all adventurers" (826). His suicide, according to *The Times*, is a kind of redemption: the man who begins his story as a "showy upstart adventurer" who must enter "society on sufferance" ends it by killing himself with "better taste than might have been expected" ("Recent" 4). Such remarks anticipated an enduring fascination with Lopez who is a more compelling figure of Judaized exile and Sartrean bad faith than the cartoonish Emilius or the opaque Melmotte—one whose saga David Skilton has likened to the ordeal of one of Trollope's most beloved characters, Josiah Crawley in *The Last Chronicle of Barset* (1866–7) ("Introduction" xix). Like comparable debates over *Madame Bovary* and *Mad Men*, the commentary on Lopez demonstrates how serialized realism of this existential bent incites passionate engagement. If these audiences do not necessarily qualify as oppositional "counterpublics" in Michael Warner's sense (*Publics* 63), neither are they reducible to passive consumers. Indeed, one is tempted to borrow a phrase from Netflix to speculate that when Trollope injected this naturalistic turn into his Palliser series, his most devoted readers, like the water-cooler publics of today, "figur[ed] out how to talk about it."

SOCIOLOGY AND THE "ONTOLOGICAL TURN"

I have proffered this discussion of seriality then and now in part to show how readily historicism crosses, not only between synchronic and diachronic time frames, but also between (on the one hand) hermeneutic practices like the geopolitical aesthetic which theorize the interrelation of human experience, aesthetic poiesis, and material history, and (on the other hand) alternatives like material culture and sociology of the book which seek to decenter the human by, for example, "wrest[ing] attention away from the fraction of any book's life cycle spent in the hands of readers" (Price, "From" 120). Indeed, my example of Trollope and *Mad Men*, may suggest that these methodological standpoints are more mutually reinforcing—perhaps even inseparable—than some strong proponents of an anti-humanist and anti-hermeneutical turn toward objects assume. The claim that Lopez is the world's first Mad Man so to speak, and the evidence necessary to support it, is no more or less positive, descriptive, interpretive or deep, than practices that draw from social sciences such as book history.

In his introduction to *New Sociologies of Literature* (2010), a special issue he co-edited with Felski, James English evokes a "multifaceted enterprise" ("Everywhere" vi). The new sociologies so called encompass the history and sociology of the book; media studies; the study of canon and field formation; the new economic criticism; and, of course, "distant" and "descriptive" reading. Nevertheless, behind this rosy ecumenicism is English's awareness of the polemical thrust of the positions most influenced by Latour.

Here it will be useful to return to my allusion to a *Methodenstreit* in the social sciences. This often strident debate originated in differences between Latour and Bourdieu, France's leading sociologist during most of the postwar period. As Willem Schinkel explains, the sociological theories of Bourdieu and Latour, have, since the 1990s, been engaged in a "clash" that has continued despite Bourdieu's death in 2002. Latour seeks "a complete redefinition" of the epistemological and ontological principles Bourdieu laid down for a critical sociology over several decades (Schinkel 707). For Latour, Bourdieu's quasi-Marxist sociology relies on overweening abstractions such as "the social" which enable sociologists to profess to know more than social actors themselves. In contrast, Latour's methodology advances the assumption that "neither society nor the social exists" (*Reassembling* 36). As the anthropologist Hylton White has argued, Latour's actor network theory (ANT) attempts to show "how various non-human actors . . . participate in creating the links or assemblages that organize pathways of action" (668). This deliberate leveling of human and non-human is offered in contrast to a critical theory that, according to Latour, is vitiated by Marx's understanding of the object as commodity. Thus, whereas Bourdieu inveighs against neoliberalism in books such as *Acts of Resistance: Against the Tyranny of the Market* (1999), Latour mocks the "paternal and arrogant attitude" of "the social scientist who sees things as they really are, and who sees it as his duty to speak on behalf of all the ignorant souls" (Schinkel 711). Moreover, since Bourdieu's materialism calls on the critic to defamiliarize "things as they appear to the 'naked eye'" (712), Latour's critique of Bourdieu parallels Best and Marcus's critique of "symptomatic" reading.

Describing Tony Bennett's essay in the *New Sociologies of Literature* special issue, English writes that Latour's ANT has helped to discredit "the explanatory power of the social" which underwrites the "now exhausted program of critique" (xv–xvi). Yet, Bennett himself is more circumspect. Although he embraces the same flat ontology one finds in Latour's actor-networks, he does so through the mediation of Jacques Rancière. According to Bennett, Rancière shares "Latour's dissent from the depth/surface model of traditional forms of sociological explanation," but "far from sharing Latour's perception that critique has run out of steam," Rancière "seeks to refound it" on a more equalitarian basis (271). Whatever one's position on the turn to ontology, Bennett's preference for a version of that project which does not advertise itself as a death knell for critique should give pause. If it partly signals a wish to stand back from a strident *Methodenstreit*, it also shows that the desire to rein in "intellectual mastery" (Bennett 271) can be acted on without denigrating "the political urge that itches so many critical sociologists" (Latour, *Reassembling* 42).

To be sure, not all ANT-influenced thinkers adopt Latour's acerbity. Love avoids this tone even while expressing a familiar Latourian concern regarding the "ethical heroism of the critic" (381). Her essay observes a surprising humanist residue: although Marxism and poststructuralism focus on material or linguistic structures, "humanist values" survive in practices such as close reading (371–2). Against this contradiction, Love recommends sociological approaches such as history of the book and data mining which "turn away from the singularity and richness of individual texts" and, thus, (presumably) curb the critic's "ethical charisma" (373–4). The style of reading she urges—"close but not deep"—uses "descriptive" methods to advance the anti-hermeneuticist agenda on the hermeneut's terrain (375). Drawing on the methods of Erving Goffman, Latour, and Louis Quéré, descriptive reading eschews "imponderables like human experience" in favor of "the real variety that is already there" (377). Her example is a reading of the murder scene in Morrison's *Beloved* which sets aside Sethe's perspective as "witness" to focus on the "flattening, dehumanizing, exterior perspective" of a prior "documentary" account that, like an actor-network, emphasizes the association between human and non-human objects (385–6).

Love's account of descriptive reading may impress even those who do not share her determination to extinguish humanist "imponderables" or critical "charisma." Whereas Felski's embrace of Latour contradicts her desire to revive humanist pedagogy, Love clearly specifies the goals of a Latourian critical practice.[26] She writes: "I play out the possibilities for a method of textual analysis that would take its cue from observation-based social sciences . . . These fields have developed practices of close attention, but, because they rely on description rather than interpretation, they do not engage the metaphysical and humanist concerns of hermeneutics" (375). For many readers, the surprise here will be the opposition of social-scientific neutrality and humanist "metaphysics." Given that she seeks to extend—not repudiate—the anti-essentialist project of poststructuralism, one wonders: Where is the "long baking process of history" in this assertion of social-scientific truth (qtd. in Foucault, "Nietzsche" 144)? What are the relations of power at stake in affirming "observation-based" disciplinary knowledge?

Love anticipates these questions when she upholds Latour's post-humanist ontology: "In place of the sociology of the social," she writes, "Latour argues that we need to develop a 'sociology of associations' that 'traces a network.' This focus on "'what the *real* world is *really* like'" is not "a naïve empiricism," because "Latour insists that empiricism is inadequate as a means of accounting for the world" (Latour, *Reassembling* 128, 117 qtd. in Love 377). In Latour's words, the "poverty" of empiricism "is not overcome by moving *away* from material experience, for instance to the 'rich human subjectivity,' but *closer* to the much variegated lives materials have to offer. It's not true that one should fight reductionism by adding some human, symbolic, subjective, or social 'aspect' to the description since reductionism . . . does not render justice to objective facts" (*Reassembling* 111–12

---

[26] Felski's arguments against suspicion seek to recuperate humanist focal points; for example, enabling students to consider "why literary texts matter" ("After" 30). Felski thus embraces Latour's flat ontology in the interest of a greater appreciation of the object of study; Love in the interest of a more depersonalized approach. Felski also stands out in criticizing Foucauldians such as Miller rather than Marxists ("Suspicious").

qtd. in Love 377). It is hard to ignore the tautology in this reasoning: Latour does not promote naïve empiricism because empiricism is inadequate; a focus on material objects is not reductionist because reductionism "does not render justice to objective facts." At bottom, Latour has nothing to certify his supposed shift from "*metaphysics* to *ontology*" beyond confident assertion: the possibility, as he puts it, that "we, in science studies, might know" (*Reassembling* 117; 112).

Latour's sociology is positivistic because it seeks resolutely to exclude abstractions from the domain of knowledge (though Latour's network is itself an abstraction woven around the premise of a "point-to-point connection" that "can be recorded empirically" [132; cf. 128–33]). Consider, for example, the positivism at work in this passage from *Reassembling the Social* (2005), excerpted from a chapter subtitled "Localizing the Global." It will be useful in reading it to recall Bourdieu's emphasis on what is "imperceptible in the moment" and Jameson's on global materialities so complex in form and long in duration that their effects exceed the grasp of individual experience. Latour writes:

> even though the question seems really odd at first—not to say in bad taste—whenever anyone speaks of a 'system,' a 'global feature,' a 'structure,' a 'society,' an 'empire,' a 'world economy,' an 'organization,' the first ANT reflex should be to ask: 'In which building? Through which bureau? Through which corridor is it accessible? Which colleagues has it been read to?. . .' Inquirers . . . will be surprised at the number of . . . conduits that pop up as soon as those queries are . . . raised. The social landscape begins to change rather quickly . . . [I]t does not produce . . . the same feeling as if they were asked to penetrate some intimidating overarching pyramid of power (*Reassembling* 183).

Latour here pits the actor-network theorist's worm's-eye attention to particular buildings, corridors, and memoranda against the world-systems theorist's birds-eye view. While the comprehensivity of world-systems analysis can be achieved only in theory, the micro-level concretion targeted by ANT posits practice itself as theory's positive achievement. One need not doubt, of course, that Latour is proffering a useful method, perhaps even a bracing tonic for some sclerotic critical habits. But what is nonetheless striking is the absence of *temporality* in his design. With its insistent focus on the tangible and localizable, ANT calls for a detailed snapshot of a set of objects in a given place: gains in clarity and focus which come courtesy of the freezing of time and the narrowing of space ("localizing the global"). Such trumping of spatial over temporal effects is the product partly of the flat ontology that secures the same status for the mortal and sentient as for objects immune to the passage of time. But it is also the effect of a definition of "the real" which privileges the plainly visible over that which eludes the surface by becoming internalized or reflexive (e.g., Bourdieu's *habitus*), occurring at a very slow pace (e.g. climate change), or operating on a spatio-temporal scale that exceeds individual perception (e.g. globalization).[27] While even detailed surface

---

[27] On Bourdieu's *habitus* which concerns the individual's development of mental and physical dispositions, see *Language* 51 and *passim*.

images will only go so far in concretizing such processes, what helps to render them in thought are the conceptual entities Latour indicts—"society," "empire," "world economy," "structure," et al.—and against which he asserts his positive criteria ("I want to be convinced that those connections exist, I want to touch the conduits, to check their solidity, to test their realism" [187]).

With no considered mechanism for theorizing the history of the assemblages it documents, ANT eternalizes a temporality of the short-term event (*l'histoire événementielle*). In doing so, it reproduces the "structural amnesia" of a television news world fixated on decontextualized accounts of the visible, synchronic, and "new."[28] Although ANT may possibly take an interest in *systems*, it has no means of exploring *systematicity*. Of course, Latour's shift from a far-reaching "pyramid of power" to a small world of visible "associations" achieves a certain liberating effect ("The social landscape begins to change rather quickly"). Yet, from a historicist perspective, ANT's flat ontology does not so much warrant equality of opportunity (as in Rancière's hope) as produce homogeneity of effect: a reduction of knowledge to the given. Hence, while ANT offers a potentially powerful tool for synchronic exploration, as a wholesale alternative to the "social" or "global," it reproduces the problems of chronic presentism and political disenchantment.

Love's essay is all the more commendable, therefore, in recognizing that descriptive reading is, ultimately, a merely partial methodology for literary analysis. That is, in the case of *Beloved*, description does not "decenter the human" in the manner of ANT for the simple reason that Morrison's depersonalized documentation and subjective witness are mutually reliant: "The flat description of the murder scene stands out in contrast to other deeper and richer moments in the novel; the blank gaze of the observer in this scene is meaningful in part because of the ethical and political commitments of the novel as a whole" (387). Thus, the documentary impulse is (to use vocabulary much-disliked by Latour) *embedded in a larger whole*.

Like Morrison's *Beloved*, serialized narratives of capitalist globalization confute the Latourian imperative to "respect . . . what is in plain view" (Felski, "After" 31). A merely descriptive reading of *Mad Men* might be dazzled by the show's acclaimed aestheticism, proffering the postmodern truism of a glamorous simulacrum beyond which nothing exists. As Don himself says, "I'm living life like there's no tomorrow, because there isn't one." A *longue durée* perspective combats this illusion of a life outside history, connecting Don's masquerade to Trollope's "secret Jew." Like Lopez and Emma, Don inhabits what Sedgwick called the "regime of the open secret." Sedgwick's essay on paranoid reading did not recant such ambitious abstractions. It was, rather, a brilliant analysis of the limited rewards of repeating critical *doxa* that just happen to be true. Like the elevator in *Inception*, moreover, *Mad Men*'s core trope of the carousel as "time machine"—its backward and forward motion taking serial viewers "around and around, and

---

[28] On the limitations of *l'histoire événementielle*, a "deceptive" temporality that is "totally lacking in time density, see Braudel 14–15.

back home again"—offers a poignant formal challenge to the "absolute reduction to the present" which plagues us (Jameson, *Antinomies* 300).

CONCLUSION

In "'Context Stinks!'" (2011), Felski applauds Latour for "blast[ing] away the cobwebs of critique and shak[ing] up a ubiquitous academic ethos of detachment, negativity, and doubt" (575). As the most humanistic of the scholars to take up Latour, she writes: "We cannot close our eyes to the historicity of artworks, and yet we sorely need alternatives to seeing them as transcendentally timeless on the one hand, and imprisoned in their moment of origin on the other" (575). Felski thus polemicizes against a synchronic historicism; if "context stinks!" (a quotation from Latour), that is because, in her view, it has been used to make "a box" out of history (576). Although I share Felski's pull toward diachronic history, I see little evidence that "a ubiquitous academic ethos" of negativity is undermining it. Thus, while Felski regards Latour as an ally in the battle to curb suspicion, it is by no means clear how his pronounced presentism, positivism, and anti-hermeneuticism will nurture the historicity she craves. The insights of theorizing the art object as a "nonhuman actor" ("Context" 576) may well be vitalizing; but one might easily follow Rancière's example, which neither misrepresents Marx's pivotal analysis of the commodity nor enjoins a reactionary standpoint on critical theory.[29] As Bill Brown observes, "human interaction with the nonhuman world of objects" is "mediated by," but not "reducible to," the "advance of consumer culture" since things "pressure . . . us to engage them as something other than mere surfaces" (12–13). For all of these reasons, I am doubtful that Latour's "realist attitude" justifies his wholesale assault on critique ("Why" 232).

Looking back at Sedgwick's essay on "paranoid reading," I am struck anew by its puissant call for "a fresh, deroutinized sense of accountability to the real" pursued through "diverse" paths of inquiry" (2). Now, as then, what we need is a committed resistance to routinization, not a new set of routines. Nineteenth-century studies strikes me as brimming with such open-ended critical enterprises: inside and outside newer fields such as book history. Long temporalities have come to the fore in the work of Wai Chee Dimock whose notion of "deep time" underwrites a transhistorical comparativism; of Franco Moretti, whose quantitative experiments explore massive archives across long swathes of time (*Graphs*); of Rob Nixon, who seeks to visibilize the time scale of climate change; and, in a different way, of Helen Small, who proposes a kind of *longue durée* for a single life span.[30]

To consider the *longue durée* on multiple scales is not to ignore either "subtle, nuanced change" or responsibility to otherness. As Susan Watkins writes in

---

[29] Though see Chapter 6 on Rancière's somewhat Jameson-like tendency to dismiss nineteenth-century realism after Flaubert.
[30] For a consideration of Moretti's recent turn to network theory for "distant reading," see Goodlad and Sartori.

an important critique of presentism, "capitalist accumulation" since Marx's day has "driven the mode of production through successive phases, punctuated by wars, crises and depressions: monopoly capitalism, the second industrial revolution and the emergence of Fordism; the welfare-state capitalism of the Cold War, and the developmentalisms . . . of the periphery; the era of finance capital, neoliberal globalization and the rise of China as workshop of the world; and the next stage, to which we are now unmistakably in the process of transition. No uniform ethos, habitus or particular way of being human is discernible across this varied landscape" (84–5). Watkins thus renders capitalist accumulation as a continuing history while simultaneously recognizing a range of heterogeneous temporalities "at work within the same chronological time." Such a world is "irreducibly pluralist: not one tonality but many" (101)—akin to the many variations on the mid-Victorian-era geopolitical aesthetic I have documented in this book. From such a view, critics of the long nineteenth century—so far from having run out of steam—have, in fact, a great deal of work to do.

I appreciate Felski's call for scholarship that respects "what is in plain view" before or in concert with the mobilizing of the critical apparatus. Describing an "embrace" of "surface" as an "ethical stance," Best and Marcus speak of the importance of "deferring to" texts "instead of mastering" them, and refusing "a depth model of truth, which dismisses surfaces as inessential and deceptive" (10). But another path to the same point might note that a self-styled mastery that misses the insights that deference would yield is merely partial and, thus, no "mastery" at all; likewise a "depth model of truth" which reflexively dismisses surface is neither deep nor true.

Rather than pit a surface-focused ethics of reading against a depth-focused politics of reading, can we not simply historicize this formulation as the expression of a certain 1980s temperament? Would it not make sense to revisit the debates between Marxism and New Historicism in light of what we have learned since that time about the need to calibrate the responsibility to otherness and the responsibility to act? This is a task that the diverse experiments of realist, Modernist, and postmodern aesthetics can surely help us to explore.

To be sure, the call to a dialectics of long and short-term history which simultaneously negotiates the disparate ethical demands of the responsibility to otherness and the responsibility to act, is no simple charge. But the task is no less urgent in the current epoch of rampant inequality and environmental hazard to name just two world-scale problems that neoliberalism only professes to solve. As respecters of the object, let us not forget our obligations to the objects of the future—that temporal beyond that no network theory can find in plain sight and no digital analysis can quantify. As for historicizing: no matter how much we may inadvertently confuse this ongoing project with some particular historicist excess, historicism cannot but be part of our critical practice. For it is that aspect of the critical enterprise which strives to illuminate the concrete conditions from which our aspirations spring and in which they either take root or fail.

Works Cited

[Anonymous] "American Disunion." *All the Year Round* (21 Dec. 1861): 295–300. Print.
[Anonymous] "Britain's Colonies—the Jewels of the Crown." *London Review and Weekly Journal of Politics, Literature, Art and Society* 9 Nov. 1861: 579–80. Print.
[Anonymous] "Chronicle of Current History." *Fraser's Magazine* Oct. 1860: 543–62. Print.
[Anonymous] "Cutting of the Koh-i-Noor." *The Times of London* 19 July 1852: 8, col. E. Print.
[Anonymous] "Cutting of the Koh-i-Noor." *The London Journal* 15 (4 Sept. 1852): 407.
[Anonymous] "Dangers in India." *Macmillan's Magazine* Mar. 1867: 412–16. Print.
[Anonymous] "Diamonds." *London Review and Weekly Journal of Politics, Society, Literature and Art* 18 Oct. 1862: 337–8. Print.
[Anonymous] "Diamond-Cutting." *Chambers Edinburgh Journal* 25 Sept 1852: 199–201. Print.
[Anonymous] "Diamond-Cutting." *Chambers Edinburgh Journal* 2 Nov. 1867: 689–91. Print.
[Anonymous] "Editor's Easy Chair." *Harper's New Monthly Magazine* 53 (1876): 141–6.
[Anonymous] "Durbar at Mysore." *The Times of London* 4 Oct. 1867: 7. Print.
[Anonymous] "*The Eustace Diamonds.*" *The Spectator* 26 Oct. 1872: 1365–6. Print.
[Anonymous] "Fenianism; and the Irish at Home and Abroad." *Blackwood's Edinburgh Magazine*. 103 (Feb. 1868): 222–41. Print.
[Anonymous] "French Literature." *The Saturday Review* 6 June 1857: 523–5. Print.
[Anonymous] "Hurry-graphs; or, Sketches of Scenery, Celebrities, and Society, taken from Life." *The Literary Gazette* 26 July 1851: 508. Print.
[Anonymous] "Indian Annexation." *The Examiner* 1 April 1865: 194.
[Anonymous] "The International Exhibition: Its Purpose and Prospects." *Blackwood's Edinburgh Magazine* 91 (April 1862): 472–88. Print.
[Anonymous] "The Koh-i-Noor, Or Mountain of Light." *Chambers Edinburgh Journal* 28 July 1849: 49–52. Print.
[Anonymous] "The Koh-i-Noor, Or Mountain of Light." *The Leader* 15 (6 July 1850): 342.
[Anonymous] "A Month in the Divorce Court." *The Englishwoman's Review and Home Newspaper* 15 Jan. 1859: 35. Print.
[Anonymous] "The Morrill Tariff." *All the Year Round* (28 December 1861): 328–31.
[Anonymous] "A Most Unpleasant." *The Times of London* 3 Nov. 1865: 7. Print.
[Anonymous] "Mr. Trollope's Prime Minister." *The Examiner* 22 July 1876: 825–6. Print.
[Anonymous] "The Negro Controversy." *The Saturday Review* 13 Oct. 1866: 446–7. Print.
[Anonymous] "The Nineteenth Century, Though it is Getting Rather Old." *The Times of London* 18 July, 1857: 9, col. D. Print.
[Anonymous] "Our Weekly Gossip." *Athenaeum* 23 Dec. 1848: 1299–300. Print.
[Anonymous] "*The Ordeal of Richard Feverel.*" *The Saturday Review* 9 July 1859: 48–49. Print.
[Anonymous] "The Prime Minister." *The Spectator.* 22 July 1876: 922–3.
[Anonymous] "The Punjab." *Chambers Edinburgh Journal* 14 Mar. 1846: 165–7. Print.

[Anonymous] "Sovereigns No. 8." *Vanity Fair* 16 April 1870. Print.
[Anonymous] W. J. "Tories Re-Cut a Crown Jewel." *The Examiner* 4 Sept. 1854: 563. Print.
Ablow, Rachel. *The Marriage of the Minds: Reading Sympathy in the Victorian Marriage Plot*. Stanford: Stanford UP, 2007. Print.
Adorno, Theodor. *Aesthetic Theory*. 1970. Trans. Robert Hullot-Kentor. London: Athlone Press, 1997. Print.
Adorno, Theodor. *Minima Moralia: Reflections on a Damaged Life*. 1951. Trans. E.F.N. Jephcott. London: Verso, 2005. Print.
Agamben, Giorgio. *Homo Sacer: Sovereign Power and Bare Life*. Trans. Daniel Heller-Roazen. Stanford: Stanford UP, 1998. Print.
Agamben, Giorgio. *Infancy and History: The Destruction of Experience*. Trans. Liz Heron. New York: Verso, 1993. Print.
Agamben, Giorgio. *State of Exception*. Trans. Kevin Attell. Chicago: U of Chicago P, 2005. Print.
Agathocleous, Tanya. *Urban Realism and the Cosmopolitan Imagination in the Nineteenth Century*. Cambridge: Cambridge UP, 2011. Print.
Agathocleous, Tanya and Jason R. Rudy. "Victorian Cosmopolitanisms: Introduction." *Victorian Literature and Culture* 38.2 (2010): 389–97. Print.
Ahmed, Sara. *Strange Encounters: Embodied Others in Post-Coloniality*. London: Routledge, 2000. Print.
Aldrich, Robert. *Colonialism and Homosexuality*. London: Routledge, 2003. Print.
Amann, Elizabeth. *Importing Madame Bovary: the Politics of Adultery*. New York: Palgrave, 2006. Print.
Amarnick, Steven. "Trollope and Anti-Semitism." Unpublished essay, 8 Sept. 2010.
Anderson, Amanda. "Cosmopolitanism, Universalism, and the Divided Legacies of Modernity." Cheah and Robbins 265–89. Print.
Anderson, Amanda. *The Powers of Distance: Cosmopolitanism and the Cultivation of Detachment*. Princeton: Princeton UP, 2001. Print.
Anderson, Amanda. "Victorian Studies and the Two Modernities." *Victorian Studies* 47.2 (2005): 195–203. Print.
Anderson, Amanda. *The Way We Argue Now: A Study in the Cultures of Theory*. Princeton: Princeton UP, 2006. Print.
Anderson, Amanda and Harry Shaw, eds. *A Companion to George Eliot*. Oxford: Wiley-Blackwell, 2013. Print.
Anderson, Benedict. *Imagined Communities: Reflections on the Origin and Spread of Nationalism*. Rev. ed. London: Verso, 1991. Print.
Anderson, Perry. "Internationalism: A Breviary." *New Left Review* 14 (2002): 5–25. Print.
Anderson, Terry. *The Movement and the Sixties: Protest America from Greensboro to Wounded Knee*. London: Oxford UP, 1996. Print.
Andrade, Susan Z. "Realism, Reception, 1968, and West Africa." Esty and Lye 289–308.
Anjaria, Ulka. *Realism in the Twentieth-Century Indian Novel: Colonial Difference and Literary Form*. Cambridge: Cambridge UP, 2012. Print.
Appadurai, Arjun. *Modernity at Large: Cultural Dimensions of Globalization*. Minneapolis: U of Minnesota P, 1996. Print.
Appiah, Kwame Anthony. *Cosmopolitanism: Ethics in a World of Strangers*. New York: Norton, 2005. Print.
Appiah, Kwame Anthony. *Ethics of Identity*. Princeton: Princeton UP, 2004. Print.
apRoberts, Ruth. *The Moral Trollope*. Athens: Ohio UP, 1971. Print.
Apter, Emily. "From Literary Channel to Narrative Chunnel." Cohen and Dever 286–94.

Apter, Emily. "Speculation and Xenophobia as Literary World Systems: the Nineteenth-Century Business Novel." McDonald and Suleiman 388–403.

Arac, Jonathan. "The Age of the Novel, the Age of Empire: Howells, James, Twain Around 1900." *Victorian World Literatures*. Ed. Priya Joshi. Spec. issue of *Yearbook of English Studies* 41.2 (2011): 94–105. Print.

Arata, Stephen. *Fictions of Loss in the Victorian Fin de Siècle: Identity and Empire*. Cambridge: Cambridge UP, 2009. Print.

Arata, Stephen. "The Occidental Tourist: *Dracula* and the Anxiety of Reverse Colonization." *Victorian Studies* 33.4 (1990): 621–45. Print.

Arendt, Hannah. *The Origins of Totalitarianism*. New York: Harcourt, Brace, Jovanovich, 1973. Print.

Armitage, David. *The Ideological Origins of the British Empire*. Cambridge: Cambridge UP, 2000. Print.

Armstrong, Nancy. *Desire and Domestic Fiction: A Political History of the Novel*. Oxford: Oxford UP, 1987. Print.

Armstrong, Paul B. "Reading India: E. M. Forster and the Politics of Interpretation." *Twentieth-Century Literature* 38.4 (1992): 365–85. Print.

Arnold, Matthew. "Anarchy and Authority." *The Cornhill Magazine, Vol. XVIII*. London: Smith, Elder, & Co., 1868. 239–56. Print.

Arnold, Matthew. "Culture and Anarchy: An Essay in Political and Social Criticism." 1867–9. Arnold, *Culture* 53–211.

Arnold, Matthew. *Culture and Anarchy and Other Writings*. Ed. Stefan Collini. New York: Cambridge UP, 1993. Print.

Arnold, Matthew. *England and the Italian Question*. (1859). Durham: Duke UP, 1953. Print.

Arnold, Matthew. "The Function of Criticism at the Present Time." 1864. Arnold, *Culture* 26–51.

Arrighi, Giovanni. *The Long Twentieth Century: Money, Power, and the Origins of Our Times*. London: Verso, 1994. Print.

Ashton, Rosemary. *George Eliot: A Life*. London: Penguin, 1998. Print.

Auerbach, Erich. *Mimesis: The Representation of Reality in Western Thought*. 1946. Trans. Willard R. Trask. Princeton: Princeton UP, 1974. Print.

Auerbach, Erich. "On the Serious Imitation of the Everyday." Flaubert, *Madame*. 423–49. Print.

Auerbach, Nina. "The Rise of the Fallen Woman." *Nineteenth-Century Fiction* 35.1 (1980): 29–52. Print.

Bachman, Maria and Don Cox, eds. *Reality's Dark Light: The Sensational Wilkie Collins*. Knoxville: U of Tennessee P, 2003. Print.

Badiou, Alain. 1998. *Ethics: An Essay on the Understanding of Evil*. Trans. Peter Hallward. London: Verso, 2001. Print.

Bagehot, Walter. *The English Constitution*. 1867. Ed. and introd. R. H. S. Crossman. Ithaca: Cornell UP, 1963. Print.

Bagehot, Walter. *Lombard Street: A Description of the Money Market*. 1873. New York: Wiley, 1999. Print.

Baguley, David. *Naturalist Fiction: The Entropic Vision*. Cambridge: Cambridge UP, 1990. Print.

Bakhtin, M. M. *The Dialogic Imagination: Four Essays*. Ed. Michael Holquist. Trans. Caryl Emerson and Holquist. Austin: U of Texas P, 1981. Print.

Bakshi, Parminder. "The Politics of Desire: E. M. Forster's Encounters with India." Davies and Wood 23–64.

Balibar, Etienne. "Ambiguous Universality." *Differences: A Journal of Feminist Cultural Studies* 7.1 (1995): 48. Print.
Balzac, Honoré de. "Author's Introduction." *The Human Comedy.* Project Gutenberg Ebook. http://www.gutenberg.org/files/1968/1968-h/1968-h.htm
Barkawi, Tarak and Mark Laffey. "Retrieving the Imperial: Empire and International Relations." *Millennium* 31.1 (2002): 109–27. Print.
Barthes, Roland. "The Reality Effect." *The Rustle of Language.* 1984. Trans. Richard Howard. Oxford: Blackwell, 1986. 141–8. Print.
Bartolovich, Crystal. "Humanities of Scale: Marxism, Surface Reading—and Milton." *PMLA* 127.1 (2012): 115–21. Print.
Baucom, Ian. *Out of Place: Englishness, Empire, and the Locations of Identity.* Princeton: Princeton UP, 1999. Print.
Baucom, Ian. *Specters of the Atlantic: Finance Capital, Slavery, and The Philosophy of History.* Durham: Duke UP, 2005. Print.
Baudelaire, Charles. "*Madame Bovary* by Gustave Flaubert." Flaubert, *Madame.* 403–11.
Bauman, Zygmunt. *Modernity and Ambivalence.* Ithaca: Cornell UP, 1991. Print.
Baumgarten, Murray. "Seeing Double: Jews in the Fiction of F. Scott Fitzgerald, Charles Dickens, Anthony Trollope, and George Eliot." *Between "Race" and Culture: Representations of "the Jew" in English and American Literature.* Ed. Bryan Cheyette. Stanford: Stanford UP, 1996. 44–61. Print.
Bayly, C.A. *Birth of the Modern World, 1789–1914.* Oxford: Wiley-Blackwell, 2003. Print.
Bayly, C.A. *Recovering Liberties: Indian Thought in the Age of Liberalism and Empire.* Cambridge: Cambridge UP, 2011.
Beasley, Edward. *Mid-Victorian Imperialists: British Gentlemen and the Empire of the Mind.* London: Routledge, 2005. Print.
Beaumont, Matthew, ed. *Adventures in Realism.* Oxford: Wiley-Blackwell, 2007. Print.
Beaumont, Matthew, "Introduction: Reclaiming Realism." Beaumont 1–12.
Beer, John. *The Achievement of E. M. Forster.* London: Chatto, 1963. Print.
Bell, Duncan. "Dissolving Distance: Technology, Space, and Empire in British Political Thought, 1770-1900." *Journal of Modern History* 77.3 (2005): 523–62. Print.
Bell, Duncan. "Empire and Imperialism." *The Cambridge History of Nineteenth Century Political Thought.* Ed. Gregory Claeys and Gareth Stedman Jones. Cambridge UP, 2001. 864–92. Print.
Bell, Duncan. *The Idea of Greater Britain: Empire and the Future of World Order, 1860–1900.* Princeton: Princeton UP, 2007. Print.
Bell, Michael Davitt. *The Problems of American Realism: Studies in the Cultural History of a Literary Idea.* Chicago: U of Chicago P, 1996. Print.
Bell, Major [T.] Evans. *The Great Parliamentary Bore.* London: Trübner & Co., 1869. Print.
Bell, Major [T.] Evans. *The Mysore Reversion. An Exceptional Case.* 2nd edition. London: Trübner & Co., 1866. Print.
Belsey, Catherine. *Critical Practice.* 1980. London: Routledge, 2002. Print.
Ben-Yishai, Ayelet. "The Fact of a Rumor: Anthony Trollope's *The Eustace Diamonds.*" *Nineteenth-Century Literature* 62.1 (2007): 88–120. Print.
Benhabib, Seyla. *Situating the Self: Gender, Community and Postmodernism in Contemporary Ethics.* London: Routledge, 1992. Print.
Benjamin. *Illuminations.* Ed. Hannah Arendt. Trans. Harry Zohn. New York: Schocken, 1978. Print.

Benjamin, Walter. "On Some Motifs in Baudelaire." 1939. Benjamin, *Illuminations* 155–200.
Benjamin, Walter. "Paris, Capital of the Nineteenth Century." *Reflections*. Ed. Peter Demetz. Trans. Edmund Jephcott. New York: Schocken, 1978. 146–62. Print.
Benjamin, Walter. "The Storyteller: Reflections on the Works of Nikolai Leskov." 1936. Benjamin, *Illuminations* 83–109.
Benjamin, Walter. "Theses on the Philosophy of History." 1940. Benjamin, *Illuminations* 253–64.
Bennett, Tony. Sociology, Aesthetics, Expertise. *New Literary History* 41.2 (2010): 253–76. Print.
Bentham, Jeremy. *An Introduction to the Principles of Morals and Legislation*. 1780. Ed. J. H. Burns and H. L. A. Hart. Oxford: Clarendon, 1996. Print.
Berman, Carolyn Vellenga. *Creole Crossings: Domestic Fiction and the Reform of Colonial Slavery*. Ithaca: Cornell UP, 2005. Print.
Berman, Jessica. *Modernist Fiction, Cosmopolitanism and the Politics of Community*. Cambridge: Cambridge UP, 2001. Print.
Bernstein, J. M. *The Philosophy of the Novel: Lukács, Marxism, and the Dialectics of Form*. Minneapolis: U of Minnesota P, 1984.
Bernstein, Susan. "The Way We Read Then: Victorian Serials by Numbers." NAVSA 2010 Conf., Montreal. Nov. 13 2010.
Best, Stephen. "On Failing to Make the Past Present." *Peripheral Realisms*. Spec. Issue of *Modern Language Quarterly* 73.3 (2013): 453–74. Print.
Best, Stephen, and Sharon Marcus. "Surface Reading: An Introduction." *The Way We Read Now*. Spec. issue of *Representations* 108.1 (2009): 1–21.
Bigelow, Gordon. "Form and Violence in Trollope's The Macdermots of Ballycloran." *Novel* 46.3 (2013): 386–405.
Birns, Nicholas. "The Empire Turned Upside Down: The Colonial Fictions of Anthony Trollope." *Ariel* 27.3 (1996): 7–23. Print.
Birns, Nicholas. "Receptacle or Reversal? Globalization Down Under in Marcus Clarke's His Natural Life." *College Literature* 32.2 (2005): 127–45.
Blumberg, Ilana. "'Unnatural Self-Sacrifice': Trollope's Ethic of Mutual Benefit." *Nineteenth-Century Literature* 58.4 (2004): 506–46. Print.
Bodenheimer, Rosemarie. *The Real Life of Mary Ann Evans: George Eliot, Her Letters and Fiction*. Ithaca: Cornell UP, 1994. Print.
Bodenheimer, Rosemarie. "A Woman of Many Names." *The Cambridge Companion to George Eliot*. Ed. George Levine. New York: Cambridge UP, 2001. 20–37. Print.
Boelhower, William. "The Rise of the New Atlantic Studies Matrix." *American Literary History* 20.1–2 (2008): 83–101. Print.
Bonaparte, Felicia. *Triptych and the Cross: Central Myths of George Eliot's Poetic Imagination*. New York: New York UP, 1979. Print.
Boone, Joseph Allen. "Modernist Maneuverings in the Marriage Plot: Breaking Ideologies of Gender and Genre in James's The Golden Bowl." *PMLA* (1986): 374–88.
Boone, Joseph Allen. *Tradition Counter Tradition: Love and the Form of Fiction*. Chicago: U of Chicago P, 1989. Print.
Bradford Booth, ed. *The Letters of Anthony Trollope*. Stanford: Stanford UP, 1983. Print.
Born, Daniel. *The Birth of Liberal Guilt in the English Novel: Charles Dickens to H. G. Wells*. Chapel Hill: U of North Carolina P, 1995. Print.
Bornstein, George. "The Colors of Zion: Black, Jewish, and Irish Nationalisms at the Turn of the Century." *Modernism/Modernity* 12.3 (2005): 369–84. Print.

Bourdieu, Pierre. *On Television*. Trans. Priscilla Parkhurst Ferguson. New York: New Press, 1998. Print.

Bourdieu, Pierre. *The Rules of Art: Genesis and Structure of the Literary Field*. Trans. Susan Emanuel. Stanford: Stanford UP, 1996. Print.

Bourdieu, Pierre, and Loïc J.D. Wacquant. *An Invitation to Reflexive Sociology*. Trans. Loïc J. D. Wacquant. Chicago: U of Chicago P, 1992. Print.

Bourget, Paul. "A Lecture at Oxford: Gustave Flaubert." Trans. C Heywood. *Fortnightly Review* 68 (1897): 152–64. Print.

Bourne, Kenneth. *The Foreign Policy of Victorian Britain, 1832–1902*. Oxford: Clarendon, 1970. Print.

Bowen, H. V. "British Conceptions of Global Empire, 1756–1783." *Journal of Imperial and Commonwealth History* 26 (1998): 1–26. Print.

Boyarin, Jonathan. "Reading Exodus into History." *Palestine and Jewish History: Criticism at the Borders of Ethnography*. Minneapolis: U of Minnesota P, 1996.

Braddon, Mary Elizabeth. *The Doctor's Wife*. 1864. Ed. Lyn Pykett. Oxford: Oxford UP, 2008. Print.

Brantlinger, Patrick. *Dark Vanishings: Discourse on the Extinction of Primitive Race, 1800–1930*. Ithaca: Cornell UP, 2003. Print.

Brantlinger, Patrick. *The Reading Lesson: The Threat of Mass Literacy in Nineteenth-Century British Fiction*. Bloomington: Indiana UP, 1998. Print.

Brantlinger, Patrick. *Rule of Darkness: British Literature and Imperialism, 1830–1914*. Ithaca: Cornell UP, 1990. Print.

Brantlinger, Patrick. *Victorian Literature and Postcolonial Studies*. Edinburgh: Edinburgh UP, 2009. Print.

Brantlinger, Patrick. "What is 'Sensational' about the 'Sensation Novel'?" *Nineteenth-Century Fiction* 37.1 (1982): 1–28. Print.

Braudel, Fernand. "History and the Social Sciences." *Economy and Society in Early Modern Europe: Essays from Annales*. Ed. Peter Burke. New York: Harper, 1972. 11–42. Print.

Bredbeck, Gregory W. "'Queer Superstitions': Forster, Carpenter, and the Illusions of (Sexual) Identity." *Queer Forster*. Martin and Piggford 29–58.

Brennan, Timothy. "Cosmopolitanism and Internationalism." *Debating Cosmopolitics*. Ed. Daniele Archibugi. London: Verso, 2003. 40–50. Print.

Briefel, Aviva. "Tautological Crimes: Why Women Can't Steal Jewels." *Novel: A Forum on Fiction* 37.1/2 (2003): 135–57. Print.

Bristow, Joseph. "Whether 'Victorian' Poetry: a Genre and Its Period." *Victorian Poetry* 42.1 (2004): 81–109. Print.

Bristow, Joseph. *Effeminate England: Homoerotic Writing after 1885*. Buckingham: Open UP, 1995. Print.

Brooks, Peter. *The Melodramatic Imagination: Balzac, Henry James, Melodrama, and the Mode of Excess*. New Haven: Yale UP, 1976. Print.

Brooks, Peter. *Realist Vision*. New Haven: Yale UP, 2005. Print.

Brown, Bill. "Now Advertising: Late James." *The Henry James Review* 30.1 (2009): 10–21. Print.

Brown, Bill. "Thing Theory." *Things*. Spec. issue of *Critical Inquiry* 28.1 (2001): 1–22. Print.

Brown, Bill. *A Sense of Things: The Object Matter of American Literature*. Chicago: U of Chicago P, 2004. Print.

Brown, Tony. "Edward Carpenter, Forster, and the Evolution of *a Room with a View.*" *ELT* 30 (1987): 279–300. Print.
Brown, Wendy. "Neo–liberalism and the End of Liberal Democracy." *Theory & Event* 7.1 (2003): n. pag. Project Muse. Web. 20 June 2011.
Brown, Wendy. "Sovereignty and the Return of the Repressed." *The New Pluralism: William Connolly and the Contemporary Global Condition.* Ed. David Campbell and Morton Schoolman. Durham: Duke UP, 2008. 250–72. Print.
Brown, Wendy. *States of Injury: Power and Freedom in Late Modernity.* Princeton: Princeton UP, 1995. Print.
Brown, Wendy. *Walled States, Waning Sovereignty.* New York: Zone Books, 2010. Print.
Brumpton, Paul R. *Security and Progress: Lord Salisbury at the India Office.* Westport: Greenwood Press, 2002. Print.
Bryer, R.A. "Accounting for the 'Railway Mania' of 1845—A Great Railway Swindle?" *Accounting, Organizations and Society* 16.5/6 (1991): 439–86. Print.
Buckton, Oliver S. *Secret Selves: Confession and Same-Sex Desire in Victorian Autobiography.* Chapel Hill: U of North Carolina P, 1998. Print.
Burke, Edmund. *Reflections on the Revolution in France.* 1790. Ed. Conor Cruise O'Brien. Harmondsworth: Penguin, 1981. Print.
Burke, Edmund. "Speech on Opening of Impeachment." 1788. *Empire and Community: Edmund Burke's Writings and Speeches on International Relations.* Ed. David P. Fidler and Jennifer M. Welsh. Boulder: Westview, 1999. 202–15. Print.
Burton, Antoinette M., ed. *After the Imperial Turn: Thinking with and through the Nation.* Durham: Duke UP, 2003. Print.
Burton, Antoinette M. *The First Anglo-Afghan Wars: A Reader.* Durham: Duke UP, 2014. Print.
Buzard, James. "'Anywhere's Nowhere': Bleak House as Autoethnography." *The Yale Journal of Criticism* 12.1 (1999): 7–39. Print.
Buzard, James. *The Beaten Track: European Tourism, Literature, and the Ways to Culture, 1800-1918.* Oxford: Oxford UP, 1993. Print.
Buzard, James. *Disorienting Fiction: The Autoethnographic Work of Nineteenth–Century British Novels.* Princeton: Princeton UP, 2005. Print.
Cain, Peter. "Radicalism, Gladstone, and the Liberal Critique of Disraelian 'Imperialism.'" *Victorian Visions of Global Order: Empire and International Relations in Nineteenth-Century Political Thought.* Cambridge: Cambridge UP, 2007. 215–38.
Calhoun, Craig. "The Class Consciousness of Frequent Travelers: Towards a Critique of Actually Existing Cosmopolitanism." *Conceiving Cosmopolitanism: Theory, Context, Practice.* Ed. Steven Vertovec and Robin Cohen. Oxford: Oxford UP, 2003. 86–109. Print.
Calvin, Jean. *Commentaries on the Four Last Books of Moses: Arranged in the Form of a Harmony,* Vol. 3. Trans. Charles W. Bingham. Edinburgh: The Calvin Translation Society, 1855. Print.
Campbell, Duncan Andrew. *English Public Opinion and the American Civil War.* London: Royal Historical Society, 2003. Print.
Cannadine, David. *G. M. Trevelyan: A Life in History.* New York: HarperCollins, 1992. Print.
Canning, Charles J. Lord. "Despatch–Viceroy to the Secretary of State." 30 April 1860. Sever, *Documents* 236–42. Print.
Capaldi, Nicholas. *John Stuart Mill: A Biography.* Cambridge: Cambridge UP, 2004. Print.

Carens, Timothy. *Outlandish English Subjects in the Victorian Domestic Novel.* New York: Palgrave, 2005. Print.

Carpenter, Edward. *The Intermediate Sex: A Study of Some Transitional Types of Men and Women.* 1906. New York: Kennerley, 1912. Print.

Carpenter, Edward. *Love's Coming-of-Age.* New York: Modern Library, 1911. Print.

Carroll, David. *George Eliot and the Conflict of Interpretations: A Reading of the Novels.* Cambridge UP, 2006. Print.

Carroll, David, ed. *George Eliot: The Critical Heritage.* 1971. New York: Routledge, 2005. Print.

Carson, Penelope. "Golden Casket or Pebbles and Trash? J.S. Mill and the Anglicist/Orientalist Controversy." Moir, Peers, Zastoupil 149–72.

Carter, Everett. "Realists and Jews." *Studies in American Fiction* 22.1 (1994): 81–92. Print.

Case, Alison. "Tasting the Original Apple: Gender and the Struggle for Narrative Authority in *Dracula*." *Narrative* 1.3 (Oct. 1993): 223–43. Print.

Caserio, Robert L. *The Novel in England, 1900–1950: History and Theory.* New York: Twayne, 1998. Print.

Casanova, Pascale. "Literature as a World." *New Left Review* 31 (Jan–Feb. 2005): 71–90.

Çelikkol, Ayşe. *Romances of Free Trade: British Literature, Laissez–Faire, and the Global Nineteenth Century.* Oxford: Oxford UP, 2011. Print.

Chakrabarty, Dipesh. *Provincializing Europe: Postcolonial Thought and Historical Difference.* Princeton: Princeton UP, 2007. Print.

Chamberlain, Muriel. *Pax Britannica? British Foreign Policy, 1789–1914.* London: Longman, 1989. Print.

Chandler, David. "International Justice." *Debating Cosmopolitics.* Ed. Daniele Archibugi. New York: Verso, 2003. 27–39. Print.

Chase, Karen and Michael Levenson. *The Spectacle of Intimacy: A Public Life for the Victorian Family.* Princeton: Princeton UP, 2000. Print.

Cheah, Pheng. "Introduction Part II: The Cosmopolitical—Today" Cheah and Robbins 20–44.

Cheah, Pheng and Bruce Robbins, eds. *Cosmopolitics: Thinking and Feeling Beyond the Nation.* Minneapolis: U of Minnesota P, 1998. Print.

Cheng, Anne Anlin. "Skins, Tattoos, and Susceptibility." Best and Marcus 98–119.

Cheyette, Bryan. *Constructions of "the Jew" in English Literature and Society: Racial Representations, 1875–1945.* Cambridge: Cambridge UP, 1996. Print.

Cheyette, Bryan and Nadia Valman. *The Image of the Jew in European Liberal Culture, 1789–1914.* Edgware: Vallentine Mitchell, 2004. Print.

Clark, Anna. *Scandal: The Sexual Politics of the British Constitution.* Princeton, Princeton UP, 2005. Print.

Clarke, John. "Dissolving the Public Realm? The Logics and Limits of Neo–Liberalism." *Journal of Social Policy* 33.1 (2004): 27–48. Print.

Claybaugh, Amanda. *The Novel of Purpose: Literature and Social Reform in the Anglo–American World.* Ithaca: Cornell UP, 2007. Print.

Cohen, Margaret. "Flaubert Lectrice: Flaubert Lady Reader." *MLN* 122.4 (2007): 746–58. Print.

Cohen, Margaret. "Introduction to the Second Edition." Flaubert, *Madame* ix–xix.

Cohen, Margaret. "International Influences." *Oxford History of the Novel in English.* Ed. John Kucich and Jenny Bourne Taylor. Vol. 3. Oxford: Oxford UP, 2012. 409–26. Print.

Cohen, Margaret. "Narratology in the Archive of Literature" Best and Marcus 51–75.

Cohen, Margaret. "Sentimental Communities." Cohen and Dever 106–32.
Cohen, Margaret and Carolyn Dever, eds. *The Literary Channel: The Inter-national Invention of The Novel*. Princeton: Princeton UP, 2002. Print.
Cohen, William A. "Trollope's Trollop." *Novel: A Forum on Fiction* 28.3 (1995): 235–56. Print.
Cohn, Bernard S. "Representing Authority in Victorian India." Hobsbawm and Ranger 165–209.
Cole, Sarah. *Modernism, Male Friendship, and the First World War*. Cambridge: Cambridge UP, 2003. Print.
Collini, Stefan. "Political Theory and the 'Science of Society' in Victorian Britain." *The Historical Journal* 23 (1980): 203–31. Print.
Collins, Wilkie. *Armadale*. 1866. Ed. John Sutherland. London: Penguin, 1995. Print.
Collins, Wilkie. *The Moonstone*. 1868. Ed. Sandra Kemp. London: Penguin, 1998. Print.
Collins, Wilkie. "A Novelist on Novel Writing." *Cassell's Saturday Journal* 4.179 (5 Mar. 1887): 355–6. Rpt. in *A Novelist on Novel Writing*. Ed. Andrew Gasson. London: The Wilkie Collins Society, 2001. Print.
Collins, Wilkie. "Portrait of an Author, Painted by his Publisher." *The Living Age, Volume LXII* 3rd ser. 6 (1859): 553–66. Print.
Collins, Wilkie. *The Woman in White*. 1859-60. Ed. John Sutherland. Oxford: Oxford UP, 1999. Print.
Connolly, William. *Pluralism*. Durham: Duke UP, 2005. Print.
Cooper, Frederick and Anna Laura Stoler, eds. *Tensions of Empire: Colonial Cultures in a Bourgeois World*. Berkeley: U of California P, 1997. Print.
Copland, Ian. *The British Raj and the Indian Princes: Paramountcy in Western India, 1857–1930*. Bombay: Orient Longman, 1982. Print.
Corbett, Mary Jean. *Allegories of Union in Irish and English Writing: 1790–1870*. Cambridge: Cambridge UP, 2000. Print.
Corner, Julian. "Trauma, Drifting, and Reconciliation in *Romola*." Levine and Turner 67–88.
"Cosmopolitan." *The Oxford English Dictionary*. 2nd ed. Oxford: Oxford UP, 1989. Print.
Cotsell, Michael. "Trollope: The International Theme." *Creditable Warriors, 1830–1876*. Vol. 3 of *English Literature and the Wider World*. Ed. Michael Cotsell. London: Ashfield, 1990. 243–56. Print.
Coundouriotis, Eleni. "Hetty and History: The Political Consciousness of *Adam Bede*." *Dickens Studies Annual* 30 (2001): 285–307. Print.
Courtemanche, Eleanor. *The 'Invisible Hand' and British Fiction, 1818–1860: Adam Smith, Political Economy, and the Genre of Realism*. New York: Palgrave, 2011. Print.
Craciun, Adriana. *British Women Writers and the French Revolution: Citizens of the World*. New York: Palgrave, 2005. Print.
Crane, Mary Thomas. "Surface, Depth, and the Spatial Imaginary: A Cognitive Reading of *The Political Unconscious*." Best and Marcus 76–97.
Crawford, Shawn. "No Time to Be Idle: The Serial Novel and Popular Imagination." *World and I* 13/11 (Nov. 1998): 323–32. Print.
Critchley, Simon. *The Ethics of Deconstruction: Derrida and Levinas*. 2nd ed. Edinburgh: Edinburgh UP, 1999. Print.
Critchley, Simon. "Introduction." *The Cambridge Companion to Levinas*. Ed. Simon Critchley and Robert Bernasconi. Cambridge: Cambridge UP, 2002.1–32. Print.

Crooks, Robert. "Reopening the Mysteries: Colonialist Logic and Cultural Difference in *The Moonstone* and *The Horse Latitudes*." *LIT: Literature Interpretation Theory* 4.3 (1993): 215–28. Print.

Crosby, Christina. "'A Taste for More': Trollope's Addictive Realism." *The New Economic Criticism: Studies at the Intersection of Literature and Economics*. Eds. Martha Woodmansee and Mark Osteen. London: Routledge, 1999. 251–61. Print.

Cross, J.W. *George Eliot's Life as Related in Her Letters and Journals*. Vol. 2. New York: Harpers, 1885. Print.

Cucullu, Lois. "Shepherds in the Parlor: Forster's Apostles, Pagans, and Native Sons." *Novel: A Forum on Fiction* 32.1 (1998): 19–50. Print.

Culler, Jonathan. "The Realism of *Madame Bovary*." *MLN* 122.4 (2007): 683–96. Print.

Cunningham, Valentine. "Anthony Trollope and Law, Laws, Legalisms and Assorted Legislations." *REAL: Yearbook of Research in English and American Literature* 18 (2002): 89–107. Print.

Dainotto, Roberto M. *Europe (in Theory)*. Durham: Duke UP, 2007. Print.

Dallas, E.S. *The Gay Science*. 2 vols. London: Chapman & Hall, 1866. Print.

Daly, Nicholas. *Literature, Technology, and Modernity, 1860-2000*. Cambridge: Cambridge UP, 2004. Print.

Daly, Nicholas. "Railway Novels: Sensation Fiction and the Modernization of the Senses." *ELH* 66.2 (Summer 1999): 461–87. Print.

Daly, Suzanne. "Indiscreet Jewels: *The Eustace Diamonds*." *Nineteenth-Century Studies* 19 (2005): 69–81. Print.

Dames, Nicholas. *Amnesiac Selves: Nostalgia, Forgetting, and British Fiction, 1810–1870*. New York: Oxford UP, 2001. Print.

Dames, Nicholas. *Physiology of the Novel: Reading, Neural Science, and the Form of Victorian Fiction*. New York: Oxford UP, 2007. Print.

Dames, Nicholas. "Trollope and the Career: Vocational Trajectories and the Management of Ambition." *Victorian Studies* 45.2 (2003): 247–78. Print.

Darwin, John. *The Empire Project: The Rise and Fall of the British World Project, 1830–1970*. Cambridge: Cambridge UP, 2009. Print.

Davidson, J. H. "Anthony Trollope and the Colonies." *Victorian Studies* 12.3 (1969): 305–30. Print.

Davies, Tony. Introduction. *A Passage to India*. Davies and Wood 1–22.

Davies, Tony and Nigel Wood, eds. *A Passage to India*. Buckingham: Open UP, 1994. Print.

Davison, Roderic H. "Britain, The International Spectrum, and the Eastern Question, 1827–1841." *New Perspectives on Turkey* 7 (1992): 15–35. Print.

Dean, Tim. Response. Queer Internationalism Panel. Modernist Studies Association Convention. Hyatt Regency Hotel, Vancouver. 24 Oct. 2004.

Dellamora, Richard. *Friendship's Bonds: Democracy and the Novel in Victorian England*. Philadelphia: U of Pennsylvania P, 2004. Print.

Dellamora, Richard. "Textual Politics/Sexual Politics." *MLQ* 54.1 (1993): 155–64. Print.

Dempster, Sarah, Grace Dent, Lucy Mangan, Mark Lawson, Sam Wollaston, and Richard Vine. "The Top 50 TV Dramas of All Time: 2–10." *The Guardian*. 11 Jan. 2010. Web. 5 Jan. 2012.

Deutsch, Gotthard. "Anti–Semitism." *Jewish Encyclopedia*. Web. 28 June 2011.

Dever, Carolyn. "The Marriage Plot and its Alternatives." J. Taylor, *Cambridge* 112–25.

Dever, Carolyn. *Death and the Mother from Dickens to Freud: Victorian Fiction and the Anxiety of Origins*. Cambridge: Cambridge UP, 1998. Print.

Dilke, Charles Wentworth. *Greater Britain*. 2 vols. London: Macmillan, 1868. Print.
Dimock, Wai Chee. *Through Other Continents: American Literature across Deep Time*. Princeton: Princeton UP, 2007. Print.
Dirks, Nicholas B. *The Scandal of Empire: India and the Creation of Imperial Britain*. Cambridge: Belknap, 2006. Print.
Disraeli, Benjamin. "Berlin Treaty, July 18 1878." Disraeli, *Selected Speeches* 179–202.
Disraeli, Benjamin. *Coningsby, or, The New Generation*. 1844. Ed. Thom Braun. London: Penguin, 1983. Print.
Disraeli, Benjamin. "Conservative and Liberal Principles (Crystal Palace), June 24 1872." Disraeli, *Selected Speeches* 523–35.
Disraeli, Benjamin. "Royal Titles Bill, March 9 1876." Disraeli, *Selected Speeches* 231–9.
Disraeli, Benjamin. *Selected Speeches of the Late Right Honourable the Earl of Beaconsfield*. Ed. T.E. Kebbel. Vol. 2. London: Longmans, Green and Co., 1882. 179–202. Print.
Doty, Alexander. "The Homosexual and the Single Girl." *Mad World: Sex, Politics, Style and the 1960s*. Ed. Lauren M.E. Goodlad, Lilya Kaganovsky, and Robert A. Rushing. Durham: Duke UP.
Drayton, Richard. "The Collaboration of Labour: Slaves, Empires, and Globalizations in the Atlantic World, c. 1600-1850." *Globalisation in World History*. Ed. A.G. Hopkins. London: Pimlico, 2002. 98–114. Print.
Duggan, Lisa. *The Twilight of Equality? Neoliberalism, Cultural Politics, and the Attack on Democracy*. Boston: Beacon, 2003. Print.
Duncan, Ian. "*The Moonstone,* the Victorian Novel, and Imperialist Panic." *Modern Language Quarterly* 55.3 (1994): 297–319. Print.
Duncan, Ian. *Modern Romance and Transformations of the Novel: The Gothic, Scott, Dickens*. Cambridge: Cambridge UP, 1992. Print.
Eagleton, Terry. *Criticism and Ideology: A Study in Marxist Literary Theory*. London: Verso, 1998. Print.
Eagleton, Terry. *The English Novel: An Introduction*. Oxford: Wiley-Blackwell, 2004. Print.
Eagleton, Terry. *Marxism and Literary Criticism*. Berkeley: U of California P, 1976. Print.
Earle, Bo. "Policing and Performing Liberal Individuality in Anthony Trollope's *The Warden*." *Nineteenth-Century Literature* 61.1 (2006): 1–31. Print.
Eisenstadt, S.N. "Multiple Modernities." *Daedalus* 129.1 (2000): 1–29. Print.
Eliot, George. *Adam Bede*. 1859. Ed. Margaret Reynolds. London: Penguin, 2008. Print.
Eliot, George. "The *Antigone* and its Moral." 1856. G. Eliot, *Selected* 243–6.
Eliot, George. *Daniel Deronda*. 1876. Ed. Terence Cave. London: Penguin, 1995. Print.
Eliot, George. *Mill on the Floss*. 1860. Ed. A.S. Byatt. London: Penguin, 1979. Print.
Eliot, George. "The Morality of *Wilhelm Meister*." 1855. G. Eliot, *Selected* 129–33.
Eliot, George. "Natural History of German Life."1856. G. Eliot, *Selected* 260–96.
Eliot, George. *Selected Critical Writings*. Ed. Rosemary Ashton. New York: Oxford UP, 2000. Print.
Eliot, George. "Silly Novels by Lady Novelists." 1856. G. Eliot, *Selected* 296–321.
Eliot, George. "Woman in France: Madame de Sablé." 1854. G. Eliot, *Selected* 37–68.
Eliot, T. S. "Wilkie Collins and Dickens." *Times Literary Supplement* 4 Aug. 1927: 525–6. Print.
Ellingson, Ter. *The Myth of the Noble Savage*. Berkeley: U of California P, 2001. Print.
Emanuel, Harry. *Diamonds and Precious Stones: their History, Value, and Distinguishing Characteristics*. London: Hotten, 1865. Print.

English, James F. "Everywhere and Nowhere: The Sociology of Literature After 'The Sociology of Literature.'" *New Sociologies of Literature*. Ed. Rita Felski and James F. English. Spec. issue of *New Literary History* 41.2 (2010): v–xxiii. Print.

Ermarth, Elizabeth. *Realism and Consensus in the English Novel*. Princeton: Princeton UP, 1983. Print.

Escobar, Arturo. *Encountering Development: The Making and Unmaking of the Third World*. 1995. Princeton: Princeton UP, 2012. Print.

Esty, Jed. *A Shrinking Island: Modernism and National Culture in England*. Princeton: Princeton UP, 2003. Print.

Esty, Jed. *Unseasonable Youth: Modernism, Colonialism, and the Fiction of Development*. New York: Oxford UP, 2011. Print.

Esty, Jed and Colleen Lye, eds. *Peripheral Realisms*. Spec. issue of *Modern Language Quarterly* 73.3 (2013): 255–485. Print.

Fabian, Johannes. *Time and The Other: How Anthropology Makes Its Object*. New York: Columbia UP, 2002. Print.

Farber, Dan. "Netflix Viewers Feast on '*House of Cards*.'" CNET. CBS Interactive Inc., 12 Feb. 2013. Web. 30 May 2013.

Felber, Lynette. "The Advanced Conservative Liberal: Victorian Liberalism and the Aesthetics of Anthony Trollope's Palliser Novels." *Modern Philology* 107.3 (2010): 421–46. Print.

Felski, Rita. "After Suspicion." *Profession* (2009): 28–35. Print.

Felski, Rita. "Context Stinks!" *Context?* Ed Rita Felski and Herbert F. Tucker. Spec. issue of *New Literary History* 42.4 (2011): 573–91. Print.

Felski, Rita. *The Gender of Modernity*. Cambridge: Harvard UP, 1995. Print.

Felski, Rita. "Suspicious Minds." *Poetics Today* 32.2 (2011): 215–34. Print.

Feltes, N.N. *Modes of Production of Victorian Novels*. Chicago: U of Chicago P, 1989. Print.

Ferguson, Frances. *Pornography, the Theory: What Utilitarianism Did to Action*. Chicago: U of Chicago P, 2004. Print.

Feuchtwanger, Edgar. "'Jew Feelings' and Realpolitik: Disraeli and the Making of Foreign and Imperial Policy." *Disraeli's Jewishness*. Ed. Todd Endelman and Tony Kushner. London: Valentine Mitchell, 2002. 180–96. Print.

Feuer, Jane, Paul Kerr and Tise Vahimagi, eds. *MTM: 'Quality Television.'* London: BFI, 1984. Print.

Findlay, Eileen Suarez. "Portable Roots: Identity and Memory in Nuyorican Life Stories, San Juan Puerto Rico, 1965–2000." lecture at U of Illinois, Urbana. 10 Mar. 2005. Address.

Fisch, Audrey. "Collins, Race, and Slavery." Bachman and Cox 313–28.

Flaubert, Gustave. Letter to Louise Colet. 16 January 1852. *The Letters of Gustave Flaubert, 1830-1857*. Ed. and Trans. Francis Steegmuller. Cambridge, MA: Harvard UP, 1980. 154–5. Print.

Flaubert, Gustave. *Madame Bovary*. 1857. Ed. Margaret Cohen. Trans. Eleanor Marx Aveling and Paul de Man. 2nd ed. New York: Norton, 2004. Print.

Fleishman, Avrom. *George Eliot's Intellectual Life*. Cambridge: Cambridge UP, 2010. Print.

Flint, Kate. "Why 'Victorian'?: Response." *Victorian Studies* 47.2 (2005): 230–39. Print.

Forman, Ross G. "Harbouring Discontent: British Imperialism through Brazilian Eyes in the Christie Affair." *An Age of Equipoise?: Reassessing Mid-Victorian Britain*. Ed. Martin Hewitt. Farnham: Ashgate, 2000. 225–44. Print.

Forster, E. M. *A Passage to India*. 1924. New York: Harcourt, 1952. Print.
Forster, E. M. *A Room with a View*. 1908. Harmondsworth: Penguin, 2000. Print.
Forster, E. M. *Arctic Summer and Other Fiction*. London: Arnold, 1980. Print.
Forster, E. M. "The Challenge of Our Time." 1946. Forster, *Two Cheers* 70–75.
Forster, E. M. "Edward Carpenter." 1944. Forster, *Two Cheers* 220–23.
Forster, E. M. *The Feminine Note in Literature; an Hitherto Unpublished Manuscript*. Ed. George Piggford. London: Woolf, 2001. Print.
Forster, E. M. *Howards End*. 1910. New York: Vintage, 1989. Print.
Forster, E. M. "Notes on the English Character." 1926. *Abinger Harvest*. New York: Harcourt, 1964. 3–14.
Forster, E. M. "Three Countries." 1959. *The Hill of Devi and Other Indian Writings*. London: Arnold, 1983. 289–99. Print.
Forster, E. M. *Two Cheers for Democracy*. 1951. Ed. Oliver Stallybrass. Harmondsworth: Penguin, 1976. Print.
Forster, E. M. "What I Believe." 1938. Forster, *Two Cheers* 81–90.
Forster, E. M. *Where Angels Fear to Tread*. 1905. New York: Vintage, 1992. Print.
Foucault, Michel. "What is Enlightenment?" *The Foucault Reader*. Ed. Paul Rainbow. New York: Random House, 1984. 32–50. Print.
Fraiman, Susan. *Unbecoming Women: British Women Writers and the Novel of Development*. New York: Columbia UP, 1994. Print.
Frank, Andre Gunder. *The Development of Underdevelopment*. Boston: New England Free Press, 1966. Print.
Franklin, J. Jeffrey. "Anthony Trollope Meets Pierre Bourdieu: The Conversion of Capital as Plot in the Mid-Victorian British Novel." *Victorian Literature and Culture* 31.2 (2003): 501–21. Print.
Fraser, Derek. *The Evolution of the British Welfare State: A History of Social Policy since the Industrial Revolution*. 2nd ed. London: MacMillan, 1984. Print.
Freeden, Michael. *The New Liberalism: An Ideology of Social Reform*. Oxford: Clarendon, 1978. Print.
Freedgood, Elaine. "E. M. Forster's Queer Nation: Taking the Closet to the Colony in *A Passage to India*." *Bodies of Writing, Bodies in Performance*. Ed. Thomas Foster et al. New York: New York UP, 1996. 123–44. Print.
Freedgood, Elaine. *The Ideas in Things: Fugitive Meaning in The Victorian Novel*. Chicago: U of Chicago P, 2006. Print.
Freedman, Jonathan. *The Temple of Culture: Assimilation and Anti-Semitism in Literary Anglo-America*. Oxford: Oxford UP, 2000. Print.
Frow, John. "Tourism and the Semiotics of Nostalgia." *October* 57 (1991): 123–51. Print.
Fryckstedt, Monica C. *Geraldine Jewsbury's Athenaeum Reviews: A Mirror of Mid-Victorian Attitudes to Fiction*. Upsala: Acta Universitatis Upsaliensis, 1986. Print.
Furbank, P. N. *E.M. Forster: A Life*. 2 vols. New York: Harcourt Brace Jovanovich, 1978. Print.
Gagnier, Regenia. "Conclusion: Gender, Liberalism and Resentment." *The Politics of Gender in Anthony Trollope's Novels*. Eds. Regenia Gagnier, Margaret Markwick and Deborah Denenholz Morse. Farnham: Ashgate, 2009. 235–48. Print.
Gagnier, Regenia. *Individualism, Decadence and Globalization: On the Relationship of Part to Whole, 1859-1920*. New York: Palgrave, 2010. Print.
Gallagher, Catherine. *The Body Economic: Life, Death, and Sensation in Political Economy and the Victorian Novel*. Princeton: Princeton UP, 2008. Print.

Gallagher, Catherine. "George Eliot and *Daniel Deronda*: the Prostitute and the Jewish Question." *Sex, Politics, and Science in the Nineteenth-Century Novel*. Ed. Ruth Bernard Yeazell. Baltimore: Johns Hopkins UP, 1991. 39–62. Print.
Gallagher, Catherine. *The Industrial Reformation of English Fiction: Social Discourse and Narrative Form, 1832-1867*. Chicago: U of Chicago P, 1985. Print.
Gallagher, Catherine. "Marxism and the New Historicism." Veeser 37–48.
Gallagher, Catherine, and Stephen Greenblatt. *Practicing New Historicism*. Chicago: U of Chicago P, 2000.
Gallagher, John, and Ronald Robinson. "The Imperialism of Free Trade." *The Economic History Review*, 6.1 (1953): 1–15. Print.
Ganguly, Keya. "The Work of Forgetting: Raymond Williams and the Problem of Experience." *Intellectual Work*. Spec. issue of *New Formations* 53. (2004): 91–102. Print.
Gardner, Philip, ed. *E. M. Forster: The Critical Heritage*. London: Routledge, 1973. Print.
Garrett, Peter K. *Gothic Reflections: Narrative Force in Nineteenth-Century Fiction*. Ithaca: Cornell UP, 2003. Print.
Garrett, Peter K. "Sensations: Gothic, Horror, Crime Fiction, Detective Fiction." *The Cambridge History of the English Novel*. Eds. Robert L. Caserio and Clement Hawes. Cambridge: Cambridge UP, 2012. 469–84. Print.
Garrett, Peter K. *The Victorian Multiplot Novel: Studies in Dialogical Form*. New Haven: Yale UP, 1980.
Geoghegan, Vincent. "Edward Carpenter's England Revisited." *History of Political Thought* 24.3 (2003): 509–27. Print.
Gikandi, Simon. *Maps of Englishness*. New York: Columbia UP, 1996. Print.
Gikandi, Simon. "Race and Cosmopolitanism." *American Literary History* 14.3 (2002): 593–615. Print.
Gilbert, Sandra M. and Susan Gubar. *The Madwoman in the Attic: The Woman Writer and the Nineteenth-Century Literary Imagination*. New Haven: Yale UP, 1979. Print.
Gilligan, Carol. *In a Different Voice: Psychological Theory and Women's Development*. Cambridge: Harvard UP, 1982. Print.
Gilmour, Robin. "Introduction." Trollope, *The Warden* vii–xxvi.
Gilroy, Paul. *Against Race: Imagining Political Culture beyond the Color Line*. Cambridge: Belknap, 2000. Print.
Gilroy, Paul. *The Black Atlantic: Modernity and Double Consciousness*. Cambridge: Harvard UP, 1993. Print.
Gilroy, Paul. '*There Ain't No Black in the Union Jack*': *The Cultural Politics of Race and Nation*. Chicago: U of Chicago P, 1991. Print.
Gitlin, Todd. *The Sixties: Years of Hope, Days of Rage*. New York: Bantam, 1987. Print.
Gladstone, W. E. "Lord Rector's Address." *Political Speeches in Scotland: November and December 1879*. Edinburgh: Andrew Elliot, 1879. 229–55.
Glassman, Bernard. *Benjamin Disraeli: The Fabricated Jew in Myth and Memory*. Lanham, Maryland: UP of American, 2002. Print.
GoGwilt. Christopher. *The Fictions of Geopolitics: Afterimages of Culture, from Wilkie Collins to Alfred Hitchcock*. Stanford: Stanford UP, 2000. Print.
Goh, Robbie B. H. "Subversive Modernity: Coleridge, Gothic Imagery, the 'Body Politic,' and the Contestation of the Romantic Nation–State." *Postcolonial Cultures and Literatures: Modernity and the (Un)Commonwealth*. Ed. Andrew Benjamin, Tony Davies and Robbie B. H. Goh. New York: Lang, 2002. 161–76. Print.
Gooch, G.P. "Imperialism." Masterman, *The Heart* 308–94.

Goodlad, Lauren M. E. "Afterword." *Television for Victorianists*. Ed. Caroline Levine. Spec. issue of *RaVoN* 63 (2013): n. pag. Web. 19 June 2014.

Goodlad, Lauren M. E. "'Character Worth Speaking of': Individuality, John Stuart Mill and the Critique of Liberalism." *Victorians Institute Journal* 26 (2008): 7–46. Print.

Goodlad, Lauren M. E. "Geopolitics and the Geopolitical Unconscious." Hewitt, *Victorian* 175–90.

Goodlad, Lauren M. E. "Liberalism and Literature." *The Oxford Handbook of Victorian Literary Culture*. Ed. Juliet John. Oxford: Oxford UP. [Forthcoming].

Goodlad, Lauren M. E. "The Only Unpardonable Sin." Weblog posting. *Kritik*. 24 June 2013. 10 Dec. 2014. <http://unitcrit.blogspot.com/2013/06/mad-world-on-kritik-mad-men-season-613.html>

Goodlad, Lauren M. E. *Victorian Literature and the Victorian State: Character and Governance in a Liberal Society*. Baltimore: Johns Hopkins UP, 2003. Print.

Goodlad, Lauren M. E. and Andrew Sartori. "The Ends of History: Introduction." *Victorian Studies* 55.4 (2013): 591–614. Print.

Goodlad, Lauren M.E., Nicholas Dames, and Carolyn Dever. *Trollopian Form*. Spec. cluster of *Literature Compass* 7.9 (2010): 861–75. Print.

Goodlad, Lauren M. E., Bruce Robbins, and Michael Rothberg. *States of Welfare*. Spec. issue of *Occasion: Interdisciplinary Studies in the Humanities* 2 (2010): n. pag. Web. 20 June 2011.

Goodlad, Lauren M.E. and Julia M. Wright. "Introduction and Keywords." *Victorian Internationalisms*. Spec. issue of *Romanticism and Victorianism on the Net* Nov. 2007: n. pag. Web. 23 Feb. 2011.

Goodlad, Lauren M.E. and Robert Rushing. "Groundhog Day." Weblog posting. *Kritik*. 1 Oct. 2010. 29 Dec. 2010. <http://unitcrit.blogspot.com/2010/10/mad-world-on-kritik-mad-men-season-413.html>.

Goodlad, Lauren M. E., Lilya Kaganovsky, and Robert A. Rushing, eds. *Mad Men, Mad World: Sex, Politics, Style, and the 1960s*. Duke UP, 2013.

Goscilo, Margaret. "Forster's Italian Comedies: Que[e]rying Heterosexuality Abroad." *Seeing Double: Revisioning Edwardian and Modernist Literature*. Ed. Carola M. Kaplan and Anne B. Simpson. New York: St. Martin's, 1996. 193–214. Print.

Goswami, Manu. "Rethinking the Modular Nation Form: Toward a Sociohistorical Conception of Nationalism." *Comparative Studies in Society and History* 44.4 (2002): 770–99. Print.

Green, Abigail. "The British Empire and the Jews: An Imperialism of Human Rights?" *Past and Present* 199.1 (2008): 175–205. Print.

Green, Anne. *Flaubert and the Historical Novel: Salammbô Reassessed*. Cambridge: Cambridge UP, 1982. Print.

Greenblatt, Stephen. "Towards a Poetics of Culture." Veeser 1–14.

[Greg, W.R.]. "The False Morality of Lady Novelists." *National Review* (Jan. 1859): 144–67. Print.

Greif, Mark. "You'll Love the Way it Makes You Feel." *London Review of Books* 30.20 (2008): 15–16. 23 Oct. 2008. Web. 29 Dec. 2010. <http://www.lrb.co.uk/v30/n20/mark-greif/youll-love-the-way-it-makes-you-feel>.

Grewal, Inderpal and Caren Kaplan. "Global Identities: Theorizing Transnational Studies of Sexuality." *GLQ: A Journal of Lesbian and Gay Studies* 7.4 (2001): 663–79.

Greiner, Donald J. "Narrative Technique in Wilkie Collins's *The Moonstone*." *Victorians Institute Journal* 3 (1974): 1–20. Print.

Hack, Daniel. "Close Reading at a Distance: The African Americanization of *Bleak House*." *Critical Inquiry* 34.4 (2008): 729–53. Print.
Hager, Kelly. *Dickens and the Rise of Divorce: The Failed Marriage-Plot and the Novel Tradition*. Farnham: Ashgate, 2010. Print.
Haight, Gordon S. *George Eliot: An Autobiography*. New York: Oxford UP, 1968. Print.
Haight, Gordon S., ed. *A Century of George Eliot Criticism*. Boston: Houghton Mifflin, 1965. Print.
Hall, Catherine. *Civilising Subjects: Metropole and Colony in the English Imagination, 1830–1867*. Chicago: U of Chicago P, 2002. Print.
Hall, Catherine. "Going a-Trolloping: Imperial Man Travels the Empire." *Gender and Imperialism*. Ed. Clare Midgley. Manchester: Manchester UP, 1998. 180–99. Print.
Hall, Catherine. "The Nation Within and Without." *Defining the Victorian Nation: Class, Race, Gender and the British Reform Act of 1867*. Ed. Catherine Hall, Keith McClelland and Jane Rendall. Cambridge: Cambridge UP, 2000. 179–233. Print.
Halperin, John. *Trollope and Politics: A Study of the Pallisers and Others*. London: Barnes, 1977. Print.
Hardt, Michael and Antonio Negri. *Empire*. Harvard: Harvard UP, 2000. Print.
Hardy, Barbara Nathan. "*Daniel Deronda*." *The Collected Essays of Barbara Hardy*. Vol. 1. Brighton, Sussex: The Harvester Press, 1987. 109–29. Print.
Hardy, Barbara Nathan. *Novels of George Eliot*. 1959. Biggleswaid: Watkiss Studios, 1994. Print.
Harvey, David. *Rebel Cities: From the Right to the City to the Urban Revolution*. London: Verso, 2012. Print.
Harvey, W.J. *The Art of George Eliot*. London: Chatto & Windus, 1961. Print.
Harvie, Christopher. *The Centre of Things: Political Fiction in Britain from Disraeli to the Present*. London: Unwin Hyman, 1991. Print.
Hawkins, Sherman. "Mr. Harding's Church Music." *ELH* 29.2 (1962): 202–23. Print.
Heilbrun, Carolyn. "Marriage Perceived: English Literature 1873–1941." *What Manner of Woman: Essays on English and American Life and Literature*. Ed. Marlene Springer. New York: New York UP, 1977. 160–83. Print.
Heine, Elizabeth. "Introduction." Forster, *Arctic* i–xxxv.
Heller, Tamar. "Afterword: *Masterpiece Theatre* and Ezra Jennings's Hair; Some Reflections on Where We've Been and Where We're Going in Collins Studies." Bachman and Cox 361–70.
Heller, Tamar. *Dead Secrets: Wilkie Collins and the Female Gothic*. New Haven: Yale UP, 1992. Print.
Hennelly, Mark M. "Detecting Collins' Diamond: From Serpentstone to Moonstone." *Nineteenth-Century Fiction* (1984): 25–47.
Henry, Nancy. *George Eliot and the British Empire*. Cambridge: Cambridge UP, 2002. Print.
Henry, Nancy. *The Life of George Eliot: A Critical Biography*. Oxford: Wiley-Blackwell, 2012. Print.
Henry, Nancy. "The *Romola* Code: 'Men of Appetites' in George Eliot's Historical Novel." *Victorian Literature and Culture* 39.2 (2011): 327–48. Print.
Hensley, Nathan. "*Armadale* and the Logic of Liberalism." *Victorian Studies* 51.4 (2009): 607–32. Print.
Hensley, Nathan. "Mr. Trollope, Lady Credit, and *The Way We Live Now*." *The Politics of Gender in Anthony Trollope's Novels: New Readings for the Twenty-First Century*. Ed.

Regenia Gagnier, Margaret Markwick, Deborah Morse. Farnham: Ashgate, 2009. 147–60. Print.

Herbert, Christopher. *Culture and Anomie: Ethnographic Imagination in the Nineteenth Century*. Chicago: U of Chicago P, 1991. Print.

Herbert, Christopher. *War of No Pity: The Indian Mutiny and Victorian Trauma*. Princeton UP, 2007. Print.

Hertz, Neil. *George Eliot's Pulse*. Stanford: Stanford UP, 2003. Print.

Heuman, Gad. "The British West Indies." A. Porter, *Oxford* 470–91.

Hewitt, Martin. *An Age of Equipoise? Reassessing Mid–Victorian Britain*. Farnham: Ashgate, 2000. Print.

Hewitt, Martin. ed. *The Victorian World*. New York: Routledge, 2012. Print.

Heywood, Christopher. "A Source For *Middlemarch*: Miss Braddon's *The Doctor's Wife* and *Madame Bovary*." *Revue de Littérature Comparée*. 44.2 (1970): 184–94. Print.

Heywood, Christopher. "French and American Sources of Victorian Realism." *Comparative Criticism: A Yearbook*. Ed. Elinor S. Shaffer. Vol. 1. Cambridge: Cambridge UP, 1979. 3 vols. 107–28. Print.

Hoad, Neville. "Arrested Development or the Queerness of Savages: Resisting Evolutionary Narratives of Difference." *Postcolonial Studies* 3.2 (2000): 133–58. Print.

Hobsbawm, Eric and Terrence Ranger, eds. *The Invention of Tradition*. Cambridge: Cambridge UP, 1984. Print.

Hobson, J. A. "The Ethics of Internationalism." *International Journal of Ethics* 17.1 (1906). 16–28. Print.

Hobson, J. A. *Imperialism: A Study*. 1902. Introd. Philip Siegelman. Ann Arbor: U of Michigan P, 1965. Print.

Hobson, J. A. *The Social Problem: Life and Work*. New York: James Pott and Company, 1902. Print.

Hollis, Patricia. "Anti-Slavery and British Working-class Radicalism in the Years of Reform." *Anti-Slavery, Religion, and Reform*. Eds. Christine Bolt and Seymour Drescher. Folkestone: W. Dawson, 1980. 294–315. Print.

Holt, Thomas C. *The Problem of Freedom: Race, Labor, and Politics in Jamaica and Britain, 1832–1938*. Baltimore: The Johns Hopkins UP, 1992. Print.

Homans, Margaret. *Royal Representations: Queen Victoria and British Culture, 1837–1876*. Chicago: U of Chicago P, 1999. Print.

Honig, Bonnie. *Antigone, Interrupted*. Cambridge: Cambridge UP, 2013. Print.

Honig, Bonnie. "Antigone's Two Laws: Greek Tragedy and the Politics of Humanism." *New Literary History* 41.1 (2010): 1–33. Print.

Honig, Bonnie. *Democracy and the Foreigner*. Princeton: Princeton UP, 2001. Print.

Hopkins, A. G., ed. *Globalization in World History*. New York: Norton, 2002. Print.

Howard, Michael. "The World According to Henry, From Metternich to Me." *Foreign Affairs*. (May/June 1994): n. pag. Web. 5 Jan. 2012.

Howells, William Dean. *My Literary Passions: Criticism and Fiction*. 1891. New York: Harper & Brothers, 1910. Print.

Hughes, J.R.T. "The Commercial Crisis of 1857." *Oxford Economic Papers* 8.2 (1956): 194–222. Print.

Hughes, Linda K. and Michael Lund. *The Victorian Serial*. Charlottesville: U of Virginia P., 1991. Print.

Humpherys, Anne. "The Scene of 'Divorce' in Nineteenth-Century English Fiction." *After Intimacy: The Culture of Divorce in the West since 1789*. Eds. Karl Leydecker and Nicholas White. New York: Peter Lang, 2007. 113–34. Print.

[Hutton, Richard Holt]. Unsigned Essay. *Spectator* 9 Dec. 1882: 1573–4. Rpt. in *Trollope: The Critical Heritage*. Ed. Donald Smalley. London: Routledge, 1969. 504–8. Print.

Hyndman, J. "Mind the Gap: Bridging Feminist and Political Geography through Geopolitics." *Political Geography* 23 (2004): 307–22. Print.

Irigaray, Luce. *An Ethics of Sexual Difference*. Trans. Carolyn Burke and Gillian C. Gill. Ithaca: Cornell UP, 1993. Print.

Itzoff, Dave. "Matthew Weiner Closes the Books on Season 4 of *Mad Men*." Weblog posting. *Arts Beat. New York Times Online*. 17 Oct. 2010. Web. 29 Dec. 2010. <http://artsbeat.blogs.nytimes.com/2010/10/17/matthew-weiner-closes-the-books-on-season-4-of-mad-men>.

Jaffe, Audrey. "Trollope in the Stock Market: Irrational Exuberance and *The Prime Minister*." *Victorian Studies* 45.1 (2002): 43–64. Print.

James, Henry. "Anthony Trollope." *Partial Portraits* 97–136.

[James, Henry]. Rev. of *Middlemarch* by George Eliot. *The Galaxy* 15 (Mar. 1873): 424–8. Print.

[James, Henry] "The Art of Fiction." *Longman's Magazine* 4.23 (Sept. 1884): 502–91. Print.

[James, Henry] "Flaubert's Temptation of St. Anthony." *The Nation* 4 June, 1874. 365–6. Print.

James, Henry. *Notes on Novelists with Some Other Notes*. New York: Scribners, 1914. 65–108. Print.

[James, Henry]. Rev. of *Lothair* by Benjamin Disraeli. *The Atlantic Monthly*. 26 (August 1870). 249–51. Print.

[James, Henry] "The Minor French Novelists." *The Galaxy* 21 (Feb. 1876): 219–33. Print.

James, Henry *Partial Portraits*. 1888. London: Macmillan, 1899. Print.

Jameson, Fredric. *Antinomies of Realism*. London: Verso, 2013. Print.

Jameson, Fredric. "Antinomies of the Realism-Modernism Debate." Afterword. Esty and Lye 475–85.

Jameson, Fredric. *A Singular Modernity*. London: Verso, 2002. Print.

Jameson, Fredric. "Cognitive Mapping." Nelson and Grossberg. 347–58. Print.

Jameson, Fredric. "Globalization and Political Strategy." *New Left Review* 4 (2000): 49–68.

Jameson, Fredric. *The Geopolitical Aesthetic: Cinema and Space in the World System*. Bloomington: Indiana UP, 1992. Print.

Jameson, Fredric. "Introduction." Lukács, *The Historical Novel* 1–8. Print.

Jameson, Fredric. "Modernism and Imperialism." *Nationalism, Colonialism, and Literature*. Ed. Eagleton, Terry, Fredric Jameson, and Edward Said. Minneapolis: U of Minnesota P, 1990. 41–66. Print.

Jameson, Fredric. "A Note on Literary Realism in Conclusion." Beaumont 261–71.

Jameson, Fredric. *The Political Unconscious: Narrative as a Socially Symbolic Act*. Ithaca: Cornell UP, 1981. Print.

Jameson, Fredric. "Postmodernism and Consumer Society." *The Anti-Aesthetic: Essays on Postmodern Culture*. Ed. Hal Foster. Townsend: Bay Press, 1983. 111–25. Print.

Jameson, Fredric. *Postmodernism, Or the Cultural Logic of Late Capitalism*. Durham: Duke UP, 1990. Print.

Jameson, Fredric. "Progress versus Utopia, Or, Can We Imagine the Future?" *Archaeologies of the Future: The Desire Called Utopia and Other Science Fictions*. London: Verso, 2005. 281–95. Print.

Jameson, Fredric. "Realism and Utopia in *The Wire*." *Criticism* 52.3–4 (2010): 359–72. Print.
Jameson, Fredric. "The Realist Floor-Plan." *On Signs*. Ed. Marshall Blonsky. Baltimore: Johns Hopkins UP, 1985. 373–83. Print.
Jameson, Fredric. *Signatures of the Visible*. New York: Routledge, 1992. Print.
Jameson, Fredric. *A Singular Modernity: Essay on the Ontology of the Present*. London: Verso, 2002. Print.
Jay, Martin. *Cultural Semantics: Keywords of Our Time*. Amherst: U of Massachusetts P, 1998. Print.
Joshi, Priya. "Globalizing Victorian Studies." *Victorian World Literatures*. Spec. issue of *The Yearbook of English Studies* 41.2 (2011): 20–40. Print.
Joshi, Priya. *In Another Country: Colonialism, Culture, and the English Novel in India*. New York: Columbia UP, 2002. Print.
Joyce, Simon. *The Victorians in the Rearview Mirror*. Columbus: Ohio UP, 2007.
Kaganovsky, Lilya. "The Missing Piece." Weblog posting. *Kritik*. 29 Jul. 2010. Web. 29 Dec. 2010. <http://unitcrit.blogspot.com/2010/07/mad-world-on-kritik-mad-men-season-41.html>.
Kalmar, Ivan Davidson and Derek Penslar, eds. *Orientalism and the Jew*. Hanover: UP of New England, 2005. Print.
Kaplan, Amy. "Exodus and the Americanization of Zionism." Presentation at the University of Illinois, Urbana-Champaign, Champaign-Urbana. 8 Nov. 2010. Public Lecture.
Kaye, Richard A. *The Flirt's Tragedy: Desire without End in Victorian and Edwardian Fiction*. Charlottesville: U of Virginia P, 2002. Print.
Keirstead, Christopher M. "Stranded at the Border: Browning, France, and the Challenge of Cosmopolitanism in *Red Cotton Night–Cap Country*." *Victorian Poetry* 43.4 (2005): 411–34. Print.
Kendrick, Walter M. "Balzac and British Realism: Mid-Victorian Theories of the Novel." *Victorian Studies* 20.1 (1976): 5–24. Print.
Kendrick, Walter M. "*The Eustace Diamonds*: The Truth of Trollope's Fiction." *ELH* 46.1 (1979): 136–57. Print.
Kermode, Frank. *The Sense of an Ending: Studies in the Theory of Fiction*. 1967. New York: Oxford UP, 2000. Print.
Kincaid, James R. *The Novels of Anthony Trollope*. Oxford: Oxford UP, 1974. Print.
King, Charles William. *The Natural History of Precious Stones and of the Precious Metals*. (1) First edition and (2) 1867 revised edition. London: Bell and Daldy, 1865. Print.
Kinoshita, Sharon. "Worlding Medieval Literature." McDonald and Suleiman 3–20.
Knight, L. A. "The Royal Titles Act and India." *The Historical Journal* 11.3 (1968): 488–507. Print.
Knoepflmacher, U.C. "The Counterworld of Victorian Fiction and *The Woman in White*." *The Worlds of Victorian Fiction*. Ed. Jerome Hamilton Buckley. Cambridge: Harvard UP, 1975. 350–70. Print.
Kostal, Rande W. *A Jurisprudence of Power. Victorian Empire and the Rule of Law*. Oxford: Oxford UP, 2008. Print.
Kriegel, Lara. "Narrating the Subcontinent in 1851: India at the Crystal Palace." *The Great Exhibition of 1851*. Ed. Louise Purbrick. Vancouver: U of British Columbia P, 2001. 146–78. Print.

Kriegel, Lara. "The Pudding and the Palace: Labor, Print Culture, and Imperial Britain in 1851." *After the Imperial Turn: Thinking with and through the Nation*. Burton 230–46.

Kucich, John. *The Power of Lies: Transgression in Victorian Fiction*. Ithaca: Cornell UP, 1994. Print.

Kucich, John. "The Unfinished Historicist Project: In Praise of Suspicion." *Victoriographies* 1.1 (2011): 58–78. Print.

Kurnick, David. "Abstraction and the Subject of Novel Reading: Drifting through *Romola*." *Novel: A Forum on Fiction* 42.3 (2009): 490–96. Print.

Kurnick, David. *Empty Houses: Theatrical Failure and the Novel*. Princeton: Princeton UP, 2012. Print.

Kurnick, David. "Unspeakable George Eliot." *Victorian Literature and Culture* 38.2 (2010): 489–509. Print.

LaCapra, Dominick. *History in Transit: Experience, Identity, Critical Theory*. Ithaca: Cornell UP, 2004. Print.

LaCapra, Dominick. *"Madame Bovary" on Trial*. Ithaca: Cornell UP, 1986. Print.

LaCapra, Dominick. "Review of *The Political Unconscious: Narrative as a Socially Symbolic Act* by Fredric Jameson." *History and Theory* 21.1 (February 1982): 83–106. Print.

Laclau, Ernesto, and Chantal Mouffe. *Hegemony and Socialist Strategy: Towards a Radical Democratic Politics*. Verso, 1985. Print.

Lambert, David and Alan Lester, eds. *Colonial Lives across the British Empire: Imperial Careering in the Long Nineteenth Century*. Cambridge: Cambridge UP, 2006. Print.

Lane, Christopher. "Forster and Sexuality." *The Cambridge Companion to E. M. Forster*. Ed. David Bradshaw. New York: Cambridge UP, 2007. 104–19. Print.

Lane, Christopher. *The Ruling Passion: British Colonial Allegory and the Paradox of Homosexual Desire*. Durham: Duke UP, 1995. Print.

Langbauer, Laurie. *Novels of Everyday Life: The Series in English Fiction, 1850–1930*. Ithaca: Cornell UP, 1999. Print.

Langland, Elizabeth. *Nobody's Angels: Middle-Class Women and Domestic Ideology in Victorian Culture*. Ithaca: Cornell UP, 1995. Print.

Latour, Bruno. "Why Has Critique Run Out of Steam? From Matters of Fact to Matters of Concern." *Critical Inquiry* 30.2 (2004): 225–48.

Latour, Bruno. *Reassembling the Social: An Introduction to Actor-Network-Theory*. Oxford: Oxford UP, 2005. Print.

Law, Graham. *Serializing Fiction in the Victorian Press*. New York: Palgrave, 2000. Print.

Law, Graham, and Andrew Maunder. *Wilkie Collins: A Literary Life*. New York: Palgrave, 2008. Print.

Law, Robin. "Abolition and Imperialism: International Law and the British Suppression of the Atlantic Slave Trade." D. Peterson 150–74.

Lazarus, Neil. *Nationalism and Cultural Practice in the Postcolonial World*. Cambridge: Cambridge UP, 1999. Print.

Leavis, F. R. "E. M. Forster." *Forster: A Collection of Critical Essays*. Ed. Malcolm Bradbury. Engelwood Cliffs, NJ: Prentice-Hall, 1966. 34–47. Print.

Leckie, Barbara. *Culture and Adultery: The Novel, the Newspaper, and the Law, 1857–1914*. Philadelphia: U of Pennsylvania P, 1999. Print.

Leighton, Mary Elizabeth, and Lisa Surridge. "The Transatlantic *Moonstone*: A Study of the Illustrated Serial in *Harper's Weekly*." *Victorian Periodicals Review* 42.3 (2009): 207–43. Print.

Lesjak, Carolyn. "Reading Dialectically." *Criticism* 55.2 (2013): 233–77. Print.

Lester, Alan. "Race and Citizenship: Colonial Inclusions and Exclusions." Hewitt, *Victorian* 381–97.
Levinas, Emmanuel. *Totality and Infinity: An Essay on Exteriority*. Trans. Alphonso Lingis. Pittsburgh: Duquesne UP, 1969. Print.
Levine, Caroline. "Formal Pasts and Formal Possibilities in Victorian Studies." *Literature Compass* 4.4 (2007): 1241–56. Print.
Levine, Caroline. "Historicism and its Limits: An Antislavery Sonnet, *Bleak House*, and *The Wire*." Unpublished essay, 10 Aug. 2010.
Levine, Caroline. *The Serious Pleasures of Suspense: Victorian Realism and Narrative Doubt*. Charlottesville: U of Virginia P, 2003. Print.
Levine, Caroline. "The Shock of the Banal." *Mad World: Sex, Politics, Style and the 1960s*. Ed. Lauren M.E. Goodlad, Lilya Kaganovsky, and Robert A. Rushing. Durham: Duke UP. 133–44.
Levine, Caroline and Mark W. Turner, eds. *From Author to Text: Re-reading George Eliot's Romola*. Farnham: Ashgate, 1998. Print.
Levine, George. "Literary Realism Reconsidered: 'The World in its Length and Breadth.'" Beaumont, *Adventures* 17–32.
Levine, George. *The Realistic Imagination: English Fiction from Frankenstein to Lady Chatterley*. Chicago: U of Chicago P, 1981. Print.
Levine, George. "*Romola* as Fable." *Critical Essays on George Eliot*. Ed. Barbara Hardy. London: Routledge, 1970. Print.
Levine, June Perry. "The Tame in Pursuit of the Savage: The Posthumous Fiction of E. M. Forster." *PMLA* 99.1 (1984): 72–88. Print.
[Lewes, George H.]. "Balzac and George Sand." *Foreign Quarterly Review* 33.66 (1844): 265–98. Print.
[Lewes, George H.]. "Continental Literati." *The Monthly Magazine* 95.545 (May 1842): 463–72. Print.
[Lewes, George H.]. "The Lady Novelists." *Westminster Review* 58 (1852): 129–41. Print.
[Lewes, George H.]. "Realism in Art: Recent German Fiction." *Westminster Review* 70 (1858): 271–87. Print.
[Lewes, George H.]. "Recent Novels: French and English." *Fraser's Magazine* 36.216 (1847): 689–95. Print.
Liftin, Karen. "Towards an Integral Perspective on World Politics: Secularism, Sovereignty and the Challenge of Global Ecology." *Millennium: Journal of International Studies* 32.1 (2003): 29–56. Print.
Lindner, Christoph. *Fictions of Commodity Culture: From the Victorian to the Postmodern*. Farnham: Ashgate, 2003. Print.
Littledale, Richard F. "New Novels." *The Star*. 3 August 1876. n.p.
Litvak, Joseph. "Jewish Geography: Trollope and the Question of Style." *Nineteenth-Century Geographies: The Transformation of Space from the Victorian Age to the American Century*. Ed. Helena Michie and Ronald R. Thomas. New Brunswick: Rutgers UP, 2003. 123–34. Print.
Lloyd, David. "Race under Representation." *Culture/Contexture: Explorations in Anthropology and Literary Studies*. Ed. E. Valentine Daniel and Jeffrey M. Peck. Berkeley: U of California P, 1996. 249–72. Print.
Loesberg, Jonathan. "Deconstruction, Historicism, and Overdetermination: Dislocations of the Marriage Plots in *Robert Elsmere* and *Dombey and Son*." *Victorian Studies* 33.3 (1990): 441–64. Print.
Loesberg, Jonathan. "The Ideology of Narrative Form in Sensation Fiction." *Representations* 13 (Winter, 1986): 115–38. Print.

Lonergan, Patrick. "The Representation of Phineas Finn: Anthony Trollope's Palliser Series and Victorian Ireland." *Victorian Literature and Culture* 32.1 (2004): 147–58. Print.
Long, David. *Towards a New Liberal Internationalism: the International Theory of J.A. Hobson*. New York: Cambridge UP, 1996. Print.
Lonoff, Sue. *Wilkie Collins and His Victorian Readers: A Study In The Rhetoric of Authorship*. New York: AMS, 1982. Print.
Loomba, Ania. *Colonialism/Postcolonialism*. New York: Routledge, 1998. Print.
Lorimer, Douglas A. *Colour, Class, and the Victorians: English Attitudes to the Negro in the Mid-Nineteenth Century*. Leicester: Leicester UP, 1978. Print.
Loshitzky, Yosefa. "National Rebirth as a Movie: Otto Preminger's *Exodus*." *National Identities* 4.2 (July 2002): 119–31. Print.
Lukács, Georg. *Essays on Realism*. Ed. Rodney Livingstone. Cambridge, MA: The MIT Press, 1983. Print.
Lukács, Georg. "Hegel's Aesthetics." 1951. Trans. David Taffel. *Graduate Faculty Philosophy Journal* 23.2 (2002): 87–124. Print.
Lukács, Georg. *The Historical Novel*. Trans. Hannah Mitchell and Stephen Mitchell. Lincoln: U of Nebraska P, 1983. Print.
Lukács, Georg. *Studies in European Realism: A Sociological Survey of the Writings of Balzac, Stendhal, Tolstoy, Gorki and Others*. Trans. Edith Bone. London: Hillway, 1950. Print.
Lynn, Martin. "British Policy, Trade, and Informal Empire in the Mid–Nineteenth Century." A. Porter, *Oxford* 101–21. Print.
Macaulay, Thomas Babington. "Lord Clive." *Historical Essays*. Ed. Charles Downer Hazen. New York: Charles Scribner's Sons, 1921. 184–264. Print.
Macaulay, Thomas Babington. "Minute of the 2nd of February, 1835: Indian Education." *Macaulay, Prose and Poetry*. Ed. G.M. Young. Cambridge: Harvard UP, 1967. 719–30. Print.
Macpherson, C. B. *The Political Theory of Possessive Individualism: Hobbes to Locke*. Oxford: Clarendon, 1962. Print.
Mahmood, Saba. *Politics of Piety: The Islamic Revival and the Feminist Subject*. Princeton: Princeton UP, 2005. Print.
Malachuk, Daniel. "*Romola* and Victorian Liberalism." *Victorian Literature and Culture* 36.1 (2008): 41–57. Print.
Malcolmson, Scott L. "The Varieties of Cosmopolitan Experience." Cheah and Robbins 233–45.
Malik, Charu. "To Express the Subject of Friendship: Masculine Desire and Colonialism in *A Passage to India*." Martin and Piggford 221–35.
Mamdani, Mahmood. *Citizen and Subject: Contemporary Africa and the Legacy of Late Colonialism*. Princeton: Princeton UP, 1996. Print.
Manavalli, Krishna. "Collins, Colonial Crime, and the Brahmin Sublime: The Orientalist Vision of a Hindu-Brahmin India in *The Moonstone*." *Comparative Critical Studies* 4.1 (2007): 67–86. Print.
Mansel, H.L. "Sensation Novels." *Quarterly Review* 113.226 (April 1863): 481–514. Print.
Mantena, Karuna. *Alibis of Empire: Henry Maine and the Ends of Liberal Imperialism*. Princeton: Princeton UP, 2010. Print.
Mantena, Karuna. "The Crisis of Liberal Imperialism." *Victorian Visions of Global Order: Empire and International Relations in Nineteenth-Century Political Thought*. Ed. Duncan Bell. Cambridge: Cambridge UP, 2007. 113–35. Print.

Marcus, Sharon. *Between Women: Friendship, Desire, and Marriage in Victorian England.* Princeton: Princeton UP, 2007. Print.

Marcus, Sharon. "Comparative Sapphism." Cohen and Dever 251–85.

Marcus, Sharon. "Same Difference? Transnationalism, Comparative Literature, and Victorian Studies." *Victorian Studies* 45.4 (2003): 677–86. Print.

Marder, Elissa. *Dead Time: Temporal Disorders in the Wake of Modernity.* Stanford: Stanford UP, 2002. Print.

Markley, A. A. "E. M. Forster's Reconfigured Gaze and the Creation of a Homoerotic Subjectivity." *Twentieth Century Literature* 47.2 (2001): 268–92. Print.

Markovitz, Stefanie. "Form Things: Looking at Genre through Victorian Diamonds." *Victorian Studies* 52.4 (2010): 591–619. Print.

Martin, Carol A. *George Eliot's Serial Fiction.* Columbus: The Ohio State UP, 1994. Print.

Martin, Robert K. "Edward Carpenter and the Double Structure of *Maurice.*" Tambling 100–14.

Martin, Robert K. "'It Must Have Been the Umbrella': Forster's Queer Begetting." Martin and Piggford 255–74.

Martin, Robert K. and George Piggford. *Queer Forster.* Chicago: U of Chicago P, 1997. Print.

Martineau, Harriet. *Suggestions Towards the Future Government of India.* 1858. *Harriet Martineau's Writing on the British Empire.* Vol. 5 *The India Question.* Ed. Deborah Logan. London: Pickering & Chatto, 2004. 169–248. Print.

Marx, John. "Modernism and the Female Imperial Gaze." *Novel: A Forum on Fiction* 32.1 (1998): 51–75. Print.

Marx, Karl. *Economic and Philosophical Manuscripts of 1844.* Ed. Dirk J. Struik. Trans. Martin Milligan. New York: International, 1964. Print.

Marx, Karl. *The Eighteenth Brumaire of Louis Bonaparte. The Marx-Engels Reader.* 2nd ed. Ed. Robert C. Tucker. New York: Norton, 1978. 594–617. Print.

Marx, Karl. "The Indian Question." *New York Tribune.* 14 August 1857. *Marxists.org.* Marxists Internet Archive, n.d. Web. 24 June 2011.

Marx, Karl. "The Story of the Life of Lord Palmerston." 1853. *New York Tribune. Marxists.org.* Marxists Internet Archive, n.d. Web. 23 Oct. 2008.

Marx, Karl. "Theses on Feuerbach." *The Marx-Engels Reader.* 2nd ed. Ed. Robert C. Tucker. New York: Norton, 1978. 143–6. Print.

Marx, Karl, and Friedrich Engels. *Manifesto of the Communist Party. The Marx–Engels Reader.* Ed. Robert C. Tucker. 2nd ed. New York: Norton, 1978. 473–500. Print.

[Masson, David]. "Politics of the Present, Foreign and Domestic." *Macmillan's Magazine* Nov. 1859: 1–10. Print.

Masterman, C.F.G., ed. *The Heart of the Empire: Discussions of Problems of Modern City Life in England.* 1901. Ed. and Introd. by Bentley B. Gilbert. Brighton: The Harvester Press, 1973. Print.

Masterman, C.F.G. Preface. Masterman vii–xii.

Masterman, C.F.G. "Review, *Daily News.*" Gardner 52–5.

Matlock, Jann. "The Limits of Reformism: The Novel, Censorship, and the Politics of Adultery in Nineteenth-Century France." *Cultural Institutions of the Novel.* Ed. Deidre Lynch and William B. Warner. Durham: Duke UP, 1996. 335–68. Print.

May, Brian. *The Modernist as Pragmatist: E. M. Forster and the Fate of Liberalism.* Columbia: U of Missouri P, 1997. Print.

McCormack, W.J. "Introduction." Trollope, *The Eustace Diamonds* xi–xxxii.

McDonald, Christie and Susan Suleiman, eds. *French Global: A New Approach to Literary History*. New York: Columbia, UP, 2011. Print.

McGowan, John. "The Turn of George Eliot's Realism." *Nineteenth-Century Fiction* 35.2 (1980): 171–92. Print.

McMaster, Juliet. *Trollope's Palliser Novels: Theme and Pattern*. New York: Oxford UP, 1978. Print.

Mehta, Jaya. "English Romance, Indian Violence." *Centennial Review* 39.3 (1995): 611–57. Print.

Mehta, Uday Singh. *Liberalism and Empire: A Study in Nineteenth-Century British Liberal Thought*. Chicago: U of Chicago P, 1999. Print.

Menke, Richard. *Telegraphic Realism: Victorian Fiction and Other Information Systems*. Stanford: Stanford UP, 2007. Print.

Meredith, George. "Belles Lettres and Art." *Westminster Review* 68.134 (Oct. 1857): 585–604. Print.

Merivale, Herman. "The Colonial Question in 1870." *Fortnightly Review*. Vol. 13. London: Chapman and Hall, 1870. 152–75. Print.

Merivale, Herman. *Lectures on Colonization and Colonies*. Vol. 2. (1870): 152–75.

Metcalf, Thomas. *Ideologies of the Raj. The New Cambridge History of India*. Vol. 3, Part 4. Ed. Gordon Johnson. Cambridge: Cambridge UP, 1995. Print.

Michie, Elsie B. "Buying Brains: Trollope, Oliphant, and Vulgar Victorian Commerce." *Victorian Studies* 44.1 (2001): 77–97. Print.

Michie, Elsie B. "The Odd Couple: Anthony Trollope and Henry James." *The Henry James Review* 27.1 (2006): 10–23. Print.

Michie, Elsie B. *Vulgar Question of Money: Heiresses, Materialism, and the Novel of Manners from Jane Austen to Henry James*. Baltimore: The Johns Hopkins UP, 2011. Print.

Michie, Helena. *Victorian Honeymoons: Journeys to the Conjugal*. Cambridge: Cambridge UP, 2006. Print.

Midgley, Clare. "Anti-Slavery and the Roots of Imperial Feminism." *Gender and Imperialism*. Ed. Clare Midgley. Manchester: Manchester UP, 1998. 161–79. Print.

Milley, Henry James Wye. "*The Eustace Diamonds* and *The Moonstone*." *Studies in Philology* 36.4 (Oct., 1939): 651–63. Print.

Mill, John Stuart. *Autobiography of John Stuart Mill*. 1873. Ed. Jack Stillinger. Boston: Riverside, 1969. Print.

Mill, John Stuart. *(C.W.) The Collected Works of John Stuart Mill*. Ed. John M. Robson. 33 vols. Toronto: U of Toronto P, 1963–91. Print.

Mill, John Stuart. "The Contest in America." 1862. *Collected Works* 21: 125–42.

Mill, John Stuart. *Considerations on Representative Government*. 1861. Amherst, NY: Prometheus, 1991. Print.

Mill, John Stuart. "The East India Company's Charter." 1852. *Collected Works* 30: 31–74. Print.

Mill, John Stuart. "East India Revenue." 1867. *Collected Works* 28: 233–6.

Mill, John Stuart. "To John Morley." 1866. *Collected Works* 16: 1202–3.

Mill, John Stuart. "Memorandum on Improvements in the Administration of India During the Last Thirty Years." 1858. *Collected Works* 30: 90–160.

Mill, John Stuart. "To Pasquale Villari." 1858. *Collected Works* 15: 560–62.

Mill, John Stuart. "Principles of Political Economy with Some of Their Applications to Social Philosophy." 1848. *Collected Works* 3.

Mill, John Stuart. "The Subjection of Women." 1869. *On Liberty; With The Subjection of Women; and Chapters on Socialism*. Ed. Stefan Collini. Cambridge: Cambridge UP, 1989. 117–219. Print.

Mill, John Stuart. *Utilitarianism and Other Essays*. 1863. Ed. Alan Ryan. New York: Penguin, 1987. Print.

Miller, Andrew H. *The Burdens of Perfection: On Ethics and Reading in Nineteenth-Century British Literature*. Ithaca: Cornell UP, 2008. Print.

Miller, Andrew H. "Lives Unled in Realist Fiction." *Representations* 98 (2007): 118–34. Print.

Miller, Andrew H. *Novels behind Glass: Commodity Culture and Victorian Narrative*. Cambridge: Cambridge UP, 1995. Print.

Miller, D. A. *The Novel and the Police*. Berkeley: U of California P, 1988. Print.

Milley, Henry J. W. "The Eustace Diamonds And The Moonstone." *Studies In Philology* 36 (1939): 651–63. Print.

Minca, Claudio. "Agamben's Geographies Of Modernity." *Political Geography* 26.1 (2007): 78–97. Print.

Mittell, Jason. "Serial Boxes: The Cultural Value of Long-Form American Television." Weblog posting. *Just TV*. 10 Jan. 2009. Web. 29 Dec. 2010. <http://justtv.wordpress.com/2010/01/20/serial-boxes/>.

Moir, Martin, Douglas Peers, and Lynn Zastrouphil, eds. *J.S. Mill's Encounter with India*. Buffalo: U of Toronto P, 1999. Print.

Monkhouse, A. N. Initialed review of *Howards End*. Gardner 123–4.

Moody-Adams, Michele M. "Gender and the Complexity of Moral Voices." *Feminist Ethics*. Ed. Claudia Card. Lawrence: UP of Kansas, 1991. 195–213. Print.

Moore, George. "Some of Balzac's Minor Pieces." *Fortnightly Review* 52 (1859): 491–504. Print.

Moore, Robin J. "Imperial India, 1858–1914." A. Porter, *Oxford* 422–46.

Moore, Robin J. "John Stuart Mill and Royal India." Moir, Peers, and Zastrouphil 87–110.

Moore, Robin J. "John Stuart Mill at East India House." *Historical Studies* 20.81 (1983): 497–519. Print.

Moretti, Franco. "Conjectures on World Literature." *New Left Review* 1 (2000): 54–68. Print.

Moretti, Franco. *Graphs, Maps, Trees: Abstract Models for Literary History*. New York: Verso, 2007. Print.

Moretti, Franco. *The Way of the World: The Bildungsroman in European Culture*. Trans. Albert Sbragia. New York: Verso, 1987. Print.

Morley, John. "England and the Annexation of Mysore." *Fortnightly Review* 6 (1866): 257–71. Print.

Morse, Deborah Denenholz. *Reforming Trollope: Race, Gender, and Englishness in the Novels of Anthony Trollope*. Farnham: Ashgate 2013. Print.

Mosse, George Lachmann. *Nationalism and Sexuality: Respectability and Abnormal Sexuality in Modern Europe*. New York: H. Fertig, 1985. Print.

Mufti, Aamir R. *Enlightenment in the Colony: The Jewish Question and the Crisis of Postcolonial Culture*. Princeton: Princeton UP, 2007. Print.

Mukherjee, Mithi. "Justice, War, and the Imperium: India and Britain in Edmund Burke's Prosecutorial Speeches in the Impeachment Trial of Warren Hastings." *Law and History Review* 23.3 (2005): 81 pars. Web. 24 June 2011.

Mukherjee, Pablo. "Introduction: Victorian World Literatures." *Victorian World Literatures*. Spec. issue of *The Yearbook of English Studies* 41.2 (2011): 1–19. Print.

Nairn, Tom. *The Enchanted Glass: Britain and its Monarchy*. London: Verso, 2011. Print.

Nardin, Jane. *Trollope and Victorian Moral Philosophy*. Athens: Ohio UP, 1996. Print.

Nayder, Lillian. "Agents of Empire in *The Woman in White*." *Victorian Newsletter* 83 (1993): 1–7. Print.

Nayder, Lillian. "Collins and Empire." J. Taylor, *Cambridge* 139–52.

Nayder, Lillian. *Wilkie Collins*. New York: Twayne Publishers, 1997. Print.

Nead, Lynda. *Victorian Babylon: People, Streets and Images in Nineteenth-Century London*. New Haven: Yale UP, 2005. Print.

Nealon, Christopher. "Reading on the Left." Best and Marcus 22–50.

Nelson, Cary, and Lawrence Grossberg, eds. *Marxism and the Interpretation of Culture*. Urbana: U of Illinois P, 1988. Print.

Nelson, Cary, and Lawrence Grossberg. "Introduction: The Territory of Marxism." Nelson and Grossberg 1–16.

Newsinger, John. *Fenianism in Mid-Victorian Britain*. London: Pluto Press, 1994. Print.

Newton, Kenneth M. *Modernizing George Eliot: The Writer as Artist, Intellectual, Proto-Modernist, Cultural Critic*. London: Bloomsbury, 2011.

Nixon, Rob. *Slow Violence and the Environmentalism of the Poor*. Cambridge: Harvard UP, 2011. Print.

Novak, Daniel. *Realism, Photography, and Nineteenth-Century Fiction*. Cambridge: Cambridge UP, 2008. Print.

Nunokawa, Jeff. *The Afterlife of Property: Domestic Security and the Victorian Novel*. Princeton: Princeton UP, 2009.

O'Brien, Patrick. "The Myth of Anglophone Succession: From British Primacy to American Hegemony." *New Left Review* 24 (2003): 113–34. Print.

O'Connor, Maura. *The Romance of Italy and the English Political Imagination*. New York: St. Martin's, 1998. Print.

Okin, Susan. "Reason and Feeling in Thinking about Justice." *Ethics* 99.2 (1989): 229–49. Print.

O'Sullivan, Sean. "Old, New, Borrowed, Blue: Deadwood and Serial Fiction." *Reading Deadwood: A Western to Swear By*. London: Tauris (2006): 115–29. Print.

Ó Tuathail, Gearóid. *Critical Geopolitics: The Politics of Writing Global Space*. Minneapolis: U of Minnesota P, 1996. Print.

Pagden, Anthony. *Peoples and Empires: A Short History of European Migration, Exploration, and Conquest, from Greece to the Present*. New York: Modern Library, 2003. Print.

Page, Norman, ed. *Wilkie Collins: The Critical Heritage*. New York: Routledge, 1974. Print.

Palmer, Beth. "Are the Victorians Still with Us? Victorian Sensation Fiction and Its Legacies in the Twenty-First Century." *Victorian Studies* 52.1 (Autumn 2009): 86–94. Print.

Palumbo-Liu, David, Bruce Robbins, and Nirvana Tanoukhi, eds. *Immanuel Wallerstein and the Problem of the World: System, Scale, Culture*. Durham: Duke UP, 2011. Print.

Palumbo-Liu, David, Bruce Robbins, and Nirvana Tanoukhi. "Introduction: The Most Important Thing Happening." Palumbo-Liu, Robbins, Tanoukhi 1–23.

Park, Hyungji. "'The Story of Our Lives': *The Moonstone*, the Mutiny and *All the Year Round*." *Negotiating India in the Nineteenth-Century Media*. Ed. David Finkelstein and Douglas M. Peers. New York: Palgrave, 2000. Print.

Parliamentary Debates, House of Commons, Deb 27, July 1857, Vol. 147, cc440–546. Web. 28 June 2011.

Parliamentary Debates, House of Commons, Deb 22, February 1867, Vol. 185, cc827–41. Web. 28 June 2011.

Parry, Benita. "Materiality and Mystification in E. M. Forster's *A Passage to India.*" *Novel: A Forum on Fiction* 31.2 (1999): 174–94. Print.

Parry, Benita. "The Politics of Representation in *A Passage to India.*" Tambling 133–50.

Paskow, Jacqueline Merriam. "Rethinking Madame Bovary's Motives for Committing Suicide." *Modern Language Review* 100.2 (2005): 323–39. Print.

Peperzak, Adriaan Theodoor. *To the Other: An Introduction to the Philosophy of Emmanuel Levinas.* West Lafayette: Purdue UP, 1993. Print.

Peters, Catherine. *The King of Inventors: A Life of Wilkie Collins.* Princeton: Princeton UP, 1993. Print.

Peterson, Derek R., ed. *Abolitionism and Imperialism in Britain, Africa, and the Atlantic.* Ed. Derek R. Peterson. Athens: Ohio UP, 2010. Print.

Peterson, Derek R. "Abolitionism and Political Thought in Britain and East Africa." Peterson 1–38.

Peterson, Richard K. "Marx, Race, and the Political Problem of Identity." *Race and Racism in Modern Philosophy.* Ed. Andrew Valls. Ithaca: Cornell UP, 2005. 235–55. Print.

Pitts, Jennifer. *A Turn to Empire: The Rise of Imperial Liberalism in Britain and France.* Princeton: Princeton UP, 2006. Print.

Plotz, John. "One-Way Traffic: George Lamming and the Portable Empire." *After the Imperial Turn: Thinking with and through the Nation.* Burton 308–23.

Plotz, John. *Portable Property: Victorian Culture on the Move.* Princeton: Princeton UP, 2009. Print.

Pocock, J.G.A. *The Machiavellian Moment: Florentine Political Thought and the Atlantic Republican Tradition.* Princeton: Princeton UP, 1975. Print.

Polan, Dana. "Invisible City." Weblog posting. *Museum of the Moving Image.* 28 Jul. 2008. 29 Dec. 2010. <http://www.movingimagesource.us/articles/invisible-city-20080728>.

Polan, Dana. *The Sopranos.* Durham: Duke UP, 2009. Print.

Poovey, Mary. *Making a Social Body: British Cultural Formation, 1830-1864.* Chicago: U of Chicago P, 1995. Print.

Popper, Nathaniel. "Diamonds as a Commodity." *The New York Times.* 14 Apr. 2012: B1+. Print.

Porter, Andrew, ed. *The Oxford History of the British Empire, Vol. 3: The Nineteenth Century.* Oxford: Oxford UP, 1999. Print.

Porter, Andrew. "Trusteeship, Anti-Slavery and Humanitarianism." A. Porter, *Oxford* 198–221.

Porter, Bernard. *The Absent-Minded Imperialists.* Oxford: Oxford UP, 2004. Print.

Porter, Bernard. *Britain, Europe and the World, 1850–1986: Delusions of Grandeur.* London: Allen & Unwin, 1987. Print.

Potolsky, Matthew. *The Decadent Republic of Letters: Taste, Politics, and Cosmopolitan Community from Baudelaire to Beardsley.* Philadelphia: U of Pennsylvania P, 2012.

Pratt, Mary Louise. *Imperial Eyes: Travel Writing and Transculturation.* New York: Routledge, 1992. Print.

Prendergast, Christopher, ed. *Cultural Materialism: On Raymond Williams.* Minneapolis: U of Minnesota P, 1995. Print.

Price, Leah. "From The History of a Book to A History of the Book" Best and Marcus. 20–38.

Proctor, Robert N. "Anti-Agate: The Great Diamond Hoax and the Semiprecious Stone Scam." *Configurations* 9.3 (2001): 381–412. Print.

Psomiades, Kathy Alexis. "Heterosexual Exchange and Other Victorian Fictions: *The Eustace Diamonds* and Victorian Anthropology." *Novel: A Forum on Fiction* 33.1 (1999): 93–118. Print.
Psomiades, Kathy Alexis. "The Marriage Plot in Theory." *Novel: A Forum on Fiction* 43.1 (2010): 51–9. Print.
Puar, Jasbir Kaur. "Circuits of Queer Mobility: Tourism, Travel, and Globalization." *GLQ* 8.1–2 (2002): 101–37. Print.
Qanungo, Bhupen. "A Study of British Relations with the Native States of India, 1858–62." *The Journal of Asian Studies* 26.2 (1967): 251–65. Print.
Rabinow, Paul. *Essays on the Anthropology of Reason*. Princeton: Princeton UP, 1996. Print.
Ragussis, Michael. *Figures of Conversion: "The Jewish Question" and English National Identity*. Durham: Duke UP, 1995. Print.
Rahman, Tariq. "A Study of the Under-Plot in E. M. Forster's *Where Angels Fear to Tread*." *Studies in English Literature* (1988): 51–69. Print.
Raleigh, John Henry. "What Scott Means to the Victorians." *Victorian Studies* 7.1 (1963): 7–34. Print.
Rancière, Jacques. *Dissensus: On Politics and Aesthetics*. Trans. Steve Corcoran. New York: Continuum, 2010. Print.
Rancière, Jacques. *The Politics of Aesthetics*. 2000. Trans. Gabriel Rockhill. London: Bloomsbury, 2013. Print.
Rancière, Jacques. "Why Emma Bovary Had to Be Killed." *Critical Inquiry* 34.2 (2008): 233–48. Print.
Rand, Gavin. "'Martial Races' and 'Imperial Subjects': Violence and Governance in Colonial India, 1857–1914." *European Review of History* 13.1 (2006): 1–20. Print.
Reynolds, David. *America, Empire of Liberty: A New History*. New York: Basic Books, 2009. Print.
Reynolds, Matthew. *The Realm of Verse 1830–1870: English Poetry in a Time of Nation-Building*. New York: Oxford UP, 2001. Print.
Richmond, Charles and Paul Smith, eds. *The Self-Fashioning of Disraeli, 1818–1851*. Cambridge: Cambridge UP, 1998. Print.
Rignall, John. *George Eliot, European Novelist*. Farnham: Ashgate, 2011. Print.
Roach, John. "James Fitzjames Stephen (1829–94)." *Journal of the Royal Asiatic Society of Great Britain and Ireland* 1.2 (1956): 1–16. Print.
Robbins, Bruce. *Feeling Global: Internationalism in Distress*. New York: New York UP, 1999. Print.
Robbins, Bruce. "The Cosmopolitan Eliot." Anderson and Shaw 400–12.
Robbins, Bruce. "Introduction Part I: Actually Existing Cosmopolitanism." Cheah and Robbins 1–19.
Robbins, Bruce. *Upward Mobility and the Common Good: Toward a Literary History of the Welfare State*. Princeton: Princeton UP, 2009. Print.
Rooney, Ellen. "Live Free or Describe: The Reading Effect and the Persistence of Form." *Differences* 21.3 (2010): 112–39. Print.
Rorty, Richard. *Achieving Our Country: Leftist Thought in Twentieth-Century America*. Cambridge: Harvard UP, 1998. Print.
Rorty, Richard. *Contingency, Irony, and Solidarity*. Cambridge: Cambridge UP, 1989. Print.
Rorty, Richard. "Justice as a Larger Loyalty." *Cosmopolitics: Thinking and Feeling beyond the Nation*. Ed. Pheng Cheah and Bruce Robbins. Minneapolis: U of Minnesota P, 1998. 45–58. Print.

Rosenbaum, S.P. "Towards a Literary History of Monteriano." *Twentieth Century Literature* 31.2-3 (1985): 180–98. Print.

Rowe, John Carlos. *The Theoretical Dimensions of Henry James*. Madison: U of Wisconsin P, 1984. Print.

Roy, Ashish. "The Fabulous Imperialist Semiotic of Wilkie Collins's *The Moonstone*." *New Literary History* 24.3 (1993): 657–81. Print.

Rubery, Matthew. *The Novelty of Newspapers: Victorian Fiction after the Invention of the News*. New York: Oxford UP, 2009. Print.

Sabin, Margery. *Dissenters and Mavericks: Writings about India in English, 1765–2000*. New York: Oxford UP, 2002. Print.

Sadleir, Michael. *Trollope: A Commentary*. Rev. ed. London: Constable, 1947. Print.

Said, Edward W. *Culture And Imperialism*. New York: A.A. Knopf: 1993. Print.

Said, Edward W. *Humanism and Democractic Criticism*. New York: Columbia UP, 2004. Print.

Said, Edward W. "Michael Walzer's Exodus and Revolution: A Canaanite Reading." *Blaming the Victims: Spurious Scholarship and the Palestinian Question*. 1986. Ed. Edward W. Said and Christopher Hitchens. London: Verso, 1988. 161–78. Print.

Said, Edward W. *Orientalism*. New York: Vintage, 1979. Print.

Saint-Beuve, Charles Augustin. "*Madame Bovary* (1857)." Flaubert, *Madame* 403–11.

Salih, Sara. *Representing Mixed Race in Jamaica and England from the Abolition Era to the Present*. New York: Routledge, 2011. Print.

Salisbury, Lord. House of Commons Debates, Official Report for 22 February 1867, vol. 185 col. 838.

Samuels, Maurice. "Jews and the Construction of French Identity from Balzac to Proust." McDonald and Suleiman 404–18.

Sanders, Andrew. *The Victorian Historical Novel, 1840–1880*. New York: St. Martin's Press, 1979. Print.

Sartori, Andrew. *Bengal in Global Concept History, Culturalism in the Age of Capital*. Chicago: Chicago UP, 2008. Print.

Sartori, Andrew. "The British Empire and its Liberal Mission." *Journal of Modern History* 78.3 (2006): 623–42. Print.

Saville, Julia F. "'Soul-Talk': Networks of Political Poetry in a Trans-Channel Literary Triangle." *Victorian Studies* 55.2 (2013): 299–308. Print.

Schivelbusch, Wolfgang. *The Railway Journey: The Industrialization and Perception of Time and Space*. Berkeley: U of California P, 1987. Print.

Schmitt, Carl. *The Concept of the Political: Expanded Edition*. Trans. George Schwab. 1927. Chicago: U of Chicago P, 2007. Print

Schoene, Berthold. *The Cosmopolitan Novel*. Edinburgh: Edinburgh UP, 2009. Print.

Schor, Naomi. *Breaking the Chain: Women, Theory, and French Realist Fiction*. New York: Columbia UP, 1995. Print.

Schor, Naomi. "Details and Decadence: End-Troping in Madame Bovary." *SubStance* 9.1.26 (1980): 27–35. Print.

Schor, Naomi. *George Sand and Idealism*. New York: Columbia UP, 1993. Print.

Schudson, Michael. *Advertising, The Uneasy Persuasion: Its Dubious Impact on American Society*. New York: Basic Books, 1984. Print.

Scott, Joan W. "The Evidence Of Experience." *Critical Inquiry* 17.4 (1991): 773–97. Print.

Sedgwick, Eve. *Epistemology of the Closet*. Berkeley: U of California P, 1991. Print.

Sedgwick, Eve. "Paranoid Reading and Reparative Reading; or, You're So Paranoid, You Probably Think This Introduction Is about You." *Novel Gazing: Queer Readings in Fiction*. Durham: Duke UP. 1–37. Print

Seed, D. "Henry James's Reading of Flaubert." *Comparative Literature Studies* 16.4 (1979): 307–17. Print.

Seeley, J. R. *The Expansion of England*. 1883. Ed. John Gross. Chicago: U of Chicago P, 1971. Print.

Semmel, Bernard. *The Liberal Ideal and The Demons of Empire: Theories of Imperialism from Adam Smith to Lenin*. Baltimore: Johns Hopkins UP, 1993. Print.

Semmel, Bernard. *The Rise of Free Trade Imperialism: Classical Political Economy, The Empire of Free Trade and Imperialism, 1750–1850*. Cambridge: Cambridge UP, 1970. Print.

Semmel, Bernard. *Jamaican Blood and Victorian Conscience: the Governor Eyre Controversy*. Boston: Houghton Mifflin, 1963. Print.

Sen, Amartya. *Development as Freedom*. New York: Knopf, 1999. Print.

Sen, Sudipta. *A Distant Sovereignty: National Imperialism and the Origins of British Difference*. New York: Routledge, 2002. Print.

Sever, Adrian, ed. *Documents and Speeches on the Indian Princely States*. Vol. 1. Delhi: B. R. Publishing Corporation, 1985. Print.

Sever, Adrian. "The Theory of Paramountcy—An Alternative View." Sever, *Documents* 28–38.

Shanley, Mary Lyndon. *Feminism, Marriage, and the Law in Victorian England, 1850–1895*. Princeton: Princeton UP, 1993. Print.

Shaw, Harry E. *Forms of Historical Fiction: Sir Walter Scott and His Successors*. Ithaca: Cornell UP, 1983. Print.

Shaw, Harry E. *Narrating Reality: Austen, Scott, Eliot*. Ithaca: Cornell UP, 1999. Print.

Shohat, Ella. "Area Studies, Gender Studies, and the Cartographies of Knowledge." *Social Text* 20.3 (2002): 67–78. Print.

Shohat, Ella. *Israeli Cinema: East/West and the Politics of Representation*. Austin: U of Texas P, 1989. Print.

Siegel, Jonah. *Haunted Museum: Longing, Travel and the Art-Romance Tradition*. Princeton: Princeton UP, 2005. Print.

Siegelman, Philip. "Introduction." Hobson, *Imperialism* v–xvi.

Simpkins, Scott. "Magical Strategies: The Supplement of Realism." *Twentieth Century Literature* 34.2 (1988): 140–54. Print.

Simpson, David. "Raymond Williams: Feeling for Structures, Voicing 'History.'" Prendergast 29–50.

Slade, Carol. "The Value of Diamonds in English Literature." *The Nature of Diamonds*. Ed. George Harlow. New York: Cambridge UP, 1998. 171–8. Print.

Small, Helen. *The Long Life*. Oxford: Oxford UP, 2007. Print.

Smalley, Barbara. *George Eliot and Flaubert: Pioneers of the Modern Novel*. Athens: Ohio UP, 1974. Print.

Smalley, Donald, ed. *Anthony Trollope: The Critical Heritage*. London: Routledge, 1969. Print.

Smith, Anna-Marie. "Neo-Eugenics: A Feminist Critique of Agamben." *States of Welfare*. Spec. issue of *Occasion* 2 (2010): n. pag. Web. 4 November 2014.

Smith, Denis Mack. *Mazzini*. New Haven: Yale UP, 1994. Print.

Smith, Goldwin. *Canada and the Canadian Question*. New York: Macmillian, 1891. Print.

Smith, Goldwin. "The Empire." *Essays on Questions of the Day, Political and Social*. Ed. Goldwin Smith. 2nd ed. New York: MacMillian, 1897. 139–96. Print.

Smith, Goldwin. *The Empire: A Series of Letters Published in The Daily News, 1862, 1863*. Oxford and London: John Henry and James Parker, 1863. Print.

Smith, Goldwin. *The United Kingdom: A Political History*. Vol. 1. New York: Macmillan, 1899. Print.

Somerville, Siobhan. "Scientific Racism and the Emergence of the Homosexual Body." *Journal of the History of Sexuality* 4.2 (1994): 243–66. Print.

Speare, Morris Edmund. *The Political Novel*. New York: Oxford UP, 1924. Print.

Stang, Richard. "The Literary Criticism of George Eliot." *PMLA* 72.5 (1957): 952–61. Print.

Steele, E.D. *Lord Salisbury: A Political Biography*. London: Routledge, 2001. Print.

[Stephen, J.F.]. "Madame Bovary." *The Saturday Review* 11 July 1857: 40–1. Print.

[Stephen, J.F.]. "Indian Criminal Procedure. To the Editor of *The Times*." *The Times of London* 1 March 1883: 8, col A. Print.

[Stephen, Leslie]. "American Humour." *Cornhill Magazine* 73 (1866): 28–43. Print.

Stephen, Leslie. *George Eliot*. London: Macmillan, 1902. Print.

Stevenson, Robert Louis. "A Note on Realism." *The Biographical Edition of the Notes of Robert Louis Stevenson: Essays of Travel and in the Art of Writing*. New York: Charles Scribner's Sons, 1911. 278–86. Print.

Stewart, Garrett. "The Foreign Offices of British Fiction." *Modern Language Quarterly* 61.1 (2000): 181–206. Print.

Stocking, George W., Jr. *Victorian Anthropology*. New York: Free, 1987. Print.

Stokes, Eric. *The English Utilitarians and India*. Delhi: Oxford UP, 1959. Print.

Stoler, Ann Laura. *Race and the Education of Desire: Foucault's* History of Sexuality *and the Colonial Order of Things*. Durham: U of North Carolina P, 1995.

Stone, H. "The Novel as Fairy Tale: Dickens' *Dombey and Son*." *English Studies* 47.1 (1966): 1–27. Print.

Stone, Wilfred. *The Cave and the Mountain: A Study of E.M. Forster*. Stanford: Stanford UP, 1966. Print.

Storey, Graham ed. The Letters of Charles Dickens, Vol. 9: 1859–1861 Oxford: Clarendon, 1997.

Suleri Goodyear, Sara. *The Rhetoric of English India*. Chicago: U of Chicago P, 1993. Print.

Super, R. H. *The Chronicler of Barsetshire: A Life of Anthony Trollope*. Ann Arbor: U of Michigan P. 1988. Print.

Sutherland, John. Introduction. Collins, *Armadale* vii–xxvii.

Sutherland, John. Introduction. Trollope, *Way* vii–xxviii.

Swaraj. Web. 5 January 2012. <http://cs.nyu.edu/kandathi/swaraj.txt>

Szalay, Michael. "The Writer as Producer; or, The Hip Figure after HBO." *Mad World: Sex, Politics, Style and the 1960s*. Ed. Lauren M.E. Goodlad, Lilya Kaganovsky, and Robert A. Rushing. Durham: Duke UP. 111–32.

Tambling, Jeremy, ed. *E. M. Forster*. New York: St. Martin's, 1995. Print.

Tanner, Tony. *Adultery and the Novel: Contract and Transgression*. Baltimore: Johns Hopkins UP, 1979. Print.

Tanner, Tony. "Trollope's *The Way We Live Now*: Its Modern Significance." *Critical Quarterly* 9.3 (1967): 256–71. Print.

Taylor, Charles. "Two Theories of Modernities." *Alternative Modernities*. Ed. Dilip Gaonkar. Durham: Duke UP, 2001. 172–97. Print.

Taylor, Jenny Bourne. *In the Secret Theatre of Home: Wilkie Collins, Sensation Narrative, and Nineteenth-Century Psychology*. New York: Routledge, 1988. Print.

Taylor, Jenny Bourne. ed. *The Cambridge Companion to Wilkie Collins*. New York: Cambridge UP, 2006. Print.

Taylor, Miles. "The 1848 Revolutions and the British Empire." *Past and Present* 166.1 (2000): 146–80. Print.

Teal, Karen Kurt. "Against 'All That Rowdy Lot': Trollope's Grudge Against Disraeli." *Victorian Newsletter* 112 (2007): 55–68. Print.

Teukolsky, Rachel. *The Literate Eye: Victorian Art Writing and Modernist Aesthetics*. Oxford: Oxford UP, 2009.

Thomas, David Wayne. "Liberal Legitimation and Communicative Action in British India: Reading Flora Annie Steel's *On the Face of the Waters*." *ELH* 76.1 (2009): 153–87.

Thomas, David Wayne. "*Romola*: Historical Narration and the Communicative Dynamics of Modernity." Anderson and Shaw 129–40.

Thomas, Ronald. "*The Moonstone*, Detective Fiction and Forensic Science." J. Taylor, *Cambridge* 65–79.

Thompson, Andrew. *George Eliot and Italy: Literary, Cultural and Political Influences from Dante to the Risorgimento*. Basingstroke: Macmillan, 1998. Print.

Thorne, Susan, "'The Conversion of Englishmen and the Conversion of the World Inseparable': Missionary Imperialism and the Language of Class in Early Industrial Britain." *Tensions of Empire: Colonial Cultures in a Bourgeois World*. Ed. Frederick Cooper and Ann Laura Stoler. Berkeley: U of California P, 1997. 239–62. Print.

Todorov, Tzvetan. *The Fantastic: A Structural Approach to a Literary Genre*. Trans. Richard Howard. Ithaca: Cornell UP, 1975. Print.

Trevelyan, G.M. *Englishmen and Italians: Some Aspects of their Relations, Past and Present*. London: Oxford UP, [1919]. Print.

Trilling, Lionel. *E. M. Forster*. 1943. New York: Harcourt, 1964. Print.

Trilling, Lionel. *The Liberal Imagination: Essays on Literature and Society*. New York: Doubleday, 1949. Print.

Trodd, Anthea. "Messages in Bottles and Collins's Seafaring Man." *SEL* 41.4 (Autumn 2001): 751–64. Print.

Trollope, Anthony. *Australia and New Zealand*. 2 vols. London, 1873. Print.

Trollope, Anthony. *An Autobiography*. 1883. Ed. David Skilton. Harmondsworth: Penguin, 1996. Print.

Trollope, Anthony. *Barchester Towers*. 1857. Eds. Frederick Page and Michael Sadleir. Oxford: Oxford UP, 2009. Print.

Trollope, Anthony. *Can You Forgive Her?* 1864–5. Ed. Andrew Swarbrick. Oxford: Oxford UP, 2008. Print.

Trollope, Anthony. *Doctor Thorne*. 1858. Ed. David Skilton. Oxford: Oxford UP, 2000. Print.

Trollope, Anthony. *The Eustace Diamonds*. 1871–3. Ed. W.J. McCormack. Oxford: Oxford UP, 1983. Print.

Trollope, Anthony. *Framley Parsonage*. 1860–61. Ed. David Skilton and Peter Miles. London: Penguin, 1985. Print.

Trollope, Anthony. *The Last Chronicle of Barset*. 1866–7. Ed. Stephen Gill. Oxford: Oxford UP, 1980. Print.

Trollope, Anthony. *Lord Palmerston*. 1882. Ed. John Halperin. New York: Arno, 1981. Print.

Trollope, Anthony. "Mr. Disraeli and the Mint." 1869. *Writings for Saint Paul's* 192–7.

Trollope, Anthony. *The New Zealander*. 1971. Ed. N. John Hall. London: Trollope Soc., 1995. Print.

Trollope, Anthony. *North America*. New York: Harper, 1862. Print.

Trollope, Anthony. "On Sovereignty." 1867. *Writings for Saint Paul's* 76–91.

Trollope, Anthony. *Phineas Finn*. 1868. Ed. Jacques Berthoud. Oxford: Oxford UP, 2008. Print.

Trollope, Anthony. *The Prime Minister*. 1876. Ed. David Skilton. Harmondsworth: Penguin, 1996. Print.

Trollope, Anthony. *South Africa*. 1878. Ed. J. H. Davidson. Cape Town: Balkema, 1973. Print.

Trollope, Anthony. *The Three Clerks*. 1858. Ed. Graham Handley. Oxford: Oxford UP, 1990. Print.

Trollope, Anthony. *The Tireless Traveler: Twenty Letters to The Liverpool Mercury*. 1875. Ed. Allen Booth. Berkeley: U of California P, 1978. Print.

Trollope, Anthony. *The Warden*. 1855. Ed. Robin Gilmour. Harmondsworth: Penguin, 1984. Print.

Trollope, Anthony. *The Way We Live Now*. 1874–5. Ed. John Sutherland. Oxford: Oxford UP, 1986. Print.

Trollope, Anthony. *The West Indies and the Spanish Main*. 1859. New York: Caroll, 1999. Print.

Trollope, Anthony. *Writings for Saint Pauls Magazine*. Ed. John Sutherland. New York: Arno, 1981. Print.

Tronto, Joan C. "Beyond Gender Difference to a Theory of Care." *Signs* 12.4 (1987): 644–63. Print.

Tronto, Joan C. "Care Ethics: Moving Forward." *Hypatia* 14.1 (1999): 112–19. Print.

Trumpener, Katie. *Bardic Nationalisms: The Romantic Novel and the British Empire*. Princeton: Princeton UP, 1997. Print.

Tucker, Herbert F. "Doughty's *The Dawn in Britain* and the Modernist Eclipse of the Victorian." *Romanticism and Victorianism on the Net* 47 (2007). Web. 1 Oct. 2009.

Tucker, Irene. "International Whiggery." *Victorian Studies* 45.4 (2003): 687–97. Print.

Tucker, Irene. *A Probable State: The Novel, the Contract, and The Jews*. Chicago: U of Chicago P, 2000. Print.

van Dam, Frederik. *The Man without Style: Victorian Liberalism and Literary Form in Anthony Trollope's Later Novels*. [Forthcoming: Edinburgh UP].

van der Pijl, Kees. "A Lockean Europe?" *New Left Review* 37 (2006): n. pag. Web. 20 June 2011.

Van Evrie, John H. *Negroes and Negro 'Slavery'; The First an Inferior Race; the Latter Its Normal Condition*. New York: Van Evrie, Horton, & Co., 1861. Print.

Varon, Jeremy, Michael S. Floey and John McMillian. "Time is an Ocean: the Past and Future of the Sixties." *The Sixties* 1.1 (2008): 1–7. Print.

Vertovec, Steven, and Robin Cohen, eds. *Conceiving Cosmopolitanism: Theory Context, and Practice*. Oxford: Oxford UP, 2002. Print.

Victoria, Alexandrina. "Proclamation by Queen Victoria." 1 November 1858. Sever, *Documents* 232–4.

Visram, Rozina. *Ayahs, Lascars and Princes: The Story of Indians in Britain, 1700-1947*. London: Pluto, 1986. Print.

Viswanathan, Gauri. *Masks of Conquest: Literary Study and British Rule in India*. New York: Columbia UP, 1989. Print.

Voskuil, Lynn M. *Acting Naturally: Victorian Theatricality and Authenticity*. Charlottesville: U of Virginia P, 2004. Print.

Voskuil, Lynn M. "Robert Fortune, *Camellia Sinensis*, and the Nineteenth-Century Global Imagination." *Nineteenth-Century Contexts* 34.1 (2012): 5–18. Print.

Walkowitz, Rebecca L. *Cosmopolitan Style: Modernism beyond the Nation*. New York: Columbia UP, 2006. Print.

Wall, Stephen. "Trollope, Balzac, and the Reappearing Character." *Essays in Criticism* 25.1 (1975): 123–44. Print.

Wallerstein, Immanuel Maurice. *Geopolitics and Geoculture: Essays on the Changing World–System*. Cambridge: Cambridge UP, 1991. Print.

Wallerstein, Immanuel Maurice. *World-Systems Analysis: An Introduction*. Durham: Duke UP, 2004. Print.

Walzer, Michael. *Exodus and Revolution*. New York: Basic Books, 1985. Print.

Ward, Stuart. "Transcending the Nation: A Global Imperial History?" *After the Imperial Turn: Thinking with and through the Nation*. Burton 44–56.

Warhol, Robyn R. *Having a Good Cry: Effeminate Feelings and Pop-culture Forms*. Columbus: The Ohio State UP, 2003. Print.

Warner, Michael. Introduction. *Fear of a Queer Planet: Queer Politics and Social Theory*. Ed. Michael Warner. Minneapolis: U of Minnesota P, 1993. vii–xxxi. Print.

Warner, Michael. *Publics and Counterpublics*. New York: Zone, 2002.

Washbrook, D. A. "India, 1818–1860: The Two Faces of Colonialism." A. Porter, *Oxford* 395–421.

Watkins, Susan. "Presentism? A Reply to T.J. Clark." *New Left Review* 74 (March–April 2012): 77–102. Print.

Watson, Tim. *Caribbean Culture and British Fiction in the Atlantic World, 1780–1870*. New York: Cambridge UP, 2008. Print.

Weinberg, Bernard. *French Realism: the Critical Reaction, 1830–1870*. New York: Modern Language Association, 1937. Print.

Weiner, Stephanie Kuduk. *Republic Politics and English Poetry, 1789–1874*. Basingstroke: Macmillan, 2005. Print.

Weissbrod, Rachel. "Exodus as a Zionist Melodrama." *Israel Studies* 4.1 (1999): 129–52. Print.

Wellek, René. "The Concept of Realism in Literary Scholarship." *Neophilologus* 45.1 (1961): 1–20.

Welsh, Alexander. *George Eliot and Blackmail*. Cambridge, MA: Harvard UP, 1985. Print.

Welsh, Alexander. *Strong Representations: Narrative and Circumstantial Evidence in England*. Baltimore: The Johns Hopkins UP, 1995. Print.

White, Stephen K. *Political Theory and Postmodernism*. Cambridge: Cambridge UP, 1991. Print.

Wicke, Jennifer. *Advertising Fictions: Literature, Advertisement & Social Reading*. New York: Columbia UP, 1988. Print.

Wihl, Gary S. "Republican Liberty in George Eliot's *Romola*." *Victorian Literature and Culture* 51.2 (2009): 247–62. Print.

Williams, Donovan. *The India Office, 1858–1869*. Hoshiarpur: Vishveshvaranand Vedic Research Institute, 1983. Print.

Williams, Eric. *British Historians and the West Indies*. 1964. New York: Scribners, 1966.

Williams, Raymond. *The Country and the City*. Oxford: Oxford UP, 1973. Print.

Williams, Raymond. *The English Novel from Dickens to Lawrence*. 1970. St. Albans: Paladin, 1974. Print.

Williams, Raymond. "Forms of English Fiction in 1848." *Writing in Society*. London: Verso, 1983. 150–65. Print.

Williams, Raymond. *Keywords: A Vocabulary of Culture and Society*. New York: Oxford UP, 1985. Print.

Williams, Raymond. "The Magic System." 1960. *Advertising & Society Review* 1.1 (2000): 170–95. Print.

Williams, Raymond. *Marxism and Literature*. Oxford: Oxford UP, 1977. Print.

Williams, Raymond. *Politics of Modernism: Against the New Conformists*. 1989. London: Verso, 2007. Print.

Wills, Adele. "Witnesses and Truth: Juridical Narratives and Dialogism in Wilkie Collins' *The Moonstone* and *The Woman in White*" *New Formations* 32 (1997): 91–8. Print.

Winnett, Susan. "Coming Unstrung: Women, Men, Narrative, and Principles of Pleasure." *PMLA* 103.3 (1990): 505–18. Print.

Wise, Tim. *Colorblind: The Rise of Post-Racial Politics and the Retreat from Racial Equity*. San Francisco: City Lights Books, 2010. Print.

[Wodyar, Kristna Raj], "From the Maharajah of Mysore to his Excellence the Right Honourable Viscount Canning and Governor General of India; dated 23 February 1861." *Accounts and Papers*. Volume 14 of 39 volumes. East India Session, 1 February—10 August 1866. Vol. 52, Papers Relating to Mysore. London: Great Britain Parliament. 1–3. Print.

Wohl, Anthony S. "Dizzi-Ben-Dizzi: Disraeli as Alien." *Journal of British Studies* 34.3 (July 1995): 375–411. Print.

Wohl, Anthony S. Message to the author. 6 Aug. 2011. Email.

Wolfson, Susan. "Reading for Form." *Modern Language Quarterly* 61.1 (2000): 1–16. Print.

Wood, Ellen Meiksins. *Empire of Capital*. London: Verso, 2003. Print.

Wood, Gordon S. *Empire of Liberty: A History of the Early Republic*. Oxford: Oxford UP, 2009. Print.

Wood, Marcus. *Slavery, Empathy, and Pornography*. New York: Oxford UP, 2003. Print.

Wood, Marcus. "Significant Silence: Where was Slave Agency in the Popular Imagery of 2007?" *Imagining Transatlantic Slavery*. Ed. Cora Kaplan and John Oldfield. New York: Palgrave, 2010. 163–90. Print.

Woolf, Virginia. "George Eliot." *The Common Reader*. 1925. New York: Harcourt, 1984. 162–72. Print.

Wynne, Deborah. *The Sensation Novel and the Victorian Family Magazine*. New York: Palgrave, 2001. Print.

Yeazell, Ruth Bernard. "Why Political Novels Have Heroines: *Sybil, Mary Barton*, and *Felix Holt*." *Novel: A Forum on Fiction* 18.2 (1985): 126–44. Print.

Young, Iris Marion. "Asymmetrical Reciprocity: On Moral Respect, Wonder, and Enlarged Thought." *Intersecting Voices: Dilemmas of Gender, Political Philosophy and Policy*. Princeton: Princeton UP, 1997. 38–59. Print.

Young, Iris Marion. *Inclusion and Democracy*. Oxford: Oxford UP, 2000. Print.

Young, Iris Marion. *Justice and the Politics of Difference*. Princeton: Princeton UP, 1990. Print.

Young, Paul. "'Carbon, Mere Carbon': the Koohinor, the Crystal Palace, and the Mission to Make Sense of British India." *Nineteenth-Century Contexts*. 29.4 (2007): 343–58. Print.

Young, Paul. *Globalization and the Great Exhibition: The Victorian New World Order*. New York: Palgrave, 2009. Print.

Young, Robert J.C. *Postcolonialism: An Historical Introduction*. Oxford: Blackwell, 2001. Print.

Young-Zook, Monica. "Wilkie Collins's Gwilt-y Conscience: Gender and Colonialism in *Armadale*." *Victorian Sensations: Essays on a Scandalous Genre*. Ed. Kimberly Harrison and Richard Fantina. Columbus: The Ohio UP, 2006. 234–45. Print.

Zastoupil, Lynn. *John Stuart Mill and India*. Stanford: Stanford UP, 1995. Print.

Zerilli, Linda M. G. "Toward A Feminist Theory Of Judgment." *Signs: Journal Of Women In Culture & Society* 34.2 (2009): 295–317. Print.

Žižek, Slavoj. "'There is no Sexual Relationship': Wagner as a Lacanian." *Richard Wagner*. Spec. issue of *New German Critique* 69 (1996): 7–35. Print.

Zola, Emile. *Le Roman expérimental. Oeuvres complètes*. Ed. Henri Mitterand. Paris: Cercle du Livre Précieux, Tome 10, 1968. Print.

Index

Ablow, Rachel, 204n. 61
Abolition/ abolitionism. *See* slavery
Adorno, Theodor, 185; on kitsch, 188–9, 191
adultery: A. Egg's triptych on, 163; and British business novel, 173; and Matrimonial Causes Act (1857), 162, 162n.1, 163, 163n. 2, 173; as breach of marriage contract, 162; as archetypally female sin, 191; as marker of naturalistic narratives of capitalist globalization, 167, 202 (as breach of sovereignty), 170; B. Leckie on, 182–3n. 33, 193; C. Baudelaire on, 168; definition of, 169–70, 170n. 14; in Chaucer's "Parson's Tale," 170n. 13; in G. Flaubert's *Madame Bovary* and *Mad Men*, 16, 265; in verse from Matthew, 170; J. Matlock on, 171; J. Rancière on, 186; M. Braddon's avoidance of 14, 173n. 21; novels of 173, (complication of) 164, 167, 175, (E. Amann on) 189, (exile, alienation, and damaged sovereignty in) 167, (female heroines of) 191, (F. Moretti on) 164, (G. Eliot's works as exemplary of) 15, 164, 167, 168, 175, 184, 192–3, 197, 201, 203, 204, 205, 206, (G. Eliot's non-naturalistic variations on) 167, (French sentimental examples of) 201, ("great" examples of) 193, (G. Flaubert's *Madame Bovary* as example of) 14, 188, 189, 191, 191–2; (G. Meredith's example of) 163, 163n. 2, (G. Meredith's review of *Madame Bovary* and) 163, (in Britain versus France) 171, (N. Hawthorne's example of) 180, (sentimental variations on) 185, 201; Reformation's expansion of adultery, 170n. 14; S. Žižek on 191–2; T. Tanner on, 168, 169, 170, 170n. 14, 170n. 15, 204. *See also* geopolitical aesthetic, adulterous; narrative of capitalist globalization, naturalistic
advertising, 264–5; as depicted in *Mad Men*, 266–7; *Mad Men*'s aestheticization of, 265; R. Williams on, 265
Afghanistan, 7, 8, 8n. 10, 70, 274
Agamben, Giorgio, 8–9, 9n. 12, 9n. 13, 39–40, 40n. 1, 111, 112; crisis of modern experience and, 144; *Infancy and History*, 113n. 5, 142, 144
Agathocleous, Tanya, 22n. 5, 29n. 16, 65, 158

Ahmed, Sara, 236n. 43, 236–237n. 45
All the President's Men (1976), 247
Albert, Prince, 138
Aldrich, Robert, 221n. 25
Althusser, Louis, 273
Amann, Elizabeth, 185, 189
AMC (American Movie Channel), 242, 285
Arac, Jonathan, 176n 26
Armstrong, Paul, 208n. 2
Anderson, Amanda, 22–3, 23n. 7, 34, 35–6, 65–6, 233n. 40, 240n. 50
Anderson, Benedict, 72
Anderson, Perry, 209
Anderson, Terry, 248
Andrade, Susan Z., 274n. 9
anglocentrism, self-universalizing as depicted in E. M. Forster's fiction, 209, 217
Anjaria, Ulka, 245, 274n. 9
annexation, 50, 52n. 22, 55. *See also* Mysore; India/Indian
anti-Semitism, 13, 213, 249n. 14; A. Trollope and, 88, 250; association of with diamonds, 140; and Don Pacifico, 71n 12. and figure of Tito in G. Eliot's *Romola*, 202; and financial narratives, 172; and J. Hobson's critique of imperialism, 213; E. Apter on, 172; growth of during B. Disraeli's rise to power, 105n. 21, 105, 249, 249n 14; growth of among liberals, 106n 22; liberal universalism and, 251; *Mad Men* and 250. *See also* Disraeli, Benjamin; Hobson, J. A.; Jews/Judaism
Antigone, 181, Hegel's interpretation of, 196n. 50; Honig on, 196n. 50; in G. Eliot's *Romola*, 181, 181n. 32
Appadurai, Arjun, 201n. 6
Appiah, Kwame Anthony, 65, 66
apRoberts, Ruth, 74n. 18
Apter, Emily, 172, 174n 23, 271
Arata, Stephen, 156, 156n. 60, 158n. 64
archeology. *See* geopolitical aesthetic
Arendt, Hannah, 145, 146, 249n. 14
Armitage, David, 1, 42
Armstrong, Nancy, 168–9n. 11, 225, 272n. 5
Armstrong, Paul B., 233
Arnold, Matthew, 210, 227; *Culture and Anarchy*, 52n. 23, 123, 123n. 20; "Function of Criticism," (E. M. Forster and) 229; notion of culture and, 111
Arrighi, Giovanni, 10n. 14
Ashton, Rosemary, 178, 195

Atlantic, black, 23–4, 34, 116; anticipated in W. Collins's *Armadale*, 115, 116, 154; W. Benjamin's *Erfahrung* and 116; *See also* Gilroy, Paul
Atlantic, studies, 21, 23–5, 26, 35; British history and, 115–6. *See also* Boelhower, William; Gilroy, Paul
Auerbach, Erich, 11, 14, 32n. 20, 37, 167, 172, 175–6, 188–9, 189n. 40, 190, 190–2, 278; on G. Flaubert's "existential realism," 286–7
Auerbach, Nina, 164, 179
Austen, Jane, 89n. 3, 175
autoethnography, 246; Barsetshire novels and, 68
Australia, 42, 69, 69n. 9; white settlement in, 77. *See also* imperialism/imperial, white settler

Babylon, as trope of naturalistic geopolitical aesthetic, 243; mid-Victorian London as, 249; modern (New York in *Mad Men* as), 253–4, 255–6 259, 267; Victorian, 252
Badiou, Alain, 239n. 47
Bagehot, Walter, 10n. 14, 43, 54n. 27, 63, 72, 74; *The English Constitution*, 47, 98, 101, 105, 105n. 20
Bakhtin, Mikhail, 28n. 13, 278
Bakshi, Parminder, 209n. 3
Balibar, Etienne, 214
Baltimore, as location of *The Wire*, 246, 246n. 10
Balzac, Honoré de, 28, 32, 33, 33n. 21, 88, 89, 89n. 3, 157, 163, 165, 165n. 4, 177, 178, 180, 185, 186, 203, 281; admiration of W. Scott, 275; as Lukácsian realist, 274; G. Lewes on, 175; J. Rancière on, 187, W. Collins on, 171
Barbados, 14; as location for W. Collins's *Armadale*, 117–8; sugar plantation complex and, 116n. 8. *See also*, Collins, Wilkie, *Armadale*
Barkawi, Tarak, 210n. 5
Barsetshire novels. *See* Trollope, Anthony
Barthes, Roland, *The Reality Effect*, 165, 277n. 13
Bartolovich, Crystal, 270, 272
Baucom, Ian, 10n. 14, 78, 106, 208n. 2, 234n. 41
Baudelaire, Charles, 5n. 5, 14, 111, 112, 113n. 5, 114, 168, 187n. 39, 188, 191
Bauman, Zygmunt, 251
Baumgarten, Murray, 83n. 27
Bayly, C. A., 1
Beasley, Edward, 98, 100
Beaumont, Matthew, 5n. 5, 29n. 16
Beer, John, 223
Bell, Duncan, 2n. 2, 4, 19, 57, 59, 60n. 32, 214

Bell, Major [T.] Evans, 48, 49n. 14, 50, 51n. 19, 52n. 21, 54, 96–7, 97n. 15
Belsey, Catherine, 165, 270
Benhabib, Seyla, 221, 238; "reversibility of perspectives" in contrast to E. M. Forster's point of view, 232, 232n. 38
Benjamin, Walter, 11, 14, 33, 85, 85n. 31, 111, 116, 133, 144n. 47, 157; crisis of modern experience and, 144; *flâneur* of, 172; N. Daly on, 112–3; M. Jay on, 112–3; "On Some Motifs in Baudelaire," 111, 114, 154; "Paris, Capital of the Nineteenth Century," 171–2; "The Storyteller," 110, 111
Bennett, Tony, 28
Bentham, Jeremy, 210
Bentinck, Lord William Henry, 49n. 14
Ben-Yishai, Ayelet, 73n. 16, 90n. 5
Berlin Conference of 1884–5, 276n. 11
Berman, Carolyn Vellenga, 119, 271
Berman, Jessica, 66n. 1
Bernstein, J., 279
Bernstein, Susan, 244n. 4
Best, Stephen and Sharon Marcus, 16, 269, 270. 3, 271, 272, 288, 293
Bigelow, Gordon, 79n. 22
Bildung/Bildungsroman, 154, 246; as dialogical form, 150, 150n. 51, in Balzac, 171, in Trollope's Palliser novels, 89. *See also* realism/realist fiction
biopolitics, 9n. 13
biopower, in W. Collins's *Armadale*, 128
Birns, Nicholas, 67n. 3, 271
Blackwood, John, 285
Bodenheimer, Rosemary, 179, 180, 180n. 31
Boelhower, William, 24–5, 26, 35, 116–7, 123
Bonaparte, Felicia, 181, 198n. 55, 200
books, history/sociology of, 38
Boone, Joseph, 169
Booth, B. A., 87
Born, Daniel, 208n. 2, 233n. 40
Bornstein, George, 253
Bourdieu, Pierre, 21, 27, 34n. 22, 81n. 25, 268, 273, 283, 290; critique of by B. Latour, 288; *The Rules of Art*, 185, 185n. 37, 187
bourgeois aesthetics, crisis of, 245–5. *See also* realism/realist fiction
Bourget, Paul, 165, 165n. 7
Bowen, H. V., 39
Boyarin, Jonathan, 254, 254n. 20
Braddon, Mary Elizabeth, 14, 206; *The Doctor's Wife* 181–2, 182n. 33
Brantlinger, Patrick, 67, 67n. 3, 69, 77, 88, 156n. 60
Braudel, Fernand, 16–7, 34n. 22; and Annales school, 283–4; F. Jameson on, 283n. 22
Bray, Caroline, 179, 180
Bray, Charles, 179

Bredbeck, Gregory W., 224n. 29
Brennan, Timothy, 85, 210n. 6
Briefel, Aviva, 90n. 5
Bright, John, 61, 119
Bristow, Joseph, 1n. 1, 221n. 25, 228, 228n. 35, 229, 230
Brooks, Peter, 147, 189, 190, 206
Brown, Bill, 135n. 36, 292
Brown, Tony, 228n. 36
Brown, Wendy, 3, 3n. 4, 4, 39–40, 40n. 1, 219n. 21
Browning, Elizabeth Barrett, 195
Browning, Robert, 66, 66n. 2
Brönte, Anne, 37
Brönte, Charlotte, 37, 179; *Jane Eyre*, 115n. 7, (resemblance of W. Collins's *Armadale* to) 127
Brönte, Emily, 36, 37
Brumpton, Paul R., 45, 49, 52, 53n. 26, 64, 105n. 20
Buckton, Oliver S., 221n. 25, 224n. 29
Burke, Edmund, 31, 44, 45–6, 46n. 9, 60; in A. Trollope's *The Eustace Diamonds*, 94–5; prosecution of W. Hastings, 95; *Reflections on the Revolution in France*, 75–6
Burns, W. L., 10n. 14
Burton, Antoinette, 8n. 10; *After the Imperial Turn*, 2n. 2; *The First Anglo-Afghan Wars*, 8n. 10
Buxton, Thomas, 119
Buzard, James, 68, 81
Byron, Lord, 254

Calhoun, Craig, 65
Campbell, Duncan Andrew, 120, 120n. 15, 121n. 17
Canada, 42, 58, 69, 274; and "Greater Britain," 57. *See also* imperialism /imperial, white settler
Cannadine, David, 215
Canning, Lord (1st Earl Canning), 41, 41n. 2, 50, 96
Capaldi, Nicholas, 122
capitalism, 11, 22–3, 40n. 1; A. Trollope's *The Eustace Diamonds* and, 106; cosmopolitanism and, 12, 67, 67n. 4, 86; depicted in *Mad Men*, 257; finance, 7, 10; E. M. Forster on, 233; gender and in E. M. Forster's *Where the Angels Fear to Tread*, 222; G. Arrighi and, 10; globalization of, 16, 30, 31, 38, 84, 85; post-19th-century history of (S. Watkins on), 293; *longue durée* of (and serialized realism), 243; multinational (F. Jameson on), 247; settler imperialism and, 78. *See also* globalization
Carens, Timothy, 151n. 52
Carlyle, Thomas, 7, 58–9, 104, 119

Carpenter, Edward, 211n. 8, 213n. 13, 223–25, 226, 227, 228, 228n. 36, 231; anti-racism of, 224, 224n. 29; developmental tropes in, 224; *Love's Coming of Age*, 224n. 29
Carroll, David, 193, 196n. 51, 203
Carson, Penelope, 46n. 10
Carter, Everett, 83n. 27, 250n. 15
Casanova, Pascale, 34n. 22
Case, Alison, 128n. 28
Caserio, Robert L., 221n. 25
Çelikkol, Ayşe, 6n. 8, 34n. 23
Central Asia, 42
Chakrabarty, Dipesh, 2, 217, 230, 231n. 37, 236n. 43, 241
Chamberlain, Muriel, 72
Chandler, David, 211n. 7
Chapman, John, 179–80
Chase, Karen, 162n. 1
Cheah, Pheng, 210n. 5
Cheng, Anne Anlin, 269n. 1
Cheyette, Bryan, 83n. 27, 85, 212, 212n. 12, 250, 251
China, 42, 274; British imperialism and, 57–8; in W. Collins's *The Woman in White*, 113
Church of England, A. Trollope and, 79
circulating libraries, 243
City of London, location for A. Trollope's *The Prime Minister*, 243
Clark, Anna, 45n. 8
Clarke, John, 3n. 4
Clerk, George Russell, 50
climate change (as long historical process), 273
Clinton, William J., 3
Clough, Arthur Hugh, 195
Cobden, Richard, 105n. 21
Cohen, Margaret, 30n. 17, 174–5, 176, 181, 184, 185, 185n. 36, 187, 193n. 42, 264n. 24, 269n. 1
Cohen, Margaret and Carolyn Dever, 14, 27, 163, 167, 174, 211
Cohen, Robin, 22
Cohen, William A., 90n. 5
Cohn, Bernard, 39, 45n. 8, 46–8, 51, 63
Cole, Sarah, 223–4
Collini, Stefan, 208n. 1, 212
Collins, Wilkie, 2, 4, 13–4, 17, 29, 37, 96, 110–4, 115–8, 119, 119–120n. 14, 120–21n. 16, 123–33, 134, 135–6, 138, 139–40, 141–4, 146–60, 177, 178, 180, 209n. 4, 269, 275n. 10, 281, as contemporary of W. Pater and C. Baudelaire, 113n. 5; as participant in literary "world-system," 274–5; Baudelairian sensibility of, 275; distaste for racism, 123; G. GoGwilt and, 111; mid-Victorian-era seriality and, 243; multi-perspectivity in fiction of, 114;

phenomenological variation on the geopolitical aesthetic of, 275; pluralized sovereignty of, 168, 239; political attitudes of, 120–1n. 16; post-raciality in fiction of, 128, 128n. 27; praise for Balzac of, 171; racially-mixed characters in fiction of, 114, 178; resistant anti-naturalism of, 168; sensational styles of fiction of, 275; travel of, 111n. 2; A. Trollope and, 110–1, 111n. 1
Works: "A Sermon for the Sepoys," 159
Antonina, 111
Armadale, 4, 14, 31, 111, 114–8, 119, 120–33; as a black Atlantic narrative; 116; assimilationist erasure in, 155; flawed execution of, 127; N. Hensley on, 130; history of transatlantic slavery in, 275; homoeroticism of, 127n. 26; post-raciality in, 125, 130–1; projection of experience onto spatial motifs in, 154; review of, 123; serialization of, 122; timing of, 119–20n. 14; travel for, 115; uncanniness of, 125, 126; U. S. Civil War and, 120; author's view of, 114–5
Black and White, 131
Miss or Mrs? 131
Poor Miss Finch, 131
The Guilty River, 131
The Moonstone 11, 13, 14, 31, 41, 42, 44, 88, 91, 95, 110, 111, 114, 115, 120, 132–3, 134, 136, 137–8, 139–40, 141–4, 146–60, 219n. 20, 221, 275, 276n. 11, 286n. 25; as anti-detective novel, 155; as multi-genre work, 114, 143, 156; as multi-sited story of experience, 149; as "mutiny" narrative, 139; as romance of Hindu otherness, 142; collective *Bildung* in, 152, 153; compared to *The Wire*, 282n. 20; conclusion of 155–6; crisis of modern experience in, 144; decolonization adumbrated in, 159–60; depiction of diamonds in compared to that of A. Trollope's *The Eustace Diamonds*, 135; descent of Jennings in, 155; I. Duncan's reading of, 158–9; essentialization of Indianness in, 136, 136n. 37; futuristic Jennings in, 157–8; Hindu ownership in, 138; Judaization of moneylender in, 142n. 43, 151n. 53; limits of detective form in, 152; logic of the "civilizing mission" as depicted in, 149; mixed-race characters in, 131; multi-voiced narration in, 143, 143n. 44, 152; multi-perspectivity of, 150; narrative art in, 147; Orientalism and, 132, 136; pluralized sovereignty in, 151; polymorphous form of, 142; post-imperial future of India in, 136;

refusal of naturalism of, 141, 142n. 43; revision of sovereign experience in, 153, 154; scientific authority in, 146–7; serialization of, 143n. 45; shift of from detective fiction to utopian romance, 153; sovereignty of India in, 134, 137–8; temporality of, 159–60; time frame of, 136; utopian dimensions of 157, 159–60; utopian romance form in, 142; vertical narration in, 143–4, 144n. 46, 152
The Woman in White, 112, 115, 123, 128n. 28, 143n. 44, 147n. 50, 152; historical experience and, 113–4
colonialism/colonization, as distinct from imperialism 8n. 11; emancipation from, 58. *See also* imperialism/imperial
Conan Doyle, Arthur, 274n. 10; *Sign of Four*, 156n. 60, 156n. 61
Connolly, William, 9n. 12, 150, 153
Conrad, Joseph, 228, 229
Conservative Party, 4, 10, 12, 51n. 18, 87; British working classes and, 63; predominance of, 61. *See also* Tory politics
Cooper, Frederick, 2n. 2
Cooper, James Fenimore, 176n. 26
Copland, Ian, 47, 51
Corbett, Mary Jean, 79n. 22
Corn Laws, 7
Corner, Julian, 202n. 57, 203–4n. 59
cosmopolitanism, 21, 22–4, 27, 35, 65–8, 214; "actually existing," 12, 23, 24; alleged control of Jewish financiers and, 212; as depicted in W. Collins's *The Moonstone*, 143, 152; as worrisome decay, 212; T. Brennan and, 85; capitalism and, 82, 83; capitalist circuits of (in A. Trollope's *The Eustace Diamonds*), 135; colonialism and, 86; definition of, 67, 67n. 4; E. M. Forster's *Howards End* and, 214; G. Eliot and, 168 (*Daniel Deronda*), 205–6; globalization and, 86; "heirloom" sovereignty and, 65; J. A. Hobson and, 212, 214; imperialism and, 71; in W. Collins's *The Woman in White*, 113; in *The Way We Live Now*, 83. 28; Irish settlers and, 79; Jews and, 82, 83, 139–40; P. Rabinow and, 116, 146; "race" and, 77, 82; realism and, 29n. 16; Romanticism and, 66n. 1; rootlessness and, 80, 81; tourism and, 216n. 18; A. Trollope and, 76, 77, 78, 85; versus internationalism, 209n. 4, 211, 212; Victorian ambivalence toward, 67; I. Young's democratic theory of, 239–40. *See also* transnationalism/transnationality
Cotsell, Michael, 67, 87
Coundouriotis, Eleni, 183n. 35

Courtemanche, Eleanor, 85
Craciun, Adriana, 66n. 1
Crane, Mary Thomas, 269n. 1
Crimean War, 7, 10, 70, 139
Critchley, Simon, 236n. 43
Crooks, Robert, 157
Crosby, Christina, 88
Cross, J. W., 178n. 28, 193
Cucullu, Lois, 228n. 35
Culler, Jonathan, 187, 190–1
Cunningham, Valentine, 73n. 16

Dainotto, Roberto, 217, 231n. 37, 271
Dalhousie, Lord (1st Marquess of Dalhousie), 41, 49, 51n. 18, 96
Dallas, E. S., 19–21
Daly, Nicholas, 92n. 8, 112, 112n. 4, 113n. 5
Damages (2007–2010), 245
Dames, Nicholas, 20n. 3, 81n. 25, 104, 147n. 50
Darwin, Charles, J. A. Hobson's notion of progress and, 213
Darwin, John, 1, 19, 194n. 46
Davidson, J. H., 67n. 3, 70, 81, 81n. 24, 87
Davies, Tony, 208n. 2
Deadwood (2004–6), 243
Dean, Tim, 221n. 21
Dellamora, Richard, 83n. 27, 221n. 25, 223, 250n. 15
democracy, 12, 55, 61, 85; British, 51, 52; E. Carpenter's writings on, 225; depicted in E. M. Forster's *Where the Angels Fear to Tread*, 223–7; E. M. Forster's romanticization of, 236; homophile discourse and, 223–7; imperialism and, 56–7; mass politics and, 105; massification of, 242–3; nineteenth-century limits of, 130n. 29; I. Young's theory of communicative, 239n. 48, 240n. 49
Dent, E. J., 215n. 17
Derby, Lord (14th Earl of Derby), 50, 53n. 24
Derrida, Jacques, notion of *différance*, 273
detective fiction, 133; P. Brooks on, 147; emerging genre of, 154; F. Jameson on, 147; in conjunction with W. Collins's *The Moonstone*, 142–3, 149, 156
Dever, Carolyn, 127n. 26, 205n. 64
Deverell, Walter, "A Pet" (1853), 260
diamonds, 133–4; as generic touchstones, 134; as modern bullion, 135; as signifier of luxury in A. Trollope's *The Eustace Diamonds*, 135; history of, 134–5, 135n 34; in W. Collins's *The Moonstone*, 135–6; Jews as dealers and cutters of, 139–40; theft of Orloff diamond, 138. *See also* Koh-i-Noor; Collins, Wilkie, *The Eustace Diamonds*, *The Moonstone*

Dickens, Charles, 30n. 17, 34n. 23, 88, 104, 115, 120n. 15, 150, 175, 182; and *All the Year Round*, 284–5; defense of E. Eyre and, 119; G. Lukács on, 177–8; R. Williams on, 178; realism of compared to *The Wire*, 282n. 20; U. S. Civil War and, 120–121n. 16
Works: *Bleak House*, 2, 173, 218, 246, 246n. 10; compared to *The Wire*, 246
David Copperfield, 174
Dombey and Son, 10n. 14, 30, 34–6; as first example of the emerging business-cum-adultery novel, 173; unconsummated adultery in, 173–4, 173n. 21; adulterous geopolitical aesthetic and, 173–4, 201; "subjunctive" space in 174
Hard Times, 174
Little Dorrit, 7, 10n. 14, 34–6, 174
Our Mutual Friend, 10n. 14, 30n. 17
The Pickwick Papers, 285
Tale of Two Cities, 177
Dilke, Charles, 39, 57–8, 60, 60n. 32, 61, 69
Dimock, Wai Chee, 292
Dirks, Nicholas, 39, 45, 45n. 8, 137n. 39
disavowal, definition of, 117n. 10; of history (in W. Collins's *Armadale*) 126; of imperialism, 152–3 (in W Collins's *The Moonstone*) 133; of racial inequality (in W. Collins's *Armadale*) 131. *See also* slavery; imperialism/imperial
Disraeli, Benjamin, 3, 5n. 5, 10, 13, 41, 41n. 2, 46, 49, 53n. 24, 64, 82–3, 96, 105n. 20, 106–7n. 23, 107n. 24, 141, 275; aestheticized arts of government of, 105; A. Trollope and, 81n. 25, 109; anti-Semitism and, 107, 249n. 14; as Chancellor of the Exchequer, 140; British Empire and, 60; author of *Coningsby*, 63; Crystal Palace speech of, 63; depicted as charlatan, 103; encounter with A. Trollope, 109; imperial policy of, 106n. 22; influence on New Imperialism of, 107, 123; likened to Koh-i-Noor's cutter, 140, 140n. 41; orientalization of, 62; Royal Titles Act (1876) and, 63; second ministry of, 106; Tory philosophy and, 63; Young England fiction and, 63. *See also* Conservative Party, New Imperialism
"distant" reading, 16, 20, 20n. 3, 36, 268, 281, 288, 292n. 30.
See also Moretti, Franco
Doctorow, E. L., *Ragtime*, 282
Don Pacifico, 69, 71n. 12, 140
Doty, Alexander, 252n. 17
Douglass, Frederick, 253
Drayton, Richard, 116n. 8, 117

Dreiser, Theodore, 165, *Sister Carrie* (1900), 275
Duggan, Lisa, 3n. 4
Dumas, Alexandre, 163
Duncan, Ian, 73, 134n. 33, 143n. 44, 156, 158–9; on W. Scott, 176; on W. Collins's *The Moonstone*, 154, 154–155n. 57, 158
Durkheim, Emile, 214

Eagleton, Terry, 28, 88, 245
East India Company, 8, 8n. 10, 8n. 11, 41, 42, 44, 45–6, 49n. 11, 66n. 2; abolition of, 53n. 24; J. S. Mill and, 53n. 26. *See also* imperialism/imperial, India/Indian
Edwardian-era, 209, 230
Egg, Augustus, 163
Egypt, 70, 274
"Eighteenth Brumaire" of Louis Napoleon, 10, 110, 128, 189. *See also* Marx, Karl
Eisenstadt, S. N., 214
Eliot, George (Marian Evans), 2, 5, 14–5, 17, 29, 31, 37, 84n. 30, 88, 150, 150n. 51, 228, 244, 269, 275n. 10, 278, 281; adultery and, 164, 175, 179, 180, 182, 192; and von Riehl's social ethnography, 178; as novelist of life, 166; as proleptic Lukácsian, 182, 207, 274–5; compared to G. Flaubert, 182; engagement with naturalism, 182 (and adulterous geopolitical aesthetic), 192; European dimensions of (J. Rignall on), 175, 175n. 24; G. Moore on, 175; German translations of, 178; influence of G. Sand and W. Scott on, 178, 178n. 28, 275; J. Ruskin's picturesque and, 178; *mauvaise foi* in, 282; mid-Victorian-era seriality and, 243; sympathy and, 104; trans-channel engagements of, 275; trip to Italy in 1860, 194; uncertain familiarity of with G. Flaubert's *Madame Bovary*, 182; union with G. Lewes, 175
Works: *Adam Bede*, 164, 164n. 3, 179, 183n. 35, 215
"The *Antigone* and its Moral," 194, 198
Daniel Deronda, 14, 37, 167, 181, 182, 193, 211, 221, 283, 286; as "country-house" novel, 172, 275; as Exodus narrative, 275, 276; as Eliot's most naturalistic novel, 167 (as well as her most utopian), 204; as example of the adulterous geopolitical aesthetic, 205–6; as philo-Semitic work, 249; C. Gallagher on, 203; global embedding of (N. Henry on), 204n. 50; gothic elements of, 205, 205n. 64; narrative splitting in, 252; nativism of (B. Robbins on), 206; serialization of, 285

Felix Holt, adulterous Mrs. Transome in, 203
Mill on the Floss, 167, 181, 205; as figurative adultery novel, 184, 201, 204; as *Bildungsroman* (J. Esty), 183; disrupting boundaries of high and low in, 186–7; drifting in, 204, 204n. 61; historicism of, 183–4
Middlemarch, 166, 181, 192, 193, 193n. 44, 205, 218; compared to *Madame Bovary* (J. Rignall on), 181–2; H. James on, 165; serialization of, 283, 285; V. Woolf on, 175n. 24
"The Morality of *Wilhelm Meister*," 80
"Natural History of German Life," 178
Romola, 4, 14, 16, 111, 167, 211, 193, 205; Antigonean moment in, 198–9; as exploration of clash between private desire and public good, 196; as problem text, 184; as female variation on the typical character, 187, 196, 197; anti-naturalism of, 142n. 43; D. Malachuk on, 195; "drifting away" in, 202, 203, 203–4n. 59; exilic subject in, 280; F. Jameson on, 202n. 57, 279–80, 280n. 16; genre fusion in, 198; Jewish exiles in, 203; mixed reception of, 167–8, 194; R.H. Hutton on, 193, 201; Romola's "marriage" to Tessa, 202, 202n. 55 (J. Morley on), 202; serialization of, 202n. 57; 283; S. Winnett on, 193, 201, 203; Tito as cosmopolitan exile in, 202 (Judaized features of), 202n. 26; Tito's adultery in, 197; utopian dimension of, 200
"Silly Novels by Lady Novelists," 164, 176, 183
The Spanish Gypsy, 205, 206n. 65
"Woman in France," 179, female adultery narrative in, 181, 192–3, 201, sustainable female *Bildung* in, 193
Eliot, T. S., 143; *The Wasteland*, 282
Ellingson, Ter, 77n. 20, 122
Ellis, Havelock, 224n. 30
Emanuel, Harry, 138
empire. *See* imperialism/imperial
Engels, Friedrich, 1, 67n. 4
English, James F., 270n. 3, 287
Enlightenment, the, 11, 21, 23, 24, 36, 38, 66; abolitionism and, 129; cosmopolitanism and, 85; ethics of, 219; gender and, 219; Governor Eyre crisis and, 60; liberalism of, 219; U. Mehta on, 130; universalism of, 43, 60, 129, 212, 214, 231, 232
Equiano, Olaudah, 117
"equipoise," mid-Victorian, 10, 10n. 14.
Erfahrung, 13–4, 132; black Atlantic experience and, 116; as utopian

imaginary, 157; "dark" in W. Collins's
fiction, 114, 129, 131 (in *Armadale*) 154
(in *The Moonstone*), 154, 155, 156–7;
definition of, 112–3; destruction of and
First World War, 144; in W. Collins's
Armadale, 114; in W. Collins's *The
Moonstone*, 160; in W. Collins's
The Woman in White, 113, 114;
integrative work of, 145; radicalizing
in W. Collins's *The Moonstone*, 157–8;
R. Williams's definition of experience
and, 144, 144–5n. 47. *See also*
Benjamin, Walter
Erlebnis, 33, 85n. 31, 144, 186; as depicted
in W. Collins's *The Moonstone*,
156; definition of, 112–13; in
W. Collins's *Armadale*, 128. *See also*
Benjamin, Walter
Ermarth, Elizabeth, 37n. 27
Escobar, Arturo, 217n. 19
Esty, Jed, 150n. 51, 211n. 10, 274n. 9;
Peripheral Realisms, 280n. 17
ethics/ethical, 109, 269; approaches to
literature, 11; capacious subject
of, 146; W. Collins's fiction and,
110; communicative, 219n. 21, (S.
Benhabib and J. Habermas), 232n.
39; connection to view (in E. Foster's
fiction), 231–3; cosmopolitan, 4,
35n. 25, 65, (K. Appiah on), 66–7,
68; E. M. Forster and, 209, 230–41,
(gendered variations on), 228–30;
embodied (in E. Carpenter's work),
224, (in E. M. Forster's fiction) 15, 235,
237–8, 239; ethico-cultural richness
(and A. Trollope), 82; failure of in
A. Trollope's *The Eustace Diamonds*,
93, 94, 108, 109; imperialism and,
43, 60, 91; in E. M. Forster's *Howards
End*, 214; internationalism and, 85,
211 (E. M. Forster's queer variation
on) 37; J. S. Mill and, 211–12; joining
of with geopolitics, 21, 26–7; kinship
ties (in E. M. Forster's fiction), 232,
(R. Rorty's expansion of), 238; of care,
219–20, 224n. 31, (in E. Carpenter's
writing), 224, (in E.M. Forster's
fiction), 218, 219, 222, 231, 238, (in
R. Rorty's internationalism), 238; of
infinite responsibility to otherness,
239; of justice (masculinism of),
220; of the self (in R. Williams and
P. Gilroy), 36; poststructuralist as well
as Enlightenment, 24, 271; priority of
(in E. Levinas's philosophy), 235–6,
236n. 43; procedural, 4; property
and, 90; responsibility to otherness
versus responsibility to act, 272–3,
293; surface reading and, 16, 293;

technocratization of, 101; Trollopian,
74n. 18 (in *The Warden*) 84; turn to in
literary studies, 4, 22–3, 239, 239n. 47;
unmooring of depicted in narratives of
capitalist globalization, 141; Victorian,
3 (in E. Dallas), 19–20.
Europe, north and south division of, 209,
217, 221, 222, (in E. M. Forster's
Where Angels Fear to Tread), 230, 237;
imperialism and, 213; R. Dainotto on,
217. *See also* southern/southerness
Exodus, Book of, 249; as focal point
for Middle East politics, 254; as
inspiration for L. Uris's novel and
O. Preminger's film 254; as inspiration
for Anglo-Saxon settlement, 254;
narratives of (in G. Eliot's *Daniel
Deronda*) 251, 275, 276 (in *Mad
Men*), 253, (in A. Trollope's *The Prime
Minister*), 249, 251; project of Jewish
nationhood and, 254; Zionism and,
254. *See also* Babylon; Jews/Judaism,
"secret Jew"
exilic subjects, in A. Trollope's fiction, 286
experience, 13, 23; G. Agamben and 9n. 12,
142 (destruction of), 111; as dialogical
concept, 145, as essentialistic category,
145, 145n. 48; Atlantic variation on
(in W. Collins's *Armadale*), 126, 131;
atrophy of (W. Benjamin on), 111;
black Atlantic, 116; crisis of modern,
144, 149, (G. Flaubert's *Madame
Bovary* on), 190n. 41; (U. Mehta on),
153 (W. Collins's fiction on), 111, 112;
evacuation of (in W. Collins's *The
Woman in White*), 113; imperialism and,
149; of Holocaust, 254; multi-voiced
in W. Collins's *The Moonstone*, 133; of
global history, 111, 112; rendered as
legible narrative (in W. Collins's *The
Moonstone*), 143; transnational, 14, 153,
171, (historical consciousness and), 247,
(in W. Collins's fiction), 111, 114, 275
(in *The Moonstone*), 153; R. Williams's
definition of, 144, 144–5n. 47. *See also
Erfahrung*; *Erlebnis*;
transnational/transnationality
Eyre, Edward John, 10, 43n. 5, 97, 119,
119–20n. 14, 123n. 19; controversy,
129; defense of, 123; prosecution
of, 131

Fabian, Johannes, 2, 217n. 19
Fabians, internationalism and, 211n. 8
Farber, Dan 286
Felber, Lynette, 89n. 4
Felski, Rita, 16, 21, 222, 268, 269–70,
270n. 3, 271, 273, 287, 291, 292, 293;
embrace of B. Latour, 289, 292

Fenianism, 43, 43n. 5, 52, 52n. 23, 60, 119
Ferguson, Frances, 187, 264, 264n. 25
Feuchtwanger, Edgar, 106n. 22
Fielding, Henry, 175
Findlay, Elaine Suarez, 80n. 23
Fisch, Audrey, 131
Flaubert, Gustave, 2, 5, 14, 84n. 30, 85, 165, 183, 205, 269, 281, 283; and sentimental novels of adultery, 185; aestheticism of compared to *Mad Men*, 245–6; as participant in a literary "world-system," 274–5; G. Lukács on, 245; letter to Louise Colet, 184, 187; Middle East travel of, 264n. 24; naturalism of, 246, 275; relationship with E. Zola, 165n. 4, trial of, 161–2, 181; turn to historical fiction (A. Green on), 184.

Works: "A Simple Heart," 33n. 21

Madame Bovary, 10, 14, 15, 16, 33n. 21, 37, 150, 161–3, 164n. 3, 164–5, 166–7, 170, 171–2, 173, 176, 179, 181–2, 184, 185, 243n. 3, 261, 264n. 24, 264n. 25, 275, 286, 287; adultery in, 188, 189, 191 (adulterous sex in), 204, 204n. 62s; as "*Kapital*, the novel" (E. Apter), 173; as powerful expression of the adulterous geopolitical aesthetic, 189; art's relation to everyday life in, 188; as naturalistic narrative, 276; B. Leckie on, 182–3n. 33; compared to G. Eliot's *Romola*, 197, 201, 204; H. James's "Preface" to, 165–6; depiction of "Modern Babylon" in, 264; Emma's failed aestheticism in (J. Rancière), 187; E. Auerbach on, 190, 190–2; evocation of failed revolution in, 171; excision of dates from, 171n. 18, 190n. 41 (E. Marder on); exilic subjectivity of Emma in, 172, 191; H. James on, 265; H. Shaw on, 189; F. Jameson on, 167, 190; J. Rancière on, 184–5, 186–9, 190; narration in (J. Culler on) 190–1; reception of, 286–7 (J. Stephen on), 161, 162, 163, (G. Meredith on), 162–3, 164; serialization of, 161, 192; sugar-plantation complex and, 191; worlding consumer culture in, 191

Salammbô, 182; G. Lukács on, 189, 190

L'Education sentimentale, 182, G. Eliot reading, 204

Flint, Kate, 1n. 1
Fontane, Theordor, 193
foreign policy, 12, 72; decline of Trollopian variation on, 82; mid-Victorian, 69–71; Palmerston and, 7; "race" and, 77–78n. 21; Trollopian, 66–8, 85–6
form, literary, 11; aesthetics and, 271; and point of view (in E. M. Forster's fiction), 231–2; dynamism of in post-1848 British fiction, 114; innovations of in W. Collins's fiction (*Armadale*), 123 (*The Moonstone*), 132, 133, 142; global genres and, 66. See also realism/realist novel

Forman, Ross G., 119n. 13
Forster, E. M., 2, 5, 15, 17, 31, 37, 195, 208–9, 214–5, 216–41, 269; as novelistic precursor to E. Levinas, 236; as postmodern ethicist, 234; as "queer" novelist, 221, 238; attention to embodiment of, 237–8; critiques of liberalism and, 29; and denaturalization of R. Rorty's family bonds, 238; depictions of view in fiction of, 216, 218–21, 229, 231–3, 234–5; exoticizing of otherness in fiction of, 236, 236n. 44; homophile discourse of friendship in fiction of, 223–7; imperial "civilizing mission" in fiction of, 221–2; internationalism of, 216; F. Jameson on, 214–5, 215n. 15; liberalism and, 208, 208n. 2; notions of gender difference of, 228–30; posthumous publications of, 218; "relaxed will" and, 284; Rortyan readings of, 233–4; G. Trevelyan and, 215–7. See also geopolitical aesthetics, "queer internationalist" variation on

Works: *A Passage to India*, 208–9n. 2, 209, 221, 225, 225n. 32, 233–4; indeterminate relation to imperialism in, 239

A Room with a View, 209, 216, 228, 228n. 36, 230, 234; influence of E. Carpenter on, 231

"Arctic Summer," 227n. 34
"Desire for a Book," 223
Howards End, 30–1, 84, 208, 208n. 2, 209, 214–5, 227n. 34, 228, 237
Maurice, 218
"Notes on the English Character," 217
The Longest Journey, 209
"The Feminine Note in Literature," 228
"The Story of a Panic," 209
"Three Countries," 215n. 17, 233
"What I Believe," 208, 231, 240n. 50
Where Angels Fear to Tread, 4, 15, 209, 215, 216, 217, 218, 221–32, 235–9, 240, 241, 284; as allegory of ethical failure, 236; as Levinasian novel, 239; breached sovereignty and, 239; depictions of view in, 237, 241; infinite responsibility depicted in, 237, 239; influence of E. Carpenter on, 224–5, 227, 228, 228n. 36, 231; limited impact of queering encounter in, 234–5; middle-class women's authority

in, 225–6, 229, 230; misogynistic dimensions of in, 226, 226n. 33, 227
Foucault, Michel, 2, 289, 187n. 39, 188; archeology of madness, 273; genealogical insights of, 271; influence of on New Historicism, 272, 272n. 6; and aesthetics of the self, 197; work on governmentality, 271n. 4
Fraiman, Susan, 150n. 51
Frank, Gunder Andre, 217n. 19
Franklin, J. Jeffrey, 81n. 25, 173n. 19
Fraser, Derek, 208n. 1
free trade, 6–8, 40, 60, 90; internationalism and, 211. *See also* imperialism/imperial
Freeden, Michael, 208n. 1
Freedgood, Elaine, 32n. 20, 115n. 7, 225n. 32, 271
Freedman, Jonathan, 83n. 27
French Revolution, 212, 247
French Second Empire, 73, 167, 171, 185, 186, 275
Freud, Sigmund, 117n. 10, 258, 258n. 22
Fryckstedt, Monica C., 203n. 58
Furbank, P N., 208, 215, 216n. 18
FX (television channel), 245

Gagnier, Regenia, 66n. 2, 83n. 27, 89n. 3, 250n. 15
Gallagher, Catherine, 168–9n. 11, 203, 272n. 5; New Historicism and, 273
Gallagher, John, and Ronald Robinson, 6n. 8
Games, Alison, 26n. 11
Ganguly, Keya, 145n. 48
Garibaldi, Giuseppe, 121, 195n. 47
Garrett, Peter, 123, 166n. 9, 205n. 64
Gaskell, Elizabeth, 36, 163
Genesis, Book of, in *Mad Men*, 253
Geoghegan, Vincent, 224n. 29
geopolitical aesthetic, 11, 21, 33, 66, 110, 273–4, 287; adulterous variation on, 164, 168–76, 192 (C. Dickens's *Dombey and Son* and G. Flaubert's *Madame Bovary* as examples of), 201, (in C. Dickens's fiction), 34n. 23, (and A. Trollope's *The Prime Minister*), 172, (in Dickens, Flaubert, Meredith, Trollope, James, Tolstoy, and Hardy), 182; and redemptive ethics, 36; archeological variation on, 9, 14, 209n. 4 (in W. Collins's *Armadale*) 114–7, 117n. 9, 118–29, 132–3, (in W. Collins's *The Moonstone*), 133; as distinct from realist antinomies (F. Jameson on), 278, 279; comparativism and 168; definition of, 9; disavowal and, 117n. 10; Edwardian-era, 230; Forsterian point of view and, 231; F. Jameson and, 9, 10, 146; G. Agamben and, 9n. 12; in W. Collins's *Armadale*, 117, 132; in W. Collins's *The Moonstone*, 150, 153; in W. Collins's *The Woman in White*, 113; in realist cinema, 247; in A. Trollope's *The Eustace Diamonds*, 101–2, 103, 105, 107; intensified variation of, 105; international variation on, 9, 37; *longue durée* history and, 268; *Mad Men's* variation on, 252; mid-Victorian-era, 114 (multiple variations of), 34n. 22, 37–8; Modernism and, 30; naturalistic variations on, 68, 243; phenomenological variation on, 9, 209n. 4 (in E. M. Forster's fiction), 221 (in W. Collins's fiction), 111, 275 (in *The Moonstone*), 132, 136, 142, 146, 154; "queer internationalist" variation on, 15, 209 (in E. M. Forster's *A Passage to India*), 233–4 (in E. M. Forster's *Where Angels Fear to Tread*), 216, 217–8, 221–3, 225–31, 234–41; racial hybridity and (in W. Collins's *Armadale*), 116; relation to Marxist and historicist theory, 271–6; serialized naturalistic variation on (in A. Trollope's *The Prime Minister*), 283–84, (in *Mad Men*), 284, 286–7; sociological variation on, 9, 12, 218 (Balzac's fiction and), 177; synchronic as well as diachronic theory of, 269; transnationality and, 65; Victorian, 1, 5, 10, 21, 27–36, 37
geopolitical unconscious, 9, 21, 31, 39, 40, 48, 64, 218; in A. Trollope's *The Eustace Diamonds*, 102–3; A. Trollope and, 110. *See also* geopolitical aesthetic; Jameson, Fredric
geopolitics, 6, 11, 17, 21, 22, 26, 27, 30, 33, 35, 37, 71, 72, 80, 170; abstracted from R. Rorty's liberal theory, 240; as depicted in A. Trollope's *The Eustace Diamonds*, 90; as depicted in W. Collins's *The Moonstone*, 152, 154; as depicted in E. M. Forster's *Where Angels Fear to Tread*, 226; critical, 6n. 7; G. GoGwilt's conception of, 111n. 3; imperial, 2–3; literary form and, 134; nineteenth-century, 7, 8, 42; "race" and, 77–8n. 21; resistance to (in E. M. Forster's fiction), 236; Tory imperial policy and, 105
Germany, unification of, 120n. 15
Gikandi, Simon, 25n. 9, 65, 78, 119
Gilbert, Sandra M., 261
Gilligan, Carol, 220, 220n. 22
Gilmour, Robin, 74n. 18
Gilroy, Paul, 23–4, 27, 28n. 13, 36, 36n. 26, 86, 115–6, 117, 155; Morant Bay rebellion and, 119; *The Black Atlantic*, 119, 126
Gissing, George, 2, 5n. 5, 10n. 14, 165
Gitlin, Todd, 248

Gladstone, William E., 105, 120, 121n. 17, 194, 215
globalization, 1, 5, 10, 19, 22–3, 31, 35, 69, 69n. 8, 135n. 36, 210; Anglo-Saxon "race" and, 59; anti-Semitism and, 140–1; captured in nineteenth-century realism, 246; Jewish "cosmopolitanism" and, 139; experiential effects of, 144; literary "world-system" and, 274; *longue durée* and, 11, 15, 85, 132; nineteenth-century Britain and, 8, 40; naturalistic effects of, 16; of capital, 11, 21, 30, 31, 38, 65, 170, 214, 246, 273; "race" and, 77–8; theory of space and time for, 283; A. Trollope and, 84; uneven developments and, 80
Goethe, Johann Wolfgang von, 170n. 14, 178, 180, 183, 183n. 34
Goffman, Erving, 289
GoGwilt, Christopher, 111, 111n. 3, 137n. 39, 143n. 44, 156n. 60
Gooch, G. P., 213n. 13
Goodlad, Lauren M. E., 1n. 1, 2, 3n. 4, 67n. 4, 73n. 15, 157n. 62, 202n. 55; 222, 245n. 6, 246n. 9, 269n. 2, 284n. 23, 292n. 30; 271, 271n. 4, 111n. 3
Goscilo, Margaret, 218
Goswami, Manu, 27, 27n. 12
governmentality. *See* imperialism/imperial; liberalism
Gramsci, Antonio, 273
Great Exhibition (1851), 8n. 11, 42, 128n. 27, 133, 138, 246; universalism of, 246n. 10
"Greater Britain," nineteenth-century notion of, 8, 11, 12, 41, 56–64, 69, 72 194n. 46; A. Trollope and, 78–79, 80, 87; as global polity, 57; and the United States, 57; genocidal outlook of, 60. *See also* Dilke, Charles; imperialism/imperial, settler; Merivale, Herman; Seeley, J. R.; Smith, Goldwin; Trollope, Anthony
Green, Abigail, 71n. 12, 140
Greg, W. R., 163
Greif, Mark, 245
Greiner, Donald J., 143, 144n. 46
Grewal, Inderpal, 210
Grossberg, Lawrence, 273
Grote, George, 122
Gubar, Susan, 261

Habermas, Jürgen, 15, 208, 220, 220n. 24, 233–234; communicative ethics of and S. Benhabib, 232n. 38
Hack, Daniel, 270
Hager, Kelly, 173
Haggard, Rider, 275n. 10
Haight, Gordon, 175n. 14, 178, 178n. 28, 179–80

Hall, Catherine, 2n. 2, 25n. 10, 43n. 5, 52, 52n. 23, 67, 71, 78, 87, 100, 106n. 22, 120n. 14, 123n. 19, 222n. 26
Halperin, John, 81n. 25, 95, 105
Hardt, Michael and Antonio Negri, 39–40, 40n. 1, 210n. 6
Hardy, Barbara, 166n. 9, 176, 204
Hardy, Thomas, 164
Harvey, David, 171
Harvey, W. J., 166, 176
Harvie, Christopher, 74n. 18, 89
Hastings, Warren, 11, 45–6, 61, 153; in A. Trollope's *The Eustace Diamonds*, 95
Hawkins, Sherman, 74n. 18
Haworth, Jill, 254
Hawthorne, Nathaniel, 164, *The Scarlet Letter*, 180
HBO (Home Box Office), 245
Hegel, G. W. F., 176, 247; influence on F. Jameson, 273
Heilbrun, Carolyn, 168–9n. 11
Heywood, Christopher, 167
heirloom. *See* sovereignty, "heirloom"
Heller, Tamar, 133n. 32, 143n. 44, 155n. 59
Hennelly, Mark 134n. 33
Henry, Nancy, 179, 194n. 46, 202n. 56, 204, 204n. 50
Hensley, Nathan, 130, 130n. 29, 132, 132n. 31, 173n. 19
Herbert, Christopher, 88n. 2
hermeneutics of suspicion, 11, 268–9, 271; R. Felski on, 270, 270n. 3
Herriton, Philip, 231
Heuman, Gad, 132
Hewitt, Martin, 10n. 14
historical novel/romance, 274, F. Jameson on, 278–82; G. Eliot's *Romola* and, 111; post-1848 decline of, 157; W. Collins and, 111. *See also* Eliot, George, *Romola*; Scott, Walter
historicism. *See* geopolitical aesthetic; New Historicism; new imperial history
Hoad, Neville, 217n. 19, 224n. 29
Hobbes, Thomas, 73, 82, 211n. 9; individualism and, 78
Hobson, J. A., 23, 83, 83n. 27, 139, 211–5, 220n. 24, 224n. 29, 237, 211
Hollis, Patricia, 222n. 26
Holt, Thomas C., 118, 119
Homans, Margaret, 63
Hong Kong, annexation of, 8
Honig, Bonnie, 85, 196n. 50; 200, 233n. 40
Hopkins, A. G., 1
Howard, Michael, 6n. 7
Howells, William Dean, 89, 193–4
Hughes, J. R. T, 173
Hughes, Linda K., 244
humanism, 85, 289
Hunt, James, 122

Index

Hunt, Thornton Leigh, 179–80
Hutton, R. H., 68, 89, 193
Huysmans, Joris-Karl, 187n. 39
Hyde Park riots (1866), 120
Hyndman, J., 1n. 1, 6n. 7

Ilbert Bill (1883), 11, 61
imperialism/imperial, 4, 6, 9, 11, 12, 22–3, 29, 41; "absent-minded" (depicted in W. Collins's *The Moonstone*), 153, 153n. 56; adventure fiction, 136; ancient Rome and, 8; anglicization and, 51–52n. 20; annexation and, 41, 41n. 2, 50, 96–7, 97n. 15; A. Trollope and, 77–82, (*The Eustace Diamonds*), 87–109, 105, 109; anti-Semitism and, 106; "blowback" of (captured in nineteenth-century realism), 246; British disavowal of, 9, 62, 273 (H. Martineau and), 152–3; "Oriental" despotism of British, 57; capitalism and, 69n. 8; "civilizing mission," 6, 11, 42, 48–9, 49n. 13, 55–6, 100, 130, 149, 213, 214, 222n. 26, (depicted in W. Collins's *Armadale*), 131, (depicted in E. M. Forster's fiction), 216, 230, 233, (in *Where the Angels Fear to Tread*), 221, 238; complicitness with (of E. M. Forster's *A Passage to India*), 239; contradictions of, 123; cosmopolitanism and, 65, 66–7; crisis of experience and, 149; crisis of sovereignty, 212; debates between "Orientalists" and liberals, 51; decline of liberal, 60–3; "dependencies," 57; E. Carpenter's critique of, 213n. 13; E. Carpenter's works and, 224, 224n. 29; "engraftment" and, 50–1; federalism and, 58; formal /formalization of, 6, 242–3; free trade and, 42; governance, 54–7; governmentality, 13, 52, 56, 64, 90, 109; "Greater Britain" and, 8, 61; J. A. Hobson and, 212–14; humanitarianism and, 119n. 13; in India, 8, 41–2; in North America, 42; "indirect" rule and, 12, 41–2, 48–9, 50, 96, 120, 137; informal, 42; invention of "heirlooms," 109; liberal (governmentality of), 88, 97, 101, 103, (U. Mehra on), 218–9, (in W. Collins's *Armadale*), 130; mentality depicted in *Mad Men* compared to Victorian, 256; J. S. Mill and, 55–6; neo-feudal style of, 62, 63; policy for, 69; portable culture of, 225; prior to Modernism, 276; reactionary political effects of, 8, 31, 39; royalty and (in A. Trollope's *The Eustace Diamonds*), 90; technocratic governmentality and, 101; territorial (as distinct from "Greater Britain"), 7, 40, 43, 55, 57, 58, 59–60, 69, 86; Tory, 47–8, 62, 88, 97; white settler, 41, 43, 48, 56, 57, 58, 69, 70, 77–9, 98–9, 102, (hostility to indigenes and), 118, 119n. 12, (relative insignificance of in France), 171. *See also* colonialism; geopolitics; "Greater Britain," liberalism; New Imperialism

India/Indian, 8, 15, 60, 69, 70, 120, 130n. 29, 274; anglicist versus orientalist views of, 46; anglicization and, 46, 118; Anglo-Mysore War and, 91; annexation of the Punjab in, 136–7, 152; A. Trollope and, 67n. 3, 87–8, 100 (and *The Eustace Diamonds*) 88; as dependency, 8, 8n. 11, 39, 58; as child-like, 55; as depicted in W. Collins's *The Moonstone*, 33, 88, 91, 133, 134, 134n. 136, 159; as "Great Parliamentary bore," 97, 98, 101, 102; as "jewel in the crown," 12; as source of raw materials, 138; British, 47–8; British misrecognition of, 149; British rule of, 63; "civilizing mission" and, 118; "declaration of independence" of, 8n. 11; deindustrialization of, 8n. 11, 42; diamonds in, 135n. 34; E. M. Forster's travel to, 215n. 16, 233 (and views on), 234; famine in Orissa (1866), 52n. 22; Ilbert Bill (1883) and, 61, 61n. 33; imperialism in (compared to Atlantic), 118; independence of, 49; "indirect" rule of, 44, 96; irreducible sovereignty of (in W. Collins's *The Moonstone*), 159; G. Smith on, 56–7, 58; J. Seeley on, 59; J. S. Mill and, 53n. 25, 53n. 26; Koh-i-Noor diamond and, 92; K. Marx's article on, 274; "princely" states of, 46n. 11, 49; *pundit* and, 32n. 20; readers in, 38, 285n. 24; realist novels in, 245; rising nationalism in, 61; romanticization of (in W. Collins's *The Moonstone*), 154; rule of, 53; secretary of State for, 44, 49; storming of Seringapatam (1799), 91; support for liberal reforms in, 62; transfer to Crown rule of, 53–4; W. Bagehot on, 54n. 27; W. Collins's "dark *Erfahrung*" and, 114.
See also New Imperialism

Indian "mutiny"/rebellion (1857–8), 7, 10, 14, 29, 31, 40, 41, 42, 43, 44, 45, 48–9, 59, 60, 70, 88, 96, 97, 113, 114, 118, 129, 137, 137n. 39, 139, 141, 152, 161, 195; H. Martineau and, 7

Indian royals, 41, 61, 95, 96, 97, 97n. 16, 97n. 16, adoption and, 96; as metropolitan types, 97–100; as represented (in W. Collins's *The Moonstone*), 137, (in A. Trollope's *The Eustace Diamonds*), 103
"indirect" British rule. *See* imperialism/imperial
Indonesia, 8, 42
internationalism, 15, 23, 85, 209, 209n. 2, 212, 216; J. Bentham and, 210; M. Cohen and C. Dever's notion of, 211; federated world governance and, 212; E. M. Forster's "queer" variation on, 234, 237 (and responsibility to otherness), 272; J. A. Hobson and, 211, 214; post-nationalism and, 210; R. Rorty on, 238; G. Trevelyan on, 217; actually existing, 210–11. *See also* ethics/ethical; Forster, E. M.; geopolitical aesthetic, "queer" internationalist variation on
Ireland/Irish, 42, 60, 61, 274; Fenianism and, 119; in A. Trollope's fiction, 77–8, 79–80, 102; likened to Africans, 122; rootless cosmopolitanism of, 79
Irigaray, Luce, 236, 239n. 47, 239n. 48; feminist theory of, 273
Isle of Man, location for W. Collins's *Armadale*, 125
Italian *Risorgimento*, 15, 121, 210, 215, 254; as background in W. Collins's *Armadale*, 127–8; as context for G. Eliot's *Romola*, 184, 195; inspiration for internationalism, 195; Palmerston on, 195n. 47
Itzkoff, Dave, 251

Jaffe, Audrey, 83
Jamaica, 10, 43, 52, 52n. 23, 57, 60–1, 97, 119, 120n. 14, 274; rebellion, 117, 152. *See also* Eyre, Edward John; Morant Bay rebellion (1865)
James, Henry, 5n. 5, 29n. 16, 31, 89n. 3, 165, 172, 203, 265; aestheticism of, 166; novelistic form (gendering of) 166, on G. Flaubert's *Madame Bovary*, 192, 264, 265 (1902 "Preface" to) 165–6, 190; on G. Eliot's *Romola*, 193, 193n. 44; "The Art of Fiction," 175n. 25; 277; A. Trollope and, 88
Jameson, Fredric, 6n. 7, 21, 21n. 4, 27, 28, 28n. 15, 29, 30, 31n. 18, 36, 59, 84, 246, 284; *A Singular Modernity*, 35n. 25, 239n. 47; *The Antinomies of Realism*, 10n. 15, 21n. 4, 35n. 25, 276–83, 284, 292; "Antinomies of the Realism-Modernism Debate," 278–9; *Archaeologies of the Future*, 112n. 4; C. Lesjak on, 272; "Cognitive Mapping," 90; *The Geopolitical Aesthetic*, 9, 113, 147, 247, 248, 271; geopolitical aesthetic and, 11, 27, 34–5, 146; geopolitical unconscious and, 21, 31; "Globalization and Political Strategy," 210n. 6; Hegelianism of, 273; hermeneutics of suspicion and, 271; historicization and, 271; history as "absent cause" and, 273; "Introduction" to *The Historical Novel*, 247; legacy of, 269, 276; minimal interest in seriality, 283; "Modernism and Imperialism," 214; on G. Flaubert, 167, 189, 192, (*bovarysme* and), 189–90; on the future of historical fiction, 280–1; on realism's "fixed-camera" view, 245; on realist mimesis, 282n. 19; on science fiction and fantasy, 282; *The Political Unconscious*, 16, 35n. 25, 146, 268, 269, 274, 275, 281; "Postmodernism and Consumer Society," 248; privileging of Modernist and romance forms, 274; "Progress versus Utopia," 157, 276; "Realism and Utopia in *The Wire*," 246n. 10, 248n. 12; "The Realist Floor-Plan," 33; responsibility to act and, 273; science fiction and, 112n. 4; *Signatures of the Visible*, 31n. 19, 247, 276–83; S. Best and S. Marcus on, 269; *Valences of the Dialectic*, 272n. 5, 280
Jay, Martin, 112
Jews/Judaism, 13, 16, 32, 85; and advance of British interests, 140; and the "Jewish Question" (A. Mufti on), 250; A. Trollope and, 71n. 12, 82–4, 89, 106–7; as dealers in diamonds, 139–40; capitalist cosmopolitanism and, 67, 172, 212, 212n. 12; commodification of heirlooms and, 141; depiction of (as exilic modern subjects), 243 (as global financiers and imperial power brokers), 139 (as "new Jews" in L. Uris's *Exodus*), 20, 254, 254n. 20, (in A. Trollope's fiction), 243 (in A. Trollope's *The Way We Live Now*), 109n. 25, (in *Mad Men*), 257–8, 259–60, (in E. Carpenter's writings), 224n. 29; dialectical relation with Englishness, 250; Don Pacifico and, 71n. 12; liberal universalism and, 255; trope of the "secret Jew," 13, 16, 249, 252, 260 (as figure of ambiguous identity in *Mad Men*), 251 (A. Trollope's ambivalence toward), 261–2; trope of the "virtual" Jew (in *Mad Men*) 84n. 30, 248, 249–53 (prevision of in G. Eliot's *Daniel Deronda*), 205–6; unstable features of

(B. Cheyette on), 250; Zionism and (as depicted in *Mad Men*), 260. *See also* anti-Semitism
Jewsbury, Geraldine, 141–2, 203, 203n. 58
Joshi, Priya, 1n. 1, 38, 285n. 24
Joyce, Simon, 274n. 9

Kaganovsky, Lilya, 260n. 23
Kalmar, Ivan Davidson, 250
Kant, Immanuel, 23, 112, 145
Kaplan, Amy, 254n. 20
Kaplan, Caren, 210
Kaye, Richard A., 274n. 9
Keirstead, Christopher M., 66n. 2
Kemp, Sandra, 156n. 61
Kendrick, Walter M., 89, 108, 179
Kermode, Frank, 265, 284
Kincaid, James R., 89n. 3
King, Charles William, 133, 135n. 34, 136, 138, 139
Kingsley, Charles, 74n. 18, 119
Kinoshita, Sharon, 275
Kipling, Rudyard, 229, 275n. 10
Knight, L. A., 47, 97, 97n. 15, 103
the Koh-i-Noor (diamond), 92, 92n. 8, 97, 141; B. Disraeli and, 139, 140, 140n 41; "gift" to Queen Victoria, 133, 136–7; history of, 133, 136–9; old-fashioned cut of, 138; recutting of, 138–9, 139n. 40, 140, 141, 152; W. Collins's *The Moonstone* and, 133, 136, 137. *See also* Trollope, Anthony, *The Eustace Diamonds*
Kostal, Rande W., 43n. 5
Kriegel, Lara, 8n. 11, 133
Kucich, John, 73n. 16, 269, 270
Kurnick, David, 168, 203–4n. 59, 205, 206n. 65, 274n. 9

Labour Party, 3n. 3
LaCapra, Dominick, 144, 272n. 5; on G. Flaubert's *Madame Bovary*, 150, 171n. 18
Laclau, Ernesto, 273, 273n. 8
Laffey, Mark, 210n. 5
Lambert, David, 2n. 2
Lane, Christopher, 221n. 25, 227, 234, 234n. 41
Langbauer, Laurie, 81n. 24, 83n. 29, 89n. 3, 107n. 24
Langland, Elizabeth, 225
Latour, Bruno, 16, 268, 269, 288, 289, 292; absence of temporality in theory of, 290; actor network theory of, 288–9, 290–1; and anti-suspicious critique, 270; post-humanist ontology of, 289–90; *Reassembling the Social*, 288, 289–91
Law, Graham, 111n. 2, 120–121n. 16, 244, 285
Law, Robin, 119n. 13
Lazarus, Neil, 24

Leachman, Cloris, 255
League of Nations, 216
Leavis, F. R., 228
Leckie, Barbara, 170n. 15, 182–3n. 33, 193
Leighton, Mary Elizabeth, 143n. 45
Lesjak, Carolyn, 270, 272
Lester, Alan, 2n. 2, 118, 119n. 12
Levinas, Emmanuel, 235–6, 237, 239, 239n. 47; infinite responsibility of, 273; reversal of ontology and ethics, 236n. 43
Levine, Caroline, 5n. 5, 28n. 14, 147n. 50, 166, 184, 193, 246
Levine, George, 73, 88, 200, 201
Levine, June Perry, 218
Levinson, Michael, 162n. 1
Lewes, George Henry, 178n. 28, and wife's adultery, 179n. 30; on art and reality, 277; on Balzac, 175; on "lady novelists," 163 (and G. Sand) 178n 29; suggestion about Savonarola's life and times, 195; translations of Balzac of, 178–9
Liberal Party, 3n. 3, 3n. 4, 58; anti-Semitism and, 106n. 22; emergence of in 1860, 194; Home Rule and, 61; invented traditions and, 63; reactionariness of, 123; split over, 61. *See also* Ireland/Irish
liberalism, 2, 3–4, 3n. 3, 6, 9, 12, 27, 39, 52, 209, 210; "advanced," 41; and support for Italian unification, 217; Anglo-Saxon exceptionalism and, 60; A. Trollope's Palliser novels and, 89n. 3; anti-imperialism and, 60; atomized and alienating in G. Eliot's *Daniel Deronda* (205); "civilizing mission" and, 100; Cold War-era (L. Trilling and), 284; crisis of (after Morant Bay rebellion), 119 (depicted in A. Trollope's *The Eustace Diamonds*); 108; disavowal of imperialism and, 60, 194–5; equalitarian norms of, 235–6; ethics of depicted (in E. M. Forster's fiction), 235 (in A. Trollope's *The Eustace Diamonds*), 90, 92–5, 101, 104 (in W. Collins's *Armadale*), 130; feminist critique of, 219, 219n. 21; E. M. Forster and, 15, 208n. 2 (as literary standard bearer for) 208, 208n. 2, 218, 237, 238 (complicated position of) 237–8, 239, 240–1; English-educated Indians and, 62; feminist political theory and, 220; foreign policy and, 69–71;free trade and, 60; gender and (depicted in A. Trollope's *The Eustace Diamonds*) 92; gendered standpoints of, 228–30; governance and, 43; imperial governmentality and, 88, 101;

imperialism and 41–3, 45, 46, 48, 50–1n. 18, 51, 58, 60, 103, 218–9; Indian rule and, 53; individualism and, 237, 284n. 23; I. Young's feminist reconstruction of, 235–6; limitations of, 60–3 (in R. Rorty's variation on), 240; J. Morley and, 52–7; J. R. Seeley and, 108; J. S. Mill and, 58–9; L. Trilling and, 208, 217–8, 219; Morley-Minto reforms in India and, 62; neo-Kantian, 219n. 21; norms of challenged (in E. M. Forster's fiction), 218; of the 1940s, 219, 219n. 21; P. Armstrong on, 233; paternalism and, 60; "queer internationalism" as alternative to, 238–41; self-critique and, 108; social democracy and, 220n. 24; technocratic governmentality and, 101; territorial empire and, 59–60; U. Mehta on, 149; universal norms of, 219 (S. Benhabib on), 235, 238 (I. Young on), 235–6, 238, 239n. 48. See also imperialism/imperial; neoliberalism; New Liberalism; sovereignty

Liberal Party, attacks on Tories, 64; support for U. S. Confederacy, 121
Liftin, Karen, 70n. 11
Limited Liability Act (1855), 173
Lindner, Christoph, 90n. 5
Littledale, Richard F., 286
Litvak, Joseph, 83n. 27, 252n. 17
Lloyd, David, 213, 217n. 230
Locke, John, 94, possessive individualism and, 70, 73, 76, 78, 93. *See also* liberalism
Loesberg, Jonathan, 130n. 29, 168
London International Exhibition (1862), 42, 140, 210
Lonergan, Patrick, 79n. 22
Long, David, 212, 212n. 11
longue durée, 5, 17, 170, 283–4, 291, 292; of nineteenth-century geopolitics, 276; history, as complement to the geopolitical aesthetic, 268. *See also* globalization
Lonoff, Sue, 142
Loomba, Anya, 8n. 11
Lorimer, Douglas A., 122, 123
Louis Napoleon (Napoleon III), 171, 186, 264n. 24
Love, Heather, 268, 288, 291
Lukács, Georg, 10, 11, 14, 15, 27, 28, 28n. 15, 31, 88, 105, 190, 243, 246, 264–5, 273, 274, 275, 276, 279; and holistic ontology of the heirloom, 177; average hero of (F. Jameson on), 280n. 16; *Essays on Realism*, 190; form and, 11; "Hegel's Aestheticism," 247; F. Jameson on, 177, 278–9; neglect of G. Eliot, 178; on historical fiction, 247; on Flaubert, 165, 189–90, 192, 194; on post-1848 crisis of bourgeois realism, 165, 245; on realist historicity, 280n. 15; on typical character, 14–5, 104, 183, 184, 247; H. Shaw on 194, 194n. 45; *The Historical Novel*, 10, 16, 90, 127, 168, 176–7, 177–8 (and A. Trollope's *The Eustace Diamonds*), 90 (and G. Eliot), 168, 182–3, 207, (H. Shaw on), 194n. 45; *Studies in European Realism*, 165, 243
Lund, Michael, 244
Lye, Colleen, 274n. 9; *Peripheral Realisms*, 280n. 17
Lynn, Martin, 6n. 8
Lytton, Robert, 1st Earl of Lytton, 12, 47, 63, 121n. 17

Macaulay, Thomas Babington, 4, 96n. 14, 98, 118, 183n. 35, 215n. 15
Machiavelli, Niccolò, 15; in G. Eliot's *Romola*, 195, 196, 197, 200, 280; J. G. A. Pocock on 196–7
Macpherson, C. B., 78, 93n. 10
Mad Men (2007–), 15–6, 37, 242–3, 269, 283, 284, 291; as historical pastiche, 245, 248; as naturalistic narrative of capitalist globalization, 245, 246; as three-decker novel, 264; breached sovereignty in, 246; capitalist realism and, 266–7; cigarette advertising in, 258–9, 258n. 22; closeted identities in, 252–3; compared to G. Flaubert's *Madame Bovary*, 246, 264–5; conscious aestheticism of, 262; depiction of global capitalism in, 257; depiction of Middle East in, 255, 259; depiction of 1960s in, 248; first three seasons of, 248; Jewish and minority characters in, 246–7, 250–2, 257–60, (use of Yiddish in), 251, 251n. 16, ("virtual" Jewishness in), 250, 252, 286; Kodak "carousel" in, 266–7; M. Greif's critique of, 245; neo-Lukácsian form of, 253; Nietzschean dimensions of, 247; protean self-fashioning in, 248; reception of, 287; E. Sedgwick's regime of the open secret and, 252; serial temporality of, 252 (rejection of hyper-modern tempo), 245; synchronization of female characters with male protagonist, 265; voted fourth best television drama, 245n. 7. *See also* serial television
Maharis, George, 255, 256
Mahmood, Saba, 240–1
Main, Alexander, 178n. 28

Malachuk, Daniel S., 195
Malcolmson, Scott, 65
Malik, Charu, 239
Mamdami, Mahmood, 61–2n. 34
Manavalli, Krishna, 136, 137n. 39
Mansel, H. L., 111
Mantel, Hilary, 282
Mantena, Karuna, 2, 39, 41, 59, 60, 62, 95
Marcus, Sharon, 1n. 1, 15, 25–6, 175–6, 271, "just reading" and, 202, 275, on marriage plots, 168. *See also* Best, Stephen and Sharon Marcus
Marder, Elissa, 190n. 41
Markovitz, Stefanie, 134
Markwick, Margaret, 89n. 3
Martin, Carol A., 283n. 21, 285
Martin, Robert K., 221, 221n. 25, 223, 228, 229, 238
Martineau, Harriet, 3, 7; *Suggestions Towards the Future Government of India*, 152–3
Marx, Eleanor, 165
Marx, John, 234n. 41
Marx, Karl, 1, 41, 67n. 4, 96, 135, 173, 214, 241, 292; on India, 274; Friedrich Engels and, 1; Hegelian revolutionary subject of, 272; influence on New Historicism, 272; *The Eighteenth Brumaire of Louis Bonaparte*, 110, 111, 128. *See also* Marxism/Marxist theory.
Marxism/Marxist theory, 28, 30, 35n. 25, 220n. 24, 274, 288, 293; E. Laclau and C. Mouffe's revision of, 273, 273n. 8; R. Williams and 36–7; relation to New Historicism and, 272; responsibility to act and, 272
Masson, David, 70–1
Masterman, C. F. G., 208, 236n. 44
Matlock, Jann, 170n. 15, 171
material culture, of serial media, 284–7
Maunder, Andrew, 111n. 2, 120–1n. 16
May, Brian, 208n. 2, 233n. 40
Mazzini, Giuseppe, 195
McCormack, W. J., 91, 95
McDonald, Christie, 34n. 22
McGowan, John, 184
McLean, Don, 254
McMaster, Juliet, 81n. 25, 94n. 13
Mehta, Jaya, 132, 133, 133n. 32, 137n. 39, 142, 156n. 60, 158, 158n. 64, 159
Mehta, Uday Singh, 2, 4, 41, 45, 45n. 8, 57, 130, 149, 153, 153n. 56, 218–9, 219n 20, 231n. 37
Meir, Golda, 255
Menke, Richard, 29n. 16
mercantilism, 8. *See also* imperialism/imperial
Meredith, George, 15, 163, 163n. 2, 169, 172, 175, 195, 215–6

Merivale, Herman, 57, 58n. 30, 98–9, 100–1, 103
Metcalf, Thomas, 41, 49, 61–3, 61n. 33, 63
metonymy, E. Freedgood on, 32n. 20; H. Shaw on, 189, 271; in realist fiction, 190, 245–6; in *The Wire*, 246
Michie, Elsie B., 72n. 14, 81n. 25, 89n. 3, 168–9n. 11, 173n. 19
Michie, Helena, 169, 271
Midgley, Clare, 119
Mill, James, 4, 51n. 18
Mill, John Stuart, 3, 4, 12, 39, 41, 42, 43n. 5, 44, 45, 49n. 13, 49n. 15, 52, 59–61, 119, 121n. 18, 123, 211–2; anti-racialist liberalism and, 58–9; anti-racist universalism of, 212; attacks on by pseudo-scientists of race, 122; *Considerations on Representative Government*, 8, 47, 53, 53n. 25, 55; J. A. Hobson and, 213; humanistic utilitarianism of, 211; imperial governance and, 54–7; India and, 53n. 25, 53n. 26; Jamaica Committee and, 60; "The Contest in America," 118, 121–2; *The Principles of Political Economy* 67n. 4; *The Subjection of Women*, 212; *Utilitarianism*, 212
Miller, Andrew H., 73n. 16, 90, 93n. 10
Miller, D. A., 111, 143, 155n. 59, 270, 272n. 5
Milley, Henry J. W., 91n. 6, 151n. 54
mimesis. *See* Auerbach, Erich; realism/realist fiction
Minca, Claudio, 6n. 7
Mineo, Sal, 254
Mitchell, David, *Cloud Atlas*, 282
Mittell, Jason, 244, 244n. 4
Modernism, 5, 9, 28n. 14, 29, 29n. 16, 33n. 21, 34, 84, 113n. 5, 134, 187, 189, 274n. 9, 278; cosmopolitanism and, 66n. 1; crisis of experience and, 111–2; diverse experiments of, 293; F. Jameson on, 247, 279, 280, 282, 282n. 19 (naturalism as precursor to), 276n. 11; F. Jameson's privileging of, 274; N. Daly on, 112; P. Bourdieu on, 185n. 37; R. Williams on, 185; stunted *Bildungsroman* and, 150n. 51
Moir, Martin, Douglas Peers, and Lynn Zastoupil, 60n. 31
Monkhouse, A. N., 228
Moody-Adams, Michele, 220n. 22
Moore, George, 5n. 5, 165, 175, 209n. 3
Moore, Robin J., 49n. 11, 61–2n.34, 62
Morant Bay rebellion (1865), 10, 43, 43n. 5, 97, 119–20, 122, 131; crisis of liberalism and, 119; L. Nayder on, 119–20n. 14. *See also* Eyre, Edward John; Jamaica
Moretti, Franco, 16, 20n. 3, 26n. 11, 27–8, 33–4, 34n. 22, 36, 164, 173, 175

Morley, Henry Forster, 120–1n. 16
Morley, John, 12, 39, 41, 42, 44, 45, 47, 49, 49n. 15, 50, 51, 51n. 20, 52–60, 61, 95, 97; as Secretary of State for India, 52, 62, review of G. Eliot's *Romola*, 202n. 55
Morris, William, 66n. 2; *News from Nowhere*, 158
Morrison, Toni, *Beloved*, 289, 291
Morse, Deborah Denenholz, 89n. 3
Mosse, George Lachman, 224n. 30
Mouffe, Chantal, 273, 273n. 8
Mufti, Aamir, 206, 250
Mughal dynasty, 45, 45n. 8, 46n. 11
Mukherjee, Mithi, 39, 45n. 8, 46
Mukherjee, Pablo, 34n. 22, 80n. 23
Mysore, debate over, 11, 12, 41, 44–5, 48–56, 61, 95, 96–7, 98, 100, 137, 152; and A. Trollope's *The Eustace Diamonds*, 95. *See also* Wodyar, Kristna Raj (Rajah of Mysore)

Nairn, Tom, 47n. 12
Nardin, Jane, 72
narration, free indirect style of in nineteenth-century realism, 260; multi-perspectival (in W. Collins's fiction), 114, 154; omniscient, 114
narratives of capitalist globalization, 14, 16; and New Imperialism, 167; and R. Williams's "country-house" novels, 172; affective logic of, 141; breached sovereignty in, 243n. 3; geopolitical aesthetic of, 243; injured sovereignty in, 141, 167; naturalistic 31, 37, 82, 89, 109, 110, 151, 243, 243n. 3, 261–2, 276; (A. Trollope's *The Eustace Diamonds* as an example of), 135, 135n. 36, (A. Trollope's *The Prime Minister* as an example of), 252, (G. Eliot's *Daniel Deronda* as an example of), 204–5, (G. Flaubert's *Madame Bovary* as an example of), 192, (*Mad Men* as an example of), 167n. 10, 246–7; A. Trollope and, 110. *See also* naturalism
nation-state. *See* sovereignty, national
naturalism, 13, 17, 32, 110, 164–5, 247n. 4; aesthetic of in *Mad Men*, 253; E. Auerbach's "existential realism" and, 280; collapse of sovereignty in, 239; cosmopolitanism and, 81n. 24; demonized boundary figures in, 157; existential realism and, 37; G. Flaubert and, 164, 280; G. Flaubert's *Madame Bovary* and A. Trollope's *The Prime Minister* as examples of, 246; W. D. Howells and, 89n. 3; in G. Flaubert, 85; in A. Trollope's *The Eustace Diamonds*, 93–4, 103; in A. Trollope's

The Way We Live Now, 104; F. Jameson on, 275, 276n. 11; G. Lukács on, 245; *Mad Men* and, 248n. 13; neoliberal subjects in, 106; neoliberalism and, 276; of *Mad Men* and *Madame Bovary*, 286; recurrent tropes of exile in, 275–6; A. Trollope and, 68, 85, 86; versus romance genres, 276; E. Zola's codification of, 246; E. Zola's deterministic mode of, 164–5, 246, (in "The Experimental Novel"), 164. *See also* realism/realist fiction
Nayder, Lillian, 119, 119n. 14, 126n. 25, 132, 142
Nead, Lynda, 249
Nealon, Christopher, 269n. 1
Nelson, Cary, 273
Newton, K.M., 175n 24
neo-feudalism. *See* New Imperialism
neoliberalism, 3, 3n. 4, 16, 20, 40, 84n. 30, 85, 284, 284n. 23; and identity as depicted in *Mad Men*, 261; P. Bourdieu's critique of, 288; definition of, 220n. 24; *Mad Men* and, 252; depiction of subject in *Mad Men*, 256; financialization of economy, 273; naturalism and, 106, 276; post-raciality and, 129
Netflix, 285–6, 287
network theory, 16. *See also* Latour, Bruno
New Criticism, 28n. 14, 274
New Historicism, 268, 270, 293; relation to Marxism and, 272
new imperial history, 11, 271
New Imperialism, the 11–12, 13, 29, 30, 31, 43, 47, 48, 51, 52, 56, 60, 62, 68, 87, 88, 123, 170, 239–40; agenda of, 64; invention of heirlooms and, 104; mass politics and, 105; neo-feudalism and, 105; A. Trollope and, 81n. 25, 106 (in *The Eustace Diamonds*), 90, 108
New Liberalism, 3n. 3, 60, 195, 208, 208n. 1, 211–8, 237; internationalism and, 15
New York City, as location for *Mad Men*, 246, 250, 255
New Zealand, 102, 274
Newman, Paul, 254, 255, 255–6
Newsinger, John, 43n. 5
Nietzsche, Friedrich, 66n. 2, 188, 289
1960s, depiction of in *Mad Men*, 248; identitarian freedom movement of, 272; waning of, according to F. Jameson, 248
Nixon, Rob, 292
Nolan, Christopher, *Inception* (2010), 282, 291
Norris, Frank, 165, 165n. 7
North Africa, French conquest of, 171
North America, 8, 12, 42, 69n. 9; white settler colonies in, 77, 83. *See also* imperialism/imperial

Northcote, Sir Stafford, 63
Nunokawa, Jeff, 34n. 23
Nussbaum, Martha, 145n. 49

Ó Tuathail, Gearoid, 6n. 7
Obama, Barack, 3
O'Brien, Patrick, 70, 244n. 4
O'Connor, Maura, 217
Okin, Susan, 220n. 24
Oliphant, Margaret, 162
Opium Wars, 7, 10
Ottoman Empire, 70
Ouida, 275n. 10

Pagden, Anthony, 42
Pakula, Alan J., 247
Palmer, Beth, 111
Palmerston, Lord (3rd Viscount Palmerston), 7, 68, 69, 71, 71n. 12, 194
Palumbo-Liu, David, 4
Park, Hyungji, 134n. 33
Parry, Benita, 208n. 2, 234n. 41, 234n. 42
Paskow, Jacqueline, 191
Pater, Walter, 113n. 5; crisis of experience and, 112
Penslar, Derek, 250
Peperzak, Adrian T., 236n. 43, 237
Peters, Catherine, 111n. 1, 115, 120n. 14, 127
Peterson, Derek R., 118n. 11
Peterson, Richard K., 272
Piggford, George, 221, 221n. 25, 228
Pitts, Jennifer, 2, 45
Plotz, John, 80n. 23, 90n. 5, 93n. 10, 133, 134, 225, 271
Pocock, J. G. A., 196–7
Polan, Dana, 246
political economy, classical, 211n. 9
polygenesis. *See* race/racialism
Poovey, Mary, 272n. 5
Popper, Nathaniel, 135n. 34
Porter, Andrew, 46n. 9, 119, 119n. 12, 119n. 13
Porter, Bernard, 7, 40, 46–8
possessive individualism. *See* Locke, John
postmodernism, 9, 30; Fredric Jameson and, 9
postnationalism, 210, 210n. 5
poststructuralism, 11, 21, 25, 27, 36, 38, 274, 289; critique of realism and, 28
Potolsky, Matthew, 274n. 9
Pratt, Mary Louise, 231n. 31
Preminger, Otto, 254, 255n. 21; *Exodus*, 259
Prendergast, Christopher, 38
Price, Leah, 269n. 1, 284, 287
Proctor, Robert N., 134, 135
Proust, Marcel, 282
providentialism, "invisible hand" and, 85
Psalm 137, 249, 252, 259, 260–1; exile and captivity in, 253; musical arrangement of, 254.
    See also Babylon; *Mad Men*.

Psomiades, Kathy, 90n. 5, 92, 93n. 10, 168–9n. 11
Puar, Jasbir, 236n. 44
Punjab, annexation of, 10. *See also* India/ Indian

"quality" television, 242, 244, 285; nineteenth-century realism and, 245
Quéré, Louis, 289
queer theory, 221n. 25

Rabinow, Paul, 25, 116, 144, 145, 146, 150
race/racialism, 69; abolitionist views of, 131n. 30; Anglo-Saxon whiteness and, 57, 60, 71, 77–8, 81n. 24, 83, 87, 117n. 10, 129, (in G. Smith), 58–9; A. Trollope and, 59, 77–8, 84, 86, 102; as feature of mid-Victorian modernity, 129; as pseudo-scientific category, 43; B. Disraeli and, 81n. 25; capitalist modernity and, 83; cosmopolitanism and, 66, 81n. 24; disavowal and, 117n. 10; extinction of "vanishing races," 77; E. Carpenter and, 224; in A. Trollope's *Framley Parsonage*, 81n. 24; Ilbert Bill and, 61n. 34; imperialism and, 48; Irishness and, 77n. 21, 79–80, 122; J. Hobson and, 213; J. Morley and, 56; 80; mixed-race characters (in W. Collins's fiction), 114, 116, 117, 131, 157, 275; "negro", 78; of Jews, 251; post-raciality (as colorblindness), 131, (in W. Collins's *Armadale*), 125, 128–9, 130–1, 132; racial pseudo-science and, 122; racialization of Atlantic experience (in W. Collins's *Armadale*), 126; structural contradictions of, 85; subversion of (in W. Collins's *The Moonstone*), 142; T. Carlyle and, 58–9; W. Collins's distaste for, 123. *See also* racism

racism, as historical process, 273; depicted in W. Collins's *Armadale*, 130–1; post-abolition increase of, 119, 119n. 12, 122, 129–30. *See also*, race /racialism
Ragussis, Michael, 13, 83n. 27, 106, 249
Rahman, Tariq, 221n. 25
Raleigh, John Henry, 178n. 28
Rancière, Jacques, 9n. 12, 29n. 16, 171, 200, 264n. 24, 288, 292; adultery and, 186–9, 190, 191; on post- Flaubert realism, 292n. 29; *The Politics of Aesthetics*, 186n. 38; "Why Emma Bovary Had to Be Killed," 186–8 ("war of Art versus Aestheticism" in *Madame Bovary*), 187, 187n. 39
Rawlinson, Sir Henry, 52n. 21, 54
Rawls, John, 220

realism/realist fiction, 4, 5, 11, 16, 28–33, 36–7, 38, 40, 64, 66, 242, 274n. 9; alleged quietism of, 73; antinomistic condition of (according to F. Jameson), 245, 247, 276; as ideologically suspect, 245; as index of historical change, 246; capitalism's *longue durée* and, 243; capitalist realism and (M. Schudson on), 264; character-driven (of A. Trollope), 110; characteristic features of in the nineteenth century, 245–6; compared to Modernism, 274; courtship and marriage plots in, 168–9; critically acclaimed televisual variations on, 245; described in *Saturday Review*, 161; details and, 166; dissolution of into other forms, 278; E. M. Forster's experiments with (in *Where Angels Fear to Tread*), 218, 235, 236–7; experimentation of, 282–3; formal and aesthetic properties of, 10, 277–8; French as compared to British, 29, 161, 164; H. Shaw on, 276–7; historical (and *Mad Men*), 253; historicity of (F. Jameson on), 278–82, (H. Shaw on), 184; idiosyncratic form of (in A. Trollope's *The Eustace Diamonds*), 105, 108–9; international encounters (in E. M. Forster's works), 221; H. James on, 277–8; G. Lewes on, 277–8; "magical" mutation of, 15, 209, 235, 236n. 45; Marxist critiques of, 166, 245, 274; mimesis and, 282n. 19; New Criticism's critique of, 166, 274; nineteenth-century, 9, 10 (compared to "quality" television), 283, 284–7; postructuralist critique of, 166, 274; reconsideration of, 245; serialized, 242; slow nineteenth-century pace of, 245; social aspect of, 188; "sociological"register of, 88, 101, 103, 104, 110 (in A. Trollope's works), 88; subjectivism of, 37; subjunctivism of, 37; T. Eagleton on, 245; structuralist critique of, 274; use of metonymy in, 245–6; V. Woolf's critique of, 274; W. Collins's fiction and (*The Moonstone*), 156, 156n. 60, (*Armadale*), 125–6n. 23; R. Wellek's definition of, 111n. 1. See also Lukács, Georg
Reed, John, 132
revolutions of 1848, 28, 29, 247; crisis of realism and, 274
Reynolds, Matthew, 195n. 48
Richardson, Samuel, *Clarissa* (1748), 143
Richmond, Charles, 105n. 20
Rifaterre, Michael, 34, 34n. 24, 35
Rignall, John, 175, 181–2, 182n. 33

Robbins, Bruce, 3n. 4, 23, 23n. 6, 24, 27, 85, 150n. 51, 206, 211; *Feeling Global*, 210n. 6
Roebuck, John Arthur, 120, 121n. 17
romance forms, F. Jameson on, 274; I. Duncan on 174n. 22; imperial variation on (in W. Collins's *The Moonstone*) 156; spatio-temporal features of, 276. See also historical novel/romance; realism/realist fiction
Rooney, Ellen, 270
rootedness. See cosmopolitanism, "heirloom" sovereignty and
Rorty, Richard, 15, 208, 208n. 2, 233, 233n. 40, 238, 239–40
Rosenbaum, S. P., 209n. 3, 215n. 17, 232n. 39
Rothberg, Michael, 3n. 4
Rousseau, Jean-Jacques, 170n. 14, 220
Rowe, John Carlos, 89n. 3
Roy, Ashish, 132, 137n. 39, 158
Royal Titles Act (1876), 6, 10, 43, 46, 63, 106
Rudy, Jason R., 22n. 5, 65
Ruskin, John, 7, 119
Russell, Lord John (1st Earl Russell), 51n. 20, 121, 121n. 17
Russia, 7, 57, 60

Sabin, Margery, 133n. 32, 155n. 59, 158n. 63
Said, Edward W., 2, 132, 210, 217, 231n. 37, 234n. 41, 254, 254n. 20; analysis of Orientalism, 273
Saint-Beuve, Charles Augustin, 161, 165
Salih, Sara, 127n. 26
Salisbury, Lord (3rd Marquess of Salisbury), 44–5, 47, 49–50, 51–2, 52n. 22, 53n. 24, 53n. 26, 54, 54n. 27, 61, 96, 97, 103, 105, 105n. 20, 121n. 17; as Secretary of State for India, 98. See also India/Indian
Salvador (1986), 247, 248
Samuels, Maurice, 172
Sand, George, 15, 275, 163, 178, 184, 185, 185n. 36, 186, 193
Sanders, Andrew, 167–8, 177n. 27
Sartori, Andrew, 2n. 2, 4, 27n. 12, 41, 42, 62, 202n. 55, 269n. 2, 292n. 30
Sartre, Jean-Paul, F. Jameson on, 279
Saville, Julia, 195
Schinkel, William, 288
Schivelbusch, Wolfang, 19
Schmitt, Carl, 20, 47; exception and, 9; *Political Theology*, 9n. 13. See also sovereignty
Schoene, Berthold, 20
Schor, Naomi, 165, 188, 189, 193n. 42, 246
Schudson, Michael, 264, 266
science fiction, 157, 247; F. Jameson and, 112n 4
Scott, Joan, 145, 145n. 48, 146

Scott, Walter, 73, 73n. 15, 157, 158, 159, 176, 178, 184, 185, 275, 281; historical fiction of, 164, 167, 274, 281 (masculinist features of), 201, 280; I. Duncan on, 176, 177; *Ivanhoe*, 14, 247, 187; "typical character" in the fiction of, 247, 282; A. Sanders on, 177n. 27; Waverley novels, 14, 281, (*Waverley*), 177, 187.
Second Reform Act (1867), 52, 53, 53n. 24, 105. See also democracy
Sedgwick, Eve Kosofsky, paranoid reading and, 268, 269, 270, 291, 292; regime of the "open secret," 252
Seed, D., 166
Seeley, J. R., 3, 7, 39, 40, 57, 60, 64, 69; "Greater Britain" and 62; India and, 59, 108; liberal
discomfiture of, 59, 108
Semmel, Bernard, 6, 6n. 8, 42, 43n. 5
Sen, Amartya, 3
Sen, Sudipta, 39
Senior, Nassau, 64
sensation fiction, 110–11, 123, 128, 130n. 29, 150, 156n. 60, 193; N. Daly on, 112n. 4; D. A. Miller on, 111; Modernism and, 111–2; U. Anjaria on, 245; transposition of Gothic conventions and, 110, 157; variety of in W. Collins, 114; *vis-à-vis* realism, 111. See also Collins, Wilkie
sense of an ending. See Kermode, Frank
Sepoy "mutiny." See Indian "mutiny"/rebellion
serial publication, 9–10, 89n. 3
serial television, 5, 16, 85
seriality/serialization, 15, 16, 37; as feature of realist narrative, 265; audiences for, 283, 285; "binging" and, 244; communal effects of, 244; dialectical movement of, 284; historicity of, 284; in/of *Mad Men*, 253; in twenty-first century television, 248 (compared to nineteenth-century novels) 243, 244; intense feelings generated by, 244; H. James's experience of, 266; C. Martin on (in G. Eliot's fiction), 283n. 21; material culture of, 284–7; mediation of naturalistic narrative and, 192; mid-Victorian era and, 242–3; non-realist genres and, 244, 244n. 4; of G. Eliot's *Middlemarch* and *Romola*, 283; of nineteenth-century realism, 260; repetitiveness of (F. Jameson on), 283; rituals of, 244; serial *habitus* and, 244; television soap operas and, 244n. 4; temporality of, 265n. 26, (versus sense of ending), 284
Seringapatam, battle of, 11, 137, 137n. 39, 152. See also Mysore, debate over

Shakespeare, William, *Othello* (1603), 284
Shanley, Mary Lyndon, 162n. 1
Shaw, Harry E., 28, 29n. 16, 32n. 20, 184, 189–90, 192, 194, 194n. 45, 271, 276, 277n. 13
Shohat, Ella, 145, 152, 254, 254n. 20
Showtime, 245
Siegel, Jonah, 209n. 3
Simon, Paul, 255
Simpkins, Scott, 237n. 45
Simpson, David, 38n. 28
Singh, Duleep, 139
Singh, Ranjit, "lion of the Punjab," 137
Skilton, David, 287
Slade, Carol, 135n. 34
slavery, 24–5, 31, 34; abolition of, 51–2n. 20, 77, as marker of British superiority, 119; abolitionist movement and, 118–9, 131n. 30 (universalism of), 129 (depicted in W. Collins's *Armadale*), 117; British disavowal of, 117n. 10; E. Williams on, 115, 117–8; global economy and, 131–132; legacy of (depicted in W. Collins's *Armadale*), 124, 126; legislation regarding, 118, 118n. 11; J. S. Mill on, 118, 121–2; M. Wood on, 117, 117n. 10; sugar plantation complex and, 116, 116n. 8, 117–8, 119n. 12, (depicted in W. Collins's *Armadale*), 131–2. See also Enlightenment, the; United States, Civil War and; universalism/universality
Small, Helen, 292
Smith, Anna-Marie, 9n. 12
Smith, Denis Mack, 195
Smith, George, 87
Smith, Goldwin, 39, 41, 43, 56–7, 61, 69; British India and, 63–4; "Greater Britain" and, 58; on corrupting effects of Indian rule, 58, 60
Smith, Paul, 105n. 20
sociological approaches to literature, 287–92
sociology, 12. See also geopolitical aesthetic
Somerville, Siobhan, 224n. 29
South Africa, 12, 42, 274; Cape Colony, 70; discovery of diamonds in, 135; Orange River in, 8
South Asia, 11, 86, 90; expanding Raj in, 247. See also India/Indian
southern/southerness, 217; R. Dainotto on, 217; E. M. Forster's fiction and, 218, (*A Passage to India*), 233; (*Where the Angels Fear to Tread*), 223, 225, 227, 229, 235; in G. Eliot's fiction, 205
sovereignty, 14, 31; anxieties over, 9, 171; apotheosis of Hindu (in W. Collins's *The Moonstone*), 136,158; breaching of, 81n. 24, 81n. 25, 82, 86, (in

R. Williams's "country-house" novels), 172, (J. A. Hobson on), 212; British, 51, 75, 78, 80; capitalism and, 40n. 1; depiction of (in W. Collins's fiction), 120 (in *The Moonstone*), 134, 134n. 33; communal, 7; constitutional monarchy and, 73; definition of, 8–9, (C. Schmitt's), 47, (W. Brown's), 40n. 1, (W. Connolly's), 150, 153; democratic, 9; eclipse of imperial, individual, and national (in W. Collins's *The Moonstone*), 150; E. M. Forster and, 239; empirical, 211n. 7; fantasy of limitless, 85; foreign policy and, 71; formal (of United Nations), 211n. 7; globalization and, 59; "heirloom" mode of, 7, 13, 32, 37, 67, 71–7, 82, 100, 106, 215, 215n. 15, 239, (in A. Trollope's fiction), 167n. 10, 275, (bourgeois marriage and), 169, (breached in *The Eustace Diamonds*), 167n. 10, 92, 93, 102 (intact in W. Collins's *The Moonstone*), 136; imperial, 4, 6, 11, 31, 39–67, 70 ("absent-minded" history of), 273 (crisis of), 212, (G. GoGwilt on), 111n. 3; (liberal crisis of after Morant Bay rebellion), 119, (makeshift), 134; Indian, 53–4, 56; individual, 7, 40, 209 (in A. Trollope's *The Eustace Diamonds*), 92–3, (in naturalistic fiction), 239; incomplete basis for (in W. Collins's *The Moonstone*, 133); juridical notion of, 211n. 7; mid-Victorian modes of, 239; monarchy and, 74n. 18; multi-sited (in W. Collins's *The Moonstone*), 153; national, 7, 15, 40, 47n. 12, 210; nominal, 97n. 15; of Indian royals, 95, 97–100; of the United Kingdom (G. Smith on), 39; of Queen Victoria, 63; outmoded ideals of, 144; pluralistic nation form of (W. Connolly on), 153; porous and pluralized, 209 (as depicted in W. Collins's *The Moonstone*), 152–5; popular, 40; post-heirloom (as depicted in W. Collins's *The Moonstone*), 142; postmodern (in W. Collins's fiction), 239; property and, 72; realist form and, 37; recutting of Koh-i-Noor and British, 138; rootedness and, 66, 67–8, 71; territorial, 42, W. Brown on, 39–40. *See also* narratives of capitalist globalization; Mysore, debates over
Spencer, Herbert, 119, 179
Staël, Madame de, 217
Stalinism, effects of on critical theory, 273
Stang, Richard, 180–1
Stendhal, 165n. 4, 178, 185

Stephen, James Fitzjames, 58; authoritarianism of, 61, 62; India and, 59; review of *Madame Bovary*, 161, 162, 163, 180
Stephen, Leslie, 193n 44; racism of, 129–30, 131
Stewart, Garrett, 30, 31n. 18, 34–6, 34n. 24, 35, 173
Stocking, George W., 77n. 20
Stone, H. 173n. 23
Stone, Oliver, 247
Stoker, Bram, 275n. 10; *Dracula* (1895), 128n. 28
Stokes, Eric, 46n. 10, 118
Stoler, Ann Laura, 2n. 2, 222n. 26
Stone, Wilfred, 216
Storey, Graham 120–1n. 16
Suez Canal, 10
Suleiman, Susan, 34n. 22
Suleri, Sara, 45n. 8, 234n. 41
Super, R. H., 67n. 3, 89n. 3
"surface reading," 16–7, 268–9, 293; neo-positivist and anti-hermeneutic dimensions of, 269; poststructuralist ethics and, 273; versus "symptomatic reading," 269, 271. *See also* Best, Stephen and Sharon Marcus
Surridge, Lisa, 143n. 45
suspicious reading. *See* hermeneutics of suspicion
Sutherland, John, 81, 115, 117, 125n. 22
Swinburne, Algernon Charles, 253
Symonds, John Addington, 223, 224

Tanner, Tony, 168, 169, 170, 170n. 14, 170n. 15, 173, 204
Taylor Charles, 214
Taylor, Jenny Bourne, 113, 117n. 9, 132, 133n. 32
Taylor, Miles, 8
Teal, Karen Kurt, 106n. 22, 109
television, news (as depoliticizing force), 268; world-systems theory and, 281; reality, 282–3
Teukolsky, Rachel, 29n. 16, 274n. 9
Thackeray, William Makepeace, 36, 174–5, G. Lukács on, 177
The Sopranos (1999–2007), 243, 244–5, 248; form of (D. Polan on), 244n. 5
The Wire (2002–2008), 243, 246; autoethnographic structure of, 246; Dickensian dimensions of, 245, 245n. 6, 246, 283; F. Jameson on, 246n. 10, 248n. 12, 282–3; seriality of, 283
Thomas, David Wayne, 93n. 11, 198
Thomas, Ronald R., 146–7, 147n. 50, 148, 155n. 58–9
Thompson, Andrew, 195n. 47
Thorne, Susan, 222n. 26
Tipu Sultan (Sultan of Mysore), 45, 49n. 15, 137, 150, 156n. 60

Todorov, Tzvetan, 125, 125–6n. 23, 155
Tolstoy, Leo, 193, 281
Tory Party. *See* Conservative Party
Tory politics, 13, 39, 48, 51–52n. 20, 52, 53, 63, 123, 284n. 23; "engraftment" and, 43; imperialism and, 41–2; race and, 43; U. S. Civil War and, 121n. 17. *See also* imperialism/imperial, governmentality
tourism, depictions of in E. M. Forster's fiction, 231, 233; J. Puar on, 236n. 44
transnationalism/transnationality, 218, "actually existing," 21, 22–7, 28, 37; W. Collins's fiction and (*Armadale*) 116, (*The Moonstone*), 132; experience and, 23, 85, 114; feminist project of, 145; fiction and, 111; global structures and, 144; globalization and, 210; Israel and (as depicted in *Mad Men*), 255–7; obligations of justice in (in I. Young's theory), 239; queer sexual desire and, 218. *See also* experience, transnational
Trevelyan, G. M., 15, 195, 208, 211n. 8, 215–7, 231
Trevelyan, R. C., 215n. 16, 237
Trilling, Lionel, 15, 20, 208, 208n. 2, 209, 218, 219, 220n. 24, 230, 240, 284
Trollope, Anthony, 2, 3, 5, 13, 16, 29, 43, 45, 57, 65–86, 110, 137, 175, 178, 244, 269, 275n. 10, 281, 283; ambivalent anti-Semitism of, 88, 250; ambivalence toward territorial imperialism, 69n. 9; Anglo-Saxon "race" and, 67, 87; as "chronicler of Barsetshire," 67–8, 78, 80; as naturalistic precursor to serialized television, 245; as participant in literary "world-system," 274–5; Balzacian qualities of his works, 88–9, 104; E. Burke and, 76; campaign speeches of, 106. 22; W. Collins and, 110–11, 111n. 1; B. Disraeli and, 106n. 22, 107, 109; ethnography and, 12; exilic characters of, 157 (Jewish and Judaized), 71n. 12, 106, 107n. 23, 286 (Lopez, Ferdinand in *The Prime Minister*), 67; failed bid for Parliament (1868), 81n. 25; figure of the "secret Jew" in his works (compared to *Mad Men*), 250, 291 (compared to G. Flaubert's *Madame Bovary*), 172; "heirloom" sovereignty and, 275 (compared to W. Collins's *The Moonstone*), 136; India and, 42; individualism and, 76; influence of W. Collins's *The Moonstone* on, 88, 91; Ireland and, 77n. 21, 102; F. Jameson on, 280n. 15; 106; "liberal" civilizing mission and, 100, 102; middle-class women and, 94; naturalism and, 105; on characterization, 104; Parliament and, 100; play of rootedness and cosmopolitanism in works of ("foreign policy"), 85; political *Bildungsroman* and, 105; possessive individualism and, 80; "race" and, 77–8, 81n. 25, 102; racialized stock figures and, 104; sociological realism and, 104; travel writings of, 12, 59, 67–8, 71, 76, 77–82, 102; variation on W. Scott's historical fiction, 275; waning of "heirloom" sovereignty and, 106, 183

Works:
An Autobiography, 71, 72, 79n. 22, 80, 82–3, 91, 98n. 17, 100, 103, 104, 106–7n. 22, 108, 111n. 1
Australia and New Zealand, 42, 67, 77, 79, 81, 87, 98
Barchester Towers, 14, 72n. 13, 72n. 14, 162, 169
Barsetshire novels, 12, 31, 71, 72–3, 72n. 13, 73n. 15, 78, 81n. 24, 82, 89, 92, 94n. 13, 100, 215, 215n. 15, 239; rootedness and, 67–8; waning heirloom history in, 177
Can You Forgive Her? 89, 100, 101
Doctor Thorne, 71, 72n. 13, 71, 94n. 12
The Duke's Children, 106n. 22
The Eustace Diamonds, 4, 13, 41, 73n. 16, 81, 82, 86, 87–109, 110, 135, 151n. 54, 154, 243n. 3, 249n. 14, 280n. 15; anti-Semitic caricature in, 250; devastation of sovereignty in, 134, 172; Judaized jewelers in, 141n. 42; unusual form of, 108–9
Framley Parsonage, 72n. 13, 81n. 24, 177
He Knew He Was Right, 14, 169n. 12
The Last Chronicle of Barset, 72n. 13, 81n. 25, 287
"Miss Sarah Jack of Spanish Town," 169n. 12
The New Zealander, 73, 73n. 15, 74n. 17, 87
North America, 67, 73, 78–9, 80, 87, 94
"On Sovereignty," 73–4
Palliser novels, 13, 81n. 25, 88–9, 89n. 3, 100, 104, 242; political *Bildungsromane* in, 89, 109
Phineas Redux, 89, 98, 104, 106, 109
The Prime Minister, 10n. 14, 14, 15, 31–3, 37, 65, 67, 81, 82–6, 89, 98, 104, 106, 110, 169, 169n. 12, 242–3, 261, 265, 280n. 15, 284, 286n. 25; as naturalistic narrative, 174, 276; effects of Tory imperialism on, 275; H. Michie on, 169; Lopez as suspected Jew in, 243; narrative splitting in, 252; reception of, 286–7
The Small House at Allington, 72n. 13
South Africa, 67, 87

The Three Clerks, 169n. 12
Tireless Traveller, 8, 77–8n. 21, 87, 100
The West Indies and the Spanish Main, 67, 76, 77, 77n. 20, 87
The Warden, 4, 67, 72–7, 78–9, 82, 92, 104, 275
The Way We Live Now, 10n. 14, 71, 82, 83n. 28, 89, 103n. 19, 109, 109n. 25, 110, 172, 204, 218, 250, 276n. 11, 286n. 25; naturalism of, 104; T. Tanner on, 172–3
Trollope, Frances, 2, 164
Trodd, Anthea, 112n. 4
Tronto, Joan C., 220, 220n. 22
Trumbo, Dalton, 255n. 21
Trumpener, Katie, 176n. 26
Tucker, Herbert F., 29n. 16, 270n. 3, 274n. 9
Turner, Mark, 184, 193

Ulrichs, K. H., 228n. 36
uncanny, as feature of archeological geopolitical aesthetic (in W. Collins's *Armadale*), 125, 126, 130; in W. Collins's *The Moonstone*, 155
United States, Civil War (1861–5), 10, 14, 73, 117, 123, 129; as context for W. Collins's *Armadale*, 120–1, 122; British attitudes towards, 120–2; "Greater Britain" and, 57; J. S. Mill on, 117, 120–1; *Trent* affair and, 121, 121n. 18; A. Trollope and, 78–9, 80
universalism/universality, enhanced in O. Preminger's *Exodus*, 255n. 21; ethics of justice and, 220; interactive, 220n. 23; figure of "new Jew" and, 255; liberal modernity and, 252; of condition of exile (in *Mad Men*), 252; of unassimilable otherness (in *Mad Men*), 286; post-abolition decline of, 119, 120, 119–20n. 14, 122, 123, 129–30; I. Young on, 226;
Uris, Leon, 254, 254n. 20; *Exodus* (discussed in *Mad Men*), 257, 259
utopia/utopian, dimension of *The Wire* (according to F. Jameson), 248
utopian romance, 133; as riven genre, 157–8; conclusion of W. Collins's *The Moonstone* and, 153, 156; in W. Collins's *The Moonstone*, 153; in *The Wire*, 282.

Valman, Nadia, 251
van Dam, Frederik, 89n. 3
van Evrie, John H., 122
Varon, Jeremy, 248
Verne, Jules, 157, 276, 276n. 11; *Le tour du monde en quatre-vingts jours* (1873), 276n. 11
Vertovek, Steven, 22

Victoria, Queen, 46, 63, 74, 87, 96, 97, 106; Proclamation of 1858, 41, 46n. 11, 47, 48, 103. *See also* Royal Titles Act (1876)
Victorian studies, 25–6, 29n. 16; field of 65–6, 292
Viswanathan, Gauri, 46n. 10, 118
Voskuil, Lynn M., 66n. 2, 105n. 20, 106

Wacquant, Loïc J. D., 21, 27
Walkowitz, Rebecca L., 66n. 1
Wall, Stephen, 89n. 3
Wallerstein, Immanuel, 6, 6n. 7, 34n. 22. *See also* world-system theory
Walzer, Michael, 254, 254n. 20
Ward, Stuart, 171n. 16
Warhol, Robin, 244
Warner, Michael, 221n. 25, 287
Washbrook, D. A., 42n. 3
Watkins, Susan, 292–3
Watson, Tim, 124n. 21, 132n. 31
Watt, Ian, 277n. 13
Weber, Max, 72n. 14, 197, 214
Wedd, Nathaniel, 208
Weiner, Matthew, 250–1, 251n. 16
Weiner, Stephanie Kuduk, 195
Weissbrod, Rachel, 254n. 20, 255n. 21
Wellek, René, 5n. 5, 111n. 1
Wellesley, Lord (1st Marquess Wellesley), 45n. 8
Wellington, Duke of, 138, 140
Wells, H. G., 276; *A Modern Utopia*, 157; *In the Days of the Comet*, 157
Welsh, Alexander, 151n. 53, 155–6, 201
West Indies, British, 12, 42, 51–2n. 20, 56, 58, 69, 102, 118–9, 124n. 21, 132n. 31; locale for W. Collins's *Armadale*, 115–6; poverty in, 122–3; sugar plantation complex and, 116n. 8. *See also* Jamaica; Morant Bay rebellion
Whig Party, 51–2n. 20. *See also* liberalism; Liberal Party
White, Stephen K., 220n. 24, 238, 272n. 5
Whitman, Walt, influence on E. Carpenter, 223–4
Wicke, Jennifer, 265
Wihl, Gary S., 196, 200
Wilde, Oscar, 113n. 5, 187n. 39; crisis of experience and, 112; *The Picture of Dorian Gray*, 261
Williams, Donovan, 49, 49n. 14, 50, 98n. 17, 100–1
Williams, Eric, 115, 117
Williams, Raymond, 11, 27, 38, 38n. 28, 145n. 48, 193, 218, 275; "Forms of English Fiction in 1848," 36–7, 153; *Keywords*, 144, 144n. 47; "Advertising: The Magic System," 265; "subjectivist" and "subjunctive" forms of, 37, 153; 174n. 22; "structure of feeling" and, 146,

281n. 18; *The Country and the City*, 30n. 17, 172, 173
Wills, Adele, 143n. 44, 152n. 55
Winnett, Susan, 193, 201, 203
Wise, Tim, 131
Wodyar, Kristna Raj (Rajah of Mysore), 41, 45, 45n. 8, 49–50, 52, 52n. 21, 54–5, 61, 96, 97, 100, 103, 120, 137
Wohl, Anthony S., 106n. 22, 107, 107n. 24, 140n. 41, 249n. 14
Wolfson, Susan, 28
Wood, Sir Charles Wood, 49–50, 51, 54, 97, 100, 121, 121n. 17. *See also* India/Indian, Secretary of State for
Wood, Ellen Meiksins, 1, 8, 78, 171, 171n. 17, 210n. 6; working classes, British, 12
Wood, Gordon, 42n. 4, 61
Wood, Marcus, 115, 117, 117n. 10
Woolf, Virginia, 245, 274
Wright, John, 1n. 1, 67n. 4
Wynne, Deborah, 143n. 45

Yeazell, Ruth Bernard, 168n. 11
Young, Iris Marion, 219n. 21, 220, 220n. 23, 220n. 24, 224n. 31, 225–6, 230, 235, 236, 236n. 43, 238, 239, 239n. 48, 240n. 49, 241; "Asymmetrical Reciprocity," 235; *Inclusion and Democracy*, 235; *Justice and the Politics of Difference*, 235; "moral humility" (compared to E. M. Forster's fiction), 232, 232n. 38, 240n. 50
Young, Paul, 1, 8n. 11, 34n. 23, 133, 134n. 33, 138
Young, Robert J. C., 212
Young-Zook, Monica, 126n. 25

Zastoupil, Lynn, 46n. 10, 60n. 31
Zephaniah, Benjamin, 254
Zerilli, Linda, 145–6, 149, 155, 159
Žižek, Slavoj, 191–2
Zola, Émile, 12, 193; as naturalist, 246, 246n. 8

Printed and bound by CPI Group (UK) Ltd, Croydon, CR0 4YY